Functional Analysis
of Problem Behavior

From Effective Assessment to Effective Support

ALAN C. REPP
Northern Illinois University

P9-CSE-443

ROBERT H. HORNER
University of Oregon

Wadsworth Publishing Company
I⊤P® An International Thomson Publishing Company

Belmont, CA • Albany, NY • Boston • Cincinnati • Johannesburg • London • Madrid • Melbourne
Mexico City • New York • Pacific Grove, CA • Scottsdale, AZ • Singapore • Tokyo • Toronto

Education Editor: Dianne Lindsay
Assistant Editor: Tangelique Williams
Marketing Manager: Becky Tollerson
Project Editors: Jennie Redwitz/
      John Walker
Print Buyer: Barbara Britton
Permissions Editor: Susan Walters
Production: Linda Jupiter,
      Jupiter Productions

Indexer: Kay Banning
Proofreader: Elinor Lindheimer
Copy Editors: Robyn Brode, Marla Greenway, Vivian Jaquette, Carol White
Illustrator: Mendocino Graphics
Cover Design: Bill Stanton
Compositor: Pre-Press Company
Printer: Webcom Limited

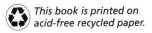

This book is printed on acid-free recycled paper.

Printed in Canada
1 2 3 4 5 6 7 8 9 10

For more information, contact Wadsworth Publishing Company, 10 Davis Drive, Belmont, CA 94002, or electronically at http://www.wadsworth.com

International Thomson Publishing Europe
Berkshire House
168-173 High Holborn
London, WC1V 7AA, United Kingdom

Nelson ITP, Australia
102 Dodds Street
South Melbourne
Victoria 3205 Australia

Nelson Canada
1120 Birchmount Road
Scarborough, Ontario
Canada M1K 5G4

International Thomson Publishing Southern Africa
Building 18, Constantia Square
138 Sixteenth Road, P.O. Box 2459
Halfway House, 1685 South Africa

International Thomson Editores
Seneca, 53
Colonia Polanco
11560 México D.F. México

International Thomson Publishing Asia
60 Albert Street #15-01
Albert Complex
Singapore 189969

International Thomson Publishing Japan
Hirakawa-cho Kyowa Building, 3F
2-2-1 Hirakawa-cho, Chiyoda-ku
Tokyo 102, Japan

Library of Congress Cataloging-in-Publication Data

Functional analysis of problem behavior : from effective assessment to effective support /
    [edited by] Alan C. Repp, Robert H. Horner.
        p.   cm. — (The Wadsworth special educator series)
    Includes bibliographical references and index.
    ISBN 0-534-34850-5 (pbk.)
    1. Behavior assessment. 2. Handicapped—Functional assessment.
    3. Behavior disorders in children—Diagnosis. I. Repp, Alan C.
    II. Horner, Robert H. III. Series
RC473.B43F85   1999
371.92—dc21
                                      98-44913

Contents

II FUNCTIONAL ASSESSMENT IN PRESCHOOL AND SCHOOL   **169**

Acknowledgments

We wish to acknowledge the extensive support of Priscilla Phillips, Terri Surratt, and Peggy Williams in the preparation of this text. We further acknowledge the impressive patience of the contributors through the protracted publication process. Our thanks also to our reviewers: James Artesani, University of Maine; Diane Browder, Lehigh University; Mary Ann Demchak, University of Nevada at Reno; and Lynne C. Ruegamer, University of Nevada at Las Vegas. Finally, we acknowledge the assistance of the editorial staff of Wadsworth Publishing in transforming this set of papers into a book.

Dedication

This book is dedicated to two groups of people. We pay tribute to those who pioneered the technology of functional analysis and established the science that made this book possible. We also dedicate the book to those people with disabilities and problem behavior who have taught us how to apply functional assessment methods with efficiency and effectiveness. The efforts of these individuals to make sense of the world around them has been the foundation for an applied technology of functional assessment.

AR/RH

Contributors

Wendy K. Berg, M.A.
The University of Iowa
University Hospital School
100 Hawkins Drive, Room 251
Iowa City, IA 52242-1011

Louis D. Burgio, Ph.D.
Applied Gerontology Program
University of Alabama
Tuscaloosa, AL 35487-0315

Edward Carr, Ph.D.
Department of Psychology
State University of New York
Stony Brook, NY 11794-2500

Linda J. Cooper, Ph.D.
Department of Pediatrics, 2525 JCP
University of Iowa Hospitals
    & Clinics
200 Hawkins Drive
Iowa City, IA 52242-1083

Teresa Daly
Emory Autism Resource Center
Department of Psychiatry
Emory University School of Medicine
718 Gatewood
Atlanta, GA 30322

K. Mark Derby, Ph.D.
Department of Special Education
Gonzaga University
AD Box 25
Spokane, WA 99258-0001

Glen Dunlap, Ph.D.
Department of Child &
    Family Studies
University of South Florida
13301 Bruce B. Downs Blvd.
Tampa, FL 33612-3899

Wayne W. Fisher
Kennedy Krieger Institute
707 North Broadway
Baltimore, MD 21205

Bud Fredericks, Ed.D.
Teaching Research
Western Oregon University
Monmouth, OR 97361

Doug Guess, Ed.D.
Life Span Institute
The University of Kansas
Lawrence, Kansas 66045

Barbara Guy, Ph.D.
Bureau of Children, Family, &
    Community Services
Iowa Department of Education
Des Moines, IA 50319

Kellie Hilker
Kennedy Krieger Institute
707 North Broadway
Baltimore, MD 21205

Robert H. Horner, Ph.D.
Specialized Training Program
University of Oregon
1235 University of Oregon
Eugene, OR 97403-1235

Brian A. Iwata, Ph.D.
Department of Psychology
The University of Florida
Gainesville, FL 32611

Susan L. Jack, M.A.
Life Span Institute, UAP
The University of Kansas at
    Parsons
Parsons, KS 67357-0738

Kathryn G. Karsh, Ed.D.
CASA of DuPage County
202 W. Willow Avenue
Wheaton, IL 60187

Lee Kern, Ph.D.
College of Education
Lehigh University
111 Research Drive
Bethlehem, PA 18015

Nancy A. Langdon, M.A.
Department of Psychology
State University of New York
Stony Brook, NY 11794-2500

Terri Lewis
Division of Gerontology and
    Geriatric Medicine
University of Alabama Medical
    School
219 Community Health Services Bldg.
Birmingham, AL 35294-2041

F. Charles Mace, Ph.D.
Children's Seashore House
3405 Civic Center Blvd.
Philadelphia, PA 19104-4302

Joyce E. Mauk
Children's Seashore House
3405 Civic Center Blvd.
Philadelphia, PA 19104

Gail G. McGee, Ph.D.
Emory Autism Resource Center
Emory University School
    of Medicine
718 Gatewood Road
Atlanta, GA 30322

Dennis D. Munk, Ed.D.
Department of Educational
    Psychology, Counseling, &
    Special Education
Northern Illinois University
De Kalb, IL 60030

Vicki Nishioka, M.A.
Work Unlimited
University of Oregon
150 SW Monroe
Corvallis, OR 97333

William O'Donohue, Ph.D.
Department of Psychology
University of Nevada, Reno
Reno, NV 89557

Stephanie M. Peck, Ph.D.
Department of Special Education
    & Rehabilitation
Utah State University
Logan, UT 84322-2865

Cathleen C. Piazza, Ph.D.
Kennedy Krieger Institute
707 North Broadway
Baltimore, MD 21205

Alan C. Repp, Ph.D.
Educational Research & Services
    Center
Northern Illinois University
DeKalb, IL 60115

Henry S. Roane, M.A.
Kennedy Krieger Institute
707 North Broadway
Baltimore, MD 21205

Sally Roberts, Ph.D.
Department of Special Education
The University of Kansas
Lawrence, Kansas 66045

Bridget A. Shore, Ph.D.
The Kennedy Krieger Institute
Pediatric Feeding Disorders Program
707 North Broadway
Baltimore, MD 21205

Richard E. Shores, Ed.D.
Life Span Institute, UAP
The University of Kansas at Parsons
Parsons, KS 67357-0738

Jeffrey R. Sprague, Ph.D.
Institute on Violence and Destructive
    Behavior
1265 University of Oregon
Eugene, OR 97403-1265

Kevin Tierney
University of Ulster
Coleraine, Northern Ireland
    BT52 1SA

H. Rutherford Turnbull, III
Department of Special Education
The University of Kansas
Lawrence, KS 66045

David P. Wacker, Ph.D.
The University of Iowa
University Hospital School
100 Hawkins Drive, Room 251
Iowa City, IA 52242-1011

Joseph H. Wehby, Ph.D.
Department of Special Education
Peabody College
Vanderbilt University
Nashville, TN 37203

Scott C. Yarbrough, M.A.
Department of Psychology
State University of New York
Stony Brook, NY 11794-2500

1

Introduction to
Functional Analysis

ALAN C. REPP
ROBERT H. HORNER

In 1934, B. F. Skinner attended a meeting of the Harvard Society of Fellows, found himself sitting next to the great mathematician and philosopher Alfred North Whitehead, and began a friendly but enthusiastic discussion of behaviorism. As they talked back and forth, Whitehead came to agree that science might be able to account for human behavior, with the exception of verbal behavior, where something else must be operative.

Whitehead ended the conversation with a friendly challenge: "Let me see you . . . account for my behavior as I sit here saying, 'No black scorpion is falling upon this table'" (Skinner, 1957, p. 457). The next day, Skinner wrote the outline for *Verbal Behavior,* near the end of which he offered a possible explanation of *why* Whitehead said those very words; and he made this guess based on what he termed a *functional analysis* of his professor's words. His analysis may be surprising to those who believe Skinner dealt only with the observable and did so only in a very sterile, experimental manner.

Instead of discussing an experiment in which he would control variables and be able to predict that Whitehead would say "a black spider is falling upon this table," or "my iced tea is warm," he attempted to explain the conditions under which Whitehead had said those particular words. This, of course, is a different and much more difficult effort, a task Skinner reasoned was considerable, but not one that could be ignored if he was trying to present a theory of human behavior.

First, he described relevant facts about the conditions under which the remarks were made: (a) the remark was emitted to make a point; (b) the remark was
meant to be problematic, precisely because it was not controlled by a present
stimulus (an antecedent); (c) the response may have been weakly determined, but
it was determined rather than free in the Freudian sense; (d) it was relevant to the
conversation; and (e) Whitehead did not agree that all human behavior was determined by outside forces.

Skinner reasoned then that the *black scorpion* meant something nonliteral; it
was a metaphorical response to the topic under discussion, and it referred to behaviorism. The word "no" was equally problematic, and Skinner addressed it in
the same way. Antecedents may have been the following: (a) Professor Whitehead
would do his best to understand Skinner's point and would interpret it in a generous way, (b) he had played a role in encouraging Skinner as a young scholar, (c)
Skinner's thinking was not typical of all young people in psychology, and (d) not
all of psychology would proffer the belief that both verbal and nonverbal behavior was determined and explained outside the skin. Therefore, no black scorpion
had fallen on the table.

Skinner's argument here was a philosophical one, as in most of his writings.
He was arguing that "cause and effect" were terms that could be replaced. "A
'cause' becomes a 'change in an independent variable' and an 'effect' a 'change in
a dependent variable.' The old 'cause and effect' connection becomes a 'functional relation.' Any condition or effect which can be shown to have an effect
must be taken into account. The behavior of the individual . . . is our 'dependent
variable'—the effect for which we are to find the cause" (Skinner, 1953, p. 35).

In his analysis of Whitehead's statement, Skinner sought the cause, but again,
he sought it not in an experimental but rather in a retrospective manner. He regarded experimentation as only one source of data for functional analysis; others
included controlled field observations (see, for example, chapters 9, 10, 11, and 12
in this book), clinical observations (see chapters 2, 3, and 7), and casual observations (Skinner, 1953).

The field of behavioral functional assessment has evolved from Skinner's many
writings, and it takes many forms, including analogue assessments, naturalistic assessments, and interviews. The characteristic it shares with general applied behavior analysis, behavior modification, or behavior therapy is that it seeks to change
behavior. However, its distinguishing characteristic is that it seeks to explain the
function of the presenting problem (such as off-task behavior) in terms of present
and past environments, and then to change the environment so that appropriate
behavior produces the same function, generally more efficiently and effectively, as
the problem behavior had been producing.

To make this point clearer, let us contrast it with two common procedures in
applied behavior analysis: overcorrection and the differential reinforcement of
other behavior (DRO). Using overcorrection with clients who frequently had
their hands in their mouths (Foxx & Azrin, 1973) or bit their hands (Barnard et
al., 1974), we might require clients to brush their teeth for an extended period
with a toothbrush that had been immersed in an oral antiseptic, and then to wipe
their lips several times with a washcloth dampened with the antiseptic. The ratio-

nale behind this procedure could be that "mouthing of objects or parts of one's body results in exposure to potentially harmful microorganisms through unhygienic oral contact" (Foxx & Azrin, 1973, p. 4). Using DRO with the same clients, we might determine the mean interval between episodes of biting, select an interval 25 percent or so smaller, provide each client a token for each of the smaller intervals in which he or she does not engage in biting, and allow the clients to exchange the tokens for favored activities (Repp & Deitz, 1975).

Using a functional assessment, we would first try to identify the conditions (setting events and antecedents) under which the biting occurred, then we would identify the consequences of biting. Having done so, we might find that biting occurred when the student could not predict what responses an upcoming task might require. An analysis of the consequences might show that problem behavior provided an escape from these unpredictable tasks, suggesting a negative reinforcement paradigm. Treatment, instead of involving a DRO program or overcorrection, would involve changing stimulus conditions associated with predictability; and we might focus on providing information to the student about the content of unfamiliar tasks or about the sequence and duration of known tasks (Flannery & Horner, 1994).

Or, analyzing the behavior of other students, we would again try to identify the conditions under which problem behavior occurred, as well as its consequences. Such an analysis might show that problem behavior occurred much more under task than under no-task conditions. However, further analysis might show that attention was 15 times more likely for problem behavior than for appropriate behavior during tasks. Thus, tasks would be serving as a discriminative stimulus for attention, suggesting a positive reinforcement hypothesis. Intervention would focus on changing reinforcement contingencies rather than on changing aspects of the task, as in Flannery and Horner (1994). Intervention would not involve a punishment procedure like overcorrection.

These two descriptions of functional analysis should demonstrate that while behaviors might be similar, and while the conditions (task presence) might be similar, a careful analysis can produce different hypotheses (negative reinforcement versus positive reinforcement) and very different interventions. Although these two studies did not show that the other hypothesis was unsuccessful (in other words, a positive reinforcement-based intervention for the first study and a negative reinforcement-based intervention for the second), an earlier study did show that contraindicated hypotheses did not generate successful interventions (Repp, Felce, & Barton, 1988).

In the last five years, there have been many studies using functional assessment procedures to change problem behavior, most or perhaps all of which are indebted to two papers. The first proposed three hypotheses for controlling self-injurious behavior (Carr, 1977); the second set the basic paradigm for an analogue functional assessment (Iwata et al., 1982). Both were with students with developmental disabilities. Most of the body of work since these papers has been with persons with developmental disabilities, and has served to validate interventions selected from a baseline assessment of the conditions under which problem behaviors occur. The purpose of this book is to present a broadened picture of functional assessment through the work of our colleagues who have moved from direct replication to systematic replication. In particular, they have shown extensions of functional assessment methodologies, procedures for better understanding the clinical process of selecting interventions, and demonstrations of the power of functional assessment applied to populations other than persons with developmental disabilities.

In the first of the three sections of the book, we have seven chapters (chapters 2 through 8) that link functional assessment to effective intervention. The first (Chapter 2, by Carr, Langdon, and Yarbrough) shows an effective procedure for staff and parents to use during assessment, one that identifies setting events, trigger stimuli, and consequences that maintain problem behavior. The second (Chapter 3 by Wacker, Cooper, Peck, Derby, and Berg) presents a method for clinicians to use in training parents and other care providers to complete analyses of both consequences of and antecedents to problem behavior. The next five chapters present some thorny problems for the field, including (a) how to predict and enhance reinforcers (Chapter 4, Piazza, Fisher, and Hilker); (b) an acknowledgment (rare to our field) that much of the behavior we treat is biologically based, and a presentation of a system for analyzing both behavioral and biological bases of problem behaviors (Chapter 5, Mace and Mauk); (c) special attention to what are the most difficult behaviors for functional analysis to address—those that are of high intensity but low frequency (Chapter 6, Sprague and Horner); (d) the problem that automatic reinforcement and private events present to the field when virtually all our studies use data from direct observation (Chapter 7, Shore and Iwata); and (e) the degree to which each of the functional assessment procedures is susceptible to threats to its reliability and validity (Chapter 8, Repp and Munk).

The second section presents five chapters (chapters 9 through 13) demonstrating functional assessment procedures in preschool and school classrooms. Topics include (a) procedures for preventing problem behaviors in preschool children (Chapter 9, McGee and Daly); (b) demonstration of assessment-based interventions for children with emotional and behavioral problems (Chapter 10, Kern and Dunlap); (c) using sequential lag analysis to assess interactions between adults and students with behavior disorders (Chapter 11, Shores, Wehby, and Jack); (d) using conditional probability tables to conduct naturalistic functional assessments of students in classrooms (Chapter 12, Repp); and (e) a review of curriculum and instructional variables that can be used to prevent or reduce problem behavior (Chapter 13, Munk and Karsh).

The third section of the book includes five chapters (chapters 14 through 18) that offer new directions for the field of functional assessment. These include (a) variations of functional assessment being used with sex offenders (Chapter 14, Fredericks and Nishioka-Evans); (b) application of functional assessment to the particular problems presented by persons with Alzheimer's disease and other age-related conditions (Chapter 15, Burgio and Lewis); (c) legal and ethical ramifications of failing to provide functional assessments (Chapter 16, Flynn, Harvey, Kaff, Sandoval, Dulek, Egnor, Mitchell, Tovar, Carter, Frey, Martin, Smith, and Turnbull); (d) implications of analyzing behavioral states rather than discrete behaviors (Chapter 17, Guess, Roberts, and Guy); and (e) considerations of what constitutes reinforcement, the sine qua non of functional assessment (Chapter 18, Tierney and O'Donohue).

Together, the chapters in this text present current advances in the use of functional assessment technology. The focus is not only on how functional assessment should be performed, but on how the resulting information should be used. As with any edited volume, the challenge is integrating the innovations of a broad body of material. To assist in this effort, we have added brief introductions to each chapter, which are intended to link chapters within sections and to highlight the unique contribution of each chapter.

We believe this book presents an expanded vision of functional assessment. Our hope is that descriptions of the basic functional assessment procedures provide those new to the field with a sound foundation in the theory, history, and techniques associated with functional assessment. The main emphasis of this book, however, is on the extension of functional analysis technology—the strategies for using functional assessment information to construct clinical interventions and extension of the contexts and conditions in which functional assessment is used. We thank our friends and colleagues for joining us in this project, and hope this combined effort proves both enjoyable and useful for the reader.

REFERENCES

Barnard, J. D., Christophersen, E. R., Altman, K., & Wolf, M. M. (1974). *Parent-mediated treatment of self-injurious behavior using overcorrection.* Paper presented at the meeting of the American Psychological Association, New Orleans.

Carr, E. G. (1977). The motivation of self-injurious behavior: A review of some hypotheses. *Psychological Bulletin, 84,* 800–816.

Flannery, K. B., & Horner, R. H. (1994). The relationship between predictability and problem behavior for students with severe disabilities. *Journal of Behavioral Education, 4,* 157–176.

Foxx, R. M., & Azrin, N. H. (1973). The elimination of autistic self-stimulatory behavior by overcorrection. *Journal of Applied Behavior Analysis, 6,* 1–4.

Iwata, B., Dorsey, M., Slifer, K., Bauman, K., & Richman, G. (1982). Toward a functional analysis of self-injury. *Analysis and Intervention in Developmental Disabilities, 2,* 3–20.

Repp, A. C., & Deitz, S. M. (1975). Reducing aggressive and self-injurious behavior of retarded children through reinforcement of other behaviors. *Journal of Applied Behavior Analysis, 7,* 313–325.

Repp, A. C., Felce, D., & Barton, L. E. (1988). Basing the treatment of stereotypic and self-abusive behaviors on hypotheses of their causes. *Journal of Applied Behavior Analysis, 21,* 281–290.

Repp, A. C., & Karsh, K. G. (1994). Hypothesis-based interventions for tantrum behaviors of persons with developmental disabilities in school settings. *Journal of Applied Behavior Analysis, 27,* 21–31.

Skinner, B. F. (1953). *Science and human behavior.* New York: Macmillan.

Skinner, B. F. (1957). *Verbal behavior.* New York: Appleton-Century-Crofts.

PART I

Linking Functional Assessment to Effective Intervention

2

Hypothesis-Based Intervention for Severe Problem Behavior

EDWARD G. CARR
NANCY A. LANGDON
SCOTT C. YARBROUGH

INTRODUCTION

This chapter begins a seven-chapter section on linking functional assessment to effective instruction. Carr's work is particularly fitting for this section, since he was the first researcher in applied behavior analysis to argue for a system in which interventionists would develop hypotheses for conditions that maintain problem behavior and then would develop interventions based on those hypotheses.

Carr, Langdon, and Yarbrough discuss functions of behavior, why most problem behaviors should not be described as "maladaptive," and methods for identifying the functions that problem behaviors serve. The method they use is functional analysis, a term they restrict to the experimental analysis of variables thought to control behavior. One example the authors provide shows how someone planning an intervention can determine which variables are worth manipulating during the intervention. The process includes (a) an interview in which the problem behavior, its triggers, and environmental reactions to it are described; (b) direct observation in a format paralleling the results of the interview; and (c) experimental manipulation in an analogue situation. Also presented are the limitations and strengths of functional analysis and assessment.

The authors then return to the logic of hypothesis-based intervention: replacing function-serving problem behavior with appropriate behavior that serves the same function. In doing so, they show the wisdom of Carr's early (1977) paper. It and this chapter show us the plan: (a) identify the setting events, the trigger stimuli, and the consequences that maintain the problem behavior; (b) develop the hypothesis; and (c) base intervention on the hypothesis. Despite the straightforwardness of the approach in the abstract, the authors set the stage for further study and procedural development by describing the difficulty in understanding complex, interacting environments.

When the famous American novelist Henry James was asked to comment on the even more famous Norwegian playwright Henrik Ibsen, he said, "His subject is always, like the subjects of all first-rate men, primarily an idea." James's comment is equally applicable to B. F. Skinner and operant behaviorism. Here, the quintessential idea, in lay terms, is that behavior has a purpose (Skinner, 1974). Deprive behaviorism of its focus on purpose and it becomes a mundane technology (Carr et al., 1990). Imbue it with functionalism (another name for purpose), and it becomes an elegant and pragmatic philosophy of human behavior (Carr, 1993).

As operant behaviorists, we eschew the use of mentalistic terms such as purpose and related terms such as intent, motivation, and goals. Instead, we prefer to speak about the variables of which behavior is a function, and we call our method for identifying these variables functional analysis. Skinner (1974) recognized that operant behaviorism was, in essence, the scientific analysis of intents, motivations, goals, and purposes. While remaining true to the root idea of behaviorism, as functional analysts we focus our efforts on understanding the function (purpose) of problem behavior. This chapter is about the methods used to achieve this understanding and the logical ways in which understanding leads to intervention.

WHICH FUNCTIONS ARE SERVED BY PROBLEM BEHAVIOR?

Problem behavior is typically not maladaptive, even though for the past three decades much published work in the area of behavior modification has described it as such. A maladaptive behavior is one that fails to provide the individual displaying it with any advantages. In fact, most instances of aggression and self-injury, for example, produce observable benefits for the people exhibiting these behaviors. Sometimes problem behavior evokes attention, nurturance, and comfort from others (Carr & McDowell, 1980; Lovaas et al., 1965; Martin & Foxx, 1973). Sometimes it helps individuals escape or avoid difficult, boring, or arduous tasks (Carr & Newsom, 1985; Carr et al., 1976, 1980). Sometimes it helps provide individuals with access to desirable tangible items and preferred activities (Derby et al., 1992; Durand & Crimmins, 1988). Finally, problem behavior may also generate sensory reinforcement, including visual, auditory, tactile, and even gustatory stimulation (Favell, McGimsey, & Schell, 1982; Rincover et. al., 1979; Rincover & Devany, 1982).

Attention seeking, task avoidance, tangible seeking, and sensory reinforcement have been the four functions most frequently described and studied in the literature to date. However, other functions have also been identified or postulated. For example, for some individuals aggression and self-injury may function to help them avoid or terminate social interactions (Taylor & Carr, 1992a, 1992b). Self-injury may also function as a form of self-addicting behavior, in that each episode of self-injury results in the release of endogenous opiates into the bloodstream, effectively producing a biological "high" (Cataldo & Harris, 1982; Sandman, 1991). Some instances of problem behavior may not even be operants. Data from animal learning experiments suggest that aggression (Azrin et al., 1964) and self-injury (Gluck et al., 1985) may sometimes function as respondents that are elicited by painful stimuli.

Certainly we have not yet identified all the purposes that problem behavior may serve, but neither have we fully realized the additional intervention opportunities that have developed as a consequence of our having identified new functions of problem behavior (Bailey & Pyles, 1989). Similarly, much empirical evidence, both systematic and anecdotal, suggests that three functions of problem behavior—namely, escape, attention seeking, and tangible or activity seeking—account for a substantial majority of problem behavior episodes related to aggression and self-injury. For this reason, we shall focus on these three functions of problem behavior.

HOW ARE FUNCTIONS IDENTIFIED?

There are three methods for identifying the functions that problem behavior serves: functional analysis, direct observation, and interview. The process of functional analysis is analogous to performing an experiment. That is, the person carrying out the experiment systematically arranges for certain situations to take place in order to determine whether problem behavior occurs consistently in those situations and not in others. In contrast, interview and direct observation are nonexperimental in nature. The assessor does not systematically arrange situations in order to see whether problem behavior is present or absent. Interview and direct observation are collectively referred to in the literature as functional assessment rather than functional analysis to highlight the fact that only the latter term involves systematic manipulation of the environment.

Traditionally, an interview consists of the person who is doing the assessment asking classroom staff, group home staff, or family members to describe the nature of the problem behavior in detail, the circumstances that triggered the onset of the problem behavior, and the reactions that such behavior evokes from others when it occurs. Sometimes the interview process involves the use of highly structured questionnaires and rating scales (e.g., Durand & Crimmins, 1988; O'Neill et al., 1990) rather than a more conversational format, but the type of information gathered is the same.

In direct observation, the assessor closely watches the individual of interest, often for a period of several weeks or more. During this time, the individual is carefully and directly observed in a variety of typical daily life situations (as opposed to analogues or simulations), particularly in those situations that were identified in the interview process as being associated with problem behavior. Let us now examine each method in turn.

Functional Analysis

As noted earlier, functional analysis is similar to experimentation. The critical feature of an experiment is that the person doing the experiment manipulates each factor that is thought to contribute to the occurrence of the problem behavior. For example, in a study by Carr, Newsom, and Binkoff (1980), teachers identified two children diagnosed with retardation whose aggressive behavior appeared to be an escape-motivated response to academic demands. To verify the notion that the purpose of the aggressive behavior was to escape from task demands, researchers needed to demonstrate two things: (a) that task demands, per se, triggered the onset of aggressive behavior and (b) that when a teacher responded to aggression by withdrawing demands, the aggressive behavior increased in frequency.

Consider Figure 2.1. For Bob, the task was merely sitting in a chair in preparation for academic work; for Sam, the task was practicing buttoning. In each case, demands were associated with high rates of aggressive behavior, whereas the absence of demands was associated with little or no aggression. By manipulating the presence versus absence of demands, researchers were able to demonstrate experimentally that demands, per se, functioned as a trigger for aggressive behavior, thereby meeting the first requirement for establishing the escape-motivated nature of the aggressive behavior.

Consider Figure 2.2. When the teacher responded to Bob's aggressive behavior by not permitting him to leave his seat (EXT), the aggressive behavior repeatedly declined to or remained at low levels. In contrast, when the teacher permitted Bob to leave his seat contingent on episodes of aggression (NEG RFT), aggression increased to high levels. By manipulating whether or not the teacher permitted Bob to escape from having to remain seated, the experimenters were able to demonstrate that withdrawal of demands (to be seated) contingent on aggressive behavior was a powerful response consequence that exacerbated the problem behavior. In this manner, they met the second requirement for demonstrating that aggression was an escape-motivated behavior.

One question that practitioners (and many scientists) repeatedly raise concerns how one would know in advance which variables are worth manipulating when carrying out a functional analysis. Thus, in the example given, how would one know that demands per se functioned as triggers for aggression, and that therefore the aggressive behavior was likely to be escape motivated? Likewise, how would one know whether to focus on attention or tangibles in a functional analysis? The answer to these questions lies in the fact that teachers told researchers that demands (in the case of Bob and Sam) appeared to be an important factor. In other words, information derived from interviews is typically the initial basis for developing hypotheses about the purpose of problem behavior.

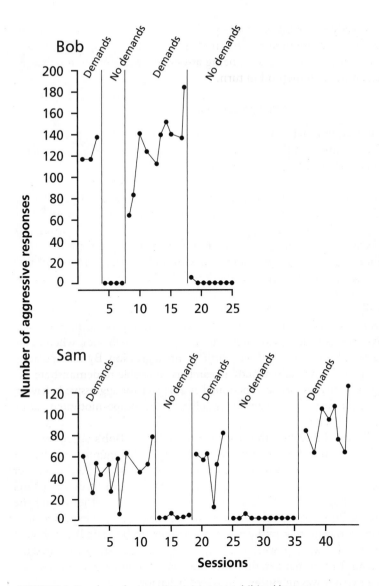

FIGURE 2.1 Number of aggressive responses exhibited by two children with intellectual disabilities during periods in which learning tasks were presented (demands) or withheld (no demands).

SOURCE: Carr, Newsom, & Binkoff, 1980. Copyright 1980 by the Society for the Experimental Analysis of Behavior. Reprinted by permission.

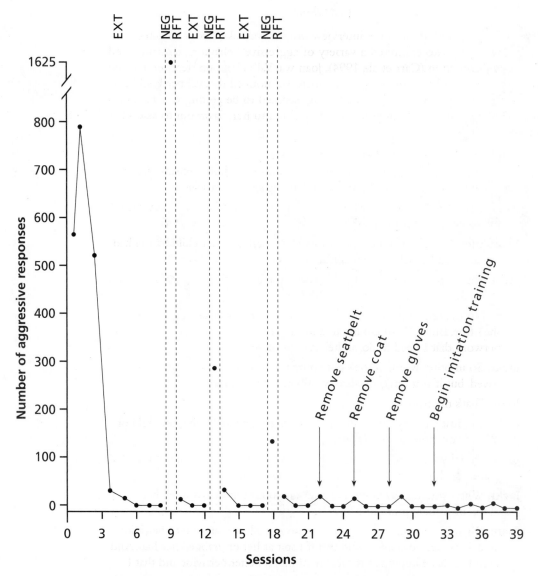

FIGURE 2.2 Number of aggressive responses per hour during several experimental conditions. During extinction (EXT), the child was not permitted to leave the demand situation contingent on aggressive behavior. During negative reinforcement (NEG RFT), the child was allowed to leave the demand situation contingent on fixed numbers of aggressive responses. From sessions 22 to 39, EXT remained in effect while the experimenter faded out his protective clothing and faded in increasingly greater numbers of imitative demands.

SOURCE: Carr, Newsom, & Binkoff, 1980. Copyright 1980 by the Society for the Experimental Analysis of Behavior. Reprinted by permission.

Interview

The following illustration of the interview process was taken from long-term research with Val, who exhibited a variety of aggressive behaviors, tantrums, and property destruction (Carr et al., 1994). Joan was Val's classroom teacher. During the first few months of the school year, Joan had noticed that Val behaved inappropriately many times each day, and things seemed to be getting worse. Therefore, Joan invited the school psychologist, Jacki, into her classroom to assess the problem. The interview went as follows:

Jacki: What is it that Val does that upsets you?

Joan: She's very disruptive and mean to the other children. Actually, she's a sweet kid, but sometimes I think she's being spiteful or jealous.

Jacki: There are lots of ways of being disruptive and mean. Would you give me some specific examples?

Joan: Sure, Val will scream or spit at me. She'll grab another child by the hair or throw all her schoolwork off her desk.

Jacki: You mentioned before that Val was sometimes spiteful or jealous. When does she act this way? All the time?

Joan: No, no, not all the time. If I'm working with her or talking with her, she's fine. But if I start talking to another child or get busy with some paperwork that I need to do, all hell will break loose.

Jacki: So in other words, if she's got your attention, she's pretty well behaved, but if you can't socialize with her, she gets angry.

Joan: That's the truth.

Jacki: I'm just curious. When she does get angry and grabs another child or spits at you, how do you react?

Joan: I'll tell you. I don't tolerate it. I lay down the law and let her know that that is not how a young lady acts in my classroom!

Jacki: When you say "lay down the law," do you mean that you tell her "No," or is there more to it?

Joan: Oh, much more. I tell her that we do not allow that kind of behavior here. I ask her how she would feel if I spit at her or grabbed her hair. And I tell her that I know she is capable of much better behavior and that I expect her to act more grown up from now on.

Jacki: How long do you talk to her like this?

Joan: Oh, not long, maybe three or four minutes.

Jacki: What is Val's reaction to all this?

Joan: Well, that's the thing that bothers me the most. Very often, she simply becomes silly and starts laughing or making funny faces at me, and then I have to lay down the law again.

Jacki: So, in fact, once Val gets off on the wrong track, you might be talking to her for much longer than three or four minutes. That must be tiring after a while.

Joan: Yes, that's why I invited you here.

Jacki: Okay, this was helpful. I have a better idea now of what's going on. Since you mentioned that there are quite a few other times when Val goes off, I'd like to talk to you about those times as well. When we're done, though, I'd like to hang out in your classroom at various times during the next two weeks so that I can observe things more directly. That will give me a much better idea of what you and Val are going through, and it will also help me to get a sense of the day-to-day routine here.

The interview, like all methods of functional assessment and analysis, focuses on three topics: a description of the problem behavior, the triggers for the problem behavior, and the reaction the problem behavior evokes from others. Traditionally, this approach has been referred to as an A–B–C (antecedents-behaviors-consequences) approach. However, by focusing on the social antecedents and social consequences of problem behavior, we wish to highlight the social role of most instances of aggression, self-injury, property destruction, and tantrums, thereby underscoring the point that the purposes of problem behavior are typically to be found in their effectiveness in influencing others to provide desired reinforcers, both positive and negative.

A few clarifying points concerning the interview are in order. First, from the standpoint of generating useful hypotheses about the purpose of Val's aggression, subjective value judgments (such as Val is "spiteful" and "jealous") are of no use because different people interpret these terms differently. There would be no way of knowing what the actual problem is, since one teacher may refer to spitting as jealous behavior, whereas a different teacher may refer to sarcastic comments as jealous behavior. No meaningful communication between intervention agents is possible until everyone is referring to the same problem behavior. That is why Jacki, the school psychologist, pressed Joan, the teacher, to translate the subjective terms (spitefulness, jealousy) into more concrete descriptors (screaming, spitting). Second, the social triggers (antecedents) must be identified in the interview. The best approach, and the one taken by Jacki, identifies social triggers for nonproblem (appropriate) behavior ("If I'm working with her . . . she's fine") as well as problem behavior ("But if I start talking to another student . . . all hell will break loose"). Identifying social triggers provides the first clues leading to hypotheses about purpose. Thus, if Val is well behaved when Joan interacts with her but poorly behaved when she does not, then it seems probable that Val's problem behavior is related to how much attention she is receiving during a given time period. If so, pursuing the issue of social reactions, as Jacki did, is appropriate. That is, Jacki began to hypothesize that Val's misbehavior may have been attention seeking. Therefore, one would expect that such behavior should influence Joan to pay more attention to Val. Jacki seized upon this possibility and questioned Joan about how she responded to Val's aggression. When Joan responded that she made lengthy speeches chastising Val contingent on Val's poor behavior, Jacki was able to see a corroborating link between the social trigger for aggression (too little attention) and the social reaction to it (much attention). In this manner, Jacki's tentative hypotheses concerning the role of attention became more certain.

From interviews, it is possible to derive many hypotheses concerning what purpose behaviors such as self-injury and aggression may serve for an individual in a given situation. Frequently, we can use the interview information in order to move directly to the design of effective interventions. However, there are at least three reasons for continuing the assessment process by carrying out direct observations as well: (a) direct observation typically generates more detailed information about the triggers and social reactions for problem behavior, which proves useful in comprehensive intervention planning; (b) the information derived from interviews sometimes proves to be inaccurate; and (c) direct observation occasionally reveals controlling variables that were overlooked during the interview.

Direct Observation

Let us continue with the example involving Val. Jacki followed up on her interview by visiting Joan's classroom for about an hour a day over a two-week period, during which she made a series of direct observations. She scattered her observations over all of the major situations that made up the classroom routine. Importantly, Jacki used the information from the interview to help guide her in selecting situations in which her observational efforts might prove the most fruitful. Thus, since Joan had told her that Val was especially likely to act up when Joan was busy with her own work or was talking to someone else, Jacki made sure to observe these situations when she visited the classroom. Figure 2.3 shows what Jacki found.

Note first that Jacki used a simple approach for recording information: She wrote down her observations on index cards using a narrative format that exactly paralleled the types of information gathered during the interview, namely, interpersonal context, behavior problem, and social reaction. In this way, Jacki was able to check quickly on the accuracy of the information obtained during the interview. Consider the top index card in Figure 2.3. Recall that during the interview, Joan had told Jacki that Val was especially likely to misbehave when Joan was talking to another student. The index card narrative shows that in fact Val did misbehave when Joan turned her attention away from Val to another student (interpersonal context). Further, Joan paid a lot of attention to Val contingent on her aggression (social reaction). Thus, direct observation appeared to confirm what Jacki had learned during the interview, namely, that Val's aggressive behavior probably served the purpose of attention seeking. The middle card in Figure 2.3 also shows a pattern of attention seeking; when Joan turned her attention away from Val to talk to a male teacher, Val again became aggressive. Finally, the bottom index card shows that when Joan was busy doing paperwork and unable to attend to Val, Val attacked another student. In each episode, Val's aggressive behavior caused one or more adults to give her their undivided attention for a period of time.

The three situations just described were not the only ones in which Val's problem behavior appeared to serve an attention-seeking function. Prolonged observation of Val eventually produced 108 problem behavior situations (all noted on index cards) involving attention. Furthermore, Val, like most people with disabilities, did not misbehave solely to get attention. In 21 additional situations, her aggression appeared to serve an escape function, and 5 more involved tangible seeking and activity seeking.

Name:	Val	Observer:	Jacki	Date:	11/12/87
General Context:	Group instruction	Time:	10:00 AM		

Interpersonal context: Joan was asking each child in turn to identify some pictures from a magazine and to tell a story about each one.

Behavior problem: Val knocked the magazine out of Joan's hand and yelled "You're stupid" to the child who had been speaking.

Social reaction: Joan angrily told Val to pick up the magazine and tried to make her apologize to the other child. When Val refused, Joan persisted for approximately 7 minutes in her efforts to get an apology.

Name:	Val	Observer:	Jacki	Date:	11/18/87
General Context:	Recess	Time:	1:45 PM		

Interpersonal context: The children were sitting on the grass near the playing field or walking around the courtyard. Joan was standing at the doorway talking to a male teacher.

Behavior problem: Val ran up to the male teacher and yelled "Hey, nubbie!" in his face. When Joan tried to intercede, Val grabbed Joan's shirt sleeve and ripped it in the struggle that followed.

Social reaction: Joan severely berated Val for about 5 minutes, telling her that she should not interrupt when people were talking to one another and that she should apologize for tearing her shirt. The male teacher repeated many of Joan's comments to Val.

Name:	Val	Observer:	Jacki	Date:	11/19/87
General Context:	Lunch	Time:	12:00 PM		

Interpersonal context: Val was seated at the lunch table with the other children. Joan was busy putting the finishing touches on some birthday cupcakes in honor of one of the children.

Behavior problem: Val suddenly yelled "I'm not hungry." When Joan turned around and made eye contact, Val pulled the hair of the birthday child while staring at Joan. As Joan approached Val to protect the other child, Val spit at Joan, cursed repeatedly, and tried to scratch Joan several times.

Social reaction: Joan pried Val's fingers off the other child and told Val that she had better start acting more grown up or nobody would want to be her friend. This theme continued for about 8 minutes.

FIGURE 2.3 Direct observation of Val's problem behavior using an index card narrative format.

SOURCE: Carr et al., 1994. Reprinted by permission.

At first, the vast amount of information concerning problem situations derived from direct observation may appear overwhelming. However, certain themes pertaining to problem behavior typically recur. Consider the 108 index cards related to Val's attention seeking. In examining these cards carefully, we found that all but five cards fell into just four themes. Specifically, 36 cards pertained to situations in which Val's performance of independent work or an activity acted as a trigger for attention-seeking aggression. In addition, 34 cards concerned situations in which the teacher turned away from Val to talk to a male adult, with the result that Val aggressed. In 25 instances, aggression appeared to be triggered when Val was required to participate in a group activity with little one-on-one attention from the teacher. Finally, eight cards described situations in which Val had to make a transition from one activity to another. The transition triggered aggressive behavior, behavior that was almost invariably followed by a large amount of attention (coaxing, pleading, scolding, and bribing) from staff members, particularly males. Thus, direct observation not only provided detailed information about the triggers for and social reactions to aggression and other problem behaviors, but also enabled the assessor to examine all the problematic situations for recurring common themes. The result was that only a small number of interventions needed to be developed, each uniquely tailored to a given theme. For example, consider the 25 situations centering on the theme of group activities. Since Val misbehaved whenever the teacher turned her attention to another student, one element of intervention involved teaching Val to ask for attention. However, since it was a group situation, Val also needed to learn to wait her turn prior to requesting attention, that is, to tolerate delayed reinforcement. The detailed direct observations outlined on the 25 index cards suggested that an intervention plan consisting of communication training, coupled with training to tolerate delay of reinforcement, would be an efficient way to deal with the group instruction theme, which was a basic element in all 25 situations.

There are two common reasons why interview information is sometimes inaccurate: (a) the interviewee describes the social reactions inaccurately and (b) the motivation (purpose) of the problem behavior changes over time. Consider the first reason. Teachers and caretakers are sometimes embarrassed to admit, for instance, that they capitulate to escape-motivated aggression. Thus, when parents are asked how they react when their child bites herself in the middle of a presumably aversive task, they answer that they make their daughter complete the task; under no circumstance do they allow her to get out of doing the required work. A direct observation shows, however, that that the parents do in fact allow their daughter to escape, contingent on aggression. Parents and teachers may not be aware of their social reactions. For example, during an interview, they may report that they ignore a child's attention-seeking aggressive behavior, when the reverse may commonly be true. For example, an adult may say, "Val, I am not going to talk to you any more as long as you are spitting. That's a terrible thing for a young lady to do. How would you like it if I did that to you? I know you can behave much better, and until you do, I'm not going to pay any attention to you." This speech does not constitute a form of ignoring, but rather is an example of the kind of one-on-one interaction that attention-seeking children often crave. Direct observation proves crucial in checking the validity or, as in this case, the invalidity of interview information.

The second reason for the inaccuracy of interviews pertains to the possibility of shifts in motivation (purpose) over time. One child with whom we worked was initially assessed as being tangible seeking in a supermarket situation. He would grab his favorite food item while waiting in line at the cash register and rip it open and consume it. If prevented from doing so, he immediately became highly aggressive. An intervention was designed that replaced such behaviors with more constructive ones. However, several months later, problem behavior began to recur. Additional direct observation showed that the purpose of the aggression had changed. The mother was so happy with the success of the first intervention that she began to shop for longer and longer periods with her son. Originally, mother and son had engaged in a brief shopping expedition, and the cashier took only a few minutes to ring up the goods and bag them. However, several months later, the number of goods purchased had become large, and the cashier took a long time to complete her work. Close direct observation showed that the child no longer tore up food packages in order to eat them. Instead, he now aggressed because waiting in line was aversive to him. There was a shift in the motivation of aggression from tangible seeking to escape seeking. Therefore, there needed to be a corresponding shift in the nature of the intervention. This example highlights a critical issue in assessment: When aspects of an individual's life change (such as work, educational activities, staff, living situations, or social relationships), as they are certain to do over time, additional functional assessments need to be carried out, because problem behavior may serve new purposes that help the individual to adjust to changing life circumstances. Assessment is not an activity that is carried out once at the beginning of an intervention; rather, it is an ongoing activity that is carried out repeatedly over time as changing conditions warrant.

The third reason we should follow up an interview with direct observation is that direct observation occasionally reveals controlling variables that were overlooked during the interview. Once again, consider Val. Months after the initial interview and observation, further direct observations were made on a day on which Val's teacher was ill and a substitute teacher had taken her place. The substitute teacher decided to ask Val to do the laundry, a task selected for Val because of plans to place her in a community residence. Val responded to the task with aggressive outbursts. When the regular teacher returned, she was asked why she had not mentioned the problem with the laundry task during the initial interview. She responded that she had long ago dropped this task because it was associated with aggressive outbursts. This example illustrates an important point that is often overlooked in carrying out assessments: Individuals with disabilities often change the behavior of others in more or less permanent ways as a consequence of their problem behavior (Carr et al., 1991; Taylor & Romanczyk, 1994). Val "taught" her teacher that any effort to make Val do the laundry would result in her having to deal with prolonged and serious bouts of aggressive behavior. Therefore, the teacher dropped the task from the curriculum. Since the task was no longer part of the curriculum at the time of the initial interview, it is hardly surprising that Val's teacher did not mention it. Frequently, severe problem behaviors of people with disabilities cause others to alter many aspects of day-to-day routines by dramatically modifying them or dropping them all together as a strategy for preventing misbehavior. These alterations may, therefore, not arise as topics during the interview, hence the necessity for long-term, ongoing direct observation. These routines are likely to be reintroduced from time to time for various reasons, thereby permitting the detection and assessment of those problem behaviors that reemerge.

STRENGTHS AND LIMITATIONS
OF FUNCTIONAL
ANALYSIS AND ASSESSMENT

Each of the three methods that we have discussed is, in principle, capable of generating hypotheses concerning the purposes of problem behavior. However, the value of each method is constrained by the circumstances under which it is carried out. Let us examine these circumstances.

Without a doubt, functional analysis constitutes the most powerful tool for identifying the purpose of problem behavior. This is so because the sources of variance are controlled experimentally, thereby permitting strong statements about which factors evoke and maintain problem behavior (that is, which factors are causal). Unfortunately, to isolate specific controlling variables, we often have to decontextualize the experimental environment. It is not possible to permit the myriad antecedent, consequent, and setting event variables that are present in the natural environments of home, school, and community to operate at the time of the analysis. The presence of multiple interacting variables would make identifying specific functions ambiguous. Therefore, in a typical functional analysis the situation is analogous in nature—it represents a simulation of the natural environment (Carr & Durand, 1985; Iwata et al., 1982). On the other hand, a simulation makes it possible to determine unambiguously whether problem behavior is a function of certain generic classes of controlling variables, such as positive reinforcement (for example, attention, tangibles) and negative reinforcement (for example, escape from tasks). Often a simulation is similar enough to the natural environment so that identifying generic classes of controlling variables leads to the development of interventions that are effective in the natural environment. For example, a child who is misbehaving in a classroom teaching situation is examined in a simulated teaching situation, and results show that the child's problem behavior is escape motivated. Interventions designed to deal with escape factors are developed and introduced in the classroom and the child's problem behavior is subsequently eliminated.

Sometimes the simulation represented by the functional analysis situation fails to identify the full range of controlling variables, so planning an intervention is hampered. For instance, in the teaching example just given, the functional analysis demonstrated the central role of negative reinforcement. The purpose of the problem behavior was to escape from demands. But does the analysis go far enough to enable effective treatment planning? Specifically, what is the individual trying to escape from (Horner, 1994)? In the natural environment, it could be the physical effort involved in responding to the demands, or the repetitiveness of the demands, or the corrective procedures used (such as negative feedback or physical prompts), or the person who is presenting the demands (such as a favorite teacher versus a disliked teacher). While negative reinforcement is involved with each of these factors, the functional analysis may nonetheless be inadequate, even though it is generically accurate. From the standpoint of treatment planning, it is important to know whether someone is escaping from physical effort or from certain corrective procedures. In the former case, one might modify the task to attenuate the amount of labor involved (at least initially). In the latter case, one might discontinue the use of negative feedback or substitute an imitative prompt for the physical prompts. The point is that generic functional analyses may themselves have to be followed up with additional analyses that provide information specific enough to enable detailed intervention planning. There is a growing recognition that functional analysis simulations may fail to adequately identify critical controlling variables (Carr, 1994; Horner, 1994; Iwata et al., 1990; Mace, 1994).

The prospect of having to carry out multiple functional analyses that progressively hone in on relevant factors is daunting in terms of both personnel and time expended. Equally daunting is the prospect that the present approach to functional analysis may fail altogether to sample entire classes of controlling variables. For example, the players in a typical simulation are the experimenter and the person being assessed: a dyad. Yet the real world is not composed solely of dyads. Consider a study by Taylor et al. (1993) involving the attention-seeking behavior of a young girl diagnosed as retarded. Low levels of adult attention sometimes occasioned problem behavior. However, the specifics of the social context emerged as the critical factor. In one context, the adult limited her attention by speaking to another child. In a second context, the adult limited her attention by speaking to another adult. Problem behavior occurred in the second context but not in the first. The problem behavior could only be fully understood when it was examined within a triadic context. The traditional dyadic simulation would have failed to identify the controlling variables and would, therefore, not have been useful as a guide for intervention planning.

Parallel cases emerge in the domain of negative reinforcement. For example, Patterson (1982) noted a relationship between teasing and aggression. If an adult and child are interacting, no aggression may be evident. However, if another child is added to the social situation and the second child teases the first, then the first may become aggressive. Here again, since the traditional dyadic simulation does not include the presence of other children, important negative reinforcement relationships would not have been identified, and intervention planning might have been compromised.

The fact that functional analysis simulations may fail to identify or sample the full range of controlling variables is not an indictment of functional analysis. Both of the examples just described could have been (and have been) subjected to rigorous functional analyses that led to usable information for planning interventions. The real issue is how one knows in advance which variables are worthy of examining by means of a functional analysis. The answer is that a combination of interview and direct observation is almost always necessary to generate meaningful hypotheses about the purpose of problem behavior, hypotheses that can later, if necessary, be tested within the framework of a functional analysis.

Sometimes, functional assessment consisting of interview or direct observation can generate hypotheses that can be used to plan successful interventions (Carr et al., 1994; Carr & Carlson, 1993; Dunlap et al., 1991; Repp et al., 1988). In the Carr et al. (1994) approach, direct observation consisted of the use of an index card narrative format. This format allowed examiners to deduce hypotheses concerning the purposes of problem behavior in various situations, and the hypotheses, in turn, led to the design of successful treatment interventions. Success was achieved in the absence of formal functional analysis. The narrative approach to direct observation is, in our experience, the one most commonly used by practitioners. However, adopting a more formal approach to direct observation— namely, a descriptive analysis—is also possible and sometimes desirable. By descriptive analysis we mean that data are taken using traditional measures of frequency, rate, and time sampling (rather than a narrative format) to generate a systematic profile of the antecedents and consequences of problem behavior. Investigators have used this assessment method to generate hypotheses about purpose, which have led to the development of successful treatment interventions (Carr & Carlson, 1993; Dunlap et al.,1991; Repp et al., 1988).

Given the limitations of functional analysis already discussed and given that functional assessment often leads to successful treatment outcomes in the absence of functional analysis, has functional analysis become an unnecessary procedure? The short answer to this question is "No." Functional analysis avoids some of the assessment difficulties stemming from child effects discussed earlier. Researchers can reintroduce situations that intervention agents had previously eliminated to determine whether these situations are indeed problematical. Functional analysis will always remain the primary tool that researchers have for demonstrating causal relationships. To make compelling demonstrations concerning cause-effect relationships, particularly in novel relationships, there is simply no known substitute for functional analysis. However, once researchers have demonstrated significant and noteworthy relationships, the question remains whether future practitioners must demonstrate, once again, those relationships that have already been rigorously identified by prior research. The purpose of research is analysis. The purpose of clinical practice is synthesis. The job of researchers is to identify for the rest of the world why problem behavior occurs and which variables are important in determining such behavior. It is the job of practitioners to sift through this large body of information, pulling out those elements that seem pertinent to the situation at hand, and then integrating (synthesizing) the relevant elements into a cohesive, functionally defined program of intervention.

We should not ask every practitioner to be a researcher; if we do, most will refuse. Why? First, because functional analysis requires a level and depth of training that relatively few practitioners have. Second, because the natural world (unlike the world of the laboratory) contains problem behavior that is under the sequential and concurrent control of multiple and often idiosyncratic antecedents, consequences, and setting events that do not easily lend themselves to the decontextualized, reductionistic analogues that are the hallmark of laboratory demonstrations. Third, because if intervention is unsuccessful, a systematic experimental analysis of the problem situation can later be carried out to definitively identify those variables that would be most fruitful in helping to design hypothesis-driven interventions.

Having made an argument against the overuse of functional analysis in clinical intervention planning, we must note that functional assessment has serious problems of its own that are as yet unresolved. Foremost among these problems is the fact that the results of descriptive analyses are sometimes not corroborated by the results of subsequent functional analyses (Lerman & Iwata, 1993; Mace & Lalli, 1991). Suppose that a situation is described in considerable detail and a hypothesis is derived that a particular set of problem behaviors is escape motivated. However, when systematic manipulations are later made as part of a functional analysis, the hypothesis is disconfirmed—the problem behavior is not demonstrated to be escape motivated.

Importantly, though, sometimes the two methods—assessment and analysis—do yield a convergence of results (Arndorfer et al., 1994; Dunlap et al., 1991; Lalli et al., 1993; Sasso et al., 1992). When is this likely to happen? The most promising research to date suggests that when both descriptive and experimental situations share many of the same stimulus features, the results obtained from examining problem behavior in the assessment stage are likely to be corroborated by the results obtained from examining problem behavior in the analysis stage. In other words, the best strategy for ensuring the ability to generalize hypotheses from descriptive analysis to experimental analysis and, more importantly, from experimental analysis to natural situations, is to be certain that relevant stimulus parameters are shared by the various situations under study. For example, a descriptive analysis carried out in the natural situation of the home may suggest that a child's aggression is maintained by maternal attention, but only when other siblings are present. If an experimental analogue is constructed in which attention is provided by a stranger who has no prior relationship with the child and if siblings are absent during the analysis, then we should not be surprised when the functional analysis fails to corroborate the descriptive analysis. On the other hand, if the relevant stimulus elements from the home (in this case, maternal presence and presence of siblings) are retained in the analogue, then we may find good corroboration. An excellent example of this strategy has been articulated by Wacker and his colleagues in their approach to outpatient functional analysis (Northup et al., 1991; Steege et al., 1989; Wacker & Steege, 1993). These investigators do not rely on preestablished analogue conditions for their evaluations. Rather, the experimental conditions are designed to reflect relevant contextual variables from the natural environment (such as current school tasks, domestic living activities, and vocational concerns). Hypotheses derived from these functional analyses are typically useful in designing effective interventions for use in the natural environment. While the convergence between functional assessment (descriptive analysis) and functional analysis is most likely to occur to the extent that they are based on situations that share multiple stimulus parameters, this convergence continues to be heuristic.

WHERE DO HYPOTHESIS-BASED ANALYSIS AND ASSESSMENT LEAD?

The end product of the analytic and assessment practices that we have been discussing is a hypothesis about the purpose (function) of the problem behavior being examined. The hypothesis statement, in turn, leads to ideas about what would constitute a plausible intervention. Within this functionalist perspective, plausible intervention never consists of simply eliminating the problem behavior. If problem behavior serves a purpose for the individual displaying it, then the intervention must provide him or her with an alternative means for achieving the purpose served by the problem behavior, thereby undermining the necessity for exhibiting the behavior as a way of influencing others. Hypothesis-based intervention thus leads inevitably to educational strategies that focus on replacing problem behavior with new, constructive behavior that better allow the individual to achieve his or her goals (Goldiamond, 1974).

Problem behavior typically serves many purposes. A person may be aggressive at home to get the attention of a parent, aggressive at school to escape academic demands, and aggressive in the supermarket to gain access to desired tangible items. Because a hypothesis-based approach usually leads to the conclusion that many different purposes are served by problem behavior, this approach also leads to the conclusion that intervention must have multiple components. Rarely is there a single, universal intervention (for example, time out, differential reinforcement of other behavior, or functional communication training) that can address all the purposes of an individual's problem behavior in all the different situations in which the problem behavior occurs. We made this point earlier when we described the index card format used in direct observation. Recall that Val showed attention-seeking problem behavior in 108 different situations, and that with only five exceptions these situations could be collapsed into just four themes involving independent work, male attention, group activities, and transitions. No single intervention could be used to address the 103 situations represented by the four themes, even though all of them were hypothesized to be based on attention seeking. Instead, each theme was addressed with an array of interventions tailored to the unique situational parameters that characterized the theme. Thus, the group activity situation was dealt with by teaching Val to request attention from the teacher (functional communication training), but only after Val had waited for her turn and the teacher was not busy (building tolerance for delayed reinforcement). This intervention strategy was not used to address the transitions theme. Here, the problem centered on Val's misbehaving when asked to terminate one activity (gym) and begin a new one (regular classroom). Val's aggression in this case was regularly followed by much male attention (for example, coaxing and pleading with Val to pick herself up off the floor where she had purposely fallen down, screaming and flailing). The strategy used to deal with this theme involved choice making. That is, school policy required Val to be accompanied from one location (the gym) to the other (the regular classroom) during transitions. Rather than waiting for Val to misbehave to get male attention, the staff hit upon the strategy of encouraging her to choose her favorite male to accompany her from one location to the other. Further, Val was taught to choose favorite topics of conversation with that male. In other words, making choices rather than demonstrating aggressiveness now consistently produced large amounts of preferred male attention. Each of the other two themes was similarly associated with its own unique intervention configuration. Since Val's aggressive behavior served several different attention-seeking functions, intervention strategies were designed that addressed the unique features of each attention-getting theme, thereby producing a multicomponent approach, an approach that contained still more components once additional escape and tangible themes were identified for Val.

EMERGING ISSUES IN
FUNCTIONAL ANALYSIS AND
ASSESSMENT: SETTING EVENTS

Let us consider the escape-motivated problem behavior that occurs in the presence of academic demands. Typically, one finds that demands do not evoke problem behavior to the same degree each day. On some days, there may be no aggression, whereas on other days aggression may occur at extremely high levels. Clearly, one would draw entirely different conclusions about the nature (purpose) of the problem behavior depending on which days one was observing. What is going on here? The answer is that broader influences on problem behavior are occurring outside of the specific analytic or assessment situation itself. These broader influences are referred to as *setting events* (Bijou & Baer, 1961). Setting events include those variables that alter ongoing stimulus-response relationships, for example, the relationship between a discriminative stimulus, such as a task demand, and the responses that that demand evokes, such as aggression versus compliance.

There are three categories of setting events: *physical, biological,* and *social* (Gardner & Sovner, 1994). Although these variables are only now beginning to be thoroughly investigated, no analysis or assessment is complete until their influence has been measured. Effective intervention planning also appears to depend on the full identification of setting event factors.

An example of a physical setting event is noise. Many children with autism, for example, are very sensitive to loud noises. Envision a situation in which a young girl with autism places her hands over her ears to minimize the aversiveness of a noisy classroom. If, during instruction, the teacher told the child to put her hands down so as to hear the instruction better, the child would be exposed, once again, to the high noise level. In this circumstance, the girl may become aggressive. On the other hand, if the teacher tolerated the girl's holding her hands over her ears, the girl would probably show no aggression. Here, noise is a setting event that determines whether or not an instructional demand evokes aggressive behavior.

An example of a biological setting event is the flu. If the young girl in our example were to come down with the flu, she may feel poorly and when confronted with demands, she may aggress. In contrast, on healthy days she may respond to the demands with cheerful compliance.

Finally, an example of a social setting event is teasing. On some days, the young girl may enter the instructional situation after having been severely teased by one or more of her classmates. She may be clearly upset. When the teacher presents the instructional demands, the girl may tear up her workbook and throw it on the floor. However, on most days she is not teased, and she may respond to the teacher's demands with cooperation. The presence or absence of a setting event (in this case, the social interaction involving teasing) can determine whether a given discriminative stimulus (instructional demand) evokes aggression or compliance.

We have barely illustrated the full range of factors that can serve as setting events for problem behavior. For example, with respect to physical setting events, factors such as environmental enrichment (Horner, 1980), transportation routes (Kennedy & Itkonen, 1993), temperature, humidity, level of lighting, clothing comfort, and odors, as well as noise level, may all be important, although few of them have been systematically investigated. A variety of biological setting events has also been implicated in the control of problem behavior (Thompson et al., 1991). These events include caffeine ingestion (Podboy & Mallory, 1977), strenuous exercise (Baumeister & MacLean 1984; Kern et al., 1982; McGimsey & Favell, 1988), urinary tract infection and constipation (Gunsett et al., 1989), allergies (Gardner, 1985), middle ear infection (deLissovoy, 1963), and menstrual discomfort (Taylor et al., 1993). Finally, social setting events include not only the teasing (Gardner et al., 1984) already mentioned, but also the presence or absence of specific people (Touchette et al., 1985), quality of staff-resident interaction (Brusca et al., 1989), classroom social structures (Repp & Karsh, 1992), crowding and population density (Boe, 1977; McAffee, 1987), and the sequencing of social activities (Brown, 1991).

The mechanisms by which setting events influence problem behavior are still being investigated. However, many of these events clearly represent *establishing operations* (Michael, 1982; Vollmer & Iwata, 1991) that is, factors that change the reinforcing or aversive properties of response consequences, thereby influencing the likelihood of problem behavior. To illustrate, consider the role of a urinary tract infection in influencing problem behavior in an instructional situation. Typically, the individual with disabilities may find the demands somewhat neutral or at most mildly aversive; therefore, the motivation for escape behavior (such as aggression) is low. However, on days when the individual has an infection, she or he may be experiencing constant burning sensations, sharp pain, and unrelenting urges to urinate. Under these circumstances, formerly nonaversive or mildly aversive demands may constitute an annoying imposition. Escape motivation rises dramatically and aggressive behavior becomes more frequent. The influence of establishing operations is, no doubt, pervasive. However, there are almost certainly other mechanisms involved in influencing the power of setting events to alter the likelihood of problem behavior. Irrespective of the mechanisms involved, setting events clearly influence the results obtained from functional assessment and analysis.

Once setting events have been identified and their influence on problem behavior measured, interventions need to be designed to deal with the events. Two prominent intervention strategies are (a) removing the setting event altogether and (b) mitigating its effects. With respect to the first strategy, consider a biological factor such as allergies. Removal of the setting event might entail the use of antihistamines. However, since drugs often do not remove symptoms completely, mitigation of the effects of the setting event might also be necessary. Here, we use the guideline that people with disabilities must be treated the same as those without disabilities. When people without disabilities have severe allergy attacks, they not only take medication in an attempt to remove the setting event altogether, but they also alter aspects of their daily routine. For example, they may schedule periods of rest. They may ask others for assistance. They may reduce their work schedule. Mitigation, for people with disabilities, should include any or all of these strategies as well. The identification of setting events has direct implications for intervention, and one of these implications concerns the need for adding new elements to whatever multicomponent intervention is under consideration.

CONCLUSION

Time and again, practitioners have reported that the most difficult aspect of intervening to reduce problem behavior is in the assessment or analytic component. That is, discovering the purposes (functions) of problem behavior is often complicated because of the variety of antecedents, consequences, and setting events that may be involved. Nonetheless, it is incumbent upon researchers and practitioners to identify these purposes, because failing to do so results in blind applications of technology, applications that are often ineffective, short lived in their effects, and usually not replicable by others. Hypothesis-driven intervention, the focus of this chapter, is an attempt to address the difficulties inherent in the use of hit-or-miss technologies. The past decade has provided ample proof that hypothesis-based intervention for severe problem behavior is here to stay.

AUTHOR NOTES

Preparation of this chapter was supported in part by Grant No. H133G20098 and Cooperative Agreement No. H133B20004 from the U.S. Department of Education. The interview on pp. 15–16 is from *Communication-based intervention for problem behavior* by E. G. Carr, L. Levin, G. McConnachie, J. I. Carlson, D. C. Kemp, and C. E. Smith, 1994, pp. 33–34. Copyright 1994 by Paul H. Brookes Publishing Co., Inc. Reprinted by permission.

Our thanks to Dr. Martin Hamburg, Executive Director, Developmental Disabilities Institute, for his generous support.

Please address all correspondence to Edward Carr, Department of Psychology, State University of New York, Stony Brook, NY 11794-2500.

REFERENCES

Arndorfer, R. E., Miltenberger, R. E., Woster, S. H., Rortvedt, A. K., & Gaffaney, T. (1994). Home-based descriptive and experimental analysis of problem behaviors in children. *Topics in Early Childhood Special Education, 14,* 64–87.

Azrin, N. H., Hutchinson, R. R., & Sallery, R. D. (1964). Pain-aggression toward inanimate objects. *Journal of the Experimental Analysis of Behavior, 7,* 223–228.

Bailey, J. S., & Pyles, D. A. M. (1989). Behavioral diagnostics. In E. Cipani (Ed.), *The treatment of severe behavior disorders* (pp. 85–107). Monographs of the *American Association on Mental Retardation, 12.*

Baumeister, A. A., & MacLean, W. E. (1984). Deceleration of self-injurious and stereotypic responding by exercise. *Applied Research in Mental Retardation, 5,* 385–393.

Bijou, S. W., & Baer, D. M. (1961). *Child development I: A systematic and empirical theory.* Englewood Cliffs, NJ: Prentice-Hall.

Boe, R. B. (1977). Economical procedures for the reduction of aggression in a residential setting. *Mental Retardation, 15,* 25–28.

Brown, F. (1991). Creative daily scheduling: A nonintrusive approach to challenging behaviors in community residences. *Journal of the Association for Persons with Severe Handicaps, 16,* 75–84.

Brusca, R. M., Nieminen, G. S., Carter, R., & Repp, A. C. (1989). The relationship of staff contact and activity to the stereotypy of children with multiple disabilities. *Journal of the Association for Persons with Severe Handicaps, 14,* 127–136.

Carr, E. G. (1993). Behavior analysis is not ultimately about behavior. *The Behavior Analyst, 16,* 47–49.

Carr, E. G. (1994). Emerging themes in the functional analysis of problem behavior. *Journal of Applied Behavior Analysis, 27,* 393–399.

Carr, E. G., & Carlson, J. I. (1993). Reduction of severe behavior problems in the community through a multicomponent treatment approach. *Journal of Applied Behavior Analysis, 26,* 157–172.

Carr, E. G., & Durand, V. M. (1985). Reducing behavior problems through functional communication training. *Journal of Applied Behavior Analysis, 18,* 111–126.

Carr, E. G., Levin, L, McConnachie, G., Carlson, J.I., Kemp, D. C., & Smith, C. E. (1994). *Communication-based intervention for problem behavior.* Baltimore: Paul H. Brookes.

Carr, E. G., & McDowell, J. J. (1980). Social control of self-injurious behavior of organic etiology. *Behavior Therapy, 11,* 402–409.

Carr, E. G., & Newsom, C. D. (1985). Demand-related tantrums: Conceptualization and treatment. *Behavior Modification, 9,* 403–426.

Carr, E. G., Newsom, C. D., & Binkoff, J. A. (1976). Stimulus control of self-destructive behavior in a psychotic child. *Journal of Abnormal Child Psychology, 4,* 139–153.

Carr, E. G., Newsom, C. D., & Binkoff, J. A. (1980). Escape as a factor in the aggressive behavior of two retarded children. *Journal of Applied Behavior Analysis, 13,* 101–117.

Carr, E. G., Robinson, S., & Palumbo, L. W. (1990). The wrong issue: Aversive versus nonaversive treatment. The right issue: Functional versus nonfunctional treatment. In A. Repp & N. Singh (Eds.), *Perspectives on the use of nonaversive and aversive interventions for persons with developmental disabilities* (pp. 361–379). Sycamore, IL: Sycamore.

Carr, E. G., Taylor, J. C., & Robinson, S. (1991). The effects of severe behavior problems in children on the teaching behavior of adults. *Journal of Applied Behavior Analysis, 24,* 523–535.

Cataldo, M. F., & Harris, J. (1982). The biological basis for self-injury in the mentally retarded. *Analysis and Intervention in Developmental Disabilities, 2,* 21–39.

DeLissovoy, V. (1963). Head banging in early childhood: A suggested cause. *Journal of Genetic Psychology, 102,* 109–114.

Derby, K. M., Wacker, D. P., Sasso, G., Northup, J., Cigrand, K., & Asmus, J. (1992). Brief functional assessment techniques to evaluate aberrant behavior in an outpatient setting: A summary of 79 cases. *Journal of Applied Behavior Analysis, 25,* 713–721.

Dunlap, G., Kern-Dunlap, L. K., Clarke, S., & Robbins, F. R. (1991). Functional assessment, curricular revision, and severe behavior problems. *Journal of Applied Behavior Analysis, 24,* 387–397.

Durand, V. M., & Crimmins, D. B. (1988). Identifying the variables maintaining self-injurious behavior. *Journal of Autism and Developmental Disorders, 18,* 99–117.

Favell, J. E., McGimsey, J. F., & Schell, R. M. (1982). Treatment of self-injury by providing alternate sensory activities. *Analysis and Intervention in Developmental Disabilities, 2,* 83–104.

Gardner, J. M. (1985). Using microcomputers to help staff reduce violent behavior. *Computers in Human Services, 1,* 53–61.

Gardner, W. I., Karan, O. C., & Cole, C. L. (1984). Assessment of setting events influencing functional capacities of mentally retarded adults with behavior difficulties. In A. S. Halpern & M. J. Fuhrer (Eds.), *Functional assessment in rehabilitation* (pp. 171–185). Baltimore: Paul H. Brookes.

Gardner, W. I., & Sovner, R. (1994). *Self-injurious behaviors: Diagnosis and treatment.* Willow Street, PA: Vida.

Gluck, J. P., Otto, M. W., & Beauchamp, A. J. (1985). Respondent conditioning of self-injurious behavior in early socially deprived rhesus monkeys. *Journal of Abnormal Psychology, 94,* 222–226.

Goldiamond, I. (1974). Towards a constructional approach to social problems. *Behaviorism, 2,* 1–84.

Gunsett, R. P., Mulick, J. A., Fernald, W. B., & Martin, J. L. (1989). Brief report: Indications for medical screening prior to behavioral programming for severely and profoundly mentally retarded clients. *Journal of Autism and Developmental Disorders, 19,* 167–172.

Horner, R. D. (1980). The effects of an environmental "enrichment" program on the behavior of institutionalized profoundly retarded children. *Journal of Applied Behavior Analysis, 13,* 473–491.

Horner, R. H. (1994). Functional assessment: Contributions and future directions. *Journal of Applied Behavior Analysis, 27,* 401–404.

Iwata, B. A., Dorsey, M. F., Slifer, K. J., Bauman, K. E., & Richman, G. S. (1982). Toward functional analysis of self-injury. *Analysis and Intervention in Developmental Disabilities, 2,* 3–20.

Iwata, B. A., Pace, G. M., Kalsher, M. J., Cowdery, G. E., & Cataldo, M. F. (1990). Experimental analysis and extinction of self-injurious escape behavior. *Journal of Applied Behavior Analysis, 23,* 11–27.

Kennedy, C. H., & Itkonen, T. (1993). Effects of setting events on the problem behavior of students with severe disabilities. *Journal of Applied Behavior Analysis, 26,* 321–327.

Kern, L., Koegel, R. L., Dyer, K., Blew, P. A., & Fenton, L. R. (1982). The effects of physical exercise on self-stimulation and appropriate responding in autistic children. *Journal of Autism and Developmental Disorders, 12,* 399–419.

Lalli, J. S., Browder, D. M., Mace, F. C., & Brown, D. K. (1993). Teacher use of descriptive analysis data to implement interventions to decrease students' problem behaviors. *Journal of Applied Behavior Analysis, 26,* 227–238.

Lerman, D. C., & Iwata, B. A., (1993). Descriptive and experimental analyses of variables maintaining self-injurious behavior. *Journal of Applied Behavior Analysis, 26,* 293–319.

Lovaas, O. I., Freitag, G., Gold, V. J., & Kassorla, I. C. (1965). Experimental studies in childhood schizophrenia: Analysis of self-destructive behavior. *Journal of Experimental Child Psychology, 2,* 67–84.

Mace, F. C. (1994). The significance and future of functional analysis methodologies. *Journal of Applied Behavior Analysis, 27,* 385–392.

Mace, F. C., & Lalli, J. S. (1991). Linking descriptive and experimental analyses in the treatment of bizarre speech. *Journal of Applied Behavior Analysis, 24,* 553–562.

Martin, P. L., & Foxx, R. M. (1973). Victim control of the aggression of an institutionalized retardate. *Journal of Behavior Therapy and Experimental Psychiatry, 4,* 161–165.

McAfee, J. K. (1987). Classroom density and the aggressive behavior of handicapped children. *Education and Treatment of Children, 10,* 134–145.

McGimsey, J. F., & Favell, J. E. (1988). The effects of increased physical exercise on disruptive behavior in retarded persons. *Journal of Autism and Developmental Disorders, 18,* 167–179.

Michael, J. (1982). Distinguishing between discriminant and motivational functions of stimuli. *Journal of the Experimental Analysis of Behavior, 37,* 149–155.

Northup, J., Wacker, D., Sasso, G., Steege, M., Cigrand, K., Cook, J., & DeRaad, A. (1991). A brief functional analysis of aggressive and alternative behavior in an outclinic setting. *Journal of Applied Behavior Analysis, 24,* 509–522.

O'Neill, R. E., Homer, R. H., Albin, R. W., Storey, K., & Sprague, J. R. (1990). *Functional analysis: A practical assessment guide.* Sycamore, IL: Sycamore.

Patterson, G. R. (1982). *Coercive family process.* Eugene, OR: Castalia.

Podboy, J. W., & Mallory, W. A. (1977). Caffeine reduction and behavior change in the severely retarded. *Mental Retardation, 15*(6), 40.

Repp, N. C., Felce, D., & Barton, L. E. (1988). Basing the treatment of stereotypic and self-injurious behaviors on hypotheses of their causes. *Journal of Applied Behavior Analysis, 21,* 281–289.

Repp, N. C., & Karsh, K. G. (1992). An analysis of a group teaching procedure for persons with developmental disabilities. *Journal of Applied Behavior Analysis, 25,* 701–712.

Rincover, A., Cook, R., Peoples, A., & Packard, D. (1979). Sensory extinction and sensory reinforcement principles for programming multiple adaptive behavior change. *Journal of Applied Behavior Analysis, 12,* 221–233.

Rincover, A, & Devaney, J. (1982). The application of sensory extinction procedures to self-injury. *Analysis and Intervention in Developmental Disabilities, 2,* 67–81.

Sandman, C. A. (1991). The opiate hypothesis in autism and self-injury. *Journal of Child and Adolescent Psychopharmacology, 1,* 237–248.

Sasso, G. M., Reimers, T. M., Cooper, L. J., Wacker, D., Berg, W., Steege, M., Kelly, L, & Allaire, A. (1992). Use of descriptive and experimental analyses to identify the functional properties of aberrant behavior in school settings. *Journal of Applied Behavior Analysis, 25,* 809–821.

Skinner, B. F. (1974). *About behaviorism.* New York: Vintage.

Steege, M. W., Wacker, D. P., Berg, W. K., Cigrand, K. K., & Cooper, L. J. (1989). The use of behavioral assessment to prescribe and evaluate treatments for severely handicapped children. *Journal of Applied Behavior Analysis, 22,* 23–33.

Taylor, J. C., & Carr, E. G. (1992a). Severe problem behaviors related to social interaction. I: Attention seeking and social avoidance. *Behavior Modification, 16,* 305–335.

Taylor, J. C., & Carr, E. G. (1992b). Severe problem behavior related to social interaction. II: A systems analysis. *Behavior Modification, 16,* 336–371.

Taylor, J. C., Sisson, L. A., McKelvey, J. L., & Trefelner, M. F. (1993). Situation specificity in attention-seeking problem behavior. *Behavior Modification, 17,* 474–497.

Taylor, J. C., & Romanczyk, R. G. (1994). Generating hypotheses about the function of student problem behavior by observing teacher behavior. *Journal of Applied Behavior Analysis, 27,* 251–265.

Taylor, D. V., Rush, D., Hetrick, W. P., & Sandman, C. A. (1993). Self-injurious behavior within the menstrual cycle of women with mental retardation. *American Journal on Mental Retardation, 97,* 659–664.

Thompson, T., Hackenberg, T., & Schaal, D. (1991). Pharmacological treatments for behavior problems in developmental disabilities. In U.S. Department of Health and Human Services, *Treatment of destructive behaviors in persons with developmental disabilities* (pp. 343–510) (NIH Publication No. 91-2410). Bethesda, MD: National Institute of Health.

Touchette, P. E., MacDonald, R. F., & Langer, S. N. (1985). A scatter plot for identifying stimulus control of problem behavior. *Journal of Applied Behavior Analysis, 18,* 343–351.

Vollmer, T. R., & Iwata, B. A. (1991). Establishing operations and reinforcement effects. *Journal of Applied Behavior Analysis, 24,* 279–291.

Wacker, D. P., & Steege, M. W. (1993). Providing outclinic services: Evaluating treatment and social validity. In S. Axelrod & R. Van Houten (Eds.), *Effective behavioral treatment: Issues and implementation* (pp. 297–319). New York: Plenum.

3

Community-Based
Functional Assessment

DAVID P. WACKER
LINDA J. COOPER
STEPHANIE M. PECK
K. MARK DERBY
WENDY K. BERG

INTRODUCTION

The analogue procedure of Carr and his associates (Chapter 2) generally uses materials (tasks) found in a person's natural environment, while the analogue procedure of Iwata and his associates (see Chapter 7) presents a greater abstraction of the natural environment. Wacker and his colleagues have been known for extending the latter approach to outpatient clinical settings. In this chapter, Wacker, Cooper, Peck, Derby, and Berg focus on how to present this methodology so that parents and other care providers can be trained to use it.

The authors focus on two approaches: (a) functional analysis, *by which they mean an analysis of the consequences of problem behavior; and (b)* structural analysis, *an analysis of antecedent conditions. Examples with two clinical populations are presented: persons with severe developmental and behavior disorders and children with mild but common behavior problems. Parents are trained and assessment is based on survey and checklist data, a phone interview, and medical chart review. Hypotheses are then developed and treatment implemented. However, because their assessments are brief, the authors stress the dynamic nature of the assessment and their willingness to change hypotheses.*

Case studies are presented showing how to move from assessment to intervention and how to incorporate parent training. This is a particularly important aspect of the chapter. As we know, behavioral change is best maintained when generalization is—and these authors are among the few researchers who are directly involving parents and other care providers who can maintain change. In addition, their replication of the procedure across settings is note-worthy. Here we have an excellent example of the systematic replication advocated by Sidman (1961) to extend our science of human behavior. With it, Wacker and his associates have provided us with a better understanding of behavior.

OVERVIEW

The functional analysis methodology described by Iwata et al., (1982) has stimulated a wide range of research. Numerous studies have supported the validity of this methodology and the utility of other forms of the procedures (for example, Carr & Durand, 1985). Overall, the analyses have proven to be quite robust (Derby et al., 1992; Sasso et al., 1992) and have been applied across a number of distinct populations (Cooper et al., 1992) and settings (Mace & Lalli, 1991; Sasso et al., 1992).

In this chapter, we present our applications of this methodology to families and care providers who live or work with individuals with behavioral problems. Our intent is to underscore how the procedures can be applied across situations, populations, and target behaviors. The conceptual (Carr, 1977) and methodological (Carr & Durand, 1985; Iwata et al., 1990) reasons for conducting pretreatment functional analyses are firmly established in the literature. Identifying the operant function of problematic behavior is a necessary step for developing effective treatments, especially reinforcer-based treatments. It is also evident to us that the most valid approach is to conduct an extended functional analysis of the target behavior (Iwata et al., 1990), meaning that potential classes of reinforcement are delivered contingently for displays of problematic behavior over multiple sessions within a single-case design. Other approaches that vary antecedents (Carr & Durand, 1985), that manipulate appropriate rather than inappropriate behavior (Cooper et al., 1992), or that are brief versions of the extended analysis (Northup et al., 1991) are often useful but require greater inference than extended functional analysis. This does not mean, however, that these approaches are not valid. In many situations they are actually preferred, given pragmatic considerations such as the amount of time available for assessment. In other situations, particularly when parents are conducting the assessment, there is an obvious need to restrict the length of the functional analysis to preclude establishing a strong reinforcement history for aberrant behavior between the parent and the child. In still other cases, the emphasis is on antecedent stimulus conditions that occasion responding, and the experimenter is willing to draw inferences based on the results of the assessment.

If one is primarily interested in the analysis of a problematic response (in other words, to study response class formation), then an extended functional analysis is almost always required. If, however, the interest is in using this methodology to identify effective treatment, then a number of variations appear to be both possible and needed. Our focus in this chapter is on this latter issue: How can we most efficiently but effectively apply this methodology with parents and other care providers? In the following sections, we provide exemplars of these applications. We begin with what we term brief experimental analyses conducted in the context of outpatient clinics. We use the term functional analysis to refer to the delivery of distinct reinforcers contingent on inappropriate behavior. We use the term structural analysis to refer to the presentation of distinct antecedent conditions. Within this context, we describe two different clinical populations and assessment approaches: clients with severe developmental and behavioral disorders (brief functional analysis) and children with more mild but also more common behavioral problems (brief structural analysis). In the second section, we describe our blending of descriptive and functional analysis procedures in home settings with very young children who have severe behavioral disorders. Finally, we discuss applications to other settings (classrooms), target behaviors (food refusal), and populations (adults in vocational settings) to further show the applicability of these procedures.

The differences among these settings, behaviors, and populations are apparent and, we hope, show the overall usefulness of the experimental analysis methodology. Of perhaps even greater importance are the points of uniformity across these situations. In all cases, parents or care providers conducted the assessments while receiving on-site coaching by trained therapists. In all cases, analogue conditions were used, either exclusively or to clarify the results obtained with other assessment procedures. Finally, the results of assessment, although of interest to us in their own right, were used primarily to assist us in the development of reinforcement-based treatments. The treatments were implemented on a long-term basis, and all required frequent but minor modifications of the type described by Cooper et al. (1992). By minor, we mean that the basic function or class of reinforcement remained constant during treatment. However, modifications were needed on how best to deliver the reinforcement contingencies and to add mild punishment procedures in conjunction with extinction and reinforcement. Although the stability of the identified function of target behavior over time warrants further research, our own findings suggest that changes in function occur infrequently, at least during short-term treatment (three to six months). Thus, as discussed by Cooper et al. (1992), the assessments that we conduct—even brief versions of experimental analysis—often have utility for initiating treatment, but behavior must also be monitored closely during treatment. In this chapter, we focus mainly on our approaches to assessment and briefly describe the treatments that were based on the assessment results. We include case examples of the approaches and provide a rationale for the components of the assessment package.

CONDUCTING BRIEF
EXPERIMENTAL ANALYSES
IN OUTPATIENT CLINICAL SETTINGS

We have previously described the history of the assessments used in our outpatient clinics in other chapters (Wacker et al., 1992; Wacker & Steege, 1993; Wacker et al., 1990) and presented the initial findings in research articles (Cooper et al., 1990; Cooper et al., 1992; Derby et al., 1992; Northup et al., 1991). In this section, we present an update of our most recent approaches and describe how parents or other care providers conduct the assessments. When reading this section, three points should be considered. First, on-site coaching is always provided. After a brief discussion of the rationale for our assessment, a trained therapist either works directly with the parent throughout the assessment (Self-Injurious and Aggressive Behavior Service) or discusses the assessment with the parent approximately every five minutes (Behavior Management Clinic). Second, the assessment is based on an extensive collection of survey and checklist data, a phone interview, and medical chart review. Each assessment is based on these descriptive measures and thus varies across children. Finally, the assessment itself is dynamic. Although we always begin with a firm plan based on hypotheses generated from the descriptive assessment, we often change our assessment depending on the behavior of the child and the reaction of the parent. The assessments are "rule governed" to the extent that they are conducted within multielement designs. However, they are also "contingency driven," meaning that the order of conditions is often dependent on observed behavior.

APPLYING BRIEF FUNCTIONAL ANALYSES WITH CLIENTS WHO DISPLAY SELF-INJURY AND AGGRESSION

With children who engage in severely aberrant behavior such as self-injury or aggression, our intent is to directly assess the operant function of problematic behavior using the brief functional analysis described by Northup et al. (1991). This methodology involves a series of rapidly changing conditions five to ten minutes in duration, with each condition providing access to a potential reinforcer contingent on aberrant behavior. Minireversals are conducted when a reinforcer is identified.

We begin the overall assessment with descriptive data collected prior to the clinic day to formulate hypotheses. Descriptive assessments involve collecting information regarding naturally occurring environmental events that are related to aberrant behavior. The information collected via descriptive assessment techniques can be used to develop hypotheses (Repp et al., 1988) regarding the function of aberrant behavior and to design analogue conditions to test these hypotheses (Lalli & Goh, 1993). Prior to the clinical evaluation, parents and other care providers are asked to complete a series of questionnaires such as the Motivation Assessment Scale (MAS) (Durand, 1988) and a modified scatterplot (Touchette, MacDonald, & Langer, 1985) that includes an antecedent-behavior-consequence (A-B-C) assessment (Bijou et al., 1968). In addition, a telephone interview is conducted to further clarify the information provided in the questionnaires. This procedure allows care providers to be directly involved in the assessment process by allowing them to specify (a) their definition of the problem behavior, (b) the antecedents that typically occasion the behavior, and (c) the consequences that typically follow the behavior.

Based on the information obtained from the descriptive assessment, we attempt to formulate hypotheses regarding the function of aberrant behavior. For example, if care providers report that aberrant behavior is observed most often when the child is ignored, we hypothesize that attention (positive reinforcement) maintains the behavior. However, if the behavior occurs most frequently when the child is required to complete a nonpreferred task, we hypothesize that escape (negative reinforcement) maintains the aberrant behavior.

Next, analogue conditions are designed to test our hypotheses. Although the specific analogue conditions conducted during the brief functional analysis are designed by clinic staff, we directly involve care providers in the functional analysis in two ways. First, care providers identify the antecedents used during the evaluation. For example, if a parent observes aberrant behavior most frequently when the child is required to complete household chores, we will use a household chore (such as folding towels) as a task demand during the evaluation. Second, whenever possible, we involve parents in the functional analysis by asking them as to serve as therapists in conducting the analogue sessions. For example, when evaluating the effects of attention, the parent typically provides attention to the child while the clinic staff "coaches" the parent.

In the next section, we provide two case examples that illustrate how families can be directly involved in conducting functional analyses. Brian provides an example of a child whose self-injury is maintained by negative reinforcement (escape), and Susan provides an example of a child whose aggression is maintained by positive reinforcement (attention).

Case Example 1: Brian

Brian, aged four years, was diagnosed with developmental delay and was referred for evaluation of self-injurious behaviors and tantrums that included head banging and hair pulling. Brian's mother reported that Brian engaged in self-injury most often when he was "frustrated" or "could not have his way." Our initial hypothesis was that Brian's self-injury was maintained by negative reinforcement (escape from nonpreferred tasks). Thus, our assessment focused on evaluating the effects of the presence and absence of task demands on Brian's behavior. During free play conditions, Brian was allowed to engage in activities of his choice, and attention was provided contingent on aberrant behavior. During demand conditions, Brian was required to participate in a nonpreferred task, and breaks from the task were provided contingent on aberrant behavior (contingent escape). In the descriptive assessment, Brian's mother identified coloring as an activity that he did not like to do at home; therefore, coloring was used as the task demand during the contingent escape conditions. During all conditions, Brian's mother provided either attention or "breaks" from coloring (depending on the condition) after each occurrence of aberrant behavior. The clinic staff coached her regarding when and how to deliver each consequence. Brian's appropriate and aberrant behavior were recorded by clinic staff using a 6-second partial interval observation system.

The results of Brian's functional analysis are provided in Figure 3.1. Self-injury and tantrums increased when he was allowed to escape the coloring task contingent on the occurrence of these behaviors. However, self-injury and

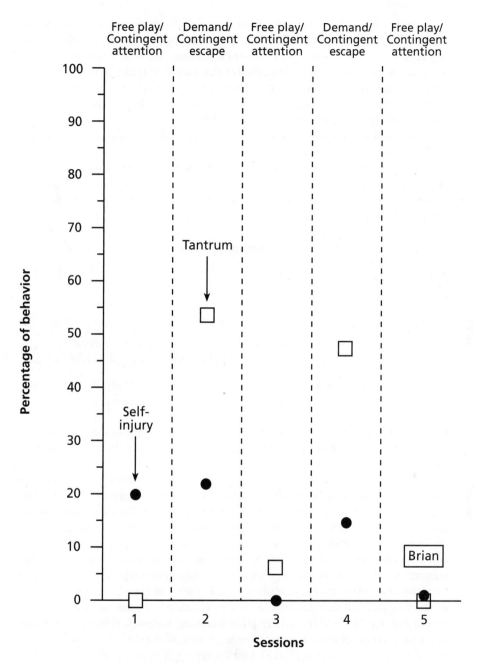

FIGURE 3.1 Results of Brian's functional analysis

tantrums rarely occurred after the first session when Brian was allowed to play with toys of his choice. This supported our hypothesis that Brian's behavior was maintained by escape from nonpreferred tasks. Based on these results, we recommended a treatment package that included providing breaks from demanding tasks contingent on appropriate forms of communication (such as signing "more," "play," or "please") and requiring Brian to continue working on the task contingent on inappropriate behavior.

In this example, Brian's mother was able to provide us with important information regarding which tasks should be used during the contingent escape condition of our analogue analysis to more closely approximate the conditions under which self-injury and tantrums typically occurred at home. Had we arbitrarily selected another task, such as picking up toys, we may not have observed self-injury or tantrums.

Case Example 2: Susan

Susan, aged 10 years, was diagnosed with developmental delay and was referred for an evaluation of aggressive behavior that included scratching, pinching, and biting others. During the descriptive assessment, Susan's mother reported that she never observed aggression as long as she was interacting with Susan, even if she required Susan to perform a difficult task. Susan's mother also reported that she observed aggression whenever her attention was diverted from Susan, such as when she was talking on the telephone or doing household chores. Based on this information, our hypothesis was that attention maintained Susan's aggression, and our assessment focused on evaluating the effects of positive reinforcement (parental attention) on Susan's aggression. Three conditions were conducted for Susan's evaluation. In the first condition, free play, Susan had continuous access to her mother's attention as she played with an activity of her choice. In the second condition, demand, Susan's mother provided continuous attention while Susan completed a difficult task. Each instance of aggression resulted in removal of both the task and her mother's attention. In the third condition, contingent attention, Susan's mother diverted her attention to the therapists until Susan engaged in aggression. Then Susan's mother provided attention in the form of reprimands or redirection ("Stop hitting me" "Why don't you go play?").

Susan engaged in aggression only when her mother provided attention contingent on the occurrence of aggression. Of equal importance was that aggression never occurred during conditions in which attention was continuously available, even when Susan was required to complete demanding tasks. These results supported our hypothesis that attention maintained Susan's aggressive behavior. Based on these results, we recommended a treatment package that included providing Susan with attention contingent on saying or signing "please" and with brief time-out for aggression.

In this example, it was important for Susan's mother to participate directly in the evaluation, because it was her attention that was reinforcing to Susan. Given that Susan had just met us, there was a possibility that our attention would not have functioned as a reinforcer for her and that we would not have observed aggression.

APPLYING BRIEF STRUCTURAL ANALYSES
WITH YOUNG CHILDREN WHO DISPLAY
TANTRUMS AND NONCOMPLIANCE

For children with milder behavioral problems, the focus of assessment is on the antecedent situations that occasion appropriate behavior, such as cooperative play or parental requests to comply. Therefore, we conduct brief structural analyses that vary the conditions under which activities or tasks are presented by a parent to the child. These conditions can involve the type of directions provided (specific or general), the amount of contact the parent has with the child, or the degree of difficulty of the task. We again provide two case examples of this approach.

Case Example 3: Chris

Chris, a three-year-old boy of average skills and development, was referred for aggression, temper tantrums, and noncompliance. Before and during Chris's clinic visit, descriptive data (parent behavior checklist, parent questionnaire developed for the clinic, and phone interview) indicated that his inappropriate behavior most frequently occurred when he did not obtain desired items (toys at home, items while in a store) and when requests were made ("Pick up your toys." "Stay in your car seat."). Discipline during "time-out" for misbehavior included discussion, such as telling him that aggression and tantrums were "not nice." His parents further reported that they typically withdrew the requests to avoid Chris's tantrums when he refused to comply. These descriptive data suggested several possible functions, including escaping demands, gaining parental attention, and gaining access to preferred toys.

In order to more directly identify conditions in which Chris displayed appropriate (compliant) as well as inappropriate (tantrums, noncompliant) behavior, we conducted a brief (45-minute) structural analysis in which we observed Chris interacting with his mother, father, and 10-month-old sister. Prior to each condition, we instructed Chris's parents regarding which tasks to present to him and which consequences to apply for inappropriate and appropriate behavior. Each condition lasted approximately five minutes and consisted of variables that we hypothesized would result in relatively high and low percentages of appropriate behavior. We recorded parent behavior using a 10-second partial interval system. This gave us a measure of the integrity with which the assessment conditions were conducted. Appropriate and inappropriate child behaviors were recorded with a 10-second momentary time-sampling recording system. By examining improvements in child behavior associated with changes in parent behavior, we could directly assess the relationship between Chris's behavior and the antecedent and consequence variables manipulated by his parents.

There were two primary differences between the evaluation used with Chris and the ones discussed previously for more aberrant behavior. First, the focus was on appropriate behavior and, specifically, on conditions that improved child behavior. Second, we attempted to develop a treatment package quickly during the initial phase of assessment and then trained the parents to practice implementing the components of the treatment package. This analysis was based on the one reported by Millard et al. (1993).

The assessment began with two control conditions in which the best and worst child behaviors were expected, respectively: (a) free play (FP) and (b) general directions/ignore (GD/IG). During the free play condition, Chris was given access to preferred activities (toys, books, crayons), and we instructed his parents to play with him (and his sister) without demands or reprimands. In the general directions/ignore condition, Chris's parents made a request of him (to pick up toys) with a general directive ("You need to clean up the room"), and ignored all of Chris's behavior by diverting their attention to his sister. We expected the best and worst behavior in these respective conditions, because the conditions represented distinct variations in the attention Chris received, the preference of the tasks, and the presence or absence of demands. We then followed these control conditions with a treatment package that involved three components: (a) specific directions on how to complete the task, (b) differential reinforcement of alternative behavior (contingent parental attention for compliance), and (c) contingent access to preferred activities for compliance (SD/DRA/PA). It was hypothesized that providing Chris with specific directives (including modeling) on how to complete the task might reduce the demands of the task by providing clearer expectations. Differential reinforcement of alternative behavior (praise) and preferred activities (playing a preferred game) provided two types of positive reinforcement for compliance.

As shown in Figure 3.2, Chris's behavior was most appropriate during free play and was least appropriate when his parents gave him a general directive to pick up toys and then ignored him. These results are important because they provided initial replication of the descriptive information. When the treatment package (SD/DRA/PA) was implemented in the third session, Chris's behavior improved, and he complied with the task request. We conducted a minireversal by reimplementing the second control condition (GD/IG) and then the treatment package in order to demonstrate control over Chris's behavior. The minireversal demonstrated control over his behavior and gave both his parents and the examiners confidence that his behavior could be controlled through the treatment package.

A trained therapist was present with Chris's parents during implementation of the treatment package on both occasions, to demonstrate the use of the treatment package and to provide immediate feedback to them. We observed that Chris's parents required the most assistance with ignoring inappropriate behavior. This observation, plus the reported use of discussion during time-out at home, led us to include a final assessment condition (general directions/discussion, GD/DIS) to simulate current behavior management at home. We informed Chris's parents of our hypothesis that their attention for inappropriate behavior may maintain its occurrence and of our desire to test the hypothesis directly with their assistance. In the general directions/discussion condition, Chris's parents were instructed to give him a general directive to pick up toys and to provide attention (discussion) only for inappropriate behavior. As expected, Chris became noncompliant, but the severity of his inappropriate behavior also increased relative to the previous GD/IG condition. When we reimplemented the treatment package, Chris again complied.

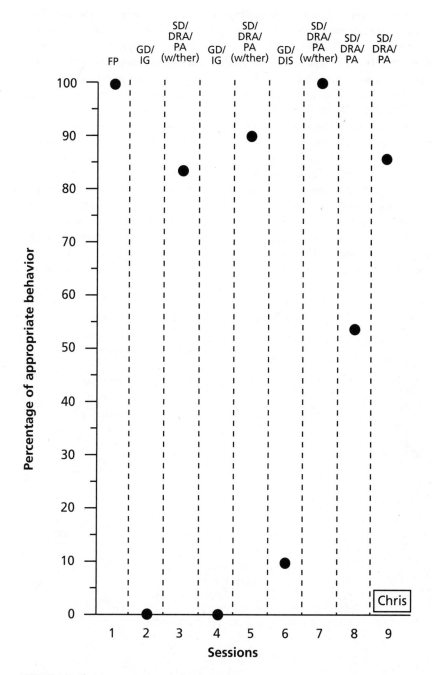

FIGURE 3.2 Chris's appropriate behavior

In the last two conditions, we again instructed Chris's parents in the use of the treatment components, and they implemented the package without the presence of a trained therapist. As shown in the figure, Chris's behavior improved across the sessions. Of note is the relatively lower percentage of appropriate behavior in the first treatment condition without the therapist present. In previous treatment conditions, Chris might have been responding to the therapist rather than to his parents; therefore, removing the therapist was important.

This assessment of Chris demonstrates the "contingency-driven" aspect of our assessment model and the importance of parental participation in the evaluation. The descriptive assessment initially led to the development of a treatment package that we tested directly. Parental response to the package led us to directly assess one component of the package (planned ignoring of inappropriate behavior) to show the parents why this component was important. Thus, in this case the parents' input was beneficial in formulating the initial treatment plan and in testing its utility. In other cases, when we are not able to formulate even a tentative treatment plan based on the results of the descriptive assessment, we hierarchically add treatment components to a package until control is established over the child's behavior.

Case Example 4: Kenneth

Kenneth, aged seven years, was referred to an outpatient clinic for tantrums and noncompliance at home and at school. He was diagnosed with average intelligence and Attention Deficit Hyperactivity Disorder. Kenneth's teacher and parents believed that Ritalin might improve his behavior; therefore, we evaluated the relative effects of Ritalin and various environmental variables on his compliance and appropriate behavior. We conducted the evaluation with Kenneth and his parents, and each condition lasted for five minutes. Prior to each condition, we showed his parents how to present instructional-level academic tasks, as well as how to deliver consequences for instances of both appropriate and inappropriate behavior.

The assessment conditions for Kenneth were arranged in a hierarchical, cumulative manner (see Table 3.1) such that the effects of both antecedent and consequent variables were evaluated sequentially by adding them into the assessment conditions, as described by Harding et al. (1994). When we identified an effective condition, we conducted an immediate reversal to determine the effects of that variable. The assessment model used with Kenneth allowed us to directly evaluate a series of intervention components, and the treatment package included only those components that were shown to be effective. We initially evaluated Kenneth without Ritalin, and we repeated the best and worst conditions after he received an appropriate dose of the medication. Without Ritalin, Kenneth displayed the most appropriate behavior when his parents gave him specific directions and choices and provided both differential reinforcement of appropriate behavior and differential reinforcement of communication (assessment condition 6). The same results occurred on medication, and thus we emphasized the need for a treatment package that included these environmental components.

Table 3.1 Environmental Assessment Conditions

Condition	Description
1. Free Play	1. Constant attention
2. General direction/Discussion	2. General instruction for task completion; discussion for inappropriate behavior
3. Specific directions/Discussion	3. Specific instruction for task completion; discussion for inappropriate behavior
4. Specific directions + Choice/Discussion	4. Same as prior condition, plus child permitted to choose various aspects of the task (which of two similar tasks to complete, order of completion)
5. Specifc directions + Choice/Differential Reinforcement of alternative behavior (DRA)	5. Same as prior condition, except attention (praise) provided only for appropriate behavior
6. Specific directions + Choice/DRA/ Differential reinforcement of communication	6. Same as prior condition, plus child given mand to request desired reinforcer (assistance, attention)

APPLYING DESCRIPTIVE, STRUCTURAL, AND FUNCTIONAL ANALYSES IN HOME SETTINGS

We approached the application of functional analysis procedures to home settings very cautiously. Although the implementation of functional analysis procedures by parents had been demonstrated in outpatient clinics, we were concerned that the analogue formats used during the assessments might overwhelm parents when the assessments were conducted in their homes. In addition, we believed that it was crucial to conduct the assessments with a limited number of response-reinforcement trials to avoid unnecessarily strengthening problematic behavior at home.

Given these concerns, we favor beginning in-home assessments with the descriptive analyses discussed by Repp et al. (1988) and Touchette et al. (1985). Repp et al. used an A–B–C (antecedent-behavior-consequence) assessment based on narrative recording to generate hypotheses concerning the function of self-injury and stereotypy. The second type of descriptive assessment is a scatterplot analysis (Touchette et al., 1985). This method involves recording the occurrence of behavior within 30-minute intervals for a 24-hour period and comparing the frequency of target behavior displayed across intervals for a specified number of days. Touchette et al. (1985) proposed that the function of behavior could be hypothesized by assessing the presence or absence of environmental events occurring during problematic intervals. These authors, like Repp et al. (1988), then showed that effective treatment could be developed based on assessment results.

Although these two descriptive assessments provide us with a way to generate hypotheses regarding the environmental events that are correlated with inappropriate behavior, they do not provide us with information regarding the functional properties of behavior (Bijou et al., 1968). If we do not match our intervention packages to an identified function of behavior, we run the risk of implementing treatments that are countertherapeutic. Therefore, to increase our confidence in the treatments prescribed, we need to conduct additional direct analyses of the environmental events hypothesized as maintaining inappropriate behavior.

As we described in the previous section, there are two distinct methodologies for assessing the function of inappropriate behavior: (a) structural analysis, based on antecedent events that set the occasion for inappropriate behavior (Carr & Durand, 1985); and (b) functional analysis, based on the assessment of consequences maintaining inappropriate behavior (Iwata et al., 1982). In our view, both versions appear to have advantages, so we use both in home settings. In our structural analysis, we evaluate the effects of varying levels of task demands, task preferences, and parental contact on child behavior. Thus, the variables believed to reinforce aberrant behavior are never delivered contingently. The advantage of the structural analysis is that we can directly assess situations that occasion aberrant behavior without requiring a large number of response-reinforcement trials from parents. In some cases, the descriptive and structural analysis results are sufficiently clear to be able to select treatment. In most cases, however, the functional analysis procedures developed by Iwata et al. (1982) or the brief functional analysis procedures developed by Northup et al. (1991) are needed to clarify which consequences maintain (reinforce) aberrant behavior. The results of the descriptive and structural analyses show us the activities that set the occasion for inappropriate behavior, but are seldom sufficient for clarifying the reinforcers.

Given the unique advantages of descriptive, structural, and functional analysis procedures, we like to incorporate each into a multiphase assessment model for home-based analyses (see Figure 3.3). There are three advantages to incorporating each of these procedures into a comprehensive assessment model. First, parents provide the primary information during the descriptive assessment, permitting us to establish a collaborative working relationship with the parents and helping us to better understand how the family functions. Second, a structural analysis allows us to evaluate the effects of presenting and removing specific antecedent events associated with the problem behavior. Third, conducting the descriptive and structural analyses first allows us to streamline the range of tasks and consequences that must be tested within the functional analysis. Thus, we minimize the amount of time and range of stimulus conditions in which the parents reinforce aberrant behavior. By incorporating all three procedures into our assessment model, we are able to generate hypotheses that can be tested quickly and directly during the functional analysis. When we have identified the reinforcer for aberrant behavior, we can "match" a treatment to the function of behavior (Iwata et al., 1990). In most cases, this match involves replacing aberrant behavior with a mending response via functional communication training (Carr & Durand, 1985).

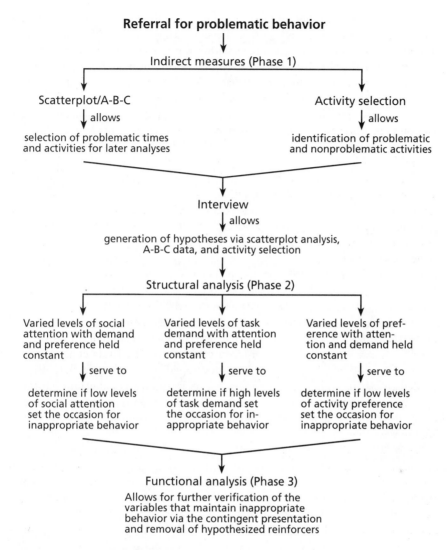

FIGURE 3.3 Assessment model for home-based procedures

The assessment process we use in home settings is described in Box 3.1 and involves three phases. In Phase 1, we conduct a descriptive assessment that includes a scatterplot (Touchette et al., 1985), an A-B-C assessment (Bijou et al., 1968), and a parent interview that identifies activities for use in later analyses. During Phase 2, we conduct a structural analysis to identify the antecedent conditions that set the occasion for problem behavior to occur. During Phase 3, we conduct a functional analysis to verify the hypotheses that were generated in Phases 1 and 2 regarding the function of aberrant behavior.

BOX 3.1   Three Phases of In-Home Assessment

Phase 1. Descriptive Assessment

Scatterplot/A-B-C analyses
To identify problematic times during the day, the parent is asked to complete the data form, shown in Figure 3.4, in which two types of descriptive measures are recorded: (a) the frequency of inappropriate behavior within 30-minute intervals between 5:00 A.M. and 11:00 P.M. and (b) a description of the antecedent and consequent events that are associated with each occurrence of problem behavior.

Activity selection
The parent is instructed to go through the child's toys to identify each toy as being high or low relative to (a) adult attention, (b) difficulty, and (c) preference. High parental attention activities and toys are those reported to typically involve one-on-one interaction between the parent and the child. Low parental attention activities and toys typically involve independent play. High demand activities and toys are those that require adult assistance to complete. Low demand activities and toys are those the child can complete without adult assistance. Highly preferred activities and toys are those that the child often plays with, and nonpreferred activities and toys are those that the child rarely plays with. Activities and toys are rated on each of these dimensions. For example, if building with blocks is reported to be an activity the child engages in independently, is easy for the child to complete, and is something the child often chooses to do, then building with blocks is categorized as a low social (LS), low demand (LD), high preference (HP) activity (thus, an LS-LD-HP task).

Phase 2: Structural Analysis

Using the information and activities obtained via the descriptive assessment, the structural analysis is used to evaluate the effects of high and low levels of parental attention, task preference, and task difficulty on child behavior. Using a multielement design, the effects of each variable are assessed by varying the level (high or low) of one variable while the remaining two variables are held constant. These assessments are conducted in 5- to 10-minute sessions, and assessment usually begins with the variable hypothesized to be the controlling behavior. If the hypothesized variable is escape from task demands, then the effects of high and low task demands are evaluated first. Thus, the level of task demands is varied while the levels of attention and preference are held constant. The

variables held constant are provided noncontingently in what we hypothesize to be the most preferred manner. When a stable pattern of behavior occurs, the next two variables are assessed sequentially in a similar manner. An example of this procedure is shown in the top panel of Figure 3.5. As shown in the figure, the effects of task demands are evaluated first by varying the level of task demands across activities, while the levels of social attention and task preference remain constant (high). Inappropriate behavior occurs most often when task demands are high. Subsequently, an evaluation of high versus low levels of attention and preference is conducted under low demand conditions. No occurrences of problematic behavior are observed when task demands remain low, regardless of the level of attention or preference, further documenting the role of task·demands as an antecedent variable for aberrant behavior.

Phase 3: Functional Analysis

Although structural analysis allows us to assess behavior within an experimental design, the function of behavior must be inferred, because consequences for inappropriate behavior are not directly assessed. For this reason, a functional analysis is used to further verify the function of inappropriate behavior. An example of a brief functional analysis is presented in the bottom panel of Figure 3.5. In this example, only four conditions (five minutes each) are needed, because the results match the structural analysis. A free play condition, consisting of the best possible combination of attention (high), preference (high), and demand (low) based on the structural analysis, is conducted as a control condition. Following the free play condition, a contingent escape condition is conducted using the task demands that set the occasion for aberrant behavior in the structural analysis. During this condition, the child is given a brief break from the task each time aberrant behavior occurs. The contingent escape condition results in high levels of aberrant behavior. A contingent attention condition is then conducted to further rule out the hypothesis that aberrant behavior is maintained by attention. During this condition, the parent ignores the child until inappropriate behavior occurs; attention is contingent on inappropriate behavior. As expected, no inappropriate behavior occurs. The contingent escape condition is then repeated, and inappropriate behavior occurs once again.

Name _____

Date _____	Frequency	Activities prior to behavior	Behavior of concern	What was your reaction?
5:00–5:30 AM				
5:30–6:00	_____			
6:00–6:30	_____			
6:30–7:00	_____			
7:00–7:30	_____			
7:30–8:00	_____			
8:00–8:30	_____			
8:30–9:00	_____			
9:00–9:30	_____			
9:30–10:00	_____			
10:00–10:30	_____			
10:30–11:00	_____			
11:00–11:30	_____			
11:30–12:00 PM	_____			
12:00–12:30	_____			
12:30–1:00	_____			
1:00–1:30	_____			
1:30–2:00	_____			
2:00–2:30	_____			
2:30–3:00	_____			
3:00–3:30	_____			
3:30–4:00	_____			
4:00–4:30	_____			
4:30–5:00	_____			
5:00–5:30	_____			
5:30–6:00	_____			
6:00–6:30	_____			
6:30–7:00	_____			
7:00–7:30	_____			
7:30–8:00	_____			
8:00–8:30	_____			
8:30–9:00	_____			
9:00–9:30	_____			
9:30–10:00	_____			
10:00–10:30	_____			
10:30–11:00	_____			

Example:

	Frequency	Activities prior to behavior	Behavior of concern	What was your reaction?
5:00–5:30 AM	__5__	Waking up	Banging head	Pick up and comfort

FIGURE 3.4 A-B-C/Scatterplot form

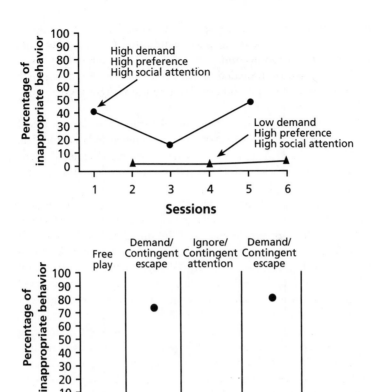

FIGURE 3.5 Assessments in sessions

The phases in Box 3.1 constitute the general guidelines we follow in conducting in-home assessments. However, as is true for the brief outpatient clinical assessments, the specific conditions conducted during each assessment are contingency driven. Here are two examples of this approach to assessment.

Case Example 5: Kathy

Kathy, a three-year-old girl diagnosed with developmental delays, was referred to the in-home intervention project by her local school staff for self-injury (hand-biting) and severe temper tantrums. Education reports indicated that Kathy had been engaging in these behaviors for about six months and that they had been increasing in frequency and intensity. Prior to our involvement, her mother's primary intervention strategy was to redirect and soothe Kathy until she stopped engaging in problem behavior. All assessment procedures were conducted by her mother with close consultation by our staff.

The descriptive phase of the evaluation lasted one week. The information that we obtained via the scatterplot/A-B-C data form indicated that self-injury occurred most often in the afternoons and was associated with returning home from preschool. This information provided us with both a time period in which to conduct future analyses and the hypothesis that attention might be maintaining Kathy's inappropriate behavior.

The structural analysis occurred over a three-week period, one day per week. The results of the structural analysis showed that task preference and demands had little effect on the occurrence of inappropriate behavior as long as parental attention remained high. Based on these results, we hypothesized that contingent attention maintained Kathy's inappropriate behavior.

Because the structural analysis showed attention to be the most prominent variable related to the occurrence of inappropriate behavior, we conducted a brief functional analysis to further test this hypothesis. The functional analysis, which we conducted in one day, consisted of five sessions five minutes long. We alternated control conditions (free play with her mother) with contingent attention conditions, in which Kathy was allowed access to preferred toys but was ignored by her mother unless inappropriate behavior occurred. For each occurrence of inappropriate behavior, Kathy's mother provided her with attention in the form of a verbal reprimand. No inappropriate behavior occurred during the free play conditions, but the frequency of Kathy's inappropriate behavior increased substantially during the attention conditions. Thus, the attention hypothesis was supported. Treatment involved two components: (a) teaching Kathy to say "want Mom" to gain her mother's attention and (b) having Kathy's mother turn away from Kathy (nonexclusionary time-out) when inappropriate behavior occurred. This treatment package resulted in a rapid increase in the mand "want Mom" and a simultaneous decrease in problem behavior. We followed Kathy's progress for several months, and no instances of inappropriate behavior were observed during the entire course of treatment.

Case Example 6: Bruce

Bruce, aged two years, was diagnosed with developmental delays and was referred to the in-home project by his local school staff for aggression, destruction, and temper tantrums. Prior to our involvement, Bruce had been placed in several foster homes since birth and had been removed from at least one foster home placement because of the severity of his inappropriate behaviors. All assessment procedures were conducted by his foster care parents with close consultation from project staff.

The results of the descriptive assessment indicated that problem behaviors occurred throughout the day across a variety of situations. The structural analysis indicated that Bruce's inappropriate behavior occurred most frequently in the presence of task demands. When we varied the level of task demands (high/low) while the levels of preference and attention were held constant, only those tasks associated with high demands occasioned inappropriate behavior. We concluded that Bruce's inappropriate behavior was maintained by escape from task demands.

During the brief functional analysis, we directly compared the effects of contingent escape from task demands and contingent social attention on inappropriate behavior. We conducted the functional analysis in six sessions, with each session lasting five minutes. The functional analysis began with free play, after which we alternated contingent attention and contingent escape conditions. Bruce's display of inappropriate behavior remained low throughout the contingent attention conditions and increased only for contingent escape.

Based on the results of our assessment, we developed an intervention that consisted of two primary components: (a) Bruce was not allowed to escape demands if he displayed inappropriate behavior and (b) we taught him to request "help" to receive parental assistance during demanding tasks. Thus, inappropriate behavior no longer resulted in desired outcomes, and we provided Bruce with an alternative behavior to escape from demanding situations. We followed Bruce for three months after treatment was implemented, and his inappropriate behavior decreased to nearly a zero occurrence with a simultaneous increase in his use of the word "help."

FURTHER APPLICATIONS OF FUNCTIONAL AND STRUCTURAL ANALYSES

In addition to applying functional and structural analyses to outpatient clinic and home settings, we have applied these procedures to other settings, such as classrooms and supported work programs. We are also continuing to apply the procedures to distinct subgroups of individuals with behavior disorders, such as children who are diagnosed with the failure to thrive. As will be obvious in our case examples, the assessments often consist of a combination of structural and functional analyses and are always contingency driven.

APPLICATION TO A CLASSROOM SETTING

Our initial application of functional analysis procedures beyond the clinical setting occurred in 1989 when we received a grant from the Iowa Bureau of Special Education (Wacker & Berg, 1989) to develop and implement proactive treatment programs in classroom settings for young children who engaged in severe forms of aberrant behavior such as self-injury and aggression (Northup et al., 1994). Although the children targeted for this project were eight years old or younger, several who had permanent facial disfigurements were at risk for more restrictive residential or educational placement because of the severity of their self-injurious or aggressive behavior. Our previous experience with similar children in clinical settings had demonstrated that the first step in developing a proactive intervention was to identify the function of aberrant behavior. Therefore, functional analysis became a critical component of this project.

We have conducted functional analyses in classroom settings for five years with students who range in age from 3 to 21 years. Throughout these years, three features of the functional analyses have remained constant: (a) The analyses have been conducted using activities and routines that are a common part of the student's school day but are conducted in an analogue format (Sasso et al., 1992), (b) the classroom teacher and associates have served as the "therapists" for the analyses, and (c) activities within the classroom have been maintained as close to the typical routine as possible. Overall, this has been an effective approach for identifying the environmental events associated with aberrant behavior and for developing a reinforcement-based treatment package that will be effective and acceptable to the teacher.

As expected, the environmental events that occur in the classroom setting are not as stable as those introduced in the clinic-based analogues. Because of this variance, we have extended the functional analyses for some children to obtain stable patterns of responding across conditions. However, we believe that these sources of variance can provide useful insights into the role of relatively subtle environmental changes on behavior.

Case Example 7: Clark

Clark, a 17-year-old male, was referred to our school-based program for a functional analysis of severe self-injury in the form of face slapping and arm biting. According to his teacher and the staff at his residential program, Clark had engaged in these behaviors since early childhood and continued to engage in high frequencies of self-injury throughout the day and evening. We conducted a functional analysis in Clark's classroom to evaluate the role of different environmental stimuli on the occurrence of aberrant behavior. We conducted five analogue assessment conditions: free play (DRA), contingent attention, contingent escape, contingent access to preferred items, and diverted attention. The free play, contingent attention, and contingent escape conditions were conducted in the same manner as described previously for the outpatient clinic and in-home assessments. Contingent access to preferred items consisted of providing Clark with a preferred item (for example, turning on a radio) for a brief interval each time he engaged in self-injury. All other behavior was ignored. In the diverted attention condition, the teacher remained in the classroom but participated in other activities. The teacher ignored all behavior. The purpose of this condition was to determine if aberrant behavior occurred in the absence of environmental or social consequences. Diverted attention, rather than an alone condition, was conducted because Clark could not be left alone in the classroom.

The results of Clark's functional analysis were confusing. Clark engaged in fairly low levels of self-injury across all but the tangible condition. His highest levels of self-injury occurred in some of the contingent escape assessment conditions. However, other contingent escape conditions resulted in near zero levels of self-injury. Further analysis showed that the contingent escape sessions with high frequencies of self-injury were conducted by a teacher associate, and the low frequency sessions were conducted by Clark's teacher. The teacher associate presented the task demands in a neutral, matter-of-fact tone of voice and did not praise Clark for compliance; the classroom teacher presented the task demands in an enthusiastic tone of voice and encouraged Clark to comply, using statements such as "I know you're a hard worker, Clark."

We hypothesized that the different request styles of the teacher and the associate accounted for the variable results observed in the contingent escape condition. We tested this hypothesis by coaching Clark's teacher to present the task demands in two ways: (a) in her usual enthusiastic style and (b) in a matter-of-fact tone of voice. By alternating the style of requests the teacher presented to Clark across a series of contingent escape sessions, we were able to confirm our hypothesis. Clark complied to task demands that were presented in an enthusiastic tone of voice but engaged in self-injury when the same task demands were presented in a more neutral manner, even when all other variables (teacher, task, and location) remained the same. The same analysis was conducted in Clark's residential center, using the same task but with direct care staff serving as therapists. The results of this analysis replicated the results achieved at school. Thus, a relatively subtle change in the analogue condition resulted in substantial changes in Clark's performance.

APPLICATION TO
SUPPORTED EMPLOYMENT

We have encountered several adults with developmental disabilities who possess marketable work skills but whose display of aberrant behavior prevents maintenance of long-term, community-based employment. We believe that these problem behaviors are influenced by the same environmental events as described in previous sections of this chapter and should also be evaluated via functional analysis procedures. Unfortunately, it is often difficult, at best, to conduct the analysis in community work settings due to pragmatic problems. For this reason, we rely more heavily on descriptive and structural analyses.

Case Example 8: Jane

Jauss (1993) used a combination of descriptive and structural analyses to evaluate environmental influences on the aberrant behavior displayed by a young woman during the work day. The analyses were conducted at the sheltered workshop that employed the woman and at a temporary community job site to evaluate the generality of the environmental effects in both sheltered and community settings.

Jane, a 28-year-old woman with moderate mental retardation, demonstrated excellent work skills when performing clerical tasks such as photocopying, address labeling, and filing. Although Jane demonstrated excellent work skills, she also engaged in high frequencies of aberrant behavior, including stereotypy, which consisted of bending over, removing her glasses, and stroking her hair every few minutes, and temper outbursts that occurred several times each day. The frequency of these behaviors significantly limited Jane's employment options. Jauss (1993) observed Jane as she performed a variety of work tasks within several set-

tings at the sheltered workshop to identify possible antecedent variables correlated with the occurrence of the problem behavior. The five variables initially targeted for evaluation included (a) the level of task difficulty, (b) Jane's apparent
preference for a task, (c) the specificity of instructions provided, (d) the social demands of the task, and (e) the presence or absence of auditory or visual distractions in the work environment. After observing Jane perform a series of tasks that
varied in these dimensions, Jauss (1993) determined that Jane's work performance
was best (high levels of accuracy and task completion and low levels of stereotypy
and having tantrums) when Jane was given a preferred task that she could perform independently. The remaining variables of specificity, social demands, and
distractions did not appear to influence Jane's task performance.

Following the completion of the descriptive assessment, Jauss conducted a
structural analysis to identify the influence of other (staff-defined) variables on
Jane's work performance within the high preference, low demand task arrangement. The following variables were evaluated within the analysis: (a) work setting
(sheltered workshop versus community work site), (b) presence of a counter to
monitor the number of work tasks completed, (c) presence of a one-minute delay
between Jane's request for assistance and the delivery of assistance, and (d) the delivery of a soft drink as a reinforcer at the end of the work period, contingent on
appropriate work performance. A job training specialist manipulated the presence
or absence of each variable. We evaluated the influence of each variable on Jane's
work performance and aberrant behavior within a reversal design. The results of
the structural analysis demonstrated that Jane's work performance was better
across both the community and the sheltered work sites when she had access to a
counter to monitor her completion of tasks, was not required to wait for more
than 10 seconds to receive assistance, and received a soft drink contingent on appropriate work behavior at the end of the work period. Given these results, Jauss
(1993) was able to identify the optimal working conditions for Jane that led to
Jane's successful placement into a clerical job at a community job site.

APPLICATION TO FOOD REFUSAL

In each of the previous examples, the analysis was conducted prior to treatment.
In some cases, however, the need for treatment is critical, precluding the use of
experimental analysis as a pretreatment assessment. In these cases, our approach is
to develop a treatment package, as described in our outpatient clinical setting
with more mild behaviors, and to follow successful treatment with a component
analysis. The component analysis is identical to the functional and structural
analyses described previously, but occurs post-treatment.

Case Example 9: Andy

Andy, a 23-month-old boy with significant development delay, had short-gut syndrome, a condition in which the intestines are too short to allow adequate absorption of nutrition. This condition was remediated by several surgeries to
lengthen his intestines. Although Andy had no known oral-motor or other physical

disorders to prevent oral food intake, he did not eat and engaged in tantrums, gagging, and spitting whenever food was presented to him orally. As a result, Andy received the majority of his nutritional needs through gastrostomy tube feedings and a central venous line.

During an in-patient evaluation, we conducted a descriptive assessment of the environmental events associated with Andy's food refusal. Baseline observations of Andy during feeding sessions with different therapists and food items revealed that Andy typically refused food offers and consumed less than 30 cc of food during a 20-minute feeding session, regardless of the therapist or food item. However, he readily accepted drinks from a sipper cup. We implemented a complex reinforcement-based treatment program that included (a) differential reinforcement of alternative behavior, in which Andy received praise and sips of water contingent on accepting an offer of food; (b) escape extinction, in which Andy was not allowed to escape a bite offer or the meal situation by refusing to eat; and (c) noncontingent access to toys during the meal to increase the overall level of socialization at mealtimes and to pair meals with preferred activities. The treatment package was effective in increasing Andy's acceptance of food, but was complex and time-consuming for his mother to implement on a routine basis at home.

We conducted a component analysis to identify which components of the treatment package we could remove without adversely affecting the number of bites Andy accepted. The two most difficult components of the treatment package, escape extinction and noncontingent access to toys, were removed and reinstated separately within a reversal design. The results of this analysis showed that both components were, indeed, critical components of the treatment package to be used at home.

SUMMARY

In this chapter, we have provided case examples of how functional and structural analyses can be used for distinct contexts, subgroups, and topographies of behavior. These analyses are often complex and can be time-consuming, because behavior is often complex and variable. However, unlike many other assessment practices, the results of these assessments lead directly to treatment. Of equal importance, the results can prevent countertherapeutic treatments—treatments that actually make the behavior worse due to inadvertent reinforcement. Thus, in our view, the amount of time and effort required to conduct a comprehensive behavioral assessment is time well spent.

Reinforcement-based treatments also take considerable amounts of time and energy to implement. We suspect that this is why treatment is changed so often and why default technologies (Iwata, 1988), such as punishment, are used so frequently. An experimental analysis can increase the confidence of care providers that the treatment they are implementing will eventually be successful. Confidence is increased because changes in behavior are directly observed during assessment. It is our view that as we continue the application of reinforcement-based treatments in a broader range of settings, subgroups, and behavior, we will need first to apply the assessment procedures of Carr & Durand (1985) and Iwata et al. (1982). As shown in the case examples presented in this chapter, we believe that it is possible to apply these procedures in most situations, and we hope that these types of applications continue to be attempted and the results disseminated.

REFERENCES

Bijou, S. W., Peterson, R. F., & Ault, M. H. (1968). A method to integrate descriptive and experimental field studies at the level of data and empirical concepts. *Journal of Applied Behavior Analysis, 1,* 175–191.

Carr, E. (1977). The motivation of self-injurious behavior: A review of some hypotheses. *Psychological Bulletin, 84,* 800–816.

Carr, E., & Durand, V. M. (1985). Reducing behavior problems through functional communication training. *Journal of Applied Behavior Analysis, 18,* 111–126.

Cooper, L. J., Wacker, D. P., Thursby, D., Plagmann, L. A., Harding, J., Millard, T., & Derby, M. (1992). Analysis of the effects of task preferences, task demands, and adult attention on child behavior in outpatient and classroom settings. *Journal of Applied Behavior Analysis, 25,* 823–840.

Cooper, L. J., Wacker, D. P., Sasso, G. M., Reimers, T. M., & Donn, L. (1990). Using parents as therapists to evaluate appropriate behavior of their children: Application to a tertiary diagnostic clinic. *Journal of Applied Behavior Analysis, 23,* 285–296.

Derby, K. M., Wacker, D. P., Sasso, G., Steege, M., Northup, J., Cigrand, K., & Asmus, J. (1992). Brief functional assessment techniques to evaluate aberrant behavior in an outpatient setting: A summary of 79 cases. *Journal of Applied Behavior Analysis, 25,* 713–721.

Durand, V. M. (1988). Motivation assessment scale. In M. Hersen & A. Bellack (Eds.), *Dictionary of behavioral assessment techniques* (pp. 309–310). Elmsford, NY: Pergamon.

Harding, J., Wacker, D., Cooper, L., Millard, T., & Jensen-Kovalan, P. (1994). Brief hierarchical assessment of potential treatment components with children in an outpatient clinic. *Journal of Applied Behavior Analysis, 27,* 291–300.

Iwata, B. (1988). The development and adoption of default technologies. *The Behavior Analyst, 11,* 149–157.

Iwata, B., Dorsey, M., Slifer, K., Bauman, K., & Richman, G. (1982). Toward a functional analysis of self-injury. *Analysis and Intervention in Developmental Disabilities, 2,* 3–20.

Iwata, B., Vollmer, T., & Zarcone, J. (1990). The experimental (functional) analysis of behavior disorders: Methodology, application, and limitations. In A. C. Repp & N. N. Singh (Eds.), *Perspective on the use of nonaversive and aversive interventions for persons with developmental disabilities* (pp. 301–330). Sycamore, IL: Sycamore.

Jauss, J. (1993). *Use of experimental analysis procedures to evaluate maintaining conditions of appropriate work behavior.* Unpublished doctoral dissertation, The University of Iowa, Iowa City, IA.

Lalli, J. S., & Goh, H. (1993). Naturalistic observation in community settings. In J. Reichle & D. Wacker (Eds.), *Communicative alternatives to challenging behavior: Integrating functional assessment and intervention strategies* (pp. 11–39). Baltimore: Paul H. Brookes.

Mace, F. C., & Lalli, J. (1991) Linking descriptive and experimental analyses in the treatment of bizarre speech. *Journal of Applied Behavior Analysis, 24,* 553–562.

Millard, T., Wacker, D., Cooper, L., Harding, J., Plagmann, L., Asmus, J., McComas, J., & Jensen-Kovalan, P. (1993). A brief component analysis of potential treatment packages in an outpatient clinic setting with young children. *Journal of Applied Behavior Analysis, 26,* 475–476.

Northup, J., Wacker, D., Berg, W., Kelly, L., Sasso, G., & DeRaad, A. (1994). The treatment of severe behavior problems in school settings using a technical assistance model. *Journal of Applied Behavior Analysis, 27,* 33–47.

Northup, J., Wacker, D., Sasso, G., Steege, M., Cigrand, K., Cook, J., & DeRaad, A. (1991). A brief functional analysis of aggressive and alternative behavior in an outclinic setting. *Journal of Applied Behavior Analysis, 24,* 509–522.

Repp, A. C., Felce, D., & Barton, L. E. (1988). Basing the treatment of stereotypic and self-injurious behavior on hypotheses of their causes. *Journal of Applied Behavior Analysis, 21,* 281–289.

Sasso, G., Reimers, T., Cooper, L., Wacker, D., Berg, W., Steege, M., Kelly, L., & Allaire, A. (1992). Use of descriptive and experimental analyses to identify the functional properties of aberrant behavior in school settings. *Journal of Applied Behavior Analysis, 25,* 809–821.

Touchette, P. E., MacDonald, R. F., & Langer, S. N. (1985). A scatter plot for identifying stimulus control of problem behavior. *Journal of Applied Behavior Analysis, 18,* 343–351.

Wacker, D., & Berg, K. (1989). *Proactive treatment model for self-injurious behavior.* Iowa Department of Education, Bureau of Special Education.

Wacker, D., Northup, J., & Cooper, L. (1992). Behavioral assessment. In D. Greydanus & M. Wolraich (Eds.), *Behavioral pediatrics* (pp. 57–68). New York: Springer-Verlag.

Wacker, D. P., & Steege, M. W. (1993). Providing outclinic services: Evaluating treatment and social validity. In R. Van Houten & S. Axelrod (Eds.), *Behavior analysis and treatment* (pp. 297–319). New York: Plenum.

Wacker, D., Steege, M., Northup, J., Reimers, T., Berg, W., & Sasso, G. (1990). Use of functional analysis and acceptability measures to assess and treat severe behavior problems: An outpatient clinic model. In A. Repp & N. Singh (Eds.), *Perspectives on the use of nonaversive and aversive interventions for persons with developmental disabilities* (pp. 349–359). Sycamore, IL: Sycamore.

4

Predicting and Enhancing the Effectiveness of Reinforcers and Punishers

CATHLEEN C. PIAZZA
WAYNE W. FISHER
HENRY S. ROANE
KELLIE HILKER

INTRODUCTION

The purpose of a functional assessment is to identify the contingencies that maintain problem behavior. Many of us use functional assessment information to develop hypotheses and then base an intervention on the chosen hypothesis. The editors and some of our colleagues argue that the intervention should consist of identifying appropriate behavior that accesses the same reinforcers the problem does, only more efficiently and effectively. The matching law of Herrnstein (1961) suggests that the individual will begin to increase the rate of appropriate behavior and decrease the rate of problem behavior when the rate of reinforcement shifts in favor of appropriate behavior. Maximization suggests that with sufficient and discriminable differences in the schedules of reinforcement for these two behaviors, the individual will maximize the amount of reinforcement by emitting only appropriate behavior.

In this context, one might view functional assessment as one method of reinforcer identification. Piazza, Fisher, Roane, and Hilker, in this fourth chapter, discuss other methods for identifying reinforcers. Because much of the work in functional assessment has been done in the field of developmental disabilities, the authors center their review in this area. They begin with the particular case these individuals present for studying sensory reinforcement, and then move to a detailed discussion of methods for predicting reinforcer effects, including preference assessments, forced choice assessments, and caregiver reports. Then they present a structured interview procedure they have developed (RAISD) and the results of work integrating it with other assessment procedures.

Other approaches, seldom brought into discussions of functional assessment, are then addressed. These include the Premack principle, response deprivation, establishing operations, the matching law, and satiation. With this chapter, the authors have moved us to consider how other methods or theories of reinforcer assessment are related to functional assessment procedures. As such, they have provided a challenge for all of us.

Reinforcement, one of the most commonly used procedures in the training of individuals with developmental disabilities, is important for two main reasons. First, reinforcers may assist in the acquisition of appropriate behaviors. For example, Koegel and Frea (1993) increased social communicative behaviors, such as eye gaze and facial expressions, in two children with autism by providing contingent access to video games. Second, reinforcers are useful in many behavior reduction programs. Vollmer et al. (1993) demonstrated decreased rates of self-injurious behavior when clients were presented with noncontingent social attention, such as praise.

The identification of reinforcing stimuli for developmentally disabled individuals may prove difficult for several reasons. First, individuals with the most severe disabilities often have limited verbal repertoires or multiple developmental impairments (sensory and motor impairments, for example) and are unable to verbally describe or emit simple responses (such as reaching) to choose reinforcers. Thus, researchers and practitioners may come to rely on arbitrarily chosen items that may or may not function as reinforcers when presented contingently (Green et al., 1988). Second, reinforcing stimuli often are idiosyncratic across people. For example, music may serve as a reinforcer for one individual, but not for another. Third, even when accurately identified, reinforcers may lose their effectiveness over time due to satiation (Egel, 1981). Finally, the occurrence of maladaptive behaviors (such as aggression or self-injury) or medical complications may limit exposure to potential reinforcing events (such as outings, social interaction, or specific foods). Therefore, some individuals with developmental disabilities may show few, if any, stimulus preferences, making it difficult to identify preferred items.

The purpose of this chapter is to provide the reader with an overview of the identification of reinforcers and punishers. Particular methods used to identify preferred stimuli and aversive events will be described. In addition, factors that influence the effectiveness of reinforcers—such as establishing operations or response effort—will be discussed.

IDENTIFICATION OF
REINFORCING STIMULI

Types of Stimuli Evaluated

The search for effective reinforcers has led investigators to examine the reinforcing potency of a variety of specific stimuli or groups of stimuli, such as food or sensory reinforcers. One of the most frequently studied categories involves the reinforcing properties of sensory stimulation. The high rate of stereotyped behaviors observed among persons with developmental disabilities has led researchers to conclude that engaging in these activities results in some reinforcing sensory consequences (Rincover et al., 1977). Sensory stimulation as a reinforcer is evidenced by (a) the lack of interest shown by some persons with developmental disabilities in alternative stimuli referred to as "social reinforcers" (Rincover & Newsom, 1985), (b) the ease of administration and availability (Pace et al., 1985), and (c) demonstration of its reinforcing properties with animals (Kish, 1966). A variety of sources of sensory stimulation—including vibratory (Fehr et al., 1979; Hogg, 1983; Johnson, Firth, & Davey, 1978), auditory (Fehr et al., 1979; Hogg, 1983; Rincover et al., 1977), visual (Hogg, 1983; Rincover et al., 1977) and proprioceptive (Rincover & Newsom, 1985) stimuli have been studied. For example, Bailey and Meyerson (1969) evaluated vibration as a reinforcer for the lever pressing of a child with profound retardation. In this investigation, a lever was mounted inside the child's crib. During baseline, lever pressing resulted in no programmed consequence. Following baseline, a vibrator was attached to the underside of the child's crib, and lever pressing resulted in 6 seconds of vibration. Stable rates of lever pressing occurred over a 21-day experimental period. During a subsequent extinction phase, lever pressing declined to baseline levels.

In addition to the evaluation of individual sensory reinforcers, the efficacy of specific reinforcers has been compared with other sensory reinforcers, and with social and edible reinforcers. Johnson, Firth, and Davey (1978) compared the effects of vibration and social praise on performance of a discrimination task with nine individuals with severe developmental disabilities. Vibration was a more potent reinforcer for eight out of the nine clients. For one individual, praise was more effective than vibration. Rincover and Newsom (1985) compared the effects of sensory and edible reinforcers on training discrimination tasks in three boys with autism. In this investigation, multiple (alternating) sensory stimuli were compared to multiple food items used as reinforcers. Comparisons also were made of single sensory and single food reinforcers. During the experimental phase, a discrimination task was presented to the child, and a reversal design was used to compare the effects of the multiple sensory reinforcers versus multiple edible reinforcers, and single edible reinforcers versus single sensory reinforcers. Multiple sensory reinforcers were superior to multiple food reinforcers in maintaining responding. Satiation occurred more quickly during the multiple food reinforcement sessions than in the multiple sensory sessions. Single edible and sensory reinforcers were equally effective in maintaining responding, and satiation occurred at approximately the same rate in the single edible and single sensory conditions.

Interest in the sensory consequences of behavior has led investigators to study the reinforcing potential of aberrant behavior such as high frequency stereotypy. The rationale for using stereotypic behavior as a reinforcer is similar to that for sensory stimuli described above. Aberrant behavior has the additional advantage of eliminating the need for external sources of reinforcement, thus increasing portability. However, one potential disadvantage would be the extent to which access to stereotypic behavior following a response results in negative side effects, such as increases in aberrant behavior. Charlop, Kurtz, and Casey (1990) evaluated the reinforcer potency of aberrant behavior such as stereotypy and echolalia for increasing the task performance of children with autism, measuring the potential side effects of this procedure in a three-experiment study. In Experiment 1, four children with autism were exposed to three experimental conditions: food reinforcement only, varied reinforcement (access to stereotypy and food), and stereotypy only. When stereotypy was used as the potential reinforcer, children were allowed or prompted to engage in stereotypic behavior following correct responding. The greatest increases in responding occurred in the access-to-stereotypy condition. In Experiment 2, evaluated reinforcers were delayed echolalia, food, and varied (echolalia and food). For one child, echolalia and varied reinforcers were about equal in effectiveness, for a second child varied reinforcers were slightly superior to echolalia, and for a third child echolalia was superior to both food and varied reinforcers. In Experiment 3, children were given access to perseverative behavior, stereotypy, or food contingent on correct responding. For two children, perseverative behavior was slightly more effective than stereotypy, and for one child, perseverative behavior was superior to either stereotypy or food in increasing responding. In general, no negative side effects (increases in stereotypies, echolalia, or perseverative behavior) were observed in postexperimental or home observations for any of the children during any phase. Other studies have supported the finding that access to stereotypic behavior can increase responding without negative side effects (Hung, 1978; Wolery, Kirk, & Gast, 1985).

Studies evaluating the reinforcing effects of specific stimuli have demonstrated that functional reinforcers can be identified for persons with disabilities. However, response to sensory reinforcement appears to be idiosyncratic across clients; thus, studies examining the effects of specific stimuli or groups of stimuli failed to delineate a clear method for predicting which stimuli would function as reinforcers for a given client. Studies examining stereotypic behavior as a reinforcer have demonstrated that such behavior can be used to reinforce other behaviors without negative side effects; however, this technique is applicable only for clients who engage in stereotypic behavior. Also, the extent to which stereotypic behavior must be restricted or prevented at other times (that is, when not being used as a reinforcer) has not been established. Thus, access to stereotypic behavior may not be motivating during learning trials if stereotypic behavior is freely available throughout the remainder of the day. If prevention of stereotypic responding is important to the success of the technique, applicability may be limited to those clients whose stereotypic behavior can be prevented when not being used as a reinforcer.

Identification of Responses to Be Reinforced

Reinforcer identification is complicated further by the difficulties in selecting an appropriate target response to evaluate reinforcer potency. Many of the same issues that affect the ability to identify preferred stimuli also affect our ability to measure reinforcing effects. That is, individuals with developmental disabilities have limited repertoires of responses, so discriminating between a motivational or a skills deficit may be difficult. The researcher, for example, must determine if the client's lack of response to a discrimination task is a function of an ineffective reinforcer or presentation of a task that is too difficult for the client to complete. In addition, individuals with multiple disabilities may be even more limited in their repertoire of responses. For example, while one client may be able to complete a color discrimination task, another client may be unable to point to an object to earn reinforcers.

Wacker et al. (1985) demonstrated that reinforcers could be identified for clients with multiple handicaps by using microswitches. Five students with profound mental retardation and multiple handicaps were given the opportunity to access stimuli (such as a fan or music) by pressing microswitches. Reinforcers were identified for each student. Responses to specific stimuli (fan or music) were idiosyncratic across students.

Dattilo (1986) used computerized assessments to evaluate reinforcer potency for three children with mental retardation. In this investigation, microswitches were connected to a computer programmed to activate sensory stimuli and to record client responses (i.e., microswitch presses). The available stimuli were music, video scenes, and a vibrating pad. A concurrent operants paradigm was used in which two switches were available during each phase. Each switch was associated with a different potential reinforcing stimulus. Each stimulus was paired with every other stimulus—one stimulus-stimulus comparison per phase, for three phases. This computerized method resulted in the identification of reinforcers for all clients.

Selecting an appropriate dependent measure for reinforcer assessment can be more difficult than one might expect. Ideally, the dependent measure should be a response with a relatively low free-operant level, clearly within the client's behavioral repertoire, and not very aversive. In our work (for example, Fisher et al., 1992), we select our dependent measures for reinforcer assessments based on informal observations made prior to beginning the reinforcer assessment. We use in-square behavior for individuals who resist sitting in chairs and in-seat behavior for clients who sit for high-preference, but not low-preference tasks. For clients who sit appropriately for most table tasks, we select a maintenance task, such as towel folding or sorting.

Methods for Predicting Reinforcer Effects

Previous research has either (a) identified stimuli as preferred without evaluating their effectiveness as reinforcers (for example, Cautela & Kastenbaum, 1967; Homme et al., 1969), or (b) identified reinforcing stimuli without assessing client preferences for those stimuli (for example, Dattilo, 1986; Wacker et al., 1985). Even though these investigations have provided useful information relative to reinforcer identification, application of the findings may be limited. Research has demonstrated that responses to specific stimuli are idiosyncratic across clients. Thus, it is possible that a large number of stimuli would need to be investigated in order to identify a reinforcing stimulus for a given individual.

In addition, it is important to distinguish between preference assessments and reinforcer assessments, because the two are not synonymous. Pace et al. (1985) evaluated a relatively large number of stimuli (16) during a preference assessment in order to identify preferred stimuli, and then the reinforcing effects of a small subset of stimuli were evaluated during the reinforcer assessment. The preference assessment is an efficient procedure for identifying potential reinforcers; however, it does not evaluate the reinforcing effects of the stimuli. The independent variable of the preference assessment involves an antecedent manipulation (for example, during each trial a stimulus is placed in front of the client) and the dependent variable is an approach response (for example, whether the client reaches for or interacts with the stimulus). Stimuli identified as highly preferred (approached during at least 80 percent of stimulus preference trials) are more likely to function as reinforcers than stimuli identified as less preferred. However, stimuli identified as highly preferred during a preference assessment do not necessarily function as reinforcers during a reinforcer assessment.

Procedures designed to identify preferred reinforcers should consist of two components. First, an assessment should be designed to evaluate preferences for multiple stimuli. Second, stimuli identified as preferred should be evaluated as reinforcers. Pace et al. (1985) developed a two-step method for assessing preferences for reinforcers. First, a preference assessment was conducted in which each of 16 stimuli was presented individually, 10 times each (for a total of 160 presentations). Approaches (such as reaches) toward each stimulus were recorded. If a client approached the stimulus within 5 seconds of its presentation, the stimulus was made available for an additional 5 seconds. If the stimulus was not approached within 5 seconds, the client was verbally prompted to touch the stimulus. If another 5 seconds elapsed, the item was removed, and a new item was presented. Preferred stimuli were defined as those approached on at least 80 percent of presentations; nonpreferred stimuli were defined as those approached on 50 percent or less of the presentations. Results demonstrated idiosyncratic responding, with four individuals responding for several stimuli on 80 percent of presentations, and two participants responding to only a few of the stimuli. Nevertheless, the preference assessment effectively identified preferred stimuli for all participants. The second step of this procedure involved the evaluation of the preferred items as reinforcers. This validation was conducted using a reversal design in which participants established a baseline rate of responding to a request, followed by responding for either a preferred or nonpreferred item (as identified in the assessment). Results demonstrated that contingent presentation of preferred stimuli increased responding relative to baseline and nonpreferred conditions. Pace et al. concluded that the assessment was an effective and simple method for identifying preferred reinforcers for individuals with severe developmental disabilities.

Despite its utility, the procedure developed by Pace et al. (1985) may have some limitations. Primarily, clients may approach all or most stimuli as an investigative response leading to multiple stimuli being identified as highly preferred (Fisher et al., 1992). In an attempt to address this limitation, Fisher et al. (1992) evaluated a variation of the preference assessment developed by Pace et al. (1985), in which individuals with severe developmental disabilities could choose between two stimuli presented concurrently. In this choice assessment, 16 stimuli were presented in pairs, and observers measured client approaches (such as reaches) toward either of the stimuli. Client approaches toward one of the two stimuli produced access to that stimulus for approximately 5 seconds. Client approaches toward both stimuli simultaneously were blocked. If 5 seconds elapsed without a client approach, the therapist would verbally prompt the client to approach an item. If another 5 seconds elapsed without an approach, both stimuli were removed, and two other stimuli were presented. The choice assessment identified stimuli as preferred—that is, approached on 80 percent of trials—for all participants.

The choice assessment was compared to the assessment developed by Pace et al. based on the outcomes for the two assessments. Results showed that all participants had items identified as preferred (approached on 80 percent of trials) in the choice assessment. In addition, the items identified as preferred in the choice assessment were also identified as preferred in the Pace et al. assessment. The Pace et al. assessment also identified several items as preferred that were not identified through the choice assessment. Next, a concurrent operants paradigm was used to compare the reinforcing effectiveness of stimuli identified as highly preferred on both assessments (that is, high-high stimuli) with stimuli identified as highly preferred on the Pace et al. assessment only (that is, approach-high stimuli). In-square or in-seat behavior was used as the dependent measure; the participants could gain access to either the high-high or the approach-high stimuli by standing in a square or sitting in a chair. Results showed that all four participants spent more time in the square or chair that contained the high-high stimuli. Thus, the choice assessment produced greater differentiation among stimuli and better predicted which stimuli would function as reinforcers when evaluated in a concurrent operants arrangement.

A number of other variations of the Pace et al. (1985) procedure have been investigated in order to improve reinforcer identification. Windsor, Piché, and Locke (1994) presented multiple stimuli to determine preferences for individuals with severe developmental disabilities. Six items were presented simultaneously to a participant over a series of five sessions, each containing ten trials. Each trial began with a therapist asking, "Which one do you want?" as the stimuli were presented. Participants were given 20 seconds to emit a selection response (for example, attempting to grasp an item). If the participant selected an item, he or she was allowed to consume the item, and the trial ended. If the participant did not respond within 20 seconds, the trial was scored as "no response" and subsequently ended. Results demonstrated that the multiple-stimulus assessment was an effective method for determining stimulus preferences. However, Windsor, Piché, and Locke did not evaluate the reinforcing efficacy of preferred stimuli.

DeLeon and Iwata (1996) evaluated an extension of the procedures described by Windsor, Piché, and Locke (1994). Whereas the latter replaced stimuli in subsequent trials following those in which they were selected, DeLeon and Iwata did not replace previously chosen stimuli. As a result, participants were required to choose among less preferred alternatives, which resulted in a more discrete ranking of preferred stimuli, based on comparisons with the less preferred stimuli. Preferred stimuli were evaluated as reinforcers through a reversal design. All participants showed increases in responding when preferred stimuli were presented contingently. DeLeon and Iwata also compared their assessment to the assessments described by Windsor, Piché, and Locke and Fisher et al. (1992) along three dimensions: (a) rank order of preferred stimuli, (b) time required for administration, and (c) number of potential reinforcers identified. For four of seven participants, all three assessments identified the same item as the most preferred. For the remaining three participants, high correlations were found between the most preferred stimuli in each assessment. The method described by Windsor, Piché, and Locke required the least amount of time to administer ($M = 16.5$ minutes), followed by the DeLeon and Iwata method ($M = 21.8$ minutes) and the choice assessment ($M = 53.3$ minutes). Finally, participants selected fewer items in the Windsor, Piché, and Locke assessment, whereas the DeLeon and Iwata and Fisher et al. assessments produced a discrete ranking of preferred stimuli.

More recently, Roane et al. (in press) developed a brief (5-minute) preference assessment in which individuals had continuous access to an array of stimuli presented simultaneously. Observers recorded the percentage of 10-second intervals that each participant manipulated any particular stimulus. Results demonstrated that all participants selected a preferred stimulus in this free-operant assessment. Preferred stimuli were assessed as reinforcers using a concurrent-operants paradigm (Fisher et al., 1992). If participants entered one square, the most-preferred stimulus was presented. If participants entered another square (control), no stimuli were presented. Results indicated that five out of six participants allocated the majority of responding toward the square associated with the most preferred stimulus. Roane et al. compared this assessment to the assessment developed by Fisher et al. Fourteen of 17 participants (82.3 percent) demonstrated similar stimulus preferences in both assessments. In addition, the average length of the Fisher et al. assessment was 21.67 minutes (range, 13.22 minutes to 34.43 minutes), whereas the Roane et al. assessment was always 5 minutes. Thus, Roane et al. identified a method of identifying stimulus preferences in a relatively brief amount of time.

Another recent extension of stimulus preference assessments involves a concurrent measurement of preference and aberrant behavior (for example, Piazza et al., 1996; Ringdahl et al., 1997). In the Piazza et al. investigation, stimuli were presented singly, and observers scored the duration of item interaction (the measure of preference) and the occurrence of problem behavior while each item was available. Thus, the assessment yielded data on stimulus preference (high or low) and the occurrence of aberrant behavior (high or low). Results demonstrated that stimuli could be classified along three dimensions: (a) high preference/high problem behavior, (b) high preference/low problem behavior, and (c) low preference/low problem behavior. Both high preference items were subsequently shown to function as reinforcers for a simple operant response (such as head turning). Ringdahl et al. also incorporated a measure of problem behavior into a preference assessment similar to that described by Roane et al. (in press). Ringdahl et al. showed that the assessment was effective at identifying preferred items that resulted in low levels of problem behavior. Thus, Piazza et al. and Ringdahl et al. developed assessments in which the ability of stimuli to compete with problem behavior was evaluated.

The verbal report of caregivers has also been investigated as a method of identifying preferred stimuli. Green et al. (1988) conducted a systematic analysis of a caregiver reports. In this investigation, client approach responses to a "standard" list of items were measured. Highly preferred items were identified for five out of seven clients based on the results of the preference assessment using the standard items. In general, items that were found to be highly preferred on the systematic preference assessment (that is, approached on 80 percent or more of trials) were found to be functional reinforcers. In addition, caregivers were asked to rank order predicted client preferences for these standard items. Correlations between caregivers' rankings of student preferences and actual student preferences (based on the results of the systematic preference assessment) were not significant. Items that caregivers predicted would be highly preferred were functional reinforcers only if the items were highly preferred in the systematic preference assessment. Finally, items that caregivers predicted would be highly preferred, but that were not approached often during the preference assessment, were not functional reinforcers. Thus, in this investigation, a caregiver report added little to the results of a systematic preference assessment.

Green et al. (1991) conducted a four-experiment investigation as follow-up to the 1988 study. Experiment 1 was a replication of their original work, in which preference assessments were conducted for six clients using a standard list of items. Preferred items were identified for five out of six clients. In addition, caregivers were asked to rank-order predicted client preferences for standard items. Caregiver opinion significantly correlated with measured preferences for two of six clients, a finding different from the original investigation. Experiment 2 evaluated the extent to which highly preferred stimuli functioned as reinforcers for nine clients. Highly preferred items (identified as highly preferred based on the results of the preference assessment and caregiver opinion) functioned as reinforcers for four clients. For four clients, highly preferred stimuli and reinforcers were not identified. For one client, the item identified as highly preferred based on the combination of the systematic preference assessment and caregiver opinion was not a functional reinforcer. In Experiment 3, caregivers were asked to independently identify potential reinforcing stimuli for six clients. Highly preferred items (based on the results of a systematic preference assessment) were identified for two out of six clients. For one client, no highly preferred items had been identified in previous assessments. Thus, for this client, caregiver opinion was useful for the identification of reinforcers. Finally, in Experiment 4 the stability of client preference over time was assessed. In this experiment, preference assessments were conducted over a variety of time intervals (4 to 28 months). A significant correlation between first and second assessment was obtained for 8 out of 12 clients, indicating that preference remained relatively stable over time.

In conclusion, several investigators have used caregiver or teacher reporting as a basis for selecting preferred stimuli. The extent to which those preferred stimuli have been found to be functional reinforcers has varied. However, the contribution of a caregiver or teacher report appears to be improved by conducting systematic preference assessments. That is, items that are highly preferred based on the results of preference assessments and caregiver reports more often function as reinforcers than items based on caregiver reports alone.

In an attempt to improve the accuracy of caregiver reporting, Fisher et al. (1996) developed a structured interview designed to be completed by caregivers—the Reinforcer Assessment for Individuals with Severe Disabilities (RAISD). The RAISD was used to have caregivers generate a list of preferred stimuli across several different stimulus domains (visual, audible, olfactory, tactile, edible, movement, social attention, and toys). Caregivers were also asked to list stimuli that could be delivered in a clinical setting (food instead of riding a pony). For example, for visual stimuli, a parent would be asked,

> "Some children really enjoy looking at things such as a mirror, bright lights, shiny objects, spinning objects, TV, etc. What are the things you think _____ most likes to watch?"

The RAISD was then used to generate a list of the most preferred stimuli based on the caregiver report, and probe questions were then asked to help better operationally define these stimuli. For example, if TV was identified as a preferred stimulus, the parent might be asked whether the child preferred (a) specific shows (such as *Barney*), (b) certain types of shows (such as cartoons or action shows), or (c) watching TV with others.

Following caregiver generation of a list of preferred stimuli, the extent to which information from the RAISD could be integrated with a choice assessment (Fisher et al., 1992) to improve reinforcer identification was evaluated. Caregivers were asked to predict the child's preference for the items by rank-ordering them from most to least preferred. These rankings were compared to the rankings produced by the choice assessment. Statistically significant correlations ($r = .32; p < .005$) were found between caregiver rankings and the results of the choice assessment when the items identified through the RAISD were used. Although significant, the correlations between the results of the RAISD and the choice assessment were low, and there were many items on which the two assessments differed (e.g., an item was highly preferred in one assessment but not in the other assessment). These results indicated that the RAISD should not be used as a substitute for a formal choice assessment, but may be used as a supplement to a preference assessment.

In the second part of this investigation, preferences for stimuli identified through the RAISD were compared to a standard set of 16 stimuli (based on the stimuli used by Pace et al., 1985). A separate choice assessment was conducted with both sets of stimuli. Highly preferred caregiver-generated and standard stimuli were identified. Subsequently, a reinforcer assessment was conducted in which participants could engage in one of two responses. For example, when the response choice consisted of sitting in one of two available chairs, one chair was associated with preferred items from the standard set of stimuli, while the other chair was associated with items generated from the RAISD. Results showed that all participants allocated more responding toward the chair associated with stimuli from the RAISD. Thus, it appeared that the RAISD was a useful method of incorporating a caregiver report of stimulus preference with a more formal preference assessment.

Identifying Reinforcers With Functional Analyses

Functional analysis is another systematic assessment that can be used to prescribe reinforcement-based treatments. The purpose of functional analysis is to identify environmental variables that influence the behavior of an individual (Skinner, 1953). Even though the term "function" refers to the environmental effects or consequences of a response, functional analysis also has been used to identify antecedent stimuli that occasion aberrant behavior (see, for example, Mace & Knight, 1986). One goal of functional analysis is to examine the extent to which antecedent and/or consequent stimuli affect a behavior's frequency, intensity, or duration. A major difference between functional analysis and other types of assessment techniques (such as interviews) is that variables hypothesized to affect the target behavior are directly manipulated using single-case experimental design procedures (Kazdin, 1982). Thus, the extent to which these variables affect the target behavior is tested experimentally. Functional analysis can be applied to reinforcer assessment: if reinforcers are identified to maintain target maladaptive behavior, then these same reinforcers can be manipulated to increase target appropriate behavior.

For example, Carr and Durand (1985) used the results of a functional analysis to teach clients to access assistance or attention by signing instead of maladaptive behavior. Steege et al. (1989) combined information from reinforcer and functional assessments to treat the self-injurious behavior of two children with developmental disabilities. For one client, self-injury was identified as self-stimulatory during a functional analysis. During treatment, the client could activate a microswitch to access a radio or a fan, items identified as reinforcers during a reinforcer assessment. Implementation of this treatment resulted in lowered rates of self-injury and high rates of microswitch pressing. For the second client, a functional analysis indicated that self-injurious behavior was maintained by escape from demands. During treatment, the child was given access to highly preferred stimuli following completion of tasks during a demand condition. Self-injury decreased following implementation of the treatment.

Predicting Reinforcer Effects Based on
Response Probabilities

Previous investigators have examined the relationship between the probability of a response and its effectiveness as a reinforcing event, developing principles that help predict the reinforcing effects of responses. One such predictor is Premack's principle. Even though reinforcers are generally classified as stimuli, Premack pointed out that reinforcers almost always involve both stimuli (M&Ms, a toy) and responses (eating the M&Ms, playing with a toy). He argued that the responses might be more important to reinforcement than the stimuli—that the reinforcing value comes from eating the M&Ms or playing with the toy rather than from the items themselves. Premack's principle states that when an individual has free access to two or more responses, responses that occur more frequently (higher probability responses) can be used to reinforce responses that occur less frequently (lower probability responses) (Premack, 1959, 1962, 1963). For example, eating dessert (a high probability response) can increase the occurrence of eating vegetables (a low probability response).

Premack's principle predicts the reinforcing effects of responses rather well. However, there are conditions under which higher probability responses do not function as reinforcers for lower probability responses (Premack, 1965), most notably when the individual gains access to a large amount of the high probability response after presenting a small amount of the low probability response. There also are conditions under which lower probability responses can function as reinforcers for higher probability responses. For example, if access to a lower probability response is restricted and provided contingent upon high amounts of a higher probability response, then the lower probability response can function as a reinforcer for the higher probability response (Eisenberger, Karpman, & Trattner, 1967). These findings have led to subsequent revisions of Premack's principle variously called response deprivation theory, disequilibrium theory, and behavioral regulation theory (Timberlake, 1984; Timberlake & Allison, 1974; Timberlake & Farmer-Dougan, 1991).

Like Premack's principle, these theories predict the reinforcing effects of responses based on the levels of responding observed during a baseline condition in which the individual has free access to all target responses concurrently. Premack's principle predicts reinforcer effects based on the relative probabilities of the target responses (based on a measurement of the relative duration of each response in a baseline condition wherein the individual has free access to all of the responses concurrently). According to Premack's principle, higher probability responses are reinforcers for lower probability responses and lower probability responses are punishers for higher probability responses. By contrast, these subsequent theories (i.e., response deprivation) predict reinforcer effects based on the restrictions imposed upon a response by a given contingency. That is, if access to either a lower or higher probability response is restricted so that it occurs less than during the free-access baseline, the response will function as a reinforcer (that is, the organism will engage in the target response to access the restricted response). If the individual is required to perform a response at levels higher than during the free-access baseline, then the response will function as a punisher.

Several investigators have applied the response deprivation hypothesis to clinical problems. For example, Kornarski et al. (1980) found that contingent access to math problems produced increases in a more probable response (coloring) or a less probable response (reading) in first-grade students. However, they also found that noncontingent access to math problems on a matched schedule resulted in similar increases in coloring and reading. Kornarski and colleagues have replicated the effects of response deprivation with individuals with developmental disabilities (Konarski, 1987; Konarski et al., 1982). In addition, Dougher (1983) used the same contingent response (coffee consumption) as a reinforcer for one response (social interaction) using response deprivation methods, and as a punisher for another response (coughing), using response satiation.

Although there are a number of advantages to reinforcement theories based on response deprivation, routine use of these procedures in most applied settings has been limited for a number of reasons. First, a substantial amount of time may be required in order to establish the free-operant levels of target behaviors in various situations. Second, it may be difficult to establish the free-operant levels of responses that are rule-governed or under instructional control. Third, all of the target responses increased in response deprivation studies have been ones that occur at some free-operant level (suggesting that there is at least some amount of automatic reinforcement associated with the response). By contrast, clinicians frequently wish to establish and strengthen new responses or responses that the client actively avoids (by noncompliance). Fourth, individuals with severe disabilities may be prompt dependent and display few free-operant responses. Finally, response deprivation appears to be an effective method of predicting reinforcer effectiveness in a given situation (such as the condition in which the free-operant baseline is established), but it is not clear to what extent the results obtained in one situation will apply in other situations.

Conditions that Affect Reinforcer Potency

The extent to which a given stimulus functions as a reinforcer may vary considerably over time and across situations. For example, going to the playground may function as a reinforcer for one response (cleaning one's room) but not another (washing windows). Edible reinforcers are generally more effective just before a meal and less effective just after a meal. The reinforcing effects of a cold drink may increase substantially immediately after consuming a bite of hot food. Being cuddled by one's father may be a more effective reinforcer with a child who has been scolded recently by his or her mother. Playing Nintendo may be an effective reinforcer for washing dishes when there is no other means available for obtaining this game, but not when Nintendo also is available contingent upon a less effortful response (starting the dishwasher). Current reinforcer assessment strategies generally do not assess this variability (or relativity) in reinforcer strength, nor do they take into account factors that produce either transient or more persistent changes in the reinforcing effects of preferred stimuli. However, the basic literature on reinforcement has produced a number of principles that help delineate conditions that increase or decrease the effectiveness of a reinforcer.

Michael (1982) coined the term "establishing operation" to describe an environmental condition or event that changes the effectiveness of a reinforcing (or punishing) stimulus. The two most investigated forms of establishing operations are deprivation (decreased availability of a reinforcer) and satiation (prolonged availability or consumption of a reinforcer). Deprivation increases and satiation decreases the effectiveness of a reinforcer. Reinforcing stimuli may vary greatly in terms of the rapidity with which deprivation occurs—for example, running out of toilet paper may lead to a trip to the store more readily than running out of cornstarch.

Similarly, satiation may occur more rapidly for some stimuli than for others. For example, the reinforcing effects of rich foods may decrease dramatically after just a few bites, whereas the reinforcing effects of video games may endure indefinitely.

Even though the importance of deprivation and satiation has been recognized in the basic operant literature, only sparse attention has been allocated to these establishing operations in the applied literature. One notable exception is an investigation by Vollmer and Iwata (1991). In this study, deprivation increased and satiation decreased performance of responses maintained on appetitive schedules using food, music, or social attention as the reinforcing stimulus. Interestingly, the lengths and levels of deprivation and satiation were similar to conditions that normally occurred in the clients' daily routines. For example, naturally occurring times of the day were used to evaluate the reinforcing effects of food under conditions of deprivation (sessions conducted just prior to lunch) and satiation (session conducted just after lunch). Music and social interaction were either presented noncontingently (satiation) or were not available (deprivation) for 15 to 30 minutes prior to each session. Across the three reinforcers, response rates were, on average, 5.5 times higher (range, 1.3 to 22.6) during deprivation conditions than during satiation conditions. These results suggest that (a) the effectiveness of a given reinforcer can vary greatly over the course of a normal day, (b) limiting access to a stimulus for a brief period prior to using it as a reinforcer can greatly increase its effectiveness, and (c) the accuracy of various reinforcer identification strategies may be affected by establishing operations like deprivation and satiation (for example, edible items may be more likely to be identified as high preference stimuli if the assessment is conducted shortly before rather than shortly after mealtimes).

One method for limiting reinforcer satiation is through reinforcer variation. Egel (1981) evaluated the extent to which varying reinforcers would result in increased acquisition and decreased reinforcer satiation. In this experiment, children were given either single edible reinforcers or varied edible reinforcers. Trials were conducted until the child satiated (that is, performance declined following repeated presentation of the reinforcer) or 125 trials. In each of the single reinforcer conditions, satiation occurred prior to the completion of 125 trials. However, in the varied reinforcement condition no declines in performance occurred during the 125 trials completed. Bowman et al. (1997) compared the reinforcing effectiveness of a single high preference stimulus versus varied reinforcers using less preferred stimuli. They found that varied reinforcement was more effective for four out of seven participants, constant reinforcement was more effective for two participants, and one participant did not demonstrate a preference for either.

The effectiveness of a reinforcer (such as food) to increase or maintain a response may be affected not only by prior availability (satiation) or unavailability (deprivation) of that specific stimulus, but also by the availability of other preferred stimuli. Situations in which multiple responses are available to an individual and each response is correlated with a different consequence are referred to as choice (Mazur, 1994), concurrent operants (Ferster & Skinner, 1957), or concurrent schedule (Herrnstein, 1961) paradigms. Because two or more reinforcers are pitted against one another in choice paradigms, they provide a direct means of comparing the relative potency of different schedules (VI 60 seconds versus VI 40 seconds), types (food versus water), or quantities (dimes versus nickels) of reinforcement (Catania, 1963). Choice paradigms may more closely approximate naturalistic situations, wherein individuals may display a variety of responses and each response may be associated with a unique consequence.

In most basic experiments on choice behavior, two topographically identical responses (such as pressing Key 1 versus Key 2) are each correlated with different variable interval schedules of reinforcement (such as Key 1 = VI 60 seconds, Key 2 = VI 40 seconds). Under such conditions, the rate of each response tends to match the amount of reinforcement available through each response. This phenomenon has been called matching—the rate of responding matches the rate of reinforcement. Herrnstein (1961) and others have developed mathematical formulas that predict reinforcer effects in choice paradigms. For example, reinforcement would be available 1.5 times more on a variable interval (VI) 40-second schedule than on a VI 60-second schedule. According to the matching law, the rate of responding associated with the VI 40-second schedule also should be 1.5 times higher than the rate of responding on the VI 60-second schedule when both schedules are in effect concurrently. By contrast, when these two schedules are in effect at different times, they tend to produce similar rates of responding. Matching has also been observed when differing amounts of reinforcement (3-second access to food versus 5-second access) are compared in a choice paradigm—that is, the rate of each response is proportional to or matches the amount of the reinforcement delivered for each response.

When two variable interval schedules are in effect in a choice paradigm, an individual tends to switch from one response to another. When two ratio schedules are in effect, individuals tend to emit only the response associated with the denser schedule. For example, if Key 1 is associated with a VR 50 schedule and Key 2 with a VR 75, over time all or almost all responding should occur on Key 1. This phenomenon has been labeled maximization—that is, the individual maximizes the amount of reinforcement received by emitting only the response associated with the denser schedule (Shimp, 1969).

From a clinical perspective, variable interval schedules appear to be most useful for comparing the relative preference of two schedules, types, or amounts of reinforcement. When variable interval schedules are used, the rate of responding generally will match the relative reinforcing value of the stimulus. For example, Neef and colleagues (for example, Neef et al., 1993; Neef, Shade, & Miller, 1994) have used concurrent VI VI schedules to assess the effects of reinforcer rate, quality, and delay, and response effort on time allocation to academic tasks among students with emotional disabilities. In general, these investigators found that time allocation matched the rate of reinforcement associated with each task when reinforcer quality, delay, and response effort were held constant. However, clients showed preferences for higher quality and more immediate reinforcers even when these reinforcers were associated with leaner reinforcement schedules.

Ratio schedules, and especially continuous reinforcement schedules (CRF), may be most useful for rapidly determining which of two schedules, types, or amounts of reinforcement is more preferred by an individual. For example, three out of four participants in the Fisher et al. (1992) study responded in a manner consistent with the maximization phenomena either immediately or within the first few sessions. It is unlikely that such rapid differential responding would have occurred had each stimulus been correlated with a variable interval schedule.

In addition, preferences observed under some ratio schedules may be abolished as reinforcement schedule requirements increase. For example, Tustin (1994) exposed one participant to increasing FR (fixed ratio) schedules of reinforcement for two qualitatively different reinforcers (visual stimulation and attention). Results showed clear changes in reinforcer preference as response requirements increased (for example, FR 20). That is, response rates that were identical under a low schedule requirement (FR 1) differed as response requirements increased. DeLeon et al. (1997) further evaluated the relationship between reinforcer preference and response effort. Preferences were assessed by increasing schedules of reinforcement over time (FR 1, FR 2, FR 5, and FR 10). Similar numbers of reinforcers were earned for each item (indicating similar preferences) under low schedule requirements; however, similarities in preferences were not replicated as schedule requirements increased.

In addition to altering schedule requirements, reinforcer preference may also be affected by changes in response effort. Shore et al. (1997) showed that participants preferred alternative forms of stimulation (such as toy play) to automatically maintained aberrant behavior when both were continuously available. In a subsequent study, however, preferences were influenced by the effort required to access the alternative reinforcement. Specifically, the effort required to access alternative reinforcement was manipulated by altering the distance between the participant and the reinforcer. Thus, participants were required to exert more effort to access alternative stimulation as the stimulus was placed further away. Results showed that small changes in reinforcer distance abolished preferences for alternative stimuli relative to aberrant behavior.

A METHOD FOR PREDICTING PUNISHMENT EFFECTS

Even though a variety of procedures are available for identifying reinforcers, few procedures are available to guide clinicians in the selection of effective punishment procedures. In cases where the clinician believes the potential benefit of a punishment procedure outweighs the potential harm, having an empirical method of punisher selection has several advantages. First, if the punishment procedure is based on an accurate method for predicting treatment effectiveness, then the probability of quickly suppressing behavior is increased. Thus the need for an individual to be repeatedly exposed to a series of potentially unpleasant, but ineffective procedures is eliminated. Rapid suppression also may be important in cases where the behavior is severe, and the individual is at significant danger to him or herself or others (for instance, further self-injury may cause blindness). Second, having an accurate method of predicting punisher effectiveness may decrease the chance that the treatment procedure will have an effect opposite of what was intended. For example, contingent restraint is sometimes selected as a treatment for self-injurious behavior, but can function to reinforce this problem behavior (see, for example, Favell, McGimsey, & Jones, 1978). Finally, effective prediction of punishment effects can result in selection of the least intrusive but most effective procedure, thus reducing the probability that resistance to treatment or habituation (Azrin & Holz, 1966) will occur as a result of exposing the client to ineffective procedures.

A method for assessing punishment effects has been evaluated by Fisher and colleagues (Chapman et al., 1993; Fisher et al., 1994a; Fisher et al., 1994b). Identification of punishers involves a two-step process similar to that used for reinforcer assessment. During the first step, stimulus avoidance assessment, the client is exposed briefly to a series of potential punishment procedures. Prior to exposure, caregivers and the client's teacher are interviewed to establish the acceptability of the potential treatment procedures. Only procedures that the caregivers find acceptable are considered for use. The potential punishment procedures are: basket hold time-out, facial screen, contingent demands, contingent exercise, tidiness training, hands down, quiet hands, chair time-out, and water mist (descriptions of the procedures appear in Fisher et al., 1994a and 1994b). One 10-minute session is conducted per procedure. Each session consists of 10 trials (that is, 10 applications of the procedure). Prior to the onset of the trial, a buzzer is sounded to signal the start of the procedure. The procedure selected for the session is then implemented for 30 seconds, followed by a 30-second break. The buzzer is used to prevent superstitious conditioning. During the sessions, observers record occurrences of avoidance movements, negative vocalizations, positive vocalizations, and escape from the procedure. Avoidance movements and negative vocalizations are used as a measure of nonpreference for the procedure. The rationale is that just as positive responding in a preference assessment (Fisher et al., 1992; Pace et al., 1985) reflects preference for a procedure, then negative responding is an indication of nonpreference for the procedure and may predict punishing effects. Escape from the procedure is used as a measure of treatment integrity and allows assessment of ease of implementation of the procedure. The avoidance movements and negative vocalizations are summed to create an avoidance index. Following completion of all sessions (that is, exposure of the child to all procedures deemed acceptable by the caregivers), the avoidance indices are compared for the procedures.

In the second step of the assessment, the punisher assessment, the behavior-suppressing effects of three procedures are compared. The procedures selected for comparison are those with the highest, median, and lowest avoidance indices based on the results of the stimulus avoidance assessment. In the first phase of the punisher assessment, a baseline is conducted to establish levels of a behavior. In the next phase, the efficacy of the three procedures is compared in a multielement design. After the effects of the three procedures have been established, a reversal to baseline is conducted. Based on the results of the punisher assessment, the most effective procedure is selected to treat the client's target maladaptive behavior.

The selected punisher is combined with a differential reinforcement procedure in a package called empirically derived consequences (EDC). The reinforcers are selected according to the procedure described above using the RAISD and a choice assessment (for example, Fisher et al., 1996). Thus far, the results for the EDC treatment package have been encouraging with the clients treated. Fisher et al. (1994a) treated two clients with severe destructive behavior (self-injury, aggression, and destruction) for whom the results of a functional analysis were equivocal. For both clients, destructive behavior decreased markedly when the EDC package was applied. Fisher et al. (1994b) also treated three children with severe pica. The pica for all clients was significantly reduced during treatment and at three, six, and nine-month follow-up. Finally, Chapman et al. (1993) treated the life-threatening pill swallowing of a young man with a dual diagnosis based on the results of a functional analysis and reinforcer and punisher assessments.

In summary, there is a growing body of literature on predicting and enhancing the effectiveness of reinforcers and punishers. In addition, there is a growing awareness regarding the relativity of reinforcer effects. A particular item, event, or activity may function as a reinforcer for one response but not another, or in one situation but not another. Similarly, reinforcer effectiveness can be affected greatly by establishing operations (such as deprivation and satiation), or the availability of alternative reinforcers (such as choices). Inclusion of these and other factors into reinforcer assessments may increase the length and complexity of our assessments, but also may improve accuracy and, hopefully, client outcome. As progress in the area of reinforcer and punisher assessment continues, we must continually balance accuracy and simplicity. As Einstein so aptly said, "Keep things as simple as possible, but no simpler."

REFERENCES

Azrin, N. H., & Holz, W. C. (1966). Punishment. In W. K. Honig (Ed.), *Operant behavior: Areas of research and application* (pp. 380–447). New York: Appleton

Bailey, J., & Meyerson, L. (1969). Vibration as a reinforcer with a profoundly retarded child. *Journal of Applied Behavior Analysis, 2,* 135–137.

Bowman, L. G., Piazza, C. C., Fisher, W. W., Hagopian, L. P., & Kogan, J. S. (1997). Assessment of preference for varied versus constant reinforcers. *Journal of Applied Behavior Analysis, 30,* 451–458.

Carr, E. G., & Durand, V. M. (1985). Reducing behavior problems through functional communication training. *Journal of Applied Behavior Analysis, 18,* 111–126.

Catania, A. C. (1963). Concurrent performances: A baseline for the study of reinforcement magnitude. *Journal of the Experimental Analysis of Behavior, 6,* 299–300.

Cautela, J. R., & Kastenbaum, R. A. (1967). A reinforcement survey for use in therapy, training, and research. *Psychological Reports, 20,* 1115–1130.

Chapman, S., Fisher, W., Piazza, C. C., & Kurtz, P. F. (1993). Functional assessment and treatment of life-threatening pill consumption in a dually-diagnosed youth. *Journal of Applied Behavior Analysis, 25,* 255–256.

Charlop, M. H., Kurtz, P. F., & Casey, F. G. (1990). Using aberrant behaviors as reinforcers for autistic children. *Journal of Applied Behavior Analysis, 23,* 163–181.

Dattilo, J. (1986). Computerized assessment of preference for severely handicapped individuals. *Journal of Applied Behavior Analysis, 19,* 445–448.

DeLeon, I. G., & Iwata, B. A. (1996). A comparison of paired and group (with and without replacement) stimulus presentation during reinforcer preference assessment. *Journal of Applied Behavior Analysis, 29,* 519–533.

DeLeon, I. G., Iwata, B. A., Goh, H. L., & Worsdell, A. S. (1997). Emergence of reinforcer preference as a function of schedule requirements and stimulus similarity. *Journal of Applied Behavior Analysis, 30,* 439–449.

Dougher, M. J. (1983). Clinical effects of response deprivation and response satiation procedures. *Behavior Therapy, 14,* 286–298.

Egel, A. L. (1981). Reinforcer variation: Implications for motivating developmentally disabled children. *Journal of Applied Behavior Analysis, 14,* 345–350.

Eisenberger, R., Karpman, M., & Trattner, J. (1967). What is the necessary and sufficient condition for reinforcement in the contingency condition? *Journal of Experimental Psychology, 74,* 342–350.

Favell, J. E., McGimsey, J. F., & Jones, M. L. (1978). The use of physical restraint in the treatment of self-injury and as positive reinforcement. *Journal of Applied Behavior Analysis, 11,* 225–241

Fehr, M. J., Wacker, D., Trezise, J., Lennon, R., & Meyerson, L. (1979). Visual, auditory, and vibratory stimulation as reinforcers for profoundly retarded children. *Rehabilitation Psychology, 26,* 201–209.

Ferster, C. B. & Skinner, B. F. (1957). *Schedules of reinforcement.* New York: Appleton-Century-Crofts.

Fisher, W. W., Piazza, C. C., Bowman, L. G., & Amari, A. (1996). Integrating caregiver report with a systematic choice assessment to enhance reinforcer identification. *American Journal on Mental Retardation, 101,* 15–25.

Fisher, W. W., Piazza, C. C., Bowman, L. G., Hagopian, L. P., & Langdon, N. A. (1994a). Empirically derived consequences: A data-based method for prescribing treatments for destructive behavior. *Research in Developmental Disabilities, 15,* 133–149.

Fisher, W., Piazza, C. C., Bowman, L. G., Hagopian, L. P., Owens, J. C., & Slevin, I. (1992). A comparison of two approaches for identifying reinforcers for persons with severe to profound disabilities. *Journal of Applied Behavior Analysis, 25,* 491–498.

Fisher, W. W., Piazza, C. C., Bowman, L. G., Kurtz, P. F., Sherer, M. R., & Lachman, S. R. (1994b). A preliminary evaluation of empirically derived consequences for the treatment of pica. *Journal of Applied Behavior Analysis, 27,* 447–457.

Green, C. W., Reid, D. H., Canipe, V. S., & Gardner, S. M. (1991). A comprehensive evaluation of reinforcer identification processes for persons with profound multiple handicaps. *Journal of Applied Behavior Analysis, 24,* 537–552.

Green, C. W., Reid, D. H., White, L. K., Halford, R. C., Brittain, D. P., & Gardner, S. M. (1988). Identifying reinforcers for persons with profound handicaps: Staff opinion versus systematic assessment of preferences. *Journal of Applied Behavior Analysis, 21,* 31–43.

Herrnstein, R. J. (1961). Relative and absolute strength of response as a function of frequency of reinforcement. *Journal of the Experimental Analysis of Behavior, 4,* 267–272.

Hogg, J. (1983). Sensory and social reinforcement of head-turning in a profoundly retarded multiply handicapped child. *British Journal of Clinical Psychology, 22,* 33–40.

Homme, L. E., Csanyi, A. P., Gonzales, M. A., & Rechs, J. R. (1969). *How to use contingency contracting in the classroom.* Champaign, IL: Research Press.

Hung, D. W. (1978). Using self-stimulation as reinforcement for autistic children. *Journal of Autism and Childhood Schizophrenia, 8,* 355–366.

Johnson, D., Firth, H., & Davey, G. C. (1978). Vibration and praise as reinforcers for mentally handicapped people. *Mental Retardation, 16,* 339–342.

Kazdin, A. G. (1982). *Single-case research designs: Methods for clinical and applied settings.* New York: Oxford.

Kish, G. B. (1966). Studies of sensory reinforcement. In W. K. Honig (Ed.), *Operant behavior: Areas of research and application.* New York: Appleton-Century-Crofts.

Koegel, R. L., & Frea, W. D. (1993). Treatment of social behavior in autism through the modification of pivotal social skills. *Journal of Applied Behavior Analysis, 26,* 369–377.

Konarski, E. A. (1987). Effects of response deprivation on the instrumental performance of mentally retarded persons. *American Journal of Mental Deficiency, 91,* 537–542.

Konarski, E. A., Crowell, C. R., Johnson, M. R., & Whitman, T. L. (1982). Response deprivation, reinforcement, and instrumental academic performance in an EMR classroom. *Behavior Therapy, 13,* 94–102.

Konarski, E. A., Johnson, M. R., Crowell, C. R., & Whitman, T. L. (1980). Response deprivation and reinforcement in applied settings: a preliminary analysis. *Journal of Applied Behavior Analysis, 13,* 595–609.

Mace, F. C., & Knight, D. (1986). Functional analysis and treatment of severe pica. *Journal of Applied Behavior Analysis, 19,* 411–416.

Mazur, J. E. (1994). *Learning and behavior.* Englewood Cliffs, New Jersey: Prentice Hall.

Michael, J. (1982). Distinguishing between discriminative and motivational functions of stimuli. *Journal of Experimental Analysis of Behavior, 37,* 149–155.

Neef, N. A., Mace, F. C., Shea, M. C., & Shade, D. (1993). Impulsivity in students with serious emotional disturbance: The interactive effects of reinforcer rate, delay, and quality. *Journal of Applied Behavior Analysis, 26,* 37–52.

Neef, N. A., Shade, D., & Miller, M. S. (1994). Assessing influential dimensions of reinforcers on choice in students with serious emotional disturbance. *Journal of Applied Behavior Analysis, 27,* 575–583.

Pace, G. M., Ivancic, M. T., Edwards, G. L., Iwata, B. A., & Page, T. J. (1985). Assessment of stimulus preference and reinforcer value with profoundly retarded individuals. *Journal of Applied Behavior Analysis, 18,* 249–255.

Piazza, C. C., Fisher, W. W., Hanley, G. P., Hilker, K., & Derby, K. M. (1996). A preliminary procedure for predicting the positive and negative effects of reinforcement-based procedures. *Journal of Applied Behavior Analysis, 29,* 137–152.

Premack, D. (1959). Toward empirical behavioral laws: I. Positive reinforcement. *Psychological Review, 66,* 219–233.

Premack, D. (1962). Reversibility of the reinforcement relation. *Science, 136,* 255–257.

Premack, D. (1963). Rate differential reinforcement in monkey manipulation. *Journal of the Experimental Analysis of Behavior, 6,* 81–89.

Premack, D. (1965). Reinforcement theory. In D. Levine (Ed.), *Nebraska symposium on motivation* (pp. 123–180). Lincoln: University of Nebraska.

Premack, D. (1971). Catching up with common sense or two sides of generalization: Reinforcement and punishment. In R. Glaser (Ed.), *The nature of reinforcement* (pp. 121–150). New York: Academic.

Rincover, A., & Newsom, C. D. (1985). The relative motivational properties of sensory and edible reinforcers in teaching autistic children. *Journal of Applied Behavior Analysis, 18,* 237–248.

Rincover, A., Newsom, C. D., Lovaas, O. I., & Koegel, R. L. (1977). Some motivational properties of sensory stimulation in psychotic children. *Journal of Applied Behavior Analysis, 24,* 312–323.

Ringdahl, J. E., Vollmer, T. R., Marcus, B. A., & Roane, H. S. (1997). An analogue evaluation of environmental enrichment: The role of stimulus preference. *Journal of Applied Behavior Analysis, 30,* 203–216.

Roane, H. S., Vollmer, T. R., Ringdahl, J. E., & Marcus, B. A. (in press). Evaluation of a brief stimulus preference assessment. *Journal of Applied Behavior Analysis.*

Shimp, C. P. (1969). Optimal behavior in free operant experiments. *Psychological Review, 76,* 97–112.

Shore, B. A., Iwata, B. A., DeLeon, I. G., Kahng, S. W., & Smith, R. G. (1997). An analysis of reinforcer substitutability using object manipulation and self-injury as competing responses. *Journal of Applied Behavior Analysis, 30,* 21–41.

Skinner, B. F. (1953). *Science and human behavior.* New York: MacMillan.

Steege, M. W., Wacker, D. P., Berg, W. K., Cigrand, K. K., & Cooper, L. J. (1989). The use of behavioral assessment to prescribe and evaluate treatment for severely handicapped children. *Journal of Applied Behavior Analysis, 22,* 23–33.

Timberlake, W. (1984). Behavior regulation and learned performance: Some misapprehensions and disagreements. *Journal of the Experimental Analysis of Behavior, 41,* 355–375.

Timberlake, W., & Allison, J. (1974). Response deprivation: An empirical approach to instrumental performance. *Psychological Review, 81,* 146–164.

Timberlake, W., & Farmer-Dougan, V. A. (1991). Reinforcement in applied settings: Figuring out ahead of time what will work. *Psychological Bulletin, 110,* 379–391.

Tustin, R. D. (1994). Preference for reinforcers under varying schedule arrangements: A behavioral economic analysis. *Journal of Applied Behavior Analysis, 27,* 439–455.

Vollmer, T. R., & Iwata, B. A. (1991). Establishing operations and reinforcement effects. *Journal of Applied Behavior Analysis, 24,* 279–291.

Vollmer, T. R., Iwata, B. A., Zarcone, J. R., Smith, R. G., & Mazaleski, J. L. (1993). The role of attention in the treatment of attention-maintained self-injurious behavior: Noncontingent reinforcement and differential reinforcement of other behavior. *Journal of Applied Behavior Analysis, 26,* 9–21.

Wacker, D. P., Berg, W. K., Wiggins, B., Muldoon, M., & Cavanaugh, J. (1985). Evaluation of reinforcer preferences for profoundly handicapped students. *Journal of Applied Behavior Analysis, 18,* 173–178.

Windsor, J., Piché, L. M., & Locke, P. A. (1994). Preference testing: A comparison of two presentation methods. *Research in Developmental Disabilities, 15,* 439–455.

Wolery, M., Kirk, K., & Gast, D. L. (1985). Stereotypic behavior as a reinforcer: Effects and side effects. *Journal of Autism and Developmental Disorders, 15,* 149–161.

5

⧉

Biobehavioral
Diagnosis and
Treatment of Self-Injury

F. CHARLES MACE
JOYCE E. MAUK

INTRODUCTION

The field of functional assessment began to be formalized with Carr's (1977) discussion of motivating factors for self-injurious behavior (SIB) and Iwata et al.'s (1982) empirical paper on assessment. Although there is a considerable medical literature on SIB, most behaviorists have addressed SIB as if it were solely environmentally based. Mace and Mauk in this chapter integrate both these approaches and present a biobehavioral model for the diagnosis and treatment of SIB.

Initially the authors review the behavioral approach, citing five subtypes. Then they review the medical approach, again citing five subtypes. With this background, they describe diagnostic procedures developed at their inpatient unit, the purpose of which is to match assessment results to diagnostic category (whether behavioral and/or medical) and then to prescribe an intervention based on that match.

In the traditional behavioral approach, a treatment based on a positive reinforcement hypothesis can exacerbate rather than help the situation if the problem behavior is in fact operating within a negative reinforcement hypothesis. This specificity is replayed in the medical approach reviewed here as the authors indicate the necessity of matching particular medications to particular diagnostic subtypes.

In presenting this approach, the authors follow the functional assessment approach we advocate, one of developing hypothesis-based interventions directly related to the assessment. However, by expanding assessment to include a medically oriented approach, they have greatly expanded our field.

Self-injurious behavior (SIB) is the most severe behavior disorder affecting persons with mental retardation. The disorder is one of the leading reasons for institutional placement, hospitalization, intensive special education programming, highly aversive treatment, and chemical and/or mechanical restraint (Favell et al., 1982a). Prevalence estimates indicate that as many as 25,000 persons in the United States suffer from extreme forms of SIB (Johnson & Day, 1992; National Institutes of Health, 1989), and the disorder is one of the leading reasons for institutional placement, hospitalization, intensive special education programming, highly aversive treatment, and chemical and/or mechanical restraint (Favell et al., 1982a). In additional to social consequence, significant medical sequelae may occur in the most severe cases, including cataracts, cauliflower ear, retinal detachment, infection, and loss of tissue.

Diagnostic systems leading to differential and effective treatments for SIB have been slow to develop and vary depending on whether the model is behavioral or biological (Cataldo & Harris, 1982; Spencer & Campbell, 1991; Iwata, Vollmer, & Zarcone, 1990; Mace, Lalli, & Shea, 1992). The literature indicates clearly that psychologists and physicians differ markedly in their approaches to the diagnosis and treatment of SIB (Amen & Singh, 1988; Cataldo & Harris, 1982; Farber, 1987; Favell et al., 1982a; Iwata et al., 1982; Iwata et al., 1990a; Mace, Lalli, & Shea, 1992; Singh & Millichamp, 1985; Spencer & Campbell, 1990). Behavioral psychologists diagnose SIB according to the type of reinforcement contingency maintaining the behavior (Iwata et al., 1982; Iwata et al., 1994). Treatment is then based on disrupting the maintaining contingency and teaching adaptive-replacement behaviors. Biologically oriented physicians, on the other hand, consider SIB to be a symptom of an underlying neurochemical imbalance, defective pain mechanism, or psychiatric disorder. Diagnosis is based on observable clinical features and pharmacological treatment is aimed at alleviating the individual's clinical symptoms as well as the SIB (Aman, 1993; Farber, 1987).

This disparity in conceptualization and approach to treatment is problematic for several reasons. First, considerable research exists to support tenets of *both* models, thus discouraging the conclusion that one model is "correct" and the other is not (Cataldo & Harris, 1982; Harris, 1992; Mace, Lalli, & Shea, 1992). Second, the type of treatment an individual with SIB receives depends, in large part, on the professional identity of the care provider, rather than on the presumed etiology of the disorder. In general, psychologists treat SIB behaviorally while physicians treat it pharmacologically. Third, no diagnostic model exists to differentiate environmentally maintained SIB from SIB that may be maintained by unspecified biological mechanisms, which would lead to the selection of effective behavioral and/or pharmacological treatments (Farber, 1987; Singh

& Millichamp, 1985). Such differentiation might help reduce the incidence of nonresponse to specific behavioral and pharmacological treatments.

We have developed and piloted a biobehavioral model for the diagnosis and treatment of self-injury that attempts to integrate key developments in the behavioral and medical literatures. The model provides a data-based method for differential diagnosis of cases of SIB. Differential diagnosis leads directly to selection of specific behavioral and/or pharmacological treatments that are matched to the individual's diagnostic classification and subtype. We begin with a brief review of the behavioral and biomedical models of self-injury, followed by a description of the biobehavioral diagnostic process and its relationship to treatment selection.

MODELS OF SELF-INJURY

Behavioral Model

Behaviorists regard SIB as a learned operant response that may or may not be modulated by specific biological conditions (Carr, 1977). These biological conditions may increase the likelihood that self-injury will emerge in a given individual's behavioral repertoire, but once the behavior does occur, it may be maintained by specific environmental responses to it. That is, predictable reactions to SIB may reinforce the behavior and give it a useful environmental function for the individual (Carr & McDowell, 1980). When self-injury is learned and maintained as a result of specific environmental responses to the behavior, it is known as *operant SIB.*

Considerable research has identified four major types of reinforcement contingencies that can maintain self-injury (Durand & Carr, 1985; Iwata et al., 1990b; Iwata et al., 1994; and Mace et al., 1992 for comprehensive reviews). These contingencies are classified as subtypes according to the kind of reinforcement process involved (positive or negative) and by the different consequences SIB produces. Positive reinforcement is the operant process by which a response or class of responses becomes more probable when it reliably produces a desirable event (a social, tangible, or sensory reinforcer). Responses become more likely through negative reinforcement when the behavior results in (a) complete avoidance of some unpleasant event, (b) a delay in the onset of an unpleasant event, (c) a reduction in the strength of the unpleasant event, or (d) removal of the unpleasant event.

Subtype 1: Positive Reinforcement by Attention   Self-injurious behavior often produces attentive reactions from care providers in the form of disapproving comments, sympathy, or redirection to an alternative activity (for example, Anderson et al., 1978). If attention is otherwise unavailable, the motivational conditions are in place for SIB to occur when, in the individual's experience, SIB has reliably resulted in attention. The potential for self-injury and other problem behaviors to be positively reinforced by attention is especially high for persons with severe disabilities. Frequently these individuals have limited adaptive repertoires and live in environments with sparse social interaction. In a recent 11-year epidemiological study of the behavioral function of SIB (Iwata et al., 1994), it was reported that SIB was maintained by attention in 27 percent of the sample population of 152 cases.

Subtype 2: Positive Reinforcement by Tangible Items For some individuals, self-injury functions to gain access to materials or activities that are otherwise unavailable to them (for example, Day et al., 1988; Durand & Crimmins, 1988; Iwata et al., 1994). The conditions that motivate such behavior include removing or restricting access to a desired object, stating that an object is contingent on certain behaviors, and observing another person's access to a particular item. Again, persons with severe disabilities and who lack adequate adaptive skills to communicate their needs are at risk for developing aberrant behaviors that can include SIB. Although several studies have now reported cases of SIB positively reinforced by tangible items (for example, Day et al., 1988; Favell, McGimsey, & Schell, 1982; Madden, Russo, & Cataldo, 1980), Iwata's epidemiological analysis reported only 3.3 percent of SIB cases with a tangible function (Iwata et al., 1994).

Subtype 3: Negative Reinforcement by Escape/Avoidance of Demands Behavior that avoids or escapes performance of self-care, academic, or vocational tasks may be maintained by negative reinforcement. The etiology of escape-maintained SIB has not been well documented. It is possible that when individuals have impaired neurological functions, significant skill deficits, or a history of impoverished teaching environments, and physical abuse associated with task performance, they may be more likely to attempt to avoid tasks (Altmeyer et al., 1987; Bachman, 1972; Carr, 1977). Escape from tasks and other unpleasant situations is the most frequently identified behavioral function for self-injury (38.1 percent of the sample population, Iwata et al., 1994).

Subtype 4: Reinforcement by Sensory Consequences Self-injurious responses can produce sensory stimulation capable of maintaining the behavior (for example, Bailey & Meyerson, 1969; Favell, McGimsey, & Schell, 1982; Iwata et al., 1994; Parrish et al., 1985; Van Houten, 1993). In some cases, the process maintaining SIB is consistent with positive reinforcement. For example, compression of the optic globe in blind individuals can cause tissue damage to the eye, but it may also stimulate the retina and produce positively reinforcing visual stimulation (Good & Hoyt, 1989). Negative reinforcement is implicated in other cases where SIB produces sensory effects that reduce or mask pain produced by medical conditions such as otitis media or increased intracranial pressure from hydrocephalus. Twenty-one percent of Iwata's study group showed response patterns consistent with sensory-maintained SIB (Iwata et al., 1994).

Subtype 5: Multiple Functions Several studies have reported cases of self-injury having multiple behavioral functions (for example, Day, Homer, & O'Neill, 1994; Iwata et al., 1994; Smith et al., 1993). For these individuals, situational variables are correlated with different consequences for SIB, resulting in SIB serving a different function depending on the circumstances (for example, an attention function during periods of low attention and an escape function during task situations). Iwata et al. (1994) reported multiply controlled SIB in 5.3 percent of the sample population.

Biomedical Model

Some children who present with self-injury and medical illnesses have experienced marked improvement in their SIB when the medical illness is treated. Examples of disorders that have been associated with SIB include otitis media, gastroesophageal reflux, and severe dental caries.

In most cases, obvious medical illness is ruled out. Several reports have postulated that disorders of neurotransmitter systems underlie SIB (Cataldo & Harris, 1982; Farber, 1987; Sandman, 1991). Our review of the literature and clinical experience suggest that there may be outwardly observable symptomatology that could correlate with different presumed disordered neurotransmitter systems. These clinical features may provide an objective basis for subtyping cases that are not responsive to operant contingencies. Additionally, medications may then be selected specifically for their known effect on the neurotransmitter systems. Logically, correcting the underlying biochemical abnormality would lead to clinical improvement.

It is possible that these observable clinical features and potential neurochemical imbalances are synonymous with accepted psychiatric disorders. However, current psychiatric diagnostic terminology is difficult to apply to individuals with severe to profound mental retardation and limited communication skills. The following subclasses are our current working model for subtyping *possibly biologic SIB*. We are currently conducting cluster analysis of the clinical features and neurochemical markers. These diagnostic features should be regarded as preliminary.

Subtype 1: Extreme Self-Inflicted Injury   Patients with this form of SIB have a history of causing themselves deep wounds that result in severe scarring, as well as experiencing accidental or self-inflicted injury that does not cause distress. A topography directed at the head may also be part of this pattern (Thompson et al., 1994). Several investigators have hypothesized that a subset of patients with SIB may be partially analgesic with congenitally pathologically altered central pain mechanisms, or may engage in SIB to produce their own opiates which may become addictive (Campbell et al., 1988; Sandman, 1991). In such cases, the mechanism maintaining SIB is similar to positive reinforcement. Reports of altered CSF B-endorphins and enkephalins in children with autism and in patients with SIB (Coid, Allolio, & Rees, 1983; Gilberg, Terenius, & Lonnerholm, 1985; Sandman, Barron, & Colman, 1990; Thompson et al., 1994) have justified medication trials of opiate antagonists (for example, naltrexone) with some success.

Subtype 2: Repetitive and Stereotypical SIB   This clinical subtype often involves hand mouthing or repeated rubbing together of body parts, with tissue damage resulting from repeated mechanical abrasion or wetting as opposed to direct severe blows as in Subtype 1. The injuries tend to be less severe, although they are prone to secondary infection. This subtype is often concurrent with a diagnosis of autism and the SIB may occur in conjunction with other non-injurious stereotypies. Stereotyped behavior is generally believed to be mediated by dopaminergic pathways as implicated by clinical responsiveness to dopamine antagonists (for example, neuroleptics) and induction of stereotypies by dopamine agonists (for example, stimulants) (Evenden, 1988). Haloperidol in low doses has been used successfully to treat this form of SIB.

Subtype 3: High-Rate SIB with Agitation if Interrupted This third subtype may be a form of compulsive behavior and may be a variation of obsessive-compulsive disorder (OCD). Various self-injurious behaviors, such as compulsive eye gouging and trichotillomania, in persons with normal intellect have been described as variants of OCD (Jenike, Baer, & Minichiello, 1990). Until recently, OCD was not recognized as a disorder of children or in persons with mental retardation, but is now believed to occur in these populations (Vitiello, Spreat, & Behar, 1989). Currently, formal psychiatric diagnosis of OCD requires the presence of "obsessions," or intrusive thoughts. However, because these internal events are not accessible in most low-functioning individuals, the compulsive nature of their SIB is presumed from its high rate and from the anxiety they exhibit following interruption of the response. Pharmacotherapy with medications used to treat OCD is indicated. Several studies (King, 1991; Bass, & Beltis, 1991; Markowitz, 1992) have shown success in treating SIB with serotonin re-uptake inhibitors such as fluoxetine and anafranil. This implicates a disorder of serotonin neurotransmitter systems in at least some cases of SIB.

Subtype 4: Co-occurrence of SIB with Agitation The fourth subtype is characterized by agitation occurring simultaneously with SIB, including screaming, aggression, running, hyperventilation, and/or tachycardia. The clinical features and target behaviors for reduction in addition to SIB in this subtype include these signs of overarousal. Some investigators have identified this high arousal state as a marker for response to lithium carbonate, which has been successfully used to treat aggression as well as SIB (Chandler, Gualtieri, & Fahs, 1988). It is possible that this clinical subtype may respond to lithium because of its "reparative effect on that system (or systems) modulating activity and arousal" (Sovner & Hurley, 1981, p. 194). Norepinephrine, a transmitter generally associated with stress and arousal and previously shown to be abnormal in adults with anxiety disorders (Sevy et al., 1989), may be involved in this subtype. Although the mechanism of lithium action is unclear, it may affect catecholamine transmission by cell membrane ATPase, or by blocking inositol triphosphate and reducing the formation of diacyglycerol and inositol triphosphate, which act as neuronal second messengers (Baraban, Worley, & Snyder, 1989). Presumably, other medications that "down tune" the norepinephrine system may also be effective (such as propranolol and clonidine).

Subtype 5: Multiple Clinical Features This subtype is assigned to individuals who present with one or more of the clinical features noted above. Observed features are prioritized based on prevalence and this hierarchy is used to guide the selection and sequencing (if necessary) of medications (see section on Treatment by Diagnostic Category).

BIOBEHAVIORAL
DIAGNOSIS AND TREATMENT

The diagnostic process described below was developed on the 10-bed inpatient unit of Children's Seashore House, a children's rehabilitation hospital located in Philadelphia, Pennsylvania. The Biobehavioral Unit is a specialized rehabilitative care facility designed for the comprehensive diagnosis and treatment of children with severe behavior disorders associated with developmental disabilities. The inpatient program lasts approximately 10 to 14 weeks and consists of three major phases: (a) Biobehavioral Diagnosis, (b) Treatment Development and Evaluation, and (c) Parent/Care Provider Training. Ongoing outpatient clinical care is also provided. The following is an overview of the first two phases of the program.

Standard Diagnostic Procedures

Although formal biobehavioral diagnosis of self-injury centers around the functional analysis and subtyping of operant contingencies and clinical features, supplemental diagnostic information is obtained from a variety of other sources. If significant unrecognized medical illnesses are discovered on pediatric examination, they are treated aggressively. The child is evaluated for the specific genetic disorders that are associated with SIB, such as Lesch-Nyhan and Cornelia deLange. Home and school environments are evaluated for stability of caregivers, adequacy of stimulating activities, and appropriateness of academic goals. Assessments of intelligence and adaptive functioning, of sensory function and psychiatric illnesses, all contribute to the diagnostic process. This information is supplemented by the use of standard instruments to assess self-injury, global functioning, and medication side effects [the Self-Injury Trauma Scale (Iwata et al., 1990); Aberrant Behavior Checklist and Abnormal Involuntary Movement Scale (National Institute of Mental Health, 1985)].

Functional Analysis

The field of applied behavior analysis has developed a diagnostic methodology, known as *functional analysis,* for classifying SIB according to the reinforcement contingencies that maintain the behavior under well-defined analogue conditions (Iwata et al., 1982). Our approach to functional analysis combines descriptive methodologies (Bijou, Peterson, & Ault, 1968) and experimental methodologies (Iwata et al., 1982), which can enhance the ecological validity of the assessment outcomes (Mace & Lalli, 1991; Mace, Lalli, & Shea, 1992).

Response patterns during functional analysis are the primary basis for the differential diagnosis of SIB as either operant, possibly biologic, or mixed operant and possibly biologic. These classifications are made following explicit decision rules concerning SIB response rates across the assessment conditions (see Differential Diagnosis and Subtyping). The following is an overview of the descriptive and experimental phases of the functional analysis.

Descriptive Phase   The goal of the descriptive phase is to identify environmental events that covary with SIB under natural conditions. During the first five days of a child's hospitalization, parents or other care providers are asked to engage in ten different naturalistic activities with their child which may be associated with the occurrence of SIB. These ten activities correspond to the four predominant reinforcement contingencies shown to be capable of maintaining SIB: positive reinforcement by attention, positive reinforcement by tangible items, negative reinforcement by escape or avoidance of demands, and automatic reinforcement by sensory consequences (Iwata et al., 1990b; Mace et al., 1991b). Examples of these activities include diverting parents' attention from the child, temporarily restricting access to a preferred item, performing an academic or daily living task, low levels of environmental stimulation, and child-directed play (a control condition). The duration of each activity varies from 10 to 30 minutes, with each activity presented a minimum of five times and in a randomized order across activities.

During each activity, data on relevant antecedent events (for example, presence/absence of task demands), SIB, appropriate child behaviors, and parental reactions to both SIB and appropriate behaviors are recorded concurrently via laptop computers. On the basis of these data, conditional rates of SIB are computed to indicate antecedent conditions correlated with more or less SIB, as well as the likelihood of specific parental reactions to SIB (the percentage of self-injurious responses followed by parental attention) (see Mace, Lalli, & Pinter-Lalli, 1991 and Mace & Lalli, 1991 for computational formulas). A successful descriptive analysis provides an empirical basis for formulating specific hypotheses concerning the environmental factors/contingencies maintaining a given child's SIB. Observation of parent–child interactions also provides information concerning specific parental responses to their child's behavior, which can be incorporated into the design of analogue conditions in the experimental phase of the functional analysis.

Experimental Phase   The goal of the experimental phase is to test the validity of the behavior-environment covariations observed in the descriptive phase. A therapist presents a patient with the four analogue experimental conditions (Iwata et al., 1982) and one additional condition based on more recent research (Wacker et al., 1990). These conditions are adapted, as necessary, on the basis of observed behavior-environment relationships recorded during the descriptive analysis to enhance the ecological validity of this phase (that is, the style of attentive reactions, specific objects or food items, and the type and mode of presenting task demands are individualized). The following conditions are then imposed during 20-minute sessions and presented in randomized order, constituting a single-subject, alternating treatments design.

During the *attention* condition, the therapist provides the child with age-appropriate toys and then diverts attention from the child. Contingent on occurrences of SIB, an attentive comment is directed to the child on a variable ratio (VR) schedule.

In the *tangible* condition, the therapist provides the child with free access to a preferred item for approximately two minutes, then states that it is time to change activities, removes the item, and prompts the child to engage in another activity (such as reading a book with the therapist). Contingent on occurrences of SIB, the therapist allows the child access to the preferred item on a VR schedule for approximately 30 seconds before returning the child to the alternative activity.

The *task* condition consists of the therapist instructing the child to perform a task using a graduated prompt hierarchy—gesture, vocal, model, physical (Cuvo, Leaf, & Borakove, 1978) and praise on a continuous reinforcement (CRF) schedule contingent on task completion. Contingent on occurrences of SIB, the therapist discontinues instruction for approximately 15 seconds and then resumes the task at the point it was interrupted.

During the *low stimulation* condition, the child is left alone in a therapy room with access to one or two toys for the duration of the session.

The final *play* condition is designed to be a *control* condition because the motivating conditions for SIB present in the other conditions are not included in the play condition. Here, the therapist interacts frequently and noncontingently with the child, presents the child with a variety of toys, and provides no instructions to manipulate the toys in any particular manner. SIB in this condition is expected to be low if the behavior is maintained by one or more environmental contingencies. Alternatively, if SIB occurs consistently in this condition, despite the absence of environmental motivations for the behavior, it is reasonable to suspect that the child's self-injury is maintained by unspecified, possibly biological, variables.

Differential Diagnosis and Subtyping

Decision Rules for Biobehavioral Classification and Operant Subtyping

The session-by-session results of the functional analysis are graphically displayed as response rates by experimental analogue condition. Diagnosis is based on the data from the last five sessions in each analogue condition to ensure stable responding in the conditions. Two behavioral psychologists independently examine the graphed results of the functional analysis and use the decision rules below to classify each patient's SIB. When disagreement on diagnosis or operant subtype occurs, the psychologists review all diagnostic information together and arrive at a consensual biobehavioral diagnosis and operant subtype. Figure 5.1 displays hypothetical data patterns from three functional analyses representing the three biobehavioral diagnostic classifications.

1. A diagnosis of *operant SIB* is given if all of the following are present (top panel of Figure 5.1):
   a. Mean response rate in the play (control) condition is ≤ 5.0 SIB/hour
   b. Mean response rate in any condition exceeds the mean response rate in the play condition by at least 10.0 SIB/hour
   c. For a given analogue condition, the percentage of overlapping data points with the play condition is ≤ 40 percent (for example, 2 out of 5).
2. A diagnosis of *mixed operant and possibly biologic SIB* is assigned if all of the following are present (bottom panel of Figure 5.1):
   a. Mean response rate in the play (control) condition is ≥ 5.0 SIB/hour
   b. Mean response rate in any condition exceeds the mean response rate in the play condition by at least 10.0 SIB/hour
   c. For a given analogue condition, the percentage of overlapping data points with the play condition is ≤ 40 percent.
3. A default diagnosis of *possibly biologic SIB* is given if neither decision rule 1 or 2 is satisfied (middle panel of Figure 5.1).

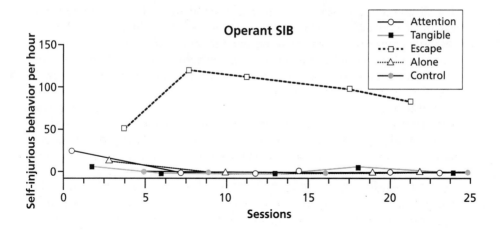

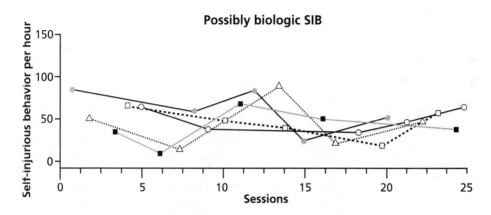

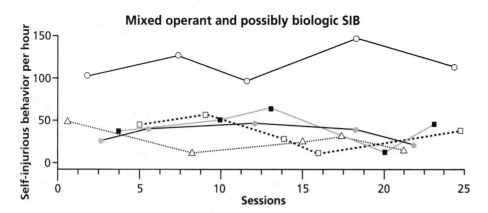

FIGURE 5.1 Hypothetical data illustrating the three major biobehavioral diagnostic classifications: Operant SIB (upper panel), Possibly biologic SIB (middle panel), and Mixed operant and possibly biologic SIB (lower panel).

The diagnosis of possibly biologic SIB is currently used when the results of the functional analysis fail to identify one or more specific environmental conditions (of those known to support SIB) that are differentially correlated with a child's self-injury. It is generally held (Iwata et al., 1982; Mace, Lalli, & Shea, 1992) that elevated rates of SIB in the play (control) condition are indicative of (a) an incomplete or incorrectly conducted functional analysis, or (b) the effects of another variable affecting SIB present in all conditions. Because such a finding provides no specific direction for behavioral intervention, these cases need further review by physicians to assess the need for medication or for the use of nonspecific techniques such as blocking or aversive interventions.

Operant SIB Subtypes   Children receiving a diagnosis of operant or mixed SIB are assigned one or more of the following subtypes that correspond to the conditions shown to be differentially elevated per the decision rules (see Figure 5.1).

Subtype 1. Positive reinforcement by attention.

Subtype 2. Positive reinforcement by tangible items.

Subtype 3. Negative reinforcement by escape/avoidance of tasks.

Subtype 4. Automatic reinforcement by sensory consequences.

Subtype 5. Multiple functions (one or more subtype).

Decision Rules for Assigning Clinical Subtypes   Children whose biobehavioral diagnosis is mixed or possibly biologic SIB are subtyped by their observable clinical features. Two developmental pediatricians independently review each patient's medical chart and history, findings from the developmental pediatric examination, and a 60-minute videotape of descriptive analysis sessions. If clear sensory consequences to the SIB are implicated, such as blindness associated with eye poking, medication is usually ruled out. If strong suspicion of a psychiatric disorder such as depression is noted, it is treated first. The remaining cases are believed to be good candidates for pharmacological treatment based on clinical features.

The physicians independently use the decision rules below to classify each child's clinical features. When disagreement on subtype occurs, the physicians review all diagnostic information together and arrive at a consensus on the clinical subtype.

1. A clinical subtype of *extreme self-inflicted tissue damage* is given if there is evidence of past or present severe self-injury (cauliflower ear, broken bones, loss of consciousness, extensive scarring or laceration with area $> 3 \times 3$ cm, and autoamputation) and one or both of the following:
   a. Lack of distress (such as crying) when inflicting injury
   b. Predilection for the head as injury site (Thompson et al., 1994)

2. A clinical subtype of *stereotypic SIB* is given if the topography of each movement is similar (stereotypic), not variable, and two or more of the following are present:
   a. Short duration between movements (1–10 seconds)
   b. Tissue damage likely only after repeated responses
   c. Co-occurring noninjurious stereotypies
   d. Diagnosis of autism or other pervasive developmental disorder

3. A clinical subtype of *high-rate SIB with agitation when interrupted* is assigned if agitation/distress occur when SIB is interrupted (such as crying, hyperventilation, aggression, pacing) and if one or more of the following is present:
   a. Mean SIB rate ≥ 100/hour
   b. SIB stops during an activity but resumes within 30 seconds of completion

4. A clinical subtype of *SIB co-occurring with agitation* is given if behavior co-occurs temporarily with agitation/aggression (such as pacing, screaming, tachycardia) and one or more of the following are present:
   a. SIB rates vary by ≥ 50 percent per session
   b. Topographies consist of self-hitting
   c. Evidence of sleep or appetite disturbance

5. A clinical subtype of *multiple features* is assigned in cases in which a child meets inclusion criteria for two or more clinical subtypes.

Interrater Reliability of the Biobehavioral Diagnostic System We have conducted a preliminary study on the interrater reliability of the diagnostic classifications. Two behavioral psychologists independently used the above decision rules to classify results of SIB functional analyses for 24 children admitted to the Unit. Using the method of exact agreement (Kazdin, 1982), interrater reliability between the psychologists was 95.8 percent (exact agreement on 23 of 24 patients). Eighteen of the 24 patients were classified as operant, with 10 of these 18 showing a single operant function and the remaining 8 having multiple operant functions. Two of the children received a classification of mixed operant and possibly biologic SIB.

Two developmental pediatricians independently assigned clinical subtypes to the six cases not diagnosed as operant SIB. There was exact agreement between raters on clinical subtypes for all six cases.

Treatment by Diagnostic Category and Subtype

The clinical importance of biobehavioral diagnosis of self-injury rests on its potential to lead to differentially effective treatment. That is, matching treatment with a diagnostic classification and subtype may result in better clinical outcomes than behavioral or pharmacological therapy independent of biobehavioral diagnosis. A principal rationale for developing the biobehavioral model is to reduce the reported incidence of nonresponse to medication and/or behavioral intervention (Iwata et al., 1994; Mace et al., 1992). Accordingly, treatment selection is based on the following assumptions derived from current research findings in the behavioral and medical literatures on SIB: (1) Operant SIB will be more responsive to behavioral treatment based on a functional analysis, alone or in combination with medication, than to medication alone; (2) Possibly biologic SIB will be more responsive to medication based on clinical subtypes, alone or in combination with behavioral treatment, than to behavioral treatment alone; and (3) Mixed operant and possibly biologic SIB will be more responsive to combined behavioral and pharmacological treatment than to either class of treatment alone.

Functional Analysis-Based Behavioral Treatment Functional analysis results for operant and mixed cases identify one or more reinforcement contingencies that

---

**BOX 5.1   Potential Intervention Strategies
Based on the Function of Self-Injury**

**Positive reinforcement
by attention**

Extinction
Provide minimal attention for self-injury
Nonexclusionary time-out contingent
on SIB

Teach appropriate requests for attention
Conversation initiation and expansion
training
Prompt noninteractional attention (for
persons with severe handicaps)

Increase the rate of noncontingent
attention

Increase opportunities for social interaction

Seating arrangements, interactive activities

**Positive reinforcement
by tangible items**

Extinction
Withhold tangible items following self-
injury

Teach appropriate request for tangible
items

Use tangible reinforcers to teach appropriate
behaviors

Increase rate of noncontingent access to
attractive materials

**Negative reinforcement by escape-
avoidance of task demands**

Extinction
Guided compliance
Continued instruction

Teach an appropriate escape response
Request assistance
Request breaks

Stimulus fading

Reduce task difficulty

Schedule frequent breaks

Increase reinforcement for task engagement

Sensory reinforcement

Sensory extinction (where possible and
practical)
Mask sensory stimulation
Response blocking

Environmental enrichment
Increased social interaction
Increased access and training with interest-
ing materials

Teach appropriate requests

Access to social interaction and materials

SOURCE: ADAPTED FROM MACE ET AL., 1992

---

maintain the child's SIB (Axelrod, 1987; Iwata et al., 1994; Mace, Lalli, & Shea, 1992). Behavioral intervention strategies can then be selected that weaken the maintaining contingency and promote the development of adaptive alternative responses to replace the function of self-injury. Three general strategies are available to accomplish this. First, reinforcement of self-injury can be discontinued (extinction). Second, alternative reinforcement, especially of the same or similar quality as that which maintains the SIB, can be arranged according to a variety of schedules of reinforcement (for example, DRO, DRA, DRL, DRH, FT, VT) to increase the frequency of adaptive behavior and further weaken the response-reinforcer relation supporting SIB. Third, a variety of stimulus–fading procedures can be used to gradually reduce the probability that certain antecedent conditions will evoke SIB (such as the gradual introduction of task demands).

Box 5.1 provides a listing of behavioral intervention strategies shown to be effective in reducing levels of self-injury. Treatment strategies are typically combined

---

BOX 5.2 Medications and Dosage Schedules Matched to Clinical Subtype of Possibly Biologic SIB

Subtype 1. Extreme self-inflicted tissue damage
Naltrexone is started initially at 0.5 mg/kg/day daily and increased to 1 mg/kg/day after 10 days (unless a clinical endpoint is reached). Dosage is increased to a maximum of 2 mg/kg/day, or until a clinical endpoint is reached.

Subtype 2. Repetitive stereotypic SIB
Haloperidol is begun at .25 mg twice per day or .025 mg/kg/day, whichever is lower. This dosage is increased by 0.25 to 0.5 mg/day every 4 days, as SIB rates indicate, to a maximum of 4 mg/day or 0.1 mg/kg/day, whichever is higher.

Subtype 3. High-rate SIB with agitation when interrupted
Fluoxetine is administered at 10 mg daily in children less than 8 years, and 20 mg daily in those older. If clinical endpoints are not reached by 4 weeks, the dosage is doubled for up to 4 additional weeks.

Subtype 4. SIB co-occurring with agitation
Propranolol is started at 10 mg three times per day for children under age 8; for children over age 8, the starting dose is 20 mg three times per day, increasing by this amount every 3 days to a maximum daily dose of 520 mg. Lithium carbonate is used as an alternative medication for those who cannot tolerate propranolol.

---

to form multicomponent interventions to maximize clinical outcome. As Box 5.1 indicates, extinction, alternative reinforcement, and stimulus fading involve different treatment procedures depending on the behavioral function of the SIB.

Medication Matched to Clinical Subtype Classification of clinical subtypes is aimed at objectively defining clusters of behavioral symptoms that may respond differentially to different SIB medications. These symptoms are believed to be mediated by disordered neurotransmitter systems and/or altered pain mechanisms, and may be ameliorated to some extent by specific medications (see review of the biomedical model of SIB). Box 5.2 lists medication choices for each clinical subtype.

All medications are administered following specific dose change decision rules. Possible medication side effects are monitored daily by observation and checklist completion.

Case Histories

Susie was a five-year-old girl with severe mental retardation, mild spastic diplegic cerebral palsy, and self-injurious behavior (head and ear banging). She also had a history of noncompliance and tantrums, especially during dressing and other self-care skills. She was nonambulatory and nonverbal, although her mother and teachers believed she understood a great deal of what was said.

On admission, Susie was noted to be significantly below the weight expected for her height, and to have chronically infected ears. Supplemental calories were given and medical treatment of her ears was begun. In the descriptive portion of the functional analysis of Susie, tantrums occurred most often during tasks, but the head hitting occurred across all conditions, including play. The head hitting occurred in association with arching behavior, crying, and tantrums. Her bio-behavioral diagnosis was possibly biologic SIB associated with agitation. Treatment with the medication propranolol was instituted, which led to a significant reduction in SIB. The task-related tantrums were treated by guided compliance and attention contingent upon task completion.

Ronald was a 15-year-old male with a long history of head hitting and leg slapping. His size and problem behaviors had led to placement in a group home. He was observed to exhibit SIB more commonly in the residence than at school, but no other pattern was recognized by his staff. This difficult behavior had re-sulted in the simultaneous administration of three psychopharmacological agents. During the descriptive analysis phase, his group home staff were observed to con-sistently respond to Ronald's SIB with comments (such as "Don't do that, you'll hurt yourself."), and sometimes with physical contact and hand holding. The experimental analysis confirmed the hypothesis that his SIB was positively re-inforced by attention. He was weaned of medications without significant increase in SIB; however, increased attempts at vocalization were noted. Treatment con-sisted of training a gesture to solicit attention from care providers. Once this ges-ture was learned, Ronald used it almost continuously, therefore the treatment was modified to include a time delay. The procedure was successfully adapted for use at his residence. Its implementation was difficult however, because it required a higher staff-client ratio, which was approved after much advocacy work on Ronald's behalf by social workers.

CONCLUDING COMMENTS

We have presented preliminary pilot data suggesting that correctly diagnosing the operant and/or possibly biologic factors maintaining an individual's SIB leads to more effective treatment (Mace & Mauk, 1994). It appears that self-injury that is maintained by positive or negative reinforcement contingencies responds prefer-entially to behavioral treatments matched to an operant function, and not to medication. Additionally, the medication responders have not responded favor-ably to generic behavioral intervention. In the past, individuals whose SIB did not respond well to first-choice interventions may have been treated with default be-havioral techniques or high doses of sedating drugs that are highly aversive and intrusive. The approach outlined in this paper represents a practical step toward reducing the reliance on default technologies by matching treatment to factors believed to be maintaining SIB for individual cases.

The model as proposed here has undergone and will undergo continual modification and refinement as more individuals are studied and our sophistica-tion increases. The subclassification system is similar to the delineation of spe-cific infectious etiologies of an infection such as pneumonia. Initially, physicians could only diagnose a pulmonary infection based on symptoms and treat symptomatically with the default strategies of antipyretics and antitussives. Advances in understanding the characteristics of the microorganisms causing pneumonia, the patient characteristics that predispose one to pneumonia, and diagnostic laboratory testing have combined to improve the morbidity and mortality of this disorder.

It should now be recognized that all individuals with SIB are not alike, and most will respond better to specific treatments than to default treatments. This proposed biobehavioral model will be further refined as new techniques in applied behavior analysis and medicine are developed, just as advances in critical care and microbiology have improved the care and treatment of pneumonia. For example, diagnostic methods that can further differentiate possibly biologic SIB cases (such as prolonged alone assessments) and the identification of specific biological markers for subsets of SIB patients may further improve response to treatment. We have also begun to extend this methodology to other behavior disorders associated with developmental disabilities.

Transdisciplinary, cooperative work should continue to facilitate our understanding of this complex disorder or disorders. It is hoped that these cooperative approaches will not only increase our understanding of SIB, but will improve the lives of individuals with this disorder.

AUTHOR NOTE

Portions of this article were previously published in *Mental Retardation and Developmental Disabilities Research Reviews,* John Wiley & Sons.

REFERENCES

Allen, K. E., & Harris, F. R. (1966). Elimination of a child's excessive scratching by training the mother in reinforcement procedures. *Behavior Research and Therapy, 4,* 79–84.

Altmeyer, B. K., Locke, B. J., Griffen, J. C., Ricketts, R. W., Williams, D. E., Mason, M., & Stark, M. T. (1987). Treatment strategies for self-injurious behavior in a large service-delivery network. *American Journal of Mental Deficiency, 91,* 333–340.

Aman, M. G. (1993). Efficacy of psychotropic drugs for reducing self-injurious behavior in the developmental disabilities. *Annals of Clinical Psychiatry, 5*(3), 171–178.

Aman, M. G., & Singh, N. N. (1988). *Psychopharmacology of the developmental disabilities.* New York: Springer-Verlag.

Anderson, L., Dancis, J., & Alpert, M. (1978). Behavioral contingencies and self-mutilation in Lesch-Nyhan disease. *Journal of Consulting and Clinical Psychology, 46,* 529–536.

Arnold, L. E., & Aman, M. G. (1991). Beta blockers in mental retardation and developmental disorders. *Journal of Child and Adolescent Psychopharmacology, 1,* 361–373.

Axelrod, S. (1987). Functional and structural analyses of behavior: Approaches leading to reduced use of punishment procedures. *Research in Developmental Disabilities, 8,* 165–178.

Bachman, J. A. (1972). Self-injurious behavior: A behavioral analysis. *Journal of Abnormal Psychology, 80,* 211–224.

Bailey, J., & Meyerson, L. (1969). Vibratory stimulation on a retardate's self-injurious behavior. *Psychological Aspects of Disability, 17,* 133–137.

Baraban, J. M., Worley, R., & Snyder, S. H. (1989). Second messenger systems and psychoactive drug action: Focus on the phosphornositide system and lithium. *American Journal of Psychiatry, 146,* 1251–1260.

Bass, J. N., & Beltis, J. (1991). Therapeutic effects of fluoxetine on naltrexone-resistant self-injurious behavior in an adolescent with mental retardation. *Journal of Chid and Adolescent Psychopharmacology, 1*(5), 331–340.

Bijou, S., Peterson, R., & Ault, M. (1968). A method to integrate descriptive and experimental field studies at the level of data and empirical concepts. *Journal of Applied Behavior Analysis, 1,* 175–191.

Campbell, M., Adams, P., Small, A., Tesch, L., & Currens, E. (1988). Naltrexone in infantile autism. *Psychopharmacology Bulletin, 24,* 135–139.

Carr, E. (1977). The motivation of self-injurious behavior: A review of some hypotheses. *Psychological Bulletin, 84,* 800–816.

Carr, E., & Durand, M. (1985). Reducing behavior problems through functional communication training. *Journal of Applied Behavior Analysis, 18,* 111–126.

Carr, E., & McDowell, J. (1980). Social control of self-injurious behavior of organic etiology. *Behavior Therapy, 11,* 402–409.

Cataldo, M., & Harris, J. (1982). The biological basis for self-injury in the mentally retarded. *Analysis and Intervention in Developmental Disabilities, 2,* 21–39.

Chandler, M., Gualtieri, C. T., & Fahs, J. J. (1988). Other psychotropic drugs: Stimulants, anti-depressants, anxiolytics, and lithium carbonate. In M.G. Aman & N.N. Singh (Eds.), *Psychopharmacology of the developmental disabilities.* New York: Springer-Verlag.

Coid, J., Allolio, B., & Rees, L. (1983). Raised plasma metenkephalin in patients who habitually mutilate themselves. *The Lancet, 3,* 545–546.

Cuvo, A., Leaf, R., & Borakove, L. (1978). Teaching janitorial skills to the mentally retarded: Acquisition, generalization, and maintenance. *Journal of Applied Behavior Analysis, 11,* 345–355.

Day, H. M., Homer, R. H., & O'Neill, R. E. (1994). Multiple functions of problem behaviors: Assessment and intervention. *Journal of Applied Behavior Analysis, 27,* 279–289.

Day, R. M., Rea, J. A., Schussler, N. G., Larsen, S. E., & Johnson, W. L. (1988). A functionally based approach to the treatment of self-injurious behavior. *Behavior Modification, 12,* 565–589.

Durand, V. M., & Carr, E. G. (1985). Self-injurious behavior: Motivating conditions and guidelines for treatment. *School Psychology Review, 14,* 171–176.

Durand, V. M., & Crimmins, D. B. (1988). Identifying variables maintaining self-injurious behavior. *Journal of Autism and Developmental Disorders, 18,* 99–117.

Durand, V. M., & Kishi, G. (1987). Reducing severe behavior problems among persons with dual sensory impairments: An evaluation of a technical assistance model. *Journal of the Association for Persons with Severe Handicaps, 12,* 2–10.

Evenden, J. (1988). Issues in behavioral pharmacology: Implications for developmental disorders. In M.G. Aman & N.N. Singh (Eds.), *Psychopharmacology of the developmental disabilities.* New York: Springer-Verlag.

Farber, J. (1987). Psychopharmacology of self-injurious behavior in the mentally retarded. *Journal of the American Academy of Child and Adolescent Psychiatry, 26,* 296–302.

Favell, J. E., Azrin, N., Baumeister, A., Carr, E., Dorsey, M., Forehand, R., Foxx, R., Lovaas, I., Rincover, A., Risley, T., Romanczyk, R., Russo, D., Schroeder, S., & Solnick, J. (1982a). The treatment of self-injurious behavior. *Behavior Therapy, 13,* 529–554.

Favell, J. E., McGimsey, J. F., & Schell, R. M. (1982b). Treatment of self-injury by providing alternate sensory activities. *Analysis and Intervention in Developmental Disabilities, 2,* 83–104.

Garvey, C. A., Gross, D., & Freeman, L. (1991). Assessing psychotropic medication side effects among children. A reliability study.

Journal of Child Adolescent Psychiatry Mental Health Nursing, 4(4), 127–131.

Gaylord-Ross, R., Weeks, M., & Lipner, C. (1980). An analysis of antecedent response, and consequence events in the treatment of self-injurious behavior. *Education and Training of the Mentally Retarded, 15,* 35–42.

Gilberg, C., Terenius, L., & Lonnerholm, G. (1985). Endorphin activity in childhood psychosis. *Archives of General Psychiatry, 42,* 780–783.

Good, W. V., & Hoyt, C. S. (1989). Behavioral correlates of poor vision in children. *International Ophthalmology Clinics, 29,* 57–60.

Harris, J. C. (1992). Neurobiological factors in self-injurious behavior. In J. K. Luiselli, J. L. Matson, & N. N. Singh (Eds.), *Self injurious behavior: Analysis. assessment and treatment.* New York: Springer-Verlag.

Horner, R. H. (1980). The effects of environmental enrichment on the behavior of institutionalized profoundly retarded children. *Journal of Applied Behavior Analysis, 13,* 473–491.

Iwata, B., Dorsey, M., Slifer, K., Bauman, K., & Richman, G. (1982). Toward a functional analysis of self-injury. *Analysis and Intervention in Developmental Disabilities, 2,* 3–20.

Iwata, B. A., Pace, G., Dorsey, M., Zarcone, J., Vollmer, T., Smith, R. G., Rodgers, T., Lerman, D., Shore, B., Mazaleski, J., Goh, H. L., Cowdery, G., Kalsher, M., McCosh, K., & Willis, K. (1994). The functions of self-injurious behavior: An experimental-epidemiological analysis. *Journal of Applied Behavior Analysis, 27,* 215–240.

Iwata, B., Pace, G., Kissel, R., Nau, P., & Farber, J. (1990a). The self-injury trauma scale: A method of quantifying surface tissue damage caused by self-injurious behavior. *Journal of Applied Behavior Analysis, 23,* 99–110.

Iwata, B., Vollmer, T., & Zarcone, J. (1990b). The experimental (functional) analysis of behavior disorders: Methodology, applications, and limitations. In A. Repp & N. Singh (Eds.), *Current perspectives in the use of non-aversive and aversive interventions with developmentally disabled persons.* Sycamore, IL: Sycamore.

Jenike, M., Baer, L., & Minichiello, W. (1990). *Obsessive compulsive disorders: Theory and management.* New York: Springer-Verlag.

Johnson, W. L., & Day, R. M. (1992). The incidence and prevalence of self-injurious behavior. In J. K. Luiselli, J. L. Matson, & N. N. Singh (Eds.), *Self-injurious behavior: Analysis, assessment, and treatment* (pp. 21–56). New York: Springer-Verlag.

Kazdin, A. (1982). *Single-case experimental designs.* New York: Oxford.

King, B. H. (1991). Fluoxetine reduced self-injurious behavior in an adolescent with mental retardation. *Journal of Child and Adolescent Psychopharmacology, 1*(5), 321–329.

Lovaas, O. I., & Simmons, J. Q. (1969). Manipulation of self-destruction in three retarded children. *Journal of Applied Behavior Analysis, 2,* 143–157.

Mace, F. C., Browder, D. M., & Hon, Y. L. (1987). Analysis of demand conditions associated with stereotypy. *Journal of Behavior Therapy and Experimental Psychiatry, 18,* 25–31.

Mace, F. C., & Knight, D. (1986). Functional analysis and treatment of severe pica. *Journal of Applied Behavior Analysis, 19,* 411–416.

Mace, F. C., & Lalli, J. S. (1991). Linking descriptive and experimental analyses in the treatment of bizarre speech. *Journal of Applied Behavior Analysis, 24,* 553–562.

Mace, F. C., Lalli, J. S., & Pinter-Lalli, E. (1991). Functional analysis and treatment of aberrant behavior. *Research in Developmental Disabilities, 12,* 155–180.

Mace, F. C., Lalli, J. S., & Shea, M. C. (1992). Functional analysis of self-injury. In J. K. Luiselli, J. L. Matson, & N. N. Singh (Eds.), *Self-injurious behavior: Analysis, assessment, and treatment* (pp. 122–152). New York: Springer-Verlag.

Mace, F. C., & Mauk, J. E. (1994). *Biobehavioral diagnosis and treatment of self-injury.* Paper presented at the Silicon Valley Symposium on Developmental Disabilities. San Jose.

Madden, N. A., Russo, D. C., & Cataldo, M. F. (1980). Environmental influences on mouthing in children with lead intoxication. *Journal of Pediatric Psychology, 5,* 207–216.

Markowitz, P. I. (1992). Effect of fluoxetine on self-injurious behavior in the developmentally disabled: A preliminary study. *Journal of Clinical Psychopharmacology, 12,* 27–31.

Mazaleski, J. L., Iwata, B. A., Rodgers, T. A., Vollmer, T. R., & Zarcone, J. R. (1994). Protective equipment as treatment for stereotypic hand mouthing: Sensory extinction or punishment effects? *Journal of Applied Behavior Analysis, 27,* 345–355.

National Institutes of Health (1985). Abnormal involuntary movement scale. *Psychopharmacology Bulletin, 21,* 845–850.

National Institutes of Health (1989). *NIH consensus development conference on the treatment of destructive behaviors in persons with developmental disabilities.* Bethesda: U.S. Department of Health and Human Services.

National Institute of Mental Health (1985).

Pace, G. M., Iwata, B. A., Edwards, G. L., & McCosh, K. C. (1986). Stimulus fading and transfer in the treatment of self-restraint and self-injurious behavior. *Journal of Applied Behavior Analysis, 19,* 381–389.

Parrish, J. M., Iwata, B. A., Dorsey, M. F., Bunck, T. J., & Slifer, K. J. (1985). Behavior analysis, program development, and transfer of control in the treatment of self-injury. *Journal of Behavior Therapy and Experimental Psychiatry, 16,* 159–168.

Ratey, J. J., Mikkelsen, E. J., Smith, G. B., Upadhyaya, A., Zuckerman, H. S., Martell, D., Sorgi, P., Polakoff, S., & Bemporad, J. (1986). Blockers in the severely and profoundly mentally retarded. *Journal of Clinical Psychopharmacology, 6,* 103–107.

Repp, A. C., & Deitz, S. M. (1974). Reducing aggressive and self-injurious behavior of institutionalized retarded children through reinforcement of other behaviors. *Journal of Applied Behavior Analysis, 7,* 313–325.

Repp, A. C., Felce, D., & Barton, L. (1988). Basing the treatment of stereotypic and self-injurious behaviors on hypotheses of their causes. *Journal of Applied Behavior Analysis, 21,* 281–289.

Rincover, A., & Devany, J. (1982). The application of sensory extinction procedures to self-injury. *Analysis and Intervention in Developmental Disabilities, 2,* 67–81.

Ruedrich, S. L., Gnush, L., & Wilson, J. (1990). Beta adrenergic blocking medications for aggressive or self-injurious mentally retarded persons. *American Journal of Mental Retardation, 95,* 110–119.

Sandman, C. (1991). The opiate hypothesis in autism and self-injury. *Journal of Child and Adolescent Psychopharmacology, 1,* 237–248.

Sandman, C. A., Barron, J. L., & Colman, H. (1990). An orally administered opiate blocker, naltrexone, attenuates self-injurious behavior. *American Journal of Mental Retardation, 95,* 93–102.

Sevy, S., Papdemitriou, G. N., Surmount, D. W., Gold, S., & Mendlwicz, J. (1989). Noradrenergic functions in generalized anxiety disorder, major depressive disorder and healthy subjects. *Biologic Psychiatry, 25,* 141–152.

Singh, N., & Millichamp, C. (1985). Pharmacological treatment of self-injurious behavior in mentally retarded persons. *Journal of Autism and Developmental Disorders, 15,* 257–267.

Smith, R. G., Iwata, B. A., Vollmer, T. R., & Zarcone, J. R. (1993). Experimental analysis and treatment of multiply controlled self-injury. *Journal of Applied Behavior Analysis, 26,* 183–196.

Sovner, R., & Hurley, A. (1981). The management of chronic behavior disorder in mentally retarded adults with lithium carbonate. *Journal of Nervous and Mental Disease, 169*(3), 191–195.

Spencer, E., & Campbell, M. (1990). Aggressiveness directed against self and others: Psychopharmacological intervention. In S. Harris & J. Handleman (Eds.), *Aversive and non-aversive interventions: Controlling life-threatening behavior by the developmentally disabled.* New York: Springer-Verlag.

Steege, M. W., Wacker, D. P., Berg, W. K., Cigrand, K. K., & Cooper, L. J. (1989). The use of behavioral assessment to prescribe and evaluate treatments for severely handicapped children. *Journal of Applied Behavior Analysis, 22,* 23–33.

Tarpley, H., & Schroeder, S. (1979). Comparison of DRO and DRI on rate of suppression of self-injurious behavior. *American Journal of Mental Deficiency, 84,* 188–194.

Thompson, T., Hackenberg, T., Cenutti, D., Baker, D., & Axtell, S. (1994). Opioid antagonist effects on self-injury in adults with mental retardation: Response form and location as determinants of medication effects. *American Journal of Mental Retardation, 99*(1), 85–102.

Van Houten, R. (1993). The use of wrist weights to reduce self-injury maintained by sensory reinforcement. *Journal of Applied Behavior Analysis, 26,* 197–203.

Vitiello, B., Spreat, S., & Behar, D. (1989). Obsessive-compulsive disorder in mentally retarded patients. *Journal of Nervous and Mental Disease, 177,* 232–236.

Vollmer, R. R., Iwata, B. A., Zarcone, J. R., Smith, R. G., & Mazaleski, J. L. (1993). The role of attention in the treatment of attention-maintained self-injurious behavior: Noncontingent reinforcement and differential reinforcement of other behavior. *Journal of Applied Behavior Analysis, 26,* 9–21.

Wacker, D., Steege, M., Northup, J., Sasso, G., Berg, W., Reimers, T., Cooper, L., Cigrand, K., & Donn, L. (1990). A component analysis of functional communication training across three topographies of severe behavior problems. *Journal of Applied Behavior Analysis, 23,* 417–430.

Weeks, M., & Gaylord-Ross, R. (1981). Task difficulty and aberrant behavior in severely handicapped students. *Journal of Applied Behavior Analysis, 14,* 449–463.

Zarcone, J. R., Iwata, B. A., Smith, R. G., Mazaleski, J. L., & Lerman, D. C. (1994). Reemergence and extinction of self-injurious escape behavior during stimulus (instructional) fading. *Journal of Applied Behavior Analysis, 27,* 307–316.

6

Low-Frequency High-Intensity Problem Behavior:

Toward an Applied Technology of Functional Assessment and Intervention

JEFFREY R. SPRAGUE
ROBERT H. HORNER

Sometimes the more measurable
drives out the most important.
RENÉ DUBOS

INTRODUCTION

One of the ironies of dealing with problem behaviors is that high-frequency behavior is often easier than low-frequency behavior to eliminate. The reason in these cases is that the person analyzing the situation has more opportunities to observe the behavior and its contingencies. Low-frequency behavior then can become a special problem for us, and low-frequency, high-intensity behavior can be especially problematic. Sprague and Horner have addressed this type of behavior, providing a model that focuses on response classes and covariation, setting events and establishing operations, and advances in measurement techniques.

All the various functional assessment procedures presented in this book are by definition intended to identify the function of problem behavior. While these procedures are able to accommodate multiple behaviors, we tend not to treat these behaviors as corelated behaviors. Instead, we treat them as semi-independent behaviors, most of which we can address with a complex program. A response class is a set of topographically different behaviors that have the same effect or function. Thus, while a behavior may be of low rate and high intensity, it may have the same function and thus be related to a behavior of high rate and low intensity.

The authors of this chapter address this relationship in several ways. First, they discuss response theory and three underlying areas of research: the matching law, behavioral allocation, and functional equivalence. Then they bring to their model a discussion of setting events or establishing operations. These are conditions or events that change the power of antecedents to exert stimulus control or of consequences to be reinforcing. Integrating these areas into something useful for intervention requires a unifying approach, which the authors see as functional assessment, and an underlying technology of data collection and analysis, seen as sequential analysis. With these unifying procedures the authors have been able to present a model by which we can study and intervene successfully with these especially problematic low-frequency, high-intensity behaviors.

Managing severe problem behavior remains among the most pressing challenges in special education and human services. Behavior that results in self-injury, injury to others, significant property damage, and impaired learning creates an obstacle to community living (Pagel & Whitling, 1978) and is a major reason for admission and readmission to state institutions (Bannerman, 1987; Tausig, 1985). A large proportion of the individuals still living in institutions (47 percent national average) exhibit severe problem behaviors (Borthwick-Duffy, Eyman, & White, 1987; Scheerenberger, 1990; White et al., 1991). In addition, while positive learning and social outcomes typically are associated with movement from institutional to community settings, patterns of reduced problem behavior are less evident (Larson & Lakin, 1989).

Significant emotional and financial costs, as well as safety factors, characterize the effects of severe problem behavior. High-intensity behaviors that result in tissue damage, property damage, or extreme disruption are described as most problematic (Borthwick-Duffy, Eyman, & White 1987), and are associated with the most intrusive interventions, including electrical stimulation, restraint, medication, and isolation (Guess et al., 1987; Lovaas & Favell, 1987). In fact, the importance of decreasing high-intensity behavior is used as justification for the use of these treatments (for example, Linscheid et al., 1990).

For some individuals, these behaviors occur unpredictably and for reasons that are unclear (Carr, 1988; Patterson, 1982). This phenomenon can be especially frustrating for families and care providers. The result is extreme stress, concern for personal safety and the safety of others, and ultimately institutionalization, more restrictive placement, or repeated failures to develop effective interventions (Bannerman, 1987; Tausig, 1985).

EXEMPLARY TREATMENT OF
SEVERE PROBLEM BEHAVIOR

A debate over the management of problem behaviors (Guess et al., 1987; National Institute of Health, 1989) has emerged from an "aversive" versus "nonaversive" division (Repp & Singh, 1990; Mulick, 1990), leading to a productive evaluation of existing assessment and intervention techniques and a discussion of which critical areas need further investigation. The focus on the use of aversive procedures has stimulated a re-evaluation of methods for assessing and treating high-intensity problem behavior. Clinicians are encouraged to use functional analysis assessment procedures, and to design interventions in response to information about the events that occasion and maintain the problem behavior (Carr et al., 1990a; Donnellan et al., 1989; Durand & Crimmins, 1987; Iwata et al., 1982; Mace et al., 1988; Meyer & Evans, 1989; Van Houten et al., 1988; Wacker et al., 1990).

New standards require that behavioral interventions be made based on the hypotheses generated by the functional analysis. Applied interventions require simultaneous manipulation of distal and immediate antecedent events, teaching appropriate behaviors that achieve the behavioral function of the problem behavior(s), and providing differential consequences for both desired and problem behaviors (Bailey & Pyles, 1989; Carr, 1988; Carr, Robinson, & Palumbo, 1990; Durand, 1990; Horner et al., 1990a; Sprague & Horner, 1992).

A range of studies utilizing both positive and aversive procedures document successful treatment of serious problem behaviors such as severe self-injury (head banging, eye poking), aggression (hitting or biting others), and property destruction (breaking furniture or windows). Classes of intervention include (a) training functionally equivalent communication behaviors (Durand, 1990; Durand & Carr, 1987; Horner & Budd, 1985), (b) removing or changing antecedent stimuli (for example, Carr & Durand, 1985; Horner et al., 1991), (c) providing competing positive and aversive consequences for desirable and problem behavior (for example, Cataldo et al., 1986; Linscheid et al., 1990), and (d) preventing serious problem behavior repertoires in young children (Dunlap, Johnson, & Robbins, 1990). The advances of the past 10 years are impressive but there is little in the current literature that provides empirically valid demonstrations of multi-element interventions in applied settings (Carr & Carlson, 1993; Lucyshyn, Olson, & Horner, 1995).

The need for an improved applied treatment technology for high-intensity behaviors has been expressed in recent analyses of behavioral interventions (Carr, Taylor, & Robinson, 1990; Helmstetter & Durand, 1991) and in federal panel reports on destructive behavior (National Institutes of Health, 1991; Reichle, 1990).

Areas needing further study include setting event and biological interactions, measurement of response intensity, the influence of challenging behavior on others, and intervention procedures for low-frequency, high-intensity behavior problems. Further, demonstrations of the utility of complex, multicomponent assessment and intervention procedures in applied community settings are needed. Each of the above areas encompasses the unique problems presented by low-frequency, high-intensity behaviors.

UNIQUE PROBLEMS OF LOW-FREQUENCY, HIGH-INTENSITY BEHAVIORS

Successful treatment of low-frequency, high-intensity behaviors will require the development of expanded alternatives to existing single-subject research methodologies. Renewed interest in response class theory, setting event analysis, and advanced measurement techniques provide the framework for an expanded model of functional assessment and intervention for this unique class of problem behavior.

The primary limitation of the existing single-subject research methodology involves the difficulty of directly manipulating conditions that effect low-frequency, high-intensity behaviors such as severe aggression, self-injury, or property destruction (i.e., setting fires). It is difficult to both assess and treat behaviors that are not manipulated easily or safely in a controlled setting (Iwata et al., 1990; Lovaas & Favell, 1987). The very nature of these behaviors resists traditional behavior analysis research designs that require relatively high-frequency behaviors for observation and diagnosis. For example, implementing a reversal design that requires repeated presentation of conditions for self-injurious head banging is ethically unacceptable, and can even result in strengthening the behavior.

The antecedent events that occasion high-intensity behaviors are extremely complex and are difficult to produce under controlled conditions (Engelmann & Colvin, 1983; Patterson, 1982). The inability to occasion a specific behavior (the dependent variable) at a relatively high rate (that is, multiple times per experimental session) creates a situation where traditional single-subject methods are not sufficiently sensitive to treatment effects. As such, long time intervals may be required to assess treatment effects, thereby increasing the chance of serious injury or the establishment of new problems (Iwata, Vollmer, & Zarcone, 1990).

There is a pressing need to develop and refine the assessment and intervention techniques to be used with individuals who perform low-frequency, high-intensity behavior. This paper outlines selected theoretical and clinical advances contributing to a comprehensive model of treatment for these behaviors. The role of response classes, setting events, and sequential analysis methods are described and integrated into a comprehensive model of assessment and intervention.

The following section outlines an emerging model for assessing and treating low-frequency, high-intensity problem behaviors, and provides applied examples of model components. Each component will be described in the following sections.

FOUNDATION: RESPONSE CLASS THEORY

There are three major theoretical foundations of the proposed model. These include research on functional response classes and response covariation, the role of setting events and establishing operations, and promising advances in objective measurement techniques. Each is described below with reference to the assessment and treatment of low-frequency, high-intensity behaviors.

Response Classes and Covariation

A response class is a set of topographically different behaviors that produce the same functional effect (Johnston & Pennypacker, 1980; Millenson & Leslie, 1979). Members of a response class are predicted to covary as consequences associated with individual members of that response class change. Thus, procedures that affect a single member of a response class should produce collateral effects on other members of the response class (Dunham & Grantmyre, 1982; Parrish et al., 1986). Discussions of the role of response classes appeared early in behavior analysis literature (Hull, 1943; Skinner, 1938). Response classes have been defined in terms of common antecedent or consequent stimulus relations (function), and in terms of topographical similarity (Baer, 1982; Johnston & Pennypacker, 1980).

Low-frequency, high-intensity behaviors typically have been defined in terms of the danger, damage, and inconvenience they impose on others. As researchers and clinicians have become more aware of the communicative function or "intent" of problem behaviors (for example, Donnellan et al., 1984; Doss & Reichle, 1991), a shift has occurred toward the classification of behavior in terms of the function it serves for the person, rather than the impact the behavior has on the teacher (Carr et al., 1993). Though researchers and teachers continue to classify behavior as "destructive," "self-injurious," or "aggressive," there is increasing reference to the purpose these behaviors serve to "obtain attention," "avoid unpleasant situations," "escape disapproval," "maintain self-stimulation," and so forth.

The emphasis on behavioral functions supports research and the common observation that a person seldom performs just a single problem behavior. Data suggest that these behaviors are not independent, but are members of a functional response class all performed to achieve a common effect. Figure 6.1 provides an illustration of multiple behaviors that may be used together or in isolation in order to achieve a functional behavioral outcome. Response class theory and research suggest that intervention should be focused on affecting the entire class, not only the individual behavior(s) that are judged as problems (Sprague & Horner, 1992). In this example, the low-frequency, high-intensity behavior (such as hitting the head, screaming) is a member of a functional response class and should be subject to the same intervention logic as lower intensity members. This recommendation differs from intervention models that emphasize sequential treatment of the most dangerous behaviors first, followed by those that are more tolerable (as in Evans & Meyer, 1985). For example, a comprehensive punishment program might be developed for low-frequency, high-intensity head hitting, while moving toward the teacher (both members of the response class "obtain attention") would be considered a low priority and ignored.

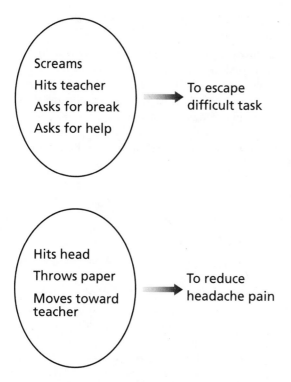

FIGURE 6.1 Two response classes

Response covariation refers to changes in the probability of one behavior being emitted as a function of changes in the probability of other behaviors. For example, it is possible to treat low-frequency, high-intensity behaviors indirectly by treating lower intensity members of the response class (Van Houten & Rolider, 1988). Response covariation is especially relevant for designing treatments to reduce serious problem behaviors (Parrish et al., 1986) and is based on three compatible lines of research. These include the matching law, behavioral allocation, and functional equivalence.

The Matching Law   Response covariation can occur as a function of the matching law (Davison & McCarthy, 1988; Herrnstein, 1970). The matching law provides a mathematical model for predicting the covariation of multiple responses based on the schedule and quality of reinforcement available for each response. (Epling & Pierce, 1990; Mace, McCurdy, & Quigley, 1990; McDowell, 1988; Myerson & Hale, 1984) and predicts that each member of a functional response class will be performed at a rate roughly equal to the relative value of the consequences produced by that response.

The matching law provides direct recommendations for the assessment and treatment of low-frequency, high-intensity behaviors. Recent applications of the matching law in applied contexts have emphasized the need to assess both the comparative frequency and quality of reinforcement available for different responses and the requirements (for example, efficiency) of the different responses (Horner & Day, 1991; Mace, McCurdy, & Quigley 1990). It is likely that lower-intensity behaviors would be performed more often as they elicit low-cost (effort) and relatively consistent (delay, schedule) reinforcement most of the time. Alternatively, low-frequency, high-intensity behaviors would pay off more consistently (every time) and immediately (no delay), but require greater effort to perform. For example, if a student asks for help in order to avoid performing a difficult task, the teacher may occasionally postpone reinforcement by requiring slightly more work. Alternatively, if the student hits the teacher and screams (low frequency and high intensity), the task is terminated immediately (and every time).

Behavioral Allocation A second, and compatible, phenomenon is behavioral allocation. Regardless of the consequences of a behavior, there is a limit to the number of responses a person can emit during a specified time period. Increases in time spent performing one behavior result in decreases in time available to perform other behaviors (Cataldo et al., 1986; Fisher et al., 1990; Parrish et al., 1986). Like the matching law, behavioral allocation emphasizes the point that many different factors affect the covariation of responses, including the decrease in opportunity to perform one behavior given occurrence of a different behavior. Interventions utilizing a behavioral allocation logic include differential reinforcement of incompatible behavior (DRI) (Tarpley & Schroeder, 1978), differential reinforcement of alternative behavior (DRA), and differential reinforcement of communication (DRC) (Carr, 1988). For example, the more often a student moves toward the teacher or throws paper to gain teacher attention (low-intensity but high-frequency behaviors), less opportunity is available to engage in head hitting (low-frequency, high-intensity behavior). Reinforcing lower intensity response class members ensures greater allocation of responding toward these more tolerable behaviors and reduces opportunity to perform the higher intensity (and less tolerable) behaviors.

Functional Equivalence A third area of research has investigated the functional equivalence of *new* response class members (Carr, 1988). Functional equivalence training is based on functional analyses that result in documentation of stimulus events that occasion and maintain problem behaviors (Bijou & Baer, 1968; Bijou, Peterson, & Ault, 1968). A new behavior is taught and added as a new response class member to the extent that it results in the same consequence as the problem behavior. The new, more desirable behavior will compete successfully with problem members of the response class only if it results in equal or greater reinforcement (the matching law) and it displaces opportunities to perform other behaviors (behavioral allocation). Teaching a low-intensity behavior that is easier to perform and results in consistent reinforcement would reduce the probability of the occurrence of low-frequency, high-intensity response class members. Empirical support for the predicted covariation associated with functional equivalence training is impressive (Durand & Crimmins, 1987; Horner & Budd, 1985; Horner et al., 1990b; Sprague & Horner, 1992; Wacker et al., 1990) but no studies to date have specifically assessed the effect on low-frequency, high-intensity behaviors.

The concepts at the foundation of response class theory that encompass response covariation, the matching law, behavioral allocation, and functional equivalence demonstrate that the magnitude and quality of concurrently available reinforcers can provide a basis for predicting which of many available behaviors will be performed at a given point in time. The type, amount, and delay in obtaining a given consequence will determine which member of a response class will be performed (Horner & Day, 1991). Assessment of the relative value of competing reinforcement in applied settings documents a critical, yet poorly understood, phenomenon in the investigation of low-frequency, high-intensity problem behaviors.

FOUNDATION:
COMPLEX STIMULUS CONTROL

Setting Events

The second theoretical underpinning focuses on the assessment and manipulation of the effect of complex and proximal or distal environmental stimuli. These have been referred to as setting events or establishing operations (Leighland, 1984; Michael, 1982; Wahler, 1975). For some time, individuals involved in direct service and clinical research have attempted to analyze the influence of these stimuli on the occurrence of problem behaviors (Chandler, Fowler, & Lubeck, 1992; Vollmer & Iwata, 1991). Research has focused on the impact of setting events on the value of immediate antecedent and consequent stimuli.

Individuals who exhibit serious problem behaviors often do so in a somewhat inconsistent manner. That is, they may respond to a situation appropriately at one time, but respond with a problem behavior at another time. Events that occur during the day may effect how the person responds to a given situation later that evening or the next morning. If the person is tired, agitated, or feeling medication effects, he or she may respond with problem behavior in a situation in which appropriate behavior is typical for him or her (being asked to complete a certain task).

Setting events have been shown to be highly correlated with certain types of problem behavior in applied contexts (Gardner et al., 1986; Horner et al., 1996; Patterson, 1982; Wahler, Leske, & Rodgers, 1979). Research has documented the influence of specific establishing operations (Chandler, Fowler, & Lubeck, 1992; Vollmer & Iwata, 1991). To date, this research has focused on describing the relationships between specific variables and stereotypical behaviors (Horner, 1980; Brusca et al., 1989), self-injurious behaviors (Schroeder et al., 1982), and aggression (Gardner, Karan, & Cole, 1984; Gardner et al., 1986). While the findings are important, research has not demonstrated the full influence of these variables within the larger context of behavioral theory (Michael, 1993: Morris, 1993).

There is a great need to further develop an applied setting event assessment methodology. Strategies have focused on use of clinical data (Reid, 1978; Gardner et al., 1986) in the form of simple event checklists. Researchers working with students who have conduct disorders (Strain & Ezzel, 1978) and aggressive families (Patterson, 1982) have discovered strong relationships between global environmental factors and the performance of problem behavior. With the exception of the work of Gardner and his colleagues (Gardner et al., 1986), little analysis has been completed in applied settings with persons with developmental disabilities who perform low-frequency, high-intensity behaviors. The potential impact of setting events theory on understanding and treating these behaviors is immense. The traditional S-R-S equation must be expanded to acknowledge the impact of setting events (complex stimulus control) and establishing operations on reinforcer value.

FOUNDATION: ASSESSMENT AND ANALYSIS STRATEGIES

The final theoretical foundation involves advances in behavioral assessment and analysis technology. Strategies for documenting the complex stimulus-response relationships described above have become increasingly more sensitive and descriptive. Research has also stressed the importance of measuring response intensity (Iwata et al., 1990; Patterson, 1982), efficiency (Horner et al., 1990b), conditional probability of individual behaviors (Carr et al., 1990), and the multiple stimulus-response relationships that exist in contexts involving low-frequency, high-intensity behaviors. Promising practices to date involve the use of the technology of functional assessment (Iwata et al., 1982; O'Neill et al., 1990) and sequential analysis of teacher-student interactions (Bakeman & Gottman, 1986; Patterson, 1982; Repp et al., 1989). Each of these strategies is described in detail below.

Functional Assessment

Functional assessment refers to the determination of the behaviors of concern, the stimulus conditions that occasion those behaviors, the consequences that are maintaining the behaviors, and the formation and testing of hypotheses regarding their function(s) (Axelrod, 1987; Carr, 1988; Durand & Crimmins, 1988; Iwata et al., l982; O'Neill et al., 1990).

Functional assessment may involve up to three activities. First, an interview is conducted with care providers to define the behaviors of concern, antecedents, consequences, and hypothesized functions of problem behavior (Durand & Crimmins, 1987; O'Neill et al., 1990). The information from the interview is then used to design in vivo observation samples (Touchette, McDonald, & Langer, 1985) or analogue manipulations (Iwata et al., 1982) that allow testing of the hypotheses. Data are then used to design interventions directly related to the function (get/obtain or escape/avoid) of the behaviors of concern. The techniques and logic of functional assessment technology can be greatly enriched with the incorporation of modern sequential analysis methods, explained below.

Sequential Analysis Methods

A technology of direct observation that allows the analysis of sequential relationships between an individual, the environment, and the persons who interact with him or her holds significant promise for increasing the efficiency and accuracy of functional assessment efforts. These techniques have been used to assess families with conduct-disordered children (Patterson, 1982), mother–infant interactions (Bakeman & Gottman, 1986), counseling interactions (Warnpold & Kim, 1989), mother–child interactions (Snyder & Patterson, 1988), institutionalized persons with mental illness (Natta et al., 1990), and, more recently, individuals with severe disabilities and problem behavior (Martens & Houk, 1989; Repp et al., 1988; Repp et al., 1989). The strategy typically involves the use of computers and software specifically designed to allow the simultaneous tracking of multiple behavior and stimulus events in a real-time context (Martens, Melier, & Springer, 1987; Repp et al., 1989). Unique outcomes include the ability to assess transitional probabilities and interactive social and environmental influences within a real-time framework. These tools represent a great improvement in observational accuracy over more traditional frequency, duration, or interval-based measures typically used in behavioral research. The result is a richer and more accurate analysis of behavioral functions and causes. Practitioners and researchers can ask more sophisticated questions regarding the role of specific antecedent and consequent stimuli and the effects of the problem behaviors on the ecology of the interaction.

Measurement of Response Efficiency and Intensity

While it is less well documented than other measurement processes, the measurement of response efficiency and intensity is an increasingly present variable for research on severe problem behaviors (Carr, 1988; Iwata et al., 1990; Patterson, 1982). Measures of efficiency are central to determining the functional equivalence of alternative behaviors (Carr, 1988; Horner & Billingsley, 1988; Horner & Day, 1991), which ensures that the alternative behavior selected to replace a problem behavior will actually replace it (Horner & Billingsley, 1988). This "competing behavior analysis" strategy is a potentially useful approach. For example, if a communication behavior is established to provide the same function as the excess behavior and intended to replace it, why then does the problem behavior decrease? Why doesn't the individual use both members of the response class? There is growing evidence that the behavior that is more efficient in terms of physical effort and schedule of reinforcement will be performed more frequently.

Evidence of this phenomenon is provided by Horner et al. (1990b), who taught a young man with mental retardation and severe problem behaviors two different communication strategies to request assistance under difficult task conditions. One strategy involved a "high effort" communication response (typing "help please" on a small calculator device) and another involved a "low effort" response (touching a single symbol). Independent ratings of videotape samples assessed the level of effort required for each response strategy. The problem

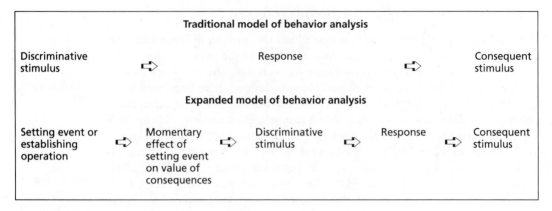

FIGURE 6.2 Expanded model of behavior analysis

behavior (aggression) was rated as being approximately equal to the "high effort" and significantly higher than the "low effort" strategy on a scale of effort expended. After training, the "low effort" communication response replaced both aggression and the "high effort" response. Though quite promising, there is a need to further test and refine our understanding of this phenomenon.

THE FRAMEWORK FOR INTERVENTION: AN EXPANDED MODEL OF BEHAVIOR ANALYSIS

The foundation concepts described above can be integrated in an expanded model for assessing and treating low-frequency, high-intensity behaviors. An illustration of the model is provided in Figure 6.2 and incorporates findings from recent work utilizing the methodologies described above. Kanfer and Phillips (1970) provided a seminal version with the SORKC model (antecedent stimulus, organismic variables, responses, contingency, and consequence). The model described here expands to include consideration of setting events and establishing operations and requires the consideration of a broader range of antecedent and consequent stimuli. The effect of individual stimuli, stimulus classes, and competing stimuli must be considered. The momentary affect of setting events on the value of available reinforcing stimuli will vary and effect the topography and function of the response an individual may perform at a given point in time. Finally, the particular response that is emitted will result in a consequence of varying value over time and as a function of the particular response emitted. The important contribution of this model is the recognition that behavior has multiple antecedent and consequent stimulus determinants and these change in value and salience over time and across contexts.

Figure 6.3 provides an illustration of an applied example of the expanded model (Horner et al., 1996). The student is presented with instructional materials

Setting events	Momentary effect of setting event on value of consequences	Antecedent stimuli	Available responses	Consequences
S_1^e Fight with peer	• Increase in value of escaping hard tasks • Decrease in value of teacher praise	S_1^D Teacher request to do task S_2^D Task materials	R_1 Scream/run R_2 Throw materials R_3 Ask for break R_4 Ask for help R_5 Perform task	• Escape hard task • Teacher praise • More work
S_2^e No breakfast	• Increase in value of food	S_3^D Teacher place-ment of snack on back table	R_6 Run to back table and grab snack	• Eat food
S_3^e Headache	• Increase in value of escaping hard tasks • Decrease in value of teacher praise • Increase in value of pain reduction • Decrease in value of completing task		R_7 Hit head R_8 Rock R_9 Sit in corner	• Reduced headache

FIGURE 6.3 An illustration of the expanded model of behavior analysis. S^e refers to setting events or establishing operations, S^D refers to discriminative stimulus, and R refers to response.

SOURCE: From Horner et al. (1996). Adapted with permission.

and a request from the teacher to complete the task. Interpreting the situation would involve the following analyses:

Component One: The Effect of
Setting Events and Establishing Operations

The first class of variables to consider are the setting events and/or establishing operations that affect the current value of available reinforcers and the ability of the student to attend to relevant antecedent stimuli. These events include temporally and proximally distant events—in this example, a fight with a peer, no breakfast, and a headache. Additional factors concurrently available in the stimulus complex of this example include a snack on the back table in the classroom and other students. These events may act independently or collectively to affect the value of different consequent stimuli and thus play a role in determining which available response is performed. In the current example, a peer fight, hunger, and a headache may change the probability that problem behaviors will be performed. The momentary effect of these setting events may increase, decrease, or have no effect on the probability of low-frequency, high-intensity behavior performance.

Component Two: The Value of Available Consequent Stimuli

The second component considers the absolute and comparative value of all possible consequent stimuli for the student. Reinforcer value occurs on a continuum. Available events may have reinforcing, aversive, or neutral values for the student at any given moment. An important recommendation for use of the model is to assess the value of consequent stimuli and the effect on the stimulus control properties of selected antecedent stimuli. The degree of stimulus control is influenced by the current value of available consequent stimuli. The most valuable consequent stimuli will be associated with stronger stimulus control of the responses associated with that consequence. An applied illustration is provided in Figure 6.3 (above).

For the student, available consequences include task avoidance, more work, teacher praise, access to food, and reduced headache pain. The teacher should anticipate different responses if the student is (a) particularly motivated to obtain teacher praise, (b) hungry, or (c) in a state of agitation (from pain) that makes escape from instruction particularly valuable.

Component Three: Antecedent Stimuli

The third level of analysis considers the available antecedent stimuli presented to the student at any given point in time. In the current example, the teacher presents the student with task materials and a request to perform the task. Some stimuli will neither increase nor decrease the probability of behavior(s). These may be stimuli such as the snack, other students in the room, or normal classroom sounds. There will be other stimuli, however, that are associated with reinforcing consequences from the student's learning history, and which function as discriminative stimuli for certain responses or response classes. In the current example, the student is presented with the combined antecedent stimulus of new task materials and a teacher request. These stimuli may occasion completing the task or behaviors that result in task avoidance. At the same time the presence of food in the classroom can occasion an appetitive response. The teacher needs to be aware that at any given moment, many stimuli (and responses) are available for the student. Many stimulus control relationships are present concurrently and the student will attend (and ultimately respond) to some or all of the available stimuli. Low-frequency, high-intensity behavior will occur if the appropriate (low-frequency) stimulus conditions exist.

Component Four: Consideration of Available Responses

The fourth component requires consideration of the range of available response options in a given stimulus context. Competition can occur between responses that result in different consequences (for example, escape from instruction versus teacher attention) and in different responses that are performed to produce a common functional effect ("throw materials" versus "ask for break"). The outcome of this competition is affected by the relative value of the competing consequent stimuli, the salience of antecedent stimuli, and the efficiency of the competing behaviors (Horner & Billingsley, 1988). In our example, available responses include screaming, running, throwing materials, asking for a break, asking for help, head hitting, rocking, grabbing the snack, or performing the task. Which response is performed will be determined by the stimulus control relationships that are competing at any one moment.

Component Five: Identification
of Response Consequences

The final consideration in the model is the type and magnitude of the consequences that result from performing a particular response. Responses will be influenced by the particular type, amount, and schedule of reinforcement available. Our student may perform the task, engage in problem behavior to avoid the task, or perform another behavior to obtain a different functional effect. The student performs minor problem behaviors often in the context of instruction; less often, the student performs very dangerous behaviors. The teacher must recognize that the consequences resulting from problem behavior performance (such as escape) are more valuable in relation to those available for task completion, and under certain low-frequency conditions a high-intensity behavior is performed to produce that effect.

The five components diagram a behavioral ecology that is in continuous transformation as setting events, antecedent stimuli, consequences, and response options change. The model is an interactive representation of the relationships between multiple stimuli and behaviors and can provide new directions for research and clinical practice. The model is particularly relevant for the analysis and treatment of low-frequency, high-intensity problem behaviors, as it provides parameters to interpret the structure of complex response classes that include those high-intensity members.

Future analyses of low-frequency, high-intensity behavior must capture the complexity and fluidity of the model described in this paper. Simple single-subject designs that emphasize control of many variables while allowing only one or a few variables to change will fail to capture this phenomenon. Clinical case study demonstrations will also be limited in the ability to empirically document these complex interactions of stimuli and responses. Methodologies that address setting events and analysis of complex stimulus and response relationships need to be refined further in order to adequately characterize these complex phenomena.

AUTHOR NOTES

Preparation of this paper was supported by Grant No. H023N10010-92 from the United States Department of Education, Office of Special Education and Rehabilitative Services. Opinions expressed are those of the authors and do not necessarily reflect those of the Department.

REFERENCES

Axelrod, S. (1987). Functional and structural analysis of behavior: Approaches leading to reduced use of punishment procedures. *Research in Developmental Disabilities, 8,* 165–178.

Baer, D. M. (1982). The imposition of structure on behavior and the demolition of behavioral structures. In D. J. Bernstein (Ed.), *Response Structure and Organization* (pp. 217–254). Lincoln: University of Nebraska.

Bailey, J. S., & Pyles, D. A. M. (1989). Behavioral diagnostics. In E. Cipani (Ed.), *The treatment of severe behavior disorders: Behavior analysis approaches* (pp. 85–107). Washington, DC: American Association on Mental Retardation.

Bakeman, R., & Gottman, J. M. (1986). *Observing interaction: An introduction to sequential analysis.* Cambridge, MA: Cambridge University.

Bannerman, S. F. (1987). *The politics of caring.* Philadelphia: The Farmer Press.

Bijou, S., & Baer, D. M. (1968). *Child development,* Vol. 2: *Universal stages of infancy.* New York: Appleton-Century-Crofts.

Bijou, S. W., Peterson, R. F., & Ault, M. H. (1968). A method to integrate descriptive and experimental field studies at the level of data and empirical concepts. *Journal of Applied Behavior Analysis, 1,* 175–191.

Borthwick-Duffy, S. A., Eyman, R. K., & White, J. F. (1987). Client characteristics and residential placement patterns. *American Journal of Mental Deficiency, 92,* 24–30.

Brusca, R. M., Nieminen, G. S., Carter, R., & Repp, A. C. (1989). The relationship of staff contact and activity to the stereotypy of children with multiple disabilities. *Journal of the Association for Persons with Severe Handicaps, 14,* 127–136.

Carr, E. G. (1988). Functional equivalence as a mechanism of response generalization. In R. H. Horner, G. Dunlap, & R. L. Koegel (Eds.), *Generalization and maintenance: Lifestyle changes in applied settings* (pp. 221–241). Baltimore: Paul H. Brookes.

Carr, E. G., & Carlson, J. L. (1993). Reduction of severe behavior problems in the community using a multicomponent treatment approach. *Journal of Applied Behavior Analysis, 26,* 157–172.

Carr, E. G., & Durand, V. M. (1985). Reducing behavior problems through functional communication training. *Journal of Applied Behavior Analysis, 18,* 111–126.

Carr, E. G., McConnachie, G., Levin, L., & Kemp, D. (1993). Communication-based treatment of severe behavior problems. In R. Van Houten & S. Axelrod (Eds.), *Behavior analysis and treatment* (pp. 231–267). New York: Plenum.

Carr, E. G., Robinson, S., & Palumbo, L. W. (1990). The wrong issue: Aversive versus nonaversive treatment. The right issue: Functional versus nonfunctional treatment. In A. C. Repp & N. N. Singh (Eds.), *Perspectives on the use of nonaversive and aversive interventions for persons with developmental disabilities* (pp. 361–379). Sycamore, IL: Sycamore.

Carr, E. G., Robinson, S., Taylor, J. C., Carlson, J. I. (1990). Positive approaches to the treatment of severe behavior problems in persons with developmental disabilities: A review and analysis of reinforcement and stimulus-based procedures. *The Association for Persons with Severe Handicaps, Monograph No. 4.* Washington, DC: National Institutes of Health.

Carr, E. G., Taylor, J. C., Carlson, J. I., & Robinson, S. (1990). Appendix B: Re-inforcement and stimulus based treatments for severe behavior problems in developmental disabilities. *Draft report of the consensus development panel on treatment of destructive behaviors in persons with developmental disabilities.* Bethesda: National Institutes of Health.

Carr, E., Taylor, J., Robinson, S. (1990). The effects of severe behavior problems in children on the teaching behavior of adults. *Journal of Applied Behavior Analysis, 24,* 523–535.

Cataldo, M. F., Ward, E. M., Russo, D. C., Riordan, M., & Bennett, D. (1986). Compliance and correlated problem behavior in children: Effects of contingent and noncontingent reinforcement. *Analysis and Intervention in Developmental Disabilities, 6,* 265–282.

Chandler, L. K., Fowler, S. A., & Lubeck, R. C. (1992). An analysis of the effects of multiple setting events on the social behavior of preschool children with special needs. *Journal of Applied Behavior Analysis, 25,* 249–264.

Davison, M., & McCarthy, D. (1988). *The Matching Law: A Research Review.* Hillsday, NJ: Lawrence, Erlbaum Associates.

Donnellan, A., LaVigna, G. W., Negri-Shoultz, N., & Fassbender, L. (1989). *Progress without punishment: Effective approaches for learners with behavior problems.* New York: Teachers College Press, Columbia University.

Donnellan, A. M., Mirenda, P. L., Mesaros, R. A., & Fassbender, L. L. (1984). Analyzing the communicative functions of aberrant behavior. *Journal of the Association for Persons with Severe Handicaps, 9,* 201–212.

Doss, S., & Reichle, J. (1991). Replacing excess behavior with an initial communicative repertoire. In J. Reichle, J. York, & J. Sigafoos (Eds.), *Implementing augmentative and alternative communication* (pp. 215–237). Baltimore: Paul H. Brookes.

Dunham, P. J., & Grantmyre, T. (1982). Changes in a multiple response repertoire during response contingent punishment and response restriction. *Journal of the Experimental Analysis of Behavior, 37,* 123–133.

Dunlap, G., Johnson, L. F., & Robbins, R. R. (1990). Preventing serious behavior support for students with emotional and behavioral challenges. In A. C. Repp & N. N. Singh (Eds.), *Perspectives on the use of nonaversive and aversive interventions for persons with developmental disabilities* (pp. 273–286). Sycamore, IL: Sycamore.

Durand, V. M. (1990). *Severe behavior problems: A functional communication training approach.* New York: Guilford.

Durand, V. M., & Carr, E. G. (1987). Social influences on self-stimulatory behavior: Analysis and treatment application. *Journal of Applied Behavior Analysis, 20,* 119–132.

Durand, V. M., & Crimmins, D. B. (1987). Assessment and treatment of psychotic speech in an autistic child. *Journal of Autism and Developmental Disorders, 17,* 17–28.

Durand, V. M., & Crimmins, D. B. (1988). Identifying the variables maintaining self-injurious behavior. *Journal of Autism and Developmental Disorders, 18,* 99–117.

Engelmann, S., & Colvin, G. (1983). *Generalized compliance training.* Austin, TX: Pro-Ed, Incorporated.

Epling, W. F., & Pierce, W. D. (1990). Laboratory to application: An experimental analysis of severe problem behavior. In A. C. Repp & N. N. Singh (Eds.), *Perspectives on the use of nonaversive and aversive interventions for persons with developmental disabilities.* Sycamore, IL: Sycamore.

Evans, I. M., & Meyer, L. H. (1985). *An educative approach to behavior problems: A practical decision model for interventions with severely handicapped learners.* Baltimore: Paul H. Brookes.

Fisher, W. W., Piazza, C. C., Cataldo, M. F., & Harell, R. (May 1990). *The effects of nonverbal communication training, communication, and punishment in the treatment of self-injury and other aberrant behavior.* Paper presented at the 16th Annual International Convention of the Association for Behavior Analysis, Nashville.

Gardner, W. I., Cole, C. L., Davidson, D. P., & Karan, O. C. (1986). Reducing aggression in individuals with developmental disabilities: An expanded stimulus control, assessment, and intervention model. *Education and Training of the Mentally Retarded, 21,* 3–12.

Gardner, W. I., Karan, O. C., & Cole, C. L. (1984). Assessment of setting events influencing functional capacities of mentally retarded adults with behavior difficulties. In A. S. Halpern & M. J. Fuhrer (Eds.), *Functional assessment in rehabilitation* (pp. 171–185). Baltimore: Paul H. Brookes.

Guess, D., Helmstetter, E., Turnbull, H. R., & Knowlton, S. (1987). *Use of aversive procedures with persons who are disabled: An historical review and critical analysis.* Seattle: The Association for Persons with Severe Handicaps.

Helmstetter, E., & Durand, V. M. (1991). Nonaversive interventions for severe behavior problems. In L. H. Meyer, C. A. Peck, & L. Brown (Eds.), *Critical issues in the lives of people with severe disabilities* (pp. 559–600). Baltimore: Paul H. Brookes.

Herrnstein, R. J. (1970). On the law of effect. *Journal of the Experimental Analysis of Behavior, 13,* 243–266.

Horner, R. H. (1980). Effects of an environmental enrichment program on the behavior of institutionalized, profoundly retarded children. *Journal of Applied Behavior Analysis, 13,* 473–491.

Horner, R. H., & Billingsley, F. F. (1988). The effect of competing behavior on the generalization and maintenance of adaptive behavior in applied settings. In R. H. Horner, G. Dunlap, & R. L. Koegel (Eds.), *Generalization and maintenance: Lifestyle changes in applied settings* (pp. 197–220). Baltimore: Paul H. Brookes.

Horner, R. H., & Budd, C. M. (1985). Acquisition of manual sign use: Collateral reduction of maladaptive behavior, and factors limiting generalization. *Education and Training of the Mentally Retarded, 20,* 39–47.

Horner, R. H., & Day, M. (1991). The effects of response efficiency on functionally equivalent, competing behaviors. *Journal of Applied Behavior Analysis, 24,* 719–732.

Horner, R. H., Day, M., Sprague, J. R., O'Brien, M. M., & Heathfield, T. L. (1991). Use of interspersed requests to reduce excess behavior. *Journal of Applied Behavior Analysis, 24*(2), 265–278.

Horner, R. H., Dunlap, G., Koegel, R. L., Carr, E. G., Sailor, W., Anderson, J., Albin, R. W., & O'Neill, R. E. (1990a). Toward a technology of "nonaversive" behavioral support. *Journal of the Association for Persons with Severe Handicaps, 15*(3), 125–132.

Horner, R. H., Sprague, J. R., O'Brien, M. M., & Heathfield, T. L. (1990b). The role of response efficiency in the reduction of problem behaviors through functional equivalence training: A case study. *Journal of the Association for Persons with Severe Handicaps, 15*(2), 91–97.

Horner, R. H., Vaughn, B., Day, H. M., & Ard, B. (1996). The relationship between setting events and problem behavior. In L. Koegel, R. L. Koegel, & G. Dunlap (Eds.), *Positive behavioral support: Including people with difficult behavior in the community* (pp. 381–402). Baltimore: Paul H. Brookes.

Hull, C. L. (1943). *Principles of behavior.* New York: Appleton-Century-Crofts.

Iwata, B. A., Dorsey, M. F., Slifer, K. J., Baumann, K. E., & Richman, G. S. (1982). Toward a functional analysis of self injury. *Analysis and Intervention in Developmental Disabilities, 2,* 3–20.

Iwata, B. A., Pace, G. M., Kissell, R. C., Nau, P. A., & Farber, J. M. (1990). The self-injury trauma (SIT) scale: A method for quantifying surface tissue damage caused by self-injurious behavior. *Journal of Applied Behavior Analysis, 23,* 99–110.

Iwata, B., Vollmer, R., & Zarcone, J. (1990). The experimental (functional) analysis of behavior disorders: Methodology, applications, and limitations. In A. C. Repp & N. N. Singh (Eds.), *Perspectives on the use of nonaversive and aversive interventions for persons with developmental disabilities* (pp. 301–330). Sycamore, IL: Sycamore.

Johnston, J. M., & Pennypacker, H. S. (1980). *Strategies and tactics of human behavioral research.* Hillsdale, NJ: Lawrence, Erlbaum Associates.

Kanfer, F. H., & Phillips, J. S. (1970). *Learning foundations of behavior therapy.* New York: Wiley.

Larson, S. A., & Lakin, K. C. (1989). Deinstitutionalization of persons with mental retardation: Behavioral outcomes. *Journal of the Association for Persons with Severe Handicaps, 14,* 324–332.

Leighland, S. (1984). On "setting events" and related concepts. *The Behavior Analyst, 7*(1), 41–45.

Linscheid, T. R., Iwata, B. A., Ricketts, R. W., Williams, D. E., & Griffin, J. C. (1990). Clinical evaluation of the Self-Injurious Behavior Inhibiting System (SIBIS). *Journal of Applied Behavior Analysis, 23*(1), 53–78.

Lovaas, I. O., & Favell, J. E. (1987). Protection for clients undergoing aversive/restrictive interventions. *Education and Treatment of Children, 10,* 311–325.

Lucyshyn, J. M., Olson, D., & Horner, R. H. (1995). Building an ecology of support: A case study of one young woman with severe problem behaviors living in the community. *Journal of the Association for Persons with Severe Handicaps, 20,* 16–30.

Mace, F. C., McCurdy, B. & Quigley, E. A. (1990). A collateral effect of reward predicted by matching theory. *Journal of Applied Behavior Analysis, 23*(2), 197–205.

Mace, C. F., Webb, R. W., Sharkey, D. M., Mattson, D. M., & Rosen, H. S. (1988). Functional analysis and treatment of bizarre speech. *Journal of Behavior Therapy and Experimental Psychiatry, 19*(4), 289–296.

Martens, B. K, & Houk, J. L. (1989). The application of Herrnstein's law of effect to disruptive and on-task behavior of a retarded adolescent girl. *Journal of the Experimental Analysis of Behavior, 51,* 17–28.

Martens, B. K., Melier, P. J., & Springer, J. (1987). *Multivariate ecological observation system* (computer program). Syracuse, NY: Syracuse University.

McDowell, J. J. (1988). Matching theory in natural human environments. *The Behavior Analyst, 11,* 95–109.

Meyer, L. M., & Evans, I. M. (1989). *Nonaversive intervention for behavior problems: A manual for home and community.* Baltimore: Paul H. Brookes.

Michael, J. L. (1982). Distinguishing between discriminative and motivational functions of stimuli. *Journal of the Experimental Analysis of Behavior, 37,* 149–155.

Michael, J. L. (1993). Establishing operations. *The Behavior Analyst, 16,* 191–206.

Millenson, J. R., & Leslie, J. C. (1979). *Principles of behavior analysis* (2nd ed.). New York: Macmillan.

Morris, E. K. (1993). Contextualism, historiography, and the history of behavior analysis. In S. C. Hayes, L. J. Hayes, H. W. Reese, & T. R. Sarbin (Eds.), *Varieties of scientific contextualism* (pp. 137–165). Reno: Context Press.

Mulick, J. A. (1990). The ideology and science of punishment in mental retardation. *American Journal on Mental Retardation, 95,* 142–156.

Myerson, J., & Hale, S. (1984). Practical implications of the matching law. *Journal of Applied Behavior Analysis, 17,* 367–380.

Natta, M. B., Holmbeck, G. N., Kupst, M. J., Pines, R. J., & Schulman, J. L. (1990). Sequences of staff-child interactions on a psychiatric inpatient unit. *Journal of Abnormal Child Psychology, 18*(1), 1–14.

National Institutes of Health (1989). *NIH consensus development conference on the treatment of destructive behaviors in persons with developmental disabilities.* Bethesda: U. S. Department of Health and Human Services.

National Institutes of Health. (1991). *Treatment of destructive behaviors in persons with developmental disabilities* (NIH Publication No. 91-2410). Bethesda: U. S. Department of Health and Human Services.

O'Neill, R. E., Horner, R. H., Albin, R. A., Storey, K. S., & Sprague, J. R. (1990). *Functional analysis: A practical assessment guide.* Pacific Grove, CA: Brooks-Cole.

Pagel, S. E., & Whitling, C. A. (1978). Mental retardation abstracts. Readmission to a state hospital for mental retarded persons: Reasons for community placement failure. *Mental Retardation, 16*(2), 164–166.

Parrish, J. M., Cataldo, M. F., Kolko, D. J., Neef, N. A., & Egel, A. L. (1986). Experimental analysis of response covariation among compliant and inappropriate behaviors. *Journal of Applied Behavior Analysis, 19,* 241–254.

Patterson, G. (1982). *Coercive family process: A social learning approach to family intervention.* Eugene: Castalia.

Reichle, J. (1990). *National working conference on positive approaches to the management of excess behavior: Final report and recommendations.* Minneapolis: University of Minnesota, Center for Residential and Community Services, Institute on Community Integration.

Reid, J. B. (Ed.). (1978). *A social learning approach to family intervention: Observation in home settings.* Eugene: Castalia.

Repp, A. C., Felce, D., Barton, L. E., & Lyle, E. (1988). Basing the treatment of stereotypic and self-injurious behaviors on hypotheses of their causes. *Journal of Applied Behavior Analysis, 21,* 281–290.

Repp, A. C., Harman, M. L., Felce, D., VanAcker, R., & Karsh, K. L. (1989). Conducting behavioral assessments on computer collected data. *Behavioral Assessment, 2,* 249–268.

Repp, A. C., & Singh, N. N. (1990). *Perspectives on the use of nonaversive and aversive interventions for persons with developmental disabilities.* Sycamore, IL: Sycamore.

Scheerenberger, R. (1990). *Public residential services for the mentally retarded: FY 1988-89.* Fairfax, VA: National Association of Superintendents of Public Residential Facilities for the Mentally Retarded.

Schroeder, S. R., Kanoy, J. R., Mulick, J. A., Rojahn, J., Thios, S. J., Stephens, M., & Hawk, B. (1982). The effects of the environment on programs for self-injurious behavior. In J. H. Hollis & C. E. Meyers (Eds.), *Life threatening behavior: Analysis and intervention* (pp. 105–159). Washington: American Association on Mental Deficiency.

Skinner, B. F. (1938). *The behavior of organisms.* New York: Appleton-Century-Crofts.

Snyder, J., & Patterson, G. R. (1988). The effects of consequences on patterns of social interaction: A quasi-experimental approach to reinforcement in natural interaction. *Child Development, 57,* 1257–1268.

Sprague, J. R., & Horner, R. H. (1992). Covariation within functional response classes: Implications for treatment of severe problem behavior. *Journal of Applied Behavior Analysis, 25,* 735–745.

Strain, P. S., & Ezzell, D. (1978). The sequence and distribution of behavioral disordered adolescents' disruptive/inappropriate behaviors: An observational study in residential settings. *Behavior Modification, 2,* 403–425.

Tarpley, H. D. & Schroeder, S. R. (1979). Comparison of DRO and DRI on rate of suppression of self-injurious behavior.

American Journal of Mental Deficiency, 84(2), 188–194.

Tausig, M. (1985). Factors in family decision-making about placement for developmentally disabled individuals. *American Journal of Mental Deficiency, 89,* 352–361.

Touchette, P., McDonald, R. F., & Langer, S. N. (1985). A scatter plot for identifying stimulus control of problem behavior. *Journal of Applied Behavior Analysis, 18,* 343–351.

Van Houten, R., Axelrod, S., Bailey, J. S., Favell, J. E., Foxx, R. M., Iwata, B. A., & Lovaas, O. I. (1988). The right to effective behavioral treatment. *The Behavior Analyst, 2,* 111–114.

Van Houten, R., & Rolider, A. (1988). Recreating the scene: An effective way to provide delayed punishment for inappropriate motor behavior. *Journal of Applied Behavior Analysis, 21,* 187–192.

Vollmer, T. R., & Iwata, B. A. (1991). Establishing operations and reinforcement effects. *Journal of Applied Behavior Analysis, 24,* 279–291.

Wacker, D. P., Steege, M. W., Northrup, J., Sasso, G., Berg, W., Reimers, T., Cooper, L., Cigrand, K., & Dunn, L. (1990). A component analysis of functional communication training across three topographies of severe behavior problems. *Journal of Applied Behavior Analysis, 23*(4), 417–430.

Wahler, R. G. (1975). Some structural aspects of deviant child behavior. *Journal of Applied Behavior Analysis, 8,* 27–42.

Wahler, R. G., Leske, G., & Rodgers, E. S. (1979). The modification of stuttering: Some response-response relationships. *Journal of Experimental Child Psychology, 9,* 411–428.

Wampold, B. E., & Kim, K. (1989). Sequential analysis applied to counseling process and outcome: A case study revisited. *Journal of Counseling Psychology, 36,* 357–364.

White, C., Lakin, K., Bruininks, R., Li, X. (1991). *Persons with mental retardation and related conditions in state-operated residential facilities: Year ending June 30, 1989 with longitudinal trends from 1950 to 1989.* Minneapolis: University of Minnesota, Center for Residential and Community Services, Institute on Community Integration.

7

⬚

Assessment and Treatment of Behavior Disorders Maintained by Nonsocial (Automatic) Reinforcement

BRIDGET A. SHORE
BRIAN A. IWATA

INTRODUCTION

Most demonstrations and experiments involving function analysis have concentrated on socially mediated contingencies—either attention or escape from a task. In this chapter, Shore and Iwata present the more difficult contingency of automatic reinforcement, reinforcement that is not socially mediated but follows automatically from the behavior (for example, moving when having had to sit still or seeing a favorite artist's picture). In general, the contingency and sometimes the behavior itself is a private event.

Such private events can either be ignored by applied behavior analysts or addressed. The authors chose to do the latter and provide in this chapter a detailed review of various procedures (for example, alter establishing operations, substitute reinforcers, increase or decrease stimulation levels, use differential reinforcement) that can be used directly or with additional analysis to address behaviors maintained by automatic reinforcement.

Private events have long presented difficulty for behavior analysts, particularly since we col-
lect most of our data by direct observation. While those conducting basic research can reason-
ably choose to concentrate only on observable events, those of us in applied behavior analysis,
and particularly those of us attempting to analyze the function of problem behavior, do not
have this restrictive choice. This chapter will hopefully push us to extend our work into the
area of automatic reinforcement.

Considerable evidence indicates that many behavior disorders (for example, aggression, property destruction, and self-injury) are maintained by social reinforcement, often in the form of attention from care providers (Day et al., 1988) or escape from task demands (Iwata et al., 1990). Yet some of these behaviors seem to persist in the absence of social consequences. For example, aerophagia (Barrett et al., 1987), bruxism (Heller & Strang, 1973), pica (Danford & Huber, 1982), rumination (Johnston et al., 1991), self-injurious behavior or SIB (Cowdery, Iwata, & Pace, 1990), trichotillomania (Rothbaum, 1992), and a number of other behaviors that sometimes are called "stereotyped mannerisms" (Baumeister & Forehand, 1973) have been observed to occur in the absence of apparent environmental consequences.

Explanations for the motivation for such behaviors vary widely. Behavior without apparent environmental motivation may be the product of subtle yet direct social contingencies such as intermittent reinforcement (Spradlin & Girardeau, 1966), indirect contingencies such as those that produce adjunctive behavior (Lerman et al., 1994), or respondent conditioning (Romanczyk, Lockshin, & O'Connor, 1992). To further complicate matters, the appearance of some behavior disorders could be attributable to unlearned reflexes stemming from either biological insult (Cataldo & Harris, 1982) or neurological dysfunction (Gedye, 1992).

In addition to the above possibilities, stereotyped behavior—to the extent that it is acquired through experience—may also be maintained by nonsocial consequences. Skinner (1953) originally introduced the term "automatic reinforcement" to emphasize the fact that behavior can be maintained by directly produced reinforcers, and several authors have used the term as a means of distinguishing between behaviors maintained by nonsocial rather than social reinforcement (for example, Derby et al., 1994; Iwata, Vollmer, & Zarcone, 1990; Van Houten, 1993; Vollmer, 1994). The problem of identifying and demonstrating functional relations when learned behavior does not enter into social contingencies is that the presumed controlling variables (if any) are difficult to observe and manipulate. For applied behavioral analysts, the problem is a practical one: How do we assess and treat behavior disorders when their controlling variables are inaccessible? The purposes of this chapter are to examine various theories accounting for the development and maintenance of such behavior, elaborate on the concept of automatic reinforcement as a maintaining contingency for certain cases of stereotypy and SIB, and describe methods for assessment and treatment.

THEORIES ON THE DEVELOPMENT
OF STEREOTYPIC BEHAVIOR

The numerous hypotheses concerning the origins and maintenance of aberrant behavior are indicative of the fact that many researchers view some behavior problems as not maintained by social reinforcement. Cataldo and Harris (1982) reviewed a number of developmental and biological factors that may contribute to the origins and maintenance of stereotypy and SIB. Certain medical syndromes, such as Leach–Nyhan, Cornelia de Lange, and Riley–Day, have been associated with a high prevalence of SIB, although these syndromes account for only a small percentage of observed SIB. Cataldo and Harris also reviewed data on the effects of social deprivation as evidence for a biological basis for SIB. Animals raised in isolation often display stereotypic behavior and SIB, suggesting that lack of stimulation during certain crucial stages of development may lead to abnormal neurological development. In fact, there is some evidence supporting this hypothesis (see Breese, Criswell, & Mueller, 1990 for a review). Fox (1967), for example, studied dogs raised in isolation and found intense behavioral arousal and abnormalities in the central nervous system (such as short latencies of evoked potentials and desynchronized EEGs).

Cataldo and Harris (1982) also proposed two physiological sources of operant reinforcement for SIB that may be found in the body's biochemical response to pain. These biochemicals are endogenous opioids (endorphins), which are almost identical in structure and function to exogenous opioids (such as morphine). Thus, two possible functions of SIB could be to activate the release of endorphins that may either produce "pleasurable" sensation (positive reinforcement) or attenuate pain (negative reinforcement). Considerable research has been conducted using the opioid antagonists Naltrexone® and Naloxone® as pharmacological interventions, based on the assumption that endogenous opioids reinforce the occurrence of self-injury. However, the results of such studies have been mixed (see Schaal & Hackenberg, 1994 for a review).

Lewis, Baumeister, and Mailman, (1987) hypothesized that stereotypy is the behavioral output of neuronal systems seriously disturbed through developmental insult. They suggested that changes in dopaminergic systems are responsible for at least some instances of excessive stereotypic behavior seen in individuals with developmental disabilities. The view that stereotypy and SIB may be the result of neurodevelopmental dysfunction has also been the basis for sensory-integration theory (Ayers, 1972), which focuses on the organization and integration of the vestibular, tactile, visual, auditory, and olfactory systems. The maturation of these systems is viewed as stage dependent: Integration at one stage is a prerequisite for further development. Thus, therapy based on this theory emphasizes physiological stimulation that provides multiple sensory input. Much of the research on sensory-integration therapy, however, contains serious methodological problems limiting the validity of the techniques if not the underlying theory (Arendt, MacLean, & Baumeister, 1988; Mason & Iwata, 1990).

Other evidence suggesting a biological basis for SIB comes from studies in which a relationship has been found between administration of certain drugs and the appearance of stereotypies or SIB in nonhumans: Innovar® with guinea pigs (Leash et al., 1973), alcohol with macaques (Chamove & Harlow, 1970), and caffeine with rats (Boyd et al., 1965). Additional support has come from studies examining intraventricularly administrated ACTH, which results in increased stereotypy in rats (Jolles, Rompa-Barendregt, & Gispen 1979). Results of these drug studies suggest that physiological activation (for example, of CNS function) can also occur from environmental events (for example, conflict, novel experiences, etc.) and may be related to the development of stereotypy and SIB.

Gedye (1992) proposed that SIB could result from involuntary muscular contractions associated with frontal lobe seizures, which produce movement patterns resembling some topographies of SIB. Gedye reviewed the records of 10 patients diagnosed with frontal lobe seizures who also exhibited SIB and concluded that not all SIB is under voluntary control (that is, a "behavioral problem"). Coulter, (1989) criticized the bases for Gedye's hypothesis, noting that (a) extreme forms of SIB are not typically found in patients with frontal lobe seizures, and (b) Gedye's subjects did not have EEG recordings to confirm the epileptic nature of the SIB.

Criticisms directed at biological theories of stereotypy and SIB have been numerous. Newsom and Lovaas (1987), for example, suggested that "it is not enough to claim to have an account of self-stimulatory behavior, then simply point in the general direction of dysregulated neuronal systems assumed to exist in humans because of some interesting animal models" (p. 261). They also pointed to the unpredictability of pharmacological interventions, the conflicting results from antagonist drug studies, and the extensive amount of data indicating that stereotypy and SIB can be treated successfully through environmental manipulation as further evidence that biological interpretations are, at best, incomplete.

Somewhat related to neurodevelopmental theories are hypotheses based on arousal modulation, which suggest that stereotypy and SIB maintain some optimal level of stimulation. There are three general corollaries to arousal theory. First, stereotypy may *increase* arousal in an under-stimulating environment. Ellis (1973) suggested that such behavior maintains a minimal level of arousal when there is limited environmental stimulation, and support for this hypothesis can be found in studies showing that "barren" environments result in higher levels of stereotypy relative to more stimulating environments (Berkson & Mason, 1963; Forehand & Baumeister, 1971; Horner, 1980; Warren & Burns, 1970). A second corollary is that stereotypy *decreases* arousal resulting from an over-stimulating environment. Studies supporting this hypothesis have examined the effects of stimuli presumed to produce physiological arousal on rates of stereotypic behavior (Berkson & Mason, 1963; Forehand & Baumeister, 1970; Hutt & Hutt, 1965; Watters & Watters, 1980). A third view is that stereotypy regulates arousal in both under- and over-stimulating environments (Berkson, 1983). Although research on these arousal hypotheses has often shown relationships between the amount of environmental stimulation and the occurrence of stereotypic behavior, it is not clear that stereotypy produces changes in arousal states (Hutt et al., 1965;

Ornitz et al., 1970; Stone, 1964). Hutt et al. (1965), for example, simultaneously monitored the EEGs and rates of stereotypic behavior of two autistic children and found increased cortical arousal when stereotypy occurred. Stone (1964), however, found that the EEG records of blind children engaging in body rocking and eye pressing were similar to those of sleeping subjects (reduced arousal). Finally, Ornitz et al. (1970) found that the EEG records of an autistic child engaging in stereotypy could not be differentiated from records when stereotypy was absent.

A hypothesis related to arousal theories is the view that stereotypic behavior produces sensory/perceptual reinforcement. Lovaas et al. (1987) proposed that the acquisition and maintenance of stereotypic behavior is a function of directly produced interoceptive and exteroceptive perceptual consequences, which can be auditory, tactile, visual, gustatorial, or vestibular in nature. Support for this hypothesis stems from several sources. First, many studies have shown that animals engage in behavior for which the only consequence is sensory input (Fowler, 1971; Kish, 1966). Results of other studies suggest that deficits in sensory stimulation may be related to stereotypy and SIB (Harlow & Harlow, 1962; Riesen, 1975). In the Riesen study, young monkeys who were deprived of physical contact and play with other monkeys displayed stereotypic behavior and self-biting, whereas monkeys who were not deprived did not display such behavior. Of greater relevance are experimental studies examining the effects of short-term sensory deprivation (for example, Sackett, 1966) and correlational research on chronic sensory deficits in individuals with developmental disabilities (for example, Thurrell & Rice, 1970), which have shown increases in hyperactivity and stereotypy. The most direct evidence can be found in studies in which environmental manipulations altered rates of stereotypy. Assuming that sensory stimulation is the source of reinforcement, attenuation of those effects should result in decreased stereotypic behavior (extinction). Through systematic removal and reintroduction of perceptual consequences (such as blindfolding to mask reinforcing effects of visual stimuli), these studies have shown extinction-like effects with stereotypic behavior (Aiken & Salzberg, 1984; Baumeister & Forehand, 1971; Rincover & Devany, 1982; Rincover, 1978; Rincover et al., 1979).

Other researchers have suggested that stereotypic behavior and some instances of SIB could be indirectly related to operant contingencies. Baumeister and Forehand (1973) proposed that nonreinforcement in situations in which reward is expected, or in which rewards are irregularly scheduled, could elicit "frustrative" behavior that is respondent in nature. (Another possible interpretation is that the "frustrative" response is operant behavior for which reinforcer removal is an establishing operation). Similarly, Spradlin and Girardeau (1966) and Kaufman and Levitt (1965) suggested that stereotypy could represent "superstitious" behavior maintained by intermittent reinforcement such as meals or attention. They found that body rocking displayed by their developmentally delayed subjects increased steadily prior to lunch and at times when institutional staff changed shifts. Findings such as these have led researchers to propose that some stereotypy is adjunctive behavior to a positive reinforcement schedule, similar to that frequently studied in basic animal research. Wieseler et al. (1988), for example, found that by altering the value of concurrent fixed-interval (FI) schedules for adaptive behavior, the frequency of stereotypic behavior increased as interval length increased. In a more recent study, Lerman et al. (1994b) compared rates of stereotypy and SIB across three schedules of food reinforcement (fixed-time versus massed and no-reinforcement controls). Results showed that for some individuals the intermittent schedule produced characteristic adjunctive responding for stereoptypic behavior but not for SIB.

In an attempt to integrate findings from these numerous sources, several theorists have suggested that stereotypy evolves through various combinations of physiological and environmental deficits. For example, Guess and Carr (1991) recently proposed a model for the development of stereotypic behavior involving three stages or "levels." During Level I (early infant development), stereotypic behavior is viewed as normal and adaptive. During Level II, developmentally delayed children continue to show patterns of stereotypic behavior as adaptive responses to under- or over-stimulation. Stereotypy at this level is viewed as a homeostatic response similar to that proposed by the arousal theories. At Level III, the behavior acquires social functions.

Finally, Romanczyk, Kistner, and Plienis (1982) offered a model combining respondent and operant conditioning to explain the emergence of SIB. They viewed SIB as respondent in nature initially (for example, associated with stressful stimulation such as loud noise or pain) but maintained subsequently through operant reinforcement. The authors speculated that stereotypy and SIB may change continually with respect to their relationship with the environment (as respondent or operant behavior), and that multiple etiological and maintaining variables are likely both within and across individuals.

Although the theories summarized here seem diverse and unrelated, many of them may be subsumed within a common framework. For example, to the extent that stereotypy and some forms of SIB are learned responses, the arousal, biological (that is, endorphin), and sensory reinforcement theories all suggest that reinforcing consequences are direct or "automatic" response products rather than stimuli presented (or removed) by others in the environment. What follows is a discussion of the concept of automatic reinforcement and its utility as a means of describing functional characteristics of stereotypy and SIB.

AUTOMATIC REINFORCEMENT

In referring to a class of behavior that includes anything from skipping a stone across the water to scratching an itch, Skinner (1953) used the term "automatic reinforcement" in reference to the maintaining contingency. Such behaviors directly produce reinforcement that is not mediated by the action of other individuals. Skinner noted that "part of the universe exists within the organism's own skin" and gave the example of an individual's response to an inflamed tooth. "How one responds to that tooth is unlike the response anyone else can make to that particular tooth, since no one else can establish the same kind of contact with it" (p. 257). Hence, some events, both antecedent and consequent, take place entirely within one's own skin and therefore constitute "private" events.

The problem is not one of acknowledging the existence of private events, but rather of observing such events and determining their influence on behavior. Thus, the utility of interpreting behavior in terms of automatic reinforcement has been a topic of considerable debate among behavior analysts (Herrnstein, 1977a, 1977b; Schnaitter, 1978; Skinner, 1977; Vaughan & Michael, 1982). What is the role of private causes in a science of behavior that has traditionally looked to the interaction between the subject and the external environment for controlling variables? The field of behavior analysis has established rigid standards for the demonstration of functional relations; prediction and control are necessary for this demonstration, and private causes present a troubling dilemma (Place, 1993).

One solution to the problem of private events has been to exclude them from scientific study because of a tradition within the scientific community requiring independent verification in the form of interobserver agreement, as well as manipulation (Schnaitter, 1978). Skinner (1953), however, argued that this position might be detrimental because a large gap would remain in our account of human behavior if we cannot explain the motivation for behavior that persists in the absence of identifiable (social) consequences. He suggested that a more appropriate way to attack the problem would be to ". . . deal with the private event, even if only as an inference" (p. 282).

Vaughan and Michael (1982) agreed with Skinner's (1953) contention that not all contingencies must be deliberately arranged by another person. Furthermore, although there has been little research on the concept of automatic reinforcement, Vaughan and Michael noted that this does not preclude the possibility of its existence. They illustrated the point using one of Skinner's examples: "The dog lover is automatically reinforced when seeing dogs" (Skinner, 1969, p. 223). By defining "looking at dogs" as the rate of page turning in a book on dogs, an experimenter could manipulate the number of pages with dogs so that "seeing dogs" did or did not occur when turning pages. The contingency could be reversed and reinstated to replicate the effect, and deprivation could be manipulated by keeping the subject away from dogs for some period of time. Thus, Vaughan and Michael pointed out that in cases in which the subject operates on the external environment, a functional relation could be demonstrated. The problem arises in cases in which the subject acts on his or her own body because "it is virtually impossible to sever the behavior from its product" (p. 224). Nevertheless, Vaughan and Michael noted that the concept of automatic reinforcement may be useful as a basis for developing methods to analyze behavior that does not produce "conspicuous environmental changes" (p. 226). Such analyses might reveal the specific stimulus properties that serve as reinforcing events and, as a result, verify that behavior is maintained by automatic reinforcement.

As a general description of a class of operant behavior, the term "automatic reinforcement" has the advantage of focusing our attention on maintaining contingencies. Thus, it seems preferable to use descriptions based on topography alone (for example, "stereotypy," "autistic mannerisms," etc.) when we suspect that the behavior of interest is a learned response but is not maintained by social consequences. In addition, it accounts for behavior maintained by both positive reinforcement (sensory stimulation) and negative reinforcement (pain attenuation). Finally, as suggested by Vaughan and Michael (1982), it may be possible to construct methods for isolating specific sources of automatic reinforcement. The result may prove beneficial to research methodology generally and to the assessment and treatment of behavior problems specifically.

CONSIDERATIONS FOR BEHAVIORAL ASSESSMENT

A number of methodologies have been developed for identifying both antecedent and consequent events associated with the occurrence of behavioral disorders. Iwata, Vollmer, and Zarcone (1990) distinguished among three general approaches to behavioral assessment: (a) indirect or anecdotal methods, which are based on a verbal report collected via interviews, checklists, or rating scales; (b) descriptive or correlational analyses, which involve direct observation of behavior and the naturalistic context(s) in which it occurs; and (c) functional or experimental analyses, in which behavior is observed under stimulus conditions that are manipulated systematically. The strengths and limitations of these approaches have been discussed in several recent reviews (Iwata, Vollmer, & Zarcone, 1990; Mace, Lalli, & Pinter-Lalli, 1991) and will not be addressed here. Instead, our focus will be on the use of multiple methodologies for assessing behavior suspected to be maintained by automatic reinforcement. Several strategies are suggested that may be helpful in determining that behavior is not maintained by social reinforcement and, subsequently, in identifying the source of stimulation that serves as automatic reinforcement. These strategies are listed in Box 7.1 and are described in greater detail below.

Insensitivity to Social Reinforcement

When the frequency of behavior seems unaffected by social consequences, automatic reinforcement might be suspected as a maintaining variable. This finding often comes as a negative outcome of assessment. For example, questionnaires and rating scales address this characteristic indirectly by asking respondents to indicate whether or not the behavior appears to function as either attention seeking or escape behavior, and negative answers to these questions suggest insensitivity to social reinforcement. Similarly, results of descriptive (direct observation) analyses may reveal the absence of any correlation between the occurrence of behavior and environmental events such as the presence of care providers, task demands,

---

**BOX 7.1   Strategies for Identifying Automatic Reinforcement
as a Maintaining Variable for Behavior Disorders**

1. *Insensitivity to Social Reinforcement:* Examine the extent to which the occurrence of behavior is unrelated to apparent social contingencies. Rule out access to attention or other preferred materials (social positive reinforcement) and escape from task demands or other aversive interactions (social negative reinforcement).

2. *Behavioral Persistence in the Absence of Social Interaction:* Conduct additional observations to verify that behavior persists in the absence of social reinforcement. Rule out the influence of subtle variables such as intermittent social

reinforcement, idiosyncratic reinforcers, multiple control adjunctive schedules, etc.

3. *Manipulation of Public Response Products:* If the behavior produces an observable consequence, attempt to manipulate the consequence so as to reveal reinforcement and/or extinction effects.

4. *Substitutability of Reinforcers:* If the behavior does not produce an observable consequence (or if that consequence is difficult to isolate or manipulate), attempt to identify substitutable reinforcers that compete with the target response.

---

and so on. (for example, Reid et al. 1993; Repp et al., 1991). Finally, attempts to isolate these potential environmental influences through controlled manipulation in a functional analysis would suggest automatic reinforcement as a maintaining variable when results are undifferentiated (for example, Van Houten, 1993; Vollmer, Marcus, & LeBlanc, 1994). As an illustration of such results from a functional analysis, Iwata et al. (1982) exposed individuals to three test conditions (Demand, a test for sensitivity to escape contingencies; Attention, a test for sensitivity to attention; and Alone, a test for automatic reinforcement) and a control (Play, which entailed noncontingent access to leisure materials and attention contingent on the absence of SIB). Figure 7.1 shows the data obtained for one of their subjects, which revealed a high degree of variability and little differentiation across the assessment conditions.

Although behavioral insensitivity to environmental changes suggests that behavior is not maintained by social reinforcement, the conclusion must be a tentative one. Other explanations for unclear assessment data include the possibility that behavior is maintained by (a) thin schedules of intermittent social reinforcement (Spradlin & Girardeau, 1966), (b) a highly idiosyncratic source of reinforcement such as a particular item (Tarpley & Schroeder, 1979), (c) any schedule of reinforcement that might induce adjunctive behavior (Lerman et al., 1994a), or (d) multiple reinforcement contingencies (Smith et al., 1993). In each of these cases, maintaining variables may not be recognized by respondents completing checklists, may not be revealed through descriptive analysis due to their irregular occurrence, or may not be controlled in a functional analysis. Thus, when behavioral episodes seem unrelated to social consequences, automatic reinforcement may appear likely as a source of maintenance, but additional information should be gathered as corroborative evidence.

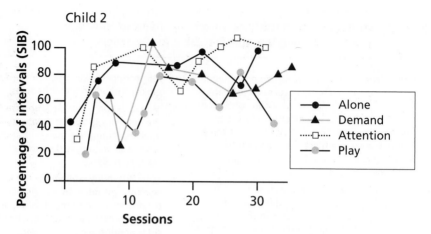

FIGURE 7.1 An example of undifferentiated assessment data suggesting that SIB is not maintained by social reinforcement

SOURCE: From Iwata et al. (1982).

Behavioral Persistence in the
Absence of Social Interaction

An obvious situation inviting a conclusion that behavior is maintained by automatic reinforcement is one in which the response occurs in the absence of social stimulation. For example, some individuals engage in repetitive behaviors such as body rocking or finger waving for extended durations of time while no one is present. Self-injurious behavior is less likely to be observed under such circumstances because care providers often intervene in an attempt to prevent physical damage resulting from the behavior, although relatively mild self-injurious responses (for example, hand mouthing) may be tolerated by care providers and occur in their absence. By contrast, aggression, due to its very nature, occurs only in social contexts. Thus, behaviors described as stereotypic (and perhaps some SIB) might be maintained by automatic reinforcement, but it is highly unlikely that aggression occurs simply because it "feels good."

Several rating scales and checklists, such as the Contingency Analysis Questionnaire (Wieseler et al., 1985), the Motivation Assessment Scale (Durand & Crimmins, 1985), and the Functional Analysis Interview Form (O'Neill et al., 1990) include specific questions related to automatic reinforcement. The relevant items from these scales are listed in Box 7.2, and we can see that their predominant emphasis is on behavioral persistence in the absence of social interaction. Three of the questions from the Motivation Assessment Scale (MAS), however, take a different focus. "Does this behavior occur repeatedly, over and over, in the same way. . . ?" seems to suggest topographical invariance as a characteristic of behavior maintained by automatic reinforcement; however, there is little empirical basis for assuming that topography and function are related in any way. Two other questions ("Does it appear to you that he or she enjoys performing this be-

---

BOX 7.2 Selected Items from Questionnaires and Rating Scales Aimed at Identifying Automatic Reinforcement as a Maintaining Contingency

Contingency Analysis Questionnaire (Wieseler et al., 1985)

- When _____ behavior occurs, the resident is either alone, or among other residents, but is unoccupied.
- When _____ behavior occurs, the resident is not involved or participating in an activity other than his own behavior.

Motivation Assessment Scale (Durand & Crimmins, 1985)

- Would this behavior occur continuously if your child was left for long periods of time (for example, one hour)?
- Does this behavior occur repeatedly, over and over, in the same way (for example, rocking back and forth for five minutes)?
- Does it appear to you that he or she enjoys performing this behavior, and would continue even if no one was around?
- When this behavior is occurring does your child seem unaware of anything else going on around him or her?

Functional Analysis Interview Form (O'Neill et al., 1989)

- Are the behavior(s) more likely, less likely, or unaffected if the individual is alone (no one present)?

---

havior. . . ?" and "When this behavior is occurring does your child seem unaware of anything else going on around him or her?") appear more relevant to functional characteristics of behavior. However, answering these questions requires a subjective judgment on the part of the respondent: An inference must be made about whether or not the individual engaging in the behavior is "enjoying it" or is "unaware."

Thus, the identification of automatic reinforcement (based on the assumption that such behavior persists in social isolation) seems to be addressed by only one or two items in currently used rating scales and checklists. In light of data from several sources indicating that inter-rater reliability is generally low for the MAS (Newton & Sturmey, 1991; Singh et al., 1993; Zarcone et al., 1991), we would agree with the suggestion of O'Neill et al. (1990) that these indirect methods are not recommended as a primary means of gathering assessment data.

Persistence of behavior in the absence of social interaction is easily observed through descriptive and functional analyses; all that is required is a condition (either naturally occurring or contrived) in which the individual is observed while alone. Examples of assessment data illustrating this point, both taken from functional analyses, are shown in Figure 7.2. In a study by Cowdery, Iwata, and Pace (1990), a boy's chronic scratching was never observed except when he was placed in a room alone and without access to leisure materials; in this condition, SIB occurred almost continuously (left panel). By contrast, Vollmer, Marcus, and LeBlanc (1994) presented a case in which a boy's multiple forms of SIB (head banging, head hitting, and hand biting) were somewhat undifferentiated across assessment conditions, yet continued to occur when the individual was exposed only to the

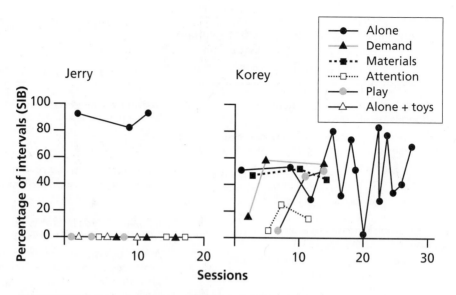

FIGURE 7.2 Examples of assessment data showing behavioral persistence in the absence of social consequences.

SOURCE: Data in the left panel are taken from Cowdery et al. (1990); data in the right panel are taken from Vollmer et al. (1994).

alone condition (right panel). Although these cases show distinct differences in responding during assessment conditions associated with social reinforcement (responding absent in the Cowdery et al. study but present in the Vollmer et al. study), their consistency lies in the finding that SIB persisted in the absence of all social consequences. Similar findings for a number of individuals were presented in a large-scale study on the functional analysis of SIB by Iwata et al. (1994).

It is highly unlikely that social contingencies can account for the continued occurrence of behavior in the absence of all social stimulation, because the effects of even subtle variables (for example, intermittent reinforcement, multiple control, other schedules that might induce adjunctive responding, etc.) are effectively ruled out. Thus, assuming that the behavior in question is an acquired performance, behavioral persistence in an alone condition strongly suggests automatic reinforcement as a maintaining contingency. However, the exact nature of the stimulus change serving as reinforcement remains unknown and can only be identified through further assessment involving systematic manipulation.

Manipulation of Public Response Products

Most if not all behavioral disorders of concern to clinicians are comprised of at least one "public" event—the response itself—and some of these behaviors also produce public outcomes when they involve manipulation of the environment (for example, spinning objects, pica). In the event that behavior produces (or can be made to produce) outcomes that are both observable and manipulable, it may be possible to identify specific sources of stimulation that serve as automatic reinforcement by arranging conditions under which those outcomes are available or unavailable. In essence, this strategy parallels one suggested earlier by Vaughan and Michael (1982), who gave the example of showing books with pictures of dogs present versus absent to a "dog lover," and subsequently measuring their effects on behavior (page turning).

Most studies of this type are based on a procedure first described by Rincover (1978) as "sensory extinction." Working with three individuals who engaged in noninjurious stereotypic behavior, he arranged conditions that apparently eliminated or attenuated stimulation produced by the response. One of the cases involved an individual who spun a plate on a table top. When a carpet, which eliminated the sound produced from plate spinning, was placed on the table top, extinction-like effects were observed. In a subsequent study (Rincover, Newsom, & Carr, 1979), similar results were obtained after disconnecting a light switch that an individual was observed to flip on and off at high rates. Both of these examples illustrate several important points with respect to the assessment of behavior maintained by automatic reinforcement.

First, although extinction was the process by which behavioral function was identified, similar information might be obtained through different means. For example, a condition comprised of noncontingent (response-independent) reinforcement might be arranged; if so, it should have a suppressive effect on behavior similar to that seen with extinction. In the case of spinning a plate (assuming that the sound alone served as reinforcement), one might spin the plate for the individual or perhaps even play an audiotape of prerecorded "plate-spinning sounds." In the case of light-switch flipping, one might arrange a condition in which lights rapidly alternated on and off independent of behavior.

Second, as illustrated in both of the above examples, behavior maintained by automatic reinforcement is somewhat unique in that there is often a close relationship between the topography of the response and the stimulation it produces. Thus, the assessment of such behavior might benefit from a careful study of response topography and consideration of likely sources of stimulation that might serve as reinforcement. However, as has been noted many times in the literature, response form per se is not a good indicator of behavioral function. Although Rincover (1978) identified the reinforcer for plate spinning as auditory in nature, it just as easily could have been visual (for example, "seeing" the plate spin), and the opposite could have been true for flipping the light switch in the Rincover et al. (1979) study. (The reinforcer could have been the sound of the switch operating rather than the visual stimulation produced by light). In addition, responses such as hand mouthing, which typically are viewed as "self-stimulatory" in nature (Rast & Jack, 1992), can be maintained by social reinforcement in the form of either attention (Vollmer et al., 1993) or escape (Mace, Browder, & Lin, 1987).

Third, the behaviors of interest produced readily observable outcomes that could be manipulated—sound from the plate in the Rincover (1978) study, and illumination from the light in the Rincover et al. (1979) study. When such manipulations are successful in altering rates of responding, one might be reasonably confident that the source of reinforcement has been identified. However, many behaviors, such as head banging, scratching, rumination, and echolalia, produce outcomes whose reinforcing effects are either not apparent or not easily manipulated. Although one can observe some public features of the response and its consequences, the exact nature of the stimulation remains, by and large, a private event. It may be possible, through the process of elimination and the use of complex preparations (such as administration of opioid antagonists with SIB), to interfere with the delivery of private stimulation. One could, for example, identify the reinforcing consequences for hand-mouthing behavior by first anesthetizing the hands. A decrease in hand mouthing would be interpreted as the outcome of extinction, but persistence of hand mouthing would suggest that stimulation to the hand was not the source of reinforcement. The mouth could then be numbed, and if hand mouthing decreased, one could infer that oral stimulation was the maintaining reinforcer. If hand mouthing persisted in both cases, a third possibility would be that stimulation to either the hand or the mouth produced reinforcement. Although this example illustrates an approach that is methodologically sound and perhaps theoretically appealing, from a clinical standpoint it is highly invasive, exceedingly complicated, and probably unnecessary. An indirect but more efficient strategy would involve identifying stimuli that serve as effective substitutes for the presumed reinforcers produced by the response.

Substitutability of Reinforcers

An extensive amount of basic research in the area of behavioral economics has examined the conditions under which preference for one reinforcer over another can be altered. In addition to studying the effects of quantitative manipulations (reinforcement schedules) on choice behavior, researchers have also examined qualitative relationships under the conceptual framework known as the "substitutability" theory (see Green & Freed, 1993 for a recent review). Substitutable reinforcers are different reinforcers that are nevertheless interchangeable under certain conditions: Given an inherent (baseline) preference for reinforcer A over reinforcer B, an increase in the "price" of reinforcer A (while the price of reinforcer B remains constant) should result in a change in preference favoring reinforcer B. To use a common example, suppose that an individual prefers grape over strawberry jam, buying twice as much grape as strawberry. If the cost of grape jam were to double, one might expect the individual to buy less grape and more strawberry; if the cost of grape jam were to quadruple, its purchase might be abolished. Thus, for substitutable reinforcers, an increase in responding for one reinforcer results in a decrease in responding for the other concurrently available reinforcer.

Although the major emphasis of research on substitutability has been on *quantitative* manipulations affecting choices between qualitatively different stimuli, the basic finding that one reinforcer effectively substitutes for (competes with) another has implications for the assessment of behavior maintained by automatic reinforcement. That is, if a source of reinforcement can be found that substitutes for stimulation produced by stereotypic behavior or SIB, the two may share common reinforcing properties. Many studies have found an inverse relationship between the availability of certain objects or types of stimulation and rates of aberrant behavior, which are indicative of a substitutability effect (for example, Bailey &

Meyerson, 1970; Berkson & Mason, 1965; Davenport & Berkson, 1963; Favell, McGimsey, & Schell, 1982). For instance, in a series of studies on the relationship between "food satiation" and rumination, Rast and colleagues demonstrated that specific characteristics of food and/or meal-related behavior, such as meal quantity (Rast et al., 1981), amount of premeal chewing (Rast et al., 1988), and caloric amount (Johnston et al., 1991), were associated with decreased rates of rumination. More recently, Goh et al. (1995) conducted a series of experiments on hand mouthing. After first determining (via functional analysis) that the behavior was not maintained by social reinforcement, Goh et al. provided noncontingent access to a variety of objects and found substitutability with eight of nine subjects (increased object manipulation and decreased hand mouthing). An interesting feature of that study was the fact that the objects could be manipulated with an individual's hands only or placed (or held) in the mouth. Data taken on both topographies indicated that a majority of subjects exhibited preference for hand-toy contact over mouth-toy contact, suggesting that the predominant reinforcer for hand mouthing was stimulation to the hand rather than to the mouth.

Although substitutable reinforcers have similar effects, their qualitative differences make it highly unlikely that they produce precisely the same stimulation (grape and strawberry jam have similar but unique tastes). Thus, substitutability per se is not always based on similar functions. For example, watching brightly colored lights might substitute for hand mouthing, even though the stimulation provided by the two activities is quite different. Nevertheless, the unique characteristics of substitutable reinforcers may be small enough to render them meaningless, and topographical similarity between reinforcers increases the likelihood that two stimuli share common reinforcing properties. In the studies just described, reinforcer substitutability and topographical similarity (between food ingestion and rumination, and between object holding and hand mouthing) strongly suggested that the substitutable reinforcers shared a common function with those suspected of maintaining behavior.

In summary, the identification of automatic reinforcement as a maintaining contingency for behavior is a difficult undertaking. Behavior that occurs in the absence of environmental consequences may nevertheless be maintained by intermittent or indirect social reinforcement. Thus, before concluding that behavior directly produces its own reinforcers, both the obvious and subtle effects of social contingencies should be ruled out. Subsequently, direct manipulation of the suspected source of reinforcement should be undertaken or, in cases in which manipulation is not possible, attempts should be made to identify substitutable reinforcers.

TREATMENT OF BEHAVIOR MAINTAINED
BY AUTOMATIC REINFORCEMENT

A variety of treatment models have been proposed over the years, and relevant to the present discussion are approaches that incorporate information about behavioral function (for example, see many of the chapters in the Repp & Singh, 1990 text, especially those by Carr, Robinson, & Palumbo; Iwata, Vollmer, & Zarcone;

Pyles & Bailey; Repp & Karsh; and Schrader & Gaylord-Ross). One of these models is derived from the basic ways in which reinforcement may be used to reduce the frequency of behavior through (a) alteration of an establishing operation, (b) extinction, or (c) differential reinforcement (Iwata et al., 1993). In addition to discussing how each of these may be applied to behavior maintained by automatic reinforcement, we will review two additional approaches—the use of protective equipment and punishment—because they have been implemented frequently in an attempt to treat behavior without apparent social motivation.

Throughout our discussion, two caveats should be noted. First, in much of the research, treatment was not based on the outcome of any formal attempt to identify behavioral function. Therefore, conclusions about the effectiveness of a given treatment for behavior maintained by automatic reinforcement are somewhat limited. A second and related problem is that, in the absence of assessment data, assumptions about the maintaining contingency for a behavior were based on topographical features of the response. Thus, in a number of studies in which "rhythmical" or "repetitive" behaviors were deemed to be "self-stimulatory" in nature, treatment effects may have been obtained through unknown mechanisms.

Alteration of Establishing Operations

Michael (1982, 1993) described a class of antecedent events having two specific influences on behavior. First, these events temporarily increase the effectiveness of a given consequence to serve as reinforcement; second, they evoke behavior that historically produced the consequence. Known as "establishing operations," these events can be arranged to both increase and decrease the motivation to engage in a particular behavior. For behavior maintained by positive reinforcement, the most common establishing operation is deprivation, and its effects are mitigated through noncontingent access to reinforcement. For behavior maintained by negative reinforcement, aversive stimulation is the typical establishing operation, and its motivational effects can be alleviated simply by eliminating the stimulation (also a form of noncontingent reinforcement). The concept of reinforcer substitutability is also relevant to a consideration of establishing operations because access to similar (substitutable) but different reinforcement might abolish the establishing effects of either deprivation or aversive stimulation.

Many studies in which behavioral suppression was observed under a condition of noncontingent reinforcement predated research on both establishing operations and reinforcer substitutability, but the relevance of these concepts to the treatment of behavior maintained by automatic reinforcement is apparent. For example, in an early demonstration, Bailey and Meyerson (1970) showed that noncontingent vibratory stimulation decreased head banging. More recently, Favell, McGimsey, & Schell (1982) provided alternative sensory activities to six individuals who engaged in SIB. In each case, selection of the objects was based on their apparent similarity to the presumed sensory consequences produced by SIB (for example, brightly colored beads and mirrors for the subjects who engaged in eye poking, large rubber balls for the subjects who engaged in hand mouthing, and popcorn for the subject who engaged in pica), and SIB decreased substantially when the alternative items were freely available.

Behaviors described as stereotypic in nature have often been observed to occur at high rates in relatively barren environments. For example, Berkson and Mason (1963) found that individuals with profound mental retardation engaged in more stereotypic behavior when placed in restrictive environments (no alternative activities or room for locomotion) than when they were placed in environments that evoked alternative activities (a playground). Similarly, Warren and Burns (1970) found that severely retarded children engaged in higher rates of repetitive behaviors during crib confinement than when they were outside the crib. More recent evidence indicating that barren environments may establish stereotypic behavior as reinforcing can be found in functional analyses comparing alone and play conditions (Iwata et al., 1994), in which some individuals (whose SIB is not maintained by social reinforcement) engage in high rates of behavior when they are left alone but low rates when leisure materials are available.

These findings suggest that if behavior occurs most frequently when an individual is deprived of access to stimulation, the appropriate intervention would consist of enriching the environment. Berkson and Mason (1965) reduced the frequency of stereotypic behaviors when they handed their subjects toys and provided them with attention. Similarly, Horner (1980) observed large decreases in a variety of inappropriate behaviors as a result of providing toys to children with profound developmental disabilities.

Enriched environments, however, are not always effective in reducing aberrant behavior. For example, Adams, Tallon, and Stangle (1980) observed somewhat lower levels of stereotypic behavior under quiet and "easy listening" music conditions than under a "television-on" condition. They also found that the addition of toys to the environment was ineffective in reducing stereotypic behavior. Thus, for some individuals, increased environmental stimulation may establish stereotypic behavior as reinforcing, in which case treatment would entail reducing stimulation.

Another approach that may reduce the motivation to engage in automatically reinforced aberrant behavior involves having individuals engage in specific antecedent activities that may produce satiation to the maintaining reinforcer. The clearest example of an apparent satiation effect can be found in the studies on rumination by Rast and colleagues described earlier (Rast et al., 1981, 1988), in which the ingestion of large portions of food led to subsequent decreases in rumination. These studies were noteworthy in that consequences produced by the alternative activity (eating food) bore close topographical resemblance to the source of reinforcement suspected of maintaining rumination (gustatory stimulation). Some studies have shown, however, that increases in activity per se may produce the same effects. For example, physical exercise has been used to decrease stereotypic behaviors (Ellis, MacLean, & Gazdag, 1989; Watters & Watters, 1980) and SIB (Baumeister & MacLean, 1984). Ellis et al. conducted 53 exercise sessions over a 16-week period with a severely developmentally disabled man, and observed reduced rates of body rocking over the course of the study. Levinson and Reid (1993) compared the effects of walking and jogging on stereotypic behavior. Results showed a temporary reduction in stereotypy following jogging but not following walking, suggesting greater satiation effects associated with the former activity. However, the results of these studies may have been due to satiation effects or simply to fatigue, and further research is needed to determine the mechanisms responsible for observed changes in behavior.

Treatment approaches based on the alteration of establishing operations are particularly attractive because their noncontingent nature makes them simple for care providers to implement relative to the rearrangement of behavioral contingencies (Vollmer, 1994). In addition, establishing operations may have significant effects on behavior regardless of whether the behavior is followed by reinforcement. Using attention-maintained behavior as an example, the noncontingent delivery of attention, which may eliminate deprivation of attention as an establishing operation, might greatly reduce the frequency of inappropriate attention-seeking behavior even if occurrences of the behavior are followed by attention. This feature of establishing operations makes their use especially pertinent to the treatment of behavior maintained by automatic reinforcement, whose reinforcers may be particularly difficult both to identify and to control.

There are, however, potential limitations in interventions based on establishing operations. First, because the alteration of an establishing operation (for example, deprivation) is usually a temporary state of affairs, one might expect to observe recurrences of the aberrant behavior when the establishing operation is again present. Second, recurrence of behavior would be exacerbated further if the maintaining contingency is not eliminated through extinction.

Extinction

Extinction of behavior maintained by automatic reinforcement requires the elimination or attenuation of stimulation directly produced by the response. As noted previously, interventions of this type have been described collectively as "sensory extinction" (Rincover, 1978). Although numerous variations of sensory extinction have been reported in the literature, the procedures seem to differ primarily in terms of the focus of manipulation. When the behavior of interest involves manipulation of the physical environment, the environment may be modified so that stimulation is reduced. Examples include carpeting a table to reduce the auditory stimulation produced by object spinning (Rincover, 1978), placing metal pins in twigs so that they would not "snap" when manipulated (Rincover, 1981), and disconnecting a light switch so that it would not operate (Rincover et al., 1979). In each of these examples, manipulations did not involve exposure of individuals to other sources of stimulation that might account for observed changes in behavior. That is, carpeting the table and disconnecting the light switch ensured that responding would only produce *less* stimulation, rather than *more* or *new* stimulation. Alternatively, when the individual acts primarily on his or her own body, extinction has involved the use of an apparatus worn by the individual which alters sensory stimulation produced by the response. Examples include goggles over the eyes (Kennedy & Souza, 1995), padded helmets on the head (Dorsey et al., 1982), vibrators on the hand (Rincover, 1978), weights on the wrist (Van Houten, 1993), and white noise delivered through headphones (Aiken & Salzberg, 1984). In each of these studies, the manipulations were associated with response reduction, which was attributed to sensory extinction. Although the interpretation is a plausible one, alternative possibilities are that (a) simply wearing the devices constituted either punishment or time-out from other sources of reinforcement, or (b) responding produced additional stimulation that served as punishment (see Mazaleski et al., 1994, for an extended discussion of this issue and for some supporting data).

Although not usually considered as such, the use of opioid antagonist drugs as treatment for SIB may represent yet another example of sensory extinction. That is, if SIB is maintained by positive reinforcement produced through the release of endorphins, pharmacologically blocking the uptake of these substances clearly functions as extinction. Although interventions of this type seem promising, few researchers have conducted functional analyses prior to treatment (Schaal & Hackenberg, 1994). Thus, it is not clear that treatment with opioid antagonists was applied to SIB maintained by automatic reinforcement. In addition, opioid antagonists may achieve their effects through two different mechanisms—extinction (by blocking the uptake of endorphins) or punishment (by decreasing the pain threshold, which is also an effect of drug administration). Further research is needed to establish both the effectiveness of opioid antagonists as treatment for SIB and the mechanism by which behavioral reduction is achieved.

The most significant limitation of sensory extinction is that it requires identification of the source of reinforcement, which may prove difficult because behaviors often produce multiple forms of stimulation. For example, hand mouthing produces tactile and gustatorial stimulation; face slapping produces tactile and auditory simulation; and object twirling produces tactile, auditory, and visual stimulation, any or all of which could be the maintaining reinforcer. Another potential problem with sensory extinction is that the procedure may be impractical (for example, eliminating visual stimulation) unless used on a temporary basis.

Differential Reinforcement

Contingent reinforcement has been used in a variety of ways in an attempt to reduce the frequency of behavior apparently maintained by automatic reinforcement. First, differential reinforcement of alternative behavior (DRA) has been applied as a supplementary procedure to increase manipulation of freely available objects. Favell, McGimsey, and Schell (1982) found that social reinforcement contingent on toy play resulted in more toy play and further reductions in hand mouthing. Lockwood and Bourland (1982) showed that, although toys affixed to an individual's wheelchair reduced SIB by approximately 50 percent, differential reinforcement for sustained toy use and the absence of finger biting was necessary to achieve clinically significant effects. Finally, Mulick et al. (1978) decreased finger picking and nail biting by differentially reinforcing independent toy play. These studies show that when alternative stimuli do not entirely substitute for those produced by aberrant behavior, additional reinforcement for the alternative may be necessary.

Another approach involves differential reinforcement of other behavior (DRO). Cowdery, Iwata, and Pace (1990), for example, showed that access to a variety of reinforcers contingent on the nonoccurrence of self-scratching was an effective intervention. Repp, Deitz, and Deitz (1976) reduced the hair twirling, hand biting, and thumb sucking behavior of three developmentally delayed children in a classroom setting by delivering praise and edible reinforcement in a DRO contingency.

A similar procedure—differential reinforcement low rates of behavior (DRL)—has also been used to decrease stereotypic behavior. Mulhern and Baumeister (1969) achieved modest reductions in stereotypic rocking in two severely developmentally delayed subjects by delivering food reinforcement contingent on reduced rates of responding. Although results of these and other studies (for example, Luiselli & Krause, 1981; Repp, Deitz, & Speir 1974) have shown positive treatment effects with DRO and DRL, the procedures do not strengthen alternative forms of behavior. This is a significant limitation in the treatment of behavior maintained by automatic reinforcement because response reduction through DRO/DRL further restricts an individual's access to highly functional sources of reinforcement (that is, those directly produced by the response). Thus, during periods of nonresponding, other behaviors may emerge that produce stimulation more aberrant or harmful than that produced by the original target response.

Because differential reinforcement often involves the delivery of arbitrary reinforcers, treatment will be ineffective unless the arbitrary reinforcers compete with (substitute for) those produced by the behavior. For example, Harris and Wolchik (1979) found that food and praise delivered in a DRO contingency were relatively ineffective in reducing hand stereotypies exhibited by four subjects. One method for enhancing reinforcer substitutability involves selecting highly preferred reinforcers. Steege et al. (1989) successfully treated subjects who engaged in stereotypy and SIB by first conducting an assessment of preference for a variety of stimuli, and then using the most preferred reinforcers in a DRO contingency.

Protective Equipment

Protective equipment resembles somewhat the use of an apparatus to produce sensory extinction. The difference is that protective equipment prevents the occurrence of behavior. Examples of this type of intervention include arm splints to prevent hand mouthing or finger biting (Ball, Campbell, & Barkermeyer, 1980; Ball et al., 1985), and hand splints and elbow braces to decrease stereotypic hand movements (Sharpe, 1992). In some cases, gradual fading of the devices is possible while maintaining low rates of behavior (Lerman et al., 1994a; Pace et al., 1986). When used noncontingently, the procedures function as restraint; when used contingently on the occurrence of the target behavior, the procedures (if effective) function as punishment. In either case, the use of such devices should be considered a short-term strategy and appropriate only with SIB that poses risk of significant tissue damage.

Punishment

When the source of stimulation for behavior maintained by automatic reinforcement cannot be identified or manipulated, or when substitutable sources of stimulation cannot be found, treatments based on establishing operations, extinction, or differential reinforcement may be ineffective. In such cases, punishment may provide a means of reducing the frequency of the target behavior until alternative reinforcers can be found and used to establish competing responses. Although intrusive when compared with other forms of intervention, punishment can be effective when the source of reinforcement for a behavior is unknown. Punishment procedures have taken a number of different forms, including (a) removal of positive reinforcement (time-out/response cost), (b) response-contingent restraint, (c) visual screening, (d) overcorrection, and (e) delivery of discrete stimuli.

Time-Out Typically defined as the removal of access to reinforcement for brief periods of times contingent on responding, time-out can be implemented by (a) removing materials, (b) removing care provider attention, (c) excluding the individual from ongoing activities, or (d) secluding the individual in a specific location (Brantner & Doherty, 1983). Although time-out has been used successfully as treatment for stereotypic behavior (Laws et al., 1971; Luiselli, 1975; Sachs, 1973), there are at least two disadvantages to the use of time-out as treatment for behavior maintained by automatic reinforcement. First, removal of an individual from reinforcing activities limits access to potentially competing reinforcers, which may actually increase rates of stereotypic behavior. Second, being in time-out affords greater opportunity to "self-stimulate."

Response-Contingent Restraint In addition to the contingent use of protective equipment, both response blocking, (Reid et al., 1993; Slifer, Iwata, & Dorsey, 1984) and brief manual restraint (Bucher, Reykdal, & Albin, 1976; Winton & Singh, 1983) have been used to suppress behavior presumed to be maintained by automatic reinforcement. The duration of response blocking is sufficiently brief so that it would appear to be relatively benign (unless it inadvertently brings behavior under social control as a result of contingent physical contact), and the advantages and disadvantages of physical restraint are similar to those found with protective equipment.

Visual Screening This procedure involves placement of a cloth or similar material over the head so that it covers the face and limits access to visual stimulation. Although its suppressive effects on behavior have been attributed primarily to time-out, the procedure may also serve as punishment via application of the screening material (Lutzker & Wesch, 1983). If the target behavior is maintained by visual stimulation, visual screening in some cases might induce sensory extinction. However, given the lack of topographical similarity between visual screening and the typical responses for which it has been used as treatment—aggressive behavior (Fremer et al., 1991), biting (Singh, 1980), face slapping (Winton, Singh, & Dawson, 1984), hand mouthing (Horton, 1987; Watson, Singh, & Winton, 1986), shoe manipulation (Barrett, Staub, & Sisson, 1983), and trichotillomania (Barmann & Vatali, 1982)—the time-out or punishment interpretations would seem most likely.

Overcorrection The "positive practice" variation of overcorrection described by Foxx and Azrin (1973), in which an individual is required to engage in postural or other motor responses as alternatives to aberrant behavior, has been used as treatment for a variety of stereotpyic responses, including bruxism (Rosenbaum & Ayllon, 1981), coprophagia (Foxx & Martin, 1975), hand waving (Wells et al., 1977, trichotillomania (Barrett & Shapiro, 1980) and vomiting (Azrin &

Wesolowski, 1975). Although the overcorrection activity involves performance of alternative behaviors, there is little evidence suggesting that it leads to an increase in the frequency of such behaviors (Libert & Forehand, 1979; Roberts et al., 1979; Wells et al., 1977). Thus, behavioral suppression through overcorrection seems to be primarily a function of punishment.

Discrete Stimuli An extensive amount of research has shown that response-contingent delivery of discrete stimuli, including ammonia held under the nose (Altman, Haavik, & Cooke, 1978, electric shock to the arm or leg (Linscheid et al., 1990), lemon juice squirted into the mouth (Sajwaj, Libet, & Agras, 1974), slaps (Koegel & Covert, 1972), tickling (Greene & Hoats, 1971), verbal reprimands (Van Houten & Doleys, 1983), and water mist sprayed in the face (Dorsey et al., 1980) can produce rapid and sometimes long-lasting response suppression. Although effective, the use of such stimuli has raised numerous objections (see Repp & Singh, 1990 for a review). First, punishment may produce indirect effects such as "emotional" responding, aggression, and generalized response suppression. Second, punishment does not strengthen alternative behaviors. Finally, the use of punishment is considered unnecessarily intrusive if behavioral suppression can be achieved through other means.

SUMMARY AND CONCLUSIONS

Most researchers and clinicians agree that not all behavior problems are maintained by social reinforcement. There is, however, considerable disagreement concerning the nature of nonsocial control, and theories have proposed numerous biological and environmental variables as either causative or maintaining factors. Given that behavior occurs within the context of a multitude of stimuli, nonsocial forms of stereotypic behavior and SIB are highly likely to be the products of both internal and external events, and well-controlled research is needed to determine the specific roles played by these events in the development and maintenance of behavior disorders. Nevertheless, to the extent that many of these behaviors are acquired performances, the concept of automatic reinforcement may provide a useful means of distinguishing between social and nonsocial reinforcement as maintaining contingencies.

Research on the assessment of behavior without apparent social motivation suggests several strategies for identifying the source of reinforcement. First, descriptive analyses may facilitate the development of subsequent functional analyses that are better suited to the identification of idiosyncratic sources of control. Second, the refinement of functional analyses will ultimately provide the control necessary to rule out these idiosyncratic influences—which may include intermittency of social reinforcement, highly unusual sources of social reinforcement, multiple control, schedule induction, and lack of discrimination—before concluding that behavior is maintained by automatic reinforcement. Finally, research should focus more carefully on isolating specific stimuli that serve as automatic reinforcement. Several lines of research suggested in this review include investigations in which sensory consequences are manipulated to produce either satiation or extinction, analyses of the relationship between response topography and function, and studies on reinforcer substitutability.

A review of the treatment literature also suggests several directions for further study. First, research is needed to identify the behavior-reducing mechanisms associated with numerous interventions described as sensory extinction. A determination of how behavior is changed may not only facilitate the development of new treatments, but also provide insight into sources of control for automatically reinforced problem behavior. Second, given that extinction of behavior maintained by automatic reinforcement may be difficult to achieve, reinforcement-based treatments will be an important component of intervention. Furthermore, when the maintaining reinforcer for behavior cannot be identified, DRO- and DRA-type procedures will almost always involve concurrent schedules of reinforcement. Therefore, more careful consideration should be given to basic research on factors affecting concurrent preference and how these factors may influence the treatment of behavior maintained by automatic reinforcement. Finally, perhaps the best current solution to the treatment of automatically reinforced problem behavior would involve the establishment of alternative responses that are themselves maintained by automatic reinforcement In the case of SIB, for example, treatment might emphasize the development of more benign stereotypic behaviors, whose reinforcing effects may be identified through a careful assessment of stimulus preference. In the case of noninjurious responses, treatment might focus on gradually shaping response topography to more closely resemble "normative" forms of stereotypy.

REFERENCES

Adams, G. L., Tallon, R. J., & Stangle, J. M. (1980). Environmental influences on self-stimulatory behavior. *American Journal of Mental Deficiency, 85,* 171–175.

Aiken, J. M., & Salzberg, C. L. (1984). The effects of a sensory extinction procedure on stereotypic sounds of two autistic children. *Journal of Autism and Developmental Disorders, 14,* 291–299.

Altman, K., Haavik, S., & Cooke, J. (1978). Punishment of self-injurious behavior in natural settings using contingent aromatic ammonia. *Behavior Research and Therapy, 46,* 529–536.

Arendt, R. E., MacLean, W. E., Jr., & Baumeister, A. A. (1988). Critique of sensory integration therapy and its application in mental retardation. *American Journal of Mental Retardation, 92,* 401–411.

Ayers, A. J. (1972). *Sensory integration and learning disorders.* Los Angeles: Western Psychological Services.

Azrin, N. H, & Wesolowski, M. D. (1975). Eliminating habitual vomiting in a retarded adult by positive practice and self-correction. *Journal of Behavior Therapy and Experimental Psychiatry, 6,* 145–148.

Bailey, J., & Meyerson, L. (1970). Effect of vibratory stimulation on a retardate's self-injurious behavior. *Psychological Aspects of Stability, 17,* 133–137.

Ball, T. S., Campbell, R., & Barkermeyer, R. (1980). Air splints applied to control self-injurious finger sucking in profoundly retarded individuals. *Journal of*

Behavior Therapy and Experimental Psychiatry, 11, 267–271.

Ball, T. S., Datta, P. C., Rios, M., & Constantine, C. (1985). Flexible arm splints in the control of a Lesch-Nyhan victim's finger biting and a profoundly retarded client's finger sucking. *Journal of Autism and Developmental Disorders, 15,* 177–184.

Barmann, B. C., & Vitali, D. L. (1982). Facial screening to eliminate trichotillomania in developmentally disabled persons. *Behavior Therapy, 13,* 735–742.

Barrett, R. P., McGonigle, J. J., Ackles, P. K., & Brukhart, J. E. (1987). Behavioral treatment of chronic aerophagia. *American Journal of Mental Deficiency, 91,* 620–625.

Barrett, R. P., & Shapiro, E. S. (1980). Treatment of stereotyped hair pulling with overcorrection: A case study with long-term follow-up. *Journal of Behavior Therapy and Experimental Psychiatry, 11,* 317–320.

Barrett, R. P., Staub, R. W., & Sisson, L. A. (1983). Treatment of compulsive rituals with visual screening: A case study with long-term follow-up. *Journal of Behavior Therapy and Experimental Psychiatry, 14,* 55–59.

Baumeister, A. A., & Forehand, R. (1971). Effects of extinction of an instrumental response on stereotyped body rocking in severe retardates. *Psychological Record, 21,* 235–240.

Baumeister, A. A., & Forehand, R. L. (1973). Stereotyped acts. In N. R. Ellis (Ed.), *International review of research in mental retardation* (pp. 55–93). New York: Academic.

Baumeister, A. A., & MacLean, W. E. (1984). Deceleration of self-injurious and stereotypic responding by exercise. *Applied Research in Mental Retardation, 5,* 385–393.

Berkson, G. (1983). Repetitive stereotyped behaviors. *American Journal of Mental Deficiency, 88,* 239–246.

Berkson, G., & Mason, W. A. (1963). Stereotyped movements of mental defectives: 3. Situational effects. *American Journal of Mental Deficiency, 68,* 409–412.

Berkson, G., & Mason, W. A. (1965). Stereotyped movements of mental defectives: 4. The effects of toys and the character of the acts. *American Journal of Mental Deficiency, 70,* 511–524.

Boyd, E. M., Dolman, M., Knight, L. M., & Sheppard, E. P. (1965). The chronic oral toxicity of caffeine. *Canadian Journal of Psychological Pharmacology, 43,* 995–1007.

Brantner, J. P., & Doherty, M. A. (1983). A review of time-out: A conceptual and methodological analysis. In S. Axelrod & J. Apsche (Eds.), *The effects of punishment on human behavior* (pp. 87–132). New York: Academic.

Breese, G. R., Criswell, H. E., & Mueller, R. A. (1990). Evidence that lack of brain dopamine during development can increase the susceptibility for aggression and self-injurious behavior by influencing D1-dopamine receptor function. *Progress in Neuro-Psychopharmacology and Biological Psychiatry, 14,* 465–480.

Bucher, B., Reykdal, B., & Albin, J. (1976). Brief physical restraint to control pica in retarded children. *Journal of Behavior Therapy and Experimental Psychiatry, 7,* 137–140.

Carr, E. G., Robinson, S., & Palumbo, L. W. (1990). The wrong issue: Aversive versus nonaversive treatment. The right issue: Functional versus nonfunctional treatment. In A. C. Repp & N. N. Singh (Eds.), *Perspectives on the use of nonaversive and aversive interventions for persons with developmental disabilities* (pp. 362–379). Sycamore, IL: Sycamore.

Cataldo, M. F., & Harris, J. (1982). The biological basis for self-injury in the mentally retarded. *Analysis and Intervention in Developmental Disabilities, 2,* 21–39.

Chamove, A. S., & Harlow, H. F. (1969). Exaggeration of self-aggression following alcohol ingestion in rhesus monkeys. *Journal of Abnormal Psychology, 15,* 207–209.

Coulter, D. L. (1989). Frontal lobe seizures: No evidence of self-injury. *American Journal on Mental Retardation, 96,* 81–84.

Cowdery, G. E., Iwata, B. A., & Pace, G. M. (1990). Effects and side effects of DRO as treatment for self-injurious behavior.

Journal of Applied Behavior Analysis, 23, 497–506.

Danford, D. E., & Huber, A. M. (1982). Pica among mentally retarded adults. *American Journal of Mental Deficiency, 87,* 141–146.

Davenport, R. K., & Berkson, G. (1963). Stereotyped movements in mental defectives: Effects of novel objects. *American Journal of Mental Deficiency, 67,* 879–882.

Day, R. M., Rea, J. A., Schussler, N. G., Larsen, S. E., & Johnson, W. L. (1988). A functionally based approach to the treatment of self-injurious behavior. *Behavior Modification, 2,* 565–589.

Derby, K. M., Wacker, D. P., Peck, S., Sasso, G., DeRaad, A., Berg, W., Asmus, J., & Ulrich, S. (1994). Functional analysis of separate topographies of aberrant behavior. *Journal of Applied Behavior Analysis, 27,* 267–278.

Dorsey, M. F., Iwata, B. A., Ong, P., & McSween, T. (1980). Treatment of self-injurious behavior using a water mist: Initial response suppression and generalization. *Journal of Applied Behavior Analysis, 13,* 343–353.

Dorsey, M. F., Iwata, B. A., Reid, D. H., & Davis, P. A. (1982). Protective equipment: Continuous and contingent application in the treatment of self-injurious behavior. *Journal of Applied Behavior Analysis, 15,* 217–230.

Durand, V. M., & Crimmins, D. B. (1985). *The Motivation Assessment Scale: An administration manual.* Unpublished manuscript, State University of New York at Albany.

Ellis, M. J. (1973). *Why people play.* Englewood Cliffs, NJ: Prentice-Hall.

Ellis, D. N., MacLean, W. E., & Gazdag, G. (1989). The effects of exercise and cardiovascular fitness on stereotyped body rocking. *Journal of Behavior Therapy and Experimental Psychiatry, 20,* 251–256.

Favell, J. E., McGimsey, J. F., & Schell, R. M. (1982). Treatment of self-injury by providing alternate sensory activities. *Analysis and Intervention in Developmental Disabilities, 2,* 83–104.

Forehand, R., & Baumeister, A. A. (1970). Effect of frustration on stereotyped body rocking. *Perceptual and Motor Skills, 31,* 894.

Forehand, R., & Baumeister, A. A. (1971). Stereotyped body rocking as a function of situation, I.Q., and time. *Journal of Clinical Psychology, 27,* 324–326.

Fowler, H. (1971). Suppression and facilitation by response contingent shock. In F.R. Brush (Ed.), *Aversive conditioning and learning* (pp. 537–604). New York: Academic.

Fox, M. W. (1967). The effects of short-term social and sensory isolation upon behavior, EEG, and averaged evoked potentials in puppies. *Physiology and Behavior, 2,* 145–151

Foxx, R. M., & Azrin, N. H. (1973). The elimination of autistic self-stimulatory behavior by overcorrection. *Journal of Applied Behavior Analysis, 6,* 1–14.

Foxx, R. M., & Martin, E. D. (1975). Treatment of scavenging behavior (coprophagy) by overcorrection. *Behavior Research and Therapy, 13,* 153–162.

Fremer, C. M., Miewald, B. K., Helsel, W. J., Lubetsky, M. J., & Hersen, M. (1991). Visual screening and carbamazepine in the treatment of a child's aggressive behavior secondary to craniopharyngioma. *Journal of Developmental and Physical Disabilities, 3,* 191–197.

Gedye, A. (1992). Anatomy of self-injurious stereotypic and aggressive movements: Evidence for involuntary explanation. *Journal of Clinical Psychology, 48,* 766–778.

Goh, H., Iwata, B. A., Shore, B. A., DeLeon, I. G., Lerman, D. C., Urich, S. M., & Amith, R. G. (1995). An analysis of the reinforcing properties of hand mouthing. *Journal of Applied Behavior Analysis, 28,* 269–284.

Green, L., & Freed, D. E. (1993). The substitutability of reinforcers. *Journal of the Experimental Analysis of Behavior, 60,* 141–158.

Greene, R. I., & Hoats, D. L. (1971). Aversive tickling: A simple conditioning technique. *Behavior Therapy, 2,* 389–393.

Guess, D., & Carr, E. (1991). Emergence and maintenance of stereotypy and self-injury. *American Journal on Mental Retardation, 96,* 299–319.

Harlow, H. F., & Harlow, M. K. (1962). Social deprivation in monkeys. *Scientific American, 207,* 136–146.

Harris, S. L., & Wolchik, S. A. (1979). Suppression of self-stimulation: Three alternative strategies. *Journal of Applied Behavior Analysis, 12,* 199–210.

Heller, R. F., & Strang, H. R. (1973). Controlling bruxism through automated aversive conditioning. *Behavior Research and Therapy, 11,* 327–329.

Herrnstein, R. J. (1977a). The evolution of behaviorism. *American Psychologist, 32,* 593–603.

Herrnstein, R. J. (1977b). Doing what comes naturally: A reply to Professor Skinner. *American Psychologist, 32,* 1013–1016.

Horner, R. D. (1980). The effects of an environmental "enrichment" program on the behavior of institutionalized profoundly retarded children. *Journal of Applied Behavior Analysis, 3,* 473–491.

Horton, S.V. (1987). Reduction of maladaptive mouthing behavior by facial screening. *Journal of Behavior Therapy and Experimental Psychiatry, 18,* 185–190.

Hutt, C., & Hutt, S. J. (1965). Stereotypies and their relation to arousal: A study of autistic children. In S. J. Hutt and C. Hutt (Eds.), *Behaviour studies in psychiatry* (pp. 175–204). London: Pergamon.

Hutt, C., Hutt, S. J., Lee, D., & Ounstead, C. A. (1965). A behavioral and electroencephalographic study of autistic children. *Journal of Psychiatric Research, 3,* 181–197.

Iwata, B. A., Dorsey, M. F., Slifer, K. J., Bauman, K. E., & Richman, G. S. (1982). Toward a functional analysis of self-injury. *Analysis and Intervention in Developmental Disabilities, 2,* 3–20.

Iwata, B. A., Pace, G. M., Dorsey, M. F., Zarcone, J. R., Vollmer, T. R., Smith, R. G., Rodgers, T. A., Lerman, D. C., Shore, B. A., Mazaleski, J. L., Goh, H., Cowdery, G. E., Kalsher, M. J., & Willis, K. D. (1994). The functions of self-injurious behavior: An experimental-epidemiological analysis. *Journal of Applied Behavior Analysis, 27,* 215–240.

Iwata, B. A., Pace, G. M., Kalsher, M. J., Cowdery, G. E., & Cataldo, M. F. (1990). Experimental analysis and extinction of self-injurious escape behavior. *Journal of Applied Behavior Analysis, 23,* 11–27.

Iwata, B. A., Vollmer, T. R., & Zarcone, J. R. (1990). The experimental (functional) analysis of behavior disorders: Methodology, applications, and limitations. In A. C. Repp & N. N. Singh (Eds.), *Perspectives on the use of nonaversive and aversive interventions for persons with developmental disabilities* (pp. 301–330). Sycamore, IL: Sycamore.

Iwata, B. A., Vollmer, T. R., Zarcone, J. R., & Rodgers, T. A. (1993). Treatment classification and selection based on behavioral function. In R. V. Houten & S. Axelrod (Eds.), *Behavior analysis and treatment* (pp. 101–125). New York: Plenum.

Johnston, J. M., Greene, K. S., Rawal, A., Vazin, T., & Winston, M. (1991). Effects of caloric level on ruminating. *Journal of Applied Behavior Analysis, 24,* 597–603.

Jolles, J., Rompa-Barendregt, J., & Gispen, W. H. (1979). ACTH-induced excessive grooming in the rat: The influence of environmental and motivational factors. *Hormones and Behavior, 12,* 60–72.

Kaufman, M. E., & Levitt, H. (1965). A study of three stereotyped behaviors in institutionalized mental defectives. *American Journal of Mental Deficiency, 69,* 467–473.

Kennedy, C. H., & Souza, G. (1995). Functional analysis and treatment of eye poking. *Journal of Applied Behavior Analysis, 28,* 27–38.

Kish, G. B. (1966). Studies of sensory reinforcement. In W. K. Honig (Ed.), *Operant behavior: Areas of research and application* (pp. 109–159). New York: Appleton-Century-Crofts.

Koegel, R. L., & Covert, A. (1972). The relationship of self-stimulation to learning in autistic children. *Journal of Applied Behavior Analysis, 5,* 381–387.

Laws, D. R., Brown, R. A., Epstein, J., & Hocking, N. (1971). Reduction of inappropriate social behavior in disturbed children by an untrained paraprofessional therapist. *Behavior Therapy, 2,* 519–533.

Leash, A. M., Beyer, R. D., & Wilber, R. G. (1973). Self-mutilation following Innovar-Vet injection in the guinea pig. *Laboratory Animal Science, 23,* 720–721.

Lerman, D. C., Iwata, B. A., Smith, R. G., & Vollmer, T. R. (1994). Restraint fading and the development of alternative behaviour in the treatment of self-restraint and self-injury. *Journal of Intellectual Disability Research, 38,* 135–148.

Lerman, D. C., Iwata, B. A., Zarcone, J. R., & Ringdahl, J. (1994). Analysis of adjunctive characteristics of self-injurious and stereotypic behavior. *Journal of Applied Behavior Analysis, 27,* 715–728.

Levinson, L. J., & Reid, G. (1993). The effects of exercise intensity on the stereotypic behaviors of individuals with autism. *Adapted Physical Activity Quarterly, 10,* 255–268.

Lewis, M. H., Baumeister, A. A., & Mailman, R. B. (1987). A neurobiological alternative to the perceptual reinforcement hypothesis of stereotyped behavior: A commentary on "self-stimulatory behavior and perceptual reinforcement." *Journal of Applied Behavior Analysis, 20,* 253–258.

Libert, A. Q., & Forehand, R. A. (1979). A component analysis of positive practice overcorrection: An examination of reeducative effects. *The Psychological Record, 29,* 219–229.

Linscheid, T. R., Iwata, B. A., Ricketts, R. W., Williams, D. E., & Griffin, J. C. (1990). Clinical evaluation of the Self-Injurious Behavior Inhibiting System (SIBIS). *Journal of Applied Behavior Analysis, 23,* 53–78.

Lockwood, K., & Bourland, G. (1982). Reduction of self-injurious behaviors by reinforcement and toy use. *Mental Retardation, 20,* 169–173.

Lovaas, I., Newsom, C., & Hickman, C. (1987). Self-stimulatory behavior and perceptual reinforcement. *Journal of Applied Behavior Analysis, 20,* 45–68.

Luiselli, J. K. (1975). The effects of multiple contingencies on the rocking behavior of a retarded child. *The Psychological Record, 25,* 559–565.

Luiselli, J. K., & Krause, S. (1981). Reduction in stereotypic behavior through a combination of DRO, cueing, and reinforcer isolation procedures. *The Behavior Therapist, 4,* 2–3.

Lutzker, J. R., & Wesch, D. (1983). Facial screening: History and critical review. *Australia and New Zealand Journal of Developmental Disabilities, 2,* 209–223.

Mace, F. C., Browder, D. M., & Lin, Y. (1987). Analysis of demand conditions associated with stereotypy. *Journal of Behavior Therapy and Experimental Psychiatry, 18,* 25–31.

Mace, F. C., Lalli, J. S., & Pinter-Lalli, E. (1991). Functional analysis and treatment of aberrant behavior. *Research in Developmental Disabilities, 12,* 155–180.

Mason, S. A., & Iwata, B. A. (1990). Artifactual effects of sensory-integrative therapy on self-injurious behavior. *Journal of Applied Behavior Analysis, 23,* 361–370.

Mazaleski, J. L., Iwata, B. A., Rodgers, T. A., Vollmer, T. R., & Zarcone, J. R. (1994). Protective equipment as treatment for stereotypic hand mouthing: Sensory extinction or punishment effects? *Journal of Applied Behavior Analysis, 27,* 345–355.

Michael, J. (1982). Distinguishing between discriminative and motivational functions of stimuli. *Journal of the Experimental Analysis of Behavior, 37,* 149–155.

Michael, J. (1993). Establishing operations. *The Behavior Analyst, 16,* 191–206.

Mulhern, T., & Baumeister, A. (1969). An experimental attempt to reduce stereotypy by reinforcement procedures. *American Journal of Mental Deficiency, 74,* 69–74.

Mulick, J. A., Hoyt, P., Rojahn, J., & Schroeder, S. (1978). Reduction of a "nervous habit" in a profoundly retarded youth by increasing toy play. *Journal of Behavior Therapy and Experimental Psychiatry, 9,* 381–385.

Newsom, C. D., & Lovaas, O. I. (1987). A neurobiological nonalternative: Rejoinder to Lewis, Baumeister, and Mailman. *Journal of Applied Behavior Analysis, 20,* 259–262.

Newton, J. T., & Sturmey, P. (1991). The Motivation Assessment Scale: Inter-rater reliability and internal consistency in a British sample. *Journal of Mental Deficiency Research, 35,* 472–474.

O'Neill, R. E., Horner, R. H., Albin, R. W., Storey, K., & Sprague, J. R. (1990). *Functional analysis of problem behavior: A practical guide.* Sycamore, IL: Sycamore.

Ornitz, E. M., Brown, M. B., Sorocky, A. D., Ritvo, E. R., & Dietrich, L. (1970). Environmental modification of autistic behavior. *Archives of General Psychiatry, 22,* 560–565.

Pace, G. M., Iwata, B. A., Edwards, G. L., & McCosh, K. C. (1986). Stimulus fading and transfer in the treatment of self-restraint and self-injurious behavior. *Journal of Applied Behavior Analysis, 19,* 381–389.

Place, U. T. (1993). A radical behaviorist methodology for the empirical investigation of private events. *Behavior and Philosophy, 21,* 25–36.

Pyles, D. A. M., & Bailey, J. S. (1990). Diagnosing severe behavior problems. In A.C. Repp & N. N. Singh (Eds.), *Perspectives on the use of nonaversive and aversive interventions for persons with developmentally disabilities* (pp. 381–401). Sycamore, IL: Sycamore.

Rast, J., & Jack, S. (1992). Mouthing. In E.A. Konarski & J.E. Favell (Eds.), *Manual for the assessment and treatment of the behavior disorders of people with mental retardation* (pp. 1–11). Morganton, NC: Western Carolina Center Foundation.

Rast, J., Johnston, J. M., Drum, C., & Conrin, J. (1981). The relation of food quantity to rumination behavior. *Journal of Applied Behavior Analysis, 14,* 121–130.

Rast, J., Johnston, J. M., Lubin, D., & Ellinger-Allen, J. (1988). Effects of pre-meal chewing on ruminative behavior. *American Journal of Mental Retardation, 93,* 67–74.

Reid, D. H., Parsons, M. B., Phillips, J. F., & Green, C. W. (1993). Reduction of self-injurious hand mouthing using response blocking. *Journal of Applied Behavior Analysis, 26,* 139–140.

Repp, A. C., Deitz, S. M., & Deitz, D. E. D. (1976). Reducing inappropriate behaviors in classrooms and in individual sessions through DRO schedules. *Mental Retardation, 15,* 11–15.

Repp, A. C., Deitz, S. M., & Speir, N. C. (1974). Reducing stereotypic responding of retarded persons by the differential reinforcement of other behaviors.

American Journal of Mental Deficiency, 79, 279–284.

Repp, A. C., & Karsh, K. G. (1990). A taxonomic approach to the nonaversive treatment of maladaptive behavior of persons with developmental disabilities. In A. C. Repp & N. N. Singh (Eds.), *Perspectives on the use of nonaversive and aversive interventions for persons with developmental disabilities* (pp. 331–347). Sycamore, IL: Sycamore.

Repp, A. C., & Singh, N. N. (Eds.). (1990). *Perspectives on the use of nonaversive and aversive interventions for persons with developmental disabilities.* Sycamore, IL: Sycamore.

Repp, A. C., Singh, N. N., Karsh, K. G., & Deitz, D. E. D. (1991). Ecobehavioural analysis of stereotypic and adaptive behaviours: Activities as setting events. *Journal of Mental Deficiency Research, 35,* 413–429.

Riesen, A. H. (1975). *The developmental neuropsychology of sensory deprivation.* New York: Academic.

Rincover, A. (1978). Sensory extinction: A procedure for eliminating self-stimulatory behavior in developmentally disabled children. *Journal of Abnormal Child Psychology, 6,* 299–310.

Rincover, A. (1981). Some directions for analysis and intervention in developmental disabilities: An editorial. *Analysis and Intervention in Developmental Disabilities, 1,* 109–115.

Rincover, A., Cook, R., Peoples, A., & Packard, C. (1979). Sensory extinction and sensory reinforcement principles for programming multiple adaptive behavior change. *Journal of Applied Behavior Analysis, 12,* 221–233.

Rincover, A., & Devany, J. (1982). The application of sensory extinction procedures to self-injury. *Analysis and Intervention in Developmental Disabilities, 2,* 67–81.

Rincover, A., Newsom, C. D., & Carr, E. G. (1979). Using sensory extinction procedures in the treatment of compulsive-like behavior of developmentally disabled children. *Journal of Consulting and Clinical Psychology, 47,* 695–701.

Roberts, P., Iwata, B. A., McSween, T. E., & Desmond, E. F., Jr. (1979). An analysis of overcorrection movements. *American Journal of Mental Deficiency, 83,* 588–594.

Romanczyk, R. G., Kistner, J. A., & Plienis, A. (1982). Self-stimulatory and self-injurious behavior: Etiology and treatment. In J. J. Steffan & P. Karoly (Eds.), *Advances in child behavior analysis and therapy* (pp. 189–254). Lexington, MA: Lexington.

Romanczyk, R. G., Lockshin, S., & O'Connor, J. (1992). Psychophysiology and issues of anxiety and arousal. In J. K. Luiselli, J. L. Matson, & N. N. Singh (Eds.), *Self-injurious behavior: Analysis, assessment, and treatment* (pp. 93–121). New York: Springer-Verlag.

Rosenbaum, M. S., & Ayllon, T. (1981). Treating bruxism with the habit-reversal technique. *Behavior Research and Therapy, 19,* 87–96.

Rothbaum, B. O. (1992). The behavioral treatment of trichotillomania. *Behavioural Psychotherapy, 20,* 85–90.

Sachs, D. A. (1973). The efficacy of time-out procedures in a variety of behavior problems. *Journal of Behavior Therapy and Experimental Psychiatry, 4,* 237–242.

Sackett, P. (1966). Monkeys reared in isolation with pictures as visual input: Evidence of an innate releasing mechanism. *Science, 154,* 140–1473.

Sajwaj, T., Libet, J., & Agras, S. (1974). Lemon-juice therapy: The control of life-threatening rumination in a six-month-old infant. *Journal of Applied Behavior Analysis, 7,* 557–563.

Schaal, D. W., & Hackenberg, T. (1994). Toward a functional analysis of drug treatment for behavior problems of people with developmental disabilities. *American Journal on Mental Retardation, 99,* 123–140.

Schnaitter, R. (1978). Private causes. *Behaviorism, 6,* 1–12.

Sharpe, P. A. (1992). Comparative effects of bilateral hand splints and an elbow orthosis on stereotypic hand movements and toy play in two children with Rett syndrome. *The American Journal of Occupational Therapy, 46,* 134–140.

Schrader, C., & Gaylord-Ross, R. (1990). The eclipse of aversive technology. In A. C. Repp & N. N. Singh (Eds.), *Perspectives on the use of nonaversive and aversive interventions for persons with developmental disabilities* (pp. 403–417). Sycamore, IL: Sycamore.

Singh, N. N. (1980). The effects of facial screening on infant self-injury. *Journal of Behavior Therapy and Experimental Psychiatry, 11,* 131–134.

Singh, N. N., Donatelli, L. S., Best, A., Williams, D. E., Barrera, F. J., Lenz, M. W., Landrum, T. J., Ellis, C. R., & Moe, T. L. (1993). Factor structure of the Motivation Assessment Scale. *Journal of Intellectual Disability Research, 37,* 65–74.

Skinner, B. F. (1953). *Science and human behavior.* New York: MacMillan.

Skinner, B. F. (1957). *Verbal behavior.* Englewood Cliffs, NJ: Prentice-Hall.

Skinner, B. F. (1969). *Contingencies of reinforcement: A theoretical analysis.* Englewood Cliffs, NJ: Prentice-Hall.

Skinner, B. F. (1977). Herrnstein and the evolution of behaviorism. *American Psychologist, 32,* 1006–1012.

Slifer, K. J., Iwata, B. A., & Dorsey, M. F. (1984). Reduction of eye gouging using a response interruption procedure. *Journal of Behavior Therapy and Experimental Psychiatry, 15,* 369–375.

Smith, R. G., Iwata, B. A., Vollmer, T. R., & Zarcone, J. R. (1993). Experimental analysis and treatment of multiply controlled self-injury. *Journal of Applied Behavior Analysis, 26,* 183–196.

Sprague, J. M., Chambers, W. W., & Stellar, E. (1961). Attentive, affective, and adaptive behavor in the cat. *Science, 133,* 165–173.

Spradlin, J. E., & Girardeau, F. L. (1966). The behavior of moderately and severely retarded persons. In N. R. Ellis (Ed.), *International review of research in mental retardation,* Vol. 1 (pp. 257–305). New York: Academic.

Steege, M. W., Wacker, D. P., Berg, W. K., Cigrand, K. K., & Cooper, L. J. (1989). The use of behavioral assessment to prescribe and evaluate treatments for severely handicapped children. *Journal of Applied Behavior Analysis, 22,* 23–33.

Stone, A. A. (1964). Consciousness: Altered levels in blind retarded children. *Psychosomatic Medicine, 26,* 14–19.

Tarpley, H. D., & Schroeder, S. R. (1979). Comparison of DRO and DRI on rate suppression of self-injurious behavior. *American Journal of Mental Deficiency, 84,* 188–194.

Thurrell, R. J., & Rice, D. G. (1970). Eye rubbing in blind children: Application of a sensory deprivation model. *Exceptional Children, 10,* 325–330.

Van Houten, R. (1993). The use of wrist weights to reduce self-injury maintained by sensory reinforcement. *Journal of Applied Behavior Analysis, 26,* 197–203.

Van Houten, R., & Doleys, D. M. (1983). Are social reprimands effective? In S. Axelrod & J. Apsche (Eds.), *The effects of punishment on human behavior* (pp. 45–70). New York: Academic.

Vaughan, M. E., & Michael, J. L. (1982). Automatic reinforcement: An important but ignored concept. *Behaviorism, 10,* 217–228.

Vollmer, T. R. (1994). The concept of automatic reinforcement: Implications for behavioral research in developmental disabilities. *Research in Developmental Disabilities, 15,* 187–207.

Vollmer, T. R., Iwata, B. A., Zarcone, J. R., Smith, R. G., & Mazaleski, J. L. (1993). Within-session patterns of self-injury as indicators of behavioral function. *Research in Developmental Disabilities, 14,* 479–492.

Vollmer, T. R, Marcus, B. A., & LeBlanc, L. (1994). Treatment of self-injury and hand mouthing following inconclusive functional analysis. *Journal of Applied Behavior Analysis, 27,* 331–344.

Warren, S. A., & Burns, N. R. (1970). Crib confinement as a factor in repetitive and stereotyped behavior in retardates. *Mental Retardation, 8,* 25–28.

Watson, J., Singh, N. N., & Winton, A. S. W. (1986). Suppressive effects of visual and facial screening on self-injurious finger sucking. *American Journal of Mental Deficiency, 90,* 526–534.

Watters, R. G., & Watters, W. E. (1980). Decreasing self-stimulatory behavior with physical exercise in a group of autistic boys. *Journal of Autism and Developmental Disorders, 10,* 379–387.

Wieseler, N. A., Hanson, R. H., Chamberlain, T. P., & Thompson, T. (1985). Functional taxonomy of stereotypic and self-injurious behavior. *Mental Retardation, 23,* 230–234.

Wieseler, N. A., Hanson, R. H., Chamberlain, T. P., & Thompson, T. (1988). Stereotypic behavior of mentally retarded adults adjunctive to a positive reinforcement schedule. *Research in Developmental Disabilities, 9,* 393–403.

Wells, K. C., Forehand, R., Hickey, K., & Green, R. (1977). Effects of a procedure derived from the overcorrection principle and nonmanipulated behavior. *Journal of Applied Behavior Analysis, 10,* 679–687.

Winton, A. S. W., & Singh, N. N. (1983). Suppression of pica using brief-duration physical restraint. *Journal of Mental Deficiency Research, 27,* 93–103.

Winton, A. S. W., Singh, N. N., & Dawson, M. J. (1984). Effects of facial screening and blindfold on self-injurious behavior. *Applied Research in Mental Retardation, 5,* 29–42.

Zarcone, J. R., Rodgers, T. A., Iwata, B. A., Rourke, D., & Dorsey, M. F. (1991). Reliability analysis of the Motivation Assessment Scale: A failure to replicate. *Research in Developmental Disabilities, 12,* 349–360.

8

Threats to Internal and External Validity of Three Functional Assessment Procedures

ALAN C. REPP
DENNIS D. MUNK

INTRODUCTION

There are numerous ways to conduct functional analyses, some of which are questionnaires, analogue assessments, naturalistic assessments, or a combination of several methods. Each of these has been cited for weaknesses, often by those using one of the other methods. In this chapter, Repp and Munk discuss general factors affecting the reliability and validity of these procedures. They use the framework provided by Campbell and Stanley (1966), analyzing each procedure for its susceptibility to four threats to internal validity, four threats to external validity, and to weaknesses relative to four constructs concerning reliability and validity.

The analysis is made in two areas: (a) the results of the assessment for each of the functional assessment procedures, and (b) the results of an intervention based on the hypothesis derived from the assessment (the intervention being considered, in effect, a measure of the criterion validity of the assessment). The effort is an attempt to identify threats to the reliability and validity of each assessment procedure in such a way that we can reduce the threats when using any procedure.

In a seminal work, Carr (1977) reviewed research on self-injurious behavior (SIB) and posited three functions for this behavior: positive reinforcement, negative reinforcement, and stimulation. Shortly thereafter, several experimental studies showed a relationship between two or more environmental conditions and SIB (for example, Carr, Newsom, & Binkoff, 1980; Carr & Newsom, 1985; Weeks & Gaylord-Ross, 1981). In each case, the researchers established conditions outside the environment in which the presenting problem was occurring, assessed behavior under those conditions, and then provided treatment in that analogue setting.

This procedure was formalized by Iwata and his colleagues (see Iwata et al., 1982; Iwata et al., 1990) who, importantly, developed a standardized means of assessing the function of behavior. This protocol established four conditions that (a) were linked to Carr's three functions as well as to a control condition, (b) would produce different rates of SIB if the behavior was under control of one of those functions, and (c) would lead logically to treatment.

An abbreviated approach to identifying the function of behavior was later developed by Durand and Crimmins (1988) in the form of a 16-item questionnaire intended to be given to staff to answer. This instrument, the Motivation Assessment Scale (MAS), sought to identify the same functions as those identified by Carr, Iwata, and their colleagues—although, as Halle and Spradlin (1993) indicated, the test assesses the conditions under which behavior occurs rather than the function of behavior. Additionally, because it was a questionnaire with items that have not since changed, it, like Iwata's functional assessment procedure, has a standardized protocol that can be analyzed across researchers, subjects, and settings. While other interview instruments have been put forward (Donnellan et al., 1984; Evans & Meyer, 1985), we will focus our discussion on the MAS because its utility has been discussed in the literature and because it is a widely recognized interview instrument.

Concurrently, a third procedure for identifying the function of behavior was being developed by various researchers (see Repp, Felce, & Barton, 1988). In this approach, the function of behavior is determined in the natural environment, and treatment is implemented directly in that assessment environment, rather than in other environments as with the analogue assessment procedure and the interview procedure. Unfortunately, because of the diverse group of researchers developing these naturalistic functional assessments, there is no standard protocol for conducting the procedure. However, learning from the shortcomings in our own work in this area (Karsh et al., 1995; Repp & Karsh, 1994), we would suggest that naturalistic functional assessment procedures should (a) assess in conditions natural to the environment, (b) assess in a sufficient number of conditions so that all three functions posited by Carr and Iwata can be addressed for each subject, (c) simultaneously evaluate the relationship between the assessment conditions and both appropriate and inappropriate behavior, and (d) base treatment on hypotheses of the function of the behavior in question, while attempting to increase the appropriate alternative behaviors addressed in the assessment.

Results with all three procedures have been mixed, although most experimental studies have identified a function that could then be addressed during an intervention phase. However, concerns regarding the appropriateness or accuracy of certain procedures have been raised (Iwata, Vollmer, & Zarcone, 1990; Repp et al., 1996). In general, these concerns are whether assessment results are both (a) stable (reliable) over time, and (b) valid representations of behavior in the natural environment.

Rather than repeat those criticisms in this paper, we will discuss general factors that may affect the reliability or validity of the three functional assessment procedures. The rationale for such a discussion is twofold. First, identifying parameters or critical variables for effective use of a method can be viewed as a natural event in the development of any approach toward assessment. For example, researchers have recently reported that functional assessment procedures sometimes fail to detect variations in behavior across different conditions, thereby failing to indicate a function for the behavior (Derby et al., 1992; Iwata et al., 1994; Vollmer, Marcus, & LeBlanc, 1994). These and other reports of failures, while uncommon, should be commended because an analysis of cases that do not follow the predictable pattern can enhance our understanding of the science of behavior (Sidman, 1960). Second, identifying variables that threaten either the validity or reliability of our methods may help us improve our procedures, as well as prompt us to report how we currently control for these threats.

Criticisms of functional assessment procedures are equivalent to discussions in other fields of the reliability and validity of assessment procedures, tests, and experimental manipulations. A commonly used system for addressing problems with reliability and validity has been established by Campbell and Stanley (1966), who discussed threats to the internal and external validity of experimental and quasi-experimental designs. Because the popularity of this listing even in behavior analysis, as evidenced by adaptations in texts by Kazdin (1982) and Johnston and Pennypacker (1993), has made it a somewhat standard approach, we will adopt it for the purpose of this paper. More specifically, we will briefly discuss four threats to internal validity, four threats to external validity, and the means by which we might address these threats.

THREATS TO INTERNAL AND
EXTERNAL VALIDITY

Campbell and Stanley (1966) discussed twelve threats to internal and external validity, eight of which we will address. Table 8.1 presents these eight, four of which concern internal validity (maturation, history, testing, and instrumentation) and four of which concern external validity (reactive effects of testing, selection bias, reactive effects of experimental arrangements, and multiple treatment interference). Additionally, the table separates the threats into those that primarily address either (a) the results of the assessment, or (b) the results of an intervention based on the hypothesis derived from the assessment (the intervention is, in effect, a measure of the criterion validity of the assessment). Finally, the table presents four constructs that may address these threats; these four are sampling validity, test-retest reliability, content validity, and predictive validity. Before discussing the threats, we will discuss the implications of these four constructs.

**Table 8.1 Threats to Internal and External
Validity of Three Functional Assessment Procedures**

	PHASE		ADDRESSING THREATS
	Results of Assessment	Results of Intervention (criterion test)	S = Sampling T-R = Test-Retest Reliability CV = Content Validity PV = Predictive Validity
Internal Validity			
Maturation	X	X	T-R
History	X		T-R
Testing	X		T-R
Instrumentation	X		T-R
External Validity			
Reactivity to testing		X	S, CV, PV
Selection biases	X		PV
Multiple-treatment interference	X		PV
Reactivity to arrangements	X		S, PV

DETECTING SOURCES OF INTERNAL AND EXTERNAL VALIDITY

Sampling

There are two sampling questions related to functional assessments: (a) do data gathered at a point in time represent behavior over the entire session, and (b) do summary data from a single session represent behavior over a longer time period? For the analogue and naturalistic functional assessments, the first question concerns intrasession reliability; that is, whether data on the function of behavior collected during one part of the assessment condition represent the occurrence of behavior during any other part of the session (Vollmer et al., 1993b). The problem is that when we collapse data (providing only a mean for each condition within a single session or a mean for an entire session if only one condition is presented), we may be missing sources of variance operating at particular times within the session. If there is an appreciable difference in the rate of behavior in, for example, the first and fourth quarter of an assessment condition, that difference may represent (a) a shift in stimulus control, (b) interference (or carryover effects) from a prior condition, or (c) behavior that is cyclical and entering an upward or downward trend due simply to the passage of time or to influences (for example, biological) other than the experimental condition presented. The problem can be addressed in a post hoc sense by reporting data per condition on a subsession basis for that condition (for example, as a quarter, or in five-minute blocks). In an ad hoc sense, the problem can be addressed by first recording behavior in the natural environment to determine whether there are patterns or cycles that repeat themselves either within sessions or days, or across days (Sidman, 1960). If there are, those repeated patterns could be a result of tight stimulus control, biological factors overriding any stimulus effects, or a combination of the two. There are at least three ways this problem can be addressed. One is by conducting the assessments at time periods that have relatively equal rates of behavior in the natural environment. In this way, any biological effects can be controlled across the several experimental conditions that might be presented. A less satisfactory means would be to report, in addition to subsession rates, the deviation between the rate in that condition and the naturally occurring rate. A third way, given sufficient repeated assessments, would be random assignment of each condition to time.

The second question—whether summary data from a single session represent rates of behavior over a longer period of time (for example, same day or different day)—concerns intersession reliability; that is, whether data collected in one session would be the same as data collected in another session representing the same condition. A problem may arise when we collect data for only one or two occasions per condition. When doing so, we cannot assess whether those data would be similarly represented in additional sessions. The problem can be addressed by repeating sessions across time, by reporting data on each session rather than just a mean across sessions for each condition, and by randomly assigning conditions across time.

Figure 8.1 presents the possible severity of the problem for the analogue and naturalistic assessments (as well as for the MAS, which will also be discussed). This figure presents four theoretical graphs of behavior constructed according to the following rules: (a) the length of the possible time is six hours (any length would be suitable for this example, but we are using six hours because it roughly represents a school day or a staff shift); (b) the six hours are divided into twenty-four units that represent 15-minute assessments; (c) one behavior pattern completes a half cycle within the six-hour period (upper panel); (d) another behavior pattern completes a full cycle within the six-hour period (upper right panel); (e) another completes two cycles (lower panel); and (f) another is random, with twenty values between the high and low points of the cycle randomly selected for each of the twenty-four, 15-minute periods (lower panel).

For each graph, the behavior represented would be operating under *extra-stimulus* or *extra-functional* control. The behavior is *not* associated with hypotheses being tested. We offer these as data representing a behavior controlled more, for example, by biological factors than by contingencies of reinforcement operating in the environment. The behavior would be entrained to a variable that would overcome those immediate contingencies.

Our effort here is to provide data on possible sampling problems for the analogue and naturalistic assessment procedures. As such, we have randomly selected times within the six hours to apply 15-minute assessments of four conditions (for positive reinforcement, negative reinforcement, stimulation, and a control) either one time each, two times each, or three times each. These data, then, would indicate the degree to which our assessments reflect the natural occurrences of the behavior. Table 8.2 presents these data, showing the mean for each condition (A, B, C, D) under one, two, or three observations of 15 minutes each, for each of the

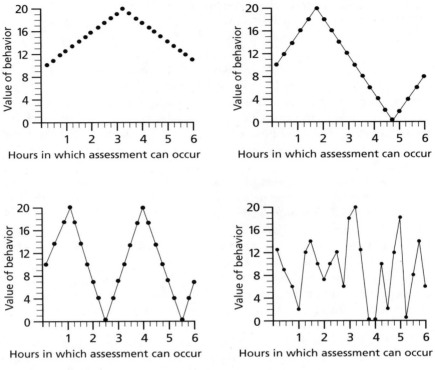

FIGURE 8.1. Four patterns representing behavior under biological control or environmental control of conditions other than those in the assessment. The y-axis represents 20 possible values of behavior (for example, rate, percent of session), while the x-axis represents six hours. The four patterns represent either 0.5, I, or 2 cycles per six hours, or a random distribution of the 20 values.

four patterns of behavior presented in Figure 8.1. Based on the suggestion that a value more than one standard deviation above the mean would identify a controlling hypothesis (for example, positive reinforcement) (Iwata et al., 1982), we then determined whether any conditions met that criterion and, as a result, suggested a controlling hypothesis. Results showed that when one observation was made, three of the four panels (0.5 cycle, 1 cycle, and random values) showed a controlling hypothesis. The point, of course, is that all three of these are false positives—the reason for the selection is due to the naturally occurring rate of behavior, not to a controlling hypothesis. Further, there were two false positives when two observations were made, and one false positive when three observations were made. This result would suggest that an assessment showing more responding in one condition than in others, when one or two observations are made, may be expected for reasons other than identification of the controlling function.

   In the analogue and naturalistic assessment procedures, an observer intervenes between the behavior of the subject and the record of that behavior, and various

Table 8.2 The Percent of Session in Which Behavior Would Be Reported as Occurring Based on Sampling Data in Figure 8.1 on One, Two, or Three Randomly Selected Occasions

Graph	ONE OBSERVATION Conditions				TWO OBSERVATIONS Conditions				THREE OBSERVATIONS Conditions			
	A	B	C	D	A	B	C	D	A	B	C	D
Upper (1 cycle)	10.83	13.32	17.47	19.96*	13.74	14.15	17.06	16.64	13.60	14.42	13.32	13.04
Upper middle (2 cycles)	1.70	13.31	19.96*	8.34	10.00	12.50*	9.17	4.19	6.68	8.89	9.45	9.99
Lower middle (3 cycles)	16.64	10.00	16.64	0.04	5.00	5.02	6.68	15.00*	7.79	8.88	11.10*	8.99
Lower (random values)	10.00	15.80*	13.30	6.70	14.98	1.27	10.83	10.42	10.00	10.55	10.28	8.33

*more than one standard deviation above the mean

procedures for promoting observer accuracy and reliability have been addressed (see Repp et al., 1988). In interview procedures, an observer also intervenes between behavior and its record. However, because the target behavior is not being recorded directly in real time, this procedure is also susceptible to sampling problems concerning the person being interviewed (even if the interviewees are accurately reporting what they have observed).

In the interview assessment procedure, unlike the other two procedures, there are two hierarchical sets of "sessions." One represents the informant's actual observations of the target behavior in the natural environment, which typically have occurred over weeks or months. As such, it is susceptible to the same problems of sampling as are the other two procedures discussed above. The other type of session represents the point at which the therapist interviews the informant. As such, the interview procedure has additional sampling problems.

For example, if the samples of direct observation were not appropriately distributed across time and conditions, the informant's impressions may not validly represent the conditions (and hence the function) under which the target behavior naturally occurs. Then, even if the point at which the informant was interviewed was properly sampled, the information from the interview may not be correct. In addition, this procedure may suffer sampling problems concerning the representativeness of each individual informant, including (a) familiarity with the setting and subject, (b) expectancy from prior experience with other subjects under a single hypothesis (for example, stimulation), (c) situational complexity, (d) recency effects from the time between the last episode of behavior and the informant's responses, and (e) intrainformant variables (for example, prior training, fatigue at time of interview).

Test-Retest Reliability

Although test-retest reliability can refer to several measures, here we mean it to refer to the particular hypothesis generated by the assessment procedure (that is, positive reinforcement, negative reinforcement, or automatic stimulation). The question becomes: Will the assessment procedure given two or more times generate the same function? The answer certainly is related to sampling, as it is affected by the adequacy of the sampling procedure. However, the term addresses the stability of the functional analysis procedure with respect to the hypothesis it generates.

For the three assessment procedures, test-retest stability can be measured by giving the assessment more than once and by comparing the functions identified on each assessment. Researchers using the analogue and naturalistic assessment procedures could use several statistics to judge the reliability. However, the most appropriate might be Cohen's kappa, for two reasons: (a) it accounts for chance agreements, and (b) it is common in the behavioral literature from which these three assessment procedures arose. The problem of chance agreement is not a trivial one, because for the two direct observation assessments there is a 33 percent probability of chance agreement between the hypothesis generated by two test administrations (25 percent for the MAS) and a 25 percent chance if a control condition is used. Researchers concerned with assessing this potential problem could provide measures of test-retest reliability for each subject being assessed.

The MAS can be assessed in a similar way (although it has been assessed in several other ways). Durand and Crimmins (1988) reported three correlational analyses with coefficients ranging from .66 to .92. However, several researchers have criticized these findings for the following reasons: (a) reliability calculations by Durand and Crimmins (1988) were based on correlational analyses rather than on an item-by-item comparison of the raters' scores (Zarcone et al., 1991); (b) reliability data were found to be less consistent than originally reported, with only 31 of 48 correlations of rank order significant at .05 level (Crawford et al., 1992); (c) reliability estimates have proven unacceptable in subsequent tests (Sigafoos, Kerr, & Roberts, 1994); and (d) agreements between two raters showed that only 16 of 55 raters agreed on the category of reinforcement maintaining behavior, none of the reliability scores based on percent agreement between raters was above 80 percent, and only 15 percent of the correlation coefficients were above .80 (Zarcone et al., 1991). Obviously one can conclude from these data that test-retest reliability should be assessed when using the MAS, and care should be taken with the reliability statistic used.

Content Validity

Content validity refers to the extent to which the instrument assesses behavior in the domain of interest. According to Suen and Ary (1989), it is the "often ignored minor difference between the intended object of measurement and what is actually being measured" (p. 166). The key question becomes: To what extent does the assessment instrument sample the domain of interest? The potential problem becomes evident when we are interested in behavior over time, occasions, environments, and so forth. If we were interested only in SIB during the Friday lunch hour, then an assessment of that hour would occupy the domain of interest for that behavior. If, on the other hand, we were interested in SIB during the school day, Monday through Friday, then such an assessment might not capture the domain. In behavioral terminology we are, of course, addressing temporal and stimulus generalization. In this case, the analogue assessment and the MAS treat the variable in the same way. Both address content validity by seeking to establish or identify a function powerful enough to overcome conflicting contributions from other aspects of the environment. Iwata has written of this problem for analogue assessments on numerous occasions, indicating that it ". . .might not reveal all the events that maintain a behavior problem in the natural environment" (Iwata, Vollmer, & Zarcone, 1990, p. 310). These authors and others (Halle & Spradlin, 1993; Mace, Lalli, & Shea, 1993; Mace & Shea, 1990) recommended careful assessment in the natural environment in order to develop more representative conditions for analogue assessments. Researchers using this approach should choose thorough samples of the conditions in the natural environment under which behavior does and does not occur, perhaps by using a scatterplot. Then, during the assessments, they might provide appropriate samplings of persons, tasks, stimulating materials, times, and so forth that might be correlated with problem behavior in the natural environment.

The MAS, as indicated, also seeks to identify a function strong enough to overcome behavioral control by particular stimuli in the environment. However, unlike researchers using analogue assessments, researchers in this area have not addressed content validity. In order to do so, researchers should include in their sample of respondents individuals who have experience with the presence and absence of the target behavior in various environments and times, and then report reliability estimates of the functions identified by these different environments.

Naturalistic functional assessment is generally considered to be much more representative of the conditions of the natural environment because, after all, the assessments are conducted in the natural environment. Although that assumption has face validity, it may not be correct. To have content validity, naturalistic functional assessments should sample the range of environmental variables, just as analogue assessments should. Again, if the domain of interest was the target behavior across, for example, the school day, five days a week, then conducting a naturalistic functional assessment only during the math activity on Monday and Tuesday may not adequately sample the domain of interest. The problem for naturalistic functional assessment is no less than it is for analogue assessments. In each case, the assessment conditions should adequately sample the domain of interest.

Predictive Validity

Predictive validity is a subtype of criterion-related validity (which is concerned with how well the level of a behavior during assessment relates to the level of that behavior in the criterion environment) (Suen & Ary, 1989). In functional assessment, predictive validity could refer to two relationships: (a) whether the relative rate of behavior in assessment predicts the rate of behavior outside the assessment environment, and (b) whether the function of behavior in the assessment environment is the same as the function of that behavior outside the assessment environment. Both questions are critical because the rate of behavior may indeed prove similar in the assessment and natural environments, whereas the function of the behavior may be different in the natural environment. Attention only to the rate of the behavior may produce an incorrect assumption that the function has remained the same. Although both are reasonable questions, we discussed the former under sampling threats; in this case, we will be referring only to the latter. In effect, functional assessment only has predictive validity if it can predict the function of behavior in the criterion environment. Clearly, this is the most important form of validity for these procedures.

All three assessment procedures have the same problem: the prediction of a function upon which intervention can be based. The question for each is: How is that prediction assessed? In most cases, it is assessed by the degree of behavior change produced by hypothesis-based intervention; validity is then inferred. However, such a test does not answer the question of whether or not any intervention would have changed behavior. That question may be answered through a multiple schedule design in which both the indicated intervention and a contraindicated one are run during the same phase (as in Repp, Felce, & Barton, 1988). While this is a good test for the psychometric properties of the assessment, it does raise practical and ethical questions about the necessity of the contraindicated treatment. For those reasons, this test may not be appropriate.

Another approach, albeit a less powerful one, is to (a) collect data in the criterion environment during naturally occurring conditions that represent each of the functions (for example, attention for positive reinforcement, tasks for negative reinforcement, and unstimulating environments for stimulation hypothesis) during both baseline and intervention, (b) define contingency tables representing these functions, and (c) determine whether the values in the contingency tables (that is, the conditional probabilities) change in the direction the hypothesis-based intervention would have predicted (see, for example, Repp & Karsh, 1994).

VARIABLES AFFECTING INTERNAL AND EXTERNAL VALIDITY

In this section, we will briefly discuss eight of the threats to validity—four of which affect internal validity and four of which affect external validity—presented by Campbell and Stanley (1966). Then, we will describe how procedures related to test-retest reliability, and sampling, content, and predictive validity can minimize threats to internal and external validity.

Threats to Internal Validity

Maturation Maturation refers to processes within the subject operating as a function of the passage of time per se (rather than to particular environmental events), and would include factors like becoming older, more hungry, or more tired (in behavioral terminology, these factors would be called setting events). In addition, maturation may be used to describe the effects of time on a behavior that occurs cyclically and is relatively independent of environmental influence.

When rates of a behavior follow a cycle or pattern that is relatively stable regardless of environmental events (such as wakefulness), the level of the behavior when measured at interval t would depend more on when behavior was measured than on the conditions that were in effect at the time of measurement (see results in Table 8.2).

History   History refers to specific events, in addition to the experimental variable, that occur between two or more sessions (Campbell & Stanley, 1966). Individuals may be exposed to specific conditions occurring between two assessment sessions or two treatment sessions that may affect responding in subsequent sessions. Such exposure might include learning new responses, changes in the contingencies maintaining the target behavior, or development of new or alternative responses. Although history has traditionally been used to describe events occurring between pretest and post-test conditions in an experiment, it can be used to consider events occurring between repeated presentations of conditions in a functional assessment, even though no independent variable has been used between tests.

Testing   Testing describes the effects of taking a test upon the scores on a second test. In a functional assessment, testing effects may include (a) intrasession changes in responding due to repeated exposure to a contingency in that assessment condition, or (b) intersession changes in responding due to exposure to setting elements (materials, people) or to contingencies in that assessment. Testing effects may reflect the subject's learning of new response rates or patterns due to exposure to a contingency or to sharpening of stimulus control resulting from repeated exposure.

Instrumentation   Traditionally, instrumentation has referred to variability in the measurement of a dependent variable due to changes in the calibration of a measuring instrument or to changes in the observers used to obtain the measurement. As described earlier, different procedures (interview, analogue, direct observation) have been used to measure levels of a target behavior under different conditions. When different functional assessment procedures are used to measure the same behavior, differences in measurements may be due to instrumentation, a problem of concurrent validity. That is, the outcomes of a functional assessment procedure may be influenced by the type of procedure used to assess behavior. In addition, changes in scores across multiple presentations of a condition (for analogue or naturalistic assessment) or multiple interviews of the same person (for the MAS) may be due to changes in the measuring instrument instead of maturation, history, or testing.

Threats to External Validity

Reactive or Interactive Effects of Testing   Reactive effects describe an increase in a subject's sensitivity or responsiveness to an experimental variable to the extent that the results obtained are unrepresentative. In functional assessment, reactive or interactive effects could result from responding controlled by unique or novel characteristics of the assessment environment. Stimuli or procedures used in the assessment situation may spuriously affect the outcome. Thus, any environmental difference between an assessment setting and the natural environment may threaten the external validity of the assessment.

Interactive Effects of Selection Biases and the Experimental Variable

The external validity of a specific functional assessment procedure may be artificially enhanced or decreased by measuring behavior occurring at certain levels on a dimension. For example, the external validity of a specific functional assessment procedure may be high only when the behavior being measured occurs at a high rate (Singh et al., 1993). Additionally, certain topographies or classes of behavior may be more accurately assessed by specific procedures. For example, the external validity of an assessment of stereotypic behavior may be highest when a specific procedure is used. While experimenters are unlikely to exercise bias in the selection of subjects, behavioral characteristics of the subjects upon which the external validity of a functional assessment procedure is based should be considered.

Multiple-Treatment Interference   Because the effects of a condition on responding are not erasable, they may influence responding in subsequent sessions under different conditions (McGonigle et al., 1987). When multiple sessions are presented intermittently throughout the day, or when experimental conditions are alternated rapidly as in an alternating treatments design, responding within a single session may be influenced by previous conditions. Examples of procedures for which multiple-treatment interference may be a threat to external validity include those which present one contingency for several minutes and then rapidly change the contingency so that (a) a behavior reinforced in the previous condition is now under extinction, or (b) a behavior previously under extinction or intermittent reinforcement is now under a dense schedule of reinforcement.

Reactive Effects of Experimental Arrangements   Reactive effects of exposure to the experimental conditions could affect the extent to which results can be generalized to nonexperimental settings. In functional assessment, reactive effects would include any effects on the level of the target behavior that are caused by elements of the assessment condition not present in the criterion environment. The potential for such reactive effects may increase concomitantly with increasing differences between the assessment setting and the criterion environment. Reactive effects in a functional assessment procedure could result in increased or decreased levels of a target behavior due to the novelty of the stimulus conditions or to contingencies present in the assessment environment.

For functional assessment procedures that involve testing in a special environment that is outside of the natural environment, external validity of the results can be assumed only if both environments are identical or variables controlling problem behavior are salient enough to override novel aspects of the assessment environment.

RELATIONSHIP OF FOUR CONSTRUCTS TO THREATS TO INTERNAL AND EXTERNAL VALIDITY

In the prior section, we briefly discussed eight threats to internal and external validity. In the section before that, we discussed the relationship of four reliability or validity constructs to functional assessment. In this section, we will discuss the relationship of those four constructs to the eight threats that are listed in Table 8.1. The discussion is summarized in Table 8.3.

Threats to Internal Validity

Maturation, or a change in responding due solely to the passage of time, is a threat to internal validity in both the assessment and intervention phases. Normally, we control for this threat through single-subject research designs. However, the assessment phase requires additional precautions to guard against maturation, which would cause the rate of behavior to be higher in one condition than in others, thus producing a Type I error (selecting one hypothesis over others when in fact there was no effect). One precaution would be to include test-retest reliability measures, calculated on the rates of behavior during repeated presentations of the same conditions. Another precaution would involve sampling procedures, in which (a) data for each condition are presented not only for overall means but also for shorter periods (for example, quarters of each session), (b) each condition's presentation is matched to times at which the behavior's rates are roughly equivalent in the natural environment, and (c) each condition is randomly assigned to its time period. For interview measures such as the MAS, the sampling and test-retest procedures discussed are appropriate for maximizing the internal validity of results for each respondent. However, further precautions are necessary in that respondents' observations must have been drawn from observations across a complete day, several days, or, preferably, weeks. When one respondent's observations are from a small or time-specific observation session, the sample must be expanded by adding respondents who have observed the subject at other times of the day, week, or month. Responses across respondents must then be compared for reliability. Variability would suggest that maturation or some other threat was operative. To minimize the effects of maturation on responding in the intervention phase, a hypothesis-based intervention should be implemented soon after assessment is completed. Lags between assessment and intervention may allow maturation to influence responding under an intervention that is based on the hypothesis identified during the functional assessment.

History, or the effect of events occurring between assessments, may threaten the internal validity of a functional assessment when exposure of a subject to novel conditions between sessions produces changes in the subject's repertoire or in the function of the target response. For example, a target response may be replaced by a functionally equivalent response, either through instruction or through surreptitious reinforcement. Test-retest measures may be used to ascertain effects of history on responding in the second through *n*th sessions. Data from two or more sessions can

Table 8.3 Recommendations for Addressing Threats to Validity

THREATS	RECOMMENDATION
1. Sampling	1. Sampling
A. Are data gathered at any point within a session reliable with regard to rate or duration to data at another point (i.e., similar to data at another point)?	A. Calculate reliability of data across blocks (e.g., 5 min) of the session on both the inappropriate and appropriate behaviors.
B. Is the rate of behavior during assessment consistent with the rate during the period in which the behavior is a problem in the natural environment?	B. Conduct the assessment at the same time of day behavior is problematic to the complaints.
C. Are data in one session comparable with data in other sessions?	C1. Calculate reliability across sessions on behavior datum (e.g., rate of responding).
	C2. Randomly assign the condition being assessed to the time of assessment (for analogue assessment only).
2. Test-Retest Reliability	2. Test-Retest Reliability
A. Is the *function* of behavior identified in one assessment session the same as the function identified in other sessions?	A. Calculate reliability on *function* using Cohen's kappa.
B. Is a new function being learned in the assessment environment?	B. Calculate reliability on *function* derived within a session by dividing into blocks of time (e.g., 5-min blocks or quartiles) to determine if a new function arises.
C. Is the identified function of behavior due to the condition being tested or to carryover effects from adjacent conditions?	C. Clearly separate the testing conditions to minimize stimulus generalization.
D. Is the measuring instrument (usually observers) reliable?	D. Calculate interobserver and/or intra-observer (using tapes) reliability.
3. Content Validity	3. Content Validity
A. Do the conditions in the assessment environment sufficiently match the natural environment to assure temporal and stimulus generalization?	A. Include in the assessment a range of environmental variables found in the environment in which the behavior is a problem.
4. Predictive Validity	4. Predictive Validity
A. Do the assessment results lead to successful intervention?	A. Determine effects using research design that allows baseline and intervention phases to be compared.
B. Would another intervention, not based on the function identified in assessment, be as effective?	B. Compare an intervention based on the indicated function (e.g., positive reinforcement) with one based on another function (e.g., negative reinforcement) (but may not be ethical).

be assessed for variability, suggesting whether new responses have been strengthened. A more potent test-retest procedure would include measurement of (a) other behaviors in addition to the target behavior, and (b) measurement of the response under alternative conditions to determine if there are changes in the function of the target behavior. A test-retest measure with only one condition testing only one hypothesis does not rule out multiple functions of a response, nor does it rule out all plausible effects of history on the validity of the assessment results.

Testing, or the effects of being assessed on scores produced in subsequent assessments, may threaten the validity of functional assessment results. Such effects would include changes in intersession responding due to repeated exposure to stimulus conditions and a contingency during the prior session. In effect, any condition in which the subject learns new contingencies would be subject to the effects of testing. Testing differs from history in that the threat arises from exposure to stimuli or contingencies presented during the assessment conditions. Recording and analyzing within-session responding, as opposed to the typical procedure of reporting only a session mean, may allow detection of testing effects due to prolonged exposure to the assessment condition as the subject is learning a new contingency. In addition, test-retest reliability scores should be provided to assess whether there are changes across repeated presentations of each condition.

Instrumentation, or variability in scores for the dependent variable as a function of changes in the measuring instrument rather than in the independent variable, can be addressed by test-retest measures. In the assessments using direct observation, this could be accomplished three ways: (a) comparing scores across two or more presentations of each condition; (b) calculating intraobserver agreement by presenting videotaped sessions several times; or (c) calculating interobserver scores for individual session data. For the MAS, test-retest measures could provide information on instrumentation by using two respondents (interobserver reliability) or by comparing the scores from a single respondent who was interviewed on several occasions (intraobserver agreement).

Threats to External Validity

Threats to external validity would include reactive or interactive effects of testing or an increase in the sensitivity to the experimental variable. Sampling, content validity, and predictive validity would all be related to this threat. Sampling problems would occur if, for example, novel adults or materials were used in the assessment and they did not exert the same degree of stimulus control that adults or materials in the natural environment did. The sampling problem would carry over to the intervention phase, again, if stimulus control was not the same for stimuli in the assessment and intervention environments. The same problem would exist for the MAS if the informant was not properly sampled from the population of possible informants. Content validity problems would also affect all three assessment procedures. Researchers and therapists should ensure that assessment variables represent the domain of interest, including environments and time. If potential sampling and content validity problems are not addressed, there may be considerable problems with the predictive validity of the assessment (that is, the function identified in the assessment may not be the same function that operates in the natural environment).

Interactive effects of selection biases with the experimental variable may also threaten external validity. For example, all three assessment procedures have been primarily used with persons with developmental disabilities, and generally in the range of severe-to-moderate retardation. Further, the procedures have been used primarily with inappropriate behaviors like self-injury, aggression, and stereotypy. There may be differences in the effectiveness of the procedures when different subjects, behavioral topographies, or behavioral classes (for example, appropriate behaviors) are chosen. Further, as Singh et al. (1993) have shown with the MAS, the rate of behavior studied may be influential. Because these procedures have primarily been used with high rate behaviors, we do not know the extent to which the results can be generalized across subjects, behaviors, rates of behaviors, and settings (see Chapter 6 by Sprague and Horner for a discussion of low rate behaviors).

Multiple-treatment interference can also affect the external validity of these assessment procedures. Although there is evidence that rapidly alternating conditions (as in assessments) can produce stimulus generalization (see McGonigle et al., 1987), we do not know the extent to which this problem can affect identification of the correct function during assessment, and thus affect predictive validity. Clearly, there should be some time between conditions during both assessment and intervention (when the latter is providing different treatments through an alternating treatments design). The problem is more difficult for the MAS during assessment, as we do not know how the respondent's judgment would be affected by the contiguous nature of the conditions in which the respondent witnessed the subject. The respondent could quite simply be confusing both conditions and rates of behaviors, particularly when these conditions followed each other rapidly and may have occurred days or weeks past.

The last threat to external validity is the reactive effects of experimental arrangements. For the direct observation assessments, the subject may react unusually to novel stimuli, either substantially increasing or decreasing the rate of the target behavior, thus producing an incorrect choice by the researcher of the hypothesis for the controlling variables. For the MAS, the same problem would hold for the situations the respondent viewed.

Reactive effects during assessment could be a product of a unique combination of stimuli found in the natural environment and those found only in the assessment environment. For example, tasks that have in the past been associated with relatively low rates of problem behavior may produce elevated levels when presented in a different setting by a novel person. In such a scenario, observers may determine a student's problem behavior is escape motivated (negative reinforcement) and recommend an intervention that addresses this function (for example, reduced task difficulty). However, upon return to the natural environment, the student may not exhibit the problem behavior when the original task is presented by a familiar staff, but may exhibit the problem behavior at other times and under different conditions.

FUTURE DIRECTIONS OF FUNCTIONAL ASSESSMENT RESEARCH

Over the past decade, our field has witnessed the development and increasingly widespread use of the powerful technology called functional assessment. While the purpose of functional assessment to identify a hypothesis of the function of a target behavior has remained universal, three variations of the assessment procedure have evolved. A common thread across interview, analogue, and naturalistic assessment procedures is an a priori assumption that a target behavior is under relatively tight stimulus control. When through a report or observation we identify stimulus conditions producing the target response, we conclude that (a) the target response is environmentally dependent and controlled by stimuli we have pinpointed, and (b) evidence of stimulus control precludes effects of other variables not assessed.

By portraying different data patterns (Figure 8.1) and results of assessments conducted on those data (Table 8.2), we have attempted to point out the role that threats to validity may play in functional assessment results. Data patterns, such as those in Figure 8.1, may appear irrespective of assessment conditions if the target response is controlled completely or partially by (a) biological influences or (b) stimuli or compound stimuli we have not assessed (see Halle & Spradlin, 1993).

We acknowledged earlier the fact that behavior analysts have discussed threats to internal and external validity of behavioral assessment and treatment procedures (see Johnston & Pennypacker, 1993; Kazdin, 1982; Sidman, 1960). Indeed, single-subject designs such as the reversal, multiple-baseline, and alternating treatments can facilitate predictive validity when we move from assessment to treatment. However, in general, single-subject designs do not account for threats to internal or external validity. Two exceptions may be (a) the alternating treatments design used by Iwata et al. (1982), in which multiple presentations of the four conditions are made, thus increasing internal validity of the results, and (b) the naturalistic functional assessment in which multiple observations are made of the conditions that could be related to each function.

In both of the above procedures, the number of observations is linked to the validity of the results. However, the goal of researchers in functional assessment appears to be to reduce the number of observations to a very small number. When this reduction is made, the false positives and the false negatives associated with assessments on data represented in Figure 8.1 can increase substantially.

In lieu of traditional single-subject designs, we would suggest creating contingency tables that show the ongoing relationship between the environment and behavior for each of the three hypotheses. For example, data in Figure 8.2 show the contingency tables for one student indicating that one hypothesis is correct and the other two are incorrect (see also Repp & Karsh, 1994). The top matrix, labeled Positive Reinforcement, indicates that appropriate behavior produced staff attention in 6 percent of occurrences, while problem behavior produced staff attention on 96 percent of occurrences. The middle matrix, entitled Negative Reinforcement, indicates that exposure to easy tasks was associated with appropriate behaviors in 53 percent of occurrences and problem behavior in the remaining 47 percent of occurrences. A similar relationship is seen between difficult tasks and appropriate or problem behaviors (that is, the probability of appropriate behavior is 0.49 while the probability of problem behavior is 0.51).

The bottom matrix, entitled Stimulation, indicates that the presence of proximate materials was associated with equivalent levels (50 percent) of adaptive and problem behavior. An identical relationship is seen for a condition of no materials and adaptive and problem behavior. Figure 8.2 presents summary data under conditions representing three hypotheses: positive reinforcement, negative reinforcement, and stimulation. Only the top matrix representing positive reinforcement

Positive reinforcement

	Appropriate behavior	Problem behavior
Attention	.06	.96
No attention	.94	.04

Negative reinforcement

	Easy task	Difficult task
Appropriate behavior	.53	.49
Problem behavior	.47	.51

Stimulation

	Proximate materials	No materials
Appropriate behavior	.50	.50
Problem behavior	.50	.50

FIGURE 8.2. Probability of problem behavior under conditions representing three controlling hypotheses: positive reinforcement, negative reinforcement, and stimulation.

suggests a functional relationship between environmental conditions and problem behavior. Although probability matrices do not always yield such clear evidence for one hypothesis, our experience has been that data will favor one hypothesis, which can be tested with further observation or by implementing an intervention and assessing effects on the level of problem behavior.

We would also caution researchers to avoid treating replication of functional assessment procedures as evidence of the validity of results. Mere replication across experimenters of the finding that analogue assessments usually identify one salient hypothesis does not validate this procedure because its identification may simply be a false positive, with the error occurring because the threats to internal validity were not controlled. A more stringent measure of validity would be the replicated choice and success of assessment-based interventions across experimenters.

CONCLUSION

Researchers knowledgeable about behavior analytic theory and application have begun to express concerns regarding the validity of some functional assessment procedures. As we have suggested, each of the three widely recognized approaches discussed in this paper are vulnerable to one or more threats. We hope that this paper will provide a framework for both testing the validity of functional assessment procedures and for describing how validity has already been established in various studies.

AUTHOR NOTE

Support for this paper was partially provided by the Office of Special and Rehabilitation Services, Grant No. H133G20098-93.

REFERENCES

Campbell, D. T., & Stanley, J. E. (1966). *Experimental and quasi-experimental designs for research*. Chicago: Rand McNally.

Carr, E. G. (1977). The motivation of self-injurious behavior: A review of some hypotheses. *Psychological Bulletin, 84,* 800–816.

Carr, E. G., & Newsom, C. D. (1985). Demand-related tantrums: Conceptualization and treatment. *Behavior Modification, 2,* 403–426.

Carr, E. G., Newsom, C. D., & Binkoff, J. A. (1980). Escape as a factor in the aggressive behavior of two retarded children. *Journal of Applied Behavior Analysis, 13,* 101–117.

Crawford, J., Brockel, B., Schauss, S., & Miltenberger, R. G. (1992). A comparison of methods for the functional assessment of stereotypic behavior. *Journal of the Association for Persons with Severe Handicaps, 17,* 77–86.

Derby, K. M., Wacker, D. P., Sasso, G., Steege, M., Northrup, J., Cigrand, K., & Asmus, J. (1992). Brief functional assessment techniques to evaluate aberrant behavior in an outpatient clinic: A summary of 79 cases. *Journal of Applied Behavior Analysis, 25,* 713–721.

Donnellan, A. M., Mirenda, P. L., Mesaros, R. A., & Fassbender, L. L. (1984). Analyzing the communicative functions of aberrant behavior. *Journal of the Association for Persons with Severe Handicaps, 9,* 201–212.

Durand, V. M., & Crimmins, D. B. (1988). Identifying the variables maintaining self-injurious behavior. *Journal of Autism and Developmental Disorders, 18,* 99–117.

Evans, I. M., & Meyer, L. H. (1985). *An educative approach to behavior problems: A practical decision model for interventions with severely handicapped learners*. Baltimore: Paul H. Brookes.

Halle, J. W., & Spradlin, J. E. (1993). Identifying stimulus control of challenging behavior: Extending the analysis. In J. Reichle & D. P. Wacker (Eds.), *Communicative alternatives to challenging behavior: Integrating functional assessment and intervention strategies* (pp. 83–109). Baltimore: Paul H. Brookes.

Iwata, B., Dorsey, M., Slifer, K., Bauman, K., & Richman, G. (1982). Toward a functional analysis of self-injury. *Analysis and Intervention in Developmental Disabilities, 2,* 320.

Iwata, B. A., Pace, G. M., Dorsey, M. F., Zarcone, J. R., Vollmer, T. R., Smith, R. G., Rodgers, T. A., Lerman, D. C., Shore, B. A., Mazaleski, J. L., Goh, H. L., Cowdery, G. E., Kalsher, J. J., McCosh, K. C., & Willis, K. D. (1994). The functions of self-injurious behavior: An experimental-epidemiological analysis. *Journal of Applied Behavior Analysis, 27,* 215–240.

Iwata, B., Pace, G., Kalsher, M., Cowdery, G., & Cataldo, M. (1990). Experimental analysis and extinction of self-injurious escape behavior. *Journal of Applied Behavior Analysis, 23,* 11–27.

Iwata, B. A., Vollmer, T. R., & Zarcone, J. R. (1990). The experimental (functional) analysis of behavior disorders: Methodology, applications, and limitations. In A. C. Repp & N. N. Singh (Eds.), *Perspectives on the use of nonaversive and aversive interventions for persons with developmental disabilities* (pp. 301–330). Sycamore, IL: Sycamore.

Johnston, J. M., & Pennypacker, H. S. (1993). *Strategies and tactics of human behavioral research* (2nd ed.). Hillsdale, NJ: Lawrence, Erlbaum Associates.

Karsh, K. G., Repp, A. C., Dahlquist, C. M., & Munk, D. (1995). In vivo functional assessment and multi-element interventions for problem behaviors of students with disabilities in classroom settings. *Journal of Behavioral Education, 5,* 189–210.

Kazdin, A. G. (1982). *Single-case research designs: Methods for clinical and applied settings.* New York: Oxford.

Mace, F. C., Lalli, J. S., & Shea, M. C. (1993). Functional analysis and treatment of self-injury. In S. Axelrod & R. Van Houten (Eds.), *Effective behavioral treatment: Issues and implementation* (pp. 122–152). New York: Plenum.

Mace, F. C., & Shea, M. C. (1990). New directions in behavior analysis for the treatment of severe behavior disorders. In S. Harris & J. Handleman (Eds.), *Advances in the treatment of severe behavior disorders* (pp. 57–79). New York: Springer-Verlag.

McGonigle, J. J., Rojahn, J., Dixon, J., & Strain, P. S. (1987). Multiple treatment interference in the alternating treatments design as a function of the inter-component interval length. *Journal of Applied Behavior Analysis, 20,* 171–178.

Repp, A. C., Felce, D., & Barton, L. (1988). Basing the treatment of stereotypic and self-injurious behaviors on hypotheses of their causes. *Journal of Applied Behavior Analysis, 21,* 281–290.

Repp, A. C., & Karsh, K. G. (1994). Hypothesis-based interventions for tantrum behaviors of persons with developmental disabilities in school settings. *Journal of Applied Behavior Analysis, 27,* 21–31.

Repp, A. C., Karsh, K. G., Munk, D., & Dahlquist, C. M. (1996). Hypothesis-based interventions: A theory of clinical decision making. In W. O'Donohue & L. Krasner (Eds.), *Theories in behavior therapy.* Washington, D.C.: American Psychological Association.

Repp, A. C., Nieminen, G. S., Olinger, E., & Brusca, R. (1988). Direct observation: Factors affecting the accuracy of observers. *Exceptional Children, 55,* 29–36.

Sidman, M. (1960). *Tactics of scientific research.* New York: Basic Books.

Sigafoos, J., Kerr, M., & Roberts, D. (1994). Interrater reliability of the Motivation Assessment Scale: Failure to replicate with aggressive behavior. *Research in Developmental Disabilities, 15,* 333–342.

Singh, N. N., Donatelli, L. S., Best, A., Williams, D. E., Barrera, F. J., Lenz, M. W., Landrum, T. J., Ellis, C. R., & Moe, T. L. (1993). Factor structure of the Motivation Assessment Scale. *Journal of Intellectual Disability Research, 37,* 65–74.

Suen, H. K., & Ary, D. (1989). *Analyzing quantitative behavioral observation data.* Hillsdale, NJ: Lawrence, Erlbaum Associates.

Vollmer, T. R., Iwata, B. A., Zarcone, J. R., Smith, R. G., & Mazaleski, J. L. (1993a). The role of attention in the treatment of attention-maintained self-injurious behavior: Noncontingent reinforcement and differential reinforcement of other behavior. *Journal of Applied Behavior Analysis, 26,* 9–21.

Vollmer, T. R., Iwata, B. A., Zarcone, J. R., Smith, R. G., & Mazaleski, J. L. (1993b). Within-session patterns of self-injury as indicators of behavioral function. *Research in Developmental Disabilities, 14,* 479–492.

Vollmer, T. R., Marcus, B. A., & LeBlanc, L., (1994). Treatment of self-injury and hand mouthing following inconclusive functional analysis. *Journal of Applied Behavioral Analysis, 27,* 331–344.

Weeks, M., & Gaylord-Ross, R. (1981). Task difficulty and aberrant behavior in severely handicapped students. *Journal of Applied Behavior Analysis, 14,* 449–463.

Zarcone, J. R., Rodgers, T. A., Iwata, B. A., Rourke, D., & Dorsey, M. F. (1991). Reliability analysis of the Motivation Assessment Scale: A failure to replicate. *Research in Developmental Disabilities, 12,* 349–360.

PART II

Functional Assessment in Preschool and School

9

※

Prevention of Problem Behaviors in Preschool Children

GAIL MCGEE
TERESA DALY

INTRODUCTION

In this section, we will present five chapters with discussions of functional assessment in preschool and school environments. The first in this set, by McGee and Daly, describes programs for preventing problem behaviors by preschool children in the Walden schools at Emory University.

Most functional assessment programs, regardless of whether they are interviews, naturalistic observation, or analogue assessments, address extant behavior problems. However, if we manipulate particular setting events, antecedents, and consequences that are associated with problem behavior, we can often prevent its occurrence. The particular program presented in this chapter assesses (a) preventive environmental arrangements, including socially mediated consequences provided by adults and peers (helping us recall Chapter 7, in which Shore and Iwata distinguished mediated from automatic reinforcement); (b) both the level of fun children are having and their preferences (see Chapter 4), identifying these factors as setting events contributing to the prevention of problem behavior; and (c) levels of engagement, showing that high levels of engagement prevent problem behavior (see the discussion by Sprague and Horner in Chapter 6 on behavioral allocation, the matching law, and functional equivalence). The chapter thus integrates points from several prior chapters while showing us a new application of functional assessment, which, if successful, would reduce the rate of problem behaviors and thus the rate of postproblem functional assessments.

Prevention is an alternative to traditional behavior management for preschool children with and without disabilities. A strategy of prevention buys time to achieve growth in fundamental social and language skills, which enables long-term prevention of problem behaviors. The priority, then, becomes one of replacement rather than reduction of problem behaviors.

A preventive approach requires program accountability for problem behaviors. The assumption is that the cause for problem behavior resides within the preschool program, and the solution will require an assessment and adjustment of program supports for more pleasant behaviors. In contrast, problem behaviors are more traditionally viewed as an intrinsic characteristic of a particular child. In behavioral programs for persons with disabilities, problem behaviors usually result in an individualized behavior reduction plan. In many early childhood programs, problem behaviors trigger a debate on what is happening in the child's home. A "blame the child" or "blame the family" perspective translates to an expectation that a child must change; in many preschools, the child must change or leave the program. A preventive approach puts the burden of change on the program.

SECONDARY PREVENTION OF SEVERE PROBLEM BEHAVIORS

For children with disabilities, proactive intervention during the toddler and preschool years is the best bet for preventing the development of problems such as harm to self or others (McGee, 1988). Early treatment does not merely extend the length of intervention. Children can most readily acquire effective language and social skills when they are young. Importantly, young children can more easily incorporate new skills as alternatives to problem behaviors, than can older children with entrenched behavioral patterns.

Children with autism are among those most likely to develop challenging behaviors at a later age. The traditional autism treatment approach has been to achieve a "tabula rasa" by first treating problem behaviors, and then addressing skill deficits. However, as more children with autism enter treatment at early ages, a marked shift in treatment priorities occurs (Dunlap & Robbins, 1991). Most of the model preschool programs for children with autism now give skill building at least initial priority over behavior reduction (for example, Harris & Handleman, 1994).

Because social development is the primary goal for young children with autism, it is extremely risky to use behavior reduction procedures that can lead to increased social avoidance. The result of multiple behavior reduction programs is often an unusually compliant child whose social vigilance may be focused on avoiding punishment. With instruction, these children tend to develop stiff or robotic social responses which occur only in specifically-trained situations. Moreover, generalization of behavior control outside the treatment context is often problematic (Powers, 1994). In contrast, the goal of a preventive approach is to preserve the natural quality of behavior, and to re-channel behavioral control to the natural contexts of a child's everyday environment.

Advantages of Problem Prevention
in Inclusive Preschools

The nationwide movement toward education of children with disabilities in less restrictive settings continues to gain momentum at the preschool level (Strain, 1990). Inclusion of children with and without disabilities presents vastly improved opportunities for social development, along with new challenges in classroom behavior management. A preventive approach is especially applicable to inclusive early childhood settings.

Behavior management procedures should be equitable across all children in an inclusive classroom. Typically, young children present a wide range of problem behaviors, which often differ only in frequency or intensity from those of children with disabilities. It's simply not justifiable to use presentation of aversives (for example, water mist in the face) when a child with autism displays a certain behavior, and a milder consequence for the same behavior in a typical child. In addition to ethical considerations, de facto segregation must be avoided. Restrictive behavior reduction procedures may signal a "difference" in the manner that teachers interact with children who have disabilities. Young classroom peers are very susceptible to influence by their teachers, and they are likely to adjust their interactions with children who have disabilities accordingly (Daly, 1993).

The social acceptability of behavior management strategies is also crucial in inclusive preschools. On one hand, behavior management plans must meet licensing and accreditation standards that mandate developmental appropriateness. Therefore, many behavior reduction procedures used commonly in programs for people with disabilities are not permissible in early childhood programs. For example, few special education programs would be viewed as excessively punitive for including feedback such as "Yuck, you have wet panties" in response to a toileting accident. Yet such a procedure may be cited as demeaning or humiliating by the licensing inspector of an early childhood program. On the other hand, a program's ability to attract the enrollment of typical children is influenced by the behavior of all children in the classroom. Most parents of typical children are new to the idea of inclusion, and they are on the lookout for signs of inappropriate behavior that could be detrimental to their child. Inclusive classrooms must be able to ensure the best behavior of all of the children, while using behavior management procedures that are palatable to all parents.

Limitations of Common Approaches to
Preschool Behavior Management

Perhaps the most practical argument for prevention is that traditional behavior management is often ineffective, in both special education and regular early childhood settings. A most troubling example of wasted time is the use of seatbelts to restrain young children with special needs. This practice is in widespread use in special education preschools around the country; little chairs with straps are commercially manufactured for this purpose. Curiously, parental consent is seldom required for restraint of young children. The following anecdote exemplifies the problem.

A 20-month-old child with profound mental retardation incites a call for technical assistance due to high levels of hand flapping and drooling. The consultant reviews the child's records, and notes that walking is the first objective in the Individualized Family Service Plan (IFSP). The second objective is learning how to play with toys. Observation of the child in her early intervention center verifies that self-stimulatory behavior is occurring at very high rates. It is also noticed that the child is seatbelted in her chair. The consultant asks if the seatbelt is needed to keep the child from falling out of her chair. The teacher responds, "Oh no, if we undid the seatbelt, she would get up and cruise along the table to get to one of the toys at the other end." In sum, she might practice her first two priority IFSP goals.

Behavior management procedures that result in wasted time come at a high cost for young children, because developmental growth can occur rapidly at young ages. For children with developmental delays, wasted time is a lost learning opportunity.

At the other end of the continuum of ineffective preschool behavior management is the use of rationales at the time of misbehavior ("You shouldn't bite Sally because it hurts her and causes a big red mark. Would you want Sally to bite you?" and so on). This is common practice in early childhood settings for normally-developing children. The use of rationales is based on a developmental literature, which contends that children cannot learn from problem behavior unless they are told why it should not continue (Zahn-Waxler, Radke-Yarrow, & King, 1979). Rationales hold tremendous appeal for parents, who want their children to learn right from wrong. However, many problem behaviors of preschool children are of the simple attention-seeking variety, and a lengthy rationale provided at the time of misbehavior can be hugely counterproductive. A teacher's attention to problem behavior can easily produce a shift that quickly escalates further problem behaviors (Sulzer-Azaroff & Mayer, 1991). The solution in this conflict between good developmental practice and sound behavioral principles (both with supporting literatures) may be found in a preventive approach to problem behaviors.

Development Site:
Walden Early Childhood Programs at Emory

The preventive behavior management strategies outlined in this chapter have evolved from nine years of research and program development at the Walden Early Childhood Programs. Many of the procedures began as practical solutions to everyday problems in a laboratory preschool, which in turn had the capability for assessment via ongoing program evaluation or formal functional analyses. Most of the procedures have also been extended for use by parents in the Walden Family Program (McGee, Jacobs, & Regnier, 1993), as well as for use with toddlers at Little Walden (McGee, Daly, & Morrier, 1993). Development work is underway to adapt preventive behavior management for a new Walden Pre-Kindergarten Program.

A distinctive feature of the Walden Preschool is its comprehensive incidental teaching approach (McGee, Daly, & Jacobs, 1994), which was a major impetus to the development of a preventive classroom management plan. In brief, incidental teaching is comprised of: (a) an environment that attracts children to desired activities; (b) child initiations that identify teachable moments; (c) teacher prompts related to children's interests; and, (d) contingent on an elaborated child response, praise and access to items of interest (Hart & Risley, 1982; McGee, Krantz, & McClannahan, 1985, 1986). Because child initiations are integral to the process of incidental teaching, behavior management procedures that suppress child initiations (such as compliance training) were not a viable option.

Another influencing feature of incidental teaching has been that classroom toys must function as both the teaching materials and the reinforcing consequences. Acquisition by children with autism improves when their responses are functional in producing potent reinforcers (Williams, Koegel, & Egel, 1981). For example, it is more effective to teach a child to use the word "ball" to get a desired ball, than to reward labeling a picture of a ball with an M&M. The importance of classroom materials as both the teaching and reinforcing stimuli has required careful attention to classroom toys, as well as to environmental arrangements that make toys attractive.

The process of incidental teaching itself serves to reduce problem behavior (Carr & Kologinsky, 1983; Koegel, Koegel & Surratt, 1992). This positive side effect of incidental teaching likely derives from the inclusion of a built-in reinforcer assessment in the incidental teaching procedure (McGee, 1992). A child thus signals that he wants a particular item by initiating (reaching or asking) for that item.

In recent years, Walden research has focused on normative and atypical development of social behavior in preschool children (McGee, 1993, 1994). Although the preschool originally enrolled approximately equal numbers of children with and without disabilities, the program has shifted to a classroom composition of 2/3 typical children and 1/3 children with autism. The research goal is to achieve an understanding of the environmental events that influence social behavior in typical preschool children, and to use this information to construct more effective social interventions for children with autism.

When social behavior is the primary concern, problem behaviors are most logically viewed as a subset of social functioning. Thus, in Walden's individualized treatment plans for children with autism, problem behaviors are not designated as a major goal area. Rather, an objective is usually specified to monitor levels of autistic behavior, and this objective is a component of the larger goal of normalized social behavior. Objectives pertaining to levels and content of engagement are also specified as subsets of social behavior, along with more obvious social objectives (for example, proximity to typical children, interactions received from children, and so on).

Preventive behavior management allows valuable early intervention time to be devoted to language and social development, the most crucial areas for all young children. The preventive procedures to follow also help ensure that children can enjoy their early childhood years. Relatively straightforward assessment strategies are presented in order of least effort. The combined preventive package follows, along with a functional analysis of the package. The logistics of managing a preventive plan are also discussed, as well as strategies to address problem behaviors when they do inevitably occur.

ASSESS PREVENTIVE ENVIRONMENTAL ARRANGEMENTS

The easiest way to prevent problem behaviors is to carefully design or engineer the environment (Twardosz, Cataldo, & Risley, 1974). By arranging furniture to prevent a racetrack, teachers may avoid nagging children to stop running. For children with autism, it is important to eliminate areas that are convenient for isolation, in both the classroom (under a tent in an unsupervised area) and on the playground (in a tunnel that others seldom use). Since requirements for developmentally appropriate best practice insist on access to privacy for children, cozy areas may be set up to afford a view for supervising teachers (such as a book corner with pillows and stuffed animals).

Child-safety gates can be used to keep children from prohibited areas (supply shelves or hallways). Preventive gates also provide wonderful teaching opportunities when a child wants to get to an interesting activity on the other side ("I want to paint, please"). Visual barriers and well-planned storage of classroom supplies prevent the need for constant behavioral corrections (the teacher's permanent marker is hidden in a box; paint is stored on high or curtained shelves, and so on).

Providing duplicates of toys is sometimes a useful means to prevent problems, especially with toddlers for whom sharing is not always realistic. When a popular toy is given to just one child, it seems only fair for other children to have access to a similar one; however, duplicate toys should be used sparingly, because overuse may preclude opportunities for sharing and turn-taking. Toy removal should be only an occasional practice, because children need to learn appropriate use of toys. However, when toys are the object of continual dispute, unsafe use, or isolative self-stimulation, it may be expedient to remove them from the classroom. Toy removal is most effectively accomplished when children are momentarily focused elsewhere (if airplanes have been sailing through the air throughout the morning, airplanes might be replaced with trucks when the children are outside for recess). When toys are removed, toy replacement is essential to avoiding an austere classroom.

Another important environmental variable is the deployment of adults. At Walden, teachers are assigned routines associated with different classroom areas, or "zones" (LeLaurin & Risley, 1972). Adults must be stationed to provide for constant view of the entire classroom. Physical separation of teachers eliminates situations in which children have to compete with adults for teacher attention. One-way observational mirrors also provide assurance that program accountability procedures are constantly in place. Walden parents and administrators can view the classrooms at any time, with no requirement to notify teachers of their presence.

Other children can also impact on problem behavior. When Walden had only a slight majority of typical children, the absence of a few typical peers could shift the atmosphere from that of a normal preschool to an institutional ambience. In fact, it has been shown that autistic behavior is less likely to occur when autistic children are in close physical proximity to typical children, in contrast to when they are near autistic children or alone (McGee, Paradis, & Feldman, 1993).

Children with autism are not likely to remain in close proximity to other children unless there are formal classroom procedures to encourage integration. At Walden, child placement is designated as a component of the Lead Teacher's responsibilities; when a child with autism is alone, the Lead Teacher may redirect the child to sit between two typical peers at an art activity, or he or she may invite several typical children to the area in which the child is playing. Whenever the Lead Teacher's performance is evaluated, he or she is rated on whether all classroom areas contain an inclusive mix of children.

Although proximity to peers is important, overcrowding of activity zones should be avoided. Zone-based staffing allows children to be distributed around the classroom. The Lead Teacher encourages children to move to sparse zones with a little "marketing." Again, the Lead Teacher is monitored and given feedback on whether children are spread around the room.

ASSESS LEVEL OF FUN
IN THE CLASSROOM

Increasing fun is the most enjoyable way to prevent problem behaviors. It is wise to interpret problem behaviors as signals that children are not having fun in ongoing classroom events, and to respond with adjustments in the curriculum or schedule. It has been suggested (Risley, 1991) that the most poorly behaved children are the most helpful to program development; these are the ones who first detect the "bugs" in a classroom's daily plan.

If everyone is acting up at Morning Circle, it is a signal that the content needs pepping up and/or that the length of the circle activity should be reduced. A disastrous nap time can be prevented by showing videos. If some children display problem behaviors every day while waiting for lunch, they may need to eat first, or the lunch schedule may be moved up, or an extra morning snack may be offered. It is obviously easier to feed hungry children than to deal with the aftermath of bad tempers.

The Walden classrooms operate with schedules of multiple, concurrent activities (O'Brien et al., 1979). Children are provided with a constant choice of activities. This format is conducive to providing lots of incidental teaching opportunities. Children also display their best behavior when they are doing what they want to do.

Importantly, multiple activities can be scheduled in overlapping time sequences so that there are as few large-group transitions as possible. Group transitions are breeding grounds for problem behavior, because they inevitably result in the need for children to "wait." At Walden, waiting is viewed as wasted time (unless an instructional plan is in place to teach waiting).

Fun classrooms require enthusiastic teachers with high energy levels. Preschoolers hugely appreciate a teacher's ability to be silly, but these personal qualities are hard to train so they are best attended to at the time of teacher selection. Moreover, even the most energetic teacher is affected by the length of "on-the-floor" teaching time. Active teachers get physically tired (and are less fun) when required to work too long. For this reason, the length of a Walden teaching shift is limited to four hours per day.

Finally, a cardinal rule at Walden is: Never get involved in a power struggle with a young child. The self-serving reason for this edict is that the child almost always wins. A young child can throw a bigger tantrum than an adult teacher. Besides, a "breaking the horse" approach is certainly not fun for the horse.

ASSESS CHILDREN'S PREFERENCES

By preschool age, virtually all typical children will clearly articulate their preferences if you ask them, and teachers should do so regularly. Another method of assessing preferences is to measure who comes to tabletop activities, and how long they stay. This teacher-collected data may be summarized as a component of a weekly program evaluation, which provides information on activities that draw an inclusive group. Less-preferred activities may then be discarded, and favored ones slated for a future repeat. For children with autism, the assessment of preferences is critically important. The complexity of reinforcer assessment became apparent in the course of pilot research taking place during Walden's first year (Farmer-Dougan & McGee, 1986). It was found that the results of a reinforcer assessment conducted in the early morning were not reliable throughout the day (a child who selected paint in a morning assessment would protest that he wanted to play with cars in the afternoon). In the interest of accomplishing preventive behavior management, Walden had to invest further research and development in the area of reinforcer potency.

There exists a literature on the topic of reinforcer potency (Egel, 1981; Ferrari & Harris, 1981; Rincover et al., 1977; Rincover & Newsom, 1985), and some research has been focused directly on reinforcer assessment (Datillo, 1986; Dyer, 1987; Green et al., 1988; Pace et al., 1985; Wacker et al., 1985). Paradoxically, if the topic is not specifically reinforcer assessment, both basic and applied studies rarely report reinforcer selection procedures. It seems safe to assume that reinforcer selection receives even less attention in busy applied settings, and treatment compromise is a likely result.

A Walden study on reinforcer assessment began as a simple "message" piece to the field: reinforcement works—but it works best if it is carefully selected (Mason et al., 1989). A multiple baseline experimental design across three children with autism was used to compare a condition of teacher-selected rewards to a condition of child-selected rewards. In the teacher-selection condition, rewards were selected by asking experienced classroom teachers, "What does Billy like to play with best?" In child-selection conditions, a systematic sensory preference assessment (adapted from Pace et al., 1985) was combined with presession miniassessments of pairs of preferred rewards. Briefly, children were presented with a comprehensive assessment to determine the category(ies) of sensory stimuli they most preferred (visual, auditory, olfactory, tactile, vestibular, gustatory, or thermal). Rewards were then selected to provide the child's preferred sensory qualities. A child who scored high on visual stimuli might then be offered a choice of a kaleidoscope or a colorful top just before the teaching session began. An important procedural feature of the study was that reinforcement was contingent on a child's correct responding, irrespective of maladaptive behaviors (eye poking, drooling, aggression).

Results showed dramatic side effects of potent child-selected reinforcers. Maladaptive behaviors were thus virtually eliminated in teaching sessions in which child-selected rewards were used as reinforcers. Given the difficulty of treating the problem behaviors of children with autism, these findings had broad implications for developing a preventive approach.

In the interest of preventing problem behaviors, it is useful to ask the following questions: When was the last comprehensive reinforcement assessment conducted? Are miniassessments conducted immediately before teaching episodes? Are materials used as rewards in good condition? (Are there working batteries? Are potato chips stale? Are all pieces of a toy available?) Children's preferences must be assessed systematically and frequently to prevent satiation and deal with individual variability across time. If children's engagement is primed with potent reinforcers (if they are not just ready to respond, but *ready* to respond), the result is focused engagement, which is incompatible with problem behaviors.

ASSESS AND MAINTAIN HIGH LEVELS OF ENGAGEMENT

Ongoing measurement of children's engagement provides an assessment of the amount of time that children are available for instruction. Classroom engagement is also the key component of a preventive behavior management plan. In a nutshell, engagement may be viewed as the primary indicator of a program's quality.

Engagement measures have been used in a variety of settings to evaluate how well programs are using the time of dependent populations (for example, Cataldo & Risley, 1974; Doke & Risley, 1972; Krantz & Risley, 1977; McClannahan & Risley, 1975). There also exists a well-formulated precedent for use of engagement as a measure of the efficacy of early intervention (McWilliam, Trivette, & Dunst, 1985).

Engagement has been defined in various ways (for example, McWilliam, 1991). Stringent definitions of on-task behavior are common in programs for persons with developmental disabilities; however, social inclusion dictates the need for an engagement measure to serve as a common denominator between groups of children. Specifically, because typical preschoolers are active organisms, the definition of engagement cannot rule out behaviors that are not "still, quiet, and docile" (Winett & Winkler, 1972). In child-centered classrooms, compliance with teacher directions is no longer the primary determinant of learning opportunities that it once was in more traditional teacher-controlled classrooms.

At Walden, preschool engagement has been broadly defined as an active focus on the environment. To be scored as engaged, the child must be doing something (emitting an overt behavior) or actively looking at something in the environment. Self-stimulatory behavior that precludes interaction with the environment (staring at his own fingers) is nonengaged, although a child may be engaged and simultaneously displaying self-stimulatory behavior (coloring a picture while sucking his thumb). Engagement is scored independently of the teacher's designated activity (a child may be scored as engaged when she is talking to another child rather than following directions to listen to a story).

Resources of the laboratory preschool permit daily videotaping of each child at random times during the day. A time-sampling data collection procedure is then used to score videotaped observations. Specifically, engagement data is recorded at-a-point-in-time in 15-second intervals. Variables of interest include overall levels of engagement, as well as the amount of time focused on toys, teachers, and other children.

The pla-check observational system (Cataldo & Risley, 1974) provides a more practical data collection format. Every child in the classroom is observed, one at a time, in one-minute intervals. Each child is scored as engaged or nonengaged at the moment of observation. A total classroom engagement score is computed by adding the number of children engaged and dividing by the total number of children present. At Walden, a pla-check is conducted weekly as part of ongoing program evaluation. In settings without the capability of extensive videotaping, more frequent pla-checks can be used to obtain individual as well as classroom engagement data.

The engagement goal should be at least 80 percent of the children's preschool day. This is an easy goal to achieve with typical children. When a typical child's engagement falls below 80 percent, it is a clear signal of a problem in the program. In contrast, it is very hard to get 80 percent engagement from many children with autism. Yet, if a child with autism is engaged only 50 percent of a six-hour preschool day, then it may be assumed that he is receiving only three hours of intervention. It is also likely that problem behaviors will be abundant.

Maintenance of high engagement by children with autism requires an optimal interface of environment, activities, reinforcer potency, and teacher behavior. The role of teacher contact in preventing problem behavior has been the focus of a considerable body of applied behavior analysis research (Sulzer-Azaroff & Mayer, 1991). Procedures for arranging Differential Reinforcement of Other (DRO) behavior (Repp, Barton, & Brulle, 1983) have emerged as the treatment of choice for the many problem behaviors that serve an attention-seeking function.

Recent descriptive analyses have shown that teachers of children with behavior disorders actually distribute their contacts in a manner quite inconsistent with a DRO (Shores et al., 1993). Teachers were most likely to provide attention for negative behaviors, and they largely ignored periods when children were behaving appropriately. Given this pattern of contact, a negative cycle of teacher-child interaction rapidly ensues.

Teachers need training, supervision, and supports to dispense their contacts most effectively. At Walden, teachers are carefully trained to make 13 to 15 child contacts in a five-minute period, and contacts must be distributed across all children in an assigned zone. Checklist-based performance appraisals for all teaching routines include a component for evaluating the rate of child contacts, and teachers are given objective feedback on their pacing. Similarly, checklist training is provided specific to implementation of DRO procedures, as shown in Figure 9.1. Teachers are trained to a criterion of two consecutive appraisals at mastery (every component completed

**Walden Performance Appraisal—Procedure for Differential
Reinforcement of Other Behaviors**

Teacher Name: _____   Mark each item: +, 0, or NA

Observer:					
Did the teacher: Date:					
1. Circulate among all children in the zone?					
2. Pace contacts at rate of 13–15 in a 5-minute observation period (tally: _____).					
3. Provide praise and incidental teaching to engaged children?					
4. Redirect children who are nonengaged more than 2 minutes?					
5. Contact children at the posted level of their need (e.g., Level 1 every circulation, Level 2 every second and third circulation, and Level 3 every third circulation)?					
6. Show enthusiasm and look cheerful when contacting children?					
7. Keep back to wall and remain vigilant?					
8. Demonstrate understanding of classroom rules and behavior management plan?					
9. Implement individualized procedures accurately?					
10. Other? (specify)					
Feedback Received? (initial)					

FIGURE 9.1 DRO teacher-training checklist

accurately). Thereafter, DRO checklists are conducted monthly, or whenever the behavior of a child or the classroom indicates a problem.

Independent engagement is the ultimate goal for all children. Each child needs enough, but not too much, contact to maintain engagement. In free-play, the Walden zone that includes the largest number of children at a given time, the teacher must make rapid-fire decisions on whom to contact at what frequency. A three-level chart is helpful to post as a cue card, designating which children to contact at what pacing. Children with chronic engagement difficulties are therefore contacted on each teacher circulation of the area (level 1), children with occasional engagement difficulties are contacted on the second and third teacher circulations (level 2), and children with stable engagement are contacted on every third teacher circulation (level 3). Depending on the child and teaching agenda, contacts may be brief praise (or smiles or pats) or they may be full-fledged teaching interactions. Teachers must be careful not to distract an engaged child to market another toy, and peer social interactions should never be interrupted.

Much research has focused on what teachers need to do, and less attention has been paid to supporting teacher efforts. A preventive plan must address the interaction of teacher contact with environment/activities/materials. To prevent problem behaviors by maintaining high engagement, a classroom system must be engineered to support teachers' selection and delivery of materials. Descriptions follow of two Walden solutions, including a toy rotation plan and hobby boxes (McGee et al., 1991).

Toy Rotation Plan

Child engagement is influenced by novelty and attraction to classroom toys, and toys lose these qualities when thrown haphazardly into the classroom. A first step in setting up the toy rotation plan was to categorize all toys on multiple dimensions. Toys were coded on dimensions of: (a) size (too many toys with little pieces keep teachers cleaning instead of teaching); (b) developmental level (a range is needed so that children at all levels can have success with toys); (c) early childhood categories (developmental appropriateness mandates that there are always manipulative, building, dramatic play, and visual-motor materials available); (d) sensory quality (a full array must be present so that all children's preferences are represented); and (e) theme (a recommended early childhood practice is to teach a topic throughout activities in a given week, such as farm animals, community helpers, vehicles, and so on).

The next step was to divide coded toys into sets (or rotations) of 10 toys. Each set was comprised of a range of sizes, developmental levels, play categories, and sensory qualities; to the extent possible, toys in a given rotation were related in thematic content. In the initial plan, toy sets were rotated in and out of the classroom one time per week. Friday morning was selected to give a preventive boost to end-of-the-week problem behaviors (all toys seem new on Monday).

Each toy rotation proceeds as follows: Toys in Set 1 and Set 2 are in the classroom one week; in the next week, Set 1 rotates out and Set 3 is brought in to combine with Set 2; and so on. The toy rotation plan, as opposed to irregular toy replacement based on teacher instinct, prevents boredom while allowing sufficient time for children to learn how to use the toys. Preplanning the available toys in a given week also helps to plan and set up teaching opportunities. For example, the Walden toy rotation plan permits new vocabulary words to be targeted weekly. Vocabulary words correspond to the toys that will be available in the classroom, and words are leveled in difficulty to specify differing developmental levels (new versus advanced language).

Hobby Boxes

Individualized materials are needed to meet the unique needs of individual children. At Walden, a "hobby box" format was developed to make it convenient for teachers to respond quickly to individual needs for materials. Each child has one (or more) hobby boxes (plastic baskets labeled with children's names). Hobby boxes are displayed on teacher-height shelves around the free-play area, within clear visibility of children. The function, contents, and method of dispensing materials varies across a color-coding system:

White Hobby Boxes The function of white hobby boxes is to store materials that will promote sustained engagement by children with chronic engagement difficulties. Each white box contains approximately five toys that a child will play with for sustained periods without direct teacher intervention. At Walden, these toys are selected by reviewing daily videotapes of the child in the classroom, but selections could be made from direct classroom observations.

The white hobby boxes are used as a backup when a child cannot be kept engaged with classroom toys. When a child with chronic engagement difficulties becomes nonengaged, the teacher redirects him to a different classroom toy. If the child continues to be nonengaged, the teacher redirects a second time to another classroom toy. If the child has still not been engaged with two redirects, the teacher offers a toy from the child's hobby box.

The procedure saves the teacher time in searching a supply room for something with which the child will play, and provides opportunities for a child to sample new toys. The risk of inadvertent reinforcement for nonengagement is not great for children with autism, for whom social contact is not initially very rewarding. Still, it is important that redirects be quick and matter-of-fact, and positive teacher contact be provided soon after the child engages in toy play. Children also learn to request their hobby box, and as a result, "box" is often a first word at Walden.

Blue Hobby Boxes Typical children (and children with autism who had no engagement difficulties) noticed the use of white hobby boxes and requested their own materials. Academic materials and small prizes were provided for them in blue hobby boxes.

Blue hobby boxes provide a nonobtrusive way to individualize academic work according to developmental readiness. Children also like the idea of having some toys that are "their own." Special prizes (such as a sticker book, Lion King figures, or crayons) are selected by each child from an array of items at a biweekly school store. Children request their blue hobby boxes whenever they want them, providing additional opportunities for child-initiated teacher interactions.

Pink Hobby Boxes Items that emit children's preferred sensory qualities, as determined by a comprehensive reinforcer assessment, are stored in pink boxes. These materials are used to build social responsivity in children with autism, at the time of initial classroom orientation and in booster sessions, as needed (Burns, 1991; McGee, 1993).

Pink hobby box items must provide brief but potent sensory stimulation. A teacher approaches a child when she is engaged, makes no demand, and delivers a noninterruptive preferred sensory input (such as ringing bells for a child who likes auditory stimuli). The teacher then departs, returning again in approximately 2½ minutes to deliver another pairing of approach and preferred sensory input. Incidental teaching is gradually introduced when the child begins to focus on (watch) teachers at near normative levels. The pink hobby box may then be used to provide a pool of potential rewards, from which miniassessments are conducted prior to one-on-one teaching sessions.

The social responsivity procedure requires that someone keep the child engaged, so that the implementing teacher can approach with a completely positive contact. Therefore, the procedure should be used in conjunction with the comprehensive preventive plan.

Functional Analysis of Materials Prevention Package

When a program assumes accountability for prevention of problem behaviors, the point of intervention is the classroom system, and the point of evaluation is classroom behavior. A weekly program evaluation (for example, O'Brien et al., 1979) provides an ongoing mechanism to assess the classroom's use of combined prevention procedures: Are children kept distributed around the room, in inclusive groups? Do children go to special art activities? Has each child with autism had a reinforcement assessment within the month? Are all teachers at mastery on the DRO performance appraisal? Objective measures of children's behavior are also needed: What are children's levels of engagement? What are the levels of autistic behaviors? How many times did children aggress towards their peers?

Program evaluation formats have been sufficient to assess and adjust the ongoing classroom prevention plan. However, a more precise functional analysis was needed to determine whether the level of effort required to implement the plan was justified by corresponding decreases in problem behaviors. Several components of the Walden prevention plan had been previously tested through functional analyses, including reinforcer assessment (Mason & McGee, 1989), zone-based staffing (LeLaurin & Risley, 1972), and DRO (Repp, Barton, & Brulle, 1983). An original report of a functional analysis of the combined procedural components represented in the Toy Rotation and Hobby Box system follows.

METHOD

Subjects

Fifteen children enrolled in the Walden preschool participated, including seven children with autism and eight typical children. Participants ranged in age from 3 years, 3 months to 6 years, 9 months (M = 4 years, 4 months). The children with autism had received independent diagnoses of autism prior to entering the program, their entry ratings on the Childhood Autism Rating Scale (Schopler et al., 1980) ranged from moderate to severe, and their entry test performance on the Stanford-Binet (form L-M or 4th Edition) ranged from untestable to an IQ of 38. Mean standardized IQ test performance for the typical children was 106 (range 94–127).

Setting and Materials

The study was conducted in the free-play area between 11:30 A.M. and 12:45 P.M. daily. Although program evaluation data for the three months prior to the study had indicated that the general frequency of problem behaviors at the preschool was quite low, the most serious problem of peer-directed physical aggression was most likely to occur in free-play around midday. The free-play area was comprised of traditional preschool centers, including areas for blocks, books, housekeeping, manipulatives, and art/writing. While in free-play, children were able to select and engage with toys and materials attractively displayed on child-size toy shelves and tables. In all conditions, standard classroom materials such as wooden blocks, dress-up clothes, books, and art materials remained available.

Measurement

Dependent Variables Negative peer-related social behaviors were the primary dependent variables, including negative affect, sharing disputes, tattling, verbal hostility, and physical aggression. Also of interest were side effects on positive social behavior, including sharing, cooperative play, and interactive play. Response definitions for negative and positive social behaviors (adapted from Guaralnick & Groom, 1987, and Daly, 1993) are in Table 9.1.

Behavioral Observations

Children in the free-play area were observed for 50 minutes each day using a partial interval recording format of 10 seconds observe/5 seconds record. Data were scored as frequency within intervals, across a total of 200 intervals daily. Observations were conducted in vivo by an observer who stood near the center of the room. Observation intervals were signaled by a tape recorder, to allow assessment of interobserver agreement.

Prior to onset of the study, chalked lines were drawn on the carpet to divide the free-play area into four quadrants. The quadrant designated for observation was rotated in a counter-clockwise direction across the 200 intervals. The quadrant assigned for the first observation of each session rotated across days. If a quadrant was empty as the signal sounded, the observer focused on the next quadrant containing children.

Interobserver Agreement Reliability data were obtained on 24 percent of sessions, distributed across conditions. The reliability observer remained within five feet of the primary observer, and they tilted scoring clipboards away from each other. Interobserver agreement (IOA) was calculated by dividing the number of agreements by the sum of agreements plus disagreements, and multiplying by 100. IOA ranged from 89 percent (interactive play) to 99 percent (all other behaviors), with a mean of 98 percent. Kappa coefficients were calculated for a more conservative estimate of scoring reliability; Kappas ranged from 0.72 (shares) to 0.95 (sharing disputes), with a mean of 0.84.

Consumer Satisfaction Teacher satisfaction with materials and ease of implementation was assessed in an informal interview at the end of each condition (week). Each of five Walden free-play teachers was asked to rate on a 5-point scale (1 = most positive, 5 = most negative) their responses to the following questions: (a) How much did you like the materials available to the children this week?; and (b) How easy was it to teach in free-play this week? Resulting responses were averaged by phase for each question.

Table 9.1 Summary of Response Definitions

Negative Peer-Related Behaviors

Negative Affect	Crying, frowning, scowling, nonstereotypic grimacing.
Sharing Disputes	Verbally or physically competing over access to a toy.
Tattling	Calling a teacher's attention to the negative behavior of a peer.
Verbal Hostility	Verbally expressing dislike or exclusion of a peer, or threatening injury.
Physical Aggression	Hitting, biting, pushing, scratching, or attempting to harm a peer.

Positive Peer-Related Social Behaviors

Sharing	Handling or offering an object to a peer.
Cooperative Play	Working with a peer to create something, or taking turns in a play activity.
Interactive Play	Conversing, helping, hugging, and other positive physical contact with a peer.

Experimental Design and Procedures

An ABCBC design was used to compare children's free-play behavior during conditions of: (A) systematic toy rotation and hobby boxes; (B) conventional toy selection and arrangement; and (C) enhanced toy rotation and hobby boxes. Throughout all conditions, the free-play teacher distributed 13 to 15 contacts across children per 5-minute interval, praising engagement and prompting language. Teachers rotated into free-play in 15-minute intervals, the usual practice in the preschool.

During the midday period, a number of simultaneous activities were offered, including free-play, lunch, and a one-to-one instructional session. Approximately 10 children were in free-play at any given time.

In all conditions, permanent classroom materials and furnishings were supplemented with 20 specially selected classroom toys, plus three to five individualized preferred toys for each child. The strategies for selection and display of toys in the free-play area varied across conditions, as follows:

Baseline (Systematic Materials Package) Conditions in the baseline phase consisted of the presence of two toy rotations and individualized hobby boxes. Because the systematic package had previously been demonstrated effective in promoting engagement (McGee et al., 1991), it represented the everyday environment in a preschool.

Each of two prearranged toy rotations included 10 toys that represented a range of sensory stimuli, sizes, play functions, and developmental levels. The toy rotations (a sample of which is shown in Table 9.2) were displayed on classroom shelves and remained fully available to children. Sets of toys were rotated on Friday morning each week.

Additionally, white and blue hobby boxes were located on teacher-height shelves around the classroom. As described previously, hobby boxes supported teacher efforts to provide children with preferred individualized materials.

Table 9.2 Classroom Materials

Sample of Two Toy Rotations

Alphabet abacus	Drums	Lincoln Logs	Perfume doll
Animal piano	Dump truck	Mirror	Shopping cart
Busy box house	Gas pump	Movie camera	Tool set
Cash register	Gears toy	Nesting cups	Train set
Doctor's kit	Grocery store	Number pegboard	Water baby

Selection by Community Survey of Preschool Teachers

Cars and trucks	Easel/paints	Magnifying glass	Tinker toys
Climber	Lego/Duplo	Pegboards	Telephones
Doctor's kit	Live plants	Puppets	Typewriter
Dolls and bed	Lotto game	Record player	Water table
Dollhouse	Magnets	Table games	Xylophone

Comparison (Conventional Toy Selection and Arrangement) In the comparison conditions, classroom toys included items recommended by 12 experienced preschool teachers from other local programs for typical children. Participating teachers were each asked to select 20 toys that they believed were most important and interesting to young children, based both on their experience and on the state licensing requirements for developmentally appropriate play materials. Teachers were encouraged to choose the toys they wished to have available for the children in their own classrooms. The 20 items most commonly cited on these surveys (also shown in Table 9.2) were assembled and displayed on toy shelves in the free-play area, replacing the toy rotations used during the systematic package.

Additionally, individualized materials were removed from the hobby boxes and arranged attractively on toy shelves and tables. An identical number of toys was thus available to children in the free-play area throughout all conditions.

Enhanced Materials Package Procedures in the enhanced package condition were similar to those in the standard package, including systematic use of toy rotations and individualized materials located in hobby boxes on teacher-height shelves. Toy rotations were carried out on a more frequent biweekly schedule, so in addition to the standard rotation of toys every Friday morning, toy rotations were also exchanged on Wednesday mornings prior to opening the classroom.

RESULTS

The overall frequency of negative peer-related social behavior varied dramatically across materials and conditions, as shown in Figure 9.2. Negative social behaviors occurred at substantially higher levels in the comparison condition, on some days occurring at twice the level of conditions in which the toy rotations and hobby

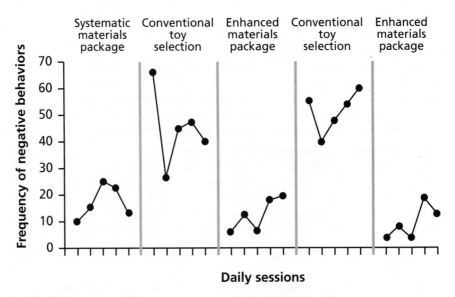

FIGURE 9.2 Frequency of negative peer-related social behaviors of preschool children during baseline (A), comparison conditions (B), and enhanced materials package (C).

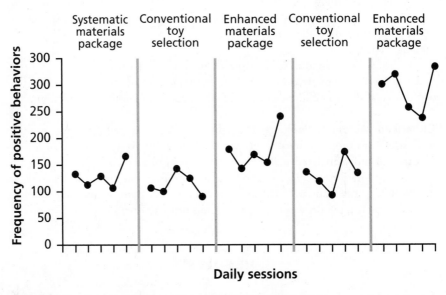

FIGURE 9.3 Frequency of positive peer-related social behaviors of preschool children during baseline (A), comparison conditions (B), and enhanced materials package (C).

boxes were in place. Analysis of individual behaviors revealed the most striking differences in the frequency of negative affect displays. An average of 24 instances per day of negative affect occurred during the comparison condition, in contrast to an average of six instances per day during the enhanced package. The daily frequency of physical aggression during the comparison condition averaged eight incidents, as compared to two incidents during the enhanced package.

The levels of positive peer-related social behavior during each condition are illustrated in Figure 9.3. The frequencies of positive social behavior were similarly high in the standard materials package and in the comparison conditions; however, there was an unanticipated increase in positive behavior during the enhanced conditions.

Teacher ratings (1 = most positive to 5 = least positive) of the materials in the comparison condition averaged 3.53, while ratings of materials in the enhanced package averaged 2.18. Teachers rated the ease of teaching in the comparison conditions at an average of 3.38, and their ratings of ease of teaching in the enhanced conditions averaged 1.54.

DISCUSSION

These findings illustrate the power of materials and environmental factors on the classroom behavior of an inclusive group of preschool-aged children. The functional analysis of classroom preventive arrangements clearly demonstrated that negative social behaviors were highest in the comparison condition, which most closely approximated the toy selection and display procedures in use in classrooms representing traditional "best practices." As a result, toy selection was based on the input of qualified and experienced teachers. There were no apparent differences in the attractiveness of materials in different conditions; however, behavior problems were lower, and children appeared happier under conditions in which a systematic plan accommodated the children's full range of interests and abilities. Novelty of toys was an integral feature of the toy rotation plan, and hobby boxes ensured a convenient mechanism for teachers to readily address children's individual preferences. The toy rotation plan and hobby boxes apparently optimize the potency of play materials, which in turn yields antecedent or preventive control over problem behaviors.

The enhanced package unexpectedly yielded uniquely high levels of positive social behavior. Positive social behaviors were actively taught and rewarded in the preschool, and consequently the levels of these behaviors were high in both baseline and comparison conditions. The more frequent rotations of toys in the enhanced package, which further increased novelty of classroom items, also functioned to create more opportunities for positive social interactions. The effect may be similar to the situation that occurs when there has been a recent classroom shopping trip; everyone is entertained and there is ample opportunity for exchange of preferred toys ("You can play with my new toy if I can play with your new toy").

It is worthwhile to note that these findings occurred in conditions of uniformly high teacher attention. This study confirms the importance of attending to the interface of environmental resources and teacher behavior when designing a preventive behavior management plan. It remains unknown what effect, if any, the environmental conditions studied would have in conditions of low teacher attention.

This study provides an example of the use of functional analysis to evaluate a preventive approach to classroom behavior management. Results also illustrate that developmental appropriateness is a necessary but insufficient condition of inclusive preschool programs. Developmental appropriateness was thus a factor in selecting items for toy rotations, but it was insufficient as a major determinant of toy selection in the comparison condition. Of practical significance, the biweekly toy rotation plan and individualized hobby boxes are amenable for use in virtually any classroom. Families have also shown these procedures are helpful at home.

LOGISTICS OF MANAGING A
PREVENTION PACKAGE

Implementation of a comprehensive prevention plan requires that resources be devoted to scheduling and maintenance of the plan. Trial and error at Walden has generated a number of practical procedures. For example, hobby box toys are labeled with children's names to facilitate cleanup, and index cards on hobby boxes list the toys that should be contained therein. Similarly, toys in the rotation plan are marked by rotation number in indelible marker. A staff member must be designated as the Materials Manager, whose responsibilities include reinforcer assessment and systematic selection of items for hobby boxes (a 10-hour per week assignment in the Walden classroom). Costs of planning and support personnel are involved, but these are less than the costs of teachers who constantly react to problem behaviors.

PROBLEM BEHAVIORS AS
TEACHING OPPORTUNITIES

The problem prevention procedures described above effectively reduce the frequency and severity of problem behaviors, but don't eliminate them altogether. Total suppression of problem behaviors is not a normative goal. When problem behaviors do occur, the key is to use them to identify teaching opportunities that will serve as future preventions.

It is essential to teach verbal alternatives to problem behaviors (Carr & Durand, 1985). The conditions that evoke problem behaviors are actually quite powerful language instruction opportunities. For example, even children with relatively new language can learn to demand desired items with phrases such as "I want" or "hobby box." Functional requests to leave an undesired activity are also learned quickly ("go" to leave morning meeting). More sophisticated means of controlling the environment with language include "trade?" (to get another child's toy), "It's mine" (to protect a toy), "I'm busy now" (to avoid an unwanted teaching interaction), and "Watch me" or "help" to gain teacher attention or assistance.

Extinction is also a powerful and greatly underused behavior management procedure (Sulzer-Azaroff & Mayer, 1991). Teachers must be trained to ignore irritating behaviors, and some acting may be required to control nonverbal reactions to problem behaviors. At Walden, aggression toward teachers is consistently ignored, and quickly eliminated.

Teachers must be trained to avoid inadvertent reinforcement of problem behaviors. It is appropriate for a teacher to ignore a child when he is whining, but care should be taken to insure that whining does not accidentally pay off (if the child needs to be directed to hobby box materials, redirection should occur during a "break" in the child's whining).

At Walden, specific problem behaviors are designated as opportunities to teach classroom rules. For example, children are consistently and matter-of-factly required to pick up toys that have been thrown. Climbing on furniture is handled with a faded guidance procedure (for example, a simple direction is given to "Put your feet on the floor"). If still not responding, the child is guided through climbing down, taking care not to provide vestibular stimulation by swinging the child down from a table). Repeated difficulties in one zone result in matter-of-fact redirection to another activity (changing to another area also changes teachers, which helps to diffuse the potential for power struggles). However, it is important that the number of rules in a classroom be kept to a short list, because a growing list of rules often indicates a breakdown of other preventive efforts.

The "felony offense" at Walden is aggression toward other children. Based on the premise that most peer aggressions are intended to get a response from the targeted child (Patterson, Littman, & Bricker, 1967), the uniform classroom consequence is two minutes apart from other children. A child who aggresses is matter-of-factly redirected to any area free of children, and given something to do (a toy she will play with, although not her most preferred toys). Peer aggressions are monitored carefully for antecedent circumstances, which are notated on a datasheet with attached pencil that is centrally located in the classroom. Repeated peer aggressions may be viewed as indicators of a breakdown in the preventive plan, or as a need for an individualized behavior change program.

INDIVIDUALIZED BEHAVIOR
MANAGEMENT PLANS

A classroom preventive approach can be compatible with direct treatment. Although the Walden peer aggression consequence (in conjunction with the preventive plan) proves effective in the large majority of situations, some children with autism may actually be rewarded by removal from other children. Experience suggests, however, that highly avoidant children are not usually the ones who have difficulties with peer aggression. In fact, peer aggressions may be an encouraging sign of peer awareness. The bottom line is that if a child shows up on the peer aggression chart with regularity, prevention efforts are redoubled, and a proactive individualized plan is developed as needed. Aside from peer aggression, the most frequent targets of Walden individualized plans are isolative or multicausal self-stimulatory behaviors.

Self-stimulatory behavior is seldom directly targeted early in treatment, and for some children it drops out given prevention and teaching. In the child's last year prior to kindergarten, residual autistic behaviors receive increased priority, in the interest of normalization for the child's future kindergarten placement.

A series of procedural safeguards limit the number of individualized treatment plans. First, program evaluation must document full operation of the prevention plan. Objective data collection and functional analysis must then be arranged. Next, a detailed individualized program must be prepared in writing, along with signed consent of parents. Administrators must also sign an agreement to provide training for implementation of the program, and initial at the time of (at least) weekly monitoring. Presentation of aversive consequences is not an option at Walden, so individualized plans must always consist of intensive teaching of alternative responses. The level of effort required to obtain an approved individualized plan helps minimize their use. By restricting individualized treatment plans to the fewest possible cases, teachers can actually remember and implement individualized procedures consistently.

CONCLUSIONS

A preventive approach buys time to teach language and social behaviors that crowd out problem behaviors or make problem behaviors unnecessary. This approach takes a lot of effort, but so do problem behaviors.

It must be acknowledged that the radically different behavior management approach at Walden doesn't always work to get rid of problem behaviors. But neither does direct treatment. The central issue is that prime skill-building time hasn't been squandered on a series of behavior reduction attempts. Although a traditional behavioral approach assumes that problem behaviors must be treated first or the child cannot attend to instruction, experience at Walden has shown that this is not the case.

A comprehensive preventive plan includes many of the accepted least restrictive behavior reduction procedures. The major difference with traditional approaches is in how problem behaviors and treatment priorities are conceptualized, and the resulting distribution of treatment time.

It may well be argued that Walden provides an "accommodating" environment that is not representative of the real world or future classrooms. For this reason, kindergarten preparation typically involves direct preparation of a child for the conditions that will be in place in the next classroom. For example, the incorporation of future classroom "schedules" has become a standard practice.

The challenge of preventive preschool behavior management is to create educational environments in which children can have fun as they learn. A commitment to prevention would require a radical overhaul in the conceptualization and design of many classrooms. Benefits would extend beyond the control of problem behaviors to vastly increased opportunities for learning. Think how good such advances would be for all preschool children. Consider how many more regular preschool settings could provide for children with special needs.

AUTHOR NOTES

Research and development activities were supported in part by Grant No. G008535122, G008019001, and H133G10162 from the National Institute on Disability and Rehabilitation Research, OSERS, U.S. Department of Education. The original functional analysis study was supported in part through a contract with the Oregon Research and Training Center for Community-Referenced, Nonaversive Behavior Management. The opinions expressed herein do not necessarily reflect the policy of the U.S. Department of Education, and no official endorsement should be inferred.

Acknowledgment is due to the Walden teachers, past and present, whose extraordinary patience has made possible these developments. Credit for input and debate on the conceptualization of this approach is owed to Todd Risley and Tom Coakley.

Correspondence may be addressed to Gail G. McGee at the Emory Autism Resource Center, 718 Gatewood Road, Department of Psychiatry and Behavioral Sciences, Emory University School of Medicine, Atlanta, Georgia 30322.

REFERENCES

Burns, J. J. (1991). Using normative data and descriptive analyses to guide and interpret social interventions. Paper presented in G. G. McGee (Chair), *Empirical support for an incidental teaching approach to early social intervention for children with autism.* Symposium presented at the annual meeting of the Association for Behavior Analysis, Atlanta.

Carr, E. G., & Durand, M. V. (1985). Reducing behavior problems through functional communication training. *Journal of Applied Behavior Analysis, 18,* 111–126.

Carr, E. G., & Kologinsky, E. (1983). Acquisition of sign language by autistic children: II. Spontaneity and generalization effects. *Journal of Applied Behavior Analysis, 16,* 297–314.

Cataldo, M. F., & Risley, T. R. (1974). Evaluation of living environments: The MAN-IFEST description of ward activities. In P. O. Davison, F. W. Clark, & C. A. Hammerlynck (Eds.), *Evaluation of behavioral programs in community, residential, and school settings.* Champaign, IL: Research Press.

Daly, T. (1993). *Comparison of typical preschoolers' behavior in mainstreamed and non-mainstreamed classrooms.* Paper presented at the biennial meeting of the Society for Research in Child Development, New Orleans.

Datillo, J. (1986). Computerized assessment of preference for severely handicapped individuals. *Journal of Applied Behavior Analysis, 19,* 445–448.

Doke, L. A., & Risley, T. R. (1972). The organization of day-care environments: Required versus optional activities. *Journal of Applied Behavior Analysis, 5,* 405–420.

Dunlap, G, & Robbins, F. R. (1991). Current perspectives in service delivery for young children with autism. *Comprehensive Mental Health Care, 1,* 177–194.

Dyer, K. I. (1987). The competition of autistic stereotyped behavior with usual and specially assessed reinforcers. *Research in Developmental Disabilities, 8,* 607–626.

Egel, A. L. (1981). Reinforcer variation: Implications for motivating developmentally disabled children. *Journal of Applied Behavior Analysis, 14,* 345–350.

Farmer-Dougan, V., & McGee, G. G. (1986). *Assessment of child-selected reinforcers in an integrated program: Effects on verbalization and engagement.* Unpublished manuscript.

Ferrari, M., & Harris, S. (1981). The limits and motivating potential of sensory stimuli as reinforcers for autistic children. *Journal of Applied Behavior Analysis, 14,* 339–343.

Green, C. W., Reid, D. H., White, L. K., Halford, R. C., Brittain, D. P., & Gardner, S. M. (1988). Identifying reinforcers for persons with profound handicaps: Staff opinion versus systematic assessment of preferences. *Journal of Applied Behavior Analysis, 21,* 32–43.

Guaralnick, M. J., & Groom, J. M. (1987). The peer relations of mildly delayed and non-handicapped preschool children in a mainstreamed playgroup. *Child Development, 58,* 1556–1572.

Harris, S. L., & Handleman, J. S. (1994). *Preschool education programs for children with autism.* New York: Pro-Ed.

Hart, B. M., & Risley, T. R. (1982). *How to use incidental teaching for elaborating language.* Lawrence, KS: H & H Enterprises.

Koegel, R. L., Koegel, L. K., & Surratt, A. (1992). Language intervention and disruptive behavior in preschool children with autism. *Journal of Autism and Developmental Disorders, 22,* 141–153.

Krantz, P., & Risley, T. R. (1977). *Behavioral ecology in the classroom.* Lawrence, KS: Center for Applied Behavior Analysis.

LeLaurin, K., & Risley, T. R. (1972). The organization of day-care environments: "Zone" versus "man-to-man" staff assignments. *Journal of Applied Behavior Analysis, 5,* 225–232.

Mason, S. A., McGee, G. G., Farmer-Dougan, V., & Risley, T. R. (1989). A practical strategy for ongoing reinforcer assessment. *Journal of Applied Behavior Analysis, 22,* 171–179.

McClannahan, L. E., & Risley, T. R. (1975). Design of living environments for nursing home residents: Increasing participation in recreation activities. *Journal of Applied Behavior Analysis, 8,* 261–268.

McGee, G. G. (1994). Environmental influences of social behavior in children with autism and typical children. In R. Koegel (Chair), *Autism: Intervention and issues related to socialization, language, disruptive behavior and families.* Symposium presented at the annual meeting of the Association for Behavior Analysis, Atlanta.

McGee, G. G. (1993). *Environmental variables affecting social development in children with autism and normally-developing children.* Invited address presented at the Child Psychiatry Grand Rounds of the Emory University School of Medicine (Division of Child Psychiatry) and Parkwood Hospital, Atlanta.

McGee, G. G. (1992). *An empirical approach to developing social interventions for children with autism.* Invited address presented at the annual meeting of the Southeastern Association for Behavior Analysis, Asheville, NC.

McGee, G. G. (1988). Early prevention of severe behavior problems. In R. Horner & G. Dunlap (Eds.), *Behavior management and community integration.* Washington, D.C.: Monograph of proceedings of a symposium invited by Madeleine Will, Assistant Secretary, Office of Special Education and Rehabilitative Services, U.S. Department of Education.

McGee, G. G., Daly, T., Izeman, S. G., Mann, L., & Risley, T. R. (1991). Use of classroom materials to promote preschool engagement. *Teaching Exceptional Children, 23,* 44–47.

McGee, G. G., Daly, T., & Jacobs, H. A. (1994). The Walden Preschool. In S. L. Harris &

J. S. Handleman (Eds.), *Preschool education programs for children with autism* (pp. 127–162). New York: Pro-Ed.

McGee, G. G., Daly, T., & Morrier, M. (1993). *Little Walden: Model treatment for children with autism.* Paper presented at the annual meeting of the Southeastern Division of Early Childhood (Council for Exceptional Children), Birmingham, AL.

McGee, G. G., Jacobs, H. A., & Regnier, M. C. (1993). Preparation of families for incidental teaching and advocacy for their children with autism. *OSERS News in Print, 5,* 9–13.

McGee, G. G., Krantz, P. J., & McClannahan, L. E. (1986). An extension of incidental teaching procedures to reading instruction for autistic children. *Journal of Applied Behavior Analysis, 19,* 147–157.

McGee, G. G., Krantz, P. J., & McClannahan, L. E. (1985). The facilitative effects of incidental teaching on preposition use by autistic children. *Journal of Applied Behavior Analysis, 18,* 17–31.

McGee, G. G., Paradis, T., & Feldman, R. S. (1993). Free effects of integration on levels of autistic behavior. *Topics in Early Childhood Special Education, 13,* 57–67.

McWilliam, R. A. (1991). *Teaching Exceptional Children, 23.*

McWilliam, R. A., Trivette, C. M., & Dunst, C. J. (1985). Behavior engagement as a measure of the efficacy of early intervention. *Analysis and Intervention in Developmental Disabilities (Special issue: Early intervention), 5,* 59–71.

O'Brien, M., Porterfield, P. J., Herbert-Jackson, E., & Risley, T. R. (1979). *The toddler center manual: A practical guide to day care for one- and two-year olds.* Baltimore: University Park Press.

Pace, G. M., Ivancic, M. T., Edwards, G. L., Iwata, B. A., & Page, T. J. (1985). Assessment of stimulus preference and reinforcer value with profoundly retarded individuals. *Journal of Applied Behavior Analysis, 18,* 249–255.

Patterson, G. R., Littman, R. A., & Bricker, W. (1967). Assertive behavior in children: A step toward a theory of aggres-sion. *Monographs of the Society for Research in Child Development, 32,* (Serial No. 113).

Powers, M. (1994). The Berkshire Hills Learning Center. In S. Harris & J. Handleman (Eds.), *Preschool education programs for children with autism.* New York: Pro-Ed.

Repp, A. C., Barton, L. E., & Brulle, A. R. (1983). A comparison of two procedures for programming the differential reinforcement of other behaviors. *Journal of Applied Behavior Analysis, 16,* 435–445.

Rincover, A., & Newsom, C. D. (1985). The relative motivational properties of sensory and edible reinforcers in teaching autistic children. *Journal of Applied Behavior Analysis, 18,* 237–248.

Rincover, A., Newsom, C. D., Lovaas, O. I., & Koegel, R. L. (1977). Some motivational properties of sensory stimulation in psychotic children. *Journal of Experimental Child Psychology, 24,* 312–323.

Risley, T. R. (1991). *Hallmarks of program quality.* Address presented at a community colloquium sponsored by the Emory Autism Resource Center, Emory University School of Medicine, Atlanta.

Schopler, E., Reichler, R. J., DeVellis, R. F., & Daly, K. (1980). Toward objective classification of childhood autism: Childhood Autism Rating Scale (CARS). *Journal of Autism and Developmental Disorders, 10,* 91–103.

Shores, R. E., Jack, S. L., Gunter, P. L., Ellis, D. N., DeBriere, T. J., & Wehby, J. H. (1993). Classroom interactions of children with behavior disorders. *Journal of Emotional and Behavioral Disorders, 1,* 27–39.

Strain, P. S. (1990). LRE for preschool children with handicaps: What we know, what we should be doing. *Journal of Early Intervention, 14,* 291–296.

Sulzer-Azaroff, E. & Mayer, G. R. (1991). *Behavior analysis for lasting change.* Philadelphia: Holt, Rinehart, & Winston.

Twardosz, S., Cataldo, M. F., & Risley, T. R. (1974). Open environment design for infant and toddler day care. *Journal of Applied Behavior Analysis, 7,* 529–549.

Wacker, D. P., Berg, W. K., Wiggins, B., Muldoon, M., & Cavanaugh, J. (1985). Evaluation of reinforcer preferences for profoundly handicapped students. *Journal of Applied Behavior Analysis, 18,* 173–178.

Williams, J. A., Koegel, R. L., & Egel, A. L. (1981). Response reinforcer relationships and improved learning in autistic children. *Journal of Applied Behavior Analysis, 14,* 53–60.

Winett, R. A., & Winkler, R. C. (1972). Current behavior modification in the classroom: Be still, be quiet, be docile. *Journal of Applied Behavior Analysis, 5,* 499–504.

Zahn-Waxler, C., Radke-Yarrow, M., & King, R. A. (1979). Child-rearing and children's prosocial initiations toward victims of distress. *Child Development, 50,* 319–330.

10

Assessment-Based Interventions for Children with Emotional and Behavioral Disorders

LEE KERN
GLEN DUNLAP

INTRODUCTION

Most functional assessment experiments published in journals involve persons with mental retardation. The last chapter discussed another group, preschool children with autism. This chapter extends our field by presenting a program for students with emotional and behavioral disorders.

Kern and Dunlap argue for assessment-based interventions, and note that such interventions can be grouped into two categories: (a) teaching functionally equivalent behaviors as alternatives to problem behaviors when assessment data indicate that specific behaviors are maintaining the problem, and (b) changing environmental stimuli when assessment data indicate that particular setting events or antecedents are exerting stimulus control over the problem behavior.

This chapter presents a case study illustrating how the authors develop specific hypotheses about controlling environmental variables and then make programmatic changes specific to those variables. It is a particularly good demonstration of reasons not to use a cookbook approach where we select reductive procedures (like time-out, DRO) from an arsenal known to us or available to us in books.

The authors conclude by discussing future directions for functional assessment, such as in-volving students in the assessment, special considerations with complex behavioral problem repertoires and environments, and functional assessment settings. As such, they continue to stretch the field's objectives, moving from continued direct replication to more systematic replication.

An exciting and important development in support programs for people with disabilities has been the emergence of interventions based on an individualized understanding of the interactions between behavior and the environment (Carr, Robinson, & Palumbo, 1990; Repp, Felce, & Barton, 1988). This development has been most apparent in the area of behavioral support (Horner et al., 1990). Functional assessment and functional analysis procedures have produced valuable insights that can be used to develop effective intervention programs for a broad range of behavioral challenges (Dunlap et al., 1993; Lennox & Miltenberger, 1989). In this chapter, we will address the use of assessment-based interventions with children who have emotional and behavioral disorders.

We are using the term "assessment-based interventions" to refer to behavioral change programs that are derived from a process of systematic assessment. The assessment process is a key component, designed to identify functional relations that describe causal interactions between stimuli or circumstances in the environment and an identified target behavior. Many authors in recent years have described useful strategies to accumulate assessment data, including surveys, interviews, direct observation and descriptive analyses, and experimental manipulations. We will not review these methods because they have been described extensively in other sources (for example, Dunlap & Kern, 1993; O'Neill et al., 1990), including many of the chapters in this book.

The objective of the assessment phase is to develop an understanding that will lead to more effective, efficient, and positive interventions. Some authors (Dunlap & Kern, 1993; Repp, Felce, & Barton, 1988) have proposed a process in which assessment data are summarized as hypothesis statements, which are then formulated as intervention components. Regardless of how the process is described, the challenge is to synthesize and interpret assessment data so that they link logically to specific intervention strategies (Horner, Sprague, & Flannery, 1993).

The interventions that are derived from functional assessments can be grouped in two categories. The first is based on assessment data that implicate specific reinforcers in the maintenance of the problem behavior. The interventions in this category include teaching functionally equivalent responses as alternatives to the problem behavior (Carr, 1988; Carr & Durand, 1985; Durand, 1990) and simply rearranging the contingencies of reinforcement, as in differential reinforcement of other behavior. The second category is derived from data that implicate antecedent, setting, and contextual events in the occurrence of problem behavior. This is an issue of stimulus control (Halle & Spradlin, 1993) and involves removal or amelioration of stimuli associated with problem behaviors, and introduction or enhancement of stimuli associated with desirable patterns of responding (for example, Singer, Singer, & Horner, 1987; Touchette,

MacDonald, & Langer, 1985; Winterling, Dunlap, & O'Neill, 1987). Both types of assessment-based interventions have been demonstrated to produce impressive effects with a variety of severe and challenging behaviors. It is important to reiterate, as many authors have emphasized (for example, Carr, Robinson, & Palumbo, 1990; Horner et al., 1990), that the effectiveness of these procedures is dependent upon the precision with which the assessment process delineates functional variables for the individual and circumstances in question.

Although the literature documenting the process and effects of functional assessment and assessment-based interventions is accumulating at an impressive rate, it has been limited largely to individuals who have developmental and intellectual disabilities. Until recently there have been very few reported applications with other populations; however, that is beginning to change (for example, Dunlap & dePerczel, 1990; Scott, 1994).

One group of children that has seemed especially appropriate for assessment-based interventions is the population generally referred to as having emotional and behavioral disorders. These children often are placed in special education programs due to their acting-out behaviors and noncompliance. These behaviors should be amenable to functional assessment procedures. In addition, a number of researchers and evaluators (for example, Knitzer, Steinberg, & Fleisch, 1990) have stated that behavioral support programs in these children's classrooms have lacked individualization and can be characterized as highly coercive.

This chapter provides a general overview of assessment-based research with children who have emotional and behavioral challenges (EBD). We begin with a description of the population and the difficulties that these children experience, and then discuss some of the few studies that have described assessment-based interventions (focusing on the most recent investigations that have explicitly identified functional relationships between these children's problem behaviors and specific variables in their environments). We conclude with a discussion of special considerations and future directions.

POPULATION CHARACTERISTICS

Children and youth described as having emotional and behavioral challenges comprise a complex group. This is partly because of inconsistencies and deficiencies in identifying them. Wide ranges in published prevalence data from a variety of service agencies underscores the problem (Koyanagi & Gaines, 1993). In a comprehensive review of prevalence studies, Brandenburg, Friedman, and Silver (1987) concluded that, at any point in time, between 14 and 19 percent of youth experience moderate or severe emotional disturbance. Each year approximately 375,000 pupils nationwide receive a label of emotionally or behaviorally disordered. This group accounts for approximately 9 percent of all children with disabilities, making it the fourth most common category.

Little data are available on personal, educational, and demographic characteristics of this group of individuals (Cullinan, Epstein, & Sabornie, 1992); however, a few recent longitudinal and epidemiologic studies have provided some marker variables. The age of onset of emotional and behavioral problems appears to be early, with the mean being six years (Friedman et al., 1988), but services are generally not provided until several years later. Almost half of these children live in single-parent homes (Freidman et al., 1988). Only one third live with both parents, compared with over two-thirds of students without disabilities (Cullinan, Epstein, & Sabornie, 1992). IQ scores typically fall in the low average range, the mean being approximately 86 (Kaufman, 1989; Valdez, Williamson, & Wagner, 1990).

As defined by Public Law 94-142, students receiving EBD services in educational settings must demonstrate deficiencies in academic performance. Indeed, available data indicates that individuals identified by school systems as EBD do experience academic challenges (for example, Ruhl & Berlinghoff, 1992). Studies report that as many as 81 percent of students described as behaviorally disordered have academic difficulties ranging from specific academic skill deficits to functional illiteracy (Cullinan, Epstein, & Lloyd, 1983).

Difficulty with social skills is also ranked as a common and severe problem among children described as EBD. Poor peer interaction is the most frequently-cited social deficit (for example, Gresham, 1982; Hollinger, 1987; Reiher, 1992). Other social skills deficits include low self-esteem or self-concept, poor relationships with adults, lack of responsibility or independence, difficulty in expressing feelings appropriately, anxiety, and trouble adjusting to change (Reiher, 1992). Additional behavioral difficulties commonly reported in this population include noncompliance, aggression, disruption, and inappropriate verbalizations (for example, Epstein, Kaufman, & Cullinan, 1985; Mattison et al., 1986).

Nationwide, segregated education has become customary with this population. Fewer than half of these students receive any of their educational instruction in regular classrooms (Foley & Epstein, 1993). Most of these students spend the majority of their time in self-contained classrooms (Cullinan et al., 1992). Almost 60 percent are served primarily in what could be considered the most restrictive educational placements. These include homebound instruction, residential school programs, alternative schools, and self-contained classrooms.

A number of studies have chronicled serious inadequacies in the educational services provided for this population. These include deficiencies in identifying children needing services (Grosenick et al., 1991), failure to provide an adequate range of services (Nelson & Pearson, 1991), and an overemphasis on behavior control with a concurrent neglect of student adjustment and learning (Knitzer et al., 1990).

School dropout data for this population are also striking. The rate of dropout for students with serious emotional disturbance is 50 percent, compared with a dropout rate of 32.5 percent for all students with disabilities. Only 42 percent graduate from high school, compared to an overall graduation rate of 56. 1 percent among all students with disabilities (National Longitudinal Transition Study of Special Education Students, 1991).

The problems these students experience in their school years do not readily dissipate, and a pattern of continued problems endures in later life (Koyanagi & Gaines, 1993). Employment difficulties are significant; only 44 percent are employed two years after leaving school, compared with 61 percent of all students. Those who do obtain employment are often unable to hold onto a job. Many become involved with the criminal justice system. Of youth out of school for two years, the arrest rate for individuals with classifications of emotional disturbance is two and a half times that of the general population. Within two years, almost 4 percent are living in correctional facilities, contrasted with only 0.3 percent of all youth with disabilities (Koyanagi & Gaines, 1993).

This data emphasizes the need to develop effective supports for these children. Although the data reveal a system that is currently failing these children, there are indications that the problems are surmountable. Sixty percent of individuals described as emotionally disturbed who completed high school were employed after two years, a rate comparable to the general population. Improving these students' educational experience ascends as a national priority (Koyanagi & Gaines, 1993). We believe that assessment-based intervention procedures provide a model for beginning to accomplish this lofty and necessary undertaking. In this chapter, we describe the preliminary applications of these strategies and propose areas of future inquiry.

ASSESSMENT-BASED INTERVENTIONS

Until recently, assessment information was rarely considered when developing specific interventions for children described as emotionally or behaviorally disordered. Most intervention programs have used standardized approaches or packages designed to teach particular skills or reduce problem behavior, without apparent regard for the individual characteristics of the student or the variables that might govern the student's existing repertoire. In a review of studies published in the last two decades in which interventions were implemented in educational settings with children identified as having behavioral or emotional challenges (Dunlap & dePerczel, 1990), only a few reports described preintervention assessment as being at all relevant to the behavior change procedures that were evaluated. Those studies reflect an effort to link interventions to assessment, and in particular, to environmental variables that might be related to the target behavior. For the most part, these studies involved direct observations of some form, and through these observations, specific variables or circumstances were associated with undesirable behavior. As a result, individualized interventions were developed, which led to improved student behavior.

In two studies, Knapczyk (1988, 1992) analyzed interactions that preceded aggressive behavior. The participants were six adolescents boys receiving special education services for students with behavioral and learning difficulties. The students were videotaped during problematic times. Evaluations of the videotapes indicated that specific events were frequently followed by aggressive behavior. For example, when peers failed to respond to a greeting or request for an object or information, aggression would follow. Following these assessments, the students were shown the videotapes and given specific feedback as well as opportunities to rehearse appropriate alternative responses to the events that typically resulted in aggression. The results of Knapczyk's analyses indicated very encouraging effects on aggression and on desirable interactions.

Bornstein, Bellack and Hersen (1980) used the Behavioral Assertiveness Test for Children to assess positive and negative assertion skills in four children with psychiatric diagnoses. Group interactions were also videotaped and rated for eye contact, hostile tone, requests for new behavior, and overall assertiveness. Social skills training was then provided in the form of role playing with feedback, modeling, and specific instructions on interpersonal situations. Rehearsal continued until criteria were met for each target behavior. This study demonstrated a social skills training approach that was based on assessments of the individual students' preintervention performance.

Behaviors related to academic activities have been targeted in a few studies. Center, Deitz, and Kaufman (1982) assessed the effects of different levels of task difficulty on the inappropriate behaviors of 15 students described as having behavior disorders. Using a series of reversal designs, they found increases in inappropriate behavior when students were given math tasks in which previous success had been below 40 percent. These effects were evident whether or not a reinforcement contingency was provided. The students' behavior improved substantially when tasks were provided in which success level had exceeded 60 percent. This finding is consistent with literature on developmental disabilities (Weeks & Gaylord-Ross, 1981) and reflects a growing emphasis on the assessment and manipulation of variables that are within the curriculum and instruction of students with challenging behaviors (for example, Dunlap et al., 1991; Munk & Repp, 1994).

Spirito et al. (1981) conducted an assessment of the progression of aggressive behaviors exhibited by a 10-year-old boy described as emotionally disturbed. Descriptions of antecedent and consequent stimuli were noted by his teacher. A review of these notes enabled the authors to rule out several variables including a specific subject, peer, activity, or time of the day; however, outbursts were generally preceded by comments about assignment difficulty. Because his assignments were commensurate with his previous performance, the authors hypothesized that the outbursts resulted from a fear of his teacher's evaluation of his school performance. Intervention consisted of a stress inoculation procedure. Results of a behavior rating scale indicated improved behavior following intervention.

In a study by Platt, Harris, and Clements (1980), the usefulness of individualized reinforcement schedules was assessed. Participants were 12 adolescents with emotional and/or learning disabilities. The density of reinforcer delivery was varied and both contingent and noncontingent reinforcement was provided. The results showed that when reinforcement was individualized, attending behavior was increased for two students. However, the other students' attending behavior was not affected by changes in the density of reinforcement when it was provided contingently versus noncontingently. The findings indicate that the effects of reinforcement differ among individuals. The authors believe contingent reinforcement may be more restrictive for some students. They also suggest that individual student characteristics need to be carefully examined, and individualized reinforcement schedules may be necessary for students who appear to be motivated primarily by extrinsic reinforcement. The results of this study underscore the importance of individualized assessment and intervention.

Truant behavior in three adolescents described as behaviorally disordered was reduced in a study by Schloss, Kane, and Miller (1981). Questionnaires were administered to parents, students, and teachers to determine variables that might be associated with truancy. Based on the results of these questionnaires, individualized interventions were developed consisting of manipulations at school to increase student satisfaction (such as communicating successful school experiences to parents, providing reinforcement for completed work), reducing reinforcement at home when students did not attend school (for example, removing television privileges, requiring school work be completed), teaching skills to improve social behavior, and providing additional courses in the student's area of interest. School attendance improved dramatically following intervention.

In each of these studies, the interventions were based on some type of assessment information. Various forms of observation helped determine the target behaviors and/or tailored the support strategies so the interventions were more individualized than they could have otherwise been. This integration of assessment data, however, has been the exception. The great majority of intervention studies with this population of children have neglected to incorporate (or report) assessment information.

RECENT RESEARCH ON
FUNCTIONAL ASSESSMENT

Although concentrated efforts to develop functional, assessment-based interventions for children with EBD have lagged behind similar advancements in developmental disabilities, there is a growing literature advocating and empirically demonstrating the efficacy of this perspective (for example, Foster-Johnson & Dunlap, 1993; Topper et al., 1994). The most recent work in this area has differed from the earlier work described above in that there is now a more explicit focus on refining and articulating the assessment process. This has been done in several ways. First, some research has focused on developing systematic assessment procedures or applying assessment procedures used with other populations to identify variables associated with target behaviors. Other research has directly manipulated aspects of the environment, thus indirectly implicating variables controlling behavior, and at the same time suggesting effective interventions. Still other research has articulated the entire operation with empirical detail on all phases of the assessment-intervention process. Examples of these endeavors are described below.

Shores, Gunter, and their colleagues (1993) delineated an assessment process called lag sequential analysis, which is used to identify variables associated with a target behavior. Using laptop computers, data are collected on a broad array of social behaviors. For example, occurrence of the following behaviors might be coded: compliance, social mends and instructional mends (to do something and to discontinue doing something), handraises, consequences, physical interactions, verbal interactions, disruptive behavior, withdrawal, talk, etc. The frequencies of each coded event and the proportion of events that precede or follow is then calculated. This analysis quantifies the probability of occurrence of each coded event that is antecedent and consequent to the behavior of interest, and referred to as a conditional probability.

Using this procedure, Shores et al. (1993) conducted an extensive analysis of the interactions between teachers and students described as having severe behavior disorders. They found that the most probable student–teacher interaction was a teacher mand followed by student compliance, most often followed by an additional teacher mand. Positive consequences were seldom delivered by teachers. The authors suggested that overall classroom interactions for these students were not positive. They recommended modifications in teacher behavior to set the stage for more positive teacher and peer interactions.

In a series of single-subject experiments conducted by Gunter et al. (1993), the methods of lag sequential analysis were used to assess events antecedent or subsequent to the disruptive behavior of two students described as having severe behavior disorders. Lag sequential analysis with the first student showed a high probability of handraises followed by disruptions, followed by teacher attention. A successful intervention was then developed consisting of quickly responding to handraising and ignoring disruptions. The lag sequential analysis conducted with the second student showed a high probability of teacher attention following disruptive student behavior. This descriptive analysis led the authors to prescribe an intervention consisting of DRI and planned ignoring; this resulted in reduced frequencies of disruptive behavior.

Cooper et al. (1990) applied functional assessment procedures in an outpatient clinic setting. They used brief functional analyses to determine variables maintaining problem behavior of children described as having conduct disorders. During 90-minute sessions, children were observed under alternating conditions: (a) difficult task requirements with high parent attention; (b) difficult task requirements with low parent attention; (c) easy task requirements with high parent attention; and (d) easy task requirements with low parent attention. Of eight participants, seven demonstrated clear differences across conditions. Based on the results of this assessment, parents were provided a description of maintaining variables, and recommendations for intervention based on the best conditions. Parent ratings indicated that these interventions were both effective and acceptable for periods up to six months following the assessments.

In our own research activities, we have explored the use of functional assessment strategies in public school settings for children with EBD since early 1991 (Dunlap & dePerczel, 1990). In several of the studies, assessments have suggested specific curricular modifications. For example, Dunlap et al. (1995) found that some children were especially disruptive during particular academic activities, but that their disruptions were dramatically reduced when the assignments were modified to incorporate the students' idiosyncratic interests. Similarly, Dunlap et al., (1994), used choice making to decrease serious problem behaviors for three students.

One report (Dunlap et al., 1993) focused most directly on the process of functional analysis; data were presented to demonstrate the feasibility and validity of functional assessment procedures in classroom settings serving children described as severely emotionally disturbed. Five elementary school children participated. A variety of assessments were conducted, including a detailed interview and direct observations in the students' classrooms. From these assessments, and with consultation from the classroom teachers, individualized hypotheses were developed for each of the students. The hypotheses were based on information from the interviews as well as direct observations, and they had to identify specific variables that could be manipulated in the classroom setting. This process led to two or three hypotheses for each participant. The hypotheses implicated a variety of contextual, antecedent, curricular, and consequence events.

Each of the hypotheses was then tested in the ongoing classroom settings through a series of reversal manipulations during which levels of individually-defined desirable and undesirable behavior were observed. The tests confirmed the validity of the hypotheses. Three hypotheses were developed for one participant, a six-year-old girl whose target behaviors were aggression, property destruction, noncompliance, and leaving the classroom. The modifications derived from the hypotheses offered the student a choice from a menu of academic tasks, incorporating preferred activities into academic tasks, and increasing praise statements and teacher proximity (Gunter et al., 1995). Each of these changes produced substantially improved behavior.

Another strategy has been to conduct intensive case studies. For example, we reported the experience of a student with multiple disabilities and very serious challenging behavior as she participated in a comprehensive functional assessment process (Dunlap & Kern, 1993; Dunlap et al., 1991). In her case, we developed and experimentally verified four hypotheses, each of which related to a feature of her curriculum. When these features were incorporated throughout her school day, her problem behavior was eliminated for the remainder of the school year. In the following paragraphs, we illustrate the process in further detail by presenting another case study (Kern et al., 1994a).

Case Illustration

The participant in this study was Eddie, an 11-year-old boy in the fifth grade who was described as having severe behavioral disorders. His tests showed above-average intelligence and he was generally a pleasant child who interacted positively with many peers and adults. However, they considered him "unable to cope with a regular classroom routine," and he displayed occasional disruptive and emotional outbursts with a consistent failure to complete academic assignments.

In developing support for Eddie, we used a two-phase process of assessment and intervention. Assessment data were gathered and used to develop hypotheses regarding undesirable classroom behavior. After testing the accuracy of the hypotheses, interventions were implemented in various academic subjects, resulting in significantly improved behavior.

During Phase I, *functional assessment,* hypotheses were developed identifying specific relations between features of Eddie's academic environment and the occurrence and nonoccurrence of undesirable behavior. To develop these hypotheses, several assessments were conducted. Descriptive data on severe behavior problems, using an A-B-C format, were collected throughout the school day. A functional assessment interview was conducted with each of Eddie's teachers. The interview was developed specifically for use in classroom settings and consisted of 22 questions designed to identify stimuli or setting events in the classroom that may have caused or maintained undesirable behavior. Finally, a Student-Assisted Functional Assessment Interview (Kern et al., 1994b) was administered to solicit information directly from Eddie regarding features of academic tasks and the classroom environment that he considered to be related to desirable and undesirable behavior.

FIGURE 10.1 Student-Assisted Functional Assessment Interview

Student _____

Date _____

Interviewer _____

SECTION I

1. In general, is your work too hard for you?	Always	Sometimes	Never
2. In general, is your work too easy for you?	Always	Sometimes	Never
3. When you ask for help appropriately, do you get it?	Always	Sometimes	Never
4. Do you think work periods for each subject are too long?	Always	Sometimes	Never
5. Do you think work periods for each subject are too short?	Always	Sometimes	Never
6. When you do seatwork, do you do better when someone works with you?	Always	Sometimes	Never
7. Do you think people notice when you do a good job?	Always	Sometimes	Never
8. Do you think you get the points or rewards you deserve when you do good work?	Always	Sometimes	Never
9. Do you think you would do better in school if you received more rewards?	Always	Sometimes	Never
10. In general, do you find your work interesting?	Always	Sometimes	Never
11. Are there things in the classroom that distract you?	Always	Sometimes	Never
12. Is your work challenging enough for you?	Always	Sometimes	Never

SECTION II

1. When do you think you have the fewest problems with _____ in school?
   (target behavior)
   Why do you not have problems during this/these time(s)?
2. When do you think you have the most problems with _____ in school?
   (target behavior)
   Why do you have problems during this/these time(s)?
3. What changes could be made so you would have fewer problems with _____?
   (target behavior)
4. What kind of rewards would you like to earn for good behavior or good school work?
5. What are your favorite activities at school?
6. What are your hobbies or interests?
7. If you had the chance, what activities would you like to do that you don't have the opportunity to do now?

Probes

SECTION III

Rate how much you like the following subjects:

	Not at all		Fair		Very much
Reading	1	2	3	4	5
Math	1	2	3	4	5
Spelling	1	2	3	4	5
Handwriting	1	2	3	4	5
Science	1	2	3	4	5
Social Studies	1	2	3	4	5
English	1	2	3	4	5
Music	1	2	3	4	5
P.E.	1	2	3	4	5
Computers	1	2	3	4	5
Art	1	2	3	4	5

SECTION IV

What do you like about Reading?

What don't you like about Reading?

What do you like about Math?

What don't you like about Math?

What do you like about Spelling?

What don't you like about Spelling?

What do you like about Handwriting?

What don't you like about Handwriting?

What do you like about Science?

What don't you like about Science?

What do you like about Social Studies?

What don't you like about Social Studies?

What do you like about English?

What don't you like about English?

What do you like about Music?

What don't you like about Music?

What do you like about P.E.?

What don't you like about P.E.?

What do you like about Computers?

What don't you like about Computers?

What do you like about Art?

What don't you like about Art?

SOURCE: Kern et al. (1994b). Reprinted with permission.

Results of the ABC data indicated undesirable behavior occurred when academic expectations were placed on Eddie. Behavior problems were absent when academic expectations were removed (during physical education, lunch, free time). These data also suggested that undesirable behavior occurred regardless of the amount of teacher attention Eddie received. A clear sequence of disruptive emotional behavior also emerged from these observations. Eddie was frequently off-task throughout academic periods. When asked to hand in assignments or when reprimanded for failing to complete assigned work, he would cry, tantrum, and sometimes engage in self-injurious responding (head hitting, hand biting). These observations suggested that one function of the undesirable behaviors was to escape from tasks. The next step was to determine specific curricular features that might influence this escape behavior.

Weekly meetings were held between the consultants and the teachers. During these meetings hypotheses were generated and discussed. Hypotheses that were not reasonable to all of the participants were discarded. For example, because Eddie stated that his work was sometimes boring, one of the consultants hypothesized that Eddie would be more engaged if he was provided a choice of academic activities. However, Eddie's teachers had observed that Eddie experienced some difficulty making decisions, that choice making did not seem to be a significant reinforcer, and it created frustration for Eddie. Therefore, this hypothesis was dismissed. In the course of these meetings, five hypotheses were generated. They are listed in Box 10, and explained below Box 10.

BOX 10   The Five Hypotheses Developed During the Functional Assessment Process for Eddie

1. Eddie is more likely to be engaged in his work when activities do not require excessive amounts of handwriting.
2. Eddie is more likely to be engaged in academic tasks that require problem-solving skills rather than drill and practice type exercises.
3. Eddie is more likely to be engaged academically when provided with multiple brief tasks during an academic session rather than a single long task.
4. Eddie is more likely to be engaged in academics when he is reminded to attend to his work instead of being left alone for the class session.
5. Eddie is more likely to be academically engaged when he is given the option of working in a study carrell rather than being required to work in the presence of visual distractions.

The first hypothesis, pertaining to handwriting, was generated from both the student and teacher interviews. Eddie stated that his least favorite subject was handwriting and that he found work easier if he could complete it orally or using a computer.

During the student interview, Eddie reported that he was often bored with his work and enjoyed learning new and different things. One of Eddie's teachers stated that he found his work redundant. This led to the second hypothesis, that Eddie would perform better if he were provided with problem solving rather than drill and practice tasks.

The third hypothesis was that improved behavior would result if Eddie was provided multiple brief tasks during academic sessions. This resulted from Eddie's report during the interview that when he liked his work he could complete it. All of Eddie's teachers also reported work completion to be a problem.

Several sources of information were used to generate the fourth hypothesis. During academic activities, Eddie was occasionally provided a timer and allotted a particular amount of time to complete his work. Observations indicated increases in engagement after the bell rang. During the teacher interview, one of Eddie's teachers indicated this procedure helped keep Eddie on-task. In addition, during the student interview Eddie stated that he had difficulty keeping his mind from wandering and that sometimes the timer helped. We thus hypothesized that Eddie would be engaged more frequently if reminded to attend to his work.

The last hypothesis, assessing the use of a study carrel, was generated from Eddie alone. During the student interview, Eddie stated that working in a carrel helped him attend to his work.

The five hypotheses were verified by conducting a series of reversal manipulations in Eddie's classrooms. The teachers decided which hypotheses would be tested in which class. In general, the hypotheses were tested by conducting one condition on one day and then switching to the contrasting condition the following day, and so on. Due to time constraints, the self-monitoring hypothesis was tested by conducting two conditions per day. The results of the reversal analyses are shown in Figure 10.2. The principal dependent measure for these analyses

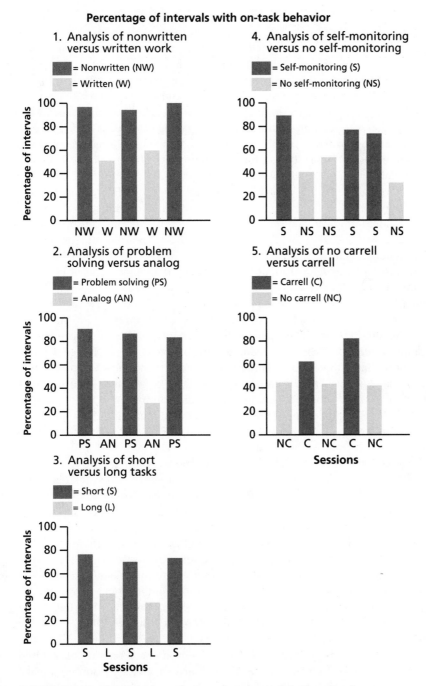

FIGURE 10.2 Results of the hypothesis-testing phase of the functional assessment process for Eddie's support program. Percentage of intervals with on-task behavior are shown for each of the five hypotheses.

SOURCE: Kern et al. (1994a). Reprinted with permission.

was on-task behavior, because this was judged to be the most sensitive (serious behavior problems did not occur with sufficient frequency) and because Eddie's essential difficulties all related to a failure to be appropriately engaged. These data indicate that each of the variables were functional influences on Eddie's behavior.

With the hypotheses confirmed, it was then time to move to Phase II, intervention. To accommodate each teacher's style of teaching and intervention preference, the interventions were individualized. Each teacher selected three of the tested hypotheses to formulate an intervention package for his or her classroom. The intervention packages were implemented in a multiple baseline fashion across classrooms. In Figure 10.3, substantial improvements are evident in Eddie's on-task behavior when the interventions were in place.

An additional measure was used to determine how much Eddie liked his academic assignments. This is an important evaluative measure for several reasons. Because epidemiological data reflect high dropout rates among this population (Koyanagi & Gaines, 1993), it seems reasonable that increasing students' enjoyment in school might help decrease this serious problem. In addition, there are interrelationships between student performance, preferences, and assessment-based interventions (for example, Foster-Johnson, Ferro, & Dunlap, 1994). To assess whether Eddie preferred the revised curriculum, he was provided a daily activity rating after each academic session. He was asked to respond to the question, "How much did you like (spelling, English, math) today?" by circling a 1, 2 or 3 rating which meant either, "I didn't like it," "It was okay," or "I liked it a lot." Eddie's ratings in all three subjects improved after intervention was implemented.

At the time of this writing, almost four years have passed since Eddie's revised curriculum was implemented. We observed Eddie continuing to make progress throughout his fifth grade school year. Eddie is now in junior high school, and he is once again attending regular classes the entire day and is doing well with a curriculum that is identical to that of his classmates.

The recent studies described here represent a more comprehensive and systematic effort to develop and apply assessment-based procedures with individuals described as having emotional or behavioral disorders. In each of the studies, specific social and/or instructional variables were identified and manipulated to improve student deportment. The assessments implicated specific environmental variables associated with desirable or undesirable classroom behavior, and these variables became the focus of the intervention plan, rather than the problem behavior. Specific procedures (punishment) traditionally used to reduce problem behaviors were thus avoided. The assessments also provided information that could be used to develop an individualized intervention for each of the participants, thus, enhancing the likelihood of desired outcomes (Carr, Robinson, & Palumbo, 1990).

Although still limited, the research now demonstrates that these procedures hold promise with this population. However, certain characteristics of children and adolescents described as emotionally and/or behaviorally disordered make them unique from other populations in which the procedures have been most frequently applied. This may warrant special adaptations and accommodations. In the next sections, we will consider some issues that pertain to the characteristics of this populations, as well as to some future directions that seem important for the continuing development of assessment-based interventions.

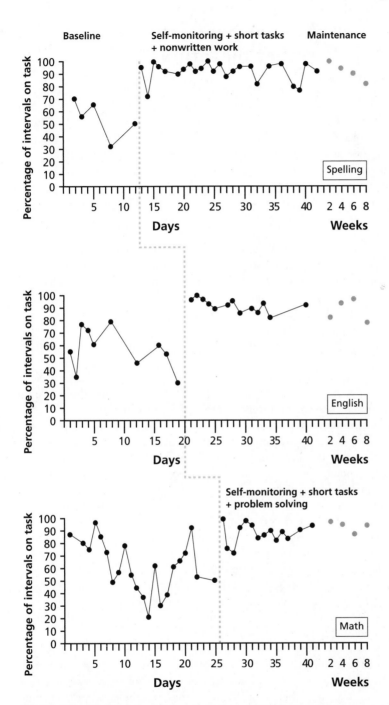

FIGURE 10.3 Results of the intervention phase for Eddie, presented as a multiple baseline across three classes. Percentage of intervals with on-task responding are shown on the ordinate.

SOURCE: Kern et al. (1994a), p. 7–19. Reprinted with permission.

SPECIAL CONSIDERATIONS AND
FUTURE DIRECTIONS

A characteristic of children with EBD that merits consideration is their ability to provide descriptions of their circumstances and behavior. Children identified as EBD generally fall close to or within the average range of intellectual functioning, are often at or near grade level in academics, and are usually able to communicate with considerable precision about a large number of topics, including their own perceptions. This has specific implications for the manner with which functional assessments are conducted.

The extensive (and seminal) research on functional assessment methodologies was conducted with individuals who had severe intellectual disabilities and were similarly challenged in communication. The assessment strategies involved direct observation and experimental or descriptive methodologies, as well as rating scales and interviews for collecting reports from knowledgeable informants. Instruments such as the Functional Analysis Interview Form (O'Neill et al., 1990) require that an adult informant describe events or conditions that may be functionally related to problem behavior. The higher level of intellectual and communicative skills characteristic of children with EBD suggest that they may be able to serve as especially well-informed participants in the functional assessment process.

We explored this possibility, and some preliminary evidence (for example, Kern et al., 1994b) supports this notion. Kern et al. (1994b) developed the Student-Assisted Functional Assessment Interview to solicit information directly from students. This instrument is reproduced in Figure 10.1. The student is asked to respond to specific questions pertaining to features of the curriculum and classroom environment that may be contributing to problem behaviors. Several questions seek to identify general functions of student behavior, such as attention ("Do you think people notice when you do a good job?"), escape ("Is your assigned work too hard?"), or tangible reinforcement ("Do you think you get the points or rewards you deserve when you do good work?"). Other questions identify specific features of academic activities and the classroom environment that might be modified to improve the student's behavior. For example, students are asked if work periods are too long, if their work is interesting, and if there are distractions in the classroom. Students are also asked to rate their preference for each school subject on a Likert-type scale. The objective of this section is to secure information that might assist in identifying distinctive aspects of the student's school day that might contribute to undesirable (and desirable) behavior.

We have administered the interview to more than 15 students labeled as having emotional or behavioral disorders. The information provided by the interview has assisted us in developing hypotheses regarding specific variables associated with problematic classroom behavior. Many of the hypotheses were later confirmed through experimental manipulations. Some student responses have been very definitive and have implicated specific classroom variables. For example, one student reported that he would do better if he could complete his most challenging work in a study carrell. Data indicated that his on-task behavior did improve when he was seated in the carrell. More often, however, student responses are less specific, and hypothesis development requires deduction. In the case study described previously, some of Eddie's responses provided during the student interview required some inference to develop hypotheses. For example, his statement that he liked his work when he could finish it was not readily translated into an hypothesis. However, it did suggest that modifications designed to provide a sense of completion might result in behavioral improvements. Thus, we hypothesized that multiple brief tasks during an academic session would be superior to a single long task. As shown in Box 10.1, this hypothesis was confirmed.

When we evaluated the input provided by one elementary school student (with EBD), we found his information much more consistent with our empirical data than were the responses provided by his teachers. Such a clear disparity may be unusual; however, the validity of a student's responses should not be surprising, especially when students are describing their preferences, including their likes and dislikes about the content and methods of the instructional curriculum, materials, classmates, and potential reinforcers. In other cases, the students' descriptions have been less reliable.

It will be useful for future research to examine the validity and usefulness of student input in the functional assessment process. It is likely that many variables would pertain, including age, communicative ability; and interest in the school environment. At this point, we believe it is appropriate and valuable to secure input directly from the student and that, at times, the input will offer unique insights. As with other sources of information, student data are included in the mix of evidence that contributes to the development of hypotheses. In this regard, the input from students should also be considered as a useful data source for purposes of program evaluation.

Another area needing further research relates to the complexity of the children's behavioral difficulties. Published research studies with this population reflect functional assessments, manipulations, and behavioral interventions conducted in only one environment and generally involving a single variable, such as one aspect of teacher-student interactions. These assessments and the corresponding interventions have resulted in behavioral improvements and it is possible that more comprehensive interventions may not have been needed. However, many individuals exhibiting emotional and behavioral difficulties have very complex and diverse needs. We currently have virtually no knowledge about the influence that learning histories might have on the vicissitudes of these children's problem behaviors, but it is very likely that children's emotional and cognitive functioning are affected in important ways by events and interactions that might now be considered historical. This is undoubtedly true for all children, but it's possible that the effects of troublesome or traumatic incidents (such as abuse) are manifested more saliently with some children who are identified as EBD. Unfortunately, research has not provided adequate information with which to understand these influences or to design assessment and intervention strategies.

Improved assessment methodologies will also need to include explicit consideration of setting events, including relatively distal events that occur outside of the school environment. For example, a child may have obtained insufficient sleep because of late-night activities in the home, a family argument may have ensued prior to school, or a student may have been in a fight on the school bus. Setting events such as these may increase the probability of undesirable behavior at school (Dadson & Horner, 1993). Given the social and psychological characteristics of these particular children (Friedman et al., 1988), it may be assumed that such circumstances could be particularly important.

The status of current research and practice in functional assessment is limited in several crucial respects. First, the assessment settings have been restricted to classrooms and clinics. These are important environments, and an understanding of the challenging behavior that occurs within these settings is undeniably useful; however, it is unusual for the difficulties exhibited by children with EBD to be confined to these settings. If a goal is to develop comprehensive support to help children resolve problems and mature into strong and fulfilled adults, then it is necessary for the enterprise of functional assessment to be expanded in scope, and include the complete array of settings and circumstances in which a child lives.

Similarly, future work in the area of functional assessment and assessment-based interventions must consider a broader array of dependent variables. The focus thus far has been on discrete problem behaviors and desirable deportment in classroom and clinic settings, including task engagement, but broader outcomes should be included. For example, Panacek-Howell (1994) argues that the needs of children with EBD can be best understood from the perspective of a social life framework, including an appreciation of the children's social networks and sources of social support. If this framework is valid, then it would benefit by strategy building for assessing and supporting children's social relationships, and for considering more explicitly such outcome measures as school placements and the nature of the children's friendships. It will also be important to pursue these assessment strategies longitudinally, because the challenges encountered by children with EBD are not transient phenomena.

SUMMARY

Children with emotional and behavioral difficulties have been treated with behavior management programs that have been characterized as highly restrictive, controlling, coercive, and punitive. Recent research in functional assessment and assessment-based interventions has demonstrated improved approaches for supporting these children. Studies thus far are encouraging, but continued and elaborated research is needed to assist these children in a comprehensive and optimally effective manner.

REFERENCES

Bornstein, M., Bellack, A. S., & Hersen, M. (1980). Social skills training for highly aggressive children: Treatment in an in-patient psychiatric setting. *Behavior Modification, 4,* 173–186.

Brandenburg, N. A., Friedman, R. M., & Silver, S. (1987). *The epidemiology of childhood psychiatric disorders: Recent prevalence findings and methodologic issues.* Tampa: Florida Mental Health Institute, University of South Florida.

Carr, E. G. (1988). Functional equivalence as a mechanism for response generalization. In R. H. Horner, G. Dunlap, R. L. Koegel (Eds.), *Generalization and maintenance: Lifestyle changes in applied settings* (pp 221–241). Baltimore: Paul H, Brookes.

Carr, E. G. (1977). The motivation of self-injurious behavior: A review of some hypotheses. *Psychological Bulletin, 84,* 800–816.

Carr, E. G., & Durand, V. M. (1985). Reducing behavioral problems through functional communication training. *Journal of Applied Behavior Analysis, 18,* 111–126.

Carr, E. G., Levin, L., McConnachie, G., Carlson, J., Kemp, D., & Smith, C. (1994). *Communication-based intervention for problem behavior: A user's guide for producing positive change.* Baltimore: Paul H. Brookes.

Carr, E. G., Robinson, S., & Palumbo, L. W. (1990). The wrong issue: Aversive versus nonaversive treatment; The right issue: Functional versus nonfunctional treatment. In A. C. Repp, & N. N. Singh (Eds.). *Perspectives on the use of aversive and nonaversive interventions for persons with developmental disabilities* (pp. 361–379). Sycamore, IL: Sycamore.

Center, D. B., Dietz, S. M., & Kaufman, M. E. (1982). Student ability, task difficulty, and inappropriate classroom behavior: A study of children with behavior disorders. *Behavior Modification, 6,* 355–374.

Cooper, L. J., Wacker, D. P., Sasso, G. M., Reimers, T. R., & Donn, L. K. (1990). Using parents as therapists to evaluate appropriate behavior of their children: Application to a tertiary diagnostic clinic. *Journal of Applied Behavior Analysis, 23,* 285–296.

Cullinan, D., Epstein, M. H., & Lloyd, J. (1983). *Behavioral disorders of children and adolescents.* Englewood Cliffs, NJ: Prentice-Hall.

Cullinan, D., Epstein, M. H., & Sabornic, E. J. (1992). Selected characteristics of a national sample of seriously emotionally disturbed adolescents. *Behavioral Disorders, 17,* 273–280.

Dadson, S., & Horner, R. H. (1993). Manipulating setting events to decrease problem behavior: A case study. *Teaching Exceptional Children, 25,* 53–55.

Dunlap, G., & dePerczel, M. (1990). *Research on positive behavioral interventions for elementary students with severe emotional and behavioral challenges* (Grant No. H023C10102). Washington D.C.: U.S. Department of Education, Office of Special Education Programs.

Dunlap, G., dePerczel, M., Clarke, S., Wilson, D., Wright, S., White, R., & Gomez, A. (1994). Choice making to promote adaptive behavior for students with emotional and behavioral challenges. *Journal of Applied Behavior Analysis, 27,* 505–518.

Dunlap, G., Foster-Johnson, L., Clarke, S., Kern, L., & Childs, K. E. (1995). Modifying activities to produce functional outcomes: Effects on the disruptive behaviors of students with disabilities. *Journal of the Association for Persons with Severe Handicaps, 20,* 248–258.

Dunlap, G., & Kern, L. (1993). Assessment and intervention for children within the instructional curriculum. In J. Reichle & D. P. Wacker (Eds.), *Communicative approaches to the management of challenging behaviors* (pp. 177–203). Baltimore: Paul H. Brookes.

Dunlap, G., Kern, L., dePerczel, M., Clarke, S., Wilson, D., Childs, K. E., White, R., & Falk, G. D. (1993). Functional analysis of classroom variables for students with emotional and behavioral disorders. *Behavioral Disorders, 18,* 275–291.

Dunlap, G., Kern-Dunlap, L., Clarke, S., Robbins, F. R. (1991). Functional assessment, curricular revision, and severe behavior problems. *Journal of Applied Behavior Analysis, 24,* 387–397.

Durand, V. M. (1990). *Functional communication training: An intervention program for severe behavior problems.* New York: Guilford.

Epstein, M. H., Kaufman, J. M., & Cullinan, D. (1985). Patterns of maladjustment among the behaviorally disordered II: Boys aged 6–11, boys aged 12–18, girls aged 6–11, and girls aged 12–18. *Behavioral Disorders, 10,* 125–135.

Foley, R. M., & Epstein, M. H. (1993). A structured instructional system for developing the school survival skills of adolescents with behavioral disorders. *Behavioral Disorders, 18,* 139–147.

Foster-Johnson, L., & Dunlap, G. (1993). Using functional assessment to develop effective, individualized interventions. *Teaching Exceptional Children, 25,* 44–50.

Foster-Johnson, L., Ferro, J., & Dunlap, G. (1994). Preferred curricular activities and reduced problem behaviors in students with intellectual disabilities. *Journal of Applied Behavior Analysis, 27,* 493–504.

Friedman, R. M., Silver, S. E., Duchnowski, A. J., Kutash, K., Eisen, M., Brandenburg, N. A., & Prange, M. (1988). *Characteristics of children with serious emotional disturbances identified by public systems as requiring services.* Tampa: Florida Mental Health Institute, University of South Florida.

Gresham, F. M. (1981). Assessment of children's social skills. *Journal of School Psychology, 19,* 120–133.

Gresham, F. M. (1982). Misguided mainstreaming: The case for social skills training with handicapped children. *Exceptional Children, 48,* 422–430.

Grosenick, J. K., George, N. L., George, M. P., & Lewis, T. J. (1991). Public school services for behaviorally disordered students: Program practices in the 1980's. *Behavioral Disorders, 16,* 87–96.

Gunter, P. L., Jack, S. L., Shores, R. E., Carrell, D. E., & Flowers, J. (1993). Lag sequential analysis as a tool for functional analysis of student disruptive behavior in classrooms. *Journal of Emotional and Behavioral Disorders, 1,* 138–148.

Gunter, P. L., Shores, R. E., Jack, S. L., Rasmussen, S., & Flowers, J. (1995). Teacher/student proximity: A strategy for classroom control through teacher movement. *Teaching Exceptional Children, 28,* 12–14.

Halle, J. W., & Spradlin, J. E. (1993). Identifying stimulus control of challenging behavior. In J. Reichle & D. P. Wacker (Eds.), *Communicative approaches to the management of challenging behaviors* (pp. 83–109). Baltimore: Paul H. Brookes.

Hollinger, J. D. (1987). Social skills for behaviorally disordered children as preparation for mainstreaming: Theory, practice, and new directions. *Remedial and Special Education, 8,* 17–27.

Horner, R. H., Dunlap, G., Koegel, R. L., Carr, E. G., Sailor, W., Anderson, J., Albin, R. W., & O'Neill, R. E. (1990). Toward a technology of "nonaversive" behavioral support. *Journal of the Association for Persons with Severe Handicaps, 15,* 125–132.

Horner, R. H., Sprague, J. R., & Flannery, B. (1993). Building functional curricula for students with severe intellectual disabilities and severe problem behaviors. In R. Van Houten & S. Axelrod (Eds.). *Effective behavioral treatment: Issues and implementation* (pp. 47–71). New York: Plenum.

Iwata, B. A., Dorsey, M. F., Slifer, K. J., Bauman, K. E., & Richman, G. S. (1994). Toward a functional analysis of self-injury. *Journal of Applied Behavior Analysis, 27,* 197–209.

Kaufman, R. (1989). *Learning and education: Psychoanalytic perspectives. Emotions and behavior monographs.* (Vol. 6). Madison: International Universities Press.

Kern, L., Childs, K. E., Dunlap, G., Clarke, S., & Falk, G. D. (1994a). Using assessment-based curricular intervention to improve the classroom behavior of a student with emotional and behavioral challenges. *Journal of Applied Behavior Analysis, 27,* 7–19.

Kern, L., Dunlap, G., Clarke, S., & Childs, K. E. (1994b). Student-assisted functional assessment interview. *Diagnostique, 19,* 29–39.

Knapczyk, D. R. (1992). Effects of developing alternative responses on the aggressive behavior of adolescents. *Behavioral Disorders, 16,* 247–263.

Knapczyk, D. R. (1988). Reducing aggressive behaviors in special and regular class settings by training alternative social responses. *Behavioral Disorders, 14,* 27–39.

Knitzer, J, Steinberg, Z., & Fleisch, B. (1990). *At the schoolhouse door: An examination of programs and policies for children with behavioral and emotional problems.* New York: Bank Street College of Education.

Koyanagi, C., & Gaines, S. (1993). *All systems failure: An examination of the results of neglecting the needs of children with serious emotional disturbance.* National Mental Health Association.

Lennox, D. B., & Miltenberger, R. G. (1989). Conducting a functional assessment of problem behavior in applied settings. *Journal of the Association for Persons with Severe Handicaps, 14,* 304–311.

Mattison, R. E., Humphrey, F. J., Kales, S. N., & Wallace, D. J. (1986). An objective evaluation of special class placement of elementary school boys with behavior problems. *Journal for Abnormal Child Psychology, 14,* 251–262.

Munk, D. D., & Repp, A. C. (1994). The relationship between instructional variables and problem behavior: A review. *Exceptional Children, 60,* 390–401.

National Longitudinal Transition Study of Special Education Students Report (1991). *Youth with disabilities: How are they doing?* Menlo Park, CA: SRI International.

Nelson, C. M., & Pearson, C. A. (1991). *Integrating services for children and youth with emotional and behavioral disorders.* Reston, VA: The Council for Exceptional Children.

Office of the Federal Register National Archives and Records Administration (1985). *Code of Federal Regulations.* Washington: U.S. Government Document Printing Office.

O'Neill, R. E., Horner, R. H., Albin, R. W., Storey, K., & Sprague, J. R. (1990). *Functional analysis of problem behavior: A practical assessment guide.* Sycamore, IL: Sycamore.

Panacek-Howell, L. (1994). *An examination of the social lives of children with serious emotional and behavioral challenges.* Unpublished doctoral dissertation. University of South Florida.

Platt, J. S., Harris, J. W., & Clements, J. E. (1980). The effects of individually-designed reinforcement schedules on attending and academic performance with behaviorally disordered adolescents. *Behavioral Disorders, 5,* 197–205.

Reiher, T. C. (1992). Identified deficits and their congruence to the IEP for behaviorally disordered students. *Behavioral Disorders, 17,* 167–177.

Repp, A. C., Felce, D., & Barton, L. (1988). Basing the treatment of stereotypic and self-injurious behavior on hypotheses of their causes. *Journal of Applied Behavior Analysis, 21,* 281–290.

Ruhl, K. L., & Berlinghoff, D. H. (1992). Research on improving behaviorally disordered students' academic performance: A review of the literature. *Behavioral Disorders, 17,* 178–190.

Schloss, P. J., Kane, M. S., & Miller, F. (1981). Truancy intervention with behavior disordered adolescents. *Behavioral Disorders, 6,* 175–179.

Scott, J. (1994). Functional assessment of learning problems. *LD Forum, 19*(2), 14–17.

Shores, R. E., Jack, S. L., Gunter, P. L., Ellis, D. N., DeBriere, T. J., & Wehby, J. H. (1993). Classroom interactions of children with behavior disorders. *Journal of Emotional and Behavioral Disorders, 1,* 27–39.

Singer, G. H., Singer, J., & Horner, R. H. (1987). Using pretask requests to increase the probability of compliance for students with severe disabilities. *Journal of the Association for Persons with Severe Handicaps, 12,* 287–291.

Spirito, A., Finch, A. J., Smith, T. L., & Cooley, W. H. (1981). Stress inoculation for anger and anxiety control: A case study with an emotionally disturbed boy. *Journal of Clinical Child Psychology, Winter,* 67–70.

Topper, K., Williams, W., Leo, K., Hamilton, R., & Fox, T. (1994). *A positive approach to understanding and addressing challenging behaviors: Supporting educators and families* to include students with emotional and behavioral difficulties in regular education. Burlington, VT: University of Vermont.

Touchette, P., MacDonald, R., & Langer, S. (1985). A scatterplot for identifying stimulus control of problem behavior. *Journal of Applied Behavior Analysis, 18,* 343–451.

Valdes, K. A., Williamson, C. L., & Wagner, M. M. (1990). *The national longitudinal transition study of special education students Vol 3: Youth categorized as emotionally disturbed.* Menlo Park, CA: SRI International.

Weeks, M., & Gaylord-Ross, R. (1981). Task difficulty and aberrant behavior in severely handicapped students. *Journal of Applied Behavior Analysis, 14,* 19–36.

Winterling, V., Dunlap, G., & O'Neill, R. E. (1987). The influence of task variation on the aberrant behavior of autistic students. *Education and Treatment of Children, 10,* 105–119.

11

Analyzing Behavior Disorders in Classrooms

RICHARD E. SHORES
JOSEPH H. WEHBY
SUSAN L. JACK

INTRODUCTION

Shores, Wehby, and Jack provide a second chapter on functional assessment for students with behavior disorders. They briefly review various assessment procedures, and then distinguish two types involving direct observation: experimental functional assessments (analogues) and descriptive functional assessments (involving naturally occurring setting events, antecedents, and consequences).

The authors then concentrate on this area and return us to one of the major points in Chapter 6, adopting more sophisticated methods of data collection and analysis, and in particular, sequential analysis methods. Shores, Wehby, and Jack discuss this procedure, which allows us to identify a sequence either based on time (for example, the latency from an antecedent to a response) or events (response B follows A, and is in turn followed by C and then D). This type of data analysis provides the authors with a means of examining the interaction sequence of students with teachers, and to assess differences in interactions within any type of sequence.

This is a sophisticated extension of functional assessment procedures, providing the basis for a more informed, data-based decision with respect to the choice of interventions. With it, the authors have extended our field, pushing us to consider new methods of data collection and analysis.

Behavior is often considered disordered when a person responds unpredictably in normal social situations. A number of authors have suggested that generalized definitions of behavior problems as internalizing or externalizing behavior are sufficient to aid in identifying students who have emotional and behavior disorders (Achenbach & Edelbrock, 1988; Eisert et al., 1989; Lerner et al., 1985; Walker et al., 1988). Externalized behavior disorders characterize students who exhibit aggression, antisocial acts, oppositional behavior, social-skill deficits, hyperactivity and/or lack of attention to task. Internalized behavior disorders characterize students who exhibit social withdrawal, anxiety, inhibited social or academic behavior, and depression. In general, both externalizing and internalizing behavior disorders are often related to students' social behavior. Social behavior is defined as behavior that is under the control of environmental stimuli or social stimuli that is emitted by another person in a dyadic exchange. This is not to say all behavior problems are directly a function of social stimuli (or lack of a functional relationship to social stimuli), but many of these behaviors are directly related to the social events in the environment (Gunter et al., 1993a; Gunter et al., 1994).

In this chapter we describe assessment procedures that are designed to collect information regarding the effects of the school environment, particularly the social environment, on students' behavior, and intended to aid in developing effective, ecologically valid interventions. Specifically, we review methods of assessing the functions of social behavior deficits and excesses in school settings. Next, we present information on the use of direct observation data and lag sequential analysis strategies to aid in developing hypotheses regarding the motivational effects of social stimuli on problem behavior. Following this discussion, we present some experimental research that tests hypotheses based on descriptive observation data. Finally, we discuss some of the issues and problems encountered using lag sequential analysis for the purpose of functional assessment.

METHODS OF ASSESSMENT

The functional assessment of problem behavior has been a growing area of behavior analysis over the last 15 years. As described in this text, the technology of functional assessment encompasses a variety of strategies, ranging from ratings obtained by significant others (Durand & Crimmins, 1988) to the experimental manipulation of aberrant behavior under contrived analog conditions (Carr & Durand, 1985; Carr, Newsom, & Binkoff, 1980; Pace et al., 1993; Weeks & Gaylord-Ross, 1981). Each of these approaches varies with regard to empirical integrity and rigor. A brief review of each can be found below.

Informant Assessments

Obtaining diagnostic information through the reports of persons in a child's environment (such as teachers or parents) is one tool that has been utilized to identify the motivating factors supporting inappropriate behavior. Reports of this nature are considered an important source of information since these persons interact with the child at some level on a routine basis (Luiselli, 1991; McMahon & Forehand, 1988). Informant assessments typically fall into two broad categories: behavioral ratings and behavioral interviews.

Behavioral Ratings   Historically, behavioral rating scales have played an influential role in our ability to assess child behavior. The simplicity associated with administering rating scales and the fact that results are easily quantifiable have made them a popular choice among researchers and practitioners (McMahon & Forehand, 1988). Scales such as the Child Behavior Checklist (Achenbach & Edelbrock, 1988) and the Revised Behavior Problem Checklist (Quay & Peterson, 1987) are among the hundreds of rating scales that have been used to classify the problem behavior of children, to identify deficits in social behavior, or to evaluate the outcomes of interventions. The major disadvantage of most rating scales, in relation to functional assessment, is that they are not designed to assess the controlling factors associated with specific topographies of problem behavior. The utility of rating scales to determine the function(s) of problem behavior is thus limited.

Durand and Crimmins (1988) attempted to incorporate the advantages of rating scales in the functional assessment process with the Motivational Assessment Scale (MAS). The MAS was designed to develop testable hypotheses regarding the controlling variables associated with self-injurious behavior. Although the utility of the MAS for analyzing low-rate behaviors such as classroom aggression is unknown, the approach represents initial attempts to broaden the traditional use of behavioral rating scales.

Behavioral Interviews   Diagnostic interviews with parents and teachers are another type of informant assessment that has been used to understand and treat child problem behavior. As with behavioral rating scales, standardized informant interviews have been used to classify children according to a prescribed set of characteristics. In some applications, interviews were designed to verbally identify the contextual variables that surround problem behavior (McMahon & Forehand, 1988; Repp, 1994). For problem behavior in classroom settings, interviews are conducted with the teacher or classroom assistant and focus on the academic and nonacademic interactions within the classroom setting. Specifically, these interviews focus on interactions between the child and teacher, child and peers, and the child and instructional materials (Dunlap et al., 1991; Dunlap et al., 1993; O'Neill et al., 1990; Sprague & Horner, 1992).

One of the more popular systematic interviews for assessing the function of problem behavior was developed at the University of Oregon by O'Neill et al. (1990). Following a standard protocol, this interview is designed to develop hypotheses regarding the motivation(s) of problem behavior based upon reports of significant others within and across settings. These hypotheses are then confirmed or denied based upon direct observation and through direct manipulation of specific variables (Repp, 1994).

Although diagnostic information from both ratings and interviews can provide relevant information regarding the nature of problem behavior, the reliability of this strategy is somewhat questionable. By relying exclusively on information from an adult who is actively involved in the child's day-to-day routine, the objectivity of the data may be affected. This is particularly pertinent given that caregivers and independent observers often disagree on the molecular interactions surrounding problem behavior (Fuchs, Fuchs, & Bahr, 1990). As noted by Fuchs and Fuchs (1989), teachers may rate behavior based on dimensions (intensity) rather than frequency. As a result, the ratings of teachers may reflect summative evaluations of children rather than identification of the molecular sequences necessary for understanding the various functions of behavior. More independent measures of controlling variables are thus typically required to lead to an effective intervention.

Direct Observation

Direct observation of problem behavior in the context of classroom settings represents the most intensive procedure for identifying the factors associated with problem behavior. The ability of researchers and practitioners to identify the controlling stimuli of high-rate problem behavior through direct observation techniques has become a highly sophisticated and precise craft. As described by several researchers (Dunlap et al., 1993; Sasso et al., 1992), direct observation approaches to functional assessment fall into two basic categories: those involving experimental manipulations of hypothesized controlling stimuli and those descriptively identifying associations between problem behavior and variables in natural environments, in this case, classrooms.

Experimental Functional Assessment   The number of studies involving the manipulation of environmental variables associated with problem behavior have increased substantially over the last 15 years (see special issue of *Journal of Applied Behavior Analysis*, Summer 1994). This expanding literature has demonstrated that specific antecedent and consequent conditions are related to serious aberrant behavior. While the experimental strategies are detailed elsewhere in this text, here we briefly summarize some of the findings. Demand situations (Carr & Durand, 1985; Carr, Newsom, & Binkoff, 1980; Day, Horner, & O'Neill, 1994), difficult tasks (Pace et al., 1993), social attention (Carr & Durand, 1985; Hagopian, Fisher, & Legacy, 1994), and tangible items (Fisher et al., 1993) are variables whose manipulation varies with the occurrence of problem behavior. As noted by Mace (1994a), the analog approach to identifying controlling stimuli has become the standard approach to functional analysis.

Advances in this technology, however, have led to the identification of problems in the functional assessment process. One major concern is that current assessment procedures may not be externally valid. The most typical functional assessments using experimental manipulations have been conducted outside classroom environments and within analog settings. Although assessment of problem behavior in standardized settings has provided some indications of the nature of severe behavior problems including aggression, the assumption that analog conditions overlap with the classroom environment is often tenuous and may hinder identification of unique situational factors that could help us understand fluctuations in levels of aggression within and across different settings (Halle & Spradlin, 1993; Mace & Shea, 1991; Reid et al., 1988). While there have been some recent investigations into the correspondence between these settings (for example, Mace & Lalli, 1991; Sasso et al., 1992), the extent to which analog and classroom environments correspond depends upon the match of the contingencies and stimuli between settings (Mace & Lalli, 1991; Sasso et al., 1992; Taylor & Romanczyk, 1994; Wehby, Symons, & Shores, 1995). If errors exist in the match between the experimental and natural environments, the extrapolation of hypotheses from analog settings for application in classroom settings may be compromised. There has thus been a recent focus on conducting experimental manipulations within classroom settings.

To a more limited extent, experimental manipulations in applied settings, such as classrooms, have achieved similar results as functional analyses in analog conditions (Durand & Carr, 1992; Repp & Karsh, 1994; Sasso et al., 1992; Wacker et al., 1990). Dunlap et al. (1991) applied functional analysis procedures to identify the conditions under which aggressive, disruptive and off-task behaviors were exhibited by a student classified as seriously emotionally disturbed. Their hypothesis and subsequent intervention were based on demands within the academic setting such as length of task. type of task (functional versus nonfunctional) and choice (preferred versus nonpreferred). Curricular modifications based on these factors produced dramatic and lasting reductions in the student's rate of problem behavior. The results suggested that functional analysis can be expanded to assess students within classroom environments; however, as the authors report, such results are not easily obtained due to the time involved in the development and testing of a hypothesis and the procedures are not easy to implement.

Subsequent research efforts by Dunlap and his colleagues have attempted to expand the application of functional analysis in classrooms for students with serious behavior disorders (SBD). Dunlap et al. (1993) demonstrated the effectiveness of interventions based on a functional analysis within the context of classroom activities for five students with SBD. While the assessment procedures were similar for each student, individualized interventions were developed that were specifically related to the functions of the aberrant behavior exhibited by each individual. The continuing research in this application of functional analysis holds promise for analyzing the behavior of students with SBD.

Despite these recent applications of functional assessment strategies in applied settings, there are still several problematic issues related to its use. One problem recently emerging in the area of assessing problem behavior has been the growing evidence that the aberrant behavior of many children and youth with SBD occurs infrequently within classrooms (Shores et al., 1993; Wehby et al., 1993; Wehby et al., 1995); yet, the behavior is serious enough to warrant attention by classroom personnel. This problem of low-rate behavior poses unique obstacles in terms of explaining the occurrence of these actions under natural conditions (Mace, 1994a). This issue is compounded because many children with mild disabilities have low rate problematic behaviors as a small part of large complex behavioral repertoires. In contrast, the majority of the functional analysis literature has dealt with persons with severe or profound developmental disabilities who have more restricted behavioral repertoires. In our view, investigating the functionality of inappropriate behavior within the context of these large behavioral repertoires is necessary. By focusing on the context of aberrant behavior within a stream of naturally occurring social interactive behavior, important operative variables within the classroom environment may be revealed that otherwise could be overlooked in an artificial analog assessment procedure (Mace, 1994b). To accomplish this, descriptive approaches to functional assessment have been applied.

Descriptive Functional Assessments   The second type of functional assessment strategy that utilizes direct observation procedures can be characterized as a descriptive study. In contrast to actively manipulating classroom variables, descriptive studies identify the naturally occurring antecedents and consequences that surround problem behavior. Correlational analyses are used to search for possible functional relations that may be operating within that environment (Sasso et al., 1992). Descriptive studies of classroom behavior have involved coding systems that represent the complex interaction patterns that characterize classroom settings (Shores et al., 1993; Strain et al., 1983; Wehby et al., 1995). Researchers have used descriptive observation techniques in a variety of ways. For instance, direct observation data were collected in natural settings to generate empirically-based hypotheses that were tested through the direct manipulation of identified variables (Dunlap et al., 1991; Lerman & Iwata, 1993; Mace & Lalli, 1991; Repp & Karsh, 1994; Sasso et al., 1992).

There have been a number of attempts to employ descriptive direct observation techniques in isolation for the purpose of functionally assessing problem behavior. Beginning with the A-B-C approach suggested by Bijou and Baer (1961) and more thoroughly outlined in what may be considered the seminal article by Bijou, Peterson, and Ault (1968), researchers have used direct observation to identify potential controlling variables within classroom environments. Early work in the use of descriptive functional assessments was conducted in homes of children with behavioral problems. One of the most comprehensive uses of descriptive data to identify the controlling variables associated with problem behavior has been the work of Patterson and his colleagues at the Oregon Social Learning Center (Patterson, 1982, 1986). Using a complex observation system, these researchers have been able to identify the coercive parent-child interactions that are common in the homes of children with emotional and behavioral disorders. In a similar fashion, Wahler and Dumas (1986) used descriptive observations to determine the functional effects of mothers' indiscriminate attention on problem behavior. These efforts have demonstrated that empirically-based hypotheses regarding the function of problem behavior can be developed from the direct observation data in home settings.

Others have used descriptive observations to identify school-based factors associated with problem behavior. Using a scatterplot approach, Touchette, MacDonald, and Langer (1985) demonstrated through case illustrations that descriptive observations could be utilized to identify stimulus conditions, such as time of day or activity, as controlling problem behavior. A series of studies (Carr, Taylor, & Robinson, 1991; Taylor & Carr, 1992; Taylor & Romanczyk, 1994) used descriptive observations to identify the maintaining variables associated with problem behavior exhibited in classrooms. For example, Taylor and Romanczyk (1994) hypothesized that problem behavior was occasioned and maintained by levels of teacher attention or lack of teacher attention. By focusing direct observations on the amount of attention distributed by teachers to children in the classroom, accurate hypotheses regarding the function of problem behavior could be generated.

Research using descriptive direct observation strategies to provide functional assessments of problem behavior in schools is promising. Although data from these descriptive observations is correlational, the resulting information provides the opportunity to develop reasonable hypotheses that can be tested through formal experimental manipulation (Dunlap et al., 1993; Mace & Lalli, 1991; Sasso et al., 1992), or through the implementation of selected interventions (Repp, Felce, & Barton, 1988). Although as Repp (1994) notes, the current research is encouraging, functional assessments need to be used in school settings to aid in developing intervention strategies that are systematic and replicable. In our efforts to implement descriptive functional assessment techniques, we have developed a complex computer-assisted data system, and applied lag sequential analysis (Bakeman & Gottman, 1986) as a tool for establishing testable hypotheses regarding the social motivation for problem behavior.

LAG SEQUENTIAL ANALYSIS PROCEDURES

The assessment of social behavior in natural settings requires data systems that can capture the social exchanges in real time with an exhaustive coding procedure, and analysis procedures that are capable of describing the sequence of the exchange. Lag sequential analysis (Bakeman & Gottman, 1986; Gottman, 1983; Gottman & Roy, 1990) is one of these procedures that is currently being used both to describe social interactions in terms of the potential antecedents and consequent events associated with prosocial and antisocial behavior, and to aid in developing hypotheses regarding functional relationships that may be used to design intervention programs. Lag sequential analysis has been employed for a number of years to study a wide variety of questions related to social interactions such as conversations (Gottman, 1983), patterns of social responding in preschool children (Hendrickson et al., 1982; Tremblay et al., 1981), family interactions (Patterson, 1982; Snyder & Patterson, 1986), and classroom interactions of students identified as severely emotionally disturbed (Jack et al., 1996; Shores et al., 1993; Simpson & Souris, 1988; Slate & Saudargas, 1987; Wehby, Symons, & Shores, 1995). Sequential analysis has also been employed to analyze setting events and ecobehavioral factors (Carta & Greenwood, 1985; Greenwood, 1991; Rotholz, Kamps, & Greenwood, 1989), and to identify potential motivation of prosocial and antisocial classroom behavior (Gunter et al., 1993; Repp & Karsh, 1994).

The use of lag sequential analysis requires that data systems are designed to be ordered sequentially in time using mutually exclusive codes. In their introductory text on lag sequential analysis, Bakeman and Gottman (1986) suggested that codes be defined as frequency (events) or duration (states) and presented several methods of independently recording each type through pencil and paper systems. With the computer technology available today, we can record both events and states concurrently. For example, in the system we use to study the classroom interactions of students with behavior disorders, we record states such as group or individual instruction, proximity of teacher, academic or nonacademic activity, and students' task engagement while concurrently recording events or responses in sequence that occur between the student and his or her peers, teacher, and/or teacher aide (see Shores et al., 1993, for details of the observation procedures).

For descriptive functional assessments, sequential analysis is a useful tool for identifying patterns of behaviors whose co-occurrence or sequence may provide some indication of the extent to which variables may be dependent upon one another. The magnitude of the dependency between variables allows for the formulation of hypotheses regarding the possible function(s) of the targeted behavior. Although several indices of sequential dependency have been identified (Gottman & Roy, 1990; Wampold, 1992; Yoder & Tapp, 1990), we will limit our discussion to conditional probabilities to describe dependent sequences for the purpose of functional assessment. Conditional probabilities are useful in that they may reflect natural contingencies of interactions, which in turn are related to the function of social behavior (Moran, Dumas, & Symons, 1992). Simply stated, conditional probabilities (CP) are the probabilities "with which a particular 'target event' occurred, relative to another 'given' event" (Bakeman & Gottman, 1986, p. 123). Thus, a CP is calculated by dividing the frequency of the "given/target" sequence by the total number of givens that occurred. Event-based conditional probabilities can be calculated within a stream of interaction. The term "lag" is used to describe the placement of the "target" behavior from the "given" condition. For instance, lag 1 would be the event that occurs immediately before or after the target behavior, and lag 2 would be the second event following or preceding the given behavior.

Conditional probabilities may be calculated on day-to-day data for individuals, or the data may be aggregated across days for individuals or groups. To assess differences in interactions by groups, the data have been aggregated for groups to describe the interaction patterns for each group (Shores et al., 1993), and aggregated by individuals within groups and to test for differences among the groups (Wehby et al., 1995). In our single subject studies, we aggregated data within each phase of the study to describe potential changes in the interaction patterns as a result of the experimental manipulations (Gunter et al., 1993b).

Descriptive Studies Using Lag Sequential Analysis

Several studies have addressed social behaviors of students with SBD in classroom environments using lag sequential analysis. Simpson and Souris (1988) presented conditional probabilities of reciprocal interactions between students and their teachers in classrooms for students with autism and for those with mild disabilities. They reported that the majority of interactions observed in these classrooms were neutral, consisting of academic interactions that involved questioning and answering. Positive interactions were infrequently initiated by students or teachers. In a similar study, Slate and Saudargas (1987) reported differential patterns of teacher attention to students with learning disabilities. The sequential data revealed that teachers seldom interacted with the students when they were engaged appropriately in academic work, and frequently responded to the students when they engaged in off-task or disruptive behaviors.

Our research has focused on the use of lag sequential analysis at two levels—descriptive and functional. In several studies we have described interaction patterns of students with and without SBD in regular and special education settings (Shores et al., 1993; Wehby, Symons, & Shores, 1995), and students with SBD in classrooms with and without the use of classroom management strategies (Jack et al., 1996). Shores et al. (1993) reported observed differences in interactions of students with and without SBD (aggressive and nonaggressive) and differences in types of interactions across placement settings (segregated and integrated classrooms). The most probable interaction sequence across all four groups of students was a teacher mand (telling the student to do something), followed by student compliance, and then followed by teacher mand or feedback. Teacher positive consequences to student appropriate behavior were seldom found across all four groups, but were more probable in segregated (such as special education) classrooms. When teachers in segregated classrooms did respond with positive consequences, those responses were significantly related to student compliance. The most probable sequence of events surrounding student disruptive behavior involved the Stop code. That is, "no social responses" were coded most often as antecedents (CP = range of .42 to .57) and as consequences (CP = range of .23 to .53) to disruptive behavior of all students observed. Further, behaviors as antecedents or subsequents to disruptive behavior were more likely to be the target students' own behavior (negative verbal or aggression) than responses by teachers or peers.

Wehby, Symons, & Shores, (1995) used sequential analysis techniques to describe the naturally occurring antecedents and consequences to aggression for 28 students with SBD. The sequential analysis of these interactions revealed that (a) few positive interactions occurred for students in either the high-aggressor or low-aggressor group, and (b) significant differences in rates of aggression (either verbal or physical aggression) were observed between the two groups. In addition, sequences of behaviors were discussed in terms of prevalence and predictive behaviors that resulted in aggression. Using sequential analysis, antecedents or consequences to aggressive behaviors could be highly prevalent (account for a high proportion of the antecedents to aggressive behavior) but have little predictive value (no conditional relation), or could be of low prevalence but highly predictive. An example of a highly prevalent/low predictive antecedent could be found in teacher interactions with target children. Teacher social commands proportionally accounted for 22 percent of the antecedents to teacher-directed aggression, but were unreliable predictors of whether a teacher social command would result in teacher-directed aggression (CP = .008). An analysis of prevalent and predictive sequences suggests that prevalent behaviors did not necessarily predict conditional (functional) relations to aggressive behavior.

Jack et al. (1996) employed lag sequential analysis to describe teachers' use of classroom management strategies and their interactions with students with SBD. The results of teacher interviews and classroom interactions revealed two groups of teachers: those who reported high use of management strategies and those who reported low use of management strategies. The data collected in this study were then reorganized to develop interaction sequences defined as positive, negative, neutral, or mixed sequences. The procedure was accomplished by identifying each sequence of interaction based on event codes recorded within the individual sequences. An interaction sequence was defined by all codes recorded between Stop codes ("Stop" indicated that no events had been coded for 10 seconds). A "positive interaction" sequence was one in which one or more codes listed as positive (praise, tangibles given, positive physical contact, etc.) were recorded within the sequence. "Negative interaction" consisted of one or more negative events being coded (aggression, negative verbal statements, disruptive behavior, etc.). "Neutral interaction" was defined by the absence of either positive or negative codes. "Mixed interaction" consisted of those sequences in which both negative and positive codes were recorded.

Reorganization of the data in this manner allowed us to examine the interaction sequences of students with their teachers, and to assess the differences in interactions within the type of sequence. There were few differences in the interaction patterns between those teachers who reported high use of management strategies and those who reported low use of management strategies. The sequence of the interactions within the type of interactions also did not differ between the groups. Significant but small differences between the two groups were found for positive interactions. The high group engaged in positive interactions for greater lengths of time than the low group, although they occurred at low rates for both groups. A positive interaction sequence was most likely initiated by a teacher giving the student an instructional command (22 percent of all positive interactions for both groups) or giving a positive consequence (17 percent and 22 percent of positive interactions for each group). When an instructional mand was given, the students were likely to follow with a compliance response (CP = .70 and .78 for each group). In both groups, "teacher positive consequence" was the response most often recorded as the termination event in the interaction sequence (CP = 28 percent and 27 percent of the positive interactions). "Negative interaction" sequences were also similar between the two groups. "Disruptive" behavior of the students was the most often recorded event to initiate (77 percent and 80 percent of all negative interactions for each group) and to terminate negative interactions (48 percent and 50 percent of negative interactions for each group). These results tended to indicate that teacher-reported use of formal behavior management strategies did not appear to affect the way in which interactions occurred in classrooms.

These studies represent an ongoing attempt to describe classroom interactions of students with behavior disorders. With detailed descriptive information provided by lag sequential analysis, we may now be better able to identify interaction sequences and potential sources of reinforcement or aversive control that may function to maintain undesirable behavior for students with SBD. This functional assessment of behavior has recently been attempted by using lag sequential analysis as a tool for developing and testing hypotheses in functional assessments of challenging classroom behavior.

Experimental Studies Using Lag Sequential Analysis

One of the first attempts to use lag sequential analysis to aid in identifying potential social stimuli that were hypothesized to control behavior was completed in a series of studies by Strain, Shores, and their colleagues. Tremblay et al. (1981) described the naturally occurring rates of social interactions of normally developing preschool children using sequential analysis procedures to identify children's social responses that had a high probability of obtaining positive responses from peers and entering into positive interactions with their peers. The data system consisted of 12 initiation codes and 3 responding codes recorded in a continuous fashion. The results indicated that the children engaged in a variety of initiating behaviors. However, four response patterns emerged as having conditional probabilities for over .60 of gaining a positive response from peers. One of these initiation responses, rough and tumble play, was significantly related to the sex of the students. It was a successful initiating response with males but not with females, and was omitted in the subsequent studies to test the functionality of these responses to aid socially withdrawn students in initiating play with peers.

In two experiments, Hendrickson et al. (1982), taught children to initiate social interactions by emitting the three social initiation responses (play organizers, shares, and assists) found in the Tremblay et al. (1981) study. In the first experiment, normally developing students were taught to initiate the prescribed responses to demonstrate that socially withdrawn students would respond reciprocally to these responses. In the second experiment, children with developmental disabilities were taught to emit the three social initiations to target students, again demonstrating that the social initiation responses were successful in gaining positive responses from their peers. These early studies indicated the potential of lag sequential analysis to identify significant patterns of social behavior in classroom environments that may lead to hypotheses for the functional analysis of social behavior.

More recently, a series of studies directly using lag sequential analysis to aid in developing functional analysis of classroom behavior disorders has been completed by our research group. Gunter et al. (1993) conducted assessments using sequential analysis to identify the social antecedents and consequences to disruptive behavior in two students with SBD. In separate studies, hypotheses were developed based on the conditional probabilities from the sequential analysis of baseline data. For one student, all disruptive behavior was most likely preceded by a "Stop code" (no social behavior) (CP = .51) or a "handraise" (CP = .37), while 73 percent of the time when the student raised his hand, it was followed by disruptive behavior. Apparently, a handraise predicted disruptive behavior. This handraise-disruptive sequence was more likely to be responded to by teachers (CP = .38) than was his handraise alone (CP = .25). These data suggested that the handraise-disruptive sequence may have been a result of extinction-induced behavior due to the schedule of teacher attention to the student's handraise. We hypothesized that increasing the teachers' responsiveness to the student's handraise and eliminating the teachers' responses to the sequence of handraise-disruptive behavior would lead to a decrease in the student's disruptive behavior. Although the results of the intervention were variable, the rate of disruptive behavior decreased by 55 percent from baseline to intervention phases, with the conditional probabilities of teacher attention to the handraise-disruption sequence decreasing to near zero.

For another student, we found that teacher attention to student disruptive behavior had high conditional probabilities, while positive attention (praise, tokens) was very low. In one experiment, disruptive behavior was followed by some form of teacher attention 54 percent of the time (combined teacher attention). In addition, teachers seldom emitted positive statements or provided other forms of positive events (such as tokens) to the student. We hypothesized that this student's disruptive behavior functioned to gain teacher attention. A simple extinction procedure was used as an intervention. In the first attempt, we were unsuccessful in decreasing the teacher's response to the student's disruptive behavior to a low level of attention. A second experiment was implemented both to decrease attention to disruptive behavior and to increase the teacher's praise statements. Since the classroom teacher had difficulty ignoring the student's disruptive behavior, a research assistant assumed the role of the teacher. A new baseline revealed that the research assistant's interactions with the student were very close to that of the teacher in the preceding study. Teacher attention still followed student disruption with a CP of .48, and his rate of praise and token delivery was slightly higher than that of the original teacher. A combination of planned ignoring of the disruptive behavior and the use of a three-minute DRI schedule of praise (to increase the rate of praise) was instituted. Reductions in the disruptive behaviors supported the social reinforcement hypothesis.

In two of the three experiments that successfully reduced inappropriate behavior, the decrease in the rate of disruptive behavior closely followed the decrease in the conditional probability of the related social stimuli. That is, across the experiments, the rates of disruptive behavior decreased by more than 50 percent and the conditional probabilities of the independent variables decreased by 40 percent or more. These results indicate the usefulness of lag sequential analysis in identifying significant stimuli related to problematic classroom behaviors.

Gunter et al. (1994) described academic interactions between a student and his teacher during an instructional period. Their interactions during a one-on-one math lesson consisted of the teacher providing written math facts on the chalkboard, the student working on the problems, and the teacher providing feedback on his performance. The student frequently engaged in disruptive or aggressive behaviors while he was working on the problems and during feedback interactions with the teacher. The analysis of the conditional probabilities of his disruptive/aggressive behaviors during a math lesson led to a negative reinforcement hypothesis: the student engaged in inappropriate behavior to escape or avoid the lesson. The intervention focused on changing the teacher's correction procedure to insure that the student would correctly respond to the academic questions by providing additional information before asking for the student's response. The results showed decreases in student negative behaviors (from .28 per minute during baseline phases to .09 per minute during intervention phases) concomitant with increases in teacher information preceding correction.

Our clinical evaluations of students with SBD continue to address the functional relationship between social stimuli and behavior in classroom environments. Often the analyses have indicated that classroom personnel were required to change the way in which they interact with students to complete a functional analysis to test the hypotheses. Controlling the behavior of teachers and others in the classroom presents a challenge for both testing the hypotheses generated by the analysis as well as for programming lasting behavior change. In one example, we found that a teacher attended to a student's disruptive behavior over 35 percent of the time, and seldom praised the student's appropriate classroom behavior (compliance or on-task). In an attempt to re-arrange these contingencies, we asked the teacher to praise the student on a specific schedule (a three-minute DRO) and respond to him less when he was disruptive. There was a strong correlation between the duration of positive and negative interactions between a teacher and student and the teacher's use of positive reinforcement contingencies. That is, when the teacher met the criterion of delivering a positive consequence once every three minutes, positive interactions occurred with the student over 30 percent of the observation session, and negative interactions occurred less than 7 percent of the time. Conversely, on days when the teacher did not meet the criterion, negative interactions occurred over 20 percent of the time, while positive interactions occurred less than 2 percent of the time. These patterns were similar for the student's rate of disruptive behavior, although they were not as dramatic. Such effects are not uncommonly observed in our ongoing efforts to understand and effectively modify teacher/student interactions.

ISSUES RELATED TO USING LAG SEQUENTIAL ANALYSIS

There are a number of issues related to using lag sequential analysis as an experimental and clinical tool in the study and treatment of social behavior. First is the difficulty encountered in obtaining reliably coded data with a system that is both extensive and inclusive enough to capture the behavior classes involved in social interaction, in sequence of their occurrence, with mutually exclusive codes. To establish interobserver reliability, two observers need to code the same event at the same time (or within a narrow window of time) to gain agreement on the system. Then, agreement on the data format to be used for analysis should be assessed. Most research studies report interobserver agreement on the events. We believe that if events (individual codes) are used for analysis, then simple event agreement is sufficient to estimate reliability of the data system. Bakeman and Gottman (1986) suggested that rather than using the percent agreement as to the occurrence on the events between each observer to estimate reliability, that Cohen's kappa be reported. Kappa statistically accounts for chance coding of events. In our research we train data collectors to a minimum of 80 percent agreement on the event codes before going to the field. Once in the field, we establish interobserver agreement again at 80 percent on the events, and we continue to take interobserver agreement data for at least 20 percent of the sessions in each classroom, for each target subject. The interobserver agreement we have obtained has been acceptable with overall agreement on events maintaining nearly 80 percent and kappa approximately .75. However, in our studies we have assessed interobserver agreement in several different ways, depending on how the data were organized. These different methods of data organization produce different statements of interobserver agreement.

In one study we obtained an average agreement on the individual codes across the course of the study of 89 percent agreement (range 62 to 100 percent) with kappa of .83. In this study (Jack et al., 1996) we organized the data into streams of interactions between students with SBD and their teachers into four types: positive, negative, neutral, and mixed sequences based on the behavior of the interactants coded by the observers. Interobserver agreement was recalculated based on the reorganization of the data. The results demonstrated that the reorganization of the data produced agreement scores that were somewhat less than agreement on individual codes. Positive interaction agreement was 58 percent, negative interaction was 85 percent, mixed interaction was 77 percent, and neutral interaction was 81 percent, with an overall agreement of 82 percent. In addition, since we reported interaction data on percent of time for the four types of interaction, we also calculated the agreement on duration by type of interaction. The results again gave a slightly different picture of the agreement between observers. Agreement was 82 percent for positive interaction, 82 percent for negative interaction, 79 percent for neutral, and 81 percent for mixed. These estimates of reliability suggest that interobserver agreement will change as a result of the organization of the data.

Another problematic reliability issue is related to the reliance on conditional probabilities to identify the relationships among the events. If the conditional probability statements are used to aid in formulating hypotheses about the potential control of social behavior, the reliability of the observed interaction sequence is needed. For example, in one of our experiments reviewed earlier (Gunter et al., 1993b) we found a conditional probability of .72 that a student's handraise was followed by disruptive behavior. Interobserver agreement was 98 percent for handraise and 98 percent for disruptive behavior. The agreement on the sequence of the handraise/disruption was 78 percent, nearly 20 percent lower than the event categories. Apparently, even small errors of agreement on events result in substantially lower agreement on the sequence of events as expressed by lag sequential analysis. Considering that 20 percent lower agreement has been found on one-step lag sequential analysis than on the event agreement, the agreement will be considerably lower than 20 percent if the analysis goes to two- or three-step lags.

Additional considerations in using lag sequential analysis, either for descriptive research or for single case functional assessment, include the stability of the conditional probabilities across time. We have taken some preliminary steps to address this issue. All subjects from archival data files for which we had at least 15 days of baseline data were selected for analysis. We submitted the conditional probabilities of two sequences that we have found to have high rates (teacher instructional and social commands followed by student compliance, and student disruptive behavior followed by teacher attention), and then tested for differences across 5, 7, 9, 12 and 15 days of data. We found no significant differences when using a Mann Whitney U test for the various sequenced pairs, indicating that for the group of nine classrooms, 5 days of data provides essentially the same conditional probabilities as do 15 days. Examining the individual graphs supported similar stability trends across time. Low-rate behavior, however, is problematic. The conditional probabilities of low-rate responses (student compliance followed by teacher positive consequence) from the same records were also examined. The probabilities were quite variable, ranging from 0 to 1.00 within and across subjects over the different lengths of time. In a separate preliminary analysis, we found that some low-rate sequences (aggression) seem to require at least 12 days of data before stability is achieved. High-rate sequences appear to be stable within about five to seven days. Low-rate sequences, on the other hand, require more samples before one can assume stability and have confidence in developing hypotheses for testing through experimental procedures.

In addition to the need to establish stability there are other problems in analyzing low-rate behavior using lag sequential analysis. Wehby et al. (1995) reported that although "teacher social commands" preceded aggressive behavior directed at teachers at a high conditional probability of .22, teacher social commands did not predict aggression (social commands followed by aggression). This is probably due to the fact that teacher social commands were emitted at a much higher rate than student aggression. One of the problems of identifying stimuli of low-rate behavior is the definitions of the events used in the analysis. Even assuming that reliability is not an issue, the operational definitions used for the coding of events are, at best, general a priori classes of behavior composed of several topographies of behavior. These generalized definitions of classes of behavior are probably not precise enough to provide predictability by lag sequential analysis.

SUMMARY

The assessment of classroom behavior disorders has moved from identifying student response typographies for classification purposes and descriptions of problematic responses, to assessment procedures that lead to developing hypotheses regarding the motivation of behavior and experimental functional analysis. The advent of computer-assisted observation procedures has facilitated the development of complex systems that are capable of providing detailed analysis. The recent research to describe interactions reported in this chapter appears to be far more sophisticated in identifying important stimuli and consequences of both prosocial and antisocial behavior than we have previously found possible with paper-and-pencil methods. Computer-assisted observation procedures using lag sequential analysis were useful in our research in describing interactions and in identifying important classes of behavior that appear to contribute to, if not control, aberrant behavior in classrooms. Such research efforts should contribute to our understanding of complex social behavior, and should enable the development of more effective intervention programs. However, there are no data to suggest that these "sophisticated" observation and analysis procedures are any more effective in developing viable hypotheses for intervention than the older paper-and-pencil method of observing the antecedents-behavior-consequences of student classroom interactions.

The use of lag sequential analysis as a tool for functional analysis of social interactions in classrooms for students with behavior disorders shows promise, even taking into account the limitations we have just discussed. The descriptive information based on the use of this tool has demonstrated several interesting points of information. For example, the low rate of teacher's attention to disruptive and socially inappropriate behavior points to the need to understand that without positive reinforcement, escape or avoidance behavior is likely to occur (Sidman,

1989). This behavior may often take the form of disruptive and even aggressive behavior, thereby increasing the excesses of behavior that are labeled disordered (Gunter et al., 1994). In addition, the descriptive studies as well as the experimental studies have indicated that teachers often respond more frequently to students' inappropriate behavior than they do to appropriate behavior. The combination of extinction of appropriate behavior and reinforcement of inappropriate behavior should increase the probabilities that a deviant social behavior pattern is well established and maintained by students' interactions in classrooms. These interactions must be a focus of intense study to provide better interventions to remediate the destructive patterns that will lead to lifelong behavior disorders (Gunter et al., 1994).

In this chapter, we have focused on the analysis of social interaction in classrooms. As stated earlier, factors other than social interactions may also may maintain or increase deviant classroom behavior. A number of factors that can lead to or maintain behavior disorders in classrooms are associated with the aversiveness of school environments that may increase escape and avoidance behavior often considered deviant (Gunter et al., 1993a). Research has shown that such factors as curricular/schedule variables (Dunlap et al., 1991), size of areas (Brown, Fox, & Brady, 1987), and before-school activities (Kennedy & Itkonen, 1993) also affect classroom behavior disorders. Wehby et al. (1995) suggested that these other factors must be incorporated into the assessment process to aid in refining the use of lag sequential analysis, including the assessment of setting events (Bijou & Baer, 1961; Dumas, 1989; Hendrickson, Gable, & Shores, 1987). As Repp (1994) stated, the continued application of functional assessment technology should be expanded to address these potentially important variables and lead us to better understand the nature and context of aberrant behavior in school settings.

REFERENCES

Achenbach, T. M., & Edelbrock, C. E. (1988). *Teacher's report form of the child behavior checklist.* Burlington: University of Vermont Department of Psychiatry.

American Psychiatric Association (1994). *Diagnostic and statistical manual of mental disorders* (4th ed.). Washington, DC: Author.

Bakeman, R., & Gottman, J. M. (1986). *Observing interaction: An introduction to sequential analysis.* New York: Cambridge University.

Bijou, S. W., & Baer, D. M. (1961). *Child development I: A systematic and empirical theory.* Englewood Cliffs, NJ: Prentice-Hall.

Bijou, S. W., Peterson, R. F., & Ault, M. H. (1968). A method to integrate descriptive and experimental field studies at the level of data and empirical concept. *Journal of Applied Behavior Analysis, 1,* 175–191.

Brown, W. H., Fox, J. J., & Brady, M. P. (1987). Effects of spatial density on 3- and 4-year-old children's socially directed behavior during freeplay: An investigation of a setting factor. *Education and Treatment of Children, 10,* 247–258.

Carr, E. G., & Durand, V. M. (1985). Reducing behavior problems through functional communication training. *Journal of Applied Behavior Analysis, 18,* 111–126.

Carr, E. G., Newsom, C., & Binkoff, J. A. (1980). Escape as a factor in the aggressive behavior of two retarded children. *Journal of Applied Behavior Analysis, 13,* 101–117.

Carr, E. G., Taylor, J. C., & Robinson, S. (l991). The effects of severe behavior problems in children on the teaching behavior of adults. *Journal of Applied Behavior Analysis, 24,* 523–535.

Carta, J. J., & Greenwood, C. R. (1985). Ecobehavioral assessment: A methodology for expanding the evaluation of early intervention programs. *Topics in Early Childhood Special Education, 5*(2), 88–104.

Day, H. M., Horner, R. H., & O'Neill, R. E. (1994). Multiple functions of problem behaviors: Assessment and intervention. *Journal of Applied Behavior Analysis, 25,* 905–916.

Dumas, J. E. (1989). Let's not forget the context in behavioral assessment. *Behavioral Assessment. 11,* 231–247.

Dunlap, G., Kern-Dunlap, L., Clark, S., & Robbins, F. R. (1991). Functional assessment, curricular revision, and severe behavior problems. *Journal of Applied Behavior Analysis, 24,* 387–397.

Dunlap, G., Kern, L., dePerczel, M., Clarke, S., Wilson, D., Childs, K. E., White, R., & Falk, G. D. (1993). Functional analysis of classroom variables for students with emotional and behavioral disorders. *Behavioral Disorders, 18,* 275–291.

Durand, V. M., & Carr, E. G. (1992). An analysis of maintenance following functional communication training. *Journal of Applied Behavior Analysis, 25,* 777–794.

Durand, V. M., & Crimmins, D. B. (1988). Identifying the variables maintaining self-injurious behavior. *Journal of Autism and Developmental Disorders, 18,* 99–117.

Eisert, D. C., Walker, H. M., Severson, H., & Block, A. (1989). Patterns of social-behavioral competence in behavior disordered preschoolers. *Early Childhood Development & Care, 41,* 139–152.

Fisher, W., Piazza, C., Cataldo, M., Harrell, R., Jefferson, G., & Conner, R. (1993). Functional communication training with and without extinction and punishment. *Journal of Applied Behavior Analysis, 26,* 23–36.

Fuchs, D., & Fuchs, L. S. (1989). Exploring effective and efficient pre-referral interventions: A component analysis of behavioral consultation. *School Psychology Review, 18,* 260–283.

Fuchs, D., Fuchs, L. S., & Bahr, M. W. (1990). Mainstream assistance teams: A scientific basis for the art of consultation. Special Issue: Enhancing the education of difficult-to-teach students in the mainstream: Federally sponsored research. *Exceptional Children, 57,* 128–139.

Gottman, J. M. (1983). How children become friends. *Monographs of the Society for Research in Child Development, 48*(3), 81–86.

Gottman, J. M., & Roy, A. (1990). *Sequential analysis: A guide for behavioral researchers.* New York: Cambridge University.

Greenwood, C. R. (1991). Longitudinal analysis of time, engagement, and achievement in at-risk versus non-risk students. *Exceptional Children, May, 57*(6), 521–535.

Gunter, P. L., Denny, R. K., Jack, S. L., Shores, R. E., & Nelson, C. M. (1993a). Aversive stimuli in academic interactions between students with serious emotional disturbance and their teachers. *Behavioral Disorders, 18,* 265–274.

Gunter, P. L., Jack, S. L., Shores, R. E., Carrell, D. E., & Flowers, J. (1993b). Lag sequential analysis as a tool for functional analysis of student disruptive behavior in classrooms. *Journal of Emotional and Behavioral Disorders, 1*(3), 138–148, 198.

Gunter, P. L., Shores, R. E., Jack, S. L., Denny, R. K., & DePaepe, P. (1994). A case study of the effects of altering instructional interactions on the disruptive behavior of a child identified with severe behavior disorders. *Education & Treatment of Children, 17,* 435–444.

Hagopian, L. P., Fisher, W. W., & Legacy, S. M. (1994). Schedule effects of noncontingent reinforcement on attention-maintained destructive behavior in identical quadruplets. *Journal of Applied Behavior Analysis, 27,* 317–325.

Halle, J. W., & Spradlin, J. E. (1993). Identifying stimulus control of challenging behavior. In J. Reichle & D. P. Wacker (Eds.), *Communicative alternatives to challenging behavior: Integrating functional assessment and intervention strategies* (pp. 83–109). Baltimore: Paul H. Brookes.

Hendrickson, J., Gable, R., & Shores, R. (1987). The ecological perspective: Setting events and behavior. *The Pointer, Spring,* 40–44.

Hendrickson, J. M., Strain, P. S., Tremblay, A., & Shores, R. E. (1982). Interactions of behaviorally handicapped children. *Behavior Modification, 6,* 323–353.

Jack, S. L., Shores, R. E., Denny, R. K., Gunter, P. L., DeBriere, T., & DePaepe, P. (1996). An analysis of the relationship of teachers' reported use of classroom management strategies on types of classroom interactions. *Journal of Behavioral Education, 6*(1), 67–87.

Kennedy, C. H., & Itkonen, T. (1993). Effects of setting events on the problem behavior of students with severe disabilities. *Journal of Applied Behavior Analysis, 26,* 321–327.

Lerman, D. C., & Iwata, B. A. (1993). Descriptive and experimental analyses of variables maintaining self-injurious behavior. *Journal of Applied Behavior Analysis, 26,* 293–319.

Lerner, J. A., Inui, T. S., Trupin, E. W., & Douglas, E. (1985). Preschool behavior can predict psychiatric disorders. *Journal of the American Academy of Child Psychiatry, 24,* 42–48.

Luiselli, J. K. (1991). Assessment-derived treatment of children's disruptive behavior disorders. *Behavior Modification, 15,* 294–309.

Mace, F. C. (1994a). The significance and future of functional analysis methodologies. *Journal of Applied Behavior Analysis, 27,* 385–392.

Mace, F. C. (1994b). Basic research needed for stimulating the development of behavioral technologies. *Journal of the Experimental Analysis of Behavior, 61,* 529–550.

Mace, F. C., & Lalli, J. S. (1991). Linking descriptive and experimental analyses in the treatment of bizarre speech. *Journal of Applied Behavior Analysis, 24,* 553–562.

Mace, F. C., & Shea, M. C. (1991). New directions in behavior analysis for the treatment of severe behavior disorders. In S. Harris & J. Handleman (Eds.), *Aversive and non-aversive interventions: Controlling life-threatening behavior by the developmentally disabled* (pp. 57–59). New York: Springer-Verlag.

McMahon, R. J., & Forehand, R. (1988). Conduct disorders. In E. J. Mash & L. G. Terdal (Eds.), *Behavioral assessment of childhood disorders* (2nd ed., pp. 105–153). New York: Guilford.

Moran, G., Dumas, J. E., & Symons, D. K. (1992). Approaches to sequential analysis and the description of contingency in behavioral interaction. *Behavioral Assessment, 14,* 65–92.

O'Neill, R., Horner, R., Albin, R., Storey, K., & Sprague, J. (1990). *Functional analysis of problem behavior: A practical assessment guide.* Sycamore, IL: Sycamore.

Pace, G. M., Iwata, B. A., Cowdery, G. E., Andree, P. J., & McIntyre, T. (1993). Stimulus fading during extinction of self-injurious escape behavior. *Journal of Applied Behavior Analysis, 26,* 205–212.

Patterson, G. R. (1982). *Coercive family process.* Eugene: Castalia.

Patterson, G. R. (1986). Performance models for antisocial boys. *American Psychologist, 41,* 432–444.

Quay, H. C., & Peterson, D. R. (1987). *Manual for the revised behavior problem checklist.* Coral Gables, FL: Author.

Reid, J. B., Baldwin, D. V., Patterson, G. R., & Dishion, T. J. (1988). Some problems relating to the assessment of childhood disorders: A role for observational data. In M. Rutter, A. H. Tuma, and I. Lann (Eds.), *Assessment and diagnosis in child and adolescent psychopathology.* New York: Guilford.

Repp, A. C. (1994). Comments on functional analysis procedures for school-based behavior problems. *Journal of Applied Behavior Analysis, 27,* 409–412.

Repp, A. C., Felce, D., & Barton, L. E. (1988). Basing the treatment of stereotypic and self-injurious behaviors on hypotheses of their causes. *Journal of Applied Behavior Analysis, 21,* 281–289.

Repp, A. C., & Karsh, K. G. (1994). Hypothesis-based interventions for tantrum behaviors of persons with developmental disabilities in school settings. *Journal of Applied Behavior Analysis, 27,* 21–31.

Rotholz, D. A., Kamps, D. M., & Greenwood, C. R. (1989). Ecobehavioral assessment and analysis in special education settings for students with autism. *The Journal of Special Education, 23,* 59–81.

Sasso, G. M., Reimers, T. M., Cooper, L. J., Wacker, D., Berg, W., Steege, M., Kelly, L., & Allaire, A. (1992). Use of descriptive and experimental analyses to identify the functional properties of aberrant behavior in school settings. *Journal of Applied Behavior Analysis, 25,* 809–821.

Shores, R. E., Jack, S. L., Gunter, P. L., Ellis, D. N., DeBriere, T. J., & Wehby, J. H. (1993). Classroom interactions of children with behavior disorders. *Journal of Emotional and Behavioral Disorders, 1,* 27–39.

Sidman, M. (1989). *Coercion and its fallout.* Boston: Authors Cooperative, Inc.

Simpson, R. L., & Souris, L. A. (1988). Reciprocity in the pupil-teacher interactions of autistic and mildly handicapped preschool children. *Behavioral Disorders, 13* (3), 159–168.

Slate, J. R., & Saudargas, R. A. (1987). Classroom behaviors of LD, seriously emotionally disturbed, and average children: A sequential analysis. *Learning Disability Quarterly, 10,* 125–134.

Snyder, J., & Patterson, G. R. (1986). Effects of consequences on patterns of social interaction: A quasi-experimental approach to reinforcement in natural interaction. *Child Development, 59,* 1257–1268.

Sprague, J. R., & Horner, R. H. (1992). Co-variations within functional response classes: Implications for treatment of severe problem behavior. *Journal of Applied Behavior Analysis, 25,* 735–745.

Strain, P. S., Lambert, D. L., Kerr, M. M., Stagg, V., & Lenkner, D. A. (1983). Naturalistic assessment of children's compliance to teacher's requests and consequences for compliance. *Journal of Applied Behavior Analysis, 16,* 243–249.

Taylor, J. C., & Carr, E. G. (1992). Severe problem behaviors related to social interaction: II. A systems analysis. *Behavior Modification, 16,* 336–371.

Taylor, J. C., & Romanczyk, R. G. (1994). Generating hypotheses about the function of student problem behavior by observing teacher behavior. *Journal of Applied Behavior Analysis, 27,* 251–265.

Touchette, P., MacDonald, R., & Langer, S. (1985). A scatter plot for identifying stimulus control of problem behaviors. *Journal of Applied Behavior Analysis, 18,* 343–351.

Tremblay, A., Strain, P. S., Hendrickson, J. M., & Shores, R. E. (1981). Social interactions of normal preschool children. *Behavior Modification, 5,* 237–253.

Wacker, D. P., Steege, M. W., Northup, J., Sasso, G., Berg, W., Reimers, T., Cooper, L., Cigrand, K., & Donn, L. (1990). A component analysis of functional communication training across three topographies of severe behavior problems. *Journal of Applied Behavior Analysis, 23,* 417–429.

Wahler, R. G., & Dumas, J. E. (1986). Maintenance factors in coercive mother-child interactions: The compliance and predictability hypothesis. *Journal of Applied Behavior Analysis, 19,* 13–22.

Walker, H. M., Severson, H. H., Stiller, B., Williams, G., Haring, N., Shinn, M., & Toddis, B. (1988). Systematic screening for pupils in the elementary age range at risk for behavior disorders: Development of trial testing of a multiple gating model. *Remedial and Special Education, 9*(3), 8–14.

Wampold, B. E. (1992) The intensive examination of social interactions. In T. R. Kratochwill & J. R. Levine (Eds.), *Single case research design and analysis: New directions for psychology and education* (pp. 93–131). Hillsdale, NJ: Lawrence Erlbaum Associates.

Weeks, M., & Gaylord-Ross, R. (1981). Task difficulty and aberrant behavior in severely handicapped students. *Journal of Applied Behavior Analysis, 14,* 449–463.

Wehby, J. H., Dodge, K. A., Valente, E., & the Conduct Problems Prevention Research Group. (1993). School behavior of first grade children identified as at-risk for development of conduct problems. *Behavioral Disorders, 19*(1), 67–78.

Wehby, J. H., Symons, F. J., & Shores, R. E. (1995). A descriptive analysis of aggressive behavior in classrooms for children with emotional and behavioral disorders. *Behavioral Disorders, 20*(2), 87–105.

Yoder, P. J., & Tapp, J. T. (1990). SATS: Sequential analysis of transcripts system. *Behavior Research Methods, Instruments, and Computers, 22,* 339–343.

12

▨

Naturalistic Functional Assessment with Regular and Special Education Students in Classroom Settings

ALAN C. REPP

INTRODUCTION

Several chapters in this book have discussed methodological variations in functional assessment, including interviews, analogue assessments, and descriptive assessments. This chapter focuses on functional assessments in schools, where in most cases analogue assessments would not be allowed but where descriptive assessments usually would be allowed.

In this chapter, Repp presents a framework for naturalistic functional assessment, in which problem behavior is analyzed during baseline, a baseline in which there are no artificial manipulations in the classroom. The rationale is that because behavior is existing under current environmental variables, our attention should be on those variables, in their natural state, in the classroom. A system is provided for analyzing mutually exclusive and exhaustive sets of setting events, antecedents, and consequences, and for analyzing data within conditional probability tables. From these tables, hypotheses are derived, and interventions are based on these hypotheses (as stressed by Kern and Dunlap).

The author uses the traditional two hypotheses (positive and negative reinforcement), but formally adds a third (sensory regulation), which he has found in his work to be as frequently involved as the reinforcement hypotheses. While the concept is similar to stimulation and some forms of automatic reinforcement as discussed by Shore and Iwata, it is more like Carr's consideration of homeostasis and formulated as the regulation of overt fine motor and gross motor activity. As such, it may emphasize formal adoption of a hypothesis that can be useful to those using functional assessment paradigms.

As indicated in Chapter 8 (Repp and Munk), we like to group the functional assessment procedures into three categories: interviews, analogue assessments, and naturalistic assessments. Each of these, of course, has variations.[1] The interview, for example, is considered by some (Durand & Crimmins, 1988) to be the functional assessment and by others (O'Neill et al., 1990) to be an information-gathering procedure that helps to identify antecedents, setting events, consequences, and behaviors that will be analyzed in the functional assessment that follows. Analogue assessments have been conducted by some (Iwata et al., 1982) to test three functions under conditions that are abstractions of the natural environment and by others (Carr, Newsom, & Binkoff, 1980) to test one particular function rather than three under conditions that are closer approximations of the natural environment.

Naturalistic assessments have also been conducted with numerous variations, and we have several excellent examples in this volume (Burgio & Lewis, 1995; Carr, Langdon, & Yarbrough, 1995; Kern & Dunlap, 1995). The primary purpose of this chapter is to provide another variation of naturalistic functional assessment, one which we have been developing over the last 10 years. A second purpose is to provide this example with a different group of persons than those with whom the procedure has generally been used. As Kern and Dunlap have explained in Chapter 10, analogue assessments began in the area of developmental disabilities with important papers by Carr, Gaylord-Weeks, Iwata, and others. Dunlap, Kern, and their colleagues (Dunlap et al., 1993, 1994; Kern et al., 1994) have made an important contribution by extending functional assessment to persons with emotional and behavioral disabilities. In this chapter, we will continue that extension by showing its use with a student labeled learning disabled (LD) and with a student not labeled and in regular education classrooms (these students serve as examples from the more than 150 students on whom we have data).

The chapter will be presented in four sections: (a) a general overview of naturalistic functional assessment, (b) the process of conducting and analyzing the data from a functional assessment, (c) the process of deriving hypothesis-based interventions, and (d) representative case studies.

---

[1]The references that follow are used as published examples; they are not meant to imply that these individuals only use these procedures or that only these individuals use these procedures.

NATURALISTIC FUNCTIONAL ASSESSMENT

Overview

Naturalistic Functional Assessment (NFA) is an assessment and intervention procedure that has been developed for natural settings rather than for analogues of those settings (Repp, Felce, & Barton, 1988; Repp & Karsh, 1990, 1994; Repp et al., 1996). The purpose of NFA is to identify the function of problem behavior from baseline data *without any artificial manipulations in the classroom*. Students are observed in their natural environment, and teachers (or parents, aides, etc.) are asked not to change anything in the way they normally conduct their activities or in the way they interact with their students. Our rationale is that if we believe that the environment is maintaining problem behavior, then an analysis of that particular environment-behavior interaction is the best way to identify the function of behavior and the specific intervention for that behavior. For this reason, we call our procedure *naturalistic functional assessment*. Baseline data are collected on student behaviors, environmental conditions (curriculum, seating arrangements), staff consequences, and setting events (fights with siblings); and the data are nested in conditional probability tables. Hypotheses are then generated for the conditions maintaining the problem behaviors, and interventions based on those hypotheses are developed that allow us to manipulate those conditions already in the environment.

NFA versus Traditional Approaches   In what we are calling the traditional behavior management approach, baseline data are collected and an intervention is selected, generally based on the experience of the interventionist (as an example, look for particular authors in the *Journal of Applied Behavior Analysis* and you will find that some invariably use punishment procedures like overcorrection while others invariably use differential reinforcement procedures). Some of the problems with this traditional approach are that (a) it does not examine the relationship between problem behavior and both the immediate (antecedents) and distal (setting events) environmental conditions; (b) it implements what may be time-intensive interventions without consideration of the function of the behavior (for example, time-out is sometimes used when the function of the behavior is to escape tasks, resulting in negative reinforcement of the problem behavior); (c) it may employ punitive interventions that are unnecessary and do not address alternative appropriate behaviors that could serve the same function as the problem behavior; and (d) it may not provide a framework by which staff can understand factors that produce and contribute to the problem behavior.

Traditional nonbehavioral approaches are even more problematic. They often look for the cause in the child, disability, or family characteristics; the thinking, unfortunately, is sometimes circular. For example, when asked to tell the reason a child is labeled A-D/HD, many teachers, parents, and others will say it is because he is hyperactive and distractable. When asked why he is hyperactive and distractable, they say it is because he is A-D/HD. In this type of pseudoexplanation, a label used to describe a set of behaviors soon becomes the reason for the behavior as well as part of the child (that is, something the child is or possesses).

The functional analysis approach, on the other hand, is based on a belief that (a) most problem behavior is environmentally dependent, and that it is related to and maintained by conditions in the environment; (b) problem behavior serves a function; (c) positive interventions can reduce and increase appropriate behavior; and (d) a program that restructures the environment can prevent problem behaviors from developing.

Functions of Behavior Behaviorists use the word *function* in several ways. Some use it to describe the environmental change that behavior causes (for example, a student disrupts class, is put in time-out, and escapes having to do the math assignment) while others use it to mean broader abstract terms (such as positive reinforcement, negative reinforcement, and stimulation). We have found that training staff to develop student-specific interventions is easier if we ask them first to identify the immediate consequence of behavior (escapes math assignment) and then translate that consequence into an abstraction (negative reinforcement). We therefore use the term function to mean positive reinforcement, negative reinforcement, and stimulation/sensory regulation.

The first two of these three are common hypotheses in the functional analysis and behavioral literatures, and we will not discuss them here. The third, however, merits some explanation because we use it in a different way than other behaviorists do. Our use of *sensory regulation* (also called *homeostasis*) is based on the *optimal stimulation* hypothesis which suggests that each individual organism has a biologically determined level of stimulation that it seeks to maintain (Zentall & Zentall, 1983). Further, the model assumes that organisms will work to optimize their level of stimulus input and arousal. In some cases, when environmental stimulation is low, organisms will behave in order to increase and thus regulate arousal states (assessed in some cases by EEG recordings). In other cases, when environmental stimulation is high, organisms may withdraw or engage in ritualized stereotyped behaviors to reduce the arousal state.

Further, the degree to which a particular environment is over- or understimulating is specific to the individual. Zentall and Zentall (1983) extended this idea to syndromes, arguing in their extensive literature review that persons labeled autistic are overstimulated and will seek to reduce the level of stimulation in many environments, while persons who are labeled hyperactive are understimulated and will seek to increase their level of stimulation in many environments.[2] In several interesting studies to test this theory with children labeled A-D/HD, they have shown, for example, that (a) A-D/HD children were more active than comparison children under a passive response condition, but that the two groups were equally active under an active response condition (Zentall & Meyer, 1987), and (b) hyperactive children were more talkative than control children during transition and nonverbal tasks but less talkative when asked to tell stories (Zentall, 1988).

Numerous studies with persons with retardation have shown that (a) when environments are barren, individuals will increase stereotyped acts, but that (b) when these environments are enriched, the same individuals will decrease

---

[2]In our language, the syndrome would be a setting event.

their stereotyped acts (Berkson & Mason, 1963; Favell, 1973; Favell, McGimsey, & Schell, 1982; Horner, 1980). Others have shown that when physical activities are made available, problem behaviors decrease (Duker et al., 1986; Sigafoos & Kerr, 1994). Further, a large literature has shown that *antecedent* aerobic exercise frequently decreases problem behavior (see review by Gabler-Halle, Halle, & Chung, 1993).

While these and many other studies have shown a relationship between activity level and problem behavior, they have not presented data in a manner that allows us to consider whether there is a moment-to-moment relationship between the two. For example, when we (Repp & Karsh, 1992) instituted a group teaching procedure that increased task responding by a factor of 4.0, eight students reduced stereotypic behavior from 45 to 10 percent of the time even though there were never any directly programmed consequences for stereotypy. While this effect suggests that the students were substituting task behaviors for stereotypies, we did not analyze the data directly to determine whether they were.

A more direct test of what we mean by sensory regulation or gross motor homeostasis has, however, been provided in two studies. In one (Repp et al., 1992) in which data were collected by computer, we made a second-by-second analysis of both stereotypies and other motor movements on 25 hours of data collection (five hours/day for five days) for each of 12 persons with retardation. Results showed that while these two classes of behavior varied in rate from day to day, the sum total of the two (the total amount of gross motor behavior) was remarkably consistent for each participant. Clearly, the individuals were substituting stereotypies for other motor movements and vice versa to maintain a constant (or homeostatic) level of movement. In a second study (Repp, Johnson, & Van Laarhoven, 1998), we measured the rate of motor movements during free-play for each of four children with developmental disabilities. We then provided two instructional sets: (a) one in which opportunities to respond matched the interresponse times shown in free-play, and (b) one in which the interresponse times did not match those in free-play but were instead approximately five times greater. All four participants engaged in much more stereotypy or other problem behaviors in the non-matched than in the matched condition. Overall motoric responding, however, remained relatively constant as the children substituted task-related behaviors for problem behaviors.

We realize that when changes in behavior increase or decrease stimulation, they could be considered examples of positive reinforcement and negative reinforcement, respectively. However, we will use *sensory regulation* in this chapter (and in our other work in functional assessment) as a third function for several reasons: (a) separating this hypothesis from positive reinforcement emphasizes the point that intervention involves the manipulation of *noncontingent* antecedent events, (b) interventions based on the positive reinforcement hypothesis usually confound stimulation (attention) with the proposed function of reinforcement, and (c) most importantly, we have found that using this function makes training much easier. Participants focus on examining the degree to which the environment occasions motoric movement during assessment and on altering the number of these environmental opportunities during intervention.

A MODEL FOR NFA

The goal of functional assessment is presented in Figure 12.1, and it is to identify a function of behavior, to develop an intervention specific for that function and that individual, and to replace the problem behavior with an appropriate behavior. During intervention, we generally

1. Provide the same consequence for the appropriate behavior that the student received for the inappropriate behavior. If that objective is not possible, then we provide a stronger, more powerful consequence for appropriate behavior than the student has been receiving for inappropriate behavior.

2. Make the consequence easier to obtain by appropriate behavior than by problem behavior.

3. Modify setting events and antecedents to promote appropriate behavior and to reduce the probability of problem behavior.

Assessment

The assessment question is, "Why do problem behaviors occur?" Because we believe most problem behaviors are environmentally dependent, we look to the environment for the answer to that question. Our first step is to identify and operationally define (a) problem behaviors and (b) appropriate behaviors that could substitute for the problem behaviors. Then we look for events that happen just before both the problem behaviors and the appropriate behaviors. These are the antecedent triggers shown in Figure 12.1.

Box 12 presents examples of antecedents and setting events that we often find in school settings. When we identify a possible antecedent (for example, passive task), we also include another antecedent, which is generally its opposite (for example, active task). We are attempting to identify antecedents for the problem behavior as well as antecedents for appropriate behavior. A common mistake in functional assessment is recording behavior during assessment under only one form of the antecedent (passive task in this example). If we did so and found a high rate of problem behavior, we could not logically link the problem to passive tasks because we do not know the rate of the behavior during either active tasks or the absence of tasks. Therefore, we suggest that each subset of the codes for antecedents (and setting events) be mutually exclusive and exhaustive.

Antecedents are those events happening just before or concurrent with the target behavior that *affect the probability of the occurrence of that behavior*. If an environmental event occurs before behavior but does not affect it, we call that event a neutral stimulus rather than an antecedent. There is another class of environmental events that does not operate on behavior quite so directly, but rather alters the probability that an antecedent will affect behavior. These are called setting events. If an antecedent does not always affect a target behavior, a setting event is probably operating. For example, if a student reacts inappropriately to a teacher's instruction today but has not done so recently, then a setting event is probably affecting the antecedent instruction. Examples could be: a peer teasing the student a few minutes

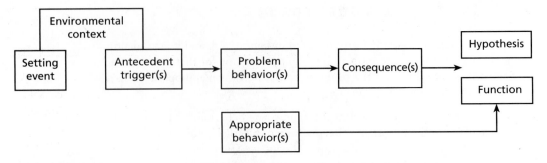

FIGURE 12.1 The goal of functional assessment is to identify the function of problem behavior; the goal of intervention is to substitute an appropriate behavior that produces the same function.

ago, a fight on the bus, fatigue, and so forth. Box 12 presents other examples that we have found in school settings.

Our last set of codes concerns consequences of the problem and the appropriate alternative behaviors. We identify these codes by making sample observations in the school while noting the consequences. Our notes, however, are guided by our three hypotheses; and because during assessment we are trying to determine the function/hypothesis, we observe what the student (a) obtains (positive reinforcement hypothesis), (b) escapes or avoids (negative reinforcement hypothesis), or (c) regulates (sensory regulation hypothesis).

Assessing the Three Hypotheses

Data Recording After determining our codes, we pilot test them in the natural environment, again asking the school personnel not to make any changes in their regular routine or ways of interacting with the student. In some cases our first set of codes will be correct; in others, we will have to make minor changes. Then we are ready for data collection.

The purpose of data collection is to identify the conditions under which behavior does and does not occur, and then develop the hypothesis describing the relationship between behavior and those conditions (in some instances, behavior may have more than one function in which case there would be more than one hypothesis). To identify these functions, we must consider the functions under which problem behavior does and does not occur. Figures 12.2, 12.3, and 12.4 emphasize that point, and present examples for the three hypotheses.

In most of our research studies, we collect data with a computer system that allows us to ask questions beyond what is needed for the functional assessment procedure. In training school personnel and university students, we use a traditional paper-and-pencil method and record using either momentary time-sampling or event recording. A variety of forms are available for data collection, but we like the Functional Analysis Observation Form provided by O'Neill et al. (1990).

This is a form with 47 columns and 10 rows, and is suitable for either momentary time-sampling (MTS) or event recording. The columns correspond to the codes, and we cluster them as setting events, antecedents, behaviors, and conse-

---

**BOX 12   Antecedents and Setting Events
Commonly Found in School Settings.**

Physiological/States

    Medication _____

    Seizures _____

    Allergies _____

    Injury _____

    Hunger _____

    Food Refusal _____

    Sleep: Lethargic. . . . . Alert

    Mood: Calm. Agitated

    Changes at home _____

    Critical incident _____

Physical Environment

    Time of Day: Early A.M.   Late A.M.
                   Early P.M.   Late P.M.

    Familiar . . . . Unfamiliar

    Small space . . . . Open space

    Barren environment . . . Enriched environment

    Restricted environment. . . . . Accessible

    Noise level: Quiet . . . . Distracting

    Density: Alone . . . . Crowded

    Music: Soothing . . . . Stimulating

    Visual input: No view . . . . View

    Layout not conducive to learning . . Conducive

Activities/Tasks

Type of Activity: Leisure   Academic   Self-help
                   Motor   Other

Materials: No materials   Shared materials
           Individual materials

Structure: Individual   Small group
          Whole class (lecture versus direct
          instruction)

Independent work

Schedule of activities:

    Predictable . . . . Unpredictable

    Free choice. . . . . Assigned

    Nonpreferred . . . . Preferred

    Easy . . . . Difficult

    Prompted . . . . Independent

    Boring/unchallenging. . . . . Novel

    Individual trials . . . . Massed trials

    No completion/follow-through . . . Completion

    No opportunities to respond. . . . Many oppor-
    tunities

    Slow pace of presentation. . . . . . . Rapid pace

    Disorganized transisitions. . Smooth transitions

Staff

    Unfamiliar . . . . Familiar

    Nonpreferred . . . . Preferred

    No proximity. . . . . Proximity

    No interactions. . . . . Frequent interactions

    Negative interactions. . . . Positive interactions

Peers

    Nonpreferred . . . . Preferred

    No proximity. . . . . Proximity

    No interaction . . . . Frequent interaction

    Inappropriate behavior. . . . . Appropriate

---

quences. The important point with respect to the codes is, again, that sets or subsets must be mutually exclusive and exhaustive. (We will show the importance of this point in the next section, Data Analysis). The rows correspond to the moment of recording. For MTS, we would use row 1 as the first observation and mark the behaviors, setting events, antecedents, and consequences occurring at that "moment" (generally a 5-second spread around the behavior to let us capture the contingency in effect); row 2 then becomes the record of the second observation, and

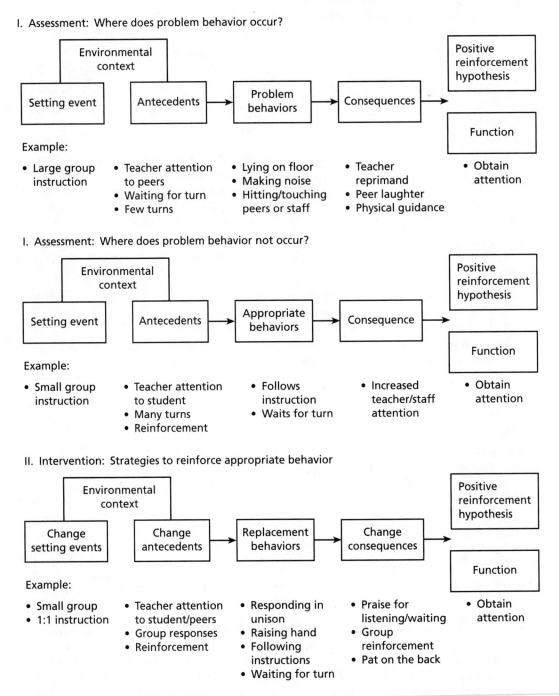

FIGURE 12.2 Example of the functional assessment and
intervention process for the positive reinforcement hypothesis.

Negative reinforcement hypothesis

I. Assessment: Where does problem behavior occur?

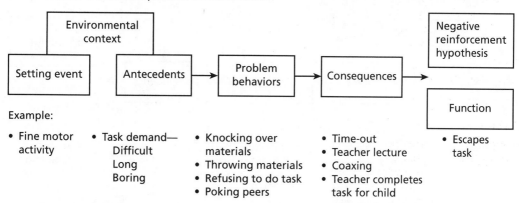

Example:

- Fine motor activity
- Task demand—
  Difficult
  Long
  Boring
- Knocking over materials
- Throwing materials
- Refusing to do task
- Poking peers
- Time-out
- Teacher lecture
- Coaxing
- Teacher completes task for child
- Escapes task

I. Attention: Where does problem behavior not occur?

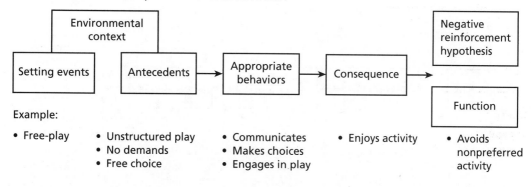

Example:

- Free-play
- Unstructured play
- No demands
- Free choice
- Communicates
- Makes choices
- Engages in play
- Enjoys activity
- Avoids nonpreferred activity

II. Intervention: Strategies to reduce aversiveness of tasks and increase appropriate behavior

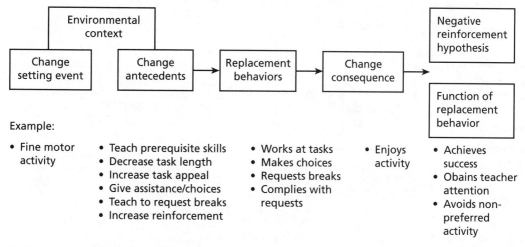

Example:

- Fine motor activity
- Teach prerequisite skills
- Decrease task length
- Increase task appeal
- Give assistance/choices
- Teach to request breaks
- Increase reinforcement
- Works at tasks
- Makes choices
- Requests breaks
- Complies with requests
- Enjoys activity
- Achieves success
- Obains teacher attention
- Avoids non-preferred activity

FIGURE 12.3 Example of the functional assessment and intervention process for the negative reinforcement hypothesis.

Stimulation hypothesis—decrease

I. Attention: Where does problem behavior occur?

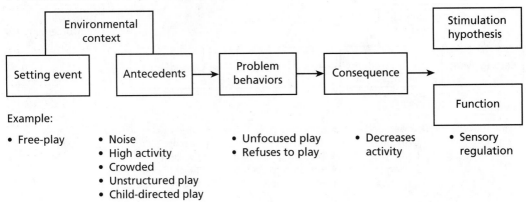

Example:

- Free-play
  - Noise
  - High activity
  - Crowded
  - Unstructured play
  - Child-directed play
- Unfocused play
- Refuses to play
- Decreases activity
- Sensory regulation

I. Attention: Where does problem behavior not occur?

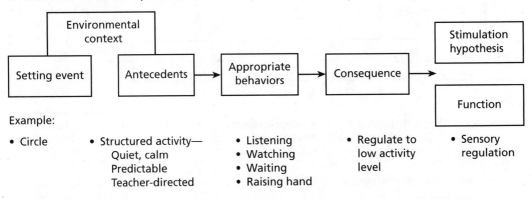

Example:

- Circle
  - Structured activity—
    Quiet, calm
    Predictable
    Teacher-directed
- Listening
- Watching
- Waiting
- Raising hand
- Regulate to low activity level
- Sensory regulation

II. Intervention: Strategies to decrease stimulation

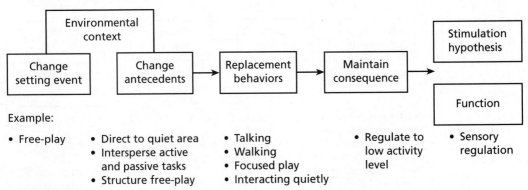

Example:

- Free-play
  - Direct to quiet area
  - Intersperse active and passive tasks
  - Structure free-play
- Talking
- Walking
- Focused play
- Interacting quietly
- Regulate to low activity level
- Sensory regulation

FIGURE 12.4 Examples of the functional assessment and intervention process for the sensory regulation hypothesis (one example to increase and one example to decrease stimulation).

Stimulation hypothesis—increase

I. Assessment: Where does problem behavior occur?

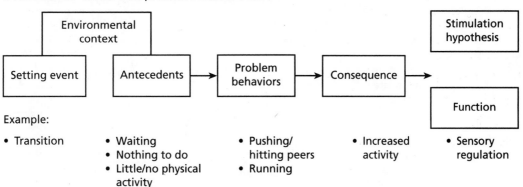

Example:

• Transition	• Waiting • Nothing to do • Little/no physical activity	• Pushing/ hitting peers • Running	• Increased activity	• Sensory regulation

I. Assessment: Where does problem behavior not occur?

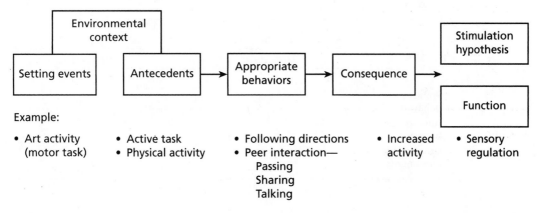

Example:

• Art activity (motor task)	• Active task • Physical activity	• Following directions • Peer interaction— Passing Sharing Talking	• Increased activity	• Sensory regulation

II. Intervention: Strategies to increase stimulation

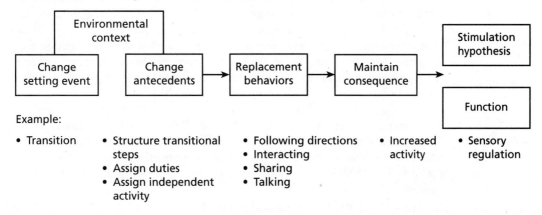

Example:

• Transition	• Structure transitional steps • Assign duties • Assign independent activity	• Following directions • Interacting • Sharing • Talking	• Increased activity	• Sensory regulation

Table 12.1 Some Generic Conditional Probability Tables for Functional Assessment

	SETTING EVENT PRESENT		SETTING EVENT ABSENT	
	ANTECEDENT		ANTECEDENT	
	Present	Absent	Present	Absent
Problem behavior				
Appropriate behavior				

	Condition			
	SE/A COMBINATION 1		ALL OTHER COMBINATIONS	
	BEHAVIOR		BEHAVIOR	
	Problem	Appropriate	Problem	Appropriate
Reinforcement				
No reinforcement				

	SETTING EVENT PRESENT				SETTING EVENT ABSENT			
	ANTECEDENT				ANTECEDENT			
	A	B	C	D	A	B	C	D
Problem behavior								
Appropriate behavior								
Other motor movements								

so forth. For event recording, we use row 1 to record codes based on the first occurrence of any, appropriate or inappropriate, behavior; row 2 becomes the record of the second occurrence of any behavior, and so forth, (O'Neill et al., 1990, have another system for event recording that allows sequences to be recorded in each row, thus saving recording sheets. We use this procedure as well; however, we refer the reader to their book, as an explanation here would be too lengthy for our present purpose).

Data Analysis The record from data collection allows us to determine the probability of behavior under settings, antecedents, and their combinations. Further, it allows us to determine the probability of each consequence for each behavior in the code. Table 12.1 presents some generic formats for analyzing the data as conditional probabilities.

The top of the three panels in this table is an initial test of the negative reinforcement hypothesis. It assesses the effect of the presence and absence of (a) a particular setting event and (b) a particular antecedent on both problem behavior and appropriate behavior. If we find that there is a higher probability of problem behavior in (a) the presence of an antecedent irrespective of the presence of a setting event, or (b) only the presence of an antecedent combined with the presence of a setting event, then we can begin to make some preliminary hypotheses. In general, we could have a (a) *negative reinforcement paradigm* in which the student is trying to escape, or we could have a (b) *positive reinforcement paradigm* in which the particular condition signals the student that more reinforcement will be available for problem behavior during that antecedent or setting event (for example, when the teacher has left and a practicum student is teaching), or a (c) *sensory regulation paradigm* in which the condition is over- or understimulating and the student is trying to regulate the level of stimulation.

The middle portion of the table represents a test of the positive reinforcement condition. The left-hand side tests the relationship between (a) appropriate and inappropriate behavior and (b) particular consequences under a *particular* setting event (presence or absence)/antecedent (presence or absence) combination. The right-hand portion tests the relationship between behavior and all other setting event/antecedent combinations. If the data show that problem behavior has too rich a schedule of reinforcement, then we would develop a positive reinforcement hypothesis. If the schedule is too rich only for a particular setting event/antecedent combination, then we would suspect that this condition exerted stimulus control by signalling the availability of reinforcement.

The lower portion of the table begins the test of the sensory regulation hypothesis. It tests the relationship between antecedents and the amount of motoric responding under each (represented by the categories: problem behavior, appropriate behavior, and other motor movements). If there is more problem behavior under a particular antecedent, we could have a *negative reinforcement hypothesis* (student is trying to escape or avoid the antecedent) or a *sensory regulation hypothesis* (student is regulating the level of stimulation). We would then go one level beneath these antecedents (they could be curriculum areas) and examine the data comparing the level of active responding in each condition, the number of opportunities to respond, the difficulty level of each curriculum area, student preparedness for each, and so forth. This information will lead us to adopt either of these two hypotheses.

Intervention

The purpose of assessment is first to propose a hypothesis for the problem behavior, and then to develop an intervention based on that hypothesis. Because we assess in the natural environment, the process of determining an intervention becomes one of rejecting certain aspects of the environment as possible sources of control. We do so by using the conditional probability tables (see Table 12.1) which allow us to reject many variables. In this section, we will present two case studies as an illustration of the process.

Case Studies We currently have data on more than 150 students, either with mild disabilities or without any disabilities.

Bill Bill is a 15-year-old in a regular education classroom. The presenting problem was talk-outs, and a set of codes was developed to address this problem. First, the teacher selected behavior codes that would form a mutually exclusive and exhaustive set. These were operationally defined and the following labels were chosen: on-task/active engagement, on-task/passive engagement, off-task/talk-outs, off-task/no talk-outs, no task present/appropriate behavior, and no task present/inappropriate behavior. The next step was to determine the antecedents. Because Bill did equally well in all academics, we did not use subject matter (such as math or English) as a category. There was some thought that the instructional condition could be relevant, so we selected the following: group instruction/lecture format, group instruction/direct instruction with choral responding, one-to-one instruction, independent seatwork, other instruction (a catch-all category), and no task present. The teacher felt that Bill came to class some days in a bad mood, and that his mood might affect his behavior. Mood was then taken as a setting event, and the teacher rated Bill's entering mood within the first five minutes of class; the categories were: especially good, average, and bad.

The teacher knew that Bill liked her and his classmates, and was unsure if he received more attention from her or his peers when he engaged in talk-outs. So, two subsets of the codes were selected: teacher attention versus no teacher attention; peer attention versus no peer attention.

Data were then collected for six days with a momentary time-sampling procedure by a school psychology intern. Data were sorted into conditional probability tables and analyzed. The first analysis was of the three possible setting events related to mood. Results showed no differentiation among the three, so the three categories were dropped from further analysis.

The next analysis was of the relationship between the five instructional conditions (treated as antecedents) and the six behavior categories. These data are presented in Table 12.2, and they show (a) that there were more *talk-outs* during *group lecture* (.18) and *no task present* (.13) than during the other four conditions (range = 0 to .04), (b) that the *group lecture* condition had less *on-task/active* responding (.08) than the other conditions (range = .38 to .82), (c) that there was more *on-task/passive behavior* during *group lecture* (.63) than during the other conditions (range = .14 to .51), and (d) that there was more total *off-task* responding during this condition (.29) than during the others (range = .03 to .13). Because there was more problem behavior under one condition than under others, these results suggest either a negative reinforcement or a sensory regulation hypothesis. However, since Bill never escaped or avoided this condition because of his talk-outs, we rejected the negative reinforcement hypothesis.

The last analysis was of the relationship between (a) *talk-outs* and *attention,* and *on-task* and *attention* during (b) *group lecture* versus the other four instructional categories combined. These data showed little more attention for talk-outs during group lecture than during the other instructional formats from (a) the teacher (.05 during group lecture versus .07 during the other formats) or from (b) the peers (.08 versus .04, respectively). In addition, although there was a difference in peer attention during group instruction (.08) versus all others (.04), we made the assumption that this difference (.04) was not sufficient to produce the difference between talk-outs in group lecture versus all other conditions. Group lecture thus

Table 12.2 Analysis of Bill's Talk-outs

	Group Instruction/ Lecture	Group Instruction/ Choral	One-to-One Instruction	Independent Seatwork	Other	No Task[1]
On-task/Active	.08	.42	.82	.79	.38	n.a.
On-task/Passive	.63	.51	.14	.18	.49	n.a.
Off-task/Talk-outs	.18	.01	.00	.00	.04	.13*
Off-task/No talk-outs	.11	.06	.04	.03	.09	.87**
No task/Appropriate	n.a.	n.a.	n.a.	n.a.	n.a.	.91
No task/Inappropriate	n.a.	n.a.	n.a.	n.a.	n.a.	.09

[1]Because there was no task present for this column, the data represent talk-outs (*) or no talk-outs (**)

	GROUP INSTRUCTION/ LECTURE		ALL OTHER	
	Talk-outs	On Task	Talk-outs	On-Task
Teacher attention	.05	.28	.07	.41
No teacher attention	.95	.72	.93	.58
Peer attention	.08	.03	.04	.06
No peer attention	.92	.97	.96	.94

did not appear to be an S^D for increased opportunity for attention to talk-outs, and this information further supported a rejection of the positive reinforcement hypothesis.

As a result, the teacher and school psychology intern concluded that sensory regulation was the most plausible hypothesis, and they instituted an intervention based upon it. The intervention consisted of (a) asking Bill a set of questions during the lecture. The questions were scripted to match the lecture, and they called for answers at approximately three times the rate at which talk-outs had been occurring; and (b) tripling the number of questions asked by the teacher of all students, including Bill. Both these procedures increased the level of active responding for Bill during this condition. Results showed a rapid decline in talk-outs to a level of .01 during the last five days of the 14-day intervention.

Carol Carol is a 14-year-old labeled with learning disabilities. Her presenting problem was a set of negative behaviors during academic periods; these included comments like "I won't do it," and movements like dropping materials to the floor. The behavior codes were *appropriate academic work* or *inappropriate academic work*. Any of the problem behaviors was unacceptable, so in an effort to ease data collection, the teacher did not want the problem behaviors separated by topography (for example, saying negative statements or dropping materials to the floor).

The teacher interviewed Carol and her parents, asking what might be the problem. None, however, identified a reason. The teacher then chose as the antecedent conditions *math, reading, English,* and *other*. There were no setting events recorded; consequences were *teacher attention* and *no teacher attention*.

Table 12.3 Analysis of Carol's Inappropriate Academic Work

	Math	Reading	English	Other
Inappropriate behavior	.16	.04	.06	.03
Appropriate behavior	.84	.96	.94	.97

	MATH		READING, ENGLISH, OTHER	
	Inappropriate Behavior	Appropriate Behavior	Inappropriate Behavior	Appropriate Behavior
Attention	.21	.19	.16	.15
No attention	.79	.81	.84	.85

	TEASING ON BUS		NO TEASING ON BUS	
	Math	Not Math	Math	Not Math
Inappropriate behavior	.41	.08	.01	.01
Appropriate behavior	.59	.92	.99	.99

Data were collected for eight days through a two-minute MTS. The observer used a recording sheet from O'Neill et al. (1990) and marked at each sampling which events were occurring. The data were sorted into conditional probability tables and analyzed; the results are presented in Table 12.3.

The first analysis, in the upper panel of Table 12.3, was of the inappropriate and appropriate behavior during the four antecedent conditions. These data showed a higher probability of inappropriate behavior during math (.16) than during the other three conditions (range = .03 to .06).

The next analysis addressed the positive reinforcement hypothesis. We wanted to know if there was a higher probability of attention during math than during the other conditions, so we analyzed the relationship between inappropriate behavior and attention during math and during all other conditions combined. These data are presented in the second panel of Table 12.3, and they show that (a) during *math* the probability of *inappropriate* behavior followed by *attention* (.21) was about the same as was the probability that *appropriate* behavior would be followed by *attention* (.19), and (b) the probability that *inappropriate* behavior would be followed by *attention* during *math* (.19) was about the same as it was during the other three antecedents (m = .16).

These results suggested that the positive reinforcement hypothesis was probably not operative because the probabilities were too similar. We also rejected the sensory regulation hypothesis because Carol had approximately the same number of opportunities to respond in all antecedent conditions; therefore, she would probably not be trying to increase motoric stimulation only during math. We were then left with the negative reinforcement hypothesis. When we examined the data on inappropriate behavior on a daily basis, we noticed considerable fluctuation in the amount of negative behaviors. These data led us to suspect that there was a setting event affecting the probability that the antecedent (math class) would be associated with more problem behavior. The teacher then talked with

Carol again, explaining the teacher's inability to help Carol because she did not know why Carol was less cooperative on certain days. Carol then confided that two boys teased her on the bus but that she had been afraid earlier to say what upset her. The teacher then asked Carol to tell her quietly each day whether or not she had been teased. We continued to collect data, but included the categories of *teasing/no teasing* as a setting event. These data are presented in the lower portion of Table 12.3 and show that there was (a) considerably more inappropriate behavior during *math* (.41) than during the other three conditions (.08) when there was *teasing* on the bus, and (b) that there was more *inappropriate* behavior during both *math* and the other conditions when there was *teasing* (.41 and .08) than when there was *no teasing* (.01 and .01). When the teacher talked more with Carol, who was quite withdrawn about the situation, she learned that Carol did her math homework and studying on her 35-minute bus trip, that teasing often lasted much of the trip, and because math was her first class she was often unprepared on the days the boys teased her.

This information suggested the negative reinforcement hypothesis (Carol was trying to avoid the math work for the day), but the intervention was directed toward the bus trip. A few changes were made on that trip, and Carol's inappropriate behavior during math lowered to .02.

CONCLUSIONS

We conduct functional assessments in the natural environment for several reasons: (a) school personnel often refuse to allow analogue conditions that are specifically intended to increase the problem behavior; (b) school staff find NFS to be relevant, and despite its research orientation, practical; (c) because we ask that nothing be changed in the natural routine, staff in many more schools than we can help ask us to help them (so the procedure appears to be reinforcing); and (d) because of the lack of environmental changes, we are likely to find an intervention in the present environment. As a result, we are more likely to achieve both maintenance and generalization effects.

In the last year, people associated with our research center have provided training either in workshops or on-site for more than 1,000 school psychologists and teachers. The reception has been very satisfying, and the feedback has been useful for making revisions in our training program. The primary concern, as with most behavioral programs, is about data collection, which teachers and/or school psychologists sometimes say they are too busy to do. Unfortunately for our educational system in general, they are often correct. In these situations, we are usually successful when we explain how to conduct momentary time samples, generally on the order of every five minutes. Because this procedure only requires checking which conditions and behaviors are occurring at a particular moment, it only consumes two to three seconds of a person's time. When the code has several-to-many members, the chart provided by O'Neill et al. (1990) has been particularly useful because recording only takes a few seconds even with 20 or 30 categories.

There is a considerable literature on time-sampling procedures, and the interested reader may want to read selected articles in the *Journal of Applied Behavior Analysis* as well as texts such as the one by Suen and Ary (1989). As the latter have indicated, authors of several articles have suggested that the critical variable for the accuracy of MTS appears to be the length of the interobservation interval, and these authors generally recommend a minute or two at most. However, because these research articles have examined accuracy within a set of finite time (for example, five 30-minute sessions), they have confounded interobservational interval, or MTS size, with the number of observations; and number, not interval size, is the critical variable. As such, we have let the school personnel choose the smallest convenient MTS size rather than telling them it must be one or two minutes. They generally seem to be willing to record enough samples, so long as recording does not interfere with other commitments; so, the objective of accuracy can be achieved. We can test for the sufficiency of data by (a) sorting data into the conditional probability tables, (b) calculating the probability, (c) adding the next day's data, and (d) seeing whether the conditional probabilities change. When they do not change over a few sessions, we probably have enough data.

In reacting to a paper presented at a conference by Brian Iwata, I said that I believed the development of the analogue functional assessment procedure was the most important development we have seen in applied behavior analysis. Its validity has been well established, and now in this book, in journal articles, and in other venues, we have seen its considerable generalization. It has quite successfully undergone systematic replication and its authors and developers should be sincerely congratulated by our entire community.

AUTHOR NOTE

This work has been supported in part by Grants No. H029K20046 and H133G20098.

REFERENCES

Berkson, G., & Mason, W. A. (1963). Stereotyped movements of mental defectives: III Situational effects. *American Journal of Mental Deficiency, 63,* 409–416.

Burgio, L. D., & Lewis, T. (1999). Gerontology and functional assessment. In A. C. Repp & R. H. Horner (Eds.), *Functional analysis of problem behavior: From effective assessment to effective support.* Belmont, CA: Wadsworth.

Carr, E. G., Langdon, N. A., & Yarbrough, S. C. (1999). Hypothesis-based intervention for severe problem behavior. In A. C. Repp & R. H. Horner (Eds.), *Functional analysis of problem behavior: From effective assessment to effective support.* Belmont, CA: Wadsworth.

Carr, E. G., Newsom, C. D., & Binkoff, J. A. (1980). Escape as a factor in the aggressive behavior of two retarded children. *Journal of Applied Behavior Analysis, 13,* 101–117.

Duker, P. C., van Druenen, C., Jol, K., & Oud, H. (1986). Determinants of maladaptive behavior of institutionalized mentally retarded individuals. *American Journal of Mental Deficiency, 91,* 51–56.

Dunlap, G., dePerczel, M., Clarke, S., Wilson, D., Wright, S., White, R., & Gomez, A. (1994). Choice making to promote adaptive behavior for students with emotional and behavioral challenges. *Journal of Applied Behavior Analysis, 27,* 505–518.

Dunlap, G., Kern, L., dePerczel, M., Clarke, S., Wilson, D., Childs, K., White, R., & Falk, G. (1993). Functional analysis of classroom variables and the responding of students with emotional and behavioral disorders. *Behavioral Disorders, 18,* 275–291.

Durand, V. M., & Crimmins, D. B. (1988). Identifying the variables maintaining self-injurious behavior. *Journal of Autism and Developmental Disorders, 18,* 99–117.

Favell, J. E. (1973). Reduction of stereotypies by reinforcement of toy play. *Mental Retardation, 11,* 21–23.

Favell, J. E., McGimsey, J. F., & Schell, R. M. (1982). Treatment of self-injury by providing alternate sensory activities. *Analysis and Intervention in Developmental Disabilities, 2,* 83–104.

Gabler-Halle, D., Halle, J. W., & Chung, Y. B. (1993). The effects of aerobic exercise on psychological and behavioral variables of individuals with developmental disabilities: A critical review. *Research in Developmental Disabilities, 14,* 359–386.

Horner, R. D. (1980). The effects of an environmental "enrichment" program on the behavior of institutionalized profoundly retarded children. *Journal of Applied Behavior Analysis, 13,* 473–491.

Iwata, B., Dorsey, M., Slifer, K., Bauman, K., & Richman, G. (1982). Toward a functional analysis of self-injury. *Analysis and Intervention in Developmental Disabilities, 2,* 3–20.

Karsh, K. G., Repp, A. C., Dahlquist, C. M., & Munk, D. (1995). In vivo functional assessment and multielement interventions for problem behaviors of students with disabilities in classroom settings. *Journal of Behavioral Education, 5,* 189–210.

Kern, L., Childs, K. E., Dunlap, G., Clarke, S., & Falk, G. D. (1994). Using assessment-based curricular intervention to improve the classroom behavior of a student with emotional and behavioral challenges. *Journal of Applied Behavior Analysis, 27,* 7–19.

Kern, L., & Dunlap, G. (1999). Assessment-based interventions for children with emotional and behavioral disorders. In A. C. Repp & R. D. Horner (Eds.), *Functional analysis of problem behavior: From effective assessment to effective support.* Belmont, CA: Wadsworth.

O'Neill, R. E., Horner, R. H., Albin, R. W., Storey, K., & Sprague, J. (1990). *Functional analysis of problem behavior: A practical assessment guide.* Sycamore, IL: Sycamore.

Repp, A. C., Felce, D., & Barton, L. E. (1988). Basing the treatment of stereotypic and self-abusive behaviors on hypotheses of their causes. *Journal of Applied Behavior Analysis, 21,* 281–290.

Repp, A. C., Johnson, J., & Van Laarhoven, T. (1998). *Matching rates of instruction to free operant rates of motor behavior to reduce problem behavior of persons with developmental disabilities: A test of the homeostasis hypothesis.* Manuscript submitted for publication.

Repp, A. C., & Karsh, K. G. (1994). Hypothesis-based interventions for tantrum behaviors of persons with developmental disabilities in school settings. *Journal of Applied Behavior Analysis, 27,* 21–31.

Repp, A. C., & Karsh, K. G. (1992). An analysis of a group teaching procedure for persons with developmental disabilities. *Journal of Applied Behavior Analysis, 25,* 701–712.

Repp, A. C., & Karsh, K. G. (1990). A taxonomy for the functional analysis of maladaptive behavior. In A. C. Repp & N. N. Singh (Eds.), *Perspectives on the use of nonaversive and aversive interventions for persons with developmental disabilities* (pp. 333–348). Sycamore, IL: Sycamore.

Repp, A. C., Karsh, K. G., Deitz, D. E. D., & Singh, N. N. (1992). A study of the homeostatic level of stereotypy and other motor movements of persons with mental handicaps. *Journal of Intellectual Disability Research, 36,* 61–75.

Repp, A. C., Karsh, K. G., Munk, D., & Dahlquist, C. M. (1996). Hypothesis-based interventions: A theory of clinical decision making. In W. O'Donohue & L. Krasner (Eds.), *Theories in behavior therapy.* Washington: American Psychological Association.

Sigafoos, J., & Kerr, M. (1994). Provision of leisure activities for the reduction of challenging behavior. *Behavioral Interventions, 9,* 43-53.

Suen, H. K., & Ary, D. (1989). *Analyzing quantitative behavioral observation data.* Hillsdale, NJ: Lawrence Erlbaum Associates.

Zentall, S. S. (1988). Production deficiencies in elicited language but not in the spontaneous verbalizations of hyperactive children. *Journal of Abnormal Child Psychology, 16,* 657–673.

Zentall, S. S., & Meyer, M. J. (1987). Self-regulation of stimulation for ADD children during reading and vigilance task performance. *Journal of Abnormal Child Psychology, 15,* 519–536.

Zentall, S. S., & Zentall, T. R. (1983). Optimal stimulation: A model of disordered activity and performance in normal and deviant children. *Psychological Bulletin, 94,* 446–471.

13

Antecedent Curriculum and Instructional Variables as Classwide Interventions for Preventing or Reducing Problem Behaviors

DENNIS D. MUNK
KATHRYN G. KARSH

INTRODUCTION

The prior four chapters in this section on functional assessment in preschool and school classrooms have presented programs developed by the four research groups. This chapter is broader, going across the results from many research groups, and it presents a review of variables that could be antecedents or setting events to problem behaviors in classrooms.

The variables discussed by Munk and Karsh are curriculum and instructional variables such as task content, predictability, and difficulty. The authors review this literature, and then tie the variables to the functional assessment hypotheses of positive reinforcement, negative reinforcement, and stimulation. In doing so, they present a schema for analyzing environments to prevent problem behaviors (see Chapter 9) as well as the means to remediate already extant problem behaviors. By addressing these variables in the baseline assessment codes (see Chapters 11 and 12), those of us working in schools can perhaps more rapidly identify relevant setting events, antecedents, and consequences for problem behaviors.

One of the most persistent and enduring challenges for researchers and practitioners who work in school settings with students who have disabilities is the identification of effective interventions for problem behaviors that interfere with learning and effective inclusion. Ultimately, problem behaviors can result in decreased interaction with the environment, isolation from peers, and more restrictive school placements and living environments (Grosenick et al., 1991; Repp & Karsh, 1990). Estimates of the proportion of the public school population that exhibits serious problem behaviors such as aggression, disruption, self-injury, and property destruction, have ranged from 2 to 30 percent with a 2 to 3 percent rate generally viewed as a conservative estimate (Kaufman, 1993; Walker & Bullis, 1990). These figures do not include students who exhibit milder, more typical classroom problem behaviors such as off-task and talking-out behaviors.

Historically, many interventions for problem behaviors in schools were chosen independently of the reasons the problem behaviors were occurring. Interventions were often directed at the student with little regard for the theories or generalized principles related to the behavior (Repp et al., 1995). Interventions were frequently based on the topography of the behavior (such as hitting), the student's disability (such as autism), and one of four approaches to intervention (behavior reduction, behavior enhancement, skills acquisition training, and stimulus-based treatments). Generally, the identification and implementation of the intervention was reactive to an intolerable level of the behavior in the classroom and the primary purpose of the intervention was to eliminate or reduce the problem behavior (Carr, Robinson, & Palumbo, 1990). The lack of success of many of these interventions may have resulted from insufficient assessment of the classroom variables maintaining these behaviors (Wehby, Symons, & Shores, 1995). Little attention was given to the classroom antecedents and consequences that preceded and followed the occurrence of the behavior or to the identification of the function of the problem behavior.

The recent emphasis on functional assessment and hypotheses for problem behaviors has directed attention toward an examination of the relationship between classroom problem behaviors and the classroom environment (Dunlap et al., 1991; Haring & Kennedy, 1990; Mace & Lalli, 1991; Sasso et al, 1992; Wehby, Symons, & Shores, 1995). For example, naturalistic functional assessment, as proposed by Repp in Chapter 12, is a procedure that assesses the relationship between student behaviors and naturally occurring antecedent conditions (type of task, grouping arrangements), consequences (staff or peer attention), and setting events (for example, allergies or fights on the school bus) in the classroom environment. Although naturalistic functional assessment may be used with little or no a priori assumptions regarding relationships between environmental variables and problem behavior, it may be expedited when specific antecedent conditions are considered. Fortunately, researchers have identified several salient features of classroom instruction that function as antecedents for problem behavior. Practitioners may consider these variables when conducting a functional assessment in a classroom setting. For example, manipulation of specific classroom antecedents such as selection of curricular activities (Dunlap et al., 1991; Kern et al., 1994), preferred tasks (Foster-Johnson, Ferro, & Dunlap, 1994), high probability requests

(Horner et al., 1991), and difficulty level of tasks (Carr & Durand, 1985) resulted in decreases in problem behavior. Manipulation of these variables is particularly promising because these antecedent (or stimulus-based) interventions have been shown to be more effective than consequence-based interventions such as differential reinforcement procedures in maintaining positive behavior change (Carr et al., 1990). In addition, these interventions can contribute to high levels of skill acquisition for students. Therefore, an instructional technology based on the manipulation of these classroom variables can be a powerful approach for reducing problem behaviors (Horner, Sprague, & Flannery, 1993).

In the following sections a proposal is made for the link between the three hypotheses for problem behavior (Carr, 1977) and antecedent curriculum and instructional variables that have resulted in reductions in problem behavior. Furthermore, it is proposed that many classroom problem behaviors can be prevented or reduced if an emphasis is placed on classwide implementation of these curriculum and instructional variables that have been shown to lead to a reduction in problem behavior. We suggest that classwide implementation of variables related to the design and delivery of instruction can be a parsimonious approach to reducing many classroom problem behaviors prior to undertaking individualized functional assessments and hypothesis-based interventions that can be both time- and staff-intensive. In our own research, we have found that problem behaviors for students could be reduced by as much as 60 percent when a classroom program that used an errorless learning procedure, a rapid pace of presentation, and union responding was implemented (Repp & Karsh, 1991, 1992).

HYPOTHESES FOR PROBLEM BEHAVIOR

Critical to the functional assessment process is the development of hypotheses that identify the relationship between the problem behavior and environmental variables that set the occasion for the behavior or maintain the behavior. Several researchers have proposed sets of hypotheses for describing the functional relationships between problem behaviors and environmental stimuli or conditions. In a seminal article, Carr (1977) identified three hypotheses for problem behavior: positive reinforcement, negative reinforcement, and stimulation. Iwata, Vollmer, & Zarcone (1990) identified the hypotheses as positive reinforcement, negative reinforcement, and automatic reinforcement.

The positive reinforcement hypothesis suggests that environmental stimuli or conditions presented contingent on the occurrence of the problem behavior will increase the probability that the behavior will recur. For example, the contingent delivery of social attention (Carr & Durand, 1985), and tangible items (Edelson, Taubman, & Lovaas, 1983) increased problem behaviors. The negative reinforcement hypothesis suggests that environmental stimuli or conditions that are removed, attenuated, or prevented contingent on the occurrence of the problem behavior will increase the probability that the behavior will recur. According to this hypothesis environmental stimuli or conditions that can be functionally related to the problem behavior are difficult tasks (Weeks & Gaylord-Ross, 1981), nonpreferred activities (Dunlap et al., 1991), and repetitive, boring tasks (Winterling, Dunlap, & O'Neill, 1987). The third hypothesis, stimulation or automatic reinforcement, suggests that the problem behavior is maintained or strengthened by the sensory consequences the behavior produces. Problem behaviors such as stereotypies and self-injurious behaviors have been reduced when the sensory feedback from these behaviors has been reduced or when appropriate behaviors are targeted to provide the same sensory feedback (Rincover, 1978; Favell, McGimsey, & Schell, 1982).

In the following sections we describe specific antecedent curriculum and instructional variables that may lead to reductions in problem behavior, and discuss how these variables may reduce or prevent problem behaviors under each of the three hypotheses described above.

DESIGN AND DELIVERY OF INSTRUCTION

Researchers have demonstrated that procedures used to select and deliver instruction influence student performance. Although many variables may influence how well students perform during instruction, several variables have been shown to not only increase correct responding, but also to reduce problem behavior (Munk & Repp, 1994). Such variables may serve the dual functions of (a) facilitating correct student responding, and (b) reducing problem behaviors exhibited during instruction.

In this section, we describe research-based procedures (variables) for facilitating correct responding and reducing problem behaviors. In the area of curriculum selection, the effects of functional (versus analog) tasks are discussed. Several variables associated with delivery of instruction are described. These variables include: (a) student (versus teacher) choice of task, (b) preferred (versus nonpreferred) tasks, (c) varied (versus same) tasks, (d) reduced (versus extended) intertrial intervals, (e) interspersed or embedded high-probability instructions, (f) reduced task difficulty, and (g) predictability of schedule.

Content as a Variable

Selection of tasks or activities that are "functional" for the student has been shown to increase on-task and correct responding while reducing problem behaviors (Dunlap et al., 1991; Kern et al., 1994). Functional tasks may be defined as those which produce immediate reinforcement for the student, and can be contrasted with analog tasks which produce, at best, reinforcement arranged by staff in the immediate environment. Functional tasks produce an immediate impact on the learner's life, rather than serving as a step in a sequence intended to "prepare" the learner to function in his or her environment.

Functional tasks are defined by their outcome, and may vary across individual learners. Dunlap et al. (1991) found that a student with severe emotional disturbance exhibited decreased problem behavior when an analog writing task was altered so that the student wrote a greeting card which she could present to her mother. The student exhibited increased on-task responding and significantly reduced problem behavior when writing produced immediate reinforcement.

Complexity of a task may also influence student performance and levels of problem behavior during instruction. Kern et al. (1994) found that a student with severe problem behaviors exhibited increased on-task responding and reduced problem behavior when a complex task requiring problem solving (reading a menu and calculating the cost, for example) was substituted for an analog, drill-and-practice task (such as completing math problems). To summarize, multistep tasks that result in a product or outcome immediately functional in the students' environment may facilitate on-task responding and an increased rate of correct responding, while reducing problem behaviors.

Student Choice of Task as a Variable

Conventional wisdom suggests that effective instruction for learners with disabilities is teacher-directed and carefully sequenced (Kameenui & Simmons, 1990). Therefore, allowing a student to select a task or activity prior to initiating a teaching session may not, upon first consideration, appear wise. However, research has shown that student choice of task may produce increased on-task responding and reduced problem behaviors by students with disabilities (Dunlap et al., 1991; Dyer, Dunlap, & Winterling, 1990; Parsons et al., 1990; Mithaug & Mar, 1980).

Studies comparing student choice with teacher assignment of tasks have involved presentation of task options prior to initiation of an instructional session or work period. Student choice therefore differs from presentation of preferred tasks (a variable to be discussed later in this chapter) in that the former provides student choice for each session, while the latter assesses student choice periodically to identify preferred tasks.

Dyer, Dunlap, & Winterling (1990) found that student choice produced significant decreases in aggression of three children with severe disabilities even though the students chose tasks in the same proportions as those assigned by the teacher. This finding suggests that opportunity to choose may, in itself, be a variable influencing task performance and problem behavior.

Task Variation as a Variable

Presenting a variety of tasks, rather than a single task of long duration, has been shown to produce increased rates of acquisition, increased levels of on-task responding during maintenance sessions, and reduced problem behaviors during instruction (Kern et al., 1994; Winterling, Dunlap, & O'Neill, 1987; Dunlap, 1984; Dunlap & Koegel, 1980). During task variation, multiple tasks are presented for relatively brief periods, often with new and maintenance tasks interspersed. The precise number and type of tasks to be presented within an instructional period (for example, 30 minutes) should be based on the learner's behavior during baseline observations. The teacher should first determine the average duration a student maintains on-task responding when a single task is presented. Next, the teacher should identify new (acquisition) and maintenance tasks to be presented in durations shorter than those associated with off-task or problem behaviors during baseline.

Reduced Intertrial Interval as a Variable

The rate at which tasks or instructions are presented may serve as a variable affecting task performance and problem behavior (Dunlap, Dyer, & Koegel, 1983; West & Sloane, 1986; Carnine, 1976). Researchers found that reducing the interval between teacher presentation of a prompt (verbal prompt, question, and so on) produced increases in the percentage of correct responding (Dunlap, Dyer, & Koegel, 1983; West & Sloane, 1986; Carnine, 1976) as well as the rate of correct responding (Repp & Karsh, 1992).

Operational definitions of fast pace (brief intertrial interval) have varied considerably, ranging from a teacher prompt delivered every 4 seconds (Dunlap, Dyer, & Koegel, 1983) to a teacher question presented every 20 seconds (West & Sloane, 1986). Undoubtedly, an ideal pace for maximizing correct responding and reducing problem behaviors during the intertrial interval will vary across students, type of task, and size of group or class. Teachers should select an appropriate pace after (a) observing the levels of problem behavior occurring during intertrial intervals at the current pace of instruction, and (b) assessing the student's ability to provide frequent, correct responses without additional instruction and feedback. In general, increasing pace of instruction is most viable on maintenance tasks or during drill and practice sessions.

Interspersal or Embedding of High-Probability Instructions as a Variable

Embedding or interspersing stimuli (such as instructions) associated with a high probability of correct responding with stimuli associated with low rates of correct responding has been shown to be an effective procedure for increasing correct responding and reducing problem behavior (Horner et al., 1991; Harchik & Putzier, 1990; Mace et al., 1988; Singer, Singer, & Horner, 1987).

Interspersal requires the teacher to first identify requests (prompts) to which the student typically responds correctly. Identification of such high-probability requests can be achieved by recording the percentage of trials in which a student responds correctly (for example, initiates work on a math worksheet) following a teacher-delivered request (for instance, "begin work on your math worksheet."). Whenever high-probability requests are delivered, reinforcement (such as verbal praise) should be delivered for each correct response. The increased density of reinforcement associated with high-probability requests may, in fact, represent the underlying mechanism for its effectiveness. That is, dense reinforcement provided for correct responding to high-probability requests may provide momentum (Mace et al., 1988) for correct responding to low-probability requests.

Exposure to Preferred Activities as a Variable

Exposing students to preferred activities has been shown to increase on-task and correct responding, and to reduce problem behaviors (Foster-Johnson, Ferro, & Dunlap, 1994; Kern et al., 1994; Cooper et al., 1992). Exposure to preferred activities involves presentation of activities that the student has (a) stated or ranked as a favorite or preferred activity (Kern et al., 1994), or (b) performed with increased rates of on-task or correct responding with relatively lower rates of problem behavior (Foster-Johnson et al., 1994; Cooper et al., 1992).

Determining preferred, as well as nonpreferred, tasks can be achieved through an interview with the student (Kern et al., 1994), or by observing the student during a variety of tasks and recording levels of on-task or correct responding, and problem behavior. Presenting preferred activities differs from allowing student choice of tasks (described previously) in that the former involves repeated presentation of stimuli or tasks identified as preferred, while the latter involves providing an opportunity to choose stimuli or tasks prior to each session.

Positive effects of scheduling and presenting access to preferred activities have been demonstrated in two procedures. In the first, preferred activities are embedded in a daily schedule of activities. Nonpreferred activities may be (a) altered so as to increase student preference, or (b) eliminated from the student's schedule. For example, Kern et al. (1994) increased a student's preference for writing tasks by altering the response modality from handwriting to typing on a computer. Upon introduction of the new requirement, the student exhibited increased on-task responding and decreased problem behavior. Eliminating nonpreferred tasks from a student's schedule should be done only after consideration of (a) the degree to which the task is functional in the student's environment, and (b) whether the task stimuli or requirements could be altered so as to decrease the aversiveness, or nonpreferred characteristics, of the task. The decision to drop a nonpreferred task should be based on an assessment of the functional role of the activity; critical skills should be dropped only when procedures for increasing student success on the task have been exhausted.

A second procedure for increasing on-task responding and decreasing problem behavior includes providing access to preferred stimuli or tasks contingent upon completion of less-preferred tasks (Cooper et al., 1992). Contingent access to preferred activities may be particularly attractive to teachers because the procedure does not require importing of extraneous reinforcers (such as edibles or tokens) and the preferred stimuli or tasks are already present, and therefore are components of the student's regular schedule. ·

Reduced Task Difficulty as a Variable

Research has demonstrated a relationship between task difficulty and problem behaviors (Carr & Durand, 1985; Weeks & Gaylord-Ross, 1981). Difficult tasks are those associated with high levels of learner errors, which typically result in high levels of corrective feedback or low rates of reinforcement for task responding.

Reducing task difficulty via within-stimulus manipulations, particularly fading, has been shown to increase correct responding and decrease problem behaviors (Weeks & Gaylord-Ross, 1981; Repp & Karsh, 1992). Stimulus fading has been incorporated into errorless teaching procedures (Terrace, 1963) that minimize learner errors. Weeks & Gaylord-Ross (1981) reduced errors and problem behaviors of a 10-year-old girl with disabilities by substituting an oversized belt for teaching belt buckling. As the girl became proficient at buckling, the size of the belt was reduced until the girl could buckle a normal belt. Repp & Karsh (1992) employed stimulus fading in a multicomponent teaching procedure, the Task Demonstration Model, which minimized errors made by learners with severe disabilities during discrimination training. These authors faded negative examples, beginning with very different negative examples that facilitated correct discriminations during initial trials. Stimulus fading procedures are unique in that learner errors are minimized without altering the instructional goal or reducing the complexity of the task.

Predictability of Schedule as a Variable

Students with disabilities, particularly those with more severe disabilities or autism, exhibit improved task performance and decreased interfering problem behaviors when the schedule and expectations for performance are predictable, modeled, or signaled.

Flannery & Horner (1994) significantly reduced the escape-motivated (negative reinforcement) problem behaviors of a 14-year-old boy with autism by describing and modeling all steps for each task in a multitask sequence. These authors also reduced escape-motivated problem behaviors of a 17-year-old student with autism by (a) combining randomly sequenced and predictably scheduled tasks and (b) incorporating a timer and printed list of tasks for the combined random/predictable schedule. Problem behaviors associated with a random schedule were significantly reduced by the intervention.

Predictability has been conceptualized as the "presentation of signals that indicate the availability of specific S → R → S relationships" (Flannery & Horner, 1994, p. 159). Procedures for increasing predictability may focus on-task features of (a) type, (b) length, and (c) sequence. Methods for increasing predictability should be geared toward the cognitive abilities of the learner. When appropriate, verbal or written presentation may suffice. For learners with more severe disabilities, pictures may be used to indicate task sequence. Task expectations may be indicated by setting a timer or presenting a finite number of stimuli or parts to be assembled or manipulated.

LINKING CURRICULUM AND INSTRUCTIONAL VARIABLES TO THREE HYPOTHESES

Earlier, we described three experimentally validated hypotheses for problem behavior: positive reinforcement; negative reinforcement; and stimulation, or automatic reinforcement. In this section, we briefly describe how the curriculum and instructional variables discussed above may reduce or prevent problem behaviors under each hypothesis.

Positive Reinforcement Hypothesis

Recall that the positive reinforcement hypothesis suggests that behavior is reinforced when it produces or results in presentation of an object or event. Tangible reinforcers include stimuli such as food items, stickers, or headphones. Social reinforcers include verbal praise, touch, eye contact, or smiling. Researchers have demonstrated that levels of an individual's problem behavior may be functionally related to staff social attention (Carr & Durand, 1985; Repp, Felce, & Barton, 1988) or the contingent presentation of toys, snacks, or manipulable objects (Durand & Crimmins, 1988).

Curriculum and instructional variables that produce increased levels of reinforcement for the learner may also affect levels of problem behavior. *Functional or complex tasks* produce more naturally-occurring reinforcement (such as social attention or a completed meal) than simple, analog tasks, and may take the place of analog tasks to increase relative rates of reinforcement for task responding. Functional or complex tasks may, in themselves, be more reinforcing to a learner who can discriminate socially valued tasks from rote, analog tasks. Interspersing functional or complex tasks may produce increased levels of task responding and a concomitant decrease in problem behaviors maintained by positive reinforcement. Examples might include disruptive, off-task behavior that functions to obtain staff or peer attention or to gain access to different, more reinforcing tasks.

The instructional variable of *reduced intertrial interval* may reduce or prevent problem behaviors maintained by positive reinforcement, particularly social attention. Reducing the interval between opportunities for a student to respond also increases the opportunities (rate) for the student to obtain positive feedback from the teacher. For reduced intertrial intervals to most effectively reduce problem behavior, the student must be able to (a) respond correctly on a high percentage of trials, and (b) receive reinforcement, particularly verbal praise, for correct responding. When these two conditions are met, the density of reinforcement available for task responding may prevent or reduce problem behaviors (such as leaving seat) maintained by positive reinforcement (teacher attention in the form of corrective feedback, for example).

Negative Reinforcement Hypothesis

Recall that the negative reinforcement hypothesis suggests that problem behaviors are maintained by avoidance or termination of an aversive stimulus or condition. In an instructional setting, aversive stimuli may include stimuli associated with specific tasks, or instruction to perform specific task requirements. Several curriculum and instructional variables may be implemented to prevent or reduce problem behaviors perceived to be maintained by negative reinforcement. Variables that effect problem behavior maintained by termination or avoidance of an instructional context may (a) reduce the aversive properties of the stimuli or task, (b) increase the density of reinforcement for task responding, or (c) a combination of the above. We are including under the negative reinforcement hypothesis variables that have been implemented in published studies to reduce escape-motivated behaviors; in fact, such variables may also produce increased reinforcement for task responding.

Functional or complex tasks were previously described as an intervention for problem behaviors maintained by positive reinforcement. Increasing or interspersing functional tasks may also reduce negatively reinforced problem behaviors in that the aversive qualities (such as repetitiveness) of analog tasks are removed. Building functional or complex tasks into the curriculum and schedule may prevent or reduce escape-motivated behaviors.

Allowing or arranging *student choice of task* may affect negatively reinforced problem behaviors by (a) allowing the learner to allocate more time to reinforcing activities and less time to aversive activities, and (b) allowing the learner to control the schedule of activities, which in itself may be reinforcing. If or when the strategy of allowing learners to choose activities is not feasible (learner does not identify a choice), providing *access to preferred activities* may be an alternative strategy. Scheduling preferred (reinforcing) tasks increases the probability of task responding, and consequently an opportunity for programmed reinforcement (such as teacher praise or points) to be obtained by the learner. No precise formula for sequencing preferred and nonpreferred tasks has been described; the frequency and duration of preferred tasks must be based on the learner's behavior and the overall goals for instruction. That is, preferred tasks are more easily and ethically substituted for less-preferred tasks when both meet the instructional goals for the learner.

Task variation, in which multiple tasks of relatively short duration are substituted for a single, relatively long duration task, may prevent or reduce negatively reinforced problem behaviors. By varying tasks, the teacher: (a) increases the probability of exposure to preferred, reinforcing tasks; and (b) prevents prolonged exposure to less-preferred tasks. Task variation thus may influence negatively reinforced problem behavior by (a) reducing exposure to aversive properties of some tasks, and (b) guaranteeing intermittent exposure to reinforcing activities.

Interspersal of high-probability instructions may prevent or reduce negatively reinforced problem behavior by temporarily increasing the density of reinforcement for task responding. Interspersal may increase task responding and provide an opportunity for the educator to reinforce the learner for responding correctly to an instruction. The action of interspersal on problem behavior differs from strategies of increasing access to preferred activities or student choice of task. In the latter strategies, the learner is exposed to reinforcing tasks, while in the former, the learner is reinforced for responding to a teacher-delivered instruction. Interspersal may produce generalized responding to teacher-delivered instructions, the result being an increase in responding to tasks previously associated with escape-motivated problem behaviors.

Predictability of schedule may reduce the aversive properties of an instructional setting by signaling the availability of reinforcement for task responding and the absence of aversive task or punishment contingencies. Providing a verbal or symbolic representation of the schedule prior to beginning an instructional sequence or modeling the steps of each task may influence negatively-reinforced problem behaviors by (a) informing the learner of task requirements that have been associated with reinforcement in past sessions, or (b) indicating the absence of novel task requirements on which the learner has a history of high rates of errors, extensive corrective feedback, or extinction.

Reduced task difficulty, as a result of within-stimulus manipulations such as fading, may affect negatively-reinforced problem behavior by reducing the aversive properties of a task previously associated with high rates of learner errors and concomitant low rates of reinforcement. Manipulating stimuli of an existing task to increase the rate of correct responses, and therefore the opportunities for educators to reinforce task responding, has been shown effective for negatively reinforced problem behavior. Within-stimulus manipulations can be used to prevent the development of problem behavior by facilitating high levels of correct responding, with associated reinforcement, from the initial presentation of the task. Termed errorless learning (Terrace, 1963), this method may prevent the onset of problem behaviors associated with difficult tasks by eliminating a defining feature of difficult tasks, high levels of learner errors.

Stimulation (Automatic Reinforcement) Hypothesis

The stimulation hypothesis suggests that maladaptive behaviors are maintained by the sensory stimulation they generate. The assumption from considerable research in biology is that a certain level of stimulation is optimal for an individual, and that an individual will engage in compensatory behaviors to maintain that optimal level. In educational settings, some individuals will engage in problem behaviors if environmental stimulation is low (Horner, 1980; Repp & Karsh, 1991; Singh & Millichamp, 1987). Two delivery variables, task variation and reduced intertrial interval, may present or reduce problem behaviors maintained by increased stimulation.

Task variation may affect levels of problem behavior if a large proportion of tasks require an active, motor response by the learner. Active responses involve motor movement, which produces sensory (proprioceptive) feedback. Active responding can be facilitated by varying tasks and stimuli so that the learner has opportunities to manipulate a variety of stimuli that affect difficult sensory modalities (tactile, visual, auditory, olfactory).

Reduced intertrial interval (rapid pace) provides increased opportunities to respond during instruction. Increasing levels of responding, particularly active responding, produces concomitant increases in sensory stimulation. Frequent task responding becomes functionally equivalent to problem behaviors used to increase stimulation (such as body rocking, repetitive vocalizations), and may therefore facilitate a reduction in the less-desirable means for modulating stimulation.

Summary

In this section, we have attempted to describe links between curriculum and instructional variables and the hypotheses for problem behavior. This linkage is summarized in Table 13.1. Such linkage is unique in that only recently have researchers (for example, Dunlap et al., 1991; Flannery & Horner, 1994; Kern et al., 1994) developed hypotheses for problem behaviors prior to manipulating one or more variables described in this paper. We have attempted to conceptually link variables and problem behaviors, recognizing the need for experimental validation in classroom settings.

Assessment of antecedent curriculum and instructional variables may precede or be incorporated into a thorough naturalistic functional assessment as described by Repp in Chapter 12. Regardless of the formal or informal procedures teachers use to identify controlling variables, Table 13.1 should guide intervention whenever the following conditions exist: (a) problem behavior has been shown more probable during instruction, rather than during noninstructional periods (free time, for example); (b) the teacher can identify a probable function (escape a task, obtain the

Table 13.1 Proposed Relationship Between Curriculum and Instructional Variables and Three Hypotheses for Problem Behavior

CURRICULUM AND INSTRUCTIONAL VARIABLES

Hypotheses for problem behavior	Functional or complex tasks		Student choice of task		Access to preferred tasks		Task variation	
	Implementation	Proposed effect	Implementation	Proposed effect	Implementation	Proposed effect	Implementation	Proposed effect
Positive reinforcement	Substitute multistep, socially valid tasks for one-step or analog tasks	Increased naturally occurring tangible and social reinforcement						
Negative reinforcement	Substitute multistep, socially valid tasks for one-step or analog tasks	Increased naturally occurring tangible and social reinforcement	Allow student to select all or some instructional activities or materials	Increasesd access to reinforcing activities and minimized exposure to nonreinforcing activities	Present intermittent exposure to highly preferred tasks	Increased access to reinforcing activities and guaranteed minimum of intermittent reinforcement	During teacher-directed instruction, present varied tasks of short duration rather than single task of long duration	Minimized exposure to nonreinforcing tasks and guaranteed minimum of intermittent reinforcement
Stimulation or automatic reinforcement							During teacher-directed instruction, present varied tasks of short duration rather than single task of long duration	Increased sensory stimulation if sensory input varies and responses are motoric

Table 13.1 Continued

CURRICULUM AND INSTRUCTIONAL VARIABLES

Hypotheses for problem behavior	Reduced intertrial interval		Interspersal of high-probability instructions		Predictability of schedule		Reduced task difficulty	
	Implementation	Proposed effect	Implementation	Proposed effect	Implementation	Proposed effect	Implementation	Proposed effect
Positive reinforcement	Reduce the interval between the end of the student's response and the initiation of the next trial	Increased opportunity for reinforcement associated with correct responding						
Negative reinforcement			Intersperse instructions to which student is likely to respond successfully with instructions to which student typically does not respond	Reduced aversiveness of an instruction by temporarily increased density of reinforcement for task responding	Present schedule of activities and task requirements at beginning of school day or class period	Reduced aversiveness of an instructional setting by signaled availability of reinforcement	Use stimulus fading procedures to increase correct responding	Increased density of reinforcement for task responding; potential reduced aversiveness of difficult task
Stimulation or automatic reinforcement	Reduce the interval between the end of the student's response and the initiation of the next trial	Increased opportunity for active responding						

Table 13.2 Antecedent Curriculum and Instructional Variables That May Be Related to Presence or Absence of Problem Behavior

1. Functional or complex tasks . . . . Analog tasks
2. Student choice of tasks . . . . Assigned tasks
3. Preferred tasks . . . . Nonpreferred tasks
4. Varied tasks . . . . Constant tasks
5. Short intertrial interval . . . . Lengthy intertrial
6. High-probability requests/instructions . . . Low probabilty requests/instructions
7. Predictable schedule . . . . Unpredictable schedule
8. Easy task . . . . Difficult task

teacher's attention, increase stimulation) for the problem behavior; and (c) the probable function of problem behavior is linked to a (probable) corresponding hypothesis of positive reinforcement, negative reinforcement, or stimulation.

Once a probable hypothesis(es) for problem behavior has been identified, the next step is to isolate specific curriculum and instructional variables that may be affecting behavior. Again, formal or informal assessment procedures may be used to determine whether problem behavior is more or less likely when a variable, or its opposite, is present. For example, problem behavior may be more probable when students choose a task or under the opposite condition of teacher-assigned tasks. Table 13.2 presents each curriculum and instructional variable, as well as its opposite.

CONCLUSIONS

Recent research on functional assessment and hypothesis-based interventions has important implications for reducing or preventing problem behaviors in classroom settings. By assessing classroom antecedents and consequences that maintain problem behaviors, researchers and practitioners may be able to identify an instructional technology that will increase student performance and reduce problem behaviors. Each of the antecedent curriculum and instructional variables identified in this chapter addresses one or more of the hypotheses for problem behavior. Classwide teacher manipulation of these variables can serve as a first-level intervention for many of the typical problem behaviors exhibited by students with disabilities in classroom environments.

Each of these variables can be viewed as a component of instruction, provides an opportunity for less obtrusive intervention, and can result in increased academic engagement and performance as well as a reduction in problem behaviors. Manipulation of these variables does not necessarily require changes in the objectives of the curriculum, the teacher:student ratio, or the number of ancillary personnel. Manipulation of these variables does include teacher-directed modifications such as changing the response mode of the task, increasing the pace of instruction, or interspersing easy and difficult tasks. While many of these instructional variables are included in teacher training programs, they are not often used by teachers in classrooms (Gunter et al., 1994).

Classwide implementation of these curriculum and instructional variables may be a parsimonious approach to reducing many of the problem behaviors exhibited by the students in the classroom without undertaking an individualized functional assessment for each student. As suggested earlier, research has shown that implementation of a comprehensive program that includes many of these instructional variables can result in significant increases in student performance and marked reductions in problem behaviors (Repp & Karsh, 1991, 1992). Research emphases must continue to be placed on the functional assessment of problem behaviors and the implementation of hypothesis-based interventions for individual students in classroom settings. However, the knowledge gained from the research on functional assessment and hypothesis-based intervention can direct our attention toward reducing problem behaviors by first designing classroom instruction to reduce the probability of the occurrence of problem behaviors. Experimental validation of the proposed link between these curriculum and instructional variables and problem behaviors is warranted.

If the curriculum and instructional variables identified in this chapter are implemented by the teacher and problem behaviors persist, then an individualized functional assessment is warranted. For example, an individualized functional assessment may indicate that changing the design and delivery of instruction according to these variables does not address the function of the problem behavior. Larger-scale changes in the curriculum (social skill training to solicit peer attention, and communication training to request assistance, for example) may be necessary in order to teach a functionally equivalent, socially valid behavior. Functional assessment may indicate that the behavior is not related to variables encompassed by curriculum or instruction but is related to idiosyncratic setting events (such as the bus ride to school), antecedents (teasing by a peer, for example) or consequences (such as access to the computer) and that a highly individualized intervention is necessary. Finally, we recognize that in some cases the severity, intensity, or durability of the behavior may demand that an individualized functional assessment and an intensive hypothesis-based intervention is the only approach to intervention for the problem behavior.

When students display problem behaviors in classroom settings it is our responsibility as researchers and practitioners to identify the classroom antecedents and consequences that maintain that behavior. The research in functional assessment has provided us with a methodology for assessing the environmental variables related to the behavior, identifying the hypothesis for the behavior; and developing a hypothesis-based intervention. If our approach to problem behavior also includes a proactive emphasis, then much of the research on functional assessment and curricular and instructional variables can be used to develop first-level, classwide interventions. Curriculum and instructional variables can be incorporated into the classroom so that problem behaviors are less likely to occur and student performance will improve.

AUTHOR NOTES

Dennis D. Munk, Northern Illinois University; Kathryn G. Karsh, Educational Research and Services Center.

This work was supported in part by Grant No. H023C00092 from the Office of Special Education Programs and Grant No. H133620098 from the National Institute on Disability and Rehabilitation Research.

Correspondence regarding this manuscript should be addressed to Dennis D. Munk, Department of Educational Psychology, Counseling, and Special Education, Northern Illinois University, DeKalb, Illinois 60115.

REFERENCES

Carnine, D. W. (1976). Effects of two teacher presentation rates on off-task behavior, answering correctly, and participation. *Journal of Applied Behavior Analysis, 9,* 199–206.

Carr, E. G. (1977). The motivation of self-injurious behavior: A review of some hypotheses. *Psychological Bulletin, 84,* 800–816.

Carr, E. G., & Durand, V. M. (1985). Reducing behavior problems through functional communication training. *Journal of Applied Behavior Analysis, 18,* 111–126.

Carr, E. G., Robinson, S., & Palumbo, L. W. (1990). The wrong issue: Aversive versus nonaversive treatment. The right issue: Functional versus nonfunctional treatment. In A. C. Repp & N. N. Singh (Eds.), *Perspectives on the use of aversive and nonaversive interventions for persons with developmental disabilities* (pp. 361–379). Sycamore, IL: Sycamore.

Carr, E. G., Robinson, S., Taylor, J. C., & Carlson, J. I. (1990). Positive approaches to the treatment of severe behavior problems in persons with developmental disabilities: A review and analysis of reinforcement and stimulus-based procedures. Monograph of the *Association for Persons with Severe Handicaps.*

Cooper, L. J., Wacker, D. P., Thurby, D., Plagmann, L. A., Harding, J., Millard, T., & Derby, M. (1992). Analysis of the effects of task preferences, task demands, and adult attention on child behavior in outpatient, and classroom settings. *Journal of Applied Behavior Analysis, 25,* 823–840.

Dunlap, G. (1984). The influence of task variation and maintenance tasks on the learning and affect of autistic children. *Journal of Experimental Child Psychology, 37,* 41–64.

Dunlap, G., Dyer, K., & Koegel, R. L. (1983). Autistic self-stimulation and intertrial interval duration. *American Journal of Mental Deficiency, 88,* 194–202.

Dunlap, G., Kern-Dunlap, L., Clarke, S., & Robbins, F. R. (1991). Functional assessment, curricular revision, and severe behavior problems. *Journal of Applied Behavior Analysis, 24,* 387–397.

Dunlap, G., & Koegel, R. L. (1980). Motivating autistic children through stimulus variation. *Journal of Applied Behavior Analysis, 13,* 619–627.

Durand, V. M., & Crimmins, D. B. (1988). Identifying the variables maintaining self-injurious behavior. *Journal of Autism and Developmental Disorders, 18,* 99–117.

Dyer, K., Dunlap, G., & Winterling, V. (1990). Effects of choice making on the serious problem behaviors of students with severe handicaps. *Journal of Applied Behavior Analysis, 23,* 515–524.

Edelson, S. M., Taubman, M. T., & Lovaas, O. I. (1983). Some social contexts of self-destructive behavior. *Journal of Abnormal Child Psychology, 11,* 299–312.

Favell, J. E., McGimsey, J. F., & Schell, R. M. (1982). Treatment of self-injury by providing alternate sensory activities. *Analysis and Intervention in Developmental Disabilities, 2,* 83–104.

Flannery, K. B., & Horner, R. H. (1994). The relationship between predictability and problem behavior for students with severe disabilities. *Journal of Behavioral Education, 14,* 157–176.

Foster-Johnson, L., Ferro, J. & Dunlap, G. (1994). Preferred curricular activities and reduced problem behaviors in students with intellectual disabilities. *Journal of Applied Behavior Analysis, 27,* 493–504.

Grosenick, J. K., George, N. L., George, M. P., & Lewis, T. J. (1991). Public school services for behaviorally disordered students: Program practices in the 1980's. *Behavioral Disorders, 16,* 87–96.

Gunter, P. L., Jack, S. L., DePaepe, P., Reed, T. M., & Harrison, J. (1994). Effects of challenging behaviors of students with EBD on teacher instructional behavior. *Preventing School Failure, 38,* 35–39.

Harchik, A. G., & Putzier, V. A. (1990). The use of high-probability requests to increase compliance with instructions to take medication. *Journal of the Association for Persons with Severe Handicaps, 15,* 40–43.

Haring, T. G., & Kennedy, C. H. (1990). Contextual control of problem behavior in students with severe disabilities. *Journal of Applied Behavior Analysis, 25,* 235–243.

Horner, R. H. (1980). The effects of an environmental "enrichment" program on the behavior of institutionalized profoundly retarded children. *Journal of Applied Behavior Analysis, 13,* 473–491.

Horner, R. H., Day, H. M., Sprague, J. R., O'Brien, M., & Heathfield, L. T. (1991). Interspersed requests: A nonaversive procedure for reducing aggression and self-injury during instruction. *Journal of Applied Behavior Analysis, 24,* 265–278.

Horner, R. D., Sprague, J. R., & Flannery, K. B. (1993). Building functional curricula for students with severe intellectual disabilities and severe behavior problems. In R. Van Houten & S. Axelrod (Eds.), *Behavior analysis and treatment* (pp. 47–71). New York: Plenum.

Iwata, B. A., Vollmer, T. R., & Zarcone, J. H. (1990). The experimental (functional) analysis of behavior disorders: Methodology, applications, and limitations. In A. C. Repp & N. N. Singh (Eds.), *Perspectives on the use of aversive and nonaversive interventions for persons with developmental disabilities* (pp. 301–330). Sycamore IL: Sycamore.

Kameenui, D. J. & Simmons, D. C. (1990). *Designing instructional strategies: The prevention of academic learning problems.* Columbus: Merrill.

Kaufman, J. M. (1993). *Characteristics of children's behavior disorders* (5th ed.). Columbus: Merrill.

Kern, L., Childs, K. E., Dunlap, G., Clarke, S., & Falk, G. D. (1994). Using assessment-based curricular interventions to improve the classroom behavior of a student with emotional and behavioral challenges. *Journal of Applied Behavior Analysis, 27,* 7–19.

Lalli, J. S., Browder, D. M., Mace, C. F. & Brown, D. K. (1993). Teacher use of descriptive analysis to implement interventions to decrease students' problem behaviors. *Journal of Applied Behavior Analysis, 26,* 227–238.

Mace, F. C., Hock, M. L., Lalli, J. S., West, B. J., Belfiore, P., Pinter, E., & Brown, D. T. (1988). Behavioral momentum in the treatment of noncompliance. *Journal of Applied Behavior Analysis, 21,* 123–141.

Mace, F. C., & Lalli, J. S. (1991). Linking descriptive and experimental analyses in the treatment of bizarre speech. *Journal of Applied Behavior Analysis, 24,* 553–562.

Mithaug, D. E., & Mar, D. K. (1980). The relation between choosing and working prevocational tasks in two severely retarded young adults. *Journal of Applied Behavior Analysis, 13,* 177–182.

Munk, D. D., & Repp, A. C. (1994). The relationship between instructional variables and problem behavior: A review. *Exceptional Children, 60,* 390–401.

Parsons, M. B., Reid, D. H., Reynolds, J., & Baumgarner, M. (1990). Effects of chosen versus assigned jobs on the work performance of persons with severe handicaps. *Journal of Applied Behavior Analysis, 23,* 253–258.

Repp, A. C., Felce, D., & Barton, L. E. (1988). Basing the treatment of stereotypic and self-injurious behaviors on hypotheses of their causes. *Journal of Applied Behavior Analysis, 21,* 281–289.

Repp, A. C. & Karsh, K. G. (1990). A taxonomy for the functional analysis of maladaptive behavior. In A. C. Repp & N. N. Singh (Eds.), *Perspectives on the use of aversive and nonaversive interventions for persons with developmental disabilities* (pp. 333–348). Sycamore, IL: Sycamore.

Repp, A. C., & Karsh, K. G. (1991). The task demonstration model: A program for teaching persons with severe disabilities. In B. Remington (Ed.), *The challenge of severe mental handicap: A behavior analytic approach* (pp. 263–282). Chichester: John Wiley.

Repp, A. C., & Karsh, K. G. (1992). An analysis of a group teaching procedure for persons with developmental disabilities. *Journal of Applied Behavior Analysis, 25,* 701–712.

Repp, A. C., & Karsh, K. G. (1994). Hypothesis-based interventions for tantrum behaviors of persons with developmental disabilities in school settings. *Journal of Applied Behavior Analysis, 27,* 21–31.

Repp, A. C., Karsh, K. G., Munk, D., & Dahlquist, C. M. (1995). Hypothesis-based interventions: A theory of clinical decision making. In W. O'Donohue & L. Krasner (Eds.). *Theories in behavior therapy* (pp. 585–608). Washington: American Psychological Association.

Rincover, A. (1978). Sensory extinction: A procedure for eliminating self-stimulatory behavior in developmentally disabled children. *Journal of Abnormal Child Psychology, 6,* 299–310.

Sasso, G. M., Reimers, T. M., Cooper, L. J., Wacker, D., Berg, W., Steege, M., Kelly, L., & Allaire, A. (1992). Use of descriptive and experimental analyses to identify the functional properties of aberrant behavior in school settings. *Journal of Applied Behavior Analysis, 25,* 809–821.

Singer, G. H., Singer, J., & Horner, R. H. (1987). Using pretask requests to increase the probability of compliance for students with severe disabilities. *Journal of the Association for Persons with Severe Handicaps, 12,* 287–291.

Singh, N. N., & Millichamp, C. J. (1987). Independent and social play among profoundly mentally retarded adults: Training maintenance, generalization and long-term follow-up. *Journal of Applied Behavior Analysis, 20,* 23–34.

Terrace, H. (1963). Discrimination learning with and without errors. *Journal of the Experimental Analysis of Behavior, 6,* 1–27.

Walker, H. M., & Bullis, M. (1990). Behavior disorders and the social context of regular class integration: A conceptual dilemma? In J. W. Lloyd, A. C. Repp, & N. N. Singh (Eds.), *The regular education initiative: Alternative perspectives on concepts. issues, and models* (pp. 75–93). Sycamore, IL: Sycamore.

Weeks, M., & Gaylord-Ross, R. (1981). Task difficulty and aberrant behavior in severely handicapped students. *Journal of Applied Behavior Analysis, 14,* 449–463.

Wehby, J. H., Symons, T. J., & Shores, R. E. (1995). A descriptive analysis of aggressive behavior in classrooms for children with emotional and behavioral disorders. *Behavioral Disorders, 20,* 87–105.

West, R. P., & Sloane, H. N. (1986). Teacher presentation rate and point delivery rate. *Behavior Modification, 10,* 267–286.

Winterling, V., Dunlap, G., & O'Neill, R. E. (1987). The influence of task variation on the aberrant behavior of autistic students. *Education and Treatment of Children, 10,* 105–119.

PART III

New Directions for
Functional Assessment

14

※

Functional Assessment for a Sex Offender Population

BUD FREDERICKS
VICKI NISHIOKA-EVANS

INTRODUCTION

The third and last section of this book presents new directions for functional assessment, including new client populations (sex offenders and gerontology), legal rights to a functional assessment, methods of study (behavioral states), and implications for reinforcement (evolution).

In the first chapter, Fredericks and Nishioka-Evans present a model for using functional assessment to design interventions for sex offenders who are living in specialized residential programs in community settings. Assessment is multilevel and includes information from others (history, reports), self-reports, plethysmography and polygraph, and observational data.

Results identify setting events and antecedents to the problem behavior as in the more traditional functional assessment procedures. However, there is a greater emphasis here on several factors, including training staff to observe chains of behaviors that lead to sex-offending acts, identifying functional deficits (lack of sexual knowledge or experience, poor social skills), and identifying thinking errors. Treatment is then tied directly to the results of assessment.

With this chapter, the authors remind us how much the development of functional assessment procedures has been restricted to the fields of mental retardation and autism. Prior chapters showed extensions to other school populations, while this chapter moves us considerably into a different perspective on the development of assessment procedures.

This chapter focuses on the use of functional assessment procedures in the treatment of adolescents with disabilities who are also sex offenders. (The term "disabilities" refers to those who are mildly mentally retarded, autistic, learning disabled, and emotionally and behaviorally disordered). The chapter discusses the types of information and various methods of assessment useful in the development of optimum treatment interventions for identified sex offenders. These methods constitute the functional assessment process, which in essence determines (a) under what circumstances a sex offender is most likely to offend, and (b) what reinforcers maintain sex offending behavior. In addition, this chapter briefly addresses the treatment of sex offenders to show the relationship between assessment and treatment.

To date, very little research has extended functional assessment procedures to the issue of sex offenses. This chapter presents efforts within the Teaching Research program to establish a model for using comprehensive functional assessment to design effective interventions for sex offenders. It is important to note that the offenders about whom we write are not incarcerated but live in specialized residential programs in community settings. They are under close supervision to ensure that the community is adequately protected. Since they live in a community rather than in an incarcerated situation, we have the opportunity to observe them in natural settings that approximate the environment in which they will function after they leave our program.

The residential settings in which these offenders reside are well staffed and serve up to five individuals in each environment. In addition, staff are available 24 hours a day to observe individuals in home, vocational, and community settings, providing comprehensive information regarding their sex-offending behaviors. Staff are trained to observe behaviors that may be precursors to offending, respond to those behaviors in a consistent manner, and record data on a continuous basis so that ongoing information is available about the individual and the effectiveness of treatment.

Both of these factors—residence within the community and an ever-present, well-trained staff—make this type of treatment program different from most sex offender treatment programs. Much that is reported in the literature about sex offender treatment is based upon information garnered in incarcerated settings or outpatient clinics. When offenders are incarcerated therapists do not have the opportunity to observe them in environments where they have access to potential victims. No women or children are present in male prisons. In outpatient clinics, the therapist is hampered in that he is almost totally reliant on self-report information from the offender.

Incidence figures regarding sex offense by adolescents vary considerably. The FBI Uniform Crime Report (United States Department of Justice, 1987) states that males under the age of 19 accounted for 19 percent of forcible rapes and 18 percent of other sex offenses in 1986. Strasburg (1984) indicates that the rate of sex offense by adolescents is increasing. Perhaps the most disturbing statistic is that reported by Elliot, Huizinga, & Morse (1985). Their research concludes that for each rape for which an adolescent was arrested, he had committed another 25 rapes that went either unreported or undetected. Since more than 60 percent of the victims of adolescents are children (Fehrenbach et al., 1986; Becker, Cunning-ham-Rathner, & Kaplan, 1986), we might assume that many sex offenses go un-reported, for it has only been in the past few years that children have been instructed to report sexual abuse.

OVERVIEW OF THE POPULATION

The term "sex offender" is one that is used in a popular sense to describe indi-viduals who commit a nonconsensual sex act against another person. In the way in which the term is used in the media and consequently the way the general public perceives the person, it becomes a global and all-inclusive descriptor. In reality, sex offenders have a variety of different profiles. The determination of an individualized profile is an essential component of both the functional assessment and treatment process.

For purposes of functional assessment, it is important to ascertain the type of sex offending that the perpetrator is liable to engage in and the type of victim he is likely to target for offense. We have chosen to categorize sex offenders in the following way:

Pedophiles: Pedophiles offend children who are prepubertal. A pedophile usu-ally focuses on one gender, although in a few cases children of both sexes can be the target.

Hebophiles: Hebophiles offend youth who have reached the age of puberty and who are not yet considered adults. Hebophiles also tend to target one gender, but again there are cases in which both sexes are victims.

Rapists: The target for rapists is usually women. Rapists may prefer a particu-lar age or type of woman and they may also be pedophiles or hebophiles. The term "rape," as used here, is any forced sexual act that can include vaginal or anal penetration or forced oral sex.

Incestuous relatives: Incest is strictly defined as sexual relations between indi-viduals who are too closely related to be legally married. Male members of the family are most often the perpetrators and their victims can be either the female or male children within the family. However, there is a growing body of evidence that indicates that incest by females against young boys occurs more frequently than was previously thought (Mayer, 1992). The popular perception of incest is that adults are the primary perpetrators. In many cases, incestuous acts are performed by adolescents with their siblings. Most young girls who have been admitted to the Teaching Research programs in Oregon have a history of being abused by a number of males in the family, including fathers, uncles, and brothers.

Stalkers: Stalkers are individuals who follow other individuals, may occasion-ally take items belonging to other individuals, and become an intrusive presence in the lives of others in general. In most states, stalkers are not cate-gorized as sex offenders because they do not actually commit a sex offense against another. We list them here because the targets of these individuals consider themselves to be harassed and in danger. Treatment of stalkers follows the same patterns as treatment of actual offenders.

Exhibitionists: Exhibitionists expose their genitals to others. They may masturbate in public. Exhibitionists may follow through with sexual acts against others if the opportunity presents itself.

In general, therefore, sex offenders represent a heterogeneous group. Most frequently, they target one sex and those of a certain age group. In some cases, all ages and sexes may be the targets. Their approaches can be subtle and persuasive, as in the case of many incestuous relationships where the child is persuaded to participate in the sexual act because of love for the family member. In other cases, the sex offense can be of a more violent nature, as in rape. The variety and types of sex offenses and the sexes and ages of the victims become important pieces of information that must figure in the construction of effective treatment.

METHODS OF ASSESSMENT

The sex offender field has not utilized the term "functional assessment," yet much of its current methodology constitutes a functional assessment in essence and would conform to the techniques described in the special edition of the *Journal of Applied Behavior Analysis* devoted to functional assessment (Neef, 1994). In other words, the methods used with sex offenders achieve the purpose of functional assessment; they determine under what circumstances the behavior is most likely to occur and what reinforcers maintain the behavior. Many of the tools used in functional assessment are used in assessing the risk that sex offenders and potential sex offenders may pose. These tools include report data from individuals who know the offender, self-report data from the individual, and observations by others of the individual in a variety of social settings. Unique to the sex offender assessment process is the use of plethysmography, to be discussed in a later section. The range of assessment methods used with sex offenders is shown in Box 14.

Information From Those Who Know the Offender

A comprehensive assessment of the sex offender includes consideration of his social history, family history, medical and psychiatric records, behavioral history, and clinical assessments. Individuals who are familiar with the offender's previous offenses should be contacted to determine the circumstances under which they occurred. A compilation of the age and gender of victims is invaluable to assist in identifying the type of victim the offender is liable to target. Details of the offense are essential to learn about the modus operandi of the offender. Does he carefully groom the victims? Were the victims known to the offender, or were they strangers? Are the offenses committed in opportunistic circumstances or is there evidence that the offenses were carefully planned? Was violence part of the offense pattern? Was the nature of the offense fondling or intercourse? What type of intercourse was it? Was some form of oral sex involved?

BOX 14   Methods of Assessment

- Information from other individuals
  - sex offender assessment
  - medical reports
  - psychiatric reports
  - neurological reports
  - social history
  - educational history
  - skill level
  - behavioral and criminal history
- Self-report information
- Plethysmography and polygraph
- Observation and data recording

Dates, times, and circumstances extraneous to the offense may be important. Were alcohol and drugs involved? Were there stressful situations in the life of the offender immediately preceding the offense?

It is important to concentrate not only upon the circumstances of previous offenses but also upon information that may help to ascertain why the person has become an offender. Therefore, interviews with individuals who are knowledgeable about the personal life of the offender may be enlightening. The history of the family may be quite helpful. What type of relationship did the offender have with his mother, father, and siblings? Was there any history of abuse? Were there previous heterosexual or homosexual relationships? Were there events in the person's life that were traumatic, or were there situations that might have had an effect on the sexuality of the individual? For instance, events during adolescence can have profound effects on an individual's perceptions of his own sexuality (other boys making fun of the size of an individual's genitalia in the physical education shower room, continual refusal of members of the opposite sex to go on dates, and so on).

Self-Report Data from the Individual

Self-report information obtained from the individual is the second form of functional assessment. Although some information from the individual may be obtained under natural circumstances, such as in routine conversations with staff, most often the information is obtained with the help of therapists trained in the treatment of sex offending. Therapists may use a number of techniques to elicit information from the offender. These therapists provide information regarding the cognitive elements of the individual's sex-offending behavior to include the thinking errors they used to avoid responsibility for their behavior, the fantasy content that underlies their acting out, and emotional factors or stressors that might be present prior to, during, and following the sex offense. Therapists may also identify previous traumas or events that might have triggered or been a causal factor for the offending behavior.

Most functional assessment information is obtained from the individual by therapists trained in the treatment of sex offending. In the gathering of information, the therapist will attempt to assist the offender in talking about his offenses, the circumstances under which they occurred, his preferences for victims, and detailed descriptions of the way in which the offender either groomed the victim or used opportunistic circumstances to offend. In addition, the therapist will probe the history of the offender to attempt to determine why the person started offending.

Staff members who work with the individual should be trained to listen carefully to the person's conversations so they may glean information about the offender. Discussion of family relationships may provide valuable information as to why offending began. Staff should be very familiar with the previous history of the individual so that they can recognize new information when it is being shared.

We cannot emphasize enough the importance of staff acquisition of information from the individual. Therapists who are treating the offender will usually have only a few hours a week with the person, but staff will be with the individual during most of the person's waking hours. If staff members are trained to be supportive, the individual may learn to trust them and may begin to share information that has not been shared with anyone else, even a trusted therapist.

Observation

In most reports of treatment of sex offenders, the offenders are incarcerated and the professionals conducting the treatment have little or no opportunity to observe the offender in natural circumstances with potential victims. Almost all treatment in such circumstances relies on self-report by the offender, the ability of the therapist to discern truth from falsity, and plethysmography, which shall be discussed in the following section. Where offenders are not incarcerated but live in the community and appear on scheduled intervals for treatment or some type of assessment, the therapist is hampered by the fact that he has little opportunity to observe the individual except in the testing and counseling situations.

The validity of self-report information from sex offenders who are developmentally disabled is further compromised because of limitations in vocabulary, communication skills, and confusion regarding time relationships. For example, the sex offender with disabilities may not know words to describe the sex-offending behavior, may not be able to match feelings to appropriate words, and may describe events that occurred in the distant past as if they had occurred recently.

In both instances—incarceration of the offender or limited contact with the offender in the community—the ability to conduct assessments that allow observation of the individual in situations where potential victims are present is, for all practical purposes, not a tool that the therapist can use. Thus, the therapist can seldom be confident that the offender is not engaging in behavior that is either offending or will lead to offending.

As such, incarceration of the offender, limited contact with the offender in the community, and communication difficulties are significant barriers for the therapist in evaluating whether the offender is engaging in behavior that is either offending or will lead to offending.

In our treatment milieu, the offender is living in the community but is under constant supervision. Staff are with or shadowing the individual at all times. Staff are also trained to be watchful for certain actions or changes in behavior that might be grooming tactics. For example, one male was observed staring, mouthing inappropriate sexual words, and making sexual hand gestures to peers when he believed adults were not looking. These behaviors were categorized as grooming tactics and appropriate behavior intervention strategies were implemented.

Staff also observe and note antecedent events that appear to trigger or precede inappropriate sexual behavior. To assist in gathering this information, Figure 14.1 shows a functional analysis interview form completed at a staff meeting for Fred. Fred is a 17-year-old individual who stands 6 feet tall and weighs over 260 pounds. He was injured in a car accident as a toddler and is certified as developmentally disordered because of traumatic brain injury. Fred was removed from his natural home at a young age due to the imprisonment of his natural father for the sexual abuse of his older siblings. At that time, Fred was reported to be out of parental control and exhibiting severe aggression, verbal threats, property damage, theft, and runaway behaviors.

The functional assessment interview was conducted with residential staff, classroom teachers, and vocational staff. Information from other medical and psychological reports were also included. The functional assessment indicated that Fred's inappropriate sexual behavior occurs at three separate levels of intensity and that these levels of behavior appear to occur as a sequence of behaviors. The Level 1 behaviors that Fred has difficulty with include staring at the genital or breast area and talking about sexual topics. If uninterrupted, Fred exhibits Level 2 behaviors, including frottage (that is, bumping into people to rub against their genital area or breasts and persistent touching without permission in nonsexual areas). If allowed to continue, Fred has exhibited Level 3 behaviors, which include inappropriate touching of small children and inappropriate explicit sexual statements.

The information on the form also indicates that Fred targets young prepubescent girls aged 12- to 14-years-old. He usually displays his behavior during active play periods in which bumping into the girls can be passed off as an accident. Settings in which he has exhibited this behavior are the swimming pool while in his mother's care, in parks, and, occasionally, during PE class at school. Previous treatments in other environments have included paying him up to $35 per week for appropriate behavior. Because of his disability he has not been adjudicated nor has he been convicted of any crimes. The recommendations are a structured behavioral program to include court sanctions and concrete rewards, sex education and social skills training, counseling, and evaluation of impulse control problems that might be related to his head injury. In addition, involvement of his parents in his treatment program is important to achieve consistent expectations regarding his sexual behavior.

In instances where staff disagree about their observations or have difficulty determining the antecedent events of an acting-out behavior, a more precise functional analysis procedure may be used. Figure 14.2 shows a form that allows the residential program staff to observe an individual's behavior in relation to the time of day, verify circumstances that the staff hypothesize might be problematic, and identify individuals who might be his targets. Frank is a 20-year-old male who exhibits the following behaviors: running away to steal items from male

Name: Fred Smith _____   Date: August 1, 1994 _____

Team: Residential staff, school teacher, Voc staff _____

Describe Target Behavior: Level 1: Staring at genital or breast area, talking about sexual topics.

Level 2: Frottage i.e., bumping into people, persistent unwanted touching of nonsexual areas, playful aggression.

Level 3: Touching genital or breast without permission.

1. Are there medical conditions or prescribed medication that influence the occurrence of the target behavior? If so, explain.

   Closed brain head injury—physician reports that the injury influences Fred's impulse control but is not responsible for inappropriate sexual or aggressive behavior. Current medication is Tegretol.

2. Is the behavior used to get something and/or avoid or escape something? Explain.

   Level 1 behavior is used to get attention from girls and to intimidate the girls. Fred uses his size to intimidate others to get his own way. Level 2 and 3 behaviors are for sexual excitement. Fred states that these girls are his girlfriends.

3. What are common triggers for the behavior, e.g., setting events, people, and schedule?

Define Events/Situations	Behavior most likely to occur	Behavior least likely to occur
Time of Day	Early morning	Nighttime—sleep hours
Settings	Swimming pool, P.E. in gym, parks, Special Olympics	Settings without prepubescent girls
Persons	Prepubescent girls 12–14 years old, sexual comments to girls and women	Men, male peers, staff, strong female staff
Activities	Sports, activity periods, unsupervised times without responsible adult	Supervised times, structured activities
Other		

4. What are warning signs or precursor behaviors that the individual may exhibit prior to the target behavior?

   Fred may demonstrate oppositional behavior to use as an excuse to "run" to a place where he will find girls or he may be overly polite to gain permission to be with girls.

5. What are reinforcers that may be maintaining the behavior?

   Sexual gratification, attention from girls. Fred does not discriminate negative from positive attention but interprets any attention from a girl as flirting.

6. What are punishers or conditions that may help remediate the behavior?

   Minimizing unsupervised access to areas with teenage, prepubescent girls. Allowing no access to activities that are loosely structured, e.g., swimming pool. Strong cues to redirect with immediate correction procedure. Behavioral accountability and juvenile court involvement.

7. What has worked or not worked in the past to treat this behavior?

   Warning or threats to stop. Fred has been charged repeatedly without prosecution or court accountability. Paying him to stop has not worked. No intervention has worked to date.

FIGURE 14.1 Functional Analysis Interview Form

8. Does the behavior change in intensity? If so, what behaviors occur in this process? Are there thinking events that maintain or strengthen the behavior?

Level	Behaviors	Thoughts	Possible Intervention
1	Persistent teasing of girls, "playful" touching on back and shoulders, animated laughter.	Fred tells himself that the girl really likes him, wants to be his girlfriend and what he is doing is okay. Everybody does it and teases like this. The girl started it anyway.	Teaching cues and reminders about boundaries. Perception checks about appropriate teasing; interpretation of response and age appropriateness of person. If girl is too young, tell Fred to leave or stop immediately.
2	Staring at genital or breast area, talking about sexual topics.	Fred tells himself that the girl really likes him and wants to have sex with him. "I know this because of how she acted and dressed. She wanted me to look at her."	Cue to remind Fred, "Fred, you are staring and she doesn't like it. It is going to get you in trouble and it needs to stop now." Remove Fred from the area.
3	Frottage, i.e., bumping into people, persistent unwanted touching of nonsexual areas, not responding to request to stop.	Fred tells himself that the girl likes to be touched and that makes it okay. He tells himself it's an accident and he tripped and fell. "It's not my fault and I didn't touch them, they brushed against me."	Remove Fred from the area immediately. Contact manager for follow-up. Explore police action.
4	Touching genital or breast without permission.	Fred tells himself that he was just playing around, they liked it and thought it was funny. When confronted, Fred states that he didn't do it, they got in my way, "I didn't mean to touch their breasts but they were wearing a two-piece swim suit so they wanted it. The other kids were telling me to do that."	Remove Fred from area. Contact manager for follow-up. Explore police action.

9. What are skills that could be taught to replace this behavior?

Appropriate approach or greeting skills, dating, responsible sexual behavior.

10. What intervention(s) does the team recommend? Identify the choices and write a description of the intervention needed.

YES/NO	Recommendations	Description
No	Behavior does not warrant intervention	
Yes	Schedule intervention	Schedule activities with same-age peers, increase level of physical activities to increase activities, enrich schedule to combat boredom.
Yes	Staff change/training	Training in teaching personal skills to Fred, behavior program, and interventions in community setting.
Yes	Medical treatment	Explore impact of closed brain injury on behavior.
Yes	Skill training program	Conversation/approach skills, personal rights, legal aspects of sexuality, appropriate responsible sexual behavior, problem solving, accepting negative feedback.
Yes	Referral for treatment	Individual sex offender treatment.
Yes	Environmental change	Select activities that limit access to children and prepubescent girls. Activities should promote interaction with same-age peers.
Yes	Behavior change or modification	Behavior intervention that reinforces appropriate conversation with peers, safe choices when in proximity of younger children, and immediate correction for Level 1 behavior to prevent possible offending behavior.

Name: Frank   Dates: August 1–7, 1994

Behavior: Stares/fixates about teenage boys, runaway to steal items.

	Frank is asked to do something he doesn't like	Shift change or change in staff persons	Visual contact with teenage neighbor Jack	Withdrawal of staff attention due to roommate	Overhears conversation about teenage boy Jack	Being denied permission to do something he likes	Unkown antecedent event
6:00–6:29 AM		10 min—Todd					
6:30–6:59							
7:00–7:29							5 min
7:30–7:59							
8:00–8:29							
8:30–8:59							
9:00–9:29						15 min—Ron 15 min—Todd	
9:30–9:59							
10:00–10:29							
10:30–10:59							
11:00–11:29						15 min—Ron	
11:30–11:59							
12:00–12:29 PM							
12:30–12:59							
1:00–1:29		10 min—Clint 20 min—Todd	5 min—Todd			5 min—Clint	
1:30–1:59							

FIGURE 14.2 Functional Analysis Observation Form

	Frank is asked to do something he doesn't like	Shift change or change in staff persons	Visual contact with teenage neighbor Jack	Withdrawal of staff attention due to roommate	Overhears conversation about teenage boy Jack	Being denied permission to do something he likes	Unkown antecedent event
2:00–2:29		Scott B/Rob H. Return vac. 8 hrs.			5½ hrs—Clint and Rob	10 min—Ron	
2:30–2:59					10 min—Clint	10 min—Clint	
3:00–3:29						25 min—Clint	
3:30–3:59						2 min—Scott B 5 min—Scott B	
4:00–4:29			45 min— Clint				
4:30–4:59							
5:00–5:29							
5:30–5:59						10 min—Todd	
6:00–6:29							
6:30–6:59			10 min—Gary				
7:00–7:29						15 min—Ron	
7:30–7:59							
8:00–8:29							
8:30–8:59							
9:00–9:29							
9:30–9:59							
10:00							

teenage boys or young, athletic-looking adults, visible tremors and staring in a fixated fashion when he is in the proximity of a teenage boy, talking repetitively about certain teenage boys, and publicly masturbating in the window when children have been present. The public masturbation was corrected by monitoring Frank in his bedroom and placing a screen outside his bedroom window that limited his view of the outside. Various staff were interviewed regarding this behavior and a variety of hypotheses were offered. Staff were unable to reach consensus about the antecedent events to the behavior; as such, the Functional Analysis Observation form was used. The purpose of the functional analysis was to determine under which conditions Frank exhibited the most intrusive behaviors (staring, running away, and theft. The results suggest that Frank exhibits his inappropriate behavior when in the presence of a specific teenage boy, when he hears conversations about this teenage boy, and when he is supervised by Todd, a young and athletic-looking staff member. Frank also appears to be more likely to run away during shift changes when staff are giving verbal updates regarding the events of the day. The recommendations that resulted from this information included no access to the teenage boy whom he is targeting, more vigilant supervision at shift change, and rescheduling staff assignments so that Todd is not working in Frank's apartment.

Observation is an essential piece of the ongoing functional assessment that occurs with the adolescents and adults for whom we provide treatment. The observation entails three major components: (a) watching the offender in situations where identified antecedent events are present, such as in visual contact with or proximity of potential victims; (b) listening carefully to verbalizations of the offender as he talks to peers, staff, and others; and (c) continuous evaluation of treatment strategies in effectively managing the sex offender's behavior.

Plethysmography

Plethysmography is the study of the variations in the size of an organ or body part because of the quantity and circulation of blood in that part. Specifically, plethysmography is most often used with males to measure the tumescence of the penis as a result of visual or auditory stimuli or both. According to Steinhauser (1989), plethysmography is the most reliable and valid means to measure deviant sexual arousal. However, plethysmography does on occasion produce false positives (the person who becomes aroused at certain pictures or auditory tapes, but yet is not an offender) and false negatives (the individual who has a history of offending, but fails to become aroused with visual or auditory stimuli). Despite these occasional difficulties, it is a valuable assessment tool.

Multilevel and Continuous Assessment

As in the functional assessment of any behavior, multilevel assessments are essential. In other words, one type of assessment does not usually provide complete information. In addition, assessment must be a continual process. As treatment of the individual progresses, not only is additional information gleaned from the reports of others who have observed him in certain situations, but also the individual reports new information to the therapist or to staff. Thus, as in all functional assessments, the more information that is accurately gathered, the clearer our understanding becomes regarding the circumstances under which the behavior occurs.

SOME COMMON CHARACTERISTICS
OF SEX OFFENDERS

Overview

Researchers in the developmental disabilities field in which the functional assessment process has blossomed have learned that behaviors seem to occur for common reasons, such as avoidance or escape from what is perceived to be an unpleasant situation or the seeking of attention. In addition, certain circumstances have been identified as probable high-risk times for the occurrence of targeted behaviors, such as during transition from one activity to another, staff shift changes, high stimulus times, or demands from others.

Likewise, the literature regarding sex offenders cites a number of characteristics or circumstances that prevail among many sex offenders. Treatment personnel should be aware of (a) a history of sexual abuse when the offender was young, (b) functional deficits in the areas of sexual knowledge and social skills, and (c) thinking errors.

History of Sexual Abuse

The incidence of sexual victimization reported by sex offenders varies considerably. Fagan and Wexler (1988) state that only 9 percent of the offenders they surveyed reported a history of sexual abuse, whereas Longo (1982) found that 47 percent of the offenders reported sexual abuse.

The connection between being sexually abused and sex offending is well established. Yet, as Aljazireh (1993) notes, there have been no reported control studies that compare those who were victimized and do not offend with those who were victims and do have a history of offending. There is also a need to correlate the age at which victimization occurred, the type of sexual abuse, and the characteristics of the perpetrator before more definitive conclusions can be drawn regarding the link between victim of sex offense and sex offender. Despite this caveat, in a survey conducted by Muster (1992) among therapists who treat sex offenders and sexual abuse victims, most thought that victimization issues should be addressed before moving on to offending issues.

Functional Deficits

Many offenders with disabilities are lacking in certain knowledge and skills, and because of this deficit, they have a tendency not to think clearly about their own sexuality and the sexuality of others. These deficits are different from the "thinking errors" discussed below although they may well be related. The functional deficits fall into two major categories: (a) lack of sexual knowledge or experience; and (b) poor social skills.

Lack of Sexual Knowledge or Experience Many offenders, during the course of their education, received little or no information regarding sexuality. They have a poor impression of their own sexuality and are not sure what obligations a responsible relationship entails. One young man, who was adjudicated because he touched a sunbathing college coed's breast, believed it was all right to do that because the movies that he had been renting from the local video store depicted men treating women in that manner. Another young man with mild mental retardation moved in with his girlfriend. He believed that the cohabitation arrangement allowed him to have sex with her "on demand." When she refused, he would rape her. After a number of such incidents, he was remanded to a sex offender treatment program.

Our experience with teaching courses on sexuality and relationships is that many youth whom one would perceive as being "street-wise" are significantly deficient in knowledge about relationships and appropriate sexual activity within relationships. In some cases, despite numerous sexual experiences, the individual may lack basic knowledge of sexual anatomy and physiology.

Some adolescents with disabilities have had little or no opportunity for the sexual talk and activities in which most other teenagers engage. Consequently, there is a dearth of adolescent sexual experience and, in some cases, a lack of appropriate fantasizing and masturbation. This stunted adolescent sexual development may cause the individual to seek other outlets for his physical needs, such as young children or same-sex peers. The same individual, given appropriate opportunities, might prefer a teenage heterosexual relationship.

Poor Social Skills Many of these individuals, and certainly most of those with disabilities, lack good social skills. The domain of social skills includes relationships and sexuality, assertiveness, appropriate communication, and self-esteem (Nishioka-Evans et al., 1983). A deficiency in social skills is a pervasive element of the sex-offending syndrome. Because of poor social skills and knowledge, individuals develop distorted thinking about others and relationships, which may lead to an offense. Poor social skills may also, for instance, cause an adolescent to be shunned or ridiculed, causing him to develop a hatred for women that may lead to rape or the need to seek sexual gratification with same-sex partners or children.

When placed in treatment, the individual may be unable to face his own actions or talk appropriately about them because of poor social skills. Thus, poor social skills have the potential not only to be a causal factor in offending but also an inhibitor to treatment.

Thinking Errors

The final characteristic found frequently among adolescents and adults with disabilities who are sex offenders is the tendency to make what are termed "thinking errors." This tendency is found not only in the offender who is mentally disabled but in most sex offenders regardless of intellectual ability. Most therapists in the field of sexual abuse identify thinking errors as common to the offender. These need to be identified, and once identified, treatment includes teaching the individual to think more clearly.

These thinking errors are delineated in various writings under different names. Haaven, Little, and Petre-Miller (1990) refer to them as "criminal self-talk statements." Each therapist's list is different, yet they embody similar behaviors. The most common are (a) lying and making evasive or misleading statements; (b) blaming others for the offense, such as poor upbringing by parents or sexual abuse suffered as a child; (c) indicating that the victim wanted the sexual act to occur; (d) making excuses or justifying why the behavior occurred; (e) indicating that he deserves to have sex and getting it is more important than anything else; and (f) minimizing the effects of the offense.

Thinking errors are undoubtedly related to poor social skills training. As was pointed out, they tend to be a causal factor in offending and an inhibitor in treatment.

TREATMENT

This chapter will not detail comprehensive treatment procedures used with offenders with disabilities who live in the community. Instead, this section on treatment focuses on the relationship between the assessment process and treatment.

Safety of the Community

When sex offenders receive their initial and intensive treatment in a community setting rather than a secure facility, the primary consideration, even before treatment considerations, is the maintenance of the safety of community members. Continuous staff surveillance guarantees this safety. Initially the offender will be accompanied or shadowed by a staff member to all community activities. As treatment progresses, the treatment team will determine the degree of freedom the offender may have.

In the last stages of the individual's treatment program, as unaccompanied movement around the community commences, the ability of the individual to manage on his own is frequently tested. These tests can best be accomplished through confederates, others who work for the agency but are unknown to the offender. Confederates function in two ways. First, they may act as observers in situations where an offense might previously have occurred, such as around young children or where members of the opposite sex are alone. (It should be emphasized that should the confederate perceive that someone is being targeted by the individual, the confederate will intervene before any harm can be done.) Secondly, confederates can attempt to entice the offender into a situation where offenses may occur, although the offender has learned from treatment that such places or activities need to be avoided.

Although staff members are providing the surveillance that keeps the community safe, they are also trained to observe the behavior of the offender and to report back anything they have observed or heard that may enhance the functional assessment information and may assist in the treatment process. In addition to surveillance, observation, and listening functions, staff members are also trained to be supportive and reinforcing to the individual. They may gently remind the offender of behaviors that will help to avoid the opportunity to offend. They provide encouragement when it is obvious the individual is trying to avoid trouble. Staff members reinforce appropriate social behavior or techniques learned in therapy.

Team Approach

We have found a team approach for treatment decisions to be most effective. The members of the team and the times they meet vary depending upon their roles. The various members of the team are (a) all residential staff who interact with the individual; (b) the vocational trainer and vocational supervisor; (c) the behavioral consultant; (d) the treatment counselor; (e) the probation or parole officer; and (f) parents, guardians, or significant others.

Residential staff meet with their supervisor weekly to review the events of the week and to discuss important incidents. Specifically, the staff's observations and insights are sought to further the functional assessment and treatment processes. This is also the time when changes to an individual's program are discussed and, if necessary, staff responses are role played.

A treatment team meeting is held every two weeks to review program progress and to assimilate additional functional assessment information that may have been gleaned from the staff, the therapist, or others. Attending this meeting are the residential supervisor, behavioral consultant, vocational personnel, and, on occasion, parents or guardians and counselors. This is the meeting in which functional assessment information is examined critically, other data are analyzed, alterations in the treatment program are decided, and the need for additional information identified.

Therapists continually feed into this process, primarily through the residential staff and, on occasion, in meetings with parents, guardians, behavioral consultants, and others. With most of the therapists, a residential supervisor or staff member may sit in the counseling session with the permission of both the counselor and the participants. Special treatment meetings are held with all the members of a team when program progress seems to be stalled or if difficulties have arisen that cannot be handled through the routine meetings.

Therapeutic Counseling

Counseling sessions with a professional trained in the treatment of sex offenders is the hub of the treatment process. The methods used in counseling are complex and varied. It is not the purpose of this chapter to discuss those methods. They are discussed in detail in such publications as Haaven, Little, & Petre-Miller (1990), Bays & Freeman-Longo (1989) and Bays, Freeman-Longo, & Hildebran (1990). Instead, we shall describe the principal elements to be achieved through the therapeutic process.

Continual Functional Assessment Therapeutic counseling provides a continual functional assessment process in that new information is periodically gained through revelations provided by the offender. This new information is then shared with the treatment team and is used to alter the treatment program if necessary.

Breaking Denial and Admission For treatment to be successful, the individual undergoing treatment should admit that he has offended and be able to describe the offenses. If there is a history of sexual abuse to the offender, part of the process is to have the individual recognize that abuse did occur and determine his attitude toward the abuser and the abuse. At this stage, the individual needs to determine whether he will confront the person who sexually abused him.

Controlling the Cycles of Urges, Fantasies, and Offending The therapist tries to determine the circumstances under which offending occurs. Since offending usually occurs as a result of a sequence of events, thoughts, circumstances, and fantasies, which seem to present a pattern of behavior, the counselor first attempts to identify that process and then to teach the individual how to break the cycle once it begins.

Developing Alternative Ways to Think and Speak Part of the cycle-breaking process is to teach the individual to stop making thinking errors. In addition, some therapists conduct social skills groups that teach social competency and thus help to alter the type of thinking that causes offending to occur.

Establishing Rules As the therapist learns more about the individual under treatment, coordination with the program will be effected to prescribe some rules that will help the person avoid the offending cycle. For instance, certain types of television programs or reading material may be proscribed. As previously indicated, when the therapist establishes these guidelines, it is up to the team to help the offender achieve the goals and follow the rules.

Building Empathy and Identifying Ways to Make Amends Part of the treatment process attempts to build empathy for victims. This is demonstrated when the offender (a) indicates that he/she is remorseful for the act, (b) is able to describe how the victim must have felt when the offense was committed, and (c) apologizes to the victim and perhaps makes some type of restitution.

Social Skills Training

Training in social skills is an essential ingredient in the treatment of those who commit sex offenses. Lunderwold and Young (1992) found that social skills training was considered as acceptable a form of treatment as incarceration or aversive therapy. Moergen, Merkel, and Brown (1990) successfully used social skills training in the treatment of an obscene phone caller. Nishioka-Evans et al. (1983) outline a potential social skills curriculum in their assessment procedures.

Aversive Therapy, Directed Masturbation, and Verbal Satiation

Aversive therapy has been used to alter sex-offending behavior. This technique most often uses plethysmography combined with various types of auditory and pictorial stimuli. Masturbatory reconditioning and verbal satiation are frequently combined. Masturbation is directed with fantasies of adults of the offender's choosing. Ejaculation is to be achieved as quickly as possible followed by 20 minutes of verbalization of deviant fantasies. Johnston, Hudson, & Marshall (1992) review data on these methods and conclude that empirical support for them is weak.

Drug Therapy

Drug therapy is a treatment methodology that is normally used with a variety of other treatments. Meyers (1991) reports successful use of Depo-Provera in conjunction with therapeutic counseling in the case of a 26-year-old man. Depo-Provera has the effect of lowering the testosterone level and thereby reducing sexual drive. The limitation is that the reduction is maintained only as long as the medication is continued.

CASE STUDIES

General

The cumulative results of successful treatment of adolescents who sexually offend is encouraging. Smith and Monastersky (1986), using subsequent referrals to a juvenile court as a measure of recidivism, found that out of 117 juveniles who had gone through an outpatient treatment program, only 17 committed sex offenses over the subsequent 17-month follow-up period. Kahn and Chambers (1991), following 221 adolescents for an average of 28.1 months, reported that 18 percent committed sex offenses again.

In this chapter we have discussed methods for functional assessment and briefly described generally accepted treatment procedures. As Davis and Leitenberg (1987) point out in their review of the literature regarding adolescent sex offenders, there are no accounts of controlled studies designed to evaluate the effectiveness of treatment packages or parts of treatment packages.

The following describes the experiences of two individuals who were referred to the Teaching Research program for sex offending. The diagnosis of the person, the offending pattern, the functional analysis process, and the treatment program are described, as well as the results achieved to date.

Alex

Alex was referred to the Teaching Research program in June 1989.

History Alex was removed from his parents' home at age two because of parental abuse and neglect. His extended family has a long history of mental illness, family dysfunction, and sex offending. He resided in various foster homes and childcare situations and was periodically returned to his parents' home between the ages of two and seven. During this time it was determined that he had been sexually abused by a number of men.

At age seven he was placed in a private residential facility. He remained there until he was 12. During his stay there, it is reported that he molested two female

children. He was then placed in the state institution for persons with mental retardation. At age 17 (almost 18) in June 1989, he was referred to the Teaching Research program.

Diagnosis   Alex had a diagnosis of schizophrenia and mental retardation. Repeated IQ tests produced scores between 60 and 70.

Presenting Behaviors   During the initial period in the Teaching Research program Alex exhibited the following behaviors:

(a) Spending long periods rocking and pacing. He seemed to be in a severe state
    of agitation.
(b) Engaging in verbal aggression, threatening to kill others.
(c) Pouting, mumbling, and being somewhat incoherent.
(d) Hearing voices and other auditory hallucinations. He frequently refused his
    medication, which exacerbated this problem.
(e) Engaging in severe incidents of property destruction, including punching
    holes in the wall and throwing objects.
(f) Running away.
(g) Engaging in a variety of sexual overtures and molestations. He exposed his
    genitalia to a female staff member, masturbated in public, made sexual com-
    ments to female staff members, and, at times, used a threatening manner. He
    committed sodomy with a male peer. He was found to be frequently groom-
    ing others (children, male and female peers, and adults) by staring intensely at
    them, being overly polite, and making sexual gestures and inappropriate sex-
    ual remarks.

Functional Assessment   The functional assessment process with Alex was
long and involved. Because of budgetary restrictions, it took the program several months to obtain approved funding for psychiatric evaluation. This was
considered essential because of (a) the diagnosis of schizophrenia; (b) the mani-
festation of hallucinations; and (c) what was observed as a cyclic behavioral pattern of six weeks of intense agitation, manifested by rocking, pacing, and violent
and angry words, followed by comparable periods of calm. At the same time,
Alex was referred to a therapist who specialized in the treatment of sex offenders for additional assistance in conducting the functional assessment. Plethysmo-
graphies and polygraphs were administered. It should be noted that several
skilled clinicians were consulted over a period of time and their conclusions
were highly consistent.

While in the Teaching Research program, staff at the residential program and
at school maintained continuous data on the presenting behaviors. In addition,
weekly staff meetings were conducted to elicit from staff information and impressions that supplemented the data that had been gathered. Behavior review team
meetings were convened biweekly to review the data and the information being
gathered from therapists. The therapist who had initially worked with Alex de-
parted after five months to take another job, a change that significantly affected

the functional assessment process, since it would take time for the subsequent therapist to build a rapport with Alex.

Functional Assessment Results   A definitive diagnosis of schizophrenia was confirmed. The hallucinations and cycles of behavior were attributed to this condition.

Initially, the sex-offending behavior was not linked with the verbal aggression and property destruction; they were treated as separate behaviors. Angry verbal aggression and property destruction seemed to occur when Alex became frustrated at not being able to do what he wanted or at being requested to do something. However, these behaviors also occurred when no consistent antecedent situations could be identified. This inability to identify causal elements in the functional assessment process was disturbing.

It was determined that the sex-offending behavior was opportunistic and occurred against any gender and any age group, although there was a decided predisposition to offend against weaker peers or children. It was believed that Alex was not capable of a sustained assault against an adult. Thus, the risk of committing rape was minimal.

As time progressed, the linkage was made between the sex offending, the pacing and rocking, verbal aggression, and property destruction. It was determined that Alex's pacing and rocking led to an agitated state and was followed or accompanied by verbal aggression or property destruction. A sex offense usually occurred at the end of the sequence of behaviors. This connection was difficult to assess at first because of the severity of the rocking and aggressive behaviors and because of the low frequency of sex-offending attempts. It was only through the process of staff and therapists working together, observing, taking data, and sharing information that a predictable behavior pattern became clear. The hypothesis that emerged was that verbal aggression and property destruction occurred to avoid tasks or when a favored activity was not available. It was further hypothesized that the verbal aggression and property destruction were antecedent to sex offending.

Treatment   The schizophrenic condition was primarily treated with medication under the direction of a physician. Over a period of two years medications including Haldol, Cogentin, and Mellaril were adjusted and changed until a combination of medications reduced the hallucinatory behavior and seemed to assist in the reduction of cyclic behavior. In addition Depo-Provera was prescribed to decrease Alex's highly sexualized behavior.

Given the hypothesis that Alex's behaviors occurred as a result of failure to get what he wanted or to avoid a task, negotiations occurred to choose tasks that he could easily do and to provide him with what he wanted at a negotiated time. These negotiations did not always work because at times his demands were impossible to satisfy or extremely unreasonable in nature. Consequently, a level system of responding to the behavior was developed for when negotiations failed. The behavior levels were defined as:

Level I: Staring, hinting to get something, ignoring others, repeating verbalizations

Level II: Negative comments, instigating others, pouting, mumbling

Level III: Rocking, throwing objects, slamming doors

Level IV: Sexual overtures, exposing himself, running away, property damage

Staff were taught to intervene at the lowest level and redirect him so that he would not progress to the next level of behaviors. A series of reinforcers was established for use when Alex successfully redirected his behavior. A brief summary of the interventions follows:

Level I Staff intervened and told Alex he could record his own data if he successfully stopped the behavior. If he was able to publicly demonstrate that he could stop the behavior, he was rewarded with staff social praise and soft drinks, extra walks, a bike ride, or a pet store outing. Other rewards were also available. He was required to stop the behavior within two minutes to earn a reward.

Level II Alex had five minutes to stop the behavior. If he failed to do so, he was placed on a structured program for the next hour in which staff instructed him to perform a series of tasks. (This process was found to be successful in breaking the cycle before it moved to the next level.) If he stopped the target behaviors within the five minutes, he was rewarded.

Levels III and IV If Alex's behavior escalated to Level III or IV behaviors, he was immediately placed on house arrest and required to perform work tasks. These tasks were assigned only as a result of Level III and IV behaviors and included scrubbing walls and picking up litter. Again, the philosophy behind this was to break the cycle before it escalated into offending behavior.

In addition, efforts were made to improve the overall quality of Alex's life. He was given the opportunity to work, was provided a rich menu of community activities, and continually received positive feedback for periods of nonexistent levels of behaviors across all three environments (school, home, and work). Staff were trained to ensure that the positive:negative ratio of interactions always exceeded a four positive to one negative ratio. Finally, Alex received intensive social skills training to assist him to function more appropriately in community, home, and school settings. These social skills were reinforced by staff on the job and during community outings.

Results When Alex left the adolescent program after three years at age 21 in November 1992, his behaviors had improved significantly.

Where initially rocking behavior was occurring for more than an hour a day, data for the five months prior to Alex's leaving the program indicated that Level III behaviors (which encompassed rocking, slamming doors, and throwing objects) had reduced to two incidents during the five-month period, one lasting one minute and the other lasting five minutes.

During the early months of 1990, Alex engaged in Level IV behaviors at least once a week, and more often three to five times a week. During the sixteen months before he left the program there were four Level IV incidents, and none that threatened anyone else in the community.

Behaviors	Pre June/July 1989*	Post November 1992*
Rocking	1.4 hours/day	0
Verbal aggression	8.2/day	.14/day
Slamming doors	2.4/day	0
Property destruction	1.1/day	0
Negative statements/instigating	5.6/day	2.1/day

*average of four weeks of behavior

FIGURE 14.3 Pre- and Postdata for Alex's Behaviors

Level I and Level II behaviors, although still occurring, were reduced to a level that was acceptable, but staff members felt more work was still needed. Figure 14.3 summarizes the pre- and postbehaviors of Alex.

Alex was transferred to an adult sex offender program for people with developmental disabilities conducted by Teaching Research where the programs developed in the adolescent program were continued. As of July 1994, Alex has now been removed from probation. He has a girlfriend. His attendance at work is erratic, but he continually returns to jobs. There have been no instances of inappropriate sexual behavior for the past year. His social skills have improved remarkably so that someone unacquainted with his history would perceive him as a polite young man who may be a little slow, but who is generally a pleasure to talk to. The linkage of aggression and sex offending is no longer present. To ensure community protection, however, he is still accompanied by staff when in the community. He may need long-range support, but there is a good prognosis that he may be able to transfer in the future to a supervised apartment program for persons with developmental disabilities.

Victor

Victor was referred to the Teaching Research program in September 1992 when he was 16 years old.

History Victor was living with his single mother when he was discovered fondling two young cousins. This fondling included pinching and hurting the cousins and violent rages when he was unable to see them take baths. Despite repeated attempts by his mother and aunt to have him stop the behavior, it continued until the mother reached out for governmental help. He has been placed on probation for these sexual molestation charges.

Prior to these incidents, which lasted for a period of two years, Victor had a history of violent episodes interspersed with reports of good school behavior and enjoyment of a job in the school cafeteria.

Diagnosis Victor is mildly mentally retarded, has few same-age friends, and gravitates towards children. He was physically abused by his father and perhaps sexually abused although he does not remember it.

Presenting Behaviors When first referred to the program, his violent behavior and potential to offend against young children were the primary behaviors. As the assessment process progressed, the staff in the program identified the following additional behaviors: lying, asking for compliments, staring, setting up of peers, blatant sexual comments, bullying behavior with peers, inappropriate sexual touching, and property damage.

Functional Assessment An intense psychosexual evaluation was done in May 1992 in which the therapist concluded that Victor was at high risk for reoffending against children. His history of violent rages was also noted, as was his tendency to bully peers. The functional assessment process continued after Victor joined the program. Staff members were instructed to maintain continual surveillance on Victor, and gradually, through observation, the additional presenting behaviors detailed above were identified. It was determined that the behaviors had one functional purpose: to intimidate and control others. This was communicated to Victor as his taking the rights of others away from them.

Treatment To assist Victor in curbing his attempts to intimidate and control, he was provided intensive social skills training, emphasizing relationships and interactions with others. He attended school where that instruction was provided. His performance was reinforced by staff in the residential, community, and vocational settings. He was employed and found the work experience to be reinforcing.

Specifically, staff members praised Victor for being cooperative and using appropriate polite social skills, such as asking for help, talking about concerns, problem solving, negotiation, and cooperation. A small group session was conducted at the end of each day with Victor and his peers in which each person would evaluate his day according to the following behaviors: being honest, keeping his own personal power, making safe choices, and respecting the rights of others. Points were awarded for achieving these behaviors and these could be traded for special events or items. The peers essentially kept each other honest in this process and would correct each other if they perceived someone was not self-evaluating accurately. Staff were also present to participate if necessary. This process assisted peers in confronting Victor's inappropriate sexual and intimidation behaviors.

If Victor engaged in any of the behaviors of inappropriate sexual behavior, threats, intimidation, aggression, sexual comments, exposure, or lying, he was required to sit at the kitchen table and identify from whom he was taking rights away, what he intended to happen, what really happened, and what he should have done instead. The intensity of the behaviors was categorized with the less intensive behaviors, requiring nothing more than the confrontation and problem-solving techniques outlined above. More serious behaviors required consequences of either chores around the home or house arrest.

Victor continues in individual and group sex offender counseling, which allows for continual refinement of his program as new aspects of his offending behavior unfold.

Results It should be pointed out that the treatment program described above was developed only two months prior to the preparation of this chapter. Under

Behaviors	Pre September/October 1992*	Post March 1993*
Inappropriate sexual touching	.28/day	0
Sexual comments	1.4/day	.28/day
Lying	2.6/day	.28/day
Threats/intimidation	3.4/day	.43/day
Aggression	.57/day	0

*average of four weeks of behavior

FIGURE 14.4 Pre- and Postdata for Victor's Behaviors

this program, Victor's offending behaviors have decreased and his prosocial behaviors have increased. The peer group process, combined with the identification that all of his behaviors were issues of power and control, have resulted in no serious sexual behaviors for the past two months, whereas previously these were frequent and dangerous. Minor incidents of sexual comments and intimidation have also significantly decreased. See Figure 14.4 for a summary of behavior data. Victor continues his treatment and the prognosis, now that the function of the behaviors has been correctly identified, is good. The therapist reports that Victor is actively seeking a same-age heterosexual relationship, that his fantasy content is acceptable, and that he is ready to move to a less restrictive setting.

Although we have to date achieved success with Alex and Victor, we must keep in mind that they have received services in a program that has as one of its goals the protection of the community; therefore, there is little opportunity for them to offend. As they return to more normal living arrangements, we cannot predict that they will not offend again. We do believe that the treatment provided them uses knowledge and skills that are currently the state of the art. However, this entire field is in its infancy. We have much to research and much to learn. Given the extent of sex offending in our culture, the requirement to learn and apply that learning should be a major public mandate.

SUMMARY

This chapter has presented the use of the functional assessment process with a sex offending population. It has described the nature of the population, the types of sex offenses, and the methods used to assess the circumstances under which sex offending occurs. A brief discussion of treatment methods has been offered. Finally, a description of the processes used with two individuals was presented.

REFERENCES

Aljazireh, L. (1993). Historical, environmental, and behavioral correlates of sexual offending by male adolescents: A critical review. *Behavioral Sciences and the Law, 11,* 423–440.

Bays, L., & Freeman-Longo, R. (1989). *Why did I do it again? Understanding my cycle of problem behaviors.* Orwell: The Safer Society.

Bays, L., Freeman-Longo, R., & Hildebran, D. D. (1990). *How can I stop? Breaking my deviant cycle.* Orwell: The Safer Society Press.

Becker, J. V., Cunningham-Rathner, J., & Kaplan, M. S. (1986). Adolescent sexual offenders: Demographics, criminal and sexual histories, and recommendations for reducing future offenses. *Journal of Interpersonal Violence, 1,* 431–445.

Davis, G. E., & Leitenberg, H. (1987). Adolescent sex offenders. *Psychological Bulletin, 101,* 417–427.

Elliot, D. S., Huizinga, D., & Morse, B. J. (1985). *The dynamics of deviant behavior: A national survey report.* Boulder: Behavioral Research Institute.

Fagan, J., & Wexler, S. (1988). Explanations of sexual assault among violent delinquents. *Journal of Adolescent Research, 3,* 363–385.

FBI Uniform Crime Report, United States Department of Justice (1987). Washington, DC: U.S. Government Document Printing Office.

Fehrenbach, P. A., Smith, W., Monastersky, C., & Deisher, R. W. (1986). Adolescent sexual offenders: Offender and offense characteristics. *American Journal of Orthopsychiatry, 56,* 225–233.

Haaven, J., Little, R., & Petre-Miller, D. (1990). *Treating intellectually disabled sex offenders.* Orwell: The Safer Society.

Johnston, P., Hudson, S. M., & Marshall, W. L. (1992). The effects of masturbatory reconditioning with nonfamilial child molesters. *Behavioral Research and Therapy, 30,* 559–561.

Kahn, T. J., & Chambers, H. J. (1991). Assessing re-offense risk with juvenile sexual offenders. *Child Welfare, LXX,* 333–345.

Longo, R. E. (1982). Sexual learning and experience among adolescent sexual offenders. *International Journal of Offender Therapy and Comparative Criminology, 26,* 235–241.

Lunderwold, D. A., & Young, L. G. (1992). Treatment acceptability ratings for sexual offenders: Effect of diagnosis and offense. *Research in Developmental Disabilities, 13,* 229–237.

Mayer, A. (1992). *Women sex offenders: Treatment and dynamics.* Holmes Beach: Learning Publications.

Meyers, B. A. (1991). Treatment of sexual offenses by persons with developmental disabilities. *American Journal on Mental Retardation, 95,* 563–569.

Moergen, S. A., Merkel, W. T., & Brown, S. (1990) The use of covert sensitization and social skills training in the treatment of an obscene telephone caller. *Journal of Behavior Therapy and Experimental Psychiatry, 21,* 269–275.

Muster, N. J. (1992). Treating the adolescent victim-turned-offender. *Adolescence, 27,* 441–450.

Neef, N. A. (Ed.). (1994). *Journal of Applied Behavior Analysis, 27*(2).

Nishioka-Evans, V., Hadden, C. K., Kraus, D., Johnson, J., Fredericks, H. D. B., & Toews, J. W. (1983). *The Teaching Research curriculum for mildly and moderately handicapped adolescents and adults: Taxonomy and assessment.* Monmouth, OR: Teaching Research Publications.

Smith, W., & Monastersky, C. (1986). Assessing juvenile sex offenders' risk for offending. *Criminal Justice and Behavior, 13,* 115-140.

Steinhauser, C. (1989). *An analysis of covert sensitization and minimal arousal conditioning: A treatment outcome study.* Unpublished doctoral dissertation, University of Chicago.

Strasburg, P. A. (1984). Recent national trends in serious juvenile crime. In R. Mathias, P. DeMuro, & R. A. Allinson (Eds.), *Violent juvenile offenders: An anthology* (pp. 5–10). San Francisco: National Council on Crime and Delinquency.

15

Gerontology and Functional Analysis

LOUIS D. BURGIO
TERRI LEWIS

INTRODUCTION

In the last chapter, Fredericks and Nishioka-Evans discussed an extension of functional assessment to another population, sex offenders. In this chapter, Burgio and Lewis discuss extension to yet another area, gerontology.

Individuals in this population often develop both excesses and deficits. Excesses include aggression, wandering, and disruptive vocalizations; deficits include many areas associated with activities of daily living. The authors provide examples of their use of functional assessment with several clients and behaviors, and in so doing provide examples of the special problems this population presents.

In their concluding remarks, they emphasize the value of functional assessment and the need to train the next generation of professionals in gerontology in this and other behavioral procedures. As we all know, Alzheimer's disease is flourishing, and we in the therapeutic and educational communities are facing considerable difficulties in trying to meet the behavioral effects of this and similar conditions. While we all work with individuals who present difficulties, the problem of successive degeneration is not one most of us face. In extending the use of functional assessment, Burgio and Lewis may have shown us one method that can help in this field.

PROBLEM BEHAVIORS IN OLDER ADULTS

Most individuals with a dementia-type illness will develop a behavior problem at some point in the course of the disease (Swearer, 1994), with these problems including both excesses and deficits. More prevalent behavior excesses include physical aggression, "wandering" (apparent aimless ambulation), and disruptive vocalization (Burgio et al., 1988). Behavior excesses have been reported in at least 50 percent of individuals diagnosed with Alzheimer's disease (Cummings et al., 1987). Research has also shown that individuals with dementia frequently display severe deficits while performing activities of daily living (ADLs) such as feeding, bathing, and dressing (Burgio et al., 1988). Although these deficits are, in part, a natural result of an illness causing dementia, gerontologists have long recognized that many demented individuals display "excess deficits" (Brody et al., 1971) (that is, symptoms of functional incapacity greater than that warranted by the actual organic impairment).

Behavior problems have been associated commonly with institutional settings such as the nursing home. However, research has shown that they are both prevalent and pervasive in community settings as well. For example, in a study of community-residing patients with Alzheimer's disease (Teri et al., 1989), all the caregivers surveyed reported the occurrence of behavior problems. Moreover, these problems were quite severe, with 22 percent of the caregivers reporting a minimum of 15 problems occurring at least twice a week (the mean number of problems reported was 10 per patient). In community settings, disruptive behaviors have been associated with poor family relationships and caregiver stress (Deimling & Bass, 1986), and, not surprisingly, behavior excesses and deficits have been shown to be predictors of institutionalization (O'Donnell et al., 1992). Behavior problems can also have a negative impact on caregivers in the nursing home. These disturbances have been associated with high levels of staff distress (Everitt et al., 1991), and they can influence the quality of staff-resident interactions. Perhaps most importantly, problem behaviors can impact the quality of care provided to nursing home residents. Staff frustration with difficult residents can result in avoiding them, consequently limiting their care (Block et al., 1987).

In summary, behavior problems are prevalent in older adults suffering from dementia and they have significant negative impact on both community and institutional caregivers. But why do these problems occur and what can be done about them?

BEHAVIORAL GERONTOLOGY
COMES OF AGE

Medicine, with its focus on organic pathology and interventions, has become a powerful force in the definition and treatment of aging (Estes & Binney, 1989). Consequently, medicine has governed the definition and treatment of behavior problems associated with senile dementia. The biomedical model has defined old age as a process of basic, inevitable, relatively immutable biological phenomena (Riley, 1981). However, because the biomedical model classifies dementia and its related effects as a purely organic disease, it has severely limited the consideration of environmental factors (Estes & Binney, 1989). As a result, the treatment of geriatric behavior problems has relied primarily upon pharmacotherapy and physical restraint (Covert, Rodrigues, & Solomon, 1977). In spite of pharmacotherapy's widespread use, a recent meta-analysis suggests that its use with neuroleptics is effective for managing behavior problems in only one of five patients receiving these drugs (Schneider, Pollock, & Lyness, 1990). Similarly, researchers have found that physical restraints can actually increase the severity of behavioral disturbances, and can be associated with increased morbidity and mortality (Evans & Strumpf, 1989).

At least three factors have contributed to the recent and growing acceptance of behavioral and environmental models of aging and interventions resulting from these models. In 1982, the Institute of Medicine published a report examining the varied linkages between health and behavior. The report emphasized that human behavior can be observed systematically, reliably, and reproducibly; it concluded that "the underlying causes [of health problems] will be identified with more certainty when the intimate interplay between genetics and environmental factors and the rich variability of individuals and societies are taken into account" (Hamburg, Elliott, & Parron, 1982, p. 4). Thus, the biomedical scientific community officially recognized in this report the contribution of environmental factors to various health problems, including the problems of older adults.

The second, and perhaps most influential event for behavioral gerontology, was the passage of the Omnibus Budget Reconciliation Act of 1987 (OBRA-87), which proposed sweeping changes in nursing home regulations (American Health Care Association, 1990). The overall impact of OBRA-87 was to encourage nursing homes to replace their long-standing custodial model with a rehabilitation model of care. Nursing homes were now required to show progress in resident functioning or to show cause as to why gains could not be made. Specific to behavioral disturbances, the regulations made using drugs for behavioral control much more difficult for the facilities. Moreover, similar to earlier regulatory changes that took place in facilities for persons with mental retardation, nursing home residents who were prescribed antipsychotic drugs for behavioral control were to receive gradual dose reductions and *behavioral interventions* in an effort to discontinue the drugs. These new regulations, although still very much a "work-in-progress," have stimulated gerontologists and clinicians to search for environmental causes and treatments for geriatric behavior problems in the nursing home.

The third impetus for the growing acceptance of behavioral gerontology was the gradual accumulation of data suggesting that behavioral interventions could be used effectively to treat a host of problem behaviors. The reader is referred to other sources for recent reviews of this treatment literature (Burgio & Bourgeois, 1992; Burgio & Burgio, 1986; Carstensen, 1988; Fisher & Carstensen, 1990). Interventions have been developed for both behavior excesses (such as physical aggression; see Vaccaro, 1988) and behavior deficits (such as low-frequency ambulation; see Burgio et al., 1986). Also, both antecedent and consequent interventions have been used successfully (Burgio & Bourgeois, 1992, p. 153–157).

The most extensive line of behavioral gerontology research has been on the problem of urinary incontinence. At this time, a number of clinical trials have been completed on the use of prompted voiding in nursing homes (Burgio et al., 1994a; Schnelle et al., 1989) and biofeedback-assisted behavioral training for cognitively intact individuals living in community settings (Burgio, Whitehead, & Engel, 1985). These studies employed control group designs (often combined with intrasubject methodology) to demonstrate the efficacy of their interventions. Their results have helped convince research funding agencies, such as the National Institutes of Health (NIH), of the tremendous potential of behavioral and environmental interventions. Consequently, a number of large studies examining behavioral treatments for geriatric problem behaviors have been funded recently by NIH.

FUNCTIONAL ASSESSMENT OF GERIATRIC BEHAVIOR PROBLEMS

In the last section, we asserted that there are sufficient data from numerous intrasubject studies and a few clinical trials suggesting the efficacy of environmental and behavioral treatments for geriatric behavior problems. Recent regulatory changes in nursing homes and a growing recognition within the biomedical sciences of the effects of environmental factors on health have created a receptive environment for behavioral gerontology. Thus, we are experiencing a period of tremendous opportunity in this area; however, this is also a time of great peril for the discipline. Very few trained behavior analysts work primarily with older populations. Consequently, much of the current research on behavioral and environmental treatments, including most of the research funded by NIH, is being conducted by research teams with little or no expertise in analyzing environment-behavior interactions. One indication of this problem is the dearth of empirical studies using functional analysis with elderly individuals.

In the following discussion of literature, we will employ the three categories of functional analysis used by Horner and his colleagues: the interview, direct observation of daily routines, and systematic environmental manipulation (Horner, 1994; O'Neill et al., 1990). Because functional analysis interviews and direct observation are often combined in the existing studies, these strategies will be discussed in a combined section.

Functional Analysis Interview and Direct Observation

Interviews and direct observations have been used in three areas of behavioral gerontology research: behavioral treatment of urinary incontinence, community caregiver training, and behavioral applications in long-term care settings.

Urinary Incontinence (UI) Contrary to common belief, UI is not a natural consequence of aging. Nevertheless, this condition becomes more prevalent with advancing age, with about 20 to 30 percent of community-dwelling elderly individuals and 50 to 60 percent of nursing home residents exhibiting UI. There are numerous physiologic, neurologic, behavioral, and environmental causes of UI: the clinical picture is complex because these factors often interact to produce the condition. A detailed discussion of the different types of UI and how causative factors interact is beyond the scope of this chapter, and the reader is referred to other sources for additional information (Burgio & Burgio, 1991). However, research in this area has used both functional analysis interviews and direct observation for detecting the controlling variables of UI, and some examples will be discussed. K. Burgio and colleagues have used functional analysis strategies in a series of treatment studies of UI in cognitively intact, community-dwelling, elderly patients (Burgio, Robinson, & Engel, 1986; Burgio, Whitehead, & Engel, 1985; Burton et al., 1988). Using carefully selected questions in a preliminary interview with patients, the interviewers in these studies elicited information that, in many cases, provided a clear picture of the controlling variables of UI.

Because the treatment strategy differs depending on the type of UI, a primary goal is to ascertain whether the patient suffers from urge or stress incontinence. These different types of UI have different etiologies and antecedents. During the interview, patients are assisted in identifying both antecedents and consequences during typical episodes of incontinence. For example, typical antecedents of urge incontinence (characterized by a sudden and uncontrollable urge to void) are sounds of running water or the sight of a toilet. Patients with stress incontinence (which occurs when bladder pressure exceeds urethral pressure) are usually able to identify specific physical activities that precede incontinence, such as coughing, sneezing, or lifting.

The next phase of the incontinence functional analysis involves daily self-recording of voiding habits and patterns of incontinence. Patients record the time and size of all voids and incontinent events, and they record the antecedent and consequence of these events. Similar functional analyses have been used to assess UI in the nursing home (Burgio et al., 1994a; Schnelle et al., 1989). However, due to the level of disability of these patients, periodic caregiver pad checks are used in place of self-monitored bladder records.

Due to frequent physical impairments of elderly individuals, and the mobility and dexterity required for successful completion of toileting, direct observation of toileting episodes is often employed in outpatient and nursing home treatment of UI. For example, Burgio et al. (1991) task-analyzed the toileting sequence and developed a rating system based on the amount of caregiver assistance required for each task component. The time needed to reach the toilet, undress, and position appropriately for voiding is measured. If any of these cannot be performed independently, note is taken of the level of assistance required and its availability in the patient's natural environment.

The final phase of assessment entails urodynamic testing with a cystometrogram. However, because this procedure involves the experimental manipulation of possible controlling variables, it will be discussed in the next section. With the use of functional assessment techniques, behavioral treatments of UI have resulted in up to 80 percent improvement in symptoms in outpatient settings; in nursing homes, approximately half of all residents with UI improve with treatment.

Community Caregiver Training As discussed above, behavioral disturbances are prevalent in community settings and are a significant stressor for individuals providing care for demented patients. Two large studies have attempted to teach behavior assessment and management skills to caregivers in an effort to manage these problems, thereby reducing caregiver stress and delaying institutionalization (Bourgeois, Burgio, & Schulz, 1993; Pinkston & Linsk, 1984a).

Elsie Pinkston's pioneering work with community caregivers, the Elderly Support Project, was summarized in a practitioner guidebook (Pinkston & Linsk, 1984b) and a research article published in the same year (Pinkston & Linsk, 1984a). This multiphase program included a three-stage functional analysis. The first stage involved a functional analysis interview in the home with family caregivers. The interview form included an analysis of potential controlling variables of problem behaviors. In the second stage, the interviewer recorded 1.5 hours of specific patient behaviors and family interactions with the patient. The observation included information on antecedents and consequences, sequence of behaviors, and characteristics of the physical environment. During the third stage, family caregivers were taught to observe and record behavior problems and possible controlling variables with the use of the Family Behavior Record data sheet (Pinkston & Linsk, 1984b, p. 30).

Pinkston and Linsk (1984a) reported results of the program with 51 families. In 94 percent of the cases, behavioral contracting, cueing, and reinforcement techniques were used. Seventy-three percent of all behavior problems improved due to the program, with self-care behaviors increasing an average of 78 percent, negative vocalizations decreasing 83 percent, and positive behaviors increasing 83 percent. A similar treatment strategy was used in a recently completed clinical trial funded by the National Institute on Aging (Bourgeois, Burgio, & Schulz, 1993). Behavioral treatment (including interview and observational functional analysis) is being compared with a caregiver affective self-management intervention and a common treatment control (information and therapeutic readings). Preliminary results suggest that caregivers are able to conduct behavioral analysis and interventions with their demented spouses, and that behavioral procedures are effective for controlling problem behaviors.

Applications in Long-Term Care Settings

The phrase "geriatric long-term care settings," though often used synonymously with nursing homes, actually includes other service delivery programs such as geriatric day care, respite care, and board and care homes (Kane & Kane, 1987). Functional analysis techniques are beginning to be used in some of these settings. For example, Lewin and Lundervold (1987) presented three case studies in a foster care setting, more commonly referred to as "board and care homes" in the gerontology literature. Board and care homes include two to eight elderly clients and one to three paraprofessional staff. The target behaviors in this study included disruptive vocalization and physical aggression. Prior to intervention, the authors employed functional analysis interviews and direct observation to assess environmental antecedents and consequences. Staff were able to decrease problematic behaviors in all three clients with this program. Lundervold and Jackson (1992) described a similar use of functional analysis in the nursing home in the case study of a 48-year-old Huntington's patient who was physically aggressive. The functional analysis suggested that the aggression was elicited by staff requests and was reinforced by negative staff attention. The intervention, consisting of a DRO and contingent five-minute physical restraint, was effective in decreasing the rate of physical aggression. Clinicians interested in the systematic application of functional analysis techniques in the nursing home are referred to chapter three of Lundervold and Lewin (1992). The authors' discussion of "Bio-Environmental Assessment" offers an excellent summary of the complex interplay between organismic and environmental variables in producing behavioral disturbances in this setting.

Two programs of nursing home research have studied naturalistic environment-behavior interactions in an effort to increase our understanding of how environmental factors influence resident behaviors (Burgio et al., 1994b; Baltes, 1988). As discussed above, gerontologists have long been aware that environmental factors contribute to the problem of "excess disability." In 1980, Margret Baltes and colleagues initiated a series of research studies examining the process of the development and maintenance of dependent and independent behaviors in nursing home residents (summarized in Baltes, 1988). They asked two main questions in their research: (a) What are the naturally existing social conditions surrounding the occurrence of dependent behaviors?; (b) Do observed temporal behavior sequences (interactions between residents and staff) have functional relevance?

To answer these questions, the authors conducted sequential observations of interactions between target residents and staff, and repeated these observations across several weeks or months. An observation code was constructed focusing on (a) overt, observable behaviors related to various categories of independent/dependent functioning by target residents; and (b) antecedent/consequent staff behaviors that either encouraged or discouraged independent and dependent resident behaviors. A Datamyte system was used to collect data and record the temporal sequence of behaviors.

These methods produced a varied and complex database, and we will herein highlight only some of the major findings pertaining to self-care interactions. Most significantly, results indicated an immediately supportive social environment for dependent self-care behaviors, whereas independent self-care behaviors were rarely followed by observable responses from the social environment. Thus, these data show that dependent behaviors were consistently followed by social reinforcement from nursing home staff, and that attempts at independence were consistently ignored.

In a series of ongoing studies, Burgio and colleagues are using a similar methodology to examine the relationship between various environmental events and the disruptive behaviors of demented residents (this methodology is summarized in Burgio et al. [1994b], which focused on disruptive vocalization [DV]). Preliminary survey research suggested that various environmental factors, including social contact, type of activity, and ambient sound, could influence the occurrence of DV. Thus, during observations residents were classified according to their location in the facility (10 codes), the activity in which they were engaged (8 codes), their social environment (4 codes), ambient sound (3 codes), use of physi-

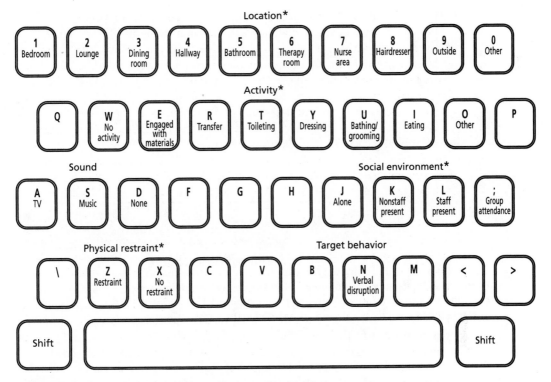

FIGURE 15.1 Behavioral and environmental categories and their event codes as displayed on the laptop computer keyboard. The asterisks denote mutually exclusive and exhaustive observation categories.

SOURCE: From Burgio et al. (1994b).

cal restraint (2 codes), and presence of verbal disruption. Real-time recording of the occurrence and temporal sequence of behavior problems and multiple environmental events requires use of laptop computer technology. A display of the categories as they appeared on the computer keyboard can be found in Figure 15.1. We employed Alan Repp's Portable Computer System for Observational Research, which allowed us to record both frequency and duration of most behavioral categories (Repp et al., 1989).

In this study, we observed 11 vocally disruptive residents during four 3-hour time blocks (8–11 A.M., 11–2 P.M., 2–5 P.M., and 5–8 P.M.) for a total of 12 hours per resident. Results showed the average occurrence of DV was 22 per hour and the average duration per occurrence was 26 seconds. Figure 15.2 indicates a significant upward linear trend in the occurrence of DV across the day. There have been frequent prior anecdotal reports of early evening increases in disruptive behaviors (Evans, 1987). Varied explanations have been proffered for this phenomenon, including increased resident disorientation due to approaching darkness ("sundowning") and lower staff-to-resident ratios during the evening shift. A Cox Proportional Hazards Regression model was used to identify environmental

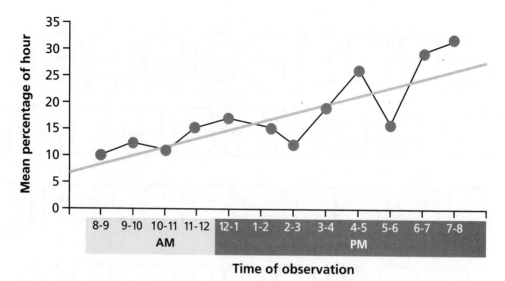

FIGURE 15.2 Mean percentage of hourly blocks of observation during which disruptive vocalization (DV) was recorded for the group of 11 participants. The solid line shows a significant upward linear trend in DV across the day.

SOURCE: From Burgio et al. (1994b).

factors that predict shorter duration and, thus, less severe DV. Results showed that the presence of other people in the immediate setting predicted shorter duration DV. This result suggests that DV is, to some extent, under attentional control. It also suggests that the therapeutic manipulation of attentional factors might have a beneficial effect on this problem behavior. An unexpected finding was that resident presence at the nursing home hairdresser also predicted shorter duration DV. Subsequent examination of our field notes uncovered a report by the hairdresser that residents were seldom vocally disruptive while under the hair dryer. The results already suggested that staff attentional factors may affect the occurrence of DV, and the hairdresser commonly provided one-on-one attention to resident "customers." However, we were also aware that the hair dryer produced a loud white noise, and that white noise generators had been used successfully in therapeutic settings to produce relaxation. Consequently, we hypothesized that the white noise produced by the hair dryer might have had a calming effect on these vocally disruptive residents, and this hypothesis resulted in an intervention that will be discussed in the next section.

Studies are currently under way examining changes in nursing home environment-behavior relationships over time (Burgio et al., 1993b), the effects of staff touch and verbal interaction on disruptive behaviors (Butler et al., 1993), and various aspects of caregiver-resident interactions during toileting (Scilley et al., 1993) and dressing (Rogers, Burgio, & Scilley, 1993).

Systematic Environmental Manipulation In 1964, Ogden Lindsley published a seminal article that proposed using the discoveries of free-operant conditioning for developing geriatric prosthetic environments (Lindsley, 1964). Lindsley asserted that, among the many possible applications of free-operant methods to geriatrics, he considered the "functional definition of stimulus, response, and reinforcement to be one of the most important" (p. 43). Thirty years later, in spite of the enormous growth of the elderly population during this time span, and although special issues on both behavioral gerontology (1986) and functional analysis (1994) have been published in the *Journal of Applied Behavior Analysis,* not a single article focusing on functional analysis with elderly individuals has been published. A computer literature search conducted by the authors using the keywords "functional analysis" and "elderly" did, however, produce a handful of articles that discussed the analysis of physical functioning in elderly individuals. This fact provides some indication of the extent of ignorance surrounding this term and the methodology outside of the discipline of behavior analysis. Yet, there has been progress even in this area in recent years.

Although not described in functional analysis terminology, K. Burgio and colleagues (Burgio, Whitehead, & Engel, 1985) manipulated environmental events under experimental conditions with systematic observation of behavior in their final phase of assessment prior to applying a behavioral treatment for UI. As discussed above, the first two phases of this functional assessment involved the detection of antecedents and consequences of stress and urge incontinence through interview and observational procedures. During this third phase, the experimenter/clinician assessed bladder (urge UI) and sphincter (stress UI) dysfunction by systematically filling the bladder with sterile water. Although the procedure is considerably more complicated than depicted in this description, the bladder is slowly filled with sterile water through a catheter until the patient reports a bladder sensation. Bladder pressure is measured with the use of an apparatus called a cystometer. If the cystometrogram (output from the cystometer) measures an uninhibited (outside of the patient's control) bladder contraction at a normal bladder capacity, the diagnosis of urge incontinence is made. To assess stress incontinence, patients are asked to stand or cough. If leakage of urine is observed during these provocative maneuvers with a normally filled bladder, a diagnosis of stress incontinence is made.

L. Burgio and colleagues received funding from the Retirement Research Foundation in 1992 to conduct a formal functional analysis of disruptive vocalization in nursing home residents (Burgio et al., 1993b). By August 1994, data collection had been completed and the results are currently being analyzed. In this chapter, we will discuss the main aspects of this study and some of the preliminary results.

Disruptive vocalization is a prevalent behavior problem in the nursing home (11 to 30 percent) that is disturbing to staff and other nursing home residents. It can result in social isolation of residents who display this problem. Until recently, little was known about the characteristics of this problem, the residents who display the problem, or the contribution of environmental factors. Most of what we know has been obtained from staff report and medical record reviews. The only existing controlled comparison study (Cariaga et al., 1991) found that disruptive vocalizers displayed greater deficits in cognitive status and ADLs than a comparison group that did not engage in this behavior. Disruptive vocalizers also displayed a higher activity level and more sleep problems.

The goal of our research was to conduct a functional analysis of possible relevant environmental events by manipulating these events under experimental conditions. In the second phase of this study, we used the information obtained from the functional analysis to select and apply an effective intervention for each resident. While designing the study, we emulated the strategy described by Iwata et al. (1982) for studying self-injurious behavior in developmentally delayed individuals.

We formed hypotheses regarding possible controlling variables of DV based on prior research findings and one common therapeutic practice that currently lacked empirical support: (a) Burgio et al. (1994b) presented preliminary data suggesting that staff attention played a role in producing DV; (b) as discussed above, the unexpected finding in this same study that resident presence at the hairdresser was associated with shorter duration DV led to a hypothesis regarding the possible therapeutic effect of white noise; (c) ongoing research by Burgio et al. (1993b) found that the presence of music in the environment was also associated with briefer duration DV; (d) various studies suggest that many nursing home residents may be experiencing sensory deprivation due to multiple sensory deficits, including impairments in sight (Cronin-Golomb et al., 1991) and hearing (Ries, 1985). Hearing impairments are particularly problematic because many hearing-impaired residents either do not have hearing aids or do not wear them. Finally, we commonly find elderly disruptive nursing home residents clutching stuffed animals that are provided to them by staff who assume that the "contact comfort" associated with the stuffed animal will soothe disruptive residents. Unfortunately, there is no empirical support for the therapeutic use of stuffed animals.

In response to these findings, we tested six stimulus conditions with 30 vocally disruptive nursing home residents. Each resident was targeted for a total of five hours of observation over a 15-day functional analysis phase. Functional analyses were completed while the residents were displaying vocally disruptive behaviors. The majority of assessment sessions were conducted between the hours of 11 A.M. and 7 P.M. Each resident was assessed three times on each of six conditions. Each condition lasted 20 minutes (four sequential five-minute segments). More specifically, condition-on (five minutes) was alternated with condition-off (five minutes) until the end of the 20-minute session. Order of condition-on and condition-off was counterbalanced. A computer-assisted data collection system, similar to that used by Burgio et al. (1994b), was employed.

Functional analyses were conducted for the following stimulus conditions:

Music. The resident's preferred music was delivered through a portable headset radio. This device was adapted by an occupational therapist to reduce slippage, maximize comfort, and prevent excessive volume.

Auditory augmentation. An inexpensive sound amplification device was firmly attached to the resident's midsection with velcro binding. Amplified ambient sounds were delivered via headphones that were placed on the resident's head. Sound volume was set according to nurses' estimate of the resident's degree of hearing impairment. The headphones were also adapted by the occupational therapist.

Teddy bear. Residents were provided with a soft teddy bear that they clutched with one or both arms.

Teddy bear plus vibration. We were aware that vibratory stimulation can function as a reinforcer for cognitively impaired, multihandicapped individuals (Bailey & Meyerson, 1969). In clinical practice, vibration has been added to soft cloth material to soothe disruptive developmentally disabled individuals. In this condition, we inserted a commercially available, battery-operated vibrator into the teddy bear so that it could be made to mildly vibrate. This device was provided to the resident and was clutched with one or both arms.

Environmental sounds. Although we considered testing audio tapes of white noise, we preferred an audio tape stimulus that would be easy for nursing home personnel to purchase if this stimulus was shown to be effective. We decided to analyze the effects of two different audio tapes: ocean sounds and a running brook. These audio tapes presented sounds that were similar to white noise, in that they were soothing and monotonous. The major difference between these environmental sound tapes was that the brook sounds were continuous, and ocean sounds were cyclic. The sounds were delivered via an adapted portable tape recorder and headphones.

Contingent social attention. This condition was similar to the attention condition used by Iwata et al. (1982); in it, an experimenter and resident were together in a room. At the beginning of the attention-on condition, the experimenter began a solitary activity until a DV occurred. Immediately contingent on a DV, the experimenter conversed with the resident for approximately 30 seconds. All other responses exhibited by the resident were ignored.

The sequential flow of the five-minute condition-on, condition-off attention periods was altered during the study. Initially, five minutes of contingent attention (condition-on) was immediately followed by the experimenter leaving the resident alone in the room for five minutes (condition-off). This sequence was repeated once within a session. However, we discovered that this procedure frequently resulted in the resident calling out for the experimenter to return during condition-off. Thus, the procedure was modified so that the five-minute conditions were run nonsequentially, and interspersed throughout the day.

Visual analysis of the intrasubject data suggests that all stimulus conditions were associated with lower percentages of DV in at least some of the residents. However, preliminary statistical analyses indicate positive group effects only for the two environmental sounds and the attention condition. Apparently, at this point, the attention condition exerted the strongest control over DV. Figure 15.3 shows data for four subjects in multielement format during the attention condition. The data suggest considerable intersubject variability. Subjects 1 and 2 show what is probably a clinically significant difference in DV in response to attention. This effect is somewhat weaker in Subject 3, and though relatively reliable, is minimal in Subject 4.

These functional analysis data were then used to make treatment decisions for each resident. If one stimulus condition was clearly exerting more control over DV than the other stimuli, staff were instructed to use that stimulus in an individualized behavioral program for the resident on the nursing unit. All the interventions

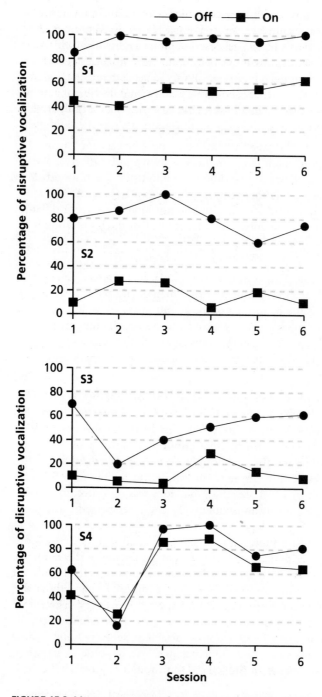

FIGURE 15.3 Mean percentage of disruptive vocalization for four subjects during the attention condition-on and condition-off in multi-element format.

(unpublished data)

that required a device (such as music) were combined with a DRO procedure. This was done because, whether or not a resident's DV was shown to be affected by attention in the functional analysis phase, the closer monitoring of residents by indigenous staff (a positive sequelae of DRO) was considered to be a desirable goal for all residents. Results of staff use of these interventions on the nursing units are not available at this time. Our clinical impression, however, is that the results are not as robust on the nursing units. If our data support this clinical impression, our inability to employ formal staff management procedures to assure appropriate use of the interventions may be responsible for the attenuated effect (Burgio & Scilley, 1994).

SUMMARY AND CONCLUSIONS

Although the need for functional definition of environment-behavior interactions in gerontology was discussed by Lindsley 30 years ago, this remains a relatively unexplored area of research. Nevertheless, this chapter shows that there has been progress in all three functional assessment strategies described by O'Neill et al. (1990). Unfortunately, this progress has occurred at a snail's pace. The developments in geriatric functional assessment have been overtaken by current and planned funded clinical trials of behavioral treatments. We are concerned that many of these experimental trials are being and will be conducted by individuals who lack the necessary training in applied behavior analysis. This result also means that the trials will most probably be conducted without the benefit of formal functional assessment strategies, severely limiting the experimenters' ability to demonstrate the efficacy of behavioral treatments. The result may be an unwarranted and premature conclusion that behavioral interventions are less than optimal treatments for geriatric behavior problems.

In their lead article to the special issue on behavioral gerontology in the *Journal of Applied Behavior Analysis,* Burgio and Burgio (1986) extended the following plea:

> The final determining factor for the future of behavioral gerontology is the number of new students who will be entering the area in coming years. . . . Behavior analysts have traditionally taken on difficult and frustrating problems and have supplied dedicated students to meet these challenges. We hope that behavioral gerontology will not prove to be the exception. (p. 21)

Eight years have passed between the writing of these lines and the writing of this study. The zeitgeist currently is more conducive to behavioral gerontology—and we are still hoping.

REFERENCES

American Health Care Association (1990). *The Long Term Care Survey: Regulations, Forms, Procedures, Guidelines.* Cat# 4697/UBP/2.5K/90. Washington: Author.

Bailey, J., & Meyerson, L. (1969). Vibration as a reinforcer with a profoundly retarded child. *Journal of Applied Behavior Analysis, 2,* 135–137.

Baltes, M. M. (1988). The etiology and maintenance of dependency in the elderly: Three phases of operant research. *Behavior Therapy, 19,* 301–319.

Block, C., Boczkowski, J., Hansen, N., & Vanderbeck, M. (1987). Nursing home consultation: Difficult residents and frustrated staff. *The Gerontologist, 27,* 443–446.

Bourgeois, M. S., Burgio, L. B., & Schulz, R. (1993). Teaching caregivers of spouses with Alzheimer's disease to modify problem behaviors in the home: Year II update. *The Gerontologist, 33* (Special Issue #1), p. 260.

Brody, E. M., Kleban, M. H., Lawton, M. P., & Silverman, H. A. (1971). Excess disabilities of mentally impaired aged: Impact of institutionalized treatment. *The Gerontologist, 11,* 124–133.

Burgio, K. L., & Burgio, L. D. (1991). The problem of incontinence. In P. Wisocki (Ed.), *Handbook of clinical behavior therapy with the elderly client.* New York: Plenum.

Burgio, K. L., Burgio, L. D., McCormick, K. A., & Engel, B. T. (1991). Assessing toileting skills and habits in an adult day care setting. *Journal of Gerontological Nursing, 17,* 32–35.

Burgio, K. L., Robinson, J. C., & Engel, B. T. (1986). The role of biofeedback in Kegel exercise training for stress urinary incontinence. *American Journal of Obstetrics and Gynecology, 154,* 58–64.

Burgio, K. L., Whitehead, W. E., & Engel, B. T. (1985). Urinary incontinence in the elderly: Bladder/sphincter biofeedback and toileting skills training. *Annals of Internal Medicine, 103,* 507–515.

Burgio, L., Scilley, K., Davis, P., & Cadman, S. (1993a). Real-time behavioral observation of disruptive behaviors in the nursing home using laptop computers. *The Gerontologist, 33* (Special Issue #1).

Burgio, L., Scilley, K., Hoar, T., Washington, C., & Tunstall, A. (1993b). Behavioral interventions for disruptive vocalizations in elderly nursing home residents with dementia. *The Gerontologist, 33* (Special Issue #1), p. 110.

Burgio, L. D., & Bourgeois, M. (1992). Treating severe behavioral disorders in geriatric residential settings. *Behavioral Residential Treatment, 7,* 145–168.

Burgio, L. D., & Burgio, K. L. (1986). Behavioral gerontology: Application of behavioral methods to the problems of older adults. *Journal of Applied Behavior Analysis, 19,* 321–328.

Burgio, L. D., Burgio, K. L., Engel, B. T., & Tice, L. M. (1986). Increasing distance and independence of ambulation in elderly nursing home patients. *Journal of Applied Behavior Analysis, 19,* 357–366.

Burgio, L. D., Jones, L. T., Butler, F., & Engel, B. T. (1988). The prevalence of geriatric behavior problems in an urban nursing home. *The Journal of Gerontological Nursing, 14,* 31–34.

Burgio, L. D., McCormick, K. A., Scheve, A. S., Engel, B. T., Hawkins, A., & Leahy, E. (1994a). The effects of changing prompted voiding schedules in the treatment of urinary incontinence in nursing home residents. *Journal of the American Geriatrics Society, 42,* 315–320.

Burgio, L. D. & Scilley, K. (1994). Caregiver performance in the nursing home: The use of staff training and management procedures. *Seminars in Speech and Language, 15,* 313–322.

Burgio, L. D., Scilley, K., Hardin, J. M., Janosky, J., Bonino, P., Slater, S. C., & Engberg, R. (1994b). Studying disruptive vocalization and contextual factors in the nursing home using computer-assisted real-time observation. *Journal of Gerontology: Psychological Science, 49,* 230–239.

Burton, J. R., Pearce, K. L., Burgio, K. L., Engel, B. T., & Whitehead, W. E. (1988). Behavioral training for urinary incontinence in elderly ambulatory patients. *Journal of the American Geriatrics Society, 36,* 693–698.

Butler, F., Burgio, L., Ung, K., & Engberg, R. (1993). Direct observation of disruptive behaviors: A longitudinal study of nursing staff-resident interactions. *The Gerontologist, 33* (Special Issue #1).

Cariaga, J., Burgio, L., Flynn, W., & Martin, D. A. (1991). A controlled study of disruptive socializations among geriatric patients residing in nursing homes. *Jour-*

nal of the American Geriatrics Society, 39, 501–507.

Carstensen, L. L. (1988). The emerging field of behavioral gerontology. Behavior Therapy, 19, 259–281.

Covert, A. B., Rodrigues, T., & Solomon, K. (1977). The use of mechanical and chemical restraints in nursing homes. Journal of the American Geriatrics Society, 25, 85–89.

Cronin-Golomb, A., Corkin, S., Rizzo, J. F., Cohen, J., Growdon, J. H., & Banks, K. (1991). Visual dysfunction in Alzheimer's disease: Relation to normal aging. Annals of Neurology, 29, 441–452.

Cummings, J. L., Miller, B., Hill, M. A., & Neshkes, R. (1987). Neuropsychiatric aspects of multi-infarct dementia and dementia of the Alzheimer type. Archives of Neurology, 44, 389–393.

Deimling, G. T., & Bass, D. M. (1986). Symptoms of mental impairment among elderly adults and their effects on family caregivers. Journal of Gerontology, 41, 778–784.

Estes, C. L., & Binney, E. A. (1989). The biomedicalization of aging: Dangers and dilemmas. The Gerontologist, 29, 587–596.

Evans, L. (1987). Sundown syndrome in institutionalized elderly. Journal of the American Geriatric Society, 35, 101–108.

Evans, L. K., & Strumpf, N. E. (1989). Tying down the elderly: A review of the literature on physical restraint. Journal of the American Geriatrics Society, 37, 65–74.

Everitt, D. E., Fields, D. R., Soumerai, S. S., & Avorn, J. (1991). Resident behavior and staff distress in the nursing homes. Journal of the American Geriatric Society, 39, 792–798.

Fisher, J. E., & Carstensen, L. L. (1990). Behavior management of the dementias. Clinical Psychology Review, 10, 611–629.

Hamburg, D. A., Elliott, G. R., & Parron, D. L. (1982). Health and behavior: Frontiers of research in the biobehavioral sciences (Institute of Medicine Publication 82-010). Washington, DC: National Academy Press.

Horner, R. H. (1994). Functional assessment: Contributions and future direc-

tions. Journal of Applied Behavior Analysis, 27, 401–404.

Iwata, B. A., Dorsey, M. F., Slifer, K. J., Bauman, K. E., & Richman, G. S. (1982). Toward a functional analysis of self-injury. Analysis and Intervention in Developmental Disabilities, 2, 3–20.

Kane, R. A., & Kane, R. L. (1987). Long-term care: Principles, programs, and policies. New York: Springer-Verlag.

Lewin, L. M., & Lundervold, D. A. (1987). Behavioral treatment of elderly in foster care homes. Adult Foster Care Journal, 1, 238–249.

Lindsley, O. (1964). Geriatric behavioral prosthetics. In R. Kastenbaum (Ed.), New thoughts on old age (pp. 41–60). New York: Springer-Verlag.

Lundervold, D. A., & Jackson, T. (1992). Use of applied behavior analysis in treating nursing home residents, Hospital and Community Psychiatry, 43, 171–173.

Lundervold, D., & Lewin, L. (1992). Behavior analysis and therapy in nursing homes (pp. 36–57). Springfield, IL: Charles C. Thomas.

O'Donnell, B. F., Drachman, D. A., Barnes, H. J., Peterson, K., Swearer, J., & Lew, R. (1992). Incontinence and troublesome behaviors predict institutionalization in dementia. Journal of Geriatric Psychiatry and Neurology, 5, 54–52.

O'Neill, R. E., Horner, R. H., Albin, R. W., Storey, K., & Sprague, J. (1990). Functional analysis of problem behavior: A practical assessment guide. Sycamore, IL: Sycamore.

Pinkston, E. M., & Linsk, N. L. (1984a). Behavioral family intervention with the impaired elderly. The Gerontologist, 24, 576–583.

Pinkston, E. M., & Linsk, N. L. (1984b). Care of the elderly: A family approach. Pergamon.

Repp, A. C., Karsh, K. G., Van Acker, R., Felce, D., & Harman, M. (1989). A computer-based system for collecting and analyzing observational data. Journal of Special Education Technology, 9, 207–216.

Ries, P. W. (1985). The demography of hearing loss. In H. Orlans (Ed.), Adjustment to adult hearing loss (pp. 3–21). San Diego: College Hill.

Riley, M. W. (1981). Health behavior of older people: Toward a new paradigm. *Health, behavior and aging: A research agenda.* Interim report, No. 5. Washington: Institute of Medicine.

Rogers, J., Burgio, L., & Scilley, K. (1993). Microcomputer use to study ADL. *The Gerontologist, 33* (Special Issue #1).

Schneider, L. S., Pollock, V. E., & Lyness, S. A. (1990). A meta-analysis of controlled trials of neuroleptic treatment in dementia. *Journal of the American Geriatrics Society, 38,* 553–563.

Schnelle, J. F., Traughber, B., Sowell, V. A., Newman, D. R., Petrilli, C. O., & Ory, M. (1989). *Journal of the American Geriatrics Society, 37,* 1051–1057.

Scilley, K., Burgio, L., Mitchell, S., & Ritchie, C. (1993). Behavioral observation of continence care activities in the nursing home using laptop computers. *The Gerontologist, 33* (Special Issue #1).

Swearer, J. M. (1994). Behavioral disturbances in dementia. In J.C. Morris (Ed.), *Handbook of dementing illnesses.* New York: Marcel Dekker.

Teri, L., Borson, S., Kiyak, H. A., & Yamagishi, M. (1989). Behavioral disturbance, cognitive dysfunction, and functional skill: Prevalence and relationship in Alzheimer's disease. *Journal of the American Geriatrics Society, 37,* 109–116.

Vaccaro, F. J. (1988). Application of operant procedures in a group of institutionalized aggressive geriatric patients. *Psychology and Aging, 3,* 22–28.

16

▨

Two Case Studies of Functional Assessment and Functional Support:

Idea Compliance, and Capacity-Building Issues

H. RUTHERFORD TURNBULL, III

INTRODUCTION

The authors of this chapter return us to school-based problems with special children. However, rather than emphasizing another method of functional assessment, they describe two cases in which students did not receive functional assessment and support services, wasted several years in which they could have received much better educational services, and sought redress under the Individuals with Disabilities Education Act (IDEA).

The success of functional assessment puts us in an interesting situation that these authors have highlighted, but that most of us have probably not considered. As this procedure has been and continues to be proven an effective way to begin treatment of behavioral excesses and deficits, professionals, advocates, parents, attorneys, and others are realizing that students with special problems may have a protected right to a functional assessment. Some states are beginning to mandate this assessment; others are considering doing so. The development of this technology has been considerable, and its ever-increasing diversity should be reinforcing to those involved in its development.

There can be little argument nowadays about the need to conduct functional assessments of students with disabilities and then to design individualized education programs based on those assessments that simultaneously build on students' strengths and remediate their needs. The wisdom of moving inexorably from effective (that is, functional) assessment to effective (that is, functional) support is memorably illustrated in the following stories about two real students. (The names of the students, their families, and their school districts have been changed in one case ["Scott Worth"] but not in the case of the other student [David Cain]. All information about them is based on interviews with their families and reviews of their school records in fall 1994).

Had functional assessment and support been provided to these students, there would have been three important differences in the outcome of these cases. First, the students' education and development would have been enhanced much sooner than it was; alternatively stated, these students' lives would not have been wasted for several years. Second, the students' claims for redress under IDEA would have been blunted; as it is, each student has experienced significant rights violations and can make successful assertions for redress under IDEA. Third, the school districts of each student would have developed a capacity to benefit not just these students but others as well.

In this chapter, we describe the students' lives, the failures of their educators to provide functional assessments and interventions, the effects of those failures on the students, the IDEA claims they can assert, and the capacity-building that should have been (or at last has been) put into place to provide functional assessments and functional supports to the students and others in special education.

THE CASE OF DAVID CAIN:
SUCCESS AT LAST

David Cain was born on September 1, 1978, to an unwed mother who exposed David to toxic substances while she was pregnant. After he was born, his mother often neglected his emotional and physical needs, and at times even physically abused him. At the age of five and a half months, David was removed from his home and placed in foster care with the Cain family in rural southeast Kansas. David arrived at the Cain home a malnourished baby who didn't cry, didn't like to be touched, and wanted to be left alone.

The Cains soon became concerned about David's health and development and took him to their pediatrician. The pediatrician assured them that David would outgrow any problems and that they should not worry. Shortly thereafter, the Cains pursued David's adoption. David officially became the Cains' son in 1980.

During David's preschool years, he was from all outward appearances a handsome, strong, and determined little boy. Yet underneath this winsome exterior was a youngster with a profound aversion to being touched and with poor or inappropriate social skills. He was confrontational to his family and friends, both physically and verbally, and hard to handle in all environments. Despite all of these challenges, his family was able to accommodate and adapt to David's unique behavior style, at least while he was very young.

Failure to Assess and Support

In 1984, at six years of age, David entered kindergarten in a school district where his father, Jim Cain, served as superintendent. During David's early education, the Cains were able to talk to David's teachers about his behavior. Together, the Cains and the teachers pursued IDEA's nondiscriminatory evaluation during David's first-grade year. The assessments indicated that David possessed a high average aptitude, with low average academic skills. Because of the discrepancy between his intelligence and his academic performance, David was diagnosed with a learning disability. David's educational records also documented behavioral concerns, including a short attention span and out-of-seat and off-task behaviors. More significant, however, were David's frequent and dramatic mood swings.

Despite these documented concerns, David was not referred for any evaluation for mental illness or serious emotional disturbance. Instead, the evaluation team recommended that David continue his education in a regular classroom with resource support in the classroom for students with specific learning disabilities.

David's new educational placement was initially successful. Both regular and special education teachers were willing and motivated to accommodate his needs in the classroom, thereby assuring a beneficial and appropriate education up to the second grade. David's second-grade teacher, however, was very rigid in her curriculum and expectations of all of her students. Unfortunately, David was not able to adapt to her teaching style and rebelled through hostile and confrontational behavior. David's family tried to collaborate with his teacher in regard to his individual educational needs, informing her about David's difficulty in relating to others, his discomfort with physical touch and contact, and his preferring to be alone rather than to socialize with his peers. All their efforts were fruitless, and David's behaviors escalated to the point where he hit his teacher.

At this point, David's teacher referred him for another comprehensive evaluation, focusing specifically on his behaviors. Following this evaluation, David was classified as having behavior disorders. Relying on the evaluation team's recommendations, David's family enrolled him in a new school, one that provided a self-contained special education classroom for students with behavior disorders.

David and his family were hopeful that this new educational placement would provide the services and support that would remediate his emotional, behavioral, and learning challenges. Again, they would be disappointed. Despite the fact that the school counselor saw David each week for one hour as a part of his educational plan during his three years in this classroom, David's emotional state and behaviors began to deteriorate, becoming unpredictable both at school and at home. Finally, by the time David was in the fifth grade, both his family and his teachers were unable to adapt to his escalating behaviors, which included extreme hostility and physical and verbal aggression toward his teachers, other authority figures, and peers.

In Jim Cain's words, "the family was in crisis over David's crisis" and ultimately made the painful and crucial decision to place David in a private psychiatric hospital, thereby throwing the family into financial and emotional upheaval. During this 120-day private hospital placement, David underwent psychological evaluations and was diagnosed as having a mental illness, bipolar mixed type. His primary treatment was medications. Although the family's insurance policy covered a portion of this hospitalization, the family's cost for the treatment was $35,000.

David was discharged to his home and returned to school, where the severity and frequency of his behaviors increased. The school attempted to reintegrate David into the classroom for students with behavioral disorders but was unsuccessful. After 10 months in school, David was readmitted to the private psychiatric hospital, where he remained for nine months. As a result of this hospitalization, the family's medical debts grew by another $120,000. Toward the later part of David's private placement, the Cains' insurance company denied further coverage for David's hospitalizations. The Cains then exhausted their personal financial resources, including selling their home, to keep David in the private hospital. Because of the enormous debt that was piling up for the Cains, they sought the assistance of the state's social and rehabilitation services agency, SRS. SRS agreed to help the Cains with David's care provided that the Cains would release David into their custody. For lack of any other way to get access to medical and educational support, the Cains relinquished David to the custody of SRS.

SRS then placed David into a state hospital for a 30-day evaluation. The evaluation determined that he was in need of psychiatric services and assistance. Based on this determination and the recommendation of staff, David was admitted as a patient at this same state facility. During one visit, Jim discovered that David was being shackled to his bed and locked in a room in order to control what the staff perceived as uncontrollable behavior. Jim vehemently opposed this form of treatment and sought a transfer out of this hospital and into a different state hospital, which he obtained only after he sought help from a state senator and the governor.

This hospital placement was as unprogressive in its approach to helping David as was the first. During his one and a half years in this institution, David received little or no psychotherapeutic or educational services.

In 1990, Jim learned about a community-based, family-directed family support program in Kansas called Keys for Networking. Together with Barbara Huff, executive director of Keys, Jim developed a service plan that would meet David's needs and allow him to return home.

Finally, in 1991, David was released to go home. SRS helped in securing services in the community for David and his family. David was enrolled in a school that was located near a mental health facility that had agreed to help with David's dual-diagnosis needs. David made an attempt to attend the public school, but again, his behavioral and mental health needs were too great to be accommodated in the school and he spent most of his days at the mental health clinic. David's family felt that he needed still more intensive mental health services, so they enrolled David in a therapeutic day facility, but this placement only lasted a week before David again was expelled.

David's family was unprepared to effectively structure David's enormous amount of free time and again turned to the state for assistance. Once again, David was admitted to a state hospital, albeit a different one. Unlike previous hospitals, however, this facility offered collaboration between the family and professionals who cared for David.

At this point David began to realize that he could effectively shape the outcomes of his own life. He also formed friendships with peers in the hospital and recognized that they were successful in leaving there and reintegrating into their communities. Finally, David received a very compelling, heartfelt letter from his mother, expressing her love for him and her deep desire for him to return home. These three developments were a turning point for David, and he began for the first time to care about his future.

Relying on David's new found self-direction, hospital staff, school professionals, family members, and the staff of Keys for Networking designed an approach whereby David would be discharged from the hospital and fully included in his home community. These collaborators recognized that David would need a fresh start in a small public school in order to succeed. Following David's enrollment in just such a school in a nearby community, these people developed an individualized educational plan. In addition to including David in regular education classes and football workouts, the plan provided for resource room tutoring, family therapy, a case manager, deliberate peer-relationship building, and additional people from the community and the local mental health center to help out when needed.

Effects on David

David's story has a successful conclusion in spite of the multiyear and multifaceted failures of educational and mental health systems to adequately provide him with the supports he needed. David was picked to play on the varsity football team as a tackle, continues to be successful in regular education (with the essential supports), maintains a part-time job, and loves spending time with his family at home. David's self-esteem is on the rise, particularly as he gets to "butt heads" with older, bigger, and more experienced football players. Something about this *mano-a-mano* combat has taught him that he has more than just physical strength—he has the courage to do battle against unfavorable odds. It also has helped his self-esteem to have been elected to the student council in his first year in this regular school, especially since he had spent most of the last four years in institutions. David is slowly getting over his feelings of being abandoned and is learning to rely on two young male paraprofessionals (paid by the school and local mental health clinic under a joint agreement) who work with him in and out of school.

Capacity-Building   What has made the difference? As Jim Cain tells it, it is a combination of a better (that is, more functional) understanding (assessment) of David and a better (that is, more functional) provision of support to him.

The difference was that people—his family, teachers, and counselors—
stopped trying to control David all the time. Instead, they helped him take

control of his own life by putting into place a system of education and therapy that he himself could affect and that increased the likelihood that he would make constructive, not destructive, choices (Cain, in Turnbull et al., 1995, p. 189).

In other words, the educators began to build on his strengths and to devise effective interventions for his learning and emotional-behavioral problems. To wit: Just before David left the hospital for his senior high school years in his local school, he declared that, more than anything else, he wanted to play football. Jim saw David's desire as the key to inclusion but only if the school district and others would collaborate with David and each other.

David began his transition out of the state hospital in the fall of his first year in senior high school. During August of that year, he spent every other night at home and at football practice. As part of his transition plan, the local mental health center employed a special education paraprofessional to help David in football practice. The team's coaches and the players regarded this man as an assistant coach, so his working with David did not distinguish him as a therapist. If, for example, David's short fuse began to burn and his behavior began to be inappropriately aggressive, "Coach" would pull David aside for some extra blocking drills.

During David's first week in school, he had to absent himself eight times during each practice. A month later, however, he had to leave practice only once a week. And by the end of the season, he never had to leave practice. As Jim tells it, making the team was David's key to self-esteem.

Yes, "Coach" had to spend about 15 hours a week with David, but the cost to the mental health center was only $100 per week. Jim, after all, had challenged the center to give him just half of what institutionalization would cost and Jim and David would do twice as well.

The clinic also conducted an in-service on David for all of his teachers. There, Jim explained that the teachers could help David best by being nonconfrontational, telling him that he has two choices, and letting him make the choice: "You can stop talking in class or you can leave, go to the counselor's office, and talk to him." As Jim put it, the teachers needed to let David know what his options were, allow him to select from among good options, and then abide by his decisions. Giving David power is important to David on short-term and long-term bases.

David's paraprofessional—his "coach"—also is available to David, on David's terms. If David believes that he needs support, he checks in with "Coach" each morning or throughout the day as necessary. If David asks for help, "Coach" gives it, staying in class with him, working with his teachers, and going to football practice or student council meetings.

In addition, the high school's three special education teachers work closely with the regular-education faculty so that David, and other students with disabilities, can take most of their classwork in regular education. The district's itinerant specialist in behavior and emotional disorders has a hands-off role insofar as David is concerned; her job is to be a resource to the high school faculty and to David's family.

The last member of David's team is a "buddy" paid for by the mental health center. This young man spends after-school time with David, shares similar interests such as sports (the companion was a college basketball player), and just "hangs out" with David, often "cruising" the main streets of the county seat in a sports car, shooting hoops, or going bowling.

The team—all of the educators, mental health center staff, David, Jim, "Coach," and David's "buddy"—meet on a fairly regular basis, usually once a month, and on those occasions when special challenges bring them together. They review what is going well, what is not, and how and what changes they need to make. Their ticket to being effective in assessing David's needs and strengths and to providing him with effective, functional support is their passionate commitment to him and their realization that they must act quickly, jointly, and largely in response to David's choices.

Acting jointly or as collaborators has been very important. The mental health clinic provides backup support and consultation to the school district, and the district and the clinic have entered into a joint agreement that shares the costs of two paraprofessionals. David's father and other family members have become equal partners with the educators and the clinic staff, not just because David's father was the district superintendent but also because David's teachers and clinicians realized how much they and David alike needed the family's insight and support. And, most important of all, David himself realized that he was on a downward spiral, that his family truly wanted him to be in the family circle and not in an institution, that they were acting to help him and not to abandon him to hospital-based care, and that he himself could affect what happened to him in the long term and in the short term. Long term, he could choose whether to act in ways that would ensure his hospitalization or his inclusion, and short term he could select time-out from classrooms or football practice instead of acting out aggressively. In fact, he could choose many of the courses of action he wanted to take, and he could control his own destiny in other ways.

In Jim Cain's words, David has "proven he is capable," and "if all of the people from the different agencies would have collaborated from the beginning, we would not have had to make the painful decisions we did" (J. Cain, oral communication, March 1994).

IDEA Violations

Without placing blame, it is helpful to examine what went wrong in David's case. The system failure (the medical model failure) was the first for the Cains, as it is for most families who have children with disabilities. When medical professionals fail to acknowledge parents' concerns, fail to give timely and functional diagnoses and evaluations, do not refer to nonmedical services, or medicalize all aspects of a disability, they foreclose any possibility of collaborative, family-centered health care.

Doctors too infrequently have been given the educational opportunities and therefore the capacity to work collaboratively with families and nonmedical service providers. Today, medical educational models are being developed and utilized at medical schools located at several different universities across the country. These state-of-the-art models include discipline-specific skills practiced within a community-based system. Care is provided within the context of the family and the system is designed to recognize family needs and collaborate on diagnosis and treatment of the child. Families need physicians to be active team members in developing comprehensive services for persons with disabilities and their family members. Cooperative learning and working together must come from a wide range of providers at the home, community, medical/health care, and public policy level (Darling, 1994; Ensher & Clark, 1986; Krahn, Hallum, & Kime, 1993; Leff & Walizer, 1992; Popper, 1990; Sharp & Lorch, 1988; DiVenere, Frankowski, & Stifler, 1992; and Crandall, Volk, & Loemaker, 1992). The shared decision making that IDEA can facilitate clearly did not occur.

There were other IDEA violations as well. First, IDEA's zero-reject rule provides that an education must be provided free to eligible students. If David's evaluation (functional assessment) and IEP (functional support) had included collaboration with mental health care providers, part of the Cains' expenses could have been covered by his educational entitlement to related services. In addition, if a comprehensive evaluation had been done and if an appropriate education in the least restrictive environment with collaborative service systems had been provided to David, the tremendous costs that his family incurred might have been avoided.

Second, IDEA carefully defines children with "specific learning disabilities" to protect against misclassifying a child as disabled. The process of identifying a child as learning disabled includes the general requirements of nondiscriminatory evaluation, multidisciplinary participation, and a number of diagnostic requirements applicable only to the category of specific learning disabilities. In addition, the definition contains exclusionary criteria, including the possible impact of emotional disturbance on a student's academic attainment.

In hindsight, it is clear that in David's case the evaluation team that first assessed him did not fully explore the documented behavioral concerns that he was exhibiting and failed to take into account his behavioral history. Indeed, the team failed to document and support their view that his history of behavior problems had no major impact on his academic attainment. We now know that these behavioral problems were the primary reason that David was struggling academically and that a learning disability classification and placement was wrong and destined to be inadequate.

Significantly, before his evaluation for behavior disorders and reclassification, David had been maintained with learning disabilities supports and services in a regular education placement. Only after he hit his teacher was he referred for a new evaluation. But the evaluation team made no effort to determine a causal relationship between the teacher's inflexibility or incompetence and David's aggression.

Third, David's right to an appropriate education depends on two components of "appropriate." An appropriate education obtains when a local educational agency follows the process requirements of evaluating a student nondiscriminatorily, relying on the evaluation in developing an IEP, and implementing the IEP (including in its implementation the documentation of progress or lack of progress toward educational goals and objectives). In David's case, his evaluation was not linked to his IEP, and his lack of progress was not documented on his IEP.

Also, an appropriate education consists of educational benefit, received through an educational program tailored to meet the individual needs of the student (*Board of Education v. Rowley,* 1982). A student is receiving a beneficial education when there is visible and realistic progress toward the established goals. In David's case the documentation that he was or was not meeting IEP goals and objectives was omitted in his IEP updates. There is no way of knowing, based on carefully gathered data (functional assessment), whether David was progressing and thereby receiving a beneficial education (functional support). This lack of documentation violates the cornerstone of a free appropriate education by not providing adequate data necessary to make appropriate adaptations to David's educational needs. Moreover, his deterioration in behavior is prima facie proof that he was not benefiting from special education. (*Board of Education v. Rowley,* 1982).

One might argue that David was provided with a free appropriate education because, before any of his hospitalizations, he had an EP reasonably calculated to enable him to receive an educational benefit. Unfortunately, this is not the case. For David to have received a benefit, he should have been progressing both academically and behaviorally. Because not only his family but also their professional advisors recommended institutionalization, it can be concluded that David was not progressing, that his LEA placement was inappropriate, and that the Cains' unilateral placement of him into an institution was necessary and should have been at district or state expense, not family expense (*Burlington School Committee v. Massachusetts Department of Education,* 1985).

In addition to recovering these expenses, the Cains could sue for compensatory education, which would come in the form of additional education past David's 21st birthday (*Burlington School Committee v. Massachusetts Department of Education,* 1985).

Fourth, IDEA's doctrine of least restrictive environment (LRE) prohibits a local education agency from placing a student in a more restrictive setting when he may be provided with an appropriate education in a less restrictive environment.

David's placement became more restrictive with each year until his needs became so critical that he had to leave his local educational placement for institutionally based psychiatric services. That is, he moved from the least to the most restrictive placement on the LRE continuum. Certain safeguards that might have prevented this movement and that might have provided a free appropriate education were not observed. For example, supplementary services were not offered when he was removed from his home school and placed in a self-contained school for students with behaviorial disorders. Perhaps if David and his family had been provided with the appropriate supports and related services, such as itinerant or consultative behavior disorder services, classroom aides, school-based social work and family therapy, and school psychological services, his subsequent inpatient placement could have been avoided.

Fifth, IDEA also provides for a family's participation in decisions about the student's education. The requirement by the state that the family must relinquish custody in order to procure payment for mental health services is in direct conflict with IDEA's principle of parent participation, but it has not yet been held illegal.

In short, David lacked functional assessments and supports, and experienced IDEA violations, for a substantial portion of his school years. In the end he benefited from family and professional understanding of his needs (functional assessment) and individual and system-wide responses (functional support). In David's case, the downward spiral was averted and success ensured, but only after wasted years, poor professional help, and multiple IDEA violations.

THE CASE OF SCOTT WORTH:
STILL WAITING FOR SUCCESS

At the time of this case study, Scott Worth was a 15-year-old eighth grader at Strong Junior High School in Heartland, Kansas, where he lived with his mother and stepfather. He had received special education services since 1981, when, at the age of three, he received his initial special education evaluation.

That evaluation identified speech and language as an area of grave concern. It also indicated that he had a very slow response time, hindering his performance on timed test items, that his math was a severe deficit area, that his reading, written language, and general knowledge were moderate deficit areas, and that he had deficits in functional academic skills including knowledge of names, addresses, phone numbers, coin values, and so on. There was no follow-up on this evaluation.

Failure to Assess and Support

Scott was re-evaluated in the fall of 1988, at the age of 10, and placed in the Daley Elementary School for his third-grade year. Daley is an open-space school, and Scott's experiences there were dismal. A year later, in the fall of 1989, the school district proposed a change in Scott's fourth-grade placement so that he could attend Sweitzer Elementary School, since he had a difficult time adjusting to the open space at Daley.

Two years passed with little progress. Then, in the early winter of 1991, Scott was re-evaluated at a university-based speech-language clinic for special education services. By now, Scott was into his fifth-grade year. The evaluation revealed that Scott's receptive and expressive language skills were still below normal limits for his age and that he had a moderate to severe language impairment characterized by poor auditory memory skills, a limited receptive and expressive vocabulary, and problems with critical thinking and abstract reasoning.

Scott was evaluated by the school psychologist in March 1991, a few months later. The evaluation revealed a 27-point difference between Scott's verbal and performance scale measures. His verbal score fell within the mental retardation range while his overall performance was in the average range. He had notable weaknesses in his ability to interpret verbal information, processed information slowly, experienced considerable difficulty in integrating and interpreting oral commands in a meaningful way, and lacked a strong vocabulary and basic fund of information.

The psychologist observed that Scott did not learn effectively through incidental learning opportunities, especially when information to be learned was presented auditorially. Rather, he required repeated exposure and practice to master and retain information and concepts.

The psychologist also noted that, although Scott was sensitive to interpersonal nuances of behavior, he experienced considerable difficulty when required to integrate information from past learning experiences for use in everyday practical problem solving. He sometimes disregarded conventional or socially acceptable solutions to common-sense problems and his responses may have reflected his inaccurate perceptions and misinterpretations of the presenting problem. His behavior appeared to serve as an indicator of his overall confusion, level of stress, or both. The psychologist further stated that Scott continued to demonstrate significant deficits in auditory memory and processing, verbal comprehension, and behavior, all of which affected his learning; that Scott continued to require considerable support services; that a more integrated multidisciplinary approach would be necessary to address Scott's needs as they affected his everyday interactions with his environment; and that this approach was preferable to a delivery model that attempted to remediate skills in isolation.

Scott's evaluation at the speech-language clinic led to his enrollment there. At the end of the 1991 school year (fifth grade for Scott), the clinic reported that Scott's prognosis for improvement was good, based on his compliance, age, parent involvement, and progress during just one semester. Clinic staff recommended that Scott be re-enrolled in two 30-minute sessions per week in the summer of 1991 and that the focus of his education be on increasing his vocabulary, improving his use and understanding of figurative language, retelling stories, and enhancing his adaptation for school work through cooperation between Scott's clinician and teachers at Sweitzer Elementary School. The clinic staff also said Scott should continue to receive oral and written language intervention and that a strategic approach to reading comprehension should be employed and supplemented with language intervention directed toward improving his vocabulary and sentence and text-level language comprehension.

When Scott was ready to go to sixth grade in the fall of 1991, staff at Sweitzer Elementary School prepared a new IEP, but it incorporated none of the recommendations made by either the school psychologist or the clinic in the winter of that very same year. His IEP goals were very general in nature and addressed (in global but not specific terms) math, reading, and written language, study skills in content areas, the ability to respond appropriately to authority figures, and participation in social situations.

Significantly, nowhere in this IEP was the use of time-out ever mentioned. Nearly six months after preparing this IEP, school staff approached Scott's mother for permission to evaluate Scott for behavioral disorders, but she refused to consent to that request. The very next day, the staff updated Scott's IEP, adding a notation that during the semester Scott had 20 "tallies," stayed after school three times, and went to time-out seven times. Scott's mother was not notified of the time-out procedure.

In October 1992 Scott's mother gave a handout to his resource teachers containing teaching suggestions for Scott. The resource teachers did not give this document to regular classroom teachers until 11 months later, in September 1993, when all of Scott's teachers were given a copy of his IEP.

Scott graduated from Sweitzer Elementary School in the summer of 1992, and in the fall of that year he enrolled in Fitzpatrick Junior High. His IEP for seventh grade indicated that his goals were to improve his study skills, improve his written language skills, respond appropriately to authority figures, and participate in social situations in structured settings. Speech-language services were listed but no speech goals appeared on the IEP. Sometime during his seventh-grade year, Scott's speech-language services were discontinued, but his mother was never notified of this change in services and his IEP was never amended accordingly. His mother earlier had inquired why the school did not implement recommendations of the 1991 school psychologist's report, but she received no answer to her inquiry.

In September 1993, when Scott was beginning eighth grade, at his mother's request all of Scott's teachers were given a copy his IEP and teaching suggestions to use for Scott. Scott's three-year re-evaluation was due for completion in March 1994. At the time of this case study it was overdue, however, and his mother reported that she had requested some extra testing, which was being completed.

IDEA Violations

At least two conclusions can be drawn from Scott's case. First, he, like David Cain, was a student whose IDEA rights were abridged by a school district's failure to effectively assess and support him. Second (unlike the David Cain case), the school district had certain options it could have exercised, but did not, to comply with IDEA and improve its own capacity for providing a free appropriate public education to Scott and other students.

Scott's rights under IDEA seem to have been violated in several major respects. His right to a nondiscriminatory evaluation (alternatively stated, a functional assessment) arguably were violated when the school in 1988 evaluated him but failed to indicate what remediations were appropriate. It is one thing to have a thorough evaluation, but without an action plan, the evaluation is nonfunctional. Indeed, it was not until 1991, when the school psychologist and the university clinic evaluated him and recommended specific, functional interventions, that Scott seems to have had an effective, functional evaluation. Moreover, Scott's mandatory three-year evaluation was overdue when this case was reviewed, despite the fact that Scott was about to transition from junior high school to senior high school and embark on a substantially different type of curriculum in a much larger and more diverse setting than his junior high school.

There were many violations to Scott's right to an appropriate education. The most significant one relates to the school district's failure to incorporate into an IEP the specific recommendations that the school psychologist and speech clinic made regarding Scott's curriculum. IDEA commands the school to link the evaluation with an intervention (IEP-based); a functional assessment and functional support must go hand in hand, but, in Scott's case, they did not.

In addition, the school did not review the IEP in a timely fashion and its compliance with the IEP was partial at best. The IEP itself was prepared in a woefully deficient manner. It expressed long-term goals, including developing social skills with peers, without stating short-term objectives to meet those goals. Some short-term objectives appeared on Scott's IEP without any commensurate long-term goals. These technical violations reflect the district's lackadaisical attitude toward IDEA compliance.

Furthermore, there is no evidence in Scott's school record to demonstrate that key school personnel, including his teachers, were aware of provisions in his IEP. For example, Scott's homework was not modified on a regular basis to accommodate his known need for special instruction. In fact, in one specific instance when Scott's mother confronted his teacher on the homework modification issue, she discovered that the teacher was unaware of the provisions in the IEP.

The district also terminated speech therapy, mandated in the IEP, on the basis of oral testimony by a school speech therapist, but without any objective criteria upon which that decision was based. Moreover, the school refused to comply with Scott's mother's reasonable request to have an independent evaluation conducted to determine the appropriateness of continued daily speech therapy.

Clearly, Scott's rights to an appropriate education were in abeyance for many years. The use of time-out, without a recommendation by the evaluation team and without approval by the IEP team and notice to his mother, violated the appropriate education rule in another respect, namely, the failure to adhere to the IEP-development process and the failure to give notice to a student's parent (*Board of Education v. Rowley,* 1982). Finally, Scott's placement into an open-pod school for third grade ensured nothing but a lack of progress, despite the fact that an appropriate education is one that is reasonably calculated to benefit a student (*Board of Education v. Rowley,* 1982).

To its credit, the district substantially complied with the least restrictive placement rule. That rule creates a rebuttable presumption that a student with a disability should be educated with nondisabled children to the greatest extent appropriate for the student. The LRE rule also provides that students may not be removed from regular education activities unless they cannot be educated successfully in regular classes even after supplementary aids and services are provided. Physical, social, and academic integration are the three components of the LRE rule (*Roncker v. Walter,* 1983; *Daniel R.R. v. State Board of Education,* 1989; *Oberti v. Board of Education,* 1992; and *Board of Education v. Holland,* 1994). Scott spent a good portion of each school day in a regular classroom and received services from a paraprofessional in order to benefit from that inclusion.

The principle of procedural due process requires the school to notify a student's parents whenever it proposes to change or refuses to change a student's placement or program. This is also a principle of parent participation. Clearly, the district violated that principle when it disregarded the notice requirements, unilaterally suspended speech-language services, and began a time-out procedure. Moreover, the procedural due process principle requires the district to consider any independent evaluation the parent may have obtained (and to pay for that evaluation under certain circumstances); in Scott's case, the independent evaluation he received at the university clinic was not taken into account by the district during his 1991–92 school year.

Finally, the principle of parent participation requires the district to not only notify the student's parents (this is a due process provision as well) but also to take good-faith efforts to involve parents in education decision making. Again, the district was in default, having failed to notify Scott's mother about the cessation of speech-language services and the use of time-out, and having failed for a year to distribute to Scott's teachers his mother's written suggestions about how to teach him effectively.

Capacity-Building

The second conclusion that can be drawn from Scott's case is that the school district clearly was not interested in building a capacity to serve Scott or other students like him. The issue here is not the abridgment of his legal rights but why they were abridged and what might have been done to comply with them.

Presumptively, complying with Scott's rights would have assured that he would have an effective or functional evaluation and an effective or functional support system, all leading to a beneficial education and successful special education outcomes.

One way to build a capacity to educate Scott and his peers effectively, and to secure their inclusion, is to adopt a five-pronged approach: analyze the issues, improve teaching practices, adopt a collaborative consultation approach, develop a collaborative team for special education of more than one student, and develop such a team for the special education of an individual student.

The district, which for a long time had been on notice that many parents were dissatisfied with its programs, should have created a task force to analyze the issues around nondiscriminatory evaluation and beneficial, appropriate special education. Its analysis should have targeted (a) the stakeholders and their interests (an "interest analysis"); (b) the barriers to and factors that facilitate effective, functional evaluations of all students and their effective, functional support and education; (c) the district's present policies and practices; (d) proposed goals, objectives, and strategies for improving evaluations and programs; (e) criteria by which a choice between goals, objectives, and strategies will be made; and (f) plans for implementing, evaluating, and using the feedback to improve the newly adopted plan.

In David Cain's case, in contrast to Scott's case, the issue analysis was never formally done but still there was an analysis, a plan of action, and eventually system-wide change. The reason for the change was that David's father, Jim, exercised his considerable powers as superintendent and his determination as a father to figure out (analyze) what David wanted (control over his life and acceptance by family and peers) and what barriers (hospitalization) and facilitating factors (football eligibility and cooperation between the mental health center and school) were part of the problem and solution.

As arcane as policy analysis is, it is indispensable to capacity-building. But no such analysis will be effective unless the teachers' capacities are at an effective level. Thus, a comprehensive and ongoing, repetitive program of in-service training of the evaluators, regular and special educators, and administrators is not only desirable, but mandated by IDEA's comprehensive system of personnel development. If the in-service program is closely linked to the barriers identified in the analysis, the district's capacities are more likely to be strengthened than not. David Cain benefited from such an in-service, conducted for the school district's staff by the mental health center and David's father, the superintendent. Scott's school district never did an in-service, although his mother was elected to the school board in Scott's seventh-grade year.

A third capacity-building technique is the collaborative consultation model. This model seeks to include students with disabilities into regular education programs by converting special education faculty into consultants to regular education faculty, rather than continuing to use special education faculty as direct-service providers and classroom teachers only for students with disabilities. Thus, special and regular educators share responsibility for jointly educating students. Again, this is the approach that David Cain's faculty is using.

David's teachers also use another capacity-building approach, namely school-based and student-focused collaborative teaming. School-based collaboration brings administrators, regular educators, and special educators together for the purpose of planning how to improve the school's services and particularly how to include students with disabilities into regular education. Student-focused collaboration is similar but is targeted at a single student, not at the entire special education student body of a particular school.

SUMMARY

What was lacking in Scott's case is exactly what was present in David's—the three ingredients that can avoid IDEA violations and secure capacity-building and system change. These are (a) a commitment to change, (b) an informed and state-of-the-art use of evaluation data for an individual student and for a district or school as a whole, and (c) an informed and state-of-the-art use of the resources of the student, the student's family, nonschool professionals, the school district, and the individual school. Stated alternatively, what was present in David's case but not in Scott's was a best-practice use of functional evaluation (of an individual and of a system) and functional support (of an individual and of his family and educators and other professionals), all undergirded by a deep-seated commitment to change.

Jim Cain says it well in his advice to school administrators:

> It's much more economical to educate students in their neighborhood schools than it is to pay for expensive out-of-home and out-of-district programs. We need funding streams to be redirected from institutional programs and into our school districts. It's entirely possible to create the support that students with the most severe emotional or behavioral challenges need in order to succeed in their own schools.

> Treat all students as individuals, because no two students are ever the same. Evaluate their strengths and weaknesses, help make their strengths stronger, and certainly help them find ways to overcome their weaknesses. It doesn't make a difference if the weakness is academic or behavioral. All of us have areas where we need to improve.

> As administrators, we're responsible for finding the right combinations for all students to be successful. If they're not successful, it means we have not yet successfully found the combination they need.

> We must believe that all children and youth can learn and behave appropriately. I'm talking about more than lip service.

We need to ask students directly what we can do to make their education work for them. We need to be able to give them the power they need and even bend our rules if necessary. We need to show them that we want them to succeed and be willing to meet them halfway. We have to stop forcing students with emotional or behavioral disorders into a corner where they have no choices and we have all the control in our hands. We must find ways for these students to get involved in extracurricular activities and to recognize that having friends is an important part of school. Many students act out because they feel alienated from their peers and on the fringe of school life. An appropriate education has to extend beyond the classroom and academic instruction.

A frequent barrier to successful inclusion is to wait until a student has a crisis to provide more individualized and personalized support. Administrators, teachers, and families must respond immediately to the first inkling that a problem is brewing. We must gather as collaborative teams and come up with creative approaches to prevent little problems from escalating into major crises which, in turn, too often lead to long-term restrictive placements. (Cain, in Turnbull et al., 1995, p. 217.)

AUTHOR NOTE

I would like to acknowledge the contributions of my students Gwen Berry, Bill Carter, Kristi Dulek, Dave Egnor, Laura Frey, Brad Harvey, Marilyn Kaff, Barbara Martin, Linda Mitchell, Jan Sandoval, Sally Morgan Smith, and Monica Tovar. Without these students taking my course, Policy Analysis in the 1994–95 academic year, this chapter would not have been written.

REFERENCES

Board of Education v. Rowley, 458 U.S. 176 (1982).

Board of Education v. Holland, 4 F.3d 1398 (9th Cir. 1994).

Burlington School Committee v. Massachusetts Department of Education, 736 F. 2d 733 (1st Cir. 1984), aff'd, 471 U.S. 359 (1985).

Cain, J. (1995). In Turnbull, A. P., Turnbull, H. R., Shank, L., and Leal, D. *Exceptional lives: Special education in today's schools.* Columbus: Merrill/Prentice-Hall.

Crandall, S. J. S., Volk, R. J., & Loemaker, V. (1992). Medical students' attitudes toward providing care for the underserved: Are we training socially responsible physicians? *Journal of the American Medical Association, 269*(19), 2519–2523.

Daniel R.R. v. State Board of Education, 874 F.2d 1036 (5th Cir. 1989).

Darling, R. (1994). *Families, physicians, and children with special health needs.* Westport, CT: Greenwood.

DiVenere, N., Frankowski, B., & Stifler, D. (1992). The medical education project: A shared learning experience incorporating the principles of family centered care in physician education. *Medical Home Newsletter, 4,* 1–3.

Ensher, G. L., & Clark, D. A. (1986). *Newborns at risk: Medical care and psychoeducational intervention.* Rockville, MD: Aspen.

Individuals with Disabilities Education Act, 20 U.S.C. Secs. 1400 et seq. (1975, as amended, 1997).

Krahn, G. L., Hallum, A., & Kime, C. (1993). Are there good ways to give 'bad news'? *Pediatrics, 91*(3), 578–582.

Leff, P.T., & Walizer, E. H. (1992). *Building the healing partnership.* Bethesda: Brookline.

Oberti v. Board of Education, 789 F. Supp. 1322 (D. N.J., 1992).

Popper, B. (1990). A parent's perspective: The changing role of parent involvement in the health care system. *Children's Health Care, 19*(4), 242–243.

Roncker v. Walter, 700 F.2d 1058 (6th Cir. 1983), *cert. denited,* 464 U.S. 864 (1983).

Sharp, M.C., & Lorch, S. C. (1988). A community outreach training program for pediatric residents and medical students. *Journal of Medical Education, 63,* 316–322.

Turnbull, A. P., Turnbull, H. R., Shank, M., & Leal, D. (1995). *Exceptional lives: Special education in today's schools.* Columbus: Merrill/Prentice-Hall.

17

Implications of Behavior State for the Assessment and Education of Students with Profound Disabilities

DOUG GUESS
SALLY ROBERTS
BARBARA GUY

INTRODUCTION

While assessment procedures in the functional analysis literature typically involve a study of the relationship between target behaviors and specific environmental events, Guess, Roberts, and Guy present a different system, one which relies on transition state analyses. In it, data are collected in real time on the behavioral states (eight observable types) of persons with severe disabilities.

The results are used to produce profiles of individuals, indicating (a) the degree to which they remain in particular states (for example, asleep-active), (b) the sequences in which they generally move from one state to another, (c) the cyclicity of sleep-awake episodes, and (d) the frequency (periodicity) with which they change states. The state data are then matched to environmental variables, resulting in a prescription for intervention. Suggestions include the external techniques that might increase activity level (for example, tactile stimulation), an assessment of the effects of medication and of nutrition, implications for the type of in-

struction that might be best for each student, and the time of day different types of instruction should be programmed.

The work in this chapter is particularly interesting from the framework of the progress of behavior analysis. At present, it is in the assessment stage, much as the classic study by Iwata et al. (1982) was. That study assessed the rate of self-injurious behavior under a control condition and three other conditions, each related to a different hypothesis. The analogue procedure has, of course, been extended and found to be very effective. The behavior state analysis is not tied to function in the same way. Rather, it suggests conditions under which states exist. The challenge for the interventionist, then, is to use that information to identify successful treatments. Following the continuing development of this procedure and the degree to which it leads directly to treatment should be interesting.

ASSESSMENT

Children and youth with profound and multiple disabilities have remained a challenge to psychologists, special educators, and other direct service providers. When testable, these individuals typically have very low scores on standardized measures of intelligence, and overall levels of development of less than six months, regardless of their chronological ages. They are typically nonverbal, have varying severity levels of sensory and motor impairments, and might display only minimal responsiveness to visual, auditory, and olfactory stimuli. Educational and clinical observations indicate problems among these individuals in their ability to maintain attentiveness and responsiveness to environmental stimuli (Ferguson, 1985; Thompson & Guess, 1989) and suggest that this phenomenon might be related to the quality and consistency of their behavior state conditions (Campbell, 1989; Helm & Simeonsson, 1989; Landesman-Dwyer & Sackett, 1978; Rainforth, 1982; Reid, Phillips, & Green, 1991; Sailor et al., 1988).

Behavior state was initially described by Wolff (1959) as a series of behavioral and physiological conditions that range from sleeping to awake and crying among infants. Helm and Simeonsson (1989) have defined states as " . . . expressions of the maturity, status, and organization of the central nervous system . . . which mediate the child's ability to respond to the environment and stimulation" (p. 203). The majority of state studies have been conducted with normally developing infants, including the extensive analysis of sleep-wake patterns (Thoman & Whitney, 1990). Although disabling conditions, per se, have not been the target of researchers, studies with premature infants (Kopp et al., 1975), infants with Down's syndrome (Prechtl, 1974), and infants exposed in the womb to alcohol (Rosett et al., 1979) and cocaine (Chasnoff et al., 1985) have all shown state patterns that vary from normal expectations (primarily indicated by inconsistent neonatal state cycles).

Our own research (Guess et al., 1988, 1990, 1991; Guess et al., 1995; Guess et al., 1993c; Guess et al., 1993a; Guy, Guess, & Ault, 1993; Roberts, 1992) indicates that state behavior has a significant influence on the alertness and responsiveness of persons with profound disabilities and, indirectly, on their learning, development, and overall quality of life. These studies started with initial pilot investigations that were designed to assess the quality of state behavior in this population (Guess et al., 1988). Later studies were conducted to identify endogenous (organismic) and exogenous (environmental) variables associated with state conditions (Guess et al., 1990), and to investigate the relationship between state and environmental events and conditions (Guess et al., 1991; Guess et al., 1993a). Data collection procedures have evolved from time sampling (Guess et al., 1988) to time interval (Guess et al., 1990) to current use of a continuous recording procedure (Guess et al., 1993b). These studies have revealed the complex impact of state on the basic alertness and responsiveness of children and youth with profound disabilities, and the importance of state to their overall development.

For our research, a state observation scale was adapted and expanded from the Neonatal Behavioral Assessment Scale (Brazelton, 1984) to accommodate much older individuals with profound mental retardation who were also presented with multiple sensory and motor impairments (including participants identified as deaf-blind and medically fragile). Table 17.1 presents the following eight state categories that evolved from our studies: Asleep-inactive; Asleep-active; Drowsy; Daze; Awake inactive-alert; Awake active-alert; Awake active/stereotypy; and Crying/agitated. Seizure activity is recorded as a separate, nonstate category.

BEHAVIOR STATE MODEL

Based upon findings from our research, a model was designed to select procedures for measuring state, and to identify variables and conditions that potentially interact with it. Our model is derived, in part, from Als's synactive theory (1982, 1986) for assessing preterm infants, Wolf's (1987) longitudinal investigations of normally developing infants, and from Helm and Simeonsson's (1989) discussion of factors that interact with state organization. The model further agrees with the observations of Korner (1972) and Helm and Simeonsson (1987) that state can be viewed as: (a) an obstacle that compromises assessment, (b) a variable that reflects the influences of endogenous and exogenous factors and conditions, and (c) a mediator that affects responsiveness to stimulation.

Our model assumes that state organization mediates attentiveness and responsiveness to environmental stimuli. Further, outcomes of this mediation are influenced by the dynamic interaction between endogenous and exogenous variables existing at the time of observation. Figure 17.1 provides a schematic of the dynamic relationship between measurable attributes of state and selected endogenous and exogenous variables. Some variables, followed by two arrows in the schematic, indicate bidirectional interaction with state organization. This implies that these variables and state behavior somewhat equally influence one another. There are other endogenous factors (for example, seizures) and exogenous variables (for example, setting/context) that have a more unidirectional influence on

Table 17.1 Definitions of Behavior State

Sleep States	S^1 Asleep-Inactive	S^2 Asleep-Active
	Person's eyes are closed. Respiration is relatively slow and regular. Exhibits little or no motor activity (startle, mouthing, brief limb/body movements).	Person's eyes are closed. Respiration is generally uneven. Sporadic movements (tossing and turning, head and limb twitching) may occur but muscle tone generally low between movements. Person may exhibit rapid eye movements (REM). Other behavior may include facial expressions (smiles, grimaces, frowns) and/or vocalizations (sighs, grunting, gurgling).
Indeterminate States	**DR Drowsy**	**DA Daze**
	Person's eyes are either open and eyelids appear "heavy" or eyes are opening/closing repeatedly. Vocalizations may occur.	Nonorientation to visual, auditory, or tactile stimuli predominates. If person's vision is intact, eyes are open and appear glassy, dull, and immobile. Motor movements (that are not orienting) may occur such as brief limb/body movements, startles. Respiration is regular.
Preferred Awake States	**A^1 Awake Inactive-Alert**	**A^2 Awake Active-Alert**
	Person's eyes are open and some active visual or auditory orientation, focusing, or tracking is displayed (oriented/focused on stimuli, turning head, eyes toward stimuli, or following stimuli). Motor movements (that are not orienting) may occur such as brief limb/body movements, startles. Demonstrates regular respiration. Vocalizations may occur.	Person attempts to engage/interact using visual, auditory, or tactile modes. If person's vision is intact, eyes are open, bright, and shiny. Visual, auditory, or tactile interaction patterns are exhibited *with* distinct fine and gross motor movements (reaching, leaning toward/away, moving toward/away, eating, touching, etc.). Vocalizations may occur.
Other Awake States	**A^2 Awake-Active/Stereotypy**	**C/A Crying/Agitated**
	Person exhibits behaviors of A^2 with movements that are self-stimulatory or stereotypical (idiosyncratic, repetitive rhythmic movements of body or body parts). Movements may include head weaving, rocking, mouthing hand or objects, arm and finger flapping.	Person may exhibit intense vocalizing, crying, or screaming. Self-injurious behavior possible. Respiration may be irregular and eyes may be open or closed. Intense motor activity possible.

state, even though more subtle interactive effects might occur. These variables are represented in the figure by single arrows pointing in the direction of state organization. The figure also acknowledges the interactive influences between all variables in the model; for example, the relationship between illness and nutrition in the endogenous component, or between assistive/adaptive devices (for example, use of communication board) and interactions with other persons in the exogenous component. Accordingly, state behavior and the endogenous and exogenous variables are all indirectly or directly interconnected within a dynamic system, implying the need for a comprehensive analytic approach.

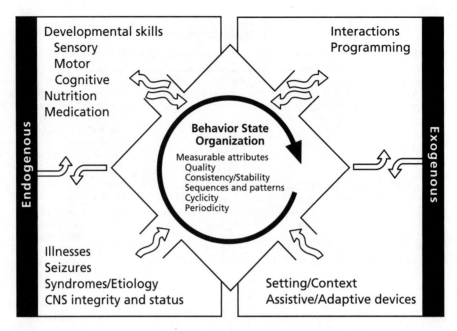

FIGURE 17.1 Schematic of the model showing the interaction of behavior state organization with endogenous and exogenous variables

APPROACHES TO BEHAVIOR STATE MEASUREMENT

Our research has measured and analyzed the five attributes of behavior state organization listed in the model. Several of these attributes have undergone multiple analyses.

State Quality

Guess et al. (1990) averaged the percent occurrences for each state across 50 students who were observed in educational settings. Results showed that, as a group, these students were observed in the awake inactive-alert and awake active-alert states 58 percent of the time. They spent the remaining 42 percent of the time in states that are not optimal for learning: asleep, drowse, daze, stereotypy, or crying/agitation. A recent study with 66 new participants (Guess et al., 1993b) supported findings from the earlier Guess et al. (1990) investigation by showing close similarity in the overall percentage of time in the eight state conditions (Guess et al., 1995). This finding is even more robust because the two studies used different procedures to record the state data, and students were observed at different time intervals. Figure 17.2 compares results from the two investigations.

These results and findings from earlier studies were used to group students by profiles that represented similar quality in state patterns. These profiles, described below, provided an independent variable for further descriptive analyses.

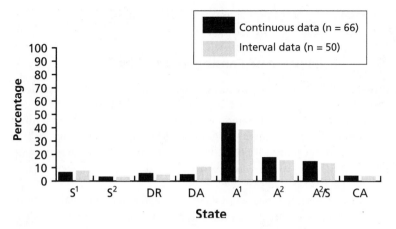

FIGURE 17.2 Graph comparing the mean percentage of time in each of eight state conditions using two different data collection procedures

Profile Group 1 Students spent at least 75 percent of the time in the educationally optimal awake inactive-alert and awake active-alert states.

Profile Group 2 These students spent at least 75 percent of the time in the awake inactive-alert and awake active-alert states, but less than 20 percent of that percentage was scored in the awake active-alert state, with at least 55 percent of the students' entire set of state scores in the awake inactive-alert state. These students thus showed considerable alert behavior, but they infrequently interacted physically with the environment.

Profile Group 3 In this group, students were observed less than 75 percent of the time in the awake inactive-alert and awake active-alert states, with more of the remaining time recorded in the stereotypy and crying/agitation states than in the sleep, drowse, and daze states. This group includes students who display considerable stereotypic behavior and/or who are often agitated. This group also includes students who engage in self-injury.

Profile Group 4 Students in this profile spent less than 75 percent of the time in the awake inactive-alert and awake active-alert states, with more of the remaining time observed in the sleep, drowse, and daze states than in the stereotypy and crying/agitation states. This profile consists of students who display a lot of asleep and drowse behavior during daytime hours.

Profile Group 5 A small number of students did not fall into any of the above profile groups and were observed to engage in a relatively large number of states without any particular focus.

It should be noted that the Guess et al. investigation (1993b) also found one participant who was observed to spend considerable time in the daze state, requiring the addition of another potential profile group. Differences in state quality between profile groups based on this study are shown in Figure 17.3.

Behavior State Consistency/Stability

Measures of state stability have been used successfully to predict later development of a disabling condition among both preterm and full-term infants (Tynan, 1986). Thoman and Whitney (1990) suggest that low state stability scores among neonates have implications for their CNS status. Although participants in our studies had confirmed neurological problems, we were interested in determining the extent to which within- and across-session state stability indices were related to the profile groups described above.

Analyses from the earlier Guess et al. (1990) research showed that students with the highest occurrences of the awake inactive-alert and awake active-alert state (Profile Groups 1 and 2) had the most within- and across-session state stability indices. Further, their state stability patterns were more stable than students who were observed to have relatively high occurrences of stereotypy and crying/agitation (Profile Group 3) and students observed with high occurrences of sleep, drowse, and daze states (Profile Group 4).

State Sequences and Patterns

In later studies, we first used five-second interval recording procedures to observe each of 25 students over a single session of about five hours (Guess et al., 1993a) and we used handheld event recorders to collect continuous data on 65 students during five-hour sessions (Guess et al., 1993b). A lag sequential analysis (Bakeman & Gottman, 1986) was used to calculate the probability that one state condition followed another across a time sequence. In using the lag sequential method, a "criterion" event (one particular state) was identified. Other events (the remaining states) were then selected as the targets. A series of transitional probabilities was then computed for the target event immediately after the criterion (lag 1), after one intervening event (lag 2), and so forth.

Figure 17.4 presents significant lag sequence patterns for five profiles in the Guess et al. (1993b) investigation. Arrows point in a direction where there is at least a 20 percent probability that one particular state will be followed directly by another. In Profile Group 1, for example, stereotypy (A^2/S), when it occurs, is often followed by the awake inactive-alert (A^1) state or the awake active-alert (A^2) state. These state sequences are similar to those described earlier for the various profile groups, and reveal state organization patterns that are not always obvious during casual observation.

State Cyclicity

Cyclicity of sleep-awake episodes has been extensively studied in neonates. Some investigators have suggested the absence of sleep-awake cycles during the first year of life (Anders & Keener, 1985), while others have shown that temporally regulated sleep-awake patterns are common among full-term (Thoman & McDowell,

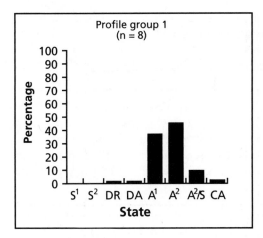

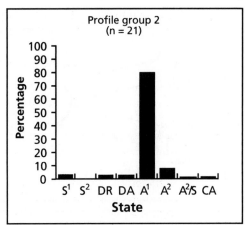

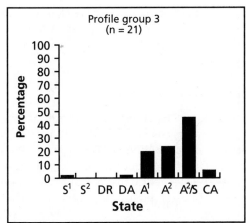

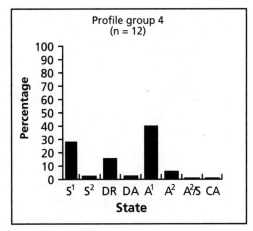

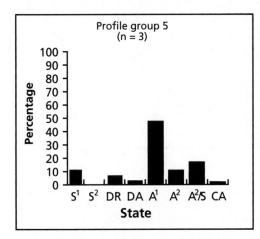

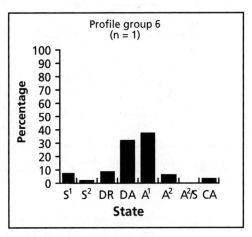

FIGURE 17.3 Mean percent of the eight behavior state conditions for each profile group

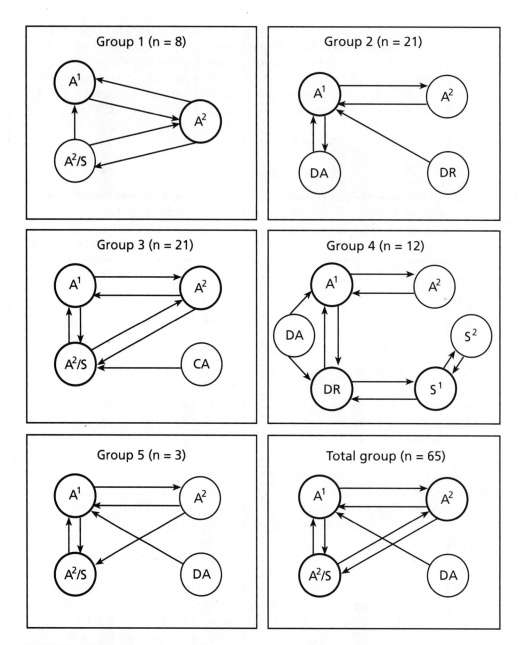

FIGURE 17.4 Diagrams showing the directions of state shifts among five profile groups.

1989) and preterm (Pugsley, Acebo, & Thoman, 1988) infants. These studies, however, are based on neonates and infants who engage in considerably longer sleep episodes during daytime hours, as compared to our participants, whose sleep states occurred less often during daytime hours, and for shorter periods of time. These findings occur even though some persons with profound disabilities are also more likely to exhibit shortened nocturnal sleep durations (Poindexter & Bihm, 1994). Nevertheless, none of the students in our studies has displayed specific state conditions that were repeated at regular intervals across time.

State Periodicity

Participants have shown rapid and varying occurrences of movement into and out of a particular state. The students observed by Guess et al. (1993b) shifted states an average of 1.28 times per minute over the five-hour observation periods. Students who had high occurrences of awake inactive-alert behavior (Profile Group 2) displayed the longest time intervals before shifting states, less than once per minute; while students with high occurrences of stereotypy and self-injury (Profile Group 3) averaged over two shifts per minute.

VARIABLES AND CONDITIONS THAT INFLUENCE STATE BEHAVIOR

The model (Figure 17.1) includes a number of variables that potentially interact with state behavior, and with each other. The mediating role of states provides interactions between these environmental events and organismic conditions.

Endogenous Variables

Unidirectional The unidirectional endogenous variables imply a mostly one-way influence on state behavior, as shown by one-direction arrows in the model given in Figure 17.1. This means that these variables likely impact state behavior to a much greater degree than the various state conditions change these variables.

Illnesses, both acute and chronic, often influence state behavior by reducing time in the awake inactive-alert and awake active-alert states. Significant changes in state quality often serve to alert teachers and caregivers of an illness among students with limited formal expressive communication modes. This variable also includes the effects of health-related conditions on state behavior. For example, a previous study (Guess et al., 1990) indicated that students who were observed for large amounts of time in the awake inactive-alert state (Profile Group 2) also required more frequent need for humidified oxygen and had more instances of choking during feeding, as did those students who spent excessive time in the sleep, daze, and drowse states (Profile Group 4). A one-year follow-up study of premature infants by Fajardo et al. (1992) found more health-related problems among subjects who displayed poor state organization during the early weeks of life.

Our studies thus far have not found that seizure activity has a significant influence on state behavior.

Another unidirectional endogenous variable is syndrome/etiology. This includes behavioral sequalae systemic to various genetic disorders found among children and youth with severe and profound disabilities. High occurrences of stereotypy, for example, are common to the Lesch-Nyhan, Cornelia de Lange, and Rett syndromes. Traumatic brain injury experienced at an older age possibly influences state in ways that differ from congenital neurological insult. An intriguing finding from an earlier study (Guess et al.,1990) suggested that a proportionally higher number of students who were observed frequently in the awake inactive-alert and awake active-alert states (Profile Group 1) experienced intraventricular hemorrhaging at birth.

It has been suggested (Thoman & Whitney, 1990) that across-time state instability among neonates has implications for CNS integrity and status. We would add to this indicator of instability the frequent state change periods observed among students in our studies. CNS integrity is a variable, however, where direct influence on state behavior can be assumed among children and youth with profound disabilities. These students almost always have impaired neurological systems.

Bidirectional   Bidirectional endogenous variables more directly interact with state and, indirectly, environmental events and conditions via state. For example, cognitive skills and exogenous factors both influence state quality. On the other hand, state quality (amount of alert versus sleep and drowse behavior) also impacts cognitive achievements as well as the quality and frequency of interactions with people.

Developmental skills important to state include, at minimum, those listed in Figure 17.1. Visual and auditory sensory perceptual skills such as localization, tracking, and scanning are important to behaviors associated with the awake inactive-alert and awake active-alert states. Participants in our studies have indicated high occurrences of sensory impairments that appear to transverse profile groups. Motor skill development (e.g., movement, rhythms, alignment) appears to be related to state quality, with a higher percentage of severe motor impairments among students observed frequently in the asleep, daze, and drowse states (Profile Group 4) and among students with a high percentage of awake inactive-alert behavior (Profile Group 2). Students with higher occurrences of stereotypy and crying/agitation states (Profile Group 3) tend to display comparatively more advanced fine motor and motility skills. At a one-year follow-up, Fajardo et al. (1992) found significantly lower scores on the Bayley motor scale among infants who had poorly organized state patterns shortly after birth, when compared to infants with well-organized neonatal state patterns.

Body alignment illustrates a bidirectional variable where motor skill development and state behavior especially interact. Guess et al. (1993a) found that the prone and sidelying positions were among several variables associated with the deep sleep state, while the seated position was among those variables that significantly co-occurred with the awake active-alert state; this finding was also indicated in a study by Landesman-Dwyer and Sackett (1978).

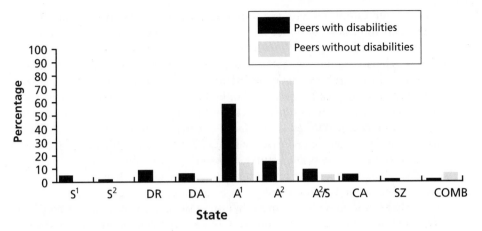

FIGURE 17.5 Average percentage of state conditions for the four preschool children with severe disabilities and their matched peers without disabilities.

Changes in state behavior appear to interact with cognitive development. Colombo and Horowitz (1987) pointed out that state variables constitute a dominant characteristic of neonatal behavior. They noted, however, that infants become less state-dependent after the age of three months. Wolff (1987) observed that emergence of increased alert activity among infants signals a point at which choice enters into the organization of their behavioral repertoire. This provides for them an avenue to behave spontaneously, rather than being stimulus-bound to state conditions. Importantly, this cognitive advancement also includes the ability to engage in concurrent states. This contrasts to an earlier developmental age in which the behavior of infants is primarily controlled by a single state. A recent study by Myers (1992) supports this observation.

Figure 17.5 from the Myers study shows, for example, state observations of four preschool children with profound disabilities and four preschool children without disabilities who were matched for chronological age, setting, and observation time periods. In addition to qualitative differences in state behavior, the matched peers without disabilities showed a higher percentage of occurrences in which two state conditions occurred simultaneously (indicated by combination on the graph). As also indicated on the graph, the matched nondisabled peers showed significantly higher percentages of time in the awake active-alert state.

Nutritional status is another endogenous variable that has a bidirectional relationship with state; it also potentially interacts with other endogenous and exogenous variables. The feeding difficulties experienced by students with profound disabilities are due to a variety or combination of factors, including chronic health problems, early negative oral experience (tube feedings, intubation, suctioning), neurological aberrations, and so on. These uniformly result in an inadequate nutritional status. Characteristics of undernourished students include lethargy, easily decreased levels of energy or stamina, and poor attention span.

From an educational point of view, inadequately nourished students may be physiologically compromised as they attempt to interact with persons or materials in the environment.

For example, Ault et al. (1994) observed a student whose weight for height was so far below recommended standards that it was not even on a standard growth chart (Ross Laboratories, 1982). Following a complete nutritional analysis, a coordinated program was made by her family and school personnel to increase caloric intake. This effort produced a weight gain of five pounds, a height increase of 1.5 inches, and positive changes in behavior state (Figure 17.6).

In two studies (Guess et al., 1990; Guess et al., 1993b), we analyzed the quality of state behavior in relation to the types and dosage levels of medications being received at the time of observation. Medications included the categories of tranquilizers, anticonvulsants, and other psychotropic and health-related drugs. Results showed that most students were receiving varying types and dosages of medications. Students with high occurrences of sleep, drowse, and daze behavior (Profile Group 4) were much more likely to receive multiple medications while some students in the crying-agitated group (Profile Group 3) received no medications. These group results do not sufficiently emphasize the fact that a specific medication change can significantly alter state behavior for individual students. Figure 17.6, for example, shows noticeable differences in state quality for a young child whose seizure medication was changed from Depakote to Dilantin, with the prescribed dosage reduced by 600 mgs. per day (Ault et al., 1994).

Exogenous Variables

Unidirectional Figure 17.1 lists two environmental variables (setting/context and assistive/adaptive devices) that likely influence state behavior among children and youth with profound disabilities. State behavior, however, does not directly dictate the quality of, or accessibility to, these conditions. Setting/context depicts environments to which children and youth with profound disabilities are allowed access, usually at the discretion of caregivers. The level of stimulation and variation in these settings influences quality of state behavior. This includes, of course, the potential stimulation provided in integrated classroom and community settings.

Assistive/adaptive devices indicate a wide range of devices and equipment that allow greater access to environmental stimulation and manipulation. Examples include: positioning equipment such as bolsters, standers, and wheelchairs; devices that enhance sensory acuity (for example, eyeglasses and hearing aids); and augmentative equipment and materials that permit or enhance expressive communication, such as switches that activate a variety of apparatuses and communication boards. Assistive/adaptive devices for students with profound disabilities are especially important for increasing time in the awake inactive-alert and awake active-alert states.

Bidirectional Interactions and programming are two critical variables that are associated with state quality and organization. Interactions comprise a host of social and physical contacts with children and youth who experience profound disabilities. These interactions occur at both the symbolic and nonsymbolic (facial

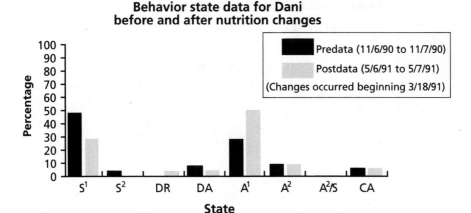

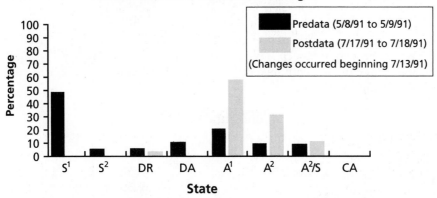

FIGURE 17.6 Changes in state behavior following changes in nutrition (top graph) and medication (bottom graph).

expressions, body movements, eye glances) levels. They involve a wide range of individuals, may be fleeting or sustained, and vary in quality and consistency. These interactions may influence the quality of state behavior, or they may be a reflection of the dominant state organization pattern for the person.

Programming is a state-related variable that encompasses numerous factors, ranging from the frequency and stimulation potential of materials accessible to these students, type of instructional procedures used in their education and treatment programs, and the content of their educational objectives. Rainforth (1982) and Simeonsson, Huntington, and Parse (1980) have noted the importance of states in the education and assessment of students with profound disabilities. Campbell (1989) discussed the need to match type of cognitive stimuli to state conditions during classroom educational programs for students with profound disabilities.

STRATEGIES AND PROCEDURES THAT
IMPROVE STATE PATTERNS

Although the number of endogenous and exogenous variables that singularly or in combination influence behavior state appears unmanageable in terms of instructional strategies, it is possible to identify from previous research those variables that often influence state. Our studies indicate that three primary variables for improving the quality of state patterns are the environment, medication, and nutrition. Within limits, medications and nutrition can be impacted by educational staff, as can environmental variables such as positioning, activity, materials, and social contacts. Systematic monitoring of these variables will provide a basis for selecting instructional strategies, as described below.

Specific strategies are presented separately for clarity, but should be considered in terms of the overall model where variables interact with each other, and with state. This means that while one factor may be of primary influence, changes in other secondary factors might also influence the entire system. For example, a student may become more alert following increased interaction with her peers. Changes in her medication or nutritional status might, however, cause a decrease in her alert time, regardless of peer contact. Additionally, certain characteristics of the type of peer contact, such as physical demands or overly active social environments, might combine with medication or nutritional influences to further decrease her time in alert states.

Environmental Variables

General environmental variables   Our previous research (Guess et al., 1991; Guess et al., 1993a) and current "best practices" indicate that there are four environmental variables most likely to interact with state. Position of the student, social contact, and type and availability of materials were variables that, when combined, were associated with either an alert or sleep state. Level of activity was also associated with state and is related to the location or environment of the student.

Group data (Guess et al., 1991; Guess et al., 1993a) indicated that prone and sidelying positions are associated with sleep, while the seated position accompanied the awake alert-active state. Further analysis indicated that individual students will have different positions that are significantly associated with various state conditions. Sidelying, however, was always associated with sleep, drowse, or daze, while the seated position was associated with the other states. On an individual basis, the prone and supine positions were associated with all of the observed state conditions. For students with limited movement, it may be even more important to monitor their positioning equipment to maintain preferred states.

Position is an important variable that might sometimes have a primary influence, and at other times may be secondary to variables such as availability and type of materials. For example, the presence of materials may not be a factor in the occurrence of sleep when students are in the sidelying position (Guess et al., 1993a), but it is important for the occurrence of awake alert-active behavior. On an individual basis, not only has the absence of materials been associated with sleep states but so has the presence of some types of materials. For some students, auditory or visual materials have been associated with sleep. For one student, the occurrence of the awake inactive-alert state was even associated with the absence of materials. Given these individual differences, it is important to note that materials are considered to be "available" only when students can actually access them. Depending on the student's available sensory modalities, materials need to be within touching distance, large enough to be seen, or loud enough to be heard. For example, sitting next to a radio tuned to a rap station would not provide available materials to a student with severe hearing impairments.

Recent practices have emphasized placing students with profound disabilities into activities with their nondisabled peers. This philosophy is partially based on the belief that enhanced opportunity will increase student interactions. While it is certain that interactions will not occur without opportunity, it is equally important to remember that opportunity alone will not ensure interactions. Accordingly, it is important to monitor social contact by examining who makes contact with students, and the types of interactions that occur.

Although there are many ways to identify the types of contact made with students having profound disabilities, one of the easiest procedures is to determine if the person is attempting to engage the students or is simply attending to them. The social contact is considered engaging if a peer or adult is attempting to directly touch or talk to the observed student. Attending occurs when the peer or adult is touching or looking at the student but direct attention is focused elsewhere. For example, pushing a wheelchair with no attempts to talk to or touch the student would be considered attending. Engaged social contact requires that the peer or adult is attempting to obtain a response from the observed student, even if none occurs.

The location or environment of the student is a variable closely related to the concept of social contact. The number and types of different environments in which students have opportunities to interact are often limited. Students with profound disabilities are dependent on others to determine "appropriate" environments for interactions to occur. Changes across or even within environments, however, may significantly affect behavior state. Indeed, changes in behavior state profiles may even demonstrate student preferences for certain environments.

Concurrent Observation of Behavior State and Environmental Variables

The form in Figure 17.7 (Guy, Ault, & Guess, 1993) is used to assess state profiles. The form represents one 7.5-minute observation period for a student. Each row (1 through 30) indicates a 15-second interval that includes 5 seconds of observation and 10 seconds of recording. Twenty observations across five days are recommended for determining a student's profile. Four observations should occur each day—early and late morning, and early and late afternoon. Observation times should differ daily, and represent a variety of activities, settings, and positions. An audio tape signaling observation and recording intervals is suggested to increase accuracy. Analysis of the 20 observation sessions has been simplified by a program designed for use on Apple lle or GS computers (Guy, Ault, & Guess, 1993). This program permits users to quickly view graphed data by state, environmental factors, time, day, and combinations of each variable.

Number _____ Date _____ Time _____ Primary Location _____

	BEHAVIOR STATE									POSITION AND LOCATION	ACTIVITY	MATERIAL (Availability)		MATERIAL (Primary modality)	SOCIAL CONTACT						
															Attending Engaging			Adult Student			
	S^1	S^2	DR	DA	A^1	A^2	A^2S	CA	SZ			Y	N		At	?	E	Ad	S		
1																					1
2																					2
3																					3
4																					4
5																					5
6																					6
7																					7
8																					8
9																					9
10																					10
11																					11
12																					12
13																					13
14																					14
15																					15
16																					16
17																					17
18																					18
19																					19
20																					20
21																					21
22																					22
23																					23
24																					24
25																					25
26																					26
27																					27
28																					28
29																					29
30																					30
	S^1	S^2	DR	DA	A^1	A^2	A^2S	CA	SZ	Targeted Skills:											

Comments: _____

FIGURE 17.7 Sample form used for collecting state and environmental data.
SOURCE: From Guy, Ault, and Guess (1993).

Specific Characteristics of Environmental Variables

The general environmental variables of position, activity, materials, and social contact may interact alone or in some combination to affect behavior state. One strategy for affecting states, described above, is to identify environmental variables that appear associated with them. Another approach is to examine the relationship of states to specific characteristics of the environmental variables.

Research in the area of sensory perception has provided information on how and why the body responds to stimuli, and the types and amounts of stimuli necessary for responding (compare Brown & Deffenbacher, 1979). Although this research has been primarily conducted with animals or persons without disabilities, there is applicability to persons with profound disabilities. One theory (Gibson, 1966) presents perception as a process of differentiating stimuli and determining those that are important to the perceiver. Perceivers may, at first, play passive roles as stimulation is imposed on them, but as they become more active in the stimulation or simply begin to react to it (for example, chewing or avoidance), the stimulation becomes "obtained"; thus the process of differentiation begins. The body's receptors and proprioceptors, originally, have specific physiological responses to various types and amounts of stimuli. As they begin to receive more stimulation and process specific connotations of the stimulation, their role develops and changes.

Receptors will require different amounts of various stimuli before they respond or recognize that the stimulus exists. For example, in order to be heard, a soft-pitched whisper will need to be louder than a low-pitched whisper. In addition, different stimuli will have different effects on the alerting system of the body. Using these types of data, environmental stimuli can be grossly classified as having either an *activating* or *soothing* effect on the system.

The systematic identification of environmental stimuli that a student finds activating or soothing will assist teachers to change states within the context of regular activities. This process should not be confused with traditional "sensory" stimulation" techniques that were not used systematically, or evaluated extensively, in educational settings. Rather, they were delivered in a nonfunctional, passive, and trial-and-error manner.

The preferred student characteristics that are integrated into regular activities should serve to excite, calm, or maintain a specific state pattern. Consider, for example, an educational goal, for a student with high occurrences of drowse behavior, to grasp a cloth and wash the face. The teacher could apply a skin freshener to the student's face using a tolerable applicator (for example, hands, cotton ball) prior to presentation of the wash cloth. The skin freshener acts as both a tactile and olfactory activator that might increase the student's level of arousal and alertness. Other techniques for attaining this goal might include the type of soap, setting, lighting, surrounding activity, and water temperature. These additions to the face-washing activity are examples of *facilitative* techniques; that is, they act as intermediary agents between the students' state and the acquisition and retention of information. These techniques may assist in the facilitation of "traditional" educational goals or, in some cases, may themselves become initial educational objectives.

A primary purpose for using facilitative techniques is to help students become active participants in educational programs. While stimulation that is passive or imposed upon students might be of some benefit, it does not allow them an opportunity to interact with the stimuli or environment. Of greater benefit is stimulation in which students are active participants. For example, while a passive range of motion is better than no range of motion, it does not encourage a student to make his or her own movements. Stimulation requiring active participation has a better chance of affecting a student's awareness of the environment, and of resulting in learning. Any stimulation provided to students should address their primary sensory modality and serve to increase their overall level of tolerance. Facilitative techniques "should match the student's current level of functioning and slightly challenge the next" (Hagen, 1981, p. 75).

The properties of environmental variables can be classified in three broad categories: (a) external, (b) motor, and (c) environmental. External facilitative techniques include strategies aimed directly at the senses. Motor facilitative techniques include bodily movement and orientation (e.g., directional tilt and type of positioning equipment). Environmental facilitative techniques are similar to external techniques, but refer to those stimuli that do not directly impact the student. Social activity level, peer interactions, classroom temperature, and lighting are all examples of environmental techniques. The categories of facilitative strategies can be implemented simultaneously. The use of movement, for example, when applying an external stimuli technique is as essential as the room atmosphere and environment. For simplicity, however, the three categories are described separately.

Types of External Techniques and Their Characteristics   There are five primary types of external facilitative techniques: tactile, auditory, smell, taste, and visual. Each type interacts with the other strategies in discrete ways. For example, the sense of taste is linked closely to the sense of smell; the senses of touch, vision, and hearing are all instrumental in the identification of objects. Activating and soothing strategies, however, are based on several specific characteristics of each type of external technique.

Table 17.2 lists specific activating and soothing characteristics of each strategy and provides examples of how they can be adapted to be functional across students and situations. Tactile characteristics can be summarized as the properties of temperature, pressure, and vibration of stimuli on the skin. This information can be of considerable use when determining materials and activities. For example, while some students may not like to play in finger paint or pudding, they might explore in shaving cream, which applies less pressure on the skin, removes more easily, and has a slightly different temperature. Or a student might respond when placed near a heating lamp, but not to a heating pad or hot water bottle placed on a body part. Although the pad and hot water bottle provide heat, they also exert pressure on the skin, whereas the lamp just provides temperature. When brushing hair, the types of brush bristles, the pressure applied, and the speed in which the brushing is done all are variables that influence student tolerance.

Smell consists of numerous categories that are not easy to classify. Henning (as reported in Brown & Deffenbacher, 1979) has divided the various fragrances into six basic areas: foul (putrid), fruity (etheral), resinous, burned, spicy, and floral (fragrant). The difficulty in classifying scents is complicated by the fact that none of these categories is exclusive. In fact, each category is composed of a range of

Table 17.2 External Facilitative Techniques

| Strategy Type | ACTIVATING TECHNIQUES | | SOOTHING TECHNIQUES | |
	Characteristics of Stimuli	Examples of Stimuli	Characteristics of Stimuli	Examples of Stimuli
Tactile	light, quick touches hard surfaces cool temperatures rough textures	skin freshener sand cool water shaving cream remove items from refrigerator	deep, lingering touches soft textures warm temperatures	warm lotion stream of water a blow dryer with a diffuser during grooming sheepskin bean bag for positioning
Smell	foul burnt spicy resinous	pine-scented cleanser coffee lemon marigolds scented soap	floral fruity	perfume
Taste	salty bitter sour	lemon water carbonated beverages bright clothes	sweet	warm pudding Kool-Aid children's toothpaste
Visual	bright-reflective light	gold or silver jewelry bright makeup (red or hot pink) extra light shined into a mirror	dull (nonreflective) dark	light pink nail polish muted clothes
Auditory	loud sharp high pitch	high tone of instruction with quick delivery crashing of pots and pans a hand mixer fast streams of water	soft muted low pitch	low tone of instruction with slow delivery computer programs without high-pitched beeps

scents that overlap each other. For example, cinnamon is considered spicy, but orange blossoms could be fruity or floral. Camphor could be considered resinous or burned, while licorice could be burned or foul.

Exposure to smells should be short in duration, pleasant to the student, and incorporated within the normal day-to-day activities. Smells can be pungent without being noxious. For example, the smells of coffee or garlic are pungent but not necessarily aversive. The natural smells of pine, lemons, or marigolds also have a stimulating effect and are not usually aversive. The selection of a scented shampoo or soap in grooming is one method of including these scents within educational activities. Another method would to be to use lemon- or pine-based cleansers when the student is participating in housekeeping tasks.

There are four basic qualities of taste. Qualities of sweet, sour, salty, and bitter are much easier to classify than those of smell. It is possible that the palatability of the food item may be of more importance than the taste. The weight, texture, and consistency of items should follow the guidelines for tactile techniques. A soothing technique, for example, would incorporate food items that are warm, thick, and soft, such as fresh pudding.

Vision can contribute greatly to a student's distinction between self and environment and has important implications in the use of facilitative techniques. Brightness, lightness, color, and contrast are the basic properties of visual stimuli. Shiny and bright items are more activating than those that are dull or nonreflective, and can be included in students' educational routines. For example, when a student is participating in setting a table, bright shiny items such as silverware can be interspersed with the setting of less shiny items. The selection of a bright shirt that is smooth in texture for dressing, the use of a red toothbrush instead of a clear plastic one, or the application of makeup and bright earrings to an adolescent girl are all examples of activating visual techniques. Even the use of bright nail polish by the student or teacher is considered an activating technique. It is also possible to accent items through the addition of light. Extra light shined into a mirror during grooming attracts a student's attention to the reflection and is considered an activating visual technique. The light can be varied in brightness or removed after the attention is secured.

Auditory stimuli can be classified into the characteristics of frequency or pitch, intensity or loudness, tone, and tempo. Pitch refers to the frequency or level of a sound (for example, soprano or alto) and tone (or timbre) is the quality characteristic of the sound. The speed of a sound is described as its tempo, while the amplitude of the sound is its intensity.

Typically, music is the first technique applied in programming, but attention to sounds also includes the voice of the programmer and properties of the items used in programming. Students do not always respond to instructions and reinforcement given in the same pitch, tone, and loudness. In the same vein, when a constant barrage of talking occurs, students may tend to "tune out." Instructions may be activating when the tone of voice is slightly higher with more emphasis and when an increase in speed of the speech pattern occurs. This emphasis should be short in duration and varied with more normal and slightly reduced speech patterns.

Sounds can be functionally incorporated throughout the day by the careful selection of materials. For example, when a student is participating in food preparation, pulling the drawer with the pots and pans in it or removing or putting the lid on the pan will make a slight cymbal-like sound. If the student is unable to do the task, with or without assistance, schedule the task to be done by another student. Help the student run the hand mixer before reaching for and releasing an ingredient. When brushing teeth, run a heavy stream of water in the sink, rather than a slight trickle; instead of running the water continuously, turn it on and off in short bursts. Consider the student's auditory preferences when selecting materials such as computer programs.

Types of Motor Techniques and Their Characteristics   Traditionally, the word "motor" has referred to gross and fine motor skills. While these skills are important to development and independence, there are components of motor movements that also relate to state conditions. Motor techniques can be employed to affect alertness and arousal. For example, in a typical physical therapy program, rocking over a ball or on a barrel might be done to promote trunk control or protective reactions. Rocking can also be a facilitative technique and, when done in a functional manner, can be a means of increasing arousal.

Table 17.3 Motor Facilitative Techniques

Strategy Type	ACTIVATING TECHNIQUES		SOOTHING TECHNIQUES	
	Characteristics of Stimuli	**Examples of Stimuli**	**Characteristics of Stimuli**	**Examples of Stimuli**
Movement	quick, static tempo frequent physical changes	swing rocking chair vacuum adaptive devices approximations of skating or tumbling	slow rhythmic, continuous tempo up and down	brushing hair with slow side-to-side motion dress with rocking motion swing rocking chair
Orientation	upright position support for head and trunk		supine, prone, and sidelying position upright position with slight backward tilt	

Movement is often discussed in terms of proprioception, kinesthesia, and vestibular stimulation. Motor facilitative techniques are discussed in terms of movement and orientation. Crucial in the use of movement strategies are the concepts of speed (acceleration or deceleration) and directional tilt (up and down, side to side, circular). Slow rhythmic motion is soothing to students while rapid motion tends to be more of an activating technique. In addition, different directions of stimulation have different results. One direction that tends to be extremely activating is an upside-down position. This position has drawbacks in its obvious lack of functionality and the difficulty in which it is obtained. An alternative substitution would be an up-and-down movement in a prone position.

The best directional tilt for movement stimulation is dependent on student preferences and educational situations. Some students may find a rapid up-and-down motion more activating than a slow side-to-side motion. Others may find a rapid back-and-forth motion more activating than an up-and-down motion.

Table 17.3 presents examples of ways to include movement strategies within functional activities. Pushing a vacuum or bending over to pick things up utilizes the vestibular system as well as the tactile system, and provides an opportunity for movement in different directions (for example, back and forth, up and down). Slightly moving a student's head in a rhythmic manner while brushing hair is another example of a functional inclusion of movement strategies. It is also possible to manipulate the student's body in a slight rocking pattern during activities such as dressing, or when repositioning.

Orientation describes the position of the student and the equipment utilized for that position as well as the directional tilt of the student. Whether the student is ambulatory or nonambulatory, the position of the student for programming is of utmost importance in the consideration of state. For example, students who are insecure in their position will expend more energy maintaining the position than on the actual program. Other students may become agitated by an uncomfortable position. The student's tolerance of the position, location, and amount of support received are all important factors to consider. Even the angle of the position and the types of sitting devices become important factors in positioning techniques. A hard surface may be activating for a certain time but can create pressure that becomes uncomfortable. A supine position with slight elevation encourages visual pursuit of the environment for some students. An upright position with a backwards tilt becomes soothing for other students. Simply supporting the head or trunk may be all that is necessary to provide the student with a sense of security and assistance to maintain a position.

Types of Environmental Techniques and Their Characteristics Environmental techniques are the physical and social elements that surround the student. The temperature of the room, the surrounding sounds, and the location of the students are all examples of environmental stimuli. Environmental techniques should not be confused with external techniques. External techniques specifically affect the outside of the body, while environmental stimuli encompass the overall effect of the external stimuli. For example, the type of lighting used in the room is an environmental stimulus, but light shined into a mirror in front of the student is an external stimulus. The temperature of the room is an example of an environmental stimulus and the temperature of an item is an example of an external stimulus.

The change of social environments has been suggested as one of the best methods of stimulation for persons with head trauma (Will, 1977) and also significantly affects the performance of persons with profound disabilities (Sailor et al., 1988). Social environmental techniques reflect the personal society of the students involved and are addressed in the social atmosphere of the setting. Social atmosphere is subtly different from the physical attributes of the setting. For example, a room in the library may have the same physical attributes as a shopping mall—furniture, lighting, and space—yet the social atmosphere is much different. A party at school may have some of the same characteristics as the county fair, but the social ambiance is different. The more socially normal an environment, the more likely the student is to respond.

People, objects, and events all contribute to social atmosphere. What are the opportunities that a student has to interact with peers with or without handicaps? Are there too many interaction opportunities for the student to feel at ease with the environment? These are the types of questions that should be asked when selecting social facilitative techniques.

Activities and items that have an effect on students' states should be chosen with the guidelines presented in the section above on activating techniques that use external stimuli (Table 17.2). Noisier, faster-paced environments are more activating than quiet, slow ones. While it is important that activities be visually and auditorially active, too much activity in an environment can overstimulate students. A simple change of physical location within a classroom may not be enough to activate state. For example, a student that is moved from a side-lyer with a mobile suspended above it to a standing table with blocks on the tray is still within the same social atmosphere of a classroom. Moving that same student into a small group for instruction can often be more activating than one-to-one instruction. Drastic contrasts in social atmosphere can be soothing for some students, dependent upon the types of physical conditions in each environment. A student in the crying/agitated state may be affected by a quiet environment while others in the same state may prefer a more active social environment.

The community provides many opportunities for applying social techniques. In a community-based job site, students with profound disabilities may not be able to complete a task. Yet the change in social environments provides students with many opportunities for increasing arousal and awareness of their surroundings.

Familiar materials and routines help students monitor their own state. For example, if a certain task is done on a consistent basis immediately prior to lunch, students may maintain an alert state in anticipation of the upcoming meal. This does not mean that materials and routines should be exactly the same from day to day. Variety is necessary, but a scheduled variety is best. For example, it is possible to have leisure time scheduled at the same time every day. Different locations, materials, and activities for leisure time add the variety. In fact, they become the soothing or activating techniques and should be selected based on the guidelines presented previously for external stimuli (Table 17.2).

The combination of physical properties that constitute the environment's physical atmosphere is similar to some types of external techniques, such as temperature and lighting. A room that is cool will have a calming effect on some students but may inhibit others. Bright lights and wide spaces may activate some students, while others may be overwhelmed. Some students may be discouraged by a dark, smelly corner but others might not be affected. Facing a student toward a window may be activating, while turning him or her toward a portion of the class may be soothing.

Differences between student needs makes it difficult to control the atmosphere of an environment for all the students. Too much of one atmospheric type will be overstimulating for one student and not stimulating enough for another. Attention to the types of atmospheric components that affect students, however, will encourage modification of environments appropriate to individual needs.

Identifying Preferred Environmental Characteristics   Once the need for decreasing or increasing state conditions has been targeted and related environmental variables have been identified, specific activating and soothing characteristics can be determined. The checklist in Figure 17.8 has been used (Guy, Ault, & Guess, 1993) as a systematic method for helping identify students' preferred characteristics. This checklist is completed for each targeted state. The observation should last for one minute and occur within the student's daily routine. For example, if the teacher and student are involved in a domestic activity and the teacher notes that the student is in a targeted state of drowse, the teacher should continue to observe the student for one minute and then complete a checklist. It is recommended that a minimum of three observations be completed for each targeted behavior.

Medication

The physical and medical characteristics of students with profound disabilities often require at least one type of medication. The therapeutic effects of these medications are often valuable, if not essential, to their lives. Medication, however, may have other less desirable effects on the behavior of these students, including the

Targeted behavior state observed _____ Student _____

External

      Tactile ❏ N/A

PRESSURE ❏ N/A	SPEED ❏ N/A	TEMPERATURE ❏ N/A		TEXTURE ❏ N/A	
❏ Light	❏ Short/Staccato	❏ Cold	❏ Neutral	❏ Soft	❏ Smooth/Slick
❏ Deep	❏ Slow/Lingering	❏ Warm	❏ Hot	❏ Rough	❏ Hard

      Smell ❏ N/A   **Taste** ❏ N/A

Fruity   Resinous

Foul ◄– – – – – – – Burnt – –◄   Salty   Spicy   Sour   Sweet

Floral   Spicy

      Auditory ❏ N/A

PITCH ❏ N/A	INTENSITY ❏ N/A	TIMBRE ❏ N/A	TEMPO ❏ N/A		SOURCE ❏ N/A	
❏ High	❏ Loud	❏ Sharp	❏ Fast	❏ Continuous	❏ Voice	❏ Other
❏ Low	❏ Soft	❏ Muted	❏ Slow	❏ Intermittent	❏ Mechanical device	

      Visual ❏ N/A

BRIGHTNESS ❏ N/A	SECONDARY LIGHT ❏ N/A		COLOR ❏ N/A			CONTRAST ❏ N/A
❏ Shiny	❏ Direct	❏ High	❏ Light	❏ Red	❏ Green	❏ High
❏ Dull	❏ Indirect	❏ Medium	❏ Neutral	❏ Blue	❏ Yellow	❏ Low
		❏ Low	❏ Dark	❏ Purple	❏ Orange	

Motor

      Movement ❏ N/A

TEMPO ❏ N/A		DIRECTION ❏ N/A		BODY COMPONENT ❏N/A		TONE ❏ N/A
❏ Slow	❏ Intermittent	❏ Up and down	❏ Back and forth	❏ Full body	❏ Head	❏ High
❏ Fast	❏ Continuous	❏ Side to side	❏ Circular	❏ Trunk	❏ Upper limbs	❏ Normal
					❏ Lower limbs	❏ Low

      Orientation ❏ N/A

POSITION ❏ N/A		TILT ❏ N/A	EQUIPMENT ❏ N/A	
❏ Sitting	❏ Standing	❏ Upright	❏ Wheelchair	❏ Corner chair
❏ Sidelying	❏ Prone	❏ Backward	❏ Tumbleform	❏ Kneeler
	❏ Supine	❏ Forward	❏ Prone stander	❏ Other person
			❏ Bean bag	❏ Other

Learning Atmosphere

      Physical atmosphere ❏ N/A

TEMPERATURE ❏ N/A		LIGHTING ❏ N/A	AROMA ❏ N/A		NOISE ❏ N/A	LOCATION CHANGE ❏ N/A	
❏ Cold	❏ Neutral	❏ Bright	❏ Foul	❏ Burnt	❏ High	❏ Primary	❏ Across room
❏ Warm	❏ Hot	❏ Normal	❏ Spicy	❏ Resinous	❏ Medium	❏ Secondary	❏ 5 ft
		❏ Dim	❏ Floral	❏ Fruity	❏ Low	❏ Community	❏ 10 ft
						❏ Outside	

      Social atmosphere ❏ N/A

PEOPLE IN ENVIRONMENT ❏ N/A (record number)	DIRECT INTERACTIONS ❏ N/A	ACTIVITY LEVEL ❏ N/A
_____ Peers	❏ Peers	❏ Fast
_____ Nonhandicapped peers	❏ Nonhandicapped peers	❏ Neutral
_____ Staff	❏ Staff	❏ Slow

FIGURE 17.8 Sample form used for collecting environmental characteristic data

SOURCE: From Guy, Ault, and Guess (1993), pp. 71–72.

General Questions

1. What state predominated throughout this observation? _____

2. Did the student remain in a particular state for relatively long periods of time (*stable*) or were there state *changes*? (Circle response) Describe the nature of the changes.

   Stable   Changes

   _____

3. List all other states that occurred during the observation. _____

   _____

4. Did any of the characteristics on this checklist change during the observation? **Y   N**

   Describe each change: _____

   _____

   Did behavior state change after/in conjunction with the environmental change? **Y   N**

   (If more than one state change, identify and list separately.)

   Initial State: _____   Subsequent State: _____

5. What was the student's position during the observation? _____

   Approximately how long was the student in this position *prior* to observation?

   _____

   Did a position change occur during the observation? **Y   N**

   Did a behavior state change after/in conjunction with the position change? **Y   N**

   Initial State: _____   Subsequent State: _____

6. Were materials available to the student? **Y   N**

   Describe material and use (see External characteristics):

			MANIPULATION OF MATERIAL					
			STUDENT			ADULT		
Material	Type of Modality(ies)	#	NA	Active	Passive	NA	Active	Passive

occurrence of nonpreferred states in education settings. Careful monitoring of medication effects by families and teachers is necessary.

Influences of medication are complicated, and extend well beyond the school day. Teachers have neither the authority to make medication decisions nor the opportunity to see that recommended changes for students are followed on a 24-hour basis. It is important, therefore, that families and educational staff work together to identify potential problems and solutions. Together they can be active participants to identify complications, including inconsistencies in administration and undesirable side effects.

Administration Analysis   There are a variety of reasons that dosage levels or administration schedules of medications prescribed for students are not properly followed. Choking, drooling, vomiting, or incomplete consumption of medications mixed with food are among the student characteristics that might result in inaccurate medication administration. If dosages are not administered as prescribed, the intended therapeutic effect of the medication might not be achieved. Depending on the medication, this might increase seizures, hyperactivity, constipation, or other unwanted behaviors.

Scheduling difficulties caused by sleep patterns, availability of the student or caregiver, and/or a misunderstanding of the directions may result in inconsistent patterns of administration. Some schedules may "clump" several administration times closely together and thus leave greater time periods between others. This might produce side effects and interaction effects between the medications. Another error occurs when double dosages are administered to "catch up" on a schedule. This might produce dosages that are too strong, increasing the likelihood of side effects such as sedation, lethargy, irritability, and gastrointestinal distress.

Instructional personnel and families can identify possible administration inaccuracies by compiling several pieces of information. Guy, Ault, and Guess (1993) present the form in Figure 17.9 to assist in the process. First, it is necessary to identify all the maintenance or episodic medications prescribed for the student. Maintenance medication is received for an extended time to address a chronic condition, such as seizures or diabetes. Episodic medication is received for treatment of a short-term or acute condition, such as an infection, cold, or allergy. Information including the prescribed dosage, the amount, and time actually received are also important in determining accuracy of administration.

Side and Interaction Effects of Medication   Students with profound disabilities often receive medications prescribed by several health care providers while taking over-the-counter medications. These medications may react singularly or together to produce behavioral effects. Common side effects include gastrointestinal distress, drowsiness, dry mouth, constipation, fluid retention, lethargy, and an increase in seizures—all of which can influence state behavior. Table 17.4 lists common names of medications received by students with profound disabilities. The table also presents the chemical name, drug category, classification, and potential side effects that impact behavior and nutritional status. Additional information in Table 17.5 describes undesirable interaction effects of multiple medications.

Name _____ Age _____

Completed by _____ Date _____

Referral (Yes or No) _____ Date of Referral _____

Administrative Analysis

Medication	M/E* Indicated Dosage	Time to Be Administered	Full Dosage Received at Time Prescribed?	Potential Side Effects with Full Dosage
_____	M/E _____	_____	Y N	_____
		_____	Y N	_____
		_____	Y N	_____
		_____	Y N	_____
_____	M/E _____	_____	Y N	_____
		_____	Y N	_____
		_____	Y N	_____
		_____	Y N	_____
_____	M/E _____	_____	Y N	_____
		_____	Y N	_____
		_____	Y N	_____
		_____	Y N	_____
_____	M/E _____	_____	Y N	_____
		_____	Y N	_____
		_____	Y N	_____
		_____	Y N	_____
_____	M/E _____	_____	Y N	_____
		_____	Y N	_____
		_____	Y N	_____
		_____	Y N	_____
_____	M/E _____	_____	Y N	_____
		_____	Y N	_____
		_____	Y N	_____
		_____	Y N	_____

*Maintainance or Episodic

FIGURE 17.9 Sample form used for collecting medication information

SOURCE: From Guy, Ault, and Guess (1993), p. 27.

Table 17.4 Common Medications and Potential Side Effects

Please note: The listing of potential side effects is not comprehensive, only those side effects which were observable and might impact nutrition or behavior were selected. A devasting side effect of Depakane, for example, is liver damage. While this side effect would eventually affect behavior, it was not listed as a side effect because the actual symptoms would not manifest themselves until the liver damage was in an advanced stage.

Brand name • Chemical name
• *Category**
(Classification)

Medications	Potential Side Effects**
Aldactone • Spironolactone • *Diuretic* (Cardiovascular medication)	[M]confusion, irregular heartbeat, nervousness, numbness or tingling in hands, feet, or lips, unusual tiredness or weakness; [R]shortness of breath, skin rash or itching
Alkets • Magnesium Oxide • *Antacid* (Gastric medication)	[M]diarrhea or laxative effect; [R]mild constipation, stomach cramps, nausea, vomiting
Alupent • Metaproterenol • *Antiasthma/Bronchodilator* (Repiratory tract medication)	chest discomfort or pain, dizziness or lightheadedness, fast heartbeat, headache, nausea, vomiting, unusual anxiety, nervousness, restlessness, severe weakness
Amoxil • Amoxicillin • *Antibacterial* (Antimicrobial)	[M]abdominal or stomach cramps, severe watery diarrhea, fever, increased thirst, increased weight loss, nausea, vomiting, unusual tiredness or weakness
Aquasol A • Vitamin A • *Vitamin A* (Vitamin)	see Vitamin A
Aspirin • Salicylate • *Analgesic* (Central nervous system medication)	[M]nausea, vomiting, stomach pain; [L/R]vomiting of blood, fever, increased thirst, increased weight loss, nausea, vomiting, skin rash, hives, or itching, unusual tiredness or weakness, wheezing
Augmentin • Amoxicillin • *Antibacterial* (Antimicrobial)	[M]abdominal or stomach cramps, watery and severe diarrhea, fever, increased thirst, increased weight loss, nausea, vomiting, unusual tiredness or weakness, skin rash, hives or itching, wheezing
Bactrim • Sulfonamide • *Antibacterial* (Antimicrobial)	[M]itching, skin rash; [L]aching of joints and muscles, difficulty in swallowing, fever, sore throat, redness, blistering, peeling, or loosening of skin, unusual tiredness or weakness; [R]blood in urine, lower back pain, pain or burning while urinating, swelling of front part of neck
Beclovent • Adrenocorticoid • *Antiasthmatic* (Respiratory tract medication)	[M]creamy-white, curdlike patches inside mouth (oral candidiasis); [R]difficulty in swallowing (monilial esophagitis), skin rash, shortness of breath (bronchospasm); [U]acne or other skin problems, back or rib pain, chills, cough, ear congestion or pain, fever, head congestion, nasal congestion, runny nose, sneezing, sore throat, decreased or blurred vision, eye pain, redness or tearing, frequent urination or increased thirst, hives, itching of skin, unusual weight gain (edema), increased susceptibility to infections, unusual tiredness or weakness, muscle weakness, nausea or vomiting, stomach pain or burning
Beconase • Adrenocorticoid • *Anti-inflammatory* (Respiratory tract medication)	[M]unusual increase in sneezing, burning, dryness or other irritation inside the nose; [L]bloody mucus or unexplained nosebleeds, crusting inside nose, sore throat; [R]shortness of breath, troubled breathing in chest, wheezing, skin rash or hives, swelling on face
Benadryl • Diphenhydramine • *Antitussive* (Respiratory tract medication)	[U/R]sore throat, fever, unusual tiredness or weakness

*The term "Category" describes therapuetic effects relevant to students with severe or profound disabilities.

Differences in frequency of occurrence of side effects are indicated by a letter preceding the correspondent symptom(s) or sign(s). **M = more frequent; **L** = less frequent; **R** = rare; **U** = unknown. If no symbol is present, no frequency estimate was stated (USP DI, 1993).

Table 17.4 Continued

Medications	Potential Side Effects**
Bio-Cal • Calcium Carbonate • *Nutritional supplement/Antacid* (Therapeutic nutrient/gastric medication)	^{M}dizziness, nausea or vomiting; ^{R}drowsiness, weakness, difficult or painful urination
Calciferol • Ergocalciferol • *Vitamin D* (Vitamin)	see Vitamin D
Ceclor • Cefaclor • *Cefalosporin* (Antimicrobial)	$^{L/R}$unusual bleeding or bruising, severe abdominal or stomach cramps and pain, abdominal tenderness, watery and severe diarrhea, fever; ^{R}allergic reactions, skin rash, joint pain, seizures
Cevalin • Ascorbic acid • *Vitamin C* (Vitamin)	see Vitamin C
Chronulac • Lactulose • *Laxative* (Gastric medication)	^{R}confusion, irregular heartbeat, muscle cramps, unusual tiredness or weakness, dizziness or lightheadedness
Colace • Docusate • *Laxative* (Gastric medication)	^{R}asthma, skin rash or itching, esophageal blockage, intestinal impaction, confusion, irregular heartbeat, muscle cramps, unusual tiredness or weakness
Cortisporin Ophthalmic • Hydrocortisone • *Anti-infective/Anti-inflammatory* (Ophthalmic agent)	no relevant observable side effect
Dantrium • Dantrolene • *Skeletal muscle relaxant* (Musculoskeletal medication)	^{L}severe diarrhea, confusion, severe constipation, convulsions, allergic dermatitis, difficult urination, mental depression
DDAVP • Desmopressin • *Antidiuretic/Antihemorrhagic* (Cardiovascular medication)	^{R}(dose-related) confusion, drowsiness, continuing headache, problems with urination, seizures, weight gain (water retention); $^{L/R}$(dose-related) abdominal or stomach cramps, flushing or redness of skin, pain in the vulva, runny or stuffy nose; pain, redness or swelling at site of injection
Depakene • Valporic Acid • *Anticonvulsant* (Central nervous system medication)	nausea, vomiting, cramping, swelling of face, tiredness, weakness, lack of coordination, easily bruised, gastroenteritis, ataxia, tremor, confusion, apathy, nystagmus
Dexedrine • Dextroamphetamine • *CNS stimulant* (Central nervous system medication)	decreased growth, nausea, dizziness, drowsiness
Diamox • Acetazolamide • *Anticonvulsant* (Central nervous system medication)	thirst, anorexia, increased urine output, drowsiness, abdominal cramping
Digoxin • Digitalis • *Antiarrhythmic* (Cardiovascular medication)	nausea, vomiting, irregular heartbeat, loss of appetite, abdominal pain, diarrhea, weakness, headache
Dilantin • Phenytoin • *Anticonvulsant* (Central nervous system medication)	gingival hyperplasia, uncontrolled movements, confusion, dizziness, ataxia, drowsiness, constipation, anorexia, nausea, vomiting
Diocto • Docusate Sodium • *Stool softener* (Gastric medication)	^{U}allergic reactions, esophageal blockage or intestinal impaction
Dulcolax • Bisacodyl • *Laxative* (Gastric medication)	no relevant observable side effect

*The term "Category" describes therapeutic effects relevant to students with severe or profound disabilities.

Differences in frequency of occurrence of side effects are indicated by a letter preceding the correspondent symptom(s) or sign(s). **M = more frequent; **L** = less frequent; **R** = rare; **U** = unkown. If no symbol is present, no frequency estimate was stated (USP DI, 1993).

Table 17.4 Continued

Medications	Potential Side Effects**
Ex-Lax • Phenolphthalein • *Laxative* (Gastric medication)	abdominal cramping
Feosol • Ferrous Sulfate • *Iron supplement* (Therapuetic nutrient)	[M]abdominal or stomach pain, cramping or soreness, allergic reaction, backache or muscle pain, chills, dizziness, fever with increased sweating, headache, nausea or vomiting
Garamycin • Gentamicin • *Antibacterial* (Antimicrobial)	[M]increased thirst, loss of appetite, nausea, vomiting, muscle twitching, numbness, seizures, tingling; any loss of hearing, ringing or buzzing, or a feeling of fullness in the ears, clumsiness, dizziness, unsteadiness; [L]skin itching, redness, rash, or swelling; [R]difficulty in breathing, drowsiness, weakness
Glyrol • Glycerin • *Diuretic* (Cardiovascular medication)	no relevant observable side effect
Intal • Cromolyn • *Antiasthma/ Antiallergic* (Respiratory tract medication)	dizziness, severe or continuing headache, joint pain or swelling, muscle pain or weakness, nausea or vomiting, skin rash, hives or itching
Klonopin • Clonazepam • *Anticonvulsant* (Central nervous system medication)	no relevant observable side effect
Lasix • Furosemide • *Diuretic* (Cardiovascular medication)	[L]unusual tiredness or weakness, nausea or vomiting, muscle cramps or pain, mood or mental changes, irregular heartbeat, increased thirst, dryness of mouth
Levoxine • Levothyroxine • *Thyroid modifier* (Hormone)	[R]severe headache, skin rash or hives
Lioresal • Baclofen • *Antispastic* (Musculoskeletal medication)	[M]drowsiness, dizziness or lightheadedness, weakness, confusion, nausea; [L/R]bloody or dark urine, chest pain, CNS toxicity (visual or auditory hallucinations, mental depression or other mood changes, ringing or buzzing in ears), allergic dermatitis (skin rash or itching), syncope (fainting), constipation, difficult or painful urination, fluid retention, frequent urge to urinate, gastrointestinal irritation, loss of appetite, stuffy nose
Maalox • Aluminum & Magnesium • *Antacid* (Gastric medication)	[M]mood or mental changes, swelling of wrist or ankles, constipation, unusual loss of weight, unusual tiredness or weakness
Mebaral • Mephobarbital • *Anticonvulsant* (Central nervous system medication)	[L]confusion, mental depression, excitement; [R]bleeding sores on lips, sore throat, fever, tiredness
Mellaril • Thioridazine • *Sedative/Hypnotic-antipsychotic* (Central nervous system medication/ autonomic medication)	[M]blurred vision; [L]chewing movements, lip smacking or puckering, puffing of cheeks, rapid or wormlike movements of tongue, uncontrolled movements of arms and legs, difficult urination; [R]difficulty breathing, fast heartbeat, fever, increased sweating, loss of bladder control, muscle stiffness, seizures, unusual tiredness or weakness, unusually pale skin
Metaprel • Metaproterenol • *Antiasthma/Bronchodilator* (Respiratory tract medication)	[M]severe chest discomfort or pain, dizziness or lightheadedness, fast heartbeat, headache, severe nausea or vomiting, severe trembling, unusual anxiety, nervousness or restlessness, blurred vision, unusual paleness and coldness of skin, weakness
Meticorten • Prednisone • *Glucocorticoid* (Anti-inflammatory/ immunosuppressant)	[L]decreased or blurred vision, decreased growth, frequent urination, increased thirst; [R]hallucinations, skin rash or hives, burning or pain at place of injection, mental depression or other mood or mental changes

*The term "Category" describes therapuetic effects relevant to students with severe or profound disabilities.

Differences in frequency of occurrence of side effects are indicated by a letter preceding the correspondent symptom(s) or sign(s). **M = more frequent; **L** = less frequent; **R** = rare; **U** = unkown. If no symbol is present, no frequency estimate was stated (USP DI, 1993).

Table 17.4 Continued

Medications	Potential Side Effects**
Minipress • Prazosin • *Antihypertensive* (Cardiovascular medication)	ᴸchest pain, dizziness, fainting, shortness of breath, weight gain (water retention), swelling of feet or lower legs; ᴿinability to control urination, numbness or tingling of hands or feet
Mylicon • Simethicone • *Antiflatulent* (Gastric medication)	no relevant observable side effect
Mysoline • Primodone • *Anticonvulsant* (Central nervous system medication)	ᴸunusual excitement or restlessness; ᴿhives, skin rash, swelling of eyelids, wheezing or tightness in chest, unusual tiredness or weakness
Narcan • Naloxone • *Analgesic/ Opioid antagonist* (Central nervous system medication)	increased sweating, nausea or vomiting, nervousness, restlessness, excitement or irritability, trembling
Neosporin Ophthalmic • Neomycin • *Antibacterial* (Ophthalmic agent)	ᴹitching, rash, redness, swelling or other sign of irritation not present before therapy; ᴸburning or stinging
Opticrom • Cromolyn • *Antiallergic* (Ophthalmic agent)	ᴿeye irritation not present before therapy including styes, severe swelling of conjunctiva
Pediazole • Erythromycin and sulfisoxasole • *Antibacterial* (Antimicrobial)	ᴸskin rash, redness, itching, stomach ache, unusual tiredness or weakness; ᴿrecurrent fainting, increased thirst, loss of appetite, nausea, vomiting, difficult breathing, sore throat and fever, unusual bleeding or bruising
Pepcid • Famotidine • *Antiulcer agent* (Gastric medication)	ᴿfast pounding heartbeat, fever, swelling of eyelids, tightness in chest, unusual bleeding or bruising, unusual severe tiredness or weakness
Peri-Colace • Casanthranol • *Laxative* (Gastric medication)	ᴿasthma, skin rash, itching, esophageal blockage, intestinal impaction
Phenobarbital • Barbiturate • *Anticonvulsant* (Central nervous system medication)	ᴸconfusion, unusual excitement; ᴿweight loss, bleeding sores on lips, chest pain, skin rash, sore throat, fever
(Phillips') Milk of Magnesia • Magnesium hydroxide • *Antacid* (Gastric medication)	ᴿmild constipation, increased thirst, dizziness or lightheadedness, unusual tiredness or weakness; ᴹdiarrhea (with overdose); ᴸnausea or vomiting, stomach cramps
Poly-Vi-Flor • Multiple vitamins and fluoride • *Multivitamin combination* (Vitamin)	ᴿskin rash, sores in the mouth and on the lips, constipation, loss of appetite, nausea or vomiting, pain and aching bones
Prednisone • Prednisone • *Glucocorticoid* (Anti-inflammatory/ Immunosuppressant)	ᴸdecreased or blurred vision, decreased growth, frequent urination, increased thirst; ᴿhallucinations, skin rash or hives, burning or pain at site of injection, mental depression or other mood or mental changes
Proventil • Albuterol • *Adrenergic bronchodilator* (Respiratory tract medication)	ᴹfast heartbeat; ᴸcoughing or other bronchial irritation, difficult or painful urination, dizziness or lightheadedness, drowsiness, dryness or irritation of mouth or throat, headache; ᴿchest discomfort or pain, increase in wheezing or difficulty in breathing; ᵁhallucinations, irregular heartbeat, mood or mental changes, flushing or redness of face or skin, nausea or vomiting, severe trembling, unusual anxiety, nervousness, or restlessness
Reglan • Metoclopramide • *Antiemetic* (Gastric medication)	ᴿ(signs of overdose) confusion; drowsiness; muscle spasms especially of jaw, neck, and back; shuffling walk, ticlike movements of the face and head, trembling or shaking of hands

*The term "Category" describes therapeutic effects relevant to students with severe or profound disabilities.

Differences in frequency of occurrence of side effects are indicated by a letter preceding the correspondent symptom(s) or sign(s). **M = more frequent; **L** = less frequent; **R** = rare; **U** = unknown. If no symbol is present, no frequency estimate was stated (USP DI, 1993).

Table 17.4 Continued

Medications	Potential Side Effects**
Riopan Plus • Simethicone and magaldrate • *Antacid* (Gastric medication)	^{M}loss of appetite, muscle weakness, unusual loss of weight, continuous feeling of discomfort, diarrhea or laxative effect; ^{L}stomach cramps, vomiting, nausea
Ritalin • Methylphenidate • *Central nervous system stimulant* (Central nervous system medication)	^{M}fast heartbeat; ^{L}chest pain, uncontrolled movements of the body, bruising, fever, joint pain, skin rash or hives; ^{R}blurred vision, convulsions, sore throat, fever, unusual tiredness or weakness
Rondec-DM • Pseudoephedrine • *Antihistaminic/Decongestant* (Respiratory tract medication)	^{U}psychotic episodes, tightness in chest
Septra • Trimethoprim and sulfamethoxazole • *Antibacterial* (Antimicrobial)	^{M}fever, itching, skin rash (hypersensitivity); ^{L}blood dyscrasias (fever and sore throat, pale skin, unusual bleeding or bruising, unusual tiredness or weakness), difficulty in swallowing; redness, blistering, peeling, or loosening of skin; ^{R}lower back pain, pain or burning while urinating, difficulty breathing
Slo-Bid • Theophylline • *Bronchodilator* (Respiratory tract medication)	^{L}heartburn, vomiting; ^{R}skin rash or hives, chest pain, dizziness, fast breathing, flushing, headache, pounding heartbeat, chill, fever, pain or swelling at site of injection; ^{R}severe headache, skin rash or hives
Suprax • Cefixime • *Antibacterial* (Antimicrobial)	$^{L/R}$unusual bleeding or bruising, severe abdominal or stomach cramps and pain, watery and severe diarrhea, fever; ^{R}allergic reactions, skin rash, itching, redness or swelling, seizures (with high doses)
Synthroid • Levothyroxine • *Thyroid modifier* (Hormone)	^{R}severe headache, skin rash or hives
Tagamet • Cimetidine • *Antacid* (Gastric medication)	^{R}sore throat, fever, unusual bleeding or bruising, unusual tiredness or weakness
Tavist • Clemastine • *Antihistaminic* (Antihistamine)	drowsiness, thickening of mucus; $^{L/R}$blurred vision, confusion, difficult or painful urination, dizziness, dryness of mouth, sore throat and fever, unusual tiredness or weakness, unusual bleeding or bruising, increased appetite or weight gain, loss of appetite, ringing or buzzing in ears, stomach upset or pain
Tegretol • Carbamazepine • *Anticonvulsant* (Central nervous system medication)	^{M}blurred vision or double vision, confusion, agitation, headache, increase in seizure frequency, nausea, vomiting, unusual drowsiness or weakness; ^{L}behavioral changes, hives, itching or skin rash; ^{R}chest pain, fainting, troubled breathing, continuous back-and-forth eye movements, trembling, uncontrolled body movements, visual hallucinations
Tetracyn • Tetracycline • *Antibiotic* (Antimicrobial)	^{M}cramps or burning of the stomach, diarrhea, sore mouth or tongue, itching of rectal or genital areas, nausea, vomiting
Theo-Dur • Theophylline • *Antiasthma/Bronchodilator* (Respiratory tract medication)	^{L}heartburn, vomiting; ^{R}skin rash or hives
Tranxene • Clorazepate • *Benzodiazepine* (Sedative/Hypnotic-anticonvulsant)	^{L}confusion, mental depression; ^{R}trouble sleeping, unusual excitement, nervousness or irritabilty, skin rash, itching
Tylenol • Acetaminophen • *Analgesic/Antipyretic* (Central nervous system medication)	^{R}difficult or painful urination, sudden increase in amount of urine, skin rash, hives or itching, unexplained sore throat and fever, unusual tiredness or weakness

*The term "Category" describes therapuetic effects relevant to students with severe or profound disabilities.

Differences in frequency of occurrence of side effects are indicated by a letter preceding the correspondent symptom(s) or sign(s). **M = more frequent; **L** = less frequent; **R** = rare; **U** = unknown. If no symbol is present, no frequency estimate was stated (USP DI, 1993).

Table 17.4 Continued

Medications	Potential Side Effects**
Valium • Diazepam • *Benzodiazepine* (Sedative/Hypnotic)	Lconfusion, mental depression, blurred vision, constipation, dizziness or lightheadedness, dryness of the mouth or increase in thirst, headache, increased bronchial secretions or watering of the mouth, nausea or vomiting, problems with urination, slurred speech
Vanceril • Beclomethasone • *Antiasthma/Bronchodilator* (Respiratory tract medication)	Mcreamy-white, curdlike patches inside mouth, cough without symptoms of infection; L/Rdry or irritated nose, mouth, tongue or throat, difficulty in swallowing, skin rash, shortness of breath, troubled breathing, tightness in chest, nausea or vomiting, back or rib pain, stomach pain or burning, muscle cramps or pain, unusual tiredness or weakness, mental depression, mood or mental changes, muscle weakness, upper respiratory tract infection (influenza, common cold, and/or sinusitis), wounds that will not heal, decreased appetite, dizziness or lightheadedness, headache
Ventolin • Albuterol • *Adrenergic bronchodilator/Antiasthma* (Respiratory tract medication)	Mfast heartbeat; Lcoughing or other bronchial irritation, difficult or painful urination, dizziness or lightheadedness, drowsiness, dryness or irritation of mouth or throat, headache; Rchest discomfort or pain, increase in wheezing or difficulty in breathing; Uirregular heartbeat, mood or mental changes, hallucinations, nausea or vomiting, unusual anxiety, nervousness, restlessness
Vitamin A (Vitamin)	acute overdose signs: bleeding from gums or sore mouth, confusion or unusual excitement, diarrhea, dizziness or drowsiness, double vision, severe headache, severe irritability, peeling of skin (especially lips and palms), seizures, severe vomiting
Vitamin B$_1$ • Thiamin • *Vitamin B* (Vitamin)	Rskin rash or itching, wheezing
Vitamin B$_6$ • Pyridoxine • *Vitamin B* (Vitamin)	no relevant observable side effect
Vitamin B$_9$ • Folic Acid • *Vitamin B* (Vitamin)	no relevant observable side effect
Vitamin C (Vitamin)	prolonged use of high doses of ascorbic acid may result in urinary tract stone formation and thus, side or lower back pain
Vitamin D (Vitamin)	no relevant observable side effect
Zantac • Rantidine • *Antiulcer agent* (Gastric medication)	Rfever, sore throat, unusual tiredness or weakness, tightness in chest, confusion; Ubreast soreness, blurred vision, joint or muscle pain
Zarontin • Ethosuximide • *Anticonvulsant* (Central nervous system medication)	Mheadache, hiccups, loss of appetite, nausea and vomiting, stomach cramps; Ldizziness, drowsiness, irritability, tiredness

*The term "Category" describes therapeutic effects relevant to students with severe or profound disabilities.

Differences in frequency of occurrence of side effects are indicated by a letter preceding the correspondent symptom(s) or sign(s). **M = more frequent; **L** = less frequent; **R** = rare; **U** = unkown. If no symbol is present, no frequency estimate was stated (USP DI, 1993).

SOURCE: From Guy, Ault, and Guess (1993), pp. 17–24.

Nutrition

Students who receive inadequate nutrition or whose bodies do not appropriately utilize nutrients may be physiologically compromised. This may reduce their alertness and interactions with persons and materials. Lethargy, decreased stamina, and poor attention span are several outcomes of poor nutrition. Severe nutritional

Table 17.5 Potential Interaction Effects of Medication Combinations

Medications	Potential Interaction Effects
Depakene and Phenobarbital	Increased CNS depression caused by increased blood concentration of Phenobarbital, decreased effect of Depakene with possible increase in seizure frequency
Dilantin and aluminum magnesium	Reduced seizure-depressing effect of Dilantin resulting in possible increase in frequency of seizures
Dilantin and antidepressants	Reduced seizure threshold, i.e., possible increase in seizure frequency
Dilantin and Bactrim	Increased depressive result of Dilantin; increase in dizziness
Dilantin and calcium	Decreased seizure-depressing effect of Dilantin by 20%
Dilantin and calcium carbonate	Reduced seizure-depressing effect of Dilantin, i.e., possible increase in seizure frequency
Dilantin and Depakene	Decreased effect of Dilantin, i.e., possible increase in seizure frequency
Dilantin and enteral; nutritional formulas	When combined with gastric feeding solutions may form non-soluble complex with Dilantin, which reduces the seizure-depressing effect of Dilantin, i.e., possible increase in seizure frequency
Dilantin and folic acid	Decreased seizure-depressing effect of Dilantin, i.e., possible increase in seizure frequency
Dilantin and Phenobarbital	Variable and unpredictable effect of both
Dilantin and Vitamin D	Decreased effect of Vitamin D or inhibition of the contribution of the vitamin to bone development, which may result in fragile bones
Librium/Valium and antacids	Delayed absorption and therapeutic effect of Librium or Valium
Phenobarbital and antidepressants	Decreased therapeutic effect of antidepressant
Phenobarbital and Haloperidol	May cause a change in the pattern and/or frequency of seizures
Phenobarbital and Tegretol	Decreased serum concentration of either one, i.e., possible increase in seizure frequency
Phenobarbital and Tylenol	Decreased effect of barbiturate; either sedating or activating
Phenobarbital and Vitamin C	Decreased effect of barbiturate, i.e., possible increase in seizure frequency Decreased absorption of Vitamin C resulting in increased requirements, which may result in susceptibility to respiratory infections
Phenobarbital and Vitamin D	Decreased effect of Vitamin D or inhibition of the contribution of the vitamin to bone development, which may result in fragile bones
Tegretol and antidepressants	Decreased anticonvulsant effect of Tegretol, i.e., possible increase in seizure frequency
Tegretol and Depakene	Decreased serum concentration of both, i.e., possible increase in seizure frequency
Tegretol and Librium/Valium	Increased effect of both, with possible enhancement of undesirable side effects
Tegretol and Tagamet	Increased plasma concentrations of Tegretol, with possible enhancement of undesirable side effects
Tegretol and Tylenol	Increased risk of liver damage (but no observable signs) Decreased therapeutic effect of Tylenol

SOURCE: USP DI, 1993. Drug Information for the Health Care Professional: 13th Edition. Rockville, MD: Pharmacopeial Convention, Inc. From Guy, Ault, and Guess (1993).

deficiency also places students at risk of developing sores, injury, gastrointestinal discomfort (such as constipation, diarrhea, or vomiting), and poor oral hygiene and skeletal structure (McCamman & Rues, 1990). Any one of these characteristics can directly impact behavior and learning.

Factors influencing nutritional intake extend beyond the classroom. Yet teachers have neither the expertise to make nutritional decisions nor the opportunity to see that recommended changes are incorporated throughout the day. Families and educational staff must, therefore, work together to identify possible nutritional risks.

There are three major areas that potentially indicate nutritional problems (McCamman & Rues, 1990): (1) overall growth and development; (2) side effects of medications; and (3) the conditions surrounding mealtimes and feeding. These three areas should be reviewed at least annually, and more frequently if a student is at risk of nutritional problems. The review should be made through the student's primary health care provider by the family, teacher, school nurse, and nutritionist.

At Risk for Growth Problems Growth is the best indicator of adequate nutrition (McCamman & Rues, 1990). Growth that is significantly above the normal range is problematic, but of particular concern are students whose weight-for-height falls below the fifth percentile and who demonstrate only a minimal growth rate over time. Because persons with profound disabilities tend to grow at different rates than their normally developing peers, a growth chart plotted just for weight-by-height should be utilized, and not the more commonly used percentile charts for boys and girls that plot weight and height by age.

In order to obtain an accurate weight, a beam scale with nondetachable weights is recommended. This type of scale is commonly found in physicians' offices and in school health offices. Larger or older students might require a sling scale or scales developed for use with a wheelchair. These scales are often available in hospitals or medical centers. A measure of weight does not provide maximum information without corresponding measures of height. Both are needed for an accurate analysis of growth. In measuring height, a metallic tape or yardstick attached to a flat wall should be used. Ideally the student must be able to stand upright. If not, measures may be taken with the student lying down, in which case it is often easier to use two people in the process. One person should hold the student's head so the eyes are vertically upward, with the crown of the head firmly against the fixed headboard. The second person should hold the student's heel, with knees and hips extended and toes pointed directly upward. Measurement should occur at the student's heels. Once height and weight measurements have been obtained, they can be plotted on a growth chart.

Students should be referred to a nutritionist if (a) weight-for-height is less than the fifth or greater than the ninety-fifth percentile; (b) a child under 12 months of age has not gained weight in one month; (c) a child between the ages of one and two years has not gained weight in three months; or (d) a youth to 15 years of age has not gained weight during the school year.

At Risk for Medications Compromising Utilization of Nutrients The body's ability to utilize nutrients might be compromised by medications (McCamman & Rues, 1990). Some medications influence food consumption by producing a change in taste, while others cause dry mouth, nausea, or a stomach ache. Any of these reactions may decrease the amount of food a student will eat, ultimately affecting nutritional status. For example, Dilantin, Phenobarbital, or Tegretol might cause alterations of food intake or utilization by the body. These three anticonvulsants interfere with Vitamin D metabolism, along with folate and calcium absorption. Other medications such as Ritalin and Dexedrine, both CNS stimulants, can cause a decrease in appetite. Theophylline, used in the treatment of asthma, increases the body's energy requirements, which can result in weight loss if not accompanied by increased food intake (Guy, Ault, & Guess, 1993).

Nonprescription medications can also affect utilization of nutrients. Aspirin can depress serum Vitamin C, as well as cause gastrointestinal irritations, nausea, and heartburn. These changes may alter the student's behavior and temperament in the classroom. Other over-the-counter medications that might affect nutrition and student behavior include antacids, such as Maalox, which might increase iron absorption, leading to constipation; and laxatives, such as mineral oil and Ex-Lax, which can cause abdominal cramping and gastrointestinal distress (Guy, Ault, & Guess, 1993; Crump, 1987).

Families and teachers have the opportunity to assist in determining whether a combination of medications might be a factor in compromising the nutritional status of a student. Additional information can be gathered by following the suggestions presented previously for monitoring medication. Referral to a nutritionist or consultation with the primary health care provider should be initiated if the student is receiving two or more of the medications for a chronic condition.

At Risk Due to Mealtime Characteristics A major factor affecting growth is simply that students do not receive sufficient calories. Limited amounts and varieties of food and personal eating characteristics affect caloric and nutritional adequacy. Table 17.6, adapted from McCamman and Rues (1990), can be used as a guideline for appropriate amounts of food for students to receive during one mealtime. This figure represents an estimate of one-fourth of the foods needed over a 24-hour period. Recognizing that appetites fluctuate, and that mealtime patterns may be inconsistent, a problem may be present when the mealtime continuously contains an inadequate amount or variety of food. Evidence of limited types and amounts of food routinely ingested during a mealtime will add information important to the first two at-risk conditions.

Hydration as a Nutritional Issue Adequate hydration is a complicated health issue that is often misunderstood, or even overlooked, as an educational consideration for students with profound disabilities. Water is present in all human tissue and is required for life, as well as the efficient or adequate functioning of the body. If a person receives insufficient amounts of water, multiple systems in the body function less efficiently, causing problems in cognitive abilities, as well as bowel, bladder, skin, and kidney functioning, among others. The symptoms of dehydration are very similar to characteristics already present among students hav-

Table 17.6 Approximate Serving Size for Height

Food Group	APPROXIMATE SERVING SIZE PER MEAL FOR HEIGHT (OR ONE-FOURTH OF DAILY NEEDS)			
	29–34"	34–37"	37–45"	45–57"
Milk	½ cup (1 oz)	¾ cup (1 oz)	¾–1 cup (1 oz)	1 cup (1½ oz)
Meat/ Legumes	¼ cup (1 oz)	¼ cup (1–2 oz)	½ cup (1½–2 oz)	1 cup (2 oz)
Bread/ Cereal	¼ cup (2 tbsp)	1/3 cup (2 tbsp)	½ cup	½–1 cup
Fruit/ Vegetables	¼ cup (2 tbsp)	¼–½ cup (2 tbsp)	½ cup (2–4 tbsp)	½ cup

SOURCE: From Guy, Ault, and Guess (1993), p. 37.

Table 17.7 Percentages of Water in Some Foods

Food Item	% Water
Milk, juice	85–90*
Infant formula	85–90*
Fruit, fresh	85–90*
Vegetables, nonstarchy	85–90*
Cereal, hot	80–85
Cereal, ready to eat	3–7
Bread	25–35
Fish, meat, poultry	40–60

*preferred

SOURCE: From Guy, Ault, and Guess (1993), p. 38.

ing profound disabilities. It is often difficult, therefore, to identify dehydration as a contributing factor. Efforts should be made, nevertheless, to identify the possibility of dehydration, given its serious health implications, as well as to recognize that students with profound disabilities generally cannot indicate thirst or independently obtain water.

Common symptoms of dehydration include drowsiness, loss of appetite, flushed skin, sunken eyes, and decreased skin turgor (fullness). Other symptoms are constipation, concentrated urine, and an increase in body temperature and pulse rate. Students who display any or all of these symptoms should have their amount of fluid intake monitored. Fluid intake can be monitored by using guidelines and being aware of foods high in water content (Table 17.7).

Dehydration is a problem that, once identified, can be easily remedied. If a student is showing signs of severe dehydration, the parents should be notified, as well as the primary care provider through the school health professional. Usually it will be determined that an increase in fluids is sufficient to address the problem of dehydration, and a plan to increase fluid intake can be implemented in the school as well as the home. In doing so, it is important to recognize that an increase in fluids does not necessarily mean an increase in *liquids*. A student's consumption of fluid can be increased by (a) more routine offerings of small sips of fluids, (b) thickening liquids for students who have difficulty swallowing and, (c) expanding the amounts of solid foods that contain large percentages of water.

Summary

The simultaneous measurement of behavior state and corresponding environmental variables will provide teachers and other educational staff the opportunity to determine instructional strategies for specific students. The addition of medication and nutrition information will assist in identifying the specific individual needs of students. The case studies presented in the following section highlight the differences between students, their state profiles, influencing exogenous and endogenous variables, and recommended instructional strategies.

CASE STUDIES

Using attributes described earlier for state quality, students can be grouped into five separate profiles. Profile Group 1 includes students who spend the majority of the time in the educationally optimal states of awake inactive-alert (A^1) and awake active-alert (A^2). Students in Profile Group 2 also spend large amounts of time in the two optimal states, but are primarily awake inactive-alert; they rarely manipulate objects. Profile Group 3 describes students who frequently engage in stereotypic (A^2/S) and/or crying and agitation (CA) behaviors, including self-injury. Students assigned to Profile Group 4 are often drowsy or sleeping, while students included in Profile Group 5 are observed to engage somewhat equally in most of the eight states.

Five students, selected from a larger sample of 66 participants (Guess et al., 1993b), will be discussed to illustrate differences in state organizational patterns across the five profile groups. Each student was observed for one five-hour session, during which continuous recording procedures were used to collect state and environmental data. Although the data recording procedures reported for the case studies are more intense than those available for classroom teachers (Guy, Ault, & Guess 1993), they serve well for a discussion of actual state organization and patterns.

Demographic, medical, and developmental characteristics are described for each student. Quality is represented by the average percentage of time the student spent in the eight states during the five-hour observation period. State organization patterns graphically depict movement across time, fluctuations between states, and change rates, which are represented by line density (the closer the lines and darker the graph, the more rapid the state changes). Data are also presented to show the total number of shifts between states across the session, the average time (in seconds) spent in a particular state prior to changing to another state, and the average time spent in the other state after the shift was made. Various environmental factors that were recorded during observation sessions are also noted.

Profile Group 1—Mark

Demographic, Medical, and Developmental Characteristics Mark was a five-year-old male attending a self-contained classroom for students with severe and profound disabilities in a regular elementary school. His profound retardation and severe spastic quadriplegia resulted from congenital cytomegolavirus (CMV) infection and microencephaly. He has a seizure disorder that is controlled by Depakene, and cortical blindness. Mark can roll from sidelying to supine, is non-ambulatory, and exhibits an external rotation deformity of the hips. Developmentally, he scored in a range from 2 months in the gross motor area to 18 months in social behavior.

Behavior State Quality Mark spent 45 percent of the time in A^1 (awake inactive-alert) and 36 percent of the time in A^2 (awake active-alert). Mark's awake inactive-alert behavior was scored for orienting, tracking, and localizing people and objects, both visually and auditorially. He was able to manipulate toys, to activate a switch attached to toys and a communication device, and to grasp his glass during mealtime. Thirteen percent of Mark's time was spent in the awake-active with stereotypy state, and 5 percent was spent crying and agitated. His stereotypic behaviors included mouthing his hands and objects, and crying/agitation was scored when he became angry and bit his hands.

Behavior State Organization Figure 17.10 illustrates Mark's behavior state pattern. This shows consistent movement between the A^1 and A^2 states, with periodic shifts to stereotypy. The very dense pattern approximately two and three-quarter hours into the observation occurred during lunch time and shows rapid movement between orienting to his food (A^1) and eating (A^2). It should also be noted that the movement between awake inactive-alert, awake active-alert, awake active-alert with stereotypy, and crying/agitation in the first and second hours of observation occurred during an activity in which he became extremely frustrated, and alternated between orienting, manipulating an object, mouthing the object or his hands, and finally biting his hands as his level of agitation increased.

Shift Data The majority of Mark's shifts between states occurred as follows: A^1 to A^2 (92 shifts), A^2 to A^1 (90 shifts), A^1 to A^2/S (66 shifts), and A^2/S to A^1 (65 shifts). He spent an average of 42 seconds in A^1 prior to shifting to another state, 55 seconds in A^2, 25 seconds in A^2/S, and 29 seconds in C/A.

Environmental Factors Mark received some type of social interaction 46 percent of the time. These interactions reflected adult engagement, however, with no observed peer interactions. This likely reflected the homogeneous nature of his

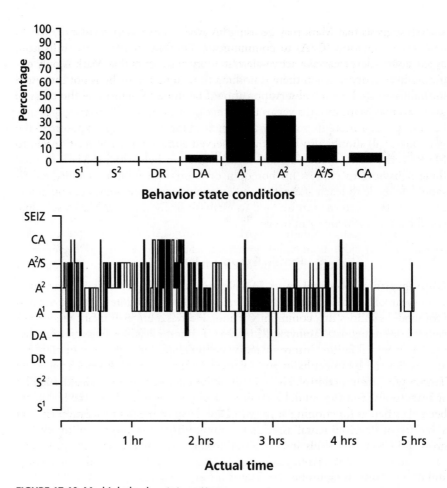

FIGURE 17.10 Mark's behavior state pattern.

classroom, where all other students evidenced an equal or greater level of disability. Fifty-three percent of his time was observed with no active social interaction by either an adult or another student. Materials were available to him 75 percent of the day and he spent the majority of the observation in a seated position (54 percent of the time) in his classroom (99 percent of the time). He changed location in the room only 1 percent of the entire five-hour observation period, and never left his primary classroom.

Instructional Implications   The identification of target states is complicated somewhat by Mark's age. Perusal of Mark's overall percentage of time in the various states might suggest decreasing the amount of time he spends in awake active-alert/stereotypy. A recent comparison of preschoolers with and without disabilities (Myers, 1992), however, indicated that comparable-age peers without disabilities spend similar amount of time engaged in stereotypical behavior. Further data analysis suggests that Mark may be using his awake active-alert/stereotypy (A^2/S) and crying agitation (C/A) to communicate. The low incidence of shifts from awake active-alert to awake active-alert/stereotypy suggests that Mark is only engaging in stereotypy when there is nothing to manipulate, or he is not interested in the materials. Further observation should be done to determine the types of materials that Mark mouths versus those that he manipulates. The types of activities and, perhaps more importantly, the length of the activities (or exposure to the same material) should also be further observed and examined in relationship to Mark's active-alert/stereotypy and crying/agitation behaviors. If Mark is using these behaviors to express his boredom or frustration with an activity, efforts should be made to teach alternative and more appropriate responses to communicate. The state patterns can be used to establish likely times in Mark's schedule when natural instruction can occur.

Profile Group 2—Jeremy

Demographic, Medical, and Developmental Characteristics Jeremy, a seven-year-old male, attended a self-contained class for children with severe and profound disabilities in a community school. He was a preterm infant who experienced severe neonatal asphyxia with secondary complications of respiratory distress, acute renal failure, intraventricular hemorrhage, and liver dysfunction. He also evidenced hydrocephalus and seizures. Jeremy receives Phenobarbital and Tegretol for seizure control. He has a severe visual impairment and, although he appears to respond to sound, his auditory acuity is considered untestable. He has been classified as functioning at the profound level of mental retardation and, on a variety of developmental assessments, ranges from the three-month level in gross and fine motor skills and cognition to the eight-month level in communication and social skills. Jeremy is nonambulatory, vocalizes and smiles frequently, and orients by turning his head and/or using an eye gaze.

Behavior State Quality Figure 17.11 shows that Jeremy was observed primarily in the awake inactive-alert state (90 percent of the time), with 9 percent of the time recorded in the awake active-alert state (A^2). While most of his time was spent in the two educationally optimal states, his profile illustrates those students who spend little time physically interacting with the environment. Jeremy's awake inactive-alert behavior included orienting to stimuli by turning his head and eyes to persons and materials at close range, smiling, and vocalizations. He placed his fist on a pressure pad, A^2 state, to activate a toy and the computer.

Behavior State Organization The graph for Jeremy in Figure 17.11 illustrates a very consistent pattern of movement between A^1 and A^2. The isolated occurrences of daze and drowse behavior were infrequent enough that they did not total even one percent of time. His graph shows relatively long periods of time spent in the A^1 state (as depicted by the long spaces of flat line between state changes). Again, the rapid movement between A^1 and A^2 at the end of the third hour of observation illustrates an eating activity.

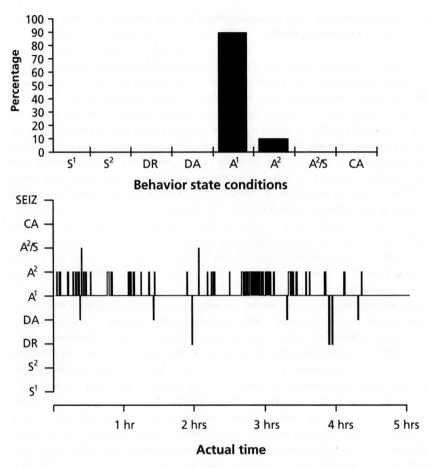

FIGURE 17.11 The average percentage of time Jeremy was observed in the eight behavior states during the five-hour observation session (top graph) and movement between states during the session (bottom graph).

Shift Data Jeremy was in the A^1 state for an average of 134 seconds before shifting into the A^2 state, where he remained for only 20 seconds before returning to A^1. These duration data explain the high percentage of time that he was observed in the A^1 state, although the total shifts between the two were nearly identical (85 shifts from A^1 to A^2; 84 shifts from A^2 to A^1).

Environmental Factors Social interaction occurred with Jeremy 44 percent of his day, while 56 percent of the time he was left alone. Within the interaction percentage, 2 percent was some type of play or instructional activity with a peer. Materials were available to Jeremy 72 percent of the time, and he spent the majority of his day (82 percent) in a seated position. He was observed in the standing and supine positions; movement, however, from one location to another occurred only 2 percent of the observation period. Jeremy spent 3 percent of his day in a secondary location (not his own classroom). This was time spent in the cafeteria, the only other location accessed.

Instructional Implications Jeremy represents students who may perhaps be the most challenging to educators. A major goal for students like Jeremy is to increase their time in the awake active-alert state. Most of them, however, have severe motor involvements that limit their voluntary movement. The onus, then, is placed on educational staff, families, and other service providers to develop simple ways for these students to voluntarily, physically interact with their environment.

Jeremy is able to access a switch, using his fist, while in a seated position. The short space of time that he is in awake active-alert before switching to another state (20 seconds) suggests that Jeremy's physical condition may affect his stamina or ability to maintain sustained contact. It is important, therefore, to present him with simple, short tasks. It may also be necessary to space tasks across the day, and to build his physical endurance and strength. For example, Jeremy's switch use occurred only in conjunction with recreational/leisure activities. Use of the switch during other types of activities, such as domestic skill training, might be used to increase his participation in functional tasks.

The use of technology with students having profound disabilities has, fortunately, increased. It should not, however, be the only opportunity that students with significant motor involvement and profound disabilities have to physically interact with objects or people. Jeremy can be provided more opportunities to physically interact by slightly altering some of his other activities. Simple caregiving tasks, such as transporting from position to position or grooming, can be used as a time for reciprocal interaction (Van Dijk, 1986; Writer, 1987). Jeremy's purposeful pressure into the body of the person who is carrying him becomes a physical interaction for him. However, in order for Jeremy to interact in this manner, other persons, especially his peers, must increase their time spent with him (that is, social contacts).

Profile Group 3—Rhonda

Demographic, Medical, and Developmental Characteristics Rhonda was 16 years of age at the time of observation. She resides in a residential facility for persons with mental retardation and received her educational programming in a school located on the grounds of this facility. Her profound mental retardation and dual sensory impairment was a result of severe head trauma and an accompanying subdural hematoma that occurred at three months of age. She has an unclassified seizure disorder that is controlled by Tegretol. Rhonda is ambulatory and engages in a variety of stereotypic behaviors, including finger flapping, body rocking, mouthing objects, head weaving, flicking her eyelashes, masturbating, and pressing her fist into her thigh and stomach. Additionally, she exhibits the following self-injurious behaviors, which were recorded as the C/A state: finger, hand, and arm biting; hitting her head with objects; slapping her thigh; and repeatedly hitting her upper lip with her finger. This last behavior has resulted in a callus that is often ulcerated. Developmental assessment indicated that Rhonda was functioning between the 12- and 24-month level.

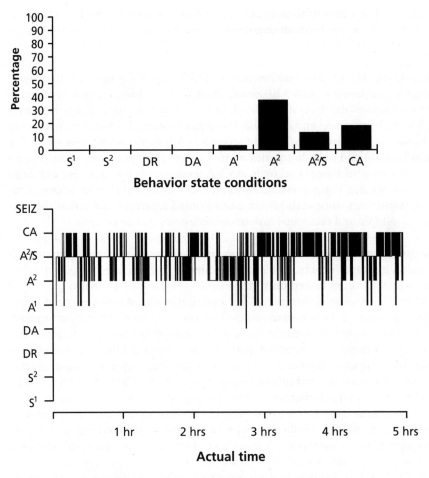

FIGURE 17.12 The average percentage of time Rhonda was observed in the eight behavior states during the five-hour observation session (top graph) and movement between states during the session (bottom graph)

Behavior State Quality Rhonda shows a state profile that displays (Figure 17.12) large amounts of stereotypic (68 percent) and self-injurious (C/A) behavior (19 percent). She spent almost no time alert and orienting (A^1) and exhibited very little awake active-alert (A^2) behavior. This means that only 12 percent of her day was spent in the two educationally optimum states of A^1 and A^2. A student with a profile like this would most likely have great difficulty acquiring information from her environment and acting on it in an appropriate manner.

Behavior State Organization As shown in Figure 17.12, Rhonda fluctuates almost continually between the A^2 and A^2/S states, and between the A^2/S and C/A states. The extreme density of the graph also indicates that she spent relatively small amounts of time in any state before moving to another. This rapid movement back and forth among states is shown clearly in the results of analysis of Rhonda's shift data.

Shift Data   The greatest number of shifts (332) occurred from A^2/S (stereotypy) to C/A (self-injury), with 330 total shifts from C/A back to A^2/S. Interaction between the A^2 and A^2/S states also showed considerable movement; there were 119 shifts between A^2 and A^2/S and 114 shifts between A^2/S and A^2. Moreover, Rhonda spent an average of only 14 seconds in A^2 before moving to another state (usually A^2/S) and only 26 seconds in A^2/S before changing states again. The average duration of time, 11 seconds, in C/A (engaging in self-injurious behavior) was even shorter. This represents, however, a self-injurious behavior of long duration or intensity, since each hit was not recorded separately, but rather they occurred in rapid and continued succession during these time periods.

Environmental Factors   The environment data for Rhonda are extremely interesting given the quality of her state profile. During the five-hour observation, social interaction occurred only 23 percent of the time. This means that for 78 percent (3 hours and 50 minutes) of her day, Rhonda was not engaged in any type of activity or social contact. While we have made no attempt in our research to determine cause and effect for a particular state profile, it is interesting to theorize as to whether her stereotypy and self-injury result from a lack of activity or attention, or perhaps the continual exhibition of these behaviors inhibits her participation in activities and interactions with others. Moreover, no social contact with peers occurred during the observation period.

Rhonda did have access to materials 67 percent of the time. Unfortunately, the lack of A^2 behavior indicates that either the materials were ignored or used inappropriately as objects for rhythmic and stereotypic behavior. She spent the majority of her time seated (87 percent) and the remaining time standing. The percentage of time in movement (6 percent) and the fact that she was ambulatory indicates that she walked about in her environment for a portion of her day. Finally, Rhonda spent 85 percent of the day in her primary classroom with only 9 percent of the time spent in a secondary location.

Instructional Implications   Obviously, the awake inactive-alert and awake active-alert states need to be increased for Rhonda, while the crying/agitated (self-injury) and awake active alert/stereotypy states should be decreased. Further analysis of Rhonda's stereotypic and self-injurious behavior is important to discover additional information, such as state sequences (compare state model in Figure 17.1) and antecedent causes. The current data do, however, have some implications for instructional strategies. Rhonda receives very little social interaction (23 percent), all with adults. In addition, the topography of her stereotypy and self-injury includes movement and quick, deep touches. This suggests that Rhonda prefers materials and activities that have activating characteristics, specifically movement and quick, deep touches. For example, using a vacuum cleaner would provide her with vestibular stimulation, quick back-and-forth movements, loud noises, and tactile vibration. More active social environments (such as community settings) would also provide her with stimulation, and could be used to increase her social contact with peers and other adults.

Typically, it would be best to present the activating strategies when Rhonda is in an awake active-alert or awake inactive-alert state. The small amounts of time she spends in these states, however, demands other strategies. It is possible that using her preferred activating techniques during A^2/S will help to decrease the behavior by providing an alternate source of stimulation. At other times, however, it may serve to overstimulate her and thus actually increase the A^2/S and C/A states. Accordingly, it is important to monitor the amounts and types of stimulation provided, and based on Rhonda's behavior, determine whether an activating or soothing characteristic is appropriate. For example, Rhonda bangs her lip with any hard object. If she is seeking deep stimulation, the removal of all hard objects might increase the intensity of her behavior, as she seeks to find other means of stimulation. Providing hard, smooth objects when doing functional tasks and patterning her into using the object appropriately is one method of introducing activating characteristics during her stereotypic behavior. If her stereotypic behavior starts to increase, materials that are soft and soothing may be necessary to help decrease the behavior.

Profile Group 4—Craig

Demographic, Medical, and Developmental Characteristics Craig was almost four years old when he was observed while attending a preschool class for children with disabilities located in a regular elementary school. He was diagnosed at age 18 months with Muscular Leukodystrophy II, a progressive neural degenerative disease. At the time of observation, Craig had no independent mobility, exhibited extreme spastic motor tone, and had declining vision and hearing. His generalized seizure activity was only partially controlled by medication. Craig's extremely fragile medical condition required gastrostomy feeding and frequent machine suctioning of respiratory mucus throughout the day. Additionally, he had periodic apneic episodes lasting almost a minute. He was taking seven different medications for both seizure control and recurring infections. Scores on developmental assessments ranged from the 1-month level in motor skills to the 21-month level in cognition.

Behavior State Quality Craig provides an example (Figure 17.13) of those students who spend large amounts of their time in educational settings sleeping and drowsy. In fact, he was fully awake and alert only 28 percent of his day, while 72 percent (2 hours and 36 minutes) of his time was spent sleeping, drowsy, or dazed. This student was so involved motorically that his A1 behavior was determined by eye shifts to stimuli and a slightly increased muscle tone.

Behavior State Organization As shown in Figure 17.13, Craig illustrates a rather complex pattern of movement among five states. He spent long periods of time sleeping and moving between the two levels of sleep (S^1 and S^2) and drowse

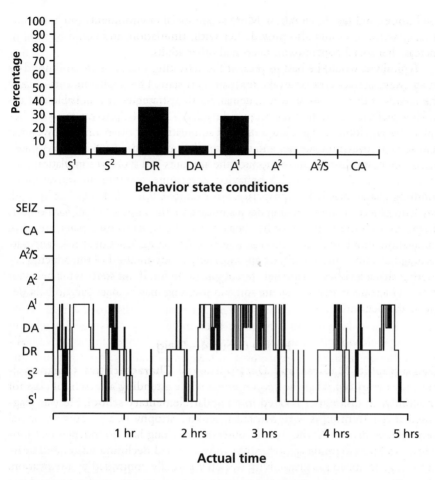

FIGURE 17.13 The average percentage of time Craig was observed in the eight behavior states during the five-hour observation session (top graph) and movement between states during the session (bottom graph).

and daze. This movement (and his behavior pattern) can be seen clearly when there is a long, straight line at S^1 followed by a rapid movement to S^2, drowse or daze, and then back to a sustained period in S^1. This illustrates his attempt to awaken and respond to a stimulus only to return, almost immediately, to a sleep state. His S^2 or active sleep was characterized by frequent startles and limb extension. It should be noted that a period of relative alertness occurred in the middle of the observation (between the second and third hours) and represented time spent in a secondary environment during a music activity.

Shift Data Shift data for Craig provide interesting information about his overall state pattern. The greatest number of shifts was seen between drowse and the other four states he exhibited (S^1, S^2, DA, and A^1). There were 82 total shifts between drowse and these other states. Additionally, he spent the shortest amount of time in drowse before moving to another state (an average of 15 seconds), while the average duration of time spent in S^1 before moving to another state was 165 seconds. Craig's movement back and forth between drowse and the sleep states, and drowse and A^1, illustrates the pivotal nature of the drowse condition for this particular state pattern. It appears very difficult for Craig to effect movement out of the pattern, particularly among the sleep and drowse states. This state organization pattern, showing extended periods of time in the sleep and indeterminate states, was likely associated with his overall medically fragile condition.

Environmental Factors   When the environmental data are examined, it is interesting to note that Craig actually received social interaction 55 percent of his day. This occurred despite the fact that 72 percent of the time he was either asleep, drowsy, or dazed. This suggests that, in spite of positive staff efforts, attempts to engage Craig's attention did little to alert him. Moreover, accessible materials were available to him for the greater part of the day (53 percent).

Craig spent 63 percent of the observation period in a seated position, with the remaining time spent supine, sidelying, or prone. As discussed earlier, while the sidelying and supine positions have been implicated as having a correlation with sleep behavior, many students do, in fact, sleep quite well in the seated position. Although sitting has been shown to have an activating effect on some students, the total array of endogenous and exogenous factors may diminish this outcome in other students. As noted above, a portion of Craig's time was spent in a secondary location (11 percent), and during 4 percent of his day, movement occurred either between positions or locations.

Instructional Implications   A large portion of Craig's sleep behavior may be attributed to the types of medication that he received. Information in Figure 17.13 indicates that there was increased A^1 state behavior between the second and third hours. This time was immediately preceded and followed by sleep. Coincidentally, Craig's medications were administered in the middle of this time slot. His medications consisted of an anticonvulsant, a sedative, two muscle relaxants, and a narcotic to reverse the respiratory depression of the other medications. While these medications are necessary, there are several things that might be done to reduce their overall effect on Craig's level of alertness. First, the primary care physician can be consulted to determine if there is any possibility of changing the types of medications administered, or the times that they are administered.

Next, Craig's state behavior in relation to environmental variables should be examined. Craig's drowsiness is a pivotal state between awake inactive-alert and deep sleep. It will be easier to move Craig to awake inactive-alert from his pivotal state of drowse than from deep sleep. For this reason, strenuous activities should be scheduled during his alert time. (Note: Activities that are strenuous for Craig may seem extremely easy to others with stronger physical skills and stamina.) Also, when Craig is seated, efforts should be made to keep him upright. If he is seated with a backwards-tilt and begins to drowse, a brief repositioning, or even just a slight movement and then replacement, might help shift him to the awake inactive-alert state. The soothing characteristics of the environment should also be analyzed to determine if they are, in fact, contributing to his sleepiness. Active social environments may help to provide Craig stimulation without demanding physical energy.

Finally, it is important to realize that there are times when Craig needs relaxation. Only careful examination of his schedule, state patterns, and responses to the environment will determine if this time needs to be spend in actual sleep or just in less strenuous activities.

Profile Group 5—Martin

Demographic, Medical, and Developmental Characteristics Martin was almost ten when he was observed in a self-contained classroom for students with severe and profound disabilities. He was a premature infant who evidenced neonatal asphyxia, respiratory difficulties, microcephalus, and failure to thrive. Repeated hospitalizations have occurred since birth for failure to thrive, pneumonia, and status epilepticus. Martin evidences severe hypotonic quadriplegia, has cerebral palsy, and is nonambulatory. In addition, he has scoliosis and takes Phenobarbital for control of generalized seizures. Although nonambulatory, he is able to roll and scoot on his back. Developmental assessments show a range from 3 months in the social area to 10 months in motor skills. Martin has a gastrostomy but receives some food orally.

Behavior State Quality Martin's state profile provides an example of a student who exhibits numerous states. Figure 17.14 graphically illustrates the occurrence of each state category, with no particular focus or predominance of any one. While 48 percent of his time was spent in A^1 and 14 percent in A^2, a considerable amount of time was also spent in S^1 and A^2/S (14 percent and 18 percent respectively). This profile is considered to be balanced because, although large amounts of time were spent in several of the states, there were not enough occurrences in any one of them for assignment to the other four groupings.

Martin's A^2 behaviors included grasping his cup, touching an adult to gain attention, and manipulating objects and himself. His A^2/S behaviors involved head weaving and rocking. Although he was tube fed, Martin received limited amounts of food and drink throughout the day (A^2 behavior).

Behavior State Organization Martin's graph (Figure 17.14) shows not only movement among all eight states, but rather rapid state changes, as indicated by the density of the lines. His activity across the day can almost be "read" by looking at the state pattern found in the continuous graph. During the first hour, with the exception of three short occurrences of daze and drowse, he moved between A^1, A^2, and A^2/S behaviors. This pattern coincided with a period of instructional programming. The second hour shows rapid movement between drowse and awake-alert behaviors with some periods of crying/agitation. Toward the end of the second hour, he finally succumbed to sleep, which lasted for approximately

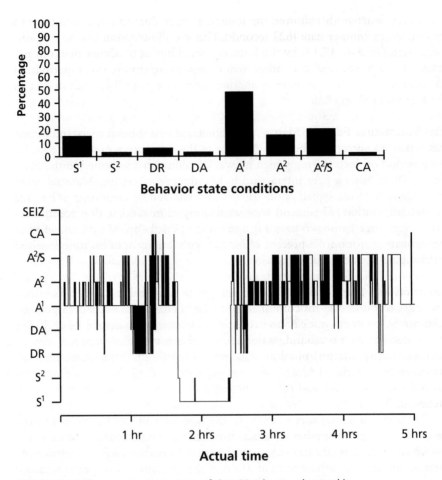

FIGURE 17.14 The average percentage of time Martin was observed in the eight behavior states during the five-hour observation session (top graph) and movement between states during the session (bottom graph).

45 minutes. Note the period immediately following sleep when he moved between the A^1, drowse, and A^2/S states. The A^1 to A^2 sequence represented his lunch time, followed again by rapid movement between A^1, A^2, and A^2/S. His day ended with sustained periods of A^2/S, A^1, and a final "burst" of crying (C/A).

Shift Data Martin's shift data further illustrate his rapid movement across the spectrum of state behaviors. The largest number of shifts occurred between A^1 and A^2/S (105), A^2/S and A^1 (99), A^2 and A^1 (74), and A^1 and A^2 (68). These data show the pivotal nature of the A^1 state, which has been described in earlier research (Guess et al., 1993a; Roberts, 1992).

Asleep-inactive (S^1) showed the longest average duration of a state prior to movement to another state (622 seconds). This was illustrated in Martin's continuous graph (Figure 17.14) by the long, sustained line at S^1. Other than this period of sleep, each of the other states showed relatively short periods of occurrence prior to movement to another state (a range of 8 seconds in daze to 39 seconds in S^2 and A^1).

Environmental Factors Martin's environmental data showed social interaction occurring 43 percent of the time. A factor in this percentage may have been his long period of sleep, during which he was left alone on a waterbed in the classroom. There was no peer interaction in his educational setting. Materials were available approximately half of the day (51 percent), and he spent most of his time in a seated position (73 percent) with small amounts in standing (9 percent), side-lying (9 percent), prone (6 percent), and supine (2 percent). Martin remained in his primary classroom 78 percent of his day with 2 percent of his time involved in changing position and/or location.

Instructional Implications The overall goal in relationship to Martin's behavior states is to increase his combined A^1 and A^2 behavior to exceed 75 percent. Ultimately, the desire is for A^2 to exceed, or at least equal, occurrences of A^1. For many students with profound disabilities, this goal is very challenging. It may be that, like Jeremy, Martin's physical skills severely limit his A^2 options. At this time, however, his combined A^1 and A^2 states occur only 62 percent of the time. We would, thus, target A1 and A2 for increase, with special attention given to A^2 behavior.

To do this, it is necessary to examine the types of activities Martin is involved in during the day. A number of factors may have accounted for sleep in the second hour. Martin might have been tired from the concentrated "programming" that occurred during the first hour. If this is the case, strenuous activities should be distributed across the day, rather than occurring all at once. Also, Martin's nutritional routine should be examined to determine if he should receive sustenance sooner. The sleep time may have occurred because it was assumed that Martin was tired, thus he was left alone with no social contact or activating materials. It may also have occurred as a result of having just received a seizure medication.

As can be seen from the graph in Figure 17.14, Martin's state behavior in the afternoon was much more active. This change could have been caused by his nap, the food, the activities, or any combination of these variables. It is interesting to note that Martin's stereotypic behavior is all related to his awake inactive-alert behavior. He never shifted to stereotypic behavior from the awake active-alert state. This suggests that Martin had certain preferences for materials and their characteristics. He would interact with them when present, but engage in stereotypy when they were not available. It may also indicate that Martin had become bored with the materials that he was given. Additional observation of the characteristics of the materials with which he interacts and the length of time that he interacts with them is necessary before determining specific teaching strategies.

SUMMARY FOR INSTRUCTIONAL STRATEGIES BASED ON STATE AND ENVIRONMENTAL FACTORS

Our model assumes that state conditions and organization mediate attentiveness and responsiveness to environmental stimuli, and that aspects of the environment as well as endogenous variables may, in turn, affect behavior states among children and youth with profound disabilities. We discussed variables that have bi-directional influences on state, and those that likely have a more unidirectional effect. The mediating role of state behavior between both endogenous and exogenous factors exists as an interconnected, dynamic system.

The measurement and analysis of state organization has been described. This included state quality and subsequent assignment to one of five profile groups. State quality depicts the percentage of time students spend in each of eight state conditions. This measurement allows for assignment into educationally relevant profile groupings, and provides educators and service providers with important information necessary to determine whether movement to more optimal states should be targeted. Organization and shift data demonstrate patterns of movement among the various states and provide a "picture" of sequences across time. These data, when paired with information about the student's environment and physical status, can be used to aid better scheduling and instructional input throughout the day.

While behavior state quality can be measured consistently and reliably by teachers or other caregivers, the characteristics of state organization (consistency and stability, sequences and patterns, and periodicity) may be more difficult to assess and analyze in classrooms. These factors are important, however, in determining an overall picture of the student's state profile as well as identifying appropriate instructional strategies for effecting state change. Further research is needed to develop procedures that will better provide this information to teachers and caregivers.

Endogenous and exogenous variables that may influence state behavior were described. The endogenous factors included the individual's developmental, nutritional, and medical status. Exogenous factors included instructional settings/contexts and potential external, motor, and environmental stimuli; such as social interaction, material availability, student position and movement, facilitative techniques with both activating and soothing characteristics, and physical atmosphere.

None of the students in the case studies presented were observed to interact with peers. Given that each was observed primarily in self-contained classrooms for students with severe and profound disabilities, opportunities were extremely limited for contact with nondisabled peers and those with disabilities who are able (motorically and verbally) to sustain interactions. Approximately one-fourth of each student's day was spent in some type of self-help or maintenance (adjusting equipment or materials) activity. These are opportunities for social engagement that must be utilized both for communication and instructional purposes. Moreover, many of the interactions occurred during a traditional 1:1 instructional training approach. It is suggested that more group instruction be used to facilitate peer interactions.

While most of these students spent the majority of time in the seated position with smaller amounts of time spent standing, supine, prone, or sidelying, it is suggested that teachers of students who have difficulty maintaining alert behavior try a variety of positions (approved for that child) to determine whether one is more activating than another. In addition, a limited amount of time was spent in position and/or location movement across the observation period. Simply changing from one position or location to another may prove to activate students who are sleepy, calm those who are agitated, or provide a diversion for those who are engaging in frequent stereotypic behaviors.

The relatively small amount of time these students spent outside of their primary educational setting is of concern. Opportunities to access other environments, particularly inclusive settings and community sites, represent "best practices" education for students with severe and profound disabilities.

While students in each profile group had access to materials, the availability varied considerably. The highest percentage of material availability was shown for the individuals in Profile Groups 1 and 2 (75 percent and 72 percent respectively). It is important to note these are the two profiles in which students exhibited predominant behavior in the two educationally optimal states of A1 and A^2. Availability of materials that are accessible to students through their primary modalities is necessary for orienting (A^1) and interactive (A^2) behavior to occur. Because of inherent difficulties presented by students with dual sensory impairments, it is critical for teachers and service providers to use materials that are accessible through the alternative modalities of touch, smell, and taste or amplified for receipt by their residual hearing and/or vision.

While all of the students profiled were medicated, the student in Profile Group 4 provided the greatest indication that both medication and nutritional status affect state behavior. Although it may be difficult to manipulate these variables, knowledge of their effects should be helpful in planning programming for students with profound disabilities. See also recent positive results from a study (Ault et al., 1995) where environmental events were manipulated to increase alertness and responsiveness among students who were observed to spend extensive periods of time in the sleep and drowse states.

State conditions exert major influence on the overall behavior of students with profound disabilities. Further, endogenous and exogenous variables, ranging from physiological and developmental status to the occurrence of a variety of environmental conditions and events, have the potential to disrupt optimal expression of state organization. Influence of these variables will surely impact the effectiveness of intervention efforts for these students and should be considered when planning and implementing appropriate instructional goals and objectives for them.

REFERENCES

Als, H. (1982). Toward a synactive theory of development: Promise for the assessment and support of infant individuality. *Infant Mental Health Journal, 3*(2), 229–243.

Als, H. (1986). A synactive model of neonatal behavioral organization: Framework for the assessment of neurobehavioral development in the premature infant and for support of infants and parents in the neonatal intensive care environment. *Physical and Occupational Therapy in Pediatrics, 6*(3/4), 3–55.

Anders, T., & Keener, M. (1985). Developmental course of nighttime and sleep-wake patterns in full-term and premature infants during the first year of life. *Sleep, 8*(3), 173–192.

Ault, M. M., Guy, B., Guess, D., Bashinski, S., & Roberts, S. (1995). Analyzing behavior state and learning environments: Application in instructional settings. *Mental Retardation, 33*(5), 304–316.

Ault, M. M., Guy, B., Rues, J., Noto, L., & Guess, D. (1994). Some educational implications for students with profound disabilities at risk for inadequate nutrition and the nontherapeutic effects of medication. *Mental Retardation, 32*(3), 200–205.

Bakeman, R., & Gottman, J. M. (1986) *Observing interaction: An introduction to sequential analysis.* Cambridge, NY: Cambridge University.

Brazelton, T. B. (1984). Neonatal behavioral assessment scale (2nd ed.). *Spastics International Medical Publications.* Philadelphia: J. B. Lippincott.

Brown, E. L., & Deffenbacher, K. (1979). *Perception and the senses.* New York: Oxford University.

Campbell, P. H. (1989). Dysfunction in posture and movement in individuals with profound disabilities: Issues and practices. In F. Brown & D. H. Lehr (Eds.), *Persons with profound disabilities: Issues and practices* (pp. 163–189). Baltimore: Paul H. Brookes.

Chasnoff, I. J., Burns, W. J., Schnoll, S. H., & Burns, K. A. (1985). Cocaine use in pregnancy. *New England Journal of Medicine, 313,* 666–669.

Colombo, J., & Horowitz, F. D. (1987). Behavioral state as a lead variable in neonatal research. *Merrill-Palmer Quarterly, 33,* 423–437.

Crump, M. (1987). *Nutrition and feeding of the handicapped child.* Boston: College-Hill.

Fajardo, B., Browning, M., Fisher, D., & Paton, J. (1992). Early state organization and follow-up over one year. *Developmental and Behavioral Pediatrics, 13*(2), 83–88.

Ferguson, D. (1985). The ideal and the real: The working out of public policy in curricula for severely handicapped students. *Remedial and Special Education, 6,* 52–60.

Gibson, J. J. (1966). *The senses considered as perceptual systems.* Boston: Houghton Mifflin.

Guess, D., Ault, M. M., Roberts, S., Struth, J., Siegel-Causey, E., Thompson, B., Bronicki, G. J., & Guy, B. (1988). Implications of biobehavioral states for the education and treatment of students with the most profoundly handicapping conditions. *Journal of the Association for Persons with Severe Handicaps, 13,* 163–174.

Guess, D., Roberts, S., Siegel-Causey, E., & Rues, J. (1995). Replication and extended analysis of behavior state, environmental events, and related variables in profound disabilities. *American Journal on Mental Retardation, 100,* 36–51.

Guess, D., Roberts, S., Siegel-Causey, E., Ault, M. M., Guy, B., Thompson, B., & Rues, J. (1991). *Investigations into the state behaviors of students with severe and profound handicapping conditions.* Lawrence: University of Kansas, Department of Special Education.

Guess, D., Roberts, S., Siegel-Causey, E., Ault, M. M., Guy, B., Thompson, B., & Rues, J. (1993a). An analysis of behavior state conditions and associated environmental variables among students with profound handicaps. *American Journal on Mental Retardation, 97,* 634–653.

Guess, D., Rues, J., Roberts, S., & Siegel-Causey, E. (1993b). *Extended Analysis of Behavior State, Environmental Events, and Related Variables Among Students with Profound Disabilities: A Final Report.* (Contract No. H133G00078). Washington: National Institute of Disability Rehabilitation and Research.

Guess, D., Siegel-Causey, E., Roberts, S., Guy, B., Mulligan-Ault, M. M., & Rues, J. (1993c). Analysis of state organizational patterns among students with profound disabilities. *Journal of the Association for Persons with Severe Handicaps, 18*(2), 93–108.

Guess, D., Siegel-Causey, E., Roberts, S., Rues, J., Thompson, B., & Siegel-Causey, D. (1990). Assessment and analysis of behavioral state and related variables among students with profoundly handicapping conditions. *Journal of the Association for Persons with Severe Handicaps, 15,* 211–230.

Guy, B., Ault, M. M., & Guess, D. (1993). *Analyzing behavior state and learning environments profile.* Project ABLE. The University of Kansas, Department of Special Education. U. S. Department of Special Education, Office of Special Education Programs (Project # H086D00013).

Guy, B., Guess, D., & Ault, M. M. (1993). Classroom procedures for the measurement of behavior state among students with profound disabilities. *Journal of the Association for Persons with Severe Handicaps, 18*(1), 52–60.

Hagan, C. (1981). Language disorders secondary to closed head injury: Diagnosis and treatment. *Topics in Language Disorders, 1,* 73–87.

Helm, J. M. & Simeonsson, R. J. (1989). Assessment of behavioral state organization. In D. B. Bailey & M. Wollery (Eds.), *Assessing infants and preschoolers with handicaps* (pp. 202–224). Columbus, OH: Merrill.

Iwata, B. A., Dorsey, M. F., Slifer, K. J., Bauman, K. E., & Richman, G. S. (1982). Toward a functional analysis of self-injury. *Analysis and Intervention in Developmental Disabilities, 2,* 3–20.

Kopp, C., Sigman, M., Parmelee, A. H., & Jeffrey, W. E. (1975). Neurological organization and visual fixation in infants at 40 weeks conceptual age. *Developmental Psychobiology, 8,* 165–170.

Korner, A. F. (1972). State as a variable, as obstacle, and as mediator of stimulation in infant research. *Merrill-Palmer Quarterly, 18,* 77–94.

Landesman-Dwyer, S., & Sackett, G. P. (1978). Behavioral changes in nonambulatory, mentally retarded individuals. In C. E. Meyers (Ed.), *Quality of life in severely and profoundly mentally retarded people: Research foundation for improvement* (Monograph No. 3) (pp. 55–144). Washington: American Association on Mental Deficiency.

McCamman, S., & Rues, J. (1990). Nutrition monitoring and supplementation. In J. C. Graff, M. M. Ault, D. Guess, M. Taylor, & B. Thompson (Eds.), *Health care for students with disabilities: An illustrated medical guide for the classroom.* Baltimore: Paul H. Brookes.

Myers, S. B. (1992). *A comparison of the behavior states of preschoolers with and without severe/profound handicaps.* Unpublished master's thesis, University of Kansas, Lawrence.

Poindexter, A. R., & Bihm, E. M. (1994). Incidence of short-sleep patterns in institutionalized individuals with profound mental retardation. *American Journal on Mental Retardation, 98*(6), 776–780.

Prechtl, H. F. R. (1974). The behavioral states of the newborn infant: A review. *Brain Research, 76,* 185–212.

Pugsley, M., Acebo, C., & Thoman, E. B. (1988). Sleep of preterm and full-term infants from home monitoring. Sixth Biennial International Conference on Infant Studies, Washington, DC, April 21-24. *Infant Behavior & Development, Special ICIS Issue, 11,* 263.

Rainforth, B. (1982). Biobehavioral state and orienting: Implications for educating profoundly retarded students. *Journal of the Association for the Severely Handicapped, 5,* 33–37.

Reid, D. H., Phillips, J. F., & Green, C. W. (1991). Teaching persons with profound multiple handicaps: A review of the effect of behavioral research. *Journal of Applied Behavior Analysis, 24,* 319–336.

Roberts, S. (1992). *An investigation and analysis of behavior state conditions and related environmental events among children and youth with multiple severe and profound disabilities.* Unpublished doctoral dissertation, University of Kansas, Lawrence.

Rosett, H. L., Snyder, P., Sander, L. W., Lee, A., Cook, P., Weiner, L., & Gould, J. (1979). Effects of maternal drinking on neonate state regulation. *Developmental Medicine and Child Neurology, 21,* 464–473.

Ross Laboratories (1982). Adapted National Center for Health Statistics physical growth percentiles. Columbus, OH.

Sailor, W., Gee, K., Goetz, L., & Graham, N. (1988). Progress in educating students with the most severe disabilities: Is there any? *Journal of the Association of the Severely Handicapped, 13,* 87–89.

Simeonsson, R. J., Huntington, G. S., & Parse, S. A. (1980). Expanding the developmental assessment of young handicapped children. *New Directions for Exceptional Children, 3,* 51–74.

Thoman, E. B., & McDowell, K. (1989). Sleep cyclicity in infants during the earliest postnatal weeks. *Physiology & Behavior, 45,* 517–522.

Thoman, E. B., & Whitney, M. P. (1990). Behavioral states in infants: Individual differences and individual analyses. In J. Colombo & J. W. Fagen (Eds.), *Individual differences in infancy* (pp. 113–135). Hillsdale, N.J: Lawrence Erbaum, Associates.

Thompson, B., Guess, D. (1989). Students who experience the most profound disabilities. In F. Brown & D. H. Lehr (Eds.), *Persons with profound disabilities: Issues and practices* (pp. 342). Baltimore: Paul H. Brookes.

Tynan, W. D. (1986). Behavioral stability predicts morbidity and mortality in infants from a neonatal intensive care unit. *Infant Behavior and Development, 9,* 71–79.

Van Dijk, J. (1986). An educational curriculum for deaf-blind multihandicapped persons. In D. Ellis (Ed.), *Sensory impairments in mentally handicapped people* (pp. 374–382). San Diego: College Hill.

Will, B. E. (1977). Methods for promoting functional recovery following brain damage. In S. R. Berenberg (Ed.), *Brain: Fetal and infant: Current research on normal and abnormal development* (pp. 330–344). The Hague: Martinus Nijhoff Medical Division.

Wolff, P. H. (1959). Observations on newborn infants. In L. J. Stone, H. T. Smith, & L. B. Murphy (Eds.), *The competent infant* (pp. 257–272). New York: Basic Books.

Wolff, P. H. (1987). *The development of behavioral states and the expression of emotions in early infancy: New proposals for investigation.* Chicago: The University of Chicago.

Writer, J. (1987). A movement-based approach to the education of students who are sensory impaired/multihandicapped. In L. Goetz, D. Guess, & K. Stremel-Campbell (Eds.), *Innovative program design for individuals with dual sensory impairments* (pp. 191–224). Baltimore: Paul H. Brookes.

18

Darwin, Skinner,
and the Concept
of Reinforcement

KEVIN TIERNEY
WILLIAM O'DONOHUE

INTRODUCTION

Those of us who believe in functional assessment tacitly support the proposition that problem behavior has been learned; it is an operant that is serving a function. Our problem as interventionists is to identify that function and then to teach the individual to substitute a different behavior that serves the same function.

But larger questions can be asked: Why does behavior develop, and why is function important to behavior? Tierney and O'Donohue answer these questions by showing the relationship between Darwinian and Skinnerian theories of behavior. Both, of course, support the concept of natural selection. In Skinner's case, natural selection refers to the consequences of selecting behavior—this is the function, then, of behavior.

The authors bring two major points to those in the field of functional assessment. In the first section, they ask us to consider why behavior shows variability across and within individuals, why behavior change endures, and why certain behaviors are selected. In the second part of this chapter, they elaborate on why certain behaviors are selected; and they do so within several contemporary accounts of reinforcements (optimal foraging theory, the probability differential hypothesis, and the molar regulatory or functional hypothesis).

With these points, the authors are asking us to consider more basic mechanisms to functional assessment. At present, while we emphasize the concept of reinforcement in teaching

*the individual functionally equivalent, appropriate alternatives to problem behavior, we ig-
nore the issue of reinforcement theory. As such, our interventions may not be optimal. By
considering the underlying reason for behavior change before we begin an assessment and an
intervention, we may become much more successful in our work.*

The work of B. F. Skinner serves as a major influence upon special education
and clinical psychology. A large part of this influence stems from the
demonstrated efficacy of interventions designed to remediate the problems
encountered in schools and clinics. A recent American Psychological Association
task force (Task Force on Promotion and Dissemination of Psychological Procedures, 1995), composed of professionals with diverse expertise and theoretical al-
liances and given the charge of identifying treatments that work, primarily
identified treatments that were behavioral.

Two questions arise from the relative success of applied behavior analysis and
behavior therapy. First, how can this apparent success be sustained, or better yet,
enhanced? That is, how can the next generation of behavioral therapies build
upon the success of this impressive body of extant work? Second, what is the
larger framework that sets a context for understanding the success of behavioral
techniques? We shall argue that these two questions are related and that the answers to both lie in a better understanding of the Darwinian basis of human behavior with its emphasis upon variation, selection, and function.

SKINNER AND DARWIN

A first glance at the work of Skinner and Darwin might suggest that the work of
each scientist has little relevance to the other's, and might actually be incompatible with it. Darwin was a biologist who dealt largely with issues such as specia-
tion and change within species over many generations. Skinner, on the other
hand, was little interested in cross-species differences and concentrated on understanding the behavior of individual organisms. However, this analysis misses important points of commonality.

Skinner, particularly in his later writings, stressed the connectedness of radical
behaviorism and the experimental analysis of behavior to Darwinian evolution.
Skinner (1963, p. 951) regarded behavioral psychology as "part of biology, a natural science for which tested and highly successful methods are available." However, biology is a large science with diverse methodologies and interests. Skinner,
without denying the importance of physiological research, did not see behavioral
psychology as dependent or subservient in any way to progress in, say, brain physiology. This is in direct contrast to biological mechanists who assert that some behavior is not really understood until it can be reduced to the physiological
mechanisms responsible for the behavior.

Skinner argued that there is a legitimate and important place for the study of the intact organism in its interaction with its environment. He argued that both physiological and psychological sets of facts are equally important. Beginning in his earliest writings (Skinner, 1938), he criticized what he believed was premature physiologizing and the "Conceptual Nervous System." Skinner (1974, p. 217) stated:

> Similarly, the effects of deprivation and satiation on behavior are not the same as the events seen through a gastric fistula. Nor is emotion, studied as behavioral predisposition, capable of being analyzed in terms appropriate to pneumographs and electrocardiographs. Both sets of facts, and their appropriate concepts, are important—but they are equally important, not dependent one upon the other.

Moreover, he argued that the work of the physiological psychologist is in an important sense dependent upon the work of the behavioral psychologist, in that the regularities discovered at the level of behavior by the behavioral psychologist are the *explanada* of the physiological psychologist.

Thus far we have briefly described the major point of tension between Skinnerians and (some) biologists. Obviously, if Skinner thought behavioral psychology was part of biology, he would have to make the case for important commonalties. The point of commonality is that the major organizing framework for biology—Darwinian evolution—is also the major organizing framework for Skinner. Skinner (1984, p. 477) stated:

> Human behavior is the joint product of (a) contingencies of survival responsible for natural selection and (b) contingencies of reinforcement responsible for the repertoires of individuals, including (c) the special contingencies maintained by an evolved social environment. Selection by consequences is a causal mode found only in living things, or in machines made by living things. It was first recognized in natural selection. Reproduction as a first consequence, led to the evolution of cells, organs, and organisms reproducing themselves under increasingly diverse conditions. The behavior functioned well, however, only under conditions similar to those under which it was selected. Reproduction under a wider range of consequences becomes possible with the evolution of processes through which organisms acquired behavior appropriate to novel environments. One of these, operant conditioning, is a second kind of selection by consequences. New responses could be strengthened by events which followed them. When the selecting consequences are the same, operant conditioning and natural selection work together redundantly. But because a species which quickly acquires behavior appropriate to an environment has less need for an innate repertoire, operant conditioning could replace as well as supplement the natural selection of behavior.

Skinner sees operant conditioning as a product of evolution and thus sees explanations of human behavior as ultimately related to biological evolution. Moreover, operant conditioning is not simply a product of evolution. It is also a process that mimics evolution—an environmental selection of behaviors. Thus, intervention efforts must analyze past and present environmental selection of behaviors in order to understand the etiology and maintenance of behavior, and must change these contingencies of reinforcement in order to elicit more desirable selections. (See Corwin & O'Donohue, 1995, for a fuller explication of the role of evolution in psychotherapy.)

Some critics of an evolutionary account may counter with this argument: Why are there still various kinds of problems (from diseases to learning disabilities), given that evolution aids organisms to become better "adapted" to their environments? This criticism is based on two major misconceptions. First, evolution is not purposive and it certainly does not have an inherent goal to produce a perfect organism. Modifications have to avoid being immediately lethal (as many mutations are) and to be somewhat better (in an appropriate cost-benefit analysis) than their competitors. This process does not produce problem-free solutions to environmental pressures, just solutions that are better than those of competitors and not immediately lethal. Second, environmental change may be very rapid and biological evolution much slower. That is, certain of our characteristics may be more suited to environmental factors that no longer exist or, in the current mix of environmental features, they may have become much less important. Eisley (1958, p. 197) nicely illustrates this point:

> [That is the] evolutionary past of every species of organism—the ghostly world of time in which animals are forever slipping from one environment to another and changing their forms and features as they go. But the marks of the passage linger, and so we come down to the present bearing the traces of all the curious tables at which our forerunners have sat and played the game of life. Our world, in short, is a marred world, an imperfect world, a never totally adjusted world, for the simple reason that it is not static. The games are still in progress and all of us, in the words of Sir Arthur Keith, bear the wounds of evolution. Our backs hurt, we have muscles which no longer move, we have hair that is not functional. All of this bespeaks another world, another game played far behind us in the past. We are indeed products of "descent with modification."

Thus, once the teleological notion that evolution aims at some sort of "perfection" is abandoned, then the numerous problems humans have in interacting with their environments pose no inconsistency with evolutionary claims.

In fact, Holland (1978, p.170) suggests that problems in environmental selection can be partly detected by behavior problems:

> I cannot overly emphasize the importance of always understanding the adaptive nature of behavior, since the problem-definers traditionally consider so much behavior maladaptive. We usually marvel at the intricate biological forms that evolve through natural selection. These astounding variations reflect generations of shifting environmental conditions. Similarly, a person's behavior reflects response contingencies. We should be as respectful and awed by these adaptations as we are of evolutionary adaptations.

That is, instead of looking at behavior problems as inexplicable nuisances, we can use these behaviors to begin an investigatory process that attempts to understand the function of the problem behavior in a perhaps very problematic environment (for example, one that includes a tantrum-reinforcing parent). The clinical investigator must understand what selection mechanisms selected out this behavior.

What are the implications of this Darwinian emphasis for the practitioner and the researcher? For Skinner's Darwinistic account to actually hold, parallels must be found for all the major mechanisms involved in evolution. We argue that the three critical processes in environmental selectionism—the generation of behavioral variability, the retention of certain modifications, and selection mechanisms—each pose important questions for the contemporary researcher and practitioner.

THE GENERATION OF
BEHAVIORAL VARIABILITY

For selection to occur, there must first be something for the environment to select. Moreover, it is advantageous if there are a variety of options posed to the environment, as a single option places all bets on one possibility. In biological evolution, genetic mutations and new genetic configurations produced by sexual reproduction result in major sources of variability. However, relatively little is understood about the mechanisms responsible for the generation of behavioral variability within the lifetime of the organism. We know some broad facts, for example that extinction produces an increase in variability (and correspondingly, that reinforcement typically produces a narrowing of variability) and that there are some species-related parameters affecting variability. However, if we better understood the factors that produce variability, we could potentially have more control over the shaping process as we could control both selection mechanisms and variability-generating mechanisms. This is a significant weakness in current operant accounts (Plotkin, 1987; Staddon, 1979). Plotkin (1987) has suggested that current operant accounts are similar to pre-Mendelian evolutionary accounts. Just as those were ignorant of the role of genetics in accounting for variability, current operant accounts are ignorant of the variability-generation devices.

A practical example of this concerns variability in children's play. Some have suggested that children's play with its unconventional, multiformed manipulations and behaviors is a good example of variability generation at work. Some of this variability makes contact with environmental contingencies so that these behaviors are chosen by a selection mechanism. This variability greatly aids in the children's learning what the environment regards as appropriate behavior. The relatively lethargic and limited play of a retarded child, however, decreases the opportunity for that child's behavior to make the same contact with extant environmental contingencies. Traditionally, the problems of the developmentally delayed have been analyzed as problems in differences in parameters affecting selection. The point here is that an additional mechanism may be involved in the impoverished behavioral repertoire: problems in mechanisms responsible for the generation of behavioral variability.

Retention Variables

There is also a need to better understand retention mechanisms. For example, in organic evolution, only characteristics that have a genetic basis can be retained. This is accomplished by the transmission of survivors' genes to the next generation. Other advantageous characteristics are simply acquired in the individual's lifetime; because of their inability to influence the retention mechanism (the genotype), they are not transmitted. Lamark thought that characteristics acquired in an individual's lifetime (say, a giraffe's neck muscles stretched due to extensive use) could be passed on to the next generation. However, Lamarkianism has been thoroughly discredited and an asymmetry is accepted such that in an individual's lifetime genes affect behavior, but behavior does not affect genes.

The question becomes this: What are the requisites for retention of experience so that the individual becomes enduringly changed? Skinner often spoke vaguely on this issue, noting simply that the organism is changed by the learning trial. But some experiences are retained and some are not. Some experiences are retained for short periods (for example, habituation effects) and others over long periods (taste aversions). What are the mechanisms responsible for these differences in retention? Can we learn to exert control over these so we can enhance retention for some individuals and perhaps shorten retention in others?

Selection Mechanisms

Selection mechanisms are better understood than the previously two discussed topics. Skinner and his followers have studied selection mechanisms extensively. However, we suggest that there have been important advances in this basic research pertaining to the analysis of baseline data that have important implications for the identification of the circumstances of reinforcement, but, at the same time, have not been adequately translated into clinical practice.

Although a reinforcer was originally defined as a response–contingent stimulus that increases the rate of the response (for example, Ferster & Skinner, 1957), the prediction of which stimuli will be reinforcing can be difficult. Reinforcing conditions that work at one time may not work at another time (perhaps due to satiation effects or to counterpreparedness). Moreover, Meehl's (1950) transsituational hypothesis (that is, a stimulus that reinforces one response will reinforce all other responses) clearly has been found to be false (Premack, 1963). Therefore, the identification of the conditions of reinforcement can be made difficult because these can change over time (as the student becomes sated), can change as a function of the behavior to be modified (Garcia & Koelling, 1966; Premack, 1963), and can be somewhat idiographic and thus change across individuals.

In practice, the most common method of identifying reinforcers has been an informal approach in which practitioners use their intuition, previous experience, and trial and error to identify potentially reinforcing stimuli (Kazdin, 1980; Konarski et al., 1980; O'Brien & Repp, 1990; Timberlake & Farmer-Dougan, 1991). In this approach, the clinician asks the question: Given what I know about this individual and the behavior to be modified, what stimuli will function as reinforcers? Thus, the clinician in this approach does not assess the circumstances of reinforcement empirically, but rather makes some a priori conjectures regarding these circumstances. Therefore, the major reason that baseline data are collected is to identify the pretreatment rate of responding, which serves as a standard by which post-treatment effects can be evaluated.

The advantage of this approach is that it requires little time and energy and is thus fairly inexpensive. The disadvantages of this approach are that (a) it is an *unsystematic* method and thus difficult to replicate; (b) the reliability of this method is unknown (it is unclear to what extent two different practitioners would identify the same reinforcing circumstances); (c) this approach is often based on depriving access to a stimulus, raising *ethical concerns*; (d) it gives no information about how to set *contingency values* (i.e., how much reinforcement should be contingent upon how much responding); and most importantly, (e) the *validity* of this approach may be questionable. There have been only a few studies that have investigated the ability of persons using this informal method to correctly identify reinforcing circumstances. All have found staff to be poor at selecting reinforcers (Green et al., 1991; Pace et al., 1985). For example, O'Brien and Repp (1990), in a review of reinforcement-based reductive procedures, found that reinforcement selection was seldom systematic and that social reinforcement was often relied upon although the outcome data indicated it was the least effective consequence. A practical goal of the remainder of this chapter is to illustrate the relevance and advantages of more contemporary accounts of the concept of reinforcement.

A MORE CONTEMPORARY ACCOUNT OF THE CONCEPT OF REINFORCEMENT

In the preceding sections, we have shown clear parallels between functional explanations in biology and those in behavioral analysis. Both share the view that the environment is the agent that shapes the organism or its behavior and that function is a key to understanding the origin of the phenomena of interest. Both evolutionary biology and behavioral analysis can offer functional accounts of apparently maladaptive features. For example, the male peacock's tail is an obvious disadvantage in terms of maintenance and the avoidance of predators. However, the tail serves to attract female peacocks and thus can be explained in terms of sexual selection (Darwin, 1871).

Similarly, there are examples of apparently maladaptive behavior by human beings that serves some short-term function for the individual. For example, self-injurious behavior by people with learning difficulties may be maintained in the short term by attention but in the long term seems maladaptive (Sasso et al., 1992).

Initially the functional explanations offered by biologists were informal or verbal. Thus, for example, in attempting to account for the prevalence of a phenotype in a population, a theorist might argue that it has a certain advantage over others and that this advantage is related to fitness. Occasionally field studies or experiments are carried out to demonstrate the advantage. Similarly, the functional approach within behavioral analysis, described thus far, has been verbal and informal. More recently there have been attempts to formalize such explanations in biology through the development of mathematical models (Maynard-Smith,

1978). This newer approach assumes that animals attempt to maximize fitness and uses mathematical techniques such as game theory and control theory to generate and test hypotheses. This formalization of functional explanations has enabled theorists to apply the approach to behaviors and life history strategies. For example, Maynard-Smith (1978) demonstrated how this general approach might usefully be employed to account for sex-ratio, gaits, and foraging strategies.

There is a clear link between the study of foraging strategies by animals in natural settings and the experimental investigation of operant behavior, as the latter may be thought of as complex, albeit artificial, foraging problems. It is not surprising that soon after the development of formal functional accounts of foraging behavior, usually referred to as optimal foraging theory, there were similar developments in the operant literature.

It is difficult to be certain that these developments in operant psychology were dependent on the developments in biology, but they have clearly benefited on at least two counts. First, mathematical frameworks have been borrowed wholesale from the behavioral ecology literature, and second, the notion that animals maximize fitness gives maximization theories in operant psychology a plausibility and credibility they might otherwise lack, as net energy gain in an experiment can act as a surrogate measure for inclusive fitness.

However, the benefits have not all been on one side. Operant procedures have enabled more rigorous tests of optimal foraging to be carried out than would have been possible from naturalistic observations alone. For example, according to Collier et al. (1986), the key assumption of optimal foraging theory is that selection has favored feeders who minimize the costs and maximize the benefits of feeding. The initiation and termination of feeding bouts, their distribution in time and space, and choice among different foods are all parameters that contribute to the cost-benefit ratio. Collier and his coworkers have demonstrated how operant procedures may be adopted to provide rigorous tests of specific hypotheses derived from optimality assumptions.

They have tested nondeprived animals living 24 hours a day in a closed economy and have used operant procedures to manipulate the procurement and handling costs of food items. Fantino (1985) has argued that this manipulative approach to testing theories has high internal validity and complements well the nonmanipulative, naturalistic approach favored by the behavioral ecologists, which is higher on external validity. Furthermore, behavioral analysis often offers proximate explanations that complement the functional explanations of behavioral ecologists.

We turn now to the adoption by behavior analysts of optimality assumptions to provide explanations for phenomena generated within the operant literature itself. This general approach has its roots in the pioneering work of David Premack in the 1960s and the early work of William Timberlake and James Allison. It received an additional impetus from the adoption by Staddon (1983) of an explicit maximization framework clearly related to developments in biology.

Premack (1965, 1971) proposed his probability differential hypothesis as an alternative to the Law of Effect. The hypothesis viewed reinforcement as a relationship between two responses and asserted that the more probable of two responses would serve as a reinforcer for the less probable. In order to measure probability, Premack measured the amount of time spent performing each response during a paired base-line condition in which both responses were freely and independently available.

Evidence for this hypothesis, often referred to as the Premack Principle, accumulated in a number of studies using both human and animal subjects performing a wide range of responses (Holstein & Hunt, 1965; Hundt & Premack, 1963; Premack, 1962, 1963, 1965, and 1971; Schaeffer, Hanna, & Rousso, 1966). The principle subsequently influenced clinical work and work settings. For example, Allen & Iwata (1980) demonstrated that daily exercise by retarded adults can be reinforced by access to a more probable response, such as game playing. O'Brien, Raynes, and Patch (1971) increased self-grooming and other routine activities by in-patient drug addicts by reinforcing them with more probable activities.

Despite the success of the Premack Principle in applied settings, evidence of its inadequacy as a complete account of the reinforcement relationship was already in the published literature. This evidence was initially provided by Premack himself (1965). He described an experiment in which rats were required to perform a low probability wheel-running response to gain access to a higher-probability drinking response. The probability differential hypothesis clearly predicts reinforcement of running in these circumstances, but no such increase was observed. The experiment used a fixed-ratio schedule that required the two responses to be performed in approximately the same ratio as had been observed under baseline conditions. Premack attributed this failure to the fact that the schedule did not produce a reduction in the contingent response.

According to Timberlake (1980), Premack had assembled all of the pieces necessary to put forward a functional theory of reinforcement. He had identified the paired baseline as a means of identifying the set point that regulates behavior. He knew that the probability differential hypothesis was correct only when the schedule and baseline ratio of the two responses were different. However, instead of focusing on this difference, he focused on the reduction in contingent responding often observed on schedules that increase instrumental responding. He merely added this as an additional condition to be fulfilled to produce reinforcement.

Subsequently, it was demonstrated that a lower-probability response can act as a reinforcer for a higher-probability response providing that a condition, later referred to as the "response deprivation condition," is satisfied (Timberlake & Allison, 1974). This condition, formalized as the response deprivation hypothesis, asserts that a schedule will produce elevation in instrumental responding if, by performing the baseline amount of the instrumental response, the subject has received less access to the contingent response than was observed under baseline conditions, that is, when

$$I/C > oi/oc$$

where I = the instrumental response requirement, C = the contingent response allocation, oi = the paired baseline level of the instrumental response, and oc = the paired baseline level of the contingent response.

Heth and Warren (1978) later identified a condition labeled response satiation, which is the converse of response deprivation and results in punishment or a decrease in instrumental responding. This condition is described thus

$$I/C < oi/oc$$

Evidence for the response deprivation and satiation hypotheses accumulated in a wide range of experiments employing both human and animal subjects (Eisenberger, Karpman, & Trattner, 1967; Heth & Warren, 1978; Allison & Timberlake, 1974; Timberlake & Allison, 1974; Miller & Wozney, 1979), and the approach has had an impact in applied settings.

Konarski and his coworkers have been largely responsible for pioneering the use of the response deprivation hypothesis in applied settings. In an early experiment, Konarski et al. (1980) demonstrated that the response deprivation hypothesis may be used to design effective teaching schedules for first graders performing academic tasks. A later study replicated these findings using educable mentally retarded children as participants (Konarski et al., 1982). In this latter study, the two responses were math and reading tasks. For three of the children, reading served as the instrumental task and for the remaining child, performing math did so. For two children, the instrumental response had a higher probability than the contingent response, and for the others, the probabilities were reversed. In all cases, the instrumental response increased in frequency when the response deprivation condition was present even when the instrumental response had a higher probability. Thus the predictions of the response deprivation hypothesis, but not those of the probability differential hypothesis, were supported in this applied context. A larger study by Konarski (1989), employing as participants 20 retarded adults performing watching and listening responses in a laboratory context, provided additional support for the response deprivation hypothesis and also for the response satiation hypothesis.

In the studies described above, only two response alternatives were available to the participants, in contrast to the circumstances usually encountered in educational settings. In response to this consideration, Aeschleman and Williams (1989) assessed the accuracy of the response deprivation hypothesis in a multiple-response environment. Their study used responses that occur in real-life settings. These included playing electronic games, coloring, doing puzzles, and playing with a toy truck. For each participant, a contingency was arranged between two activities that satisfied the response deprivation condition. In Phase 1 a high-probability alternative activity was made available independent of the schedule responses throughout the sessions, whereas in Phase 2 a low-probability response was available. In general, the results supported the response deprivation hypothesis. However, the reinforcing effect of the schedule was diminished in Phase 1 by the presence of a freely available alternative response. The results extend the application of the response deprivation hypothesis. However, the effect of the freely available response alternative cannot readily be anticipated by the hypothesis and requires further consideration. It will be shown that such an effect can readily be anticipated by the formal models to be described later.

Dougher (1983) has shown how the response deprivation hypothesis may be used in psychiatric settings. Two adults with diagnoses of schizophrenia served as participants in the study. One condition in the study was designed to meet the response deprivation condition while another was designed to meet the response satiation condition. In the former condition, a contingency was arranged between appropriate verbalizations and coffee drinking, so that to obtain a baseline level of coffee drinking, the participants had to exceed their baseline level of appropriate talk. This produced an increase in the target behavior. The second condition was arranged so that if the participants engaged in baseline levels of inappropriate verbalizations, they were required to consume an amount of coffee far in excess of their baseline levels. This produced a decrease in inappropriate verbalizations. Thus a punishment effect was obtained without the use of a noxious stimulus.

More recently, O'Donohue, Plaud, & Hecker (1992) demonstrated that a positive reinforcement regime consistent with the response deprivation hypothesis was effective in increasing time spent outside the home in a long-term homebound agoraphobic woman.

Implicit in the response deprivation hypothesis and the response satiation hypothesis is the view that the function of responding on a schedule is an attempt to preserve some aspect of baseline responding. Both conditions have in common the property that they prevent subjects from simultaneously performing the amounts of contingent and instrumental responses observed under baseline conditions. This view of schedule responding has been formalized by a number of authors whose general approach has been described as molar regulatory or functional (Timberlake, 1980; Rachlin, 1978; Staddon, 1979).

The key assumption of these functional approaches to reinforcement is that the mix of behaviors observed under baseline conditions is in some way an optimal or preferred mix and that the function of behavior observed under schedule constraints is to approach as closely as possible that preferred mix.

Of the models mentioned, only one will be dealt with in some detail for illustrative purposes, Staddon's regulatory model (1979). This has been chosen for a number of reasons. First, it is intuitively simple and is readily described. Second, Staddon's work is clearly derived from biological considerations. The simplest of Staddon's models, the static regulatory model (1983), assumes that animals pressing a lever for food attempt to regulate net energy intake. This has an obvious justification in evolutionary terms. However, in generating a more general model of responding under schedule constraints, Staddon has extended the concept of regulation to other responses and has, to some extent, stretched the evolutionary plausibility of his argument.

The minimum-distance model (Staddon, 1979) takes as its starting point the view that the mix of behaviors observed in a baseline is an optimal mix. Theoretically the model can be extended to any number of responses, but in practice it has been restricted to a consideration of just two or three, the instrumental and contingent responses and sometimes a category that includes all other responses. Here we will consider the two response versions.

In Figure 18.1 are represented the rate of two activities, the instrumental response X and the contingent response Y.

The model assumes that an animal will respond under schedule constraints (in the case of a ratio schedule, the line $Y = aX$ where $a =$ the ratio requirement) in a manner that minimizes the algebraic distance to the baseline point (X_0, Y_0). Thus the objective function $C(X,Y)$ that is minimized is given by

$$C(X,Y) = [(X_0 - X) + (Y_0 - Y)]$$

where (X_0, Y_0) are the coordinates of the free behavior point. The square root can be dispensed with, as the extrema of a power function are the same as those of the function itself, yielding

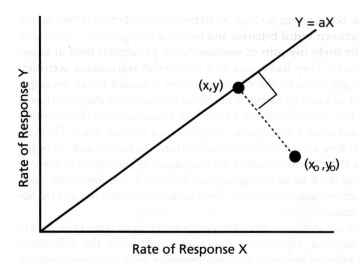

FIGURE 18.1 Hypothetical behavioral space depicting adjustment to a ratio schedule (the line Y = aX). Baseline responding is represented by (X_0, Y_0) and responding on the schedule by (X, Y).

$$C(X,Y) = [(X_0-X) + (Y_0-Y)]$$

When subjected to the constraints of a range of ratio schedules, this function predicts a response function that is a circle of diameter equal to the distance from the origin to the free behavior point. This predicts a bitonic function for ratio schedules, which corresponds reasonably well with empirically derived functions (see Staddon, 1979, 1983).

Predictions can be further improved by taking into account the reasonable assumption that deviations along the two axes should not be weighted equally, yielding the equation

$$X(X,Y) = a(X_0-X) + b(Y_0-Y)$$

Further improvements to the model's fit may be achieved by adding a third category of responding—all other responses. This modification is particularly helpful in describing interval schedule functions.

The incorporation of a third category of responding enables the model to anticipate the response substitution effects reported by Aeschleman and Williams (1989).

The approach to schedule responding described thus far has clear applications in applied contexts. However, these applications are limited to some extent by the need to gather stable baseline data prior to the introduction of schedule restrictions. While this is possible in many applied settings, such as institutions and educational environments, it is not possible in all contexts. For example, it is not always practical to carry out extensive observations on clients who attend therapy on a sessional basis. Some recent findings by Bernstein and Michael (1990) on the correspondence between verbal behavior and behavior may provide a solution to this problem. In this study, five pairs of volunteer adult participants lived in an experimental apartment. They had access to a number of recreational activities. Their levels of engagement in these activities were recorded for an extensive baseline period. In addition to carrying out these baseline recordings, Bernstein and Michael also obtained self-reports of levels of engagement in the activities. These were obtained using a sliding scale mounted on a wooden frame. The scale was 20 centimeters long and labelled "none of the time" to the left and "all of the time" to the right. Participants indicated the proportion of time spent in the two activities by moving the scale to the appropriate location. It was found that there was a reasonable correspondence between these participants' estimates and the actual behavioral measures.

Predictions for the outcome of contingency restrictions were then generated using the response deprivation hypothesis and either the behavioral recordings or the subjects' estimates. In many instances, both measures made the same predictions for the outcome of imposed contingency restrictions at a later stage of the experiment. However, where there were discrepancies, predictions derived from behavioral measures were superior to those derived from the self-reports. The concerns of Bernstein and Michael were primarily theoretical. They were concerned with the general issue of the correspondence between verbal behavior and other behaviors. However, if the measurement procedures they described can be refined and improved, they may provide a solution to the problem caused by the difficulty of carrying out extensive baseline observations in many client groups.

CONCLUSION

Darwinian evolution provides a context in which to understand human behavior. Skinner explicitly appeals to the notion of environmental selection in both his constructs of the contingencies of survival and the contingencies of reinforcement. There are many important unanswered questions concerning a more complete selectionist account of human behavior. However, it is clear that the next generation of behavioral interventionists can profit by utilizing more contemporary accounts of reinforcement.

AUTHOR NOTE

This work was supported in part by Grant No. H023C40063 from the U.S. Department of Education, Office of Special Education.

REFERENCES

Aeschleman, S. R., & Williams, M. L. (1989). A test of the response deprivation hypothesis in a multiple-response context. *American Journal on Mental Retardation, 93,* 345–353.

Allen, L. D., & Iwata, B. (1980). Reinforcing exercise maintenance: Using high rate activities. *Behaviour Modification, 4,* 337–354.

Allison, J., & Timberlake, W. (1974). Instrumental and contingent saccharin licking in rats: Response deprivation and reinforcement. *Learning and Motivation, 5,* 231–247.

Bernstein, D. J., & Michael, R. L. (1990). The utility of verbal and behavioral estimates of value. *Journal of the Experimental Analysis of Behavior, 54,* 173–184.

Collier, G. H., Johnson, D. F., Hill, W. L., & Kaufman, L. W. (1986). The economics of the law of effect. *Journal of the Experimental Analysis of Behavior, 46,* 113–136.

Corwin, J. V., & O'Donohue, W. (1995). Evolutionary theory and behavior therapy. In W. O'Donohue & L. Krasner (Eds.), *Theories in behavior therapy.* Washington: American Psychological Association.

Darwin, C. (1871). *The descent of man and selection in relation to sex.* London: John Murray.

Dougher, M. J. (1983). Clinical effects of response deprivation and response satiation procedures. *Behavior Therapy, 14,* 286–298.

Eiseley, L. (1958). *Darwin's century.* New York: Doubleday.

Eisenberger, R., Karpman, M., & Trattner, J. (1967). What is the necessary and sufficient condition for reinforcement in the contingency situation? *Journal of Experimental Psychology, 74(3),* 342–350.

Fantino, E. (1985). Behavior analysis and behavioral ecology: A synergistic coupling. *The Behavior Analyst, 8,* 151–157.

Ferster, C. B., & Skinner, B. F. (1957). *Schedules of reinforcement.* New York: Appleton-Century-Crofts.

Garcia, J., & Koelling, R. A. (1966). Relation of cue to consequence in avoidance learning. *Psychologic Science, 4,* 123–124.

Green, C. W., Reid, D. H., Canipe, V. S., & Gardner, S. M. (1991). A comprehensive evaluation of reinforcer identification processes for persons with profound retardation. *Journal of Applied Behavior Analysis, 24,* 537–552.

Heth, C. D. & Warren, A. G. (1978). Response deprivation and response satiation as determinants of instrumental performance: Some data and theory. *Animal Learning and Behaviour, 6,* 294–300.

Holland, J. G. (1978). Behaviorism: Part of the problem or part of the solution? *Journal of Applied Behavior Analysis, 11,* 163–174.

Holstein, S. B. & Hunt, A. (1965). Reinforcement of intracranial brain stimulation by licking. *Psychonomic Science, 3,* 17–18.

Hundt, A. G. & Premack, D. (1963). Running is both a positive and negative reinforcer. *Science, 142,* 1087–1088.

Kazdin, A. E. (1980). *Behavior modification in applied settings.* Homewood, IL: Dorsey.

Konarski, E. A. (1989). Towards a functional approach to learned performance. *American Journal on Mental Retardation, 93,* 360–362.

Konarski, E. A., Crowell, C. R., Johnson, M. R., & Whitman, T. L. (1982). Response deprivation, reinforcement and instrumental academic performance in an EMR classroom. *Behavior Therapy, 13,* 94–102.

Konarski, E. A., Johnson, M. R., Crowell, C. R., & Whitman, T. L. (1980). Response deprivation and reinforcement in applied settings: A preliminary analysis. *Journal of Applied Behavior Analysis, 13,* 595–609.

Maynard-Smith, J. (1978). Optimization theory in evolution. *Annual Review of Ecological Systems, 9,* 31–56.

Meehl, P. E. (1950). On the circularity of the law of effect. *Psychological Bulletin, 45,* 52–75.

Miller, M., & Wozney, M. (1979). Conservation in behaviour. *Journal of Experimental Psychology: General, 108,* 4–34.

O'Brien, J. S., Raynes, A. E., & Patch, V. D. (1971). An operant reinforcement system to improve ward behavior in inpatient drug addicts. *Journal of Behavior Therapy and Experimental Psychiatry, 2,* 239–242.

O'Brien, S., & Repp, A. C. (1990). Reinforcement-based reductive procedures: A review of 20 years of their use with persons with severe or profound retardation. *Journal of the Association for Persons with Severe Handicaps, 15,* 148–159.

O'Donohue, W. T., Plaud, J. J., & Hecker, J. E. (1992). The possible function of positive reinforcement in home-bound agoraphobia: A case study. *Journal of Behavior Therapy and Experimental Psychiatry, 23,* 303–312.

Pace, G., Ivancic, J., Edwards, G., Iwata, B., & Page, T. (1985). Assessment of stimulus preference and reinforcer value with profoundly retarded individuals. *Journal of Applied Behavior Analyses, 18,* 249–255.

Plotkin, H. (1987). The evolutionary analogy in Skinner's writings. In S. Modgil & C. Modgil (Eds.), *B. F. Skinner: Consensus and controversy* (pp. 139–149). New York: Falmer.

Premack, D. (1962). Reversibility of the reinforcement relation. *Science, 136,* 255–257

Premack, D. (1963). Rate-differential reinforcement in monkey manipulation. *Journal of the Experimental Analysis of Behavior, 6,* 81–89.

Premack, D. (1965). Reinforcement Theory. In D. Levine (Ed.), *Nebraska symposium on motivation (Vol. 13).* Lincoln: University of Nebraska.

Premack, D. (1971). Catching up with common sense, on two sides of a generalization: Reinforcement and punishment. In R. Glaser (Ed.), *The nature of reinforcement.* New York: Academic.

Rachlin, H. (1978). A molar theory of reinforcement schedules. *Journal of Experimental Analysis of Behavior, 30,* 345–360.

Sasso, G. M., Reimers, T. M., Cooper, L. J., Wacker, W. B., Steege, M., Kelly, L., & Allaire, A. (1992). Use of descriptive and experimental analysis to identify the functional properties of operant behavior in school settings. *Journal of Applied Behavioral Analysis, 25,* 809–821.

Schaeffer, R. W., Hanna, B., & Rousso, P. (1966). Positive reinforcement: A test of the Premack Theory. *Psychonomic Science, 4,* 7–8.

Skinner, B. F. (1938). *The behavior of organisms.* New York: Appleton-Century-Crofts.

Skinner, B. F. (1963). Behaviorism at fifty. *Science, 140,* 951–958.

Skinner, B. F. (1974). About behaviorism. New York: Alfred A. Knopf.

Skinner, B. F. (1984) Selection by consequences. *Behavioral and Brain Sciences, 7*(4), 477–510.

Staddon, J. E. R. (1979). Operant behaviour as adaptation to constraint. *Journal of Experimental Psychology: General, 108,* 48–67.

Staddon, J. E. R. (1983). *Adaptive behavior and learning.* Cambridge: Cambridge University.

Task Force on Promotion and Dissemination of Psychological Procedures (1995). Training in and Dissemination of empirically-validated psychological treatments: Report and Recommendations. *The Clinical Psychologist, 48,* 3–27.

Timberlake, W. (1980). A molar equilibrium theory of learned performance. In G. W. Bower (Ed.), *The psychology of learning and motivation (Vol. 14).* New York: Academic Press.

Timberlake, W., & Allison, J. (1974). Response deprivation: An empirical approach to instrumental performance. *Psychological Review, 81,* 146–164.

Timberlake, W., & Farmer-Dougan, V. A. (1991). Reinforcement in applied settings: Figuring out ahead of time what will work. *Psychological Bulletin, 110,* 379–391.

Index